American
Republics

American Republics

A CONTINENTAL HISTORY

OF THE UNITED STATES,

1783–1850

ALAN TAYLOR

W. W. NORTON & COMPANY
Independent Publishers Since 1923

FRONTISPIECE IMAGE

"War News from Mexico," 1848, by Richard Caton Woodville. This image represented the intense public interest in the war and the prominence of newspapers in public life. But Woodville feared for the Union as a consequence of the victories. In the right foreground he placed a pair of African Americans in ragged clothing to convey the salience of slavery in the war's causes and consequences. To the left, a careless listener drops a lighted match into a barrel to suggest the incendiary results that the conquest could bring. Library of Congress, LC-DIG-pga-03891.

For information about permission to reproduce selections from this book, write to Permissions, W. W. Norton & Company, Inc., 500 Fifth Avenue, New York, NY 10110

For information about special discounts for bulk purchases, please contact W. W. Norton Special Sales at specialsales@wwnorton.com or 800-233-4830

Manufacturing by LSC Communications Harrisonburg
Book design by Chris Welch Design
Production manager: Julia Druskin

Library of Congress Cataloging-in-Publication Data

Names: Taylor, Alan, 1955– author.
Title: American republics : a continental history of the United States, 1783–1850 / Alan Taylor.
Description: First edition. | New York : W. W. Norton & Company, [2021] | Includes bibliographical references and index.
Identifiers: LCCN 2021003043 | ISBN 9781324005797 (hardcover) | ISBN 9781324005803 (epub)
Subjects: LCSH: United States—History—1783-1865 | United States—Territorial expansion—History—19th century.
Classification: LCC E301 .T39 2021 | DDC 973.3/18—dc23
LC record available at https://lccn.loc.gov/2021003043

W. W. Norton & Company, Inc., 500 Fifth Avenue, New York, N.Y. 10110
www.wwnorton.com

W. W. Norton & Company Ltd., 15 Carlisle Street, London W1D 3BS

1 2 3 4 5 6 7 8 9 0

For the members of the Haynes Seminar

And in Memory of Elizabeth "Wendy" Hazard

CONTENTS

LIST OF MAPS AND ILLUSTRATIONS

Maps

— NORTH AMERICA, 1783 —

HUDSON BAY CO.

BRITISH NORTH AMERICA

NEWFOUNDLAND

GREAT LAKES

ST. JOHN

Quebec
VERMONT
Montreal

NOVA SCOTIA
Halifax

Contested by Indian confederacy

Claimed by Spain

Mississippi R.

NY   NH   Boston
            MA
Niagara   RI
Detroit   CT
Philadelphia   New York
                NJ
            DE

CALIFORNIA

Ohio R.

MD
VA

KENTUCKY
TENNESSEE   NC

UNITED
STATES

NEW
MEXICO   • Santa Fe   LOUISIANA

Bermuda

SC
GA   Charleston

Natchez   Savannah

ATLANTIC
OCEAN

New Orleans   FLORIDA

NEW
SPAIN   Gulf of Mexico

BAHAMAS

Havana

PACIFIC
OCEAN

Mexico City   Veracruz

Port-au-Prince

0 Miles   800

BELIZE   JAMAICA   ST. DOMINGUE

LESSER
ANTILLES

0 Kilometers   800

Caribbean Sea

© 2020 Jeffrey L. Ward

In 1783, the United States had expansive bounds, reaching north to the Great
Lakes, south to Florida, and west to the Mississippi, but the new country
lacked possession and control of that claim. To the north and west, a rival
confederacy of Native peoples defended their homelands, with the help of British
garrisons at Niagara and Detroit. To the south and west, the Spanish Empire
also claimed the territory between Tennessee and Florida. "North America, 1783,"
by Jeffrey L. Ward.

— North America, 1806 —

Nootka

HUDSON BAY CO.

BRITISH NORTH AMERICA

Columbia R.

OREGON
COUNTRY

Snake R.

LOWER
CANADA

Quebec

NEWFOUNDLAND

PRINCE EDWARD IS.

CAPE BRETON IS.

NOVA SCOTIA
Halifax

GREAT LAKES

Fort Mandan

Montreal

UPPER
CANADA

NEW BRUNSWICK

VT

LEWIS AND CLARK

MICHIGAN
TERR.

York

NY

NH

Boston

MA

RI

DISTRICT OF
LOUISIANA

Mississippi R.

INDIANA
TERR.

PA
Philadelphia

OH

CT
New York

NJ

DE

NEW
MEXICO

Santa Fe

St.Louis

MD

VA

Washington, DC

KY

UNITED
STATES

TN

NC

Bermuda

SC

MISSISSIPPI
TERR.

GA

Charleston

TEXAS

Savannah

ORLEANS
TERRITORY

New Orleans

FLORIDA

ATLANTIC

OCEAN

NEW
SPAIN

Gulf of Mexico

BAHAMAS

Havana

PACIFIC
OCEAN

Mexico City

Veracruz

Port-au-Prince

LESSER
ANTILLES

0 Miles   800

BELIZE

JAMAICA

HAITI

0 Kilometers   800

Caribbean Sea

© 2020 Jeffrey L. Ward

By 1806, the United States had secured and begun to settle the contested
border zones of 1783 after shattering the Indian confederacy and inducing
the British and Spanish to recede. In 1803, American leaders obtained the
Louisiana Territory, including New Orleans at the mouth of the Mississippi.
This purchase stretched the Union's territorial claims westward to the
Rocky Mountains, but almost all of that land remained in the possession
of Native peoples. The Americans, British, and Spanish all claimed the
Oregon Country. "North America, 1806," by Jeffrey L. Ward.

— NORTH AMERICA, 1845 —

VANCOUVER IS.
~54°40'~
HUDSON BAY CO.
NEWFOUNDLAND

OREGON
COUNTRY
BRITISH NORTH AMERICA
PRINCE EDWARD IS.
CAPE BRETON IS.

GREAT LAKES
Quebec City
CANADA
NOVA SCOTIA
Halifax

OREGON TRAIL
WISCONSIN
TERR.
Montreal
VT
ME
NEW BRUNSWICK

IOWA
TERRITORY
Toronto
N.Y.
NH
MA
Boston

CALIFORNIA TRAIL
MI
PA
RI
CT

Sutter's Fort
OREGON TRAIL
IL
IN
OH
Philadelphia
New York
NJ

CALIFORNIA
MD
DE

INDIAN TERRITORY
MO
VA
Washington, DC

NEW
MEXICO
•Santa Fe
KY
NC
UNITED
STATES

AR
TN
SC
Bermuda

Rio Grande
MS
AL
GA
Charleston

TX
LA
Savannah

REPUBLIC
OF MEXICO
New Orleans
FL
ATLANTIC
OCEAN

Monterrey •
Gulf of Mexico
BAHAMAS

Havana

PACIFIC
OCEAN
Mexico City
Veracruz
YUCATAN
Port-au-Prince •
LESSER
ANTILLES

0 Miles   800
BELIZE
JAMAICA
HAITI

0 Kilometers   800
GUATEMALA
HONDURAS
Caribbean Sea
© 2020 Jeffrey L. Ward

By 1845, the United States had removed most Native peoples from east of the
Mississippi to "Indian Territory" west of Arkansas and Missouri. In 1845 the
United States annexed Texas, shown here with the region's borders as defined
by Mexico. The United States provoked a war by extending those bounds south
and west to the Rio Grande and to include Santa Fe. The United States and
the British Empire still disputed sovereignty over the Oregon Country. "North
America, 1845," by Jeffrey L. Ward.

— NORTH AMERICA, 1850 —

In 1846, the United States divided the Oregon Country with the British
Empire and launched a war with Mexico that conquered the Southwest and
California, extending American power to the Pacific. "North America, 1850," by
Jeffrey L. Ward.

Liberty is but an empty name, a mere burlesque,
if we fear to speak the truth.

—ZEPHANIAH KINGSLEY, JR., 1826

PREFACE

American Republics presents a history of the United States from 1783 to 1850. Meant as a concise introduction, *American Republics* offers basic coverage of some conventional topics. These include Alexander Hamilton's financial program; Thomas Jefferson's attempt to retrench the federal government; Andrew Jackson's war on the national bank; and efforts by Frederick Douglass and Sojourner Truth to realize a more democratic and inclusive nation by challenging the slave system.

In addition to this general coverage, *American Republics* examines America's troubled relationships with its neighbors: the British and Spanish Empires, many Indian nations, and the independent republics of Haiti and Mexico. The survival of the Union seemed to depend on expanding settlements to accommodate a growing population and thereby alleviate internal tensions between East and West, North and South. But if the Union grew unevenly, benefiting one region at the expense of others, the tenuous balance of power within could collapse into disunion and civil war. American leaders also sought to control efforts by dissident groups to break away from the United States to create new, alternative republics in the vast interior of the continent. More than one republic contended for the future of North America.

Built on an unstable foundation of rival regions and an ambiguous constitution, the United States was far from united before 1850. We misunderstand our political origins if we read the post–Civil War nation back onto the early republic. Not yet a nation, the early United States was a loose union of states, with regional leaders persistently at odds over just how strong their bonds should be. Those divisions became morally charged after 1815 as reformers promoted a more inclusive citizenry by challenging slavery and the subordination of women. Although deeply rooted in our history, white supremacy has also had many critics pushing for a more egalitarian nation.

A sequel to *American Colonies: The Settling of North America* and *American Revolutions: A Continental History, 1750–1804*, this new book explores United States history on a continental scale. My witty friend Sarah Pearsall advised that I give *American Revolutions* the subtitle of "colonize harder" in tribute to the *Die Hard* and *Die Harder* movies starring Bruce Willis. In that vein, *American Republics* should be "colonize hardest." That subtitle would fit a period when the United States invaded Canada, Florida, Texas, much of Mexico, sought to stifle Haiti, ousted most of the Native peoples living east of the Mississippi, and began to impose reservations on western Indians.

By 1850 the United States had swept its claims across the continent to the Pacific coast—but it did so with far less confidence than we usually recognize. The nation's leaders sought elusive security against the internal divisions of an unstable union of disparate states, potential slave revolts, resistance by neighbors, especially Native peoples, and the fission by discontented groups, including Mormons, seeking to make their own countries on the frontiers of settlement. That pervasive, driving fear of dissolution debunks the optimistic certainty of "Manifest Destiny" as the most misleading phrase ever offered to explain American expansion. This book makes the case for the manifest divisions, instability, and uncertainty of the early United States.

American Republics

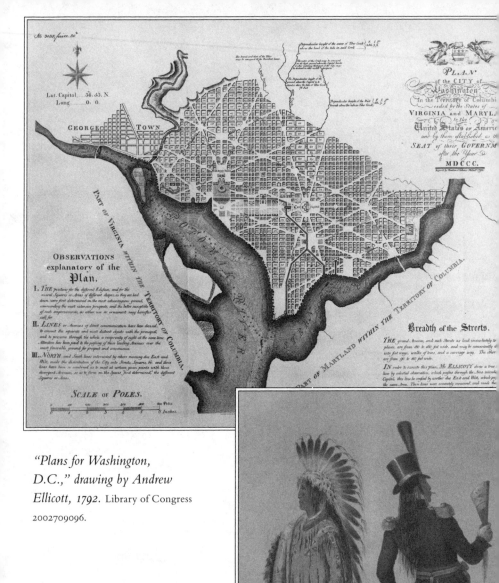

"Plans for Washington, D.C.," drawing by Andrew Ellicott, 1792. Library of Congress 2002709096.

"Wi-jun-jon (the Light), Going to and Returning from Washington," engraving by Currier & Ives after George Catlin, 1837–1839. This Assiniboine chief suffered assassination upon returning to his people. Library of Congress 98507921.

INTRODUCTION

During the early nineteenth century, Washington, D.C., displayed grand ambitions within a ragged reality. Laid out in forest and tobacco fields during the 1790s, the city had an elaborate paper plan of wide avenues and big blocks, but most lots remained filled with alder bushes, shrub-oak trees, brick kilns, shanties, and construction scraps. Monumental stone edifices—White House, Capitol, War Department, Post Office, and Patent Office—sprouted near scattered wooden houses built in haste. Rooting pigs, grazing cows, and hissing geese scavenged along muddy streets. For want of a municipal water or sewage system, filth collected in the many low-lying swamps, which promoted deadly outbreaks of malaria and dysentery. In 1841, Joel Poinsett of South Carolina described the city's grand Mall as, in fact, a "Sahara of solitude and waste—appropriated as a cow pasture and frog pond, and decorated with a stone-cutter's yard, a slaughter-house, and pig-pens."[1]

Used to the grand cities of European monarchies, diplomats and visitors struggled to make sense of the raw capital of a new republic, where, a Briton said, most residents "live like bears, brutalized and stupefied." President Jefferson did keep bears, brought back by the Lewis and Clark expedition, in cages on the lawn of the White House. The Briton added, "Never was so magnificent a design for a capital so wretchedly and shabbily executed." Visiting in 1842, the novelist Charles Dickens called Washington, "the City of Magnificent Intentions," with "spacious avenues, that begin in nothing, and lead nowhere." A worldly Portuguese diplomat thought that every man was "born with a bag of follies" and spent life emptying it, save for George Washington, who had the smallest of bags and dispensed no follies until he chose the site for a capital and "emptied the whole of it in this city."[2]

A crude and rustic capital suited Thomas Jefferson, who became president in 1801 and favored a limited federal government. Distrusting big cities as sources of turmoil, crime, and corruption, Jefferson believed that governing a republic would work best in a backwater like Washington, removed from concentrations of wealth and extremes of poverty. In 1801, the capital had a minimal bureaucracy, with just 153 federal employees, including the president. The number doubled by 1830, but that lagged behind the nation's population growth of 150 percent. Jefferson and his successor, James Madison, declined to invest in improving the city's muddy, potholed streets and rickety bridges. Frustrated in his ambitions, the city's first planner dismissed the place as a "mere contemptible hamlet."[3]

Although a republic's capital, Washington limited the citizenship of inhabitants, deprived then of the right to vote for members of Congress. Determined to control the district, Congress allowed the residents to elect a city council but not a mayor—whom the president appointed. And Congress could veto any act of the council. A Washingtonian described the residents as "a collection of slaves in the bosom of a nation of freemen." Poorly governed, the city bred a weak sense of community among the newly assembled inhabitants, who feuded over boundaries, roads, and land speculations. In 1800, a treasury secretary concluded, "The people are poor, and . . . they live like fishes by eating each other."[4]

Washington lagged behind the leading American cities of the northeast. At 3,210 inhabitants in 1800, the capital had only a tenth of the population of Philadelphia or New York. Washington grew to 50,000 by 1850, but it still paled when compared to New York, which had 800,000 people and housed the nation's leading banks and brokerage firms. London served as Britain's center of trade as well as government, but the United States separated political and economic elites in different cities. Unlike other capitals, early Washington lacked a university, art museum (other than the Capitol), or grand theater for opera and high-brow plays. In 1827 a newcomer found the white residents divided by class into leading politicians, other genteel folk, and common artisans and tradesmen. He considered the "three classes . . . almost as distinct from each other as the *castes* of the Hindoos." While denying the power of class in public life, Americans practiced it with a vengeance in private circles.[5]

By political design, Washington lay within the Upper South: nestled beside the Potomac River on the margins of Virginia, the powerhouse state of the early United States. Most of the residents came from the South, and southern pastimes—horse racing, gambling, cockfighting, and dueling—prevailed to the dismay of pious New Englanders. Northern folk also dreaded the searing heat and deadly malaria of summer in the capital.[6]

A third of Washington's people were enslaved, which reassured southerners of their clout in the Union. Slaves built the grand buildings and did menial work in homes, hotels, restaurants, laundries, stables, and brothels. The city's poor whites resented working beside rented slaves, blaming them (rather than their masters) for depressing wages. While boasting of their own freedom, whites watched coffles of shackled slaves pass through the streets to holding pens and auction blocks. Washington served as a key transit center for the interstate trade that moved enslaved people from the Upper South to the booming cotton plantations of the Lower South. In 1802, the city's grand jurors regretted the scenes "of wretchedness and human degradation, disgraceful to our character of a free government." But they could not and would not abolish a market essential to their practice of slavery.[7]

The city's largest edifice, the Capitol, housed Congress and a patriotic collection of art meant to inspire national pride. The rotunda featured iconic paintings of triumphs during the American Revolution: the Declaration of Independence, British military surrenders at Saratoga and Yorktown, and George Washington resigning his command to Congress. Statues, reliefs, and paintings also celebrated the triumph of civilization over (allegedly) savage and vanishing Indians. In contrast to that profusion of caricatured Natives, the Capitol had virtually no art depicting African Americans, denying them a place in the imagined nation. During the 1830s, the entrances obtained huge statues representing War, Peace, Hope, and Justice. In 1842, vandals broke off an arm from Justice, which seemed symbolic in a Union committed to expanding slavery and crushing Indians.[8]

Located within the War Department, the Indian Office displayed Native ornaments, weapons, and dresses as well as portraits of 150 chiefs painted during their visits to the city. The collectors practiced a sort of rescue anthropology, for they regarded Indians as doomed to vanish, with help from the War Department. But a Kentucky congressman protested and blocked spending further public money "for the pictures of these wretches."[9]

To impress Indians, the government hosted chiefs to exchange speeches, make treaties, and receive alcohol, swords, genteel clothing, American flags, and silver medals. If Washington seemed paltry to Europeans, the city struck Natives as huge and confusing, with complex buildings beyond anything they had known. Nor had Natives ever seen such crowds of gawking, grabby, and jabbering strangers who crowded around chiefs as curiosities. One delegation of chiefs complained of being "dogged by the crowd which continually besets and torments them." At the Navy Yard and on warships in the river, their hosts displayed and fired cannons to demonstrate American might. That prowess seemed all the more ominous when Native visitors caught sight of so many Black people in chains: warnings of a potential fate for defeated Indians. The visits often disappointed American expectations because Indians back home scoffed at returning chiefs telling of immense buildings and great cannon. One listening Assiniboine became outraged at the stories, so he shot and killed a returning chief, known as the Light.[10]

Union

The Capitol reflected a precious but imperiled union of fractious states. In December 1833, Benjamin Brown French began work as a clerk for the House of Representatives. Shocked by angry debates, French wondered, "*Will it always be the capitol of my happy country? I fear the seeds are already sown whose fruit will be disunion, but God forbid it.*" Six years later, French had heard so many threats and seen so much violence in Congress that he felt like "a mourner following my Country to its grave."[11]

The Union of American states originated in fear during the Revolution. Patriots had to unite, not just to defeat the British and Loyalists, but also to avoid killing one another in civil wars. The citizens lacked a common identity as Americans, for most felt greater allegiance and affection for their home states. A Massachusetts leader noted, "Instead of feeling as a nation, a state is our country. We look with indifference, often with hatred, fear, and aversion to the other states." Patriots worried that their diverse and fractious states would clash over boundaries and trade, replicating the wars that so often bloodied Europe. To preserve free government on a continental scale, Americans needed the Union.[12]

But Americans also feared that their federal government might become too powerful and tyrannical. Having resisted Britain's centralizing might, many citizens balked at creating a consolidated nation. They supported a union just strong enough to help the states but not powerful enough to subordinate them. While the pressures of the Revolutionary War had pulled the states together, a dread of central power kept pushing them apart. Consequently, the nation became both cherished and feared by citizens. In 1830 an interstate convention of Episcopalians sought to write a "prayer for the whole people." A committee proposed "O Lord, bless our nation," but this drew "so many objections" that the convention replaced "nation" with "union."[13]

During the early nineteenth century, Americans revered their

Union, but that was not the same thing as a shared nationalism. Indeed, union enabled citizens to avoid fully bonding as Americans. Where nationalism asserted a common identity, union operated as a framework for cooperation by citizens who primarily identified with their own state. Vague enough to command devotion from the nation's far corners, the Union aroused anxieties that some other region's politicians would distort it for unfair advantage. Union seemed especially precious because it was so vague and vulnerable.[14]

After winning independence, Americans still felt insecure, dreading that a foreign power would exploit disaffected elements within the new Union. Citizens knew that their country had dangerous fault lines within. Indians and enslaved people might ally with the British or Spanish Empire to overthrow the United States. Worse still, foreigners might exploit jealousies between the states to provoke disunion and civil war. Enemies without combining with foes within could shatter the Union that preserved free government and internal peace.[15]

Fear drove American leaders to expand deep into the continent to push rival empires farther away from the United States. Americans hoped that distance would weaken imperial efforts to rally Indians and provoke slave revolts—or promote secession by a restive region. Federal leaders also distrusted their own settlers, who might break away to join another empire or form their own, rival republic. Prior to the 1840s, Americans lacked confidence in any supposed "Manifest Destiny" to dominate the continent. On the contrary, anxious leaders pushed expansion to reduce the vulnerability of the United States to internal divisions.[16]

Aggressive expansion especially appealed to slaveholders. Because enslaved people could escape and seek haven beyond America's borders, slavery was an insecure property. By joining the Union, southerners gained legal rights to retrieve runaway slaves from northern states. But slaves could still seek freedom by escaping across borders to reach Spanish and British colonies. Slaveholders sought American expansion not simply to add plantations but also to subtract places where enslaved people could flee. Otherwise, masters would lose more slaves to flight and might lose their own lives in revolts by slaves rising up to get away across any nearby border. A leading newspaper editor, John B. Jones, considered slavery "the weak point of our Union—that which exposes it to [the] most danger from foreign and domestic foes." Expansion, however, might diffuse America's enslaved population and reduce their supposed menace, while preserving their economic benefit to masters.[17]

But Americans also worried that an expanding union would grow too big, breeding an imbalance of power that favored one region at the expense of another. Then secession would break up the Union and drench the continent in American blood. By expanding in search of security, Americans could provoke, unwittingly, a civil war between North and South—or East versus West.[18]

Americans regarded their republican Union as a precious but always-imperiled experiment. Although everyone professed to revere the Union, Americans differed over how to govern that Union. After 1815, many northern leaders promoted a unifying American nationalism that could sustain a stronger federal government ruled by the majority. But many other Americans, especially in the South, feared national consolidation as a tyrannical vehicle for oppressing a minority region.

Congress convened diverse men from different states and competing parties. Compelled to work together in tight spaces, they became hypersensitive to signs of disrespect and bullying from colleagues of another region. Rather than unify a nation, Congress became a cockpit that bred regional resentment. When leaders felt mistreated by a majority in Congress, they threatened disunion. During the 1830s, Congressman Henry Clay warned his peers to "pause at the edge of the precipice, before the fearful and dangerous leap to be taken into the yawning abyss below, from which none who ever take it shall return in safety."[19]

A politician had to justify any measure as meant to defend a vulnerable Union. In 1846, President James K. Polk vetoed a bill to fund public works, thereby pleasing southerners while irritating Yankees. Polk asserted that he did so because federal funding would "engender sectional feelings and prejudices calculated to disturb the harmony of the Union." Similarly, when John C. Calhoun pushed to amend the Constitution to protect the South as a minority region, he claimed to defend the Union by preventing southern alienation from a "consolidated" nation.[20]

Capitals

By expanding in search of security, the United States clashed with other empires and republics. They too erected capitals in bids to display power and appear enduring. Although most Indians dispersed authority among many chiefs and disparate villages, a few Native peoples responded to American expansion by adopting their own republican governments. During the 1820s, Cherokees built a new national capital, New Echota, in a bid to win diplomatic respect from the United States.[21]

Adapting settler architecture, New Echota featured wood-frame or squared-log structures with glass windows. The whitewashed buildings hosted institutions familiar to Americans: supreme court, legislative hall, newspaper, church, post office, school, workshops, stores, and taverns. The prime builder promised construction "in the most fashionable manner equal to that of New York or Baltimore." A visitor from New England praised New Echota as "an interesting and pleasant place." But our primary source for New Echota comes from notes taken in 1832 by a surveyor sent by Georgia to enable settlers to displace Indians. Georgians promptly destroyed New Echota, substituting cotton plantations worked by enslaved people. Ultimately, neither Georgia nor the United States could accept any Indian republic in the way of American expansion.[22]

To the north, the Canadian provinces remained British colonies, including Upper Canada (now Ontario) and Lower Canada (Quebec). In 1796, Governor John Graves Simcoe located the capital of Upper Canada at York (now Toronto) on the northwest shore of Lake Ontario. During the American Revolution, Simcoe had commanded a Loyalist regiment, and he remained unreconciled to defeat. Despising republicanism and the United States, he expected renewed war during the 1790s, so he chose York as relatively secure from American attack, but the abrupt move to a forested site outraged many colonists. One complained, "York never was intended by nature for a metropolis; and . . . nothing but the caprice and obstinacy of General Simcoe raised it to that Dignity." As a British colony rather than an American republic, Upper Canada had a governor who could shift a capital without consulting his legislature.[23]

Simcoe designed York as a Loyalist bastion against republican expansion, naming the town after his royal patron, the Duke of York. The principle streets also honored royalty: King, Queen, Duke, Duchess, Prince, Frederick, and Caroline. Seeking to make Upper Canada more like the mother country than the United States, Simcoe secured the gradual emancipation of slavery. That law barred the importation of slaves and freed those born after 1793 when they reached the age of twenty-five.[24]

Despite imperial origins, early York was even more rustic, isolated, and backward than its republican counterpart, Washington, D.C. At first, York grew slowly, housing only 336 people in 1801, when a visitor described a village of 100 houses "just emerging from the woods." People derided the town as "Little York" or "Muddy York." A local joke said that a man stooped to pick up a hat from soggy King Street only to discover that the owner had sunk to his forehead in the mud.[25]

British officials disliked York as a frosty backwater where laborers and imported goods were scarce and expensive. A newcomer from temperate Ireland declared, "The heat of Summer is insupportable & the Cold of Winter Intollerable. There are many instances of Persons being frozen to death." At night, wolves preyed on sheep and pigs, while mosquitoes drank human blood. Simcoe's wife found it

"scarcely possible, to write or use my hands, which are always occupied in killing them or driving them away."[26]

York grew faster after 1804, thanks to improved roads and a surge
of new settlers in the hinterland. In 1807 a visitor expressed "sentiments of wonder, on beholding a town which may be termed handsome, reared as if by enchantment, in the midst of a wilderness." York
had several houses "which display a considerable degree of taste," but
the provincial Parliament building remained incomplete with two
brick wings, one for each house, but without the planned dome to
link them.[27]

In April 1813, American troops invaded Canada and briefly occupied York, torching Parliament and looting the stores. York proved
less defensible than Simcoe had predicted. That plundering and burning precedent inspired the British to seize and abuse Washington,
D.C., in revenge a year later. Capitals were unstable and vulnerable
in North America.[28]

After peace returned in 1815, York recovered and prospered thanks
to many immigrants arriving from Scotland and Ireland. Renamed
Toronto in 1834, the city had 9,250 inhabitants, becoming Upper
Canada's leading city. Visiting in 1842, Dickens praised Toronto as
"full of life and motion, bustle, business, and improvement. The
streets are well paved, and lighted with gas; the houses are large and
good, the shops excellent." Dickens had bestowed no such praise on
Washington.[29]

Unlike Washington, Mexico City was populous, grand, and in a
sublime setting. Fanny Calderón de la Barca, the wife of a Spanish
ambassador, praised "the superb valley of Mexico, celebrated in all
parts of the world, with its framework of magnificent mountains,
its snow-crowned volcanoes, great lakes, and fertile plains." The
American diplomat Joel Poinsett thought that Mexico City "at a distance . . . surpasses in appearance any other city in North America"
owing to "the size and magnificence of the churches" replete with
"towers and spires."[30]

Mexico City was also ancient, beginning as Tenochtitlan, the capital of the rich and mighty Aztec Empire that had dazzled Spanish *conquistadores* as grander than any city in Spain. Destroying Tenochtitlan in a bloody conquest, they built Mexico City from the stones of ruined palaces and sacred pyramids. The victors imposed a grid of square blocks between straight streets, with the central plaza bounded on one side by a palace for the king's viceroy who ruled over "New Spain." Another side of the plaza had a vast Gothic cathedral, begun in 1573, with "two lofty, ornamented towers" and external walls displaying stray Aztec reliefs, including an immense, circular calendar. Calderón de la Barca praised the interior as "immensely rich in gold, silver, and jewels" as well as "some good paintings."[31]

After the revolution of 1821, the Mexican republic reinterpreted this imperial complex—rather than create a new capital from scratch as the United States did. The revolutionaries removed a huge equestrian statue of a Spanish king from the central square but put it up elsewhere. The republic's president claimed the viceregal palace, renamed the Palacio Nacional, and the cathedral enjoyed centrality in a nation that retained Catholicism as the state religion. The plaza's southwest corner featured the Parián, a public market of shops and stalls filled with flowers, poultry, fruits, and vegetables. Poinsett praised the profusion as "greater than I had seen in any market in Europe or America."[32]

With 124,000 inhabitants in 1813, Mexico City was twenty times bigger than Washington, D.C.—and about forty times grander. Poinsett described the public buildings and churches as "vast and splendid," providing "an air of grandeur . . . wanting in the cities of the United States." A German intellectual, Alexander von Humboldt, thought the city's statues and Baroque palaces "would appear to advantage in the finest streets of Paris, Berlin and [St.] Petersburg."[33]

A sensual capital, Mexico City rang with bells and cheers and teemed with color and pageantry—beside poverty and grime. Indian peasants rowed boats decorated with flowers and laden with vegetables along canals to market. Religious, military, and festive processions often filled the streets with exulting and flashy crowds. Attending bull fights in the arena, Calderón de la Barca praised the "extraordinary variety of brilliant costumes, all lighted up by the eternally deep blue sky" of the high altitude. Common folk wore multicolored serapes, soldiers donned yellow capes, and priests had black cloaks, white surplices, and "large shovel hats." Gentlemen paraded in gold-embroidered coats and hats, with silver buttons and stirrups, and red velvet capes. Attending genteel parties, she marveled at the "display of diamonds and pearls, silks, satins, blondes and velvets" worn by ladies. Within the legislative hall, Calderón de la Barca declared that the "flourish of trumpets" and elaborate uniforms characterized "as anti-republican-looking an assembly as I ever beheld." But she added, "The utmost decorum and tranquility prevailed."[34]

Mexico City had an array of cultural institutions created during the colonial era. "No city of the new continent, without even excepting those of the United States, can display such great and solid scientific establishments as the capital of Mexico," marveled Humboldt. The United States had nothing to match Mexico's Academy of Fine Arts, National Botanic Garden, National University, and School of Mines. Founded in 1551, the university was the oldest in the Americas.[35]

But these institutions suffered from funding cuts after the long wars of independence devastated the country and impoverished the new republic. The grand architecture became seedy from neglect. In 1839, Calderón de la Barca described the national palace as "immense and handsome but ill-kept" and the theater as "on a magnificent scale" but "neglected and falling to ruin." After political turbulence destroyed the Parián, the republic replaced the market with the foundation for a heroic monument to Mexican independence, known as the Zocalo, but the bankrupt government could not afford to complete it, thereby creating a symbol of Mexico's unfulfilled ambitions.[36]

Racial beliefs shaped both Washington and Mexico City but did so in contrasting ways. The American republic favored a racial binary with the free white majority claiming equal rights with one another while dominating African Americans held in slavery. The United

States had reduced Indians to small numbers pushed to the margins, but Native peoples were three-fifths of Mexicans, while mixed-race people composed another fifth, reducing whites to the final fifth. Mexican republicans claimed to have dissolved all racial distinctions into a common citizenship, but whites still monopolized wealth and power.[37]

Although almost all Mexicans were legally free, they suffered from a greater inequality of wealth than did white Americans. Humboldt estimated that the capital had the richest families in the Americas and at least 20,000 homeless "wretches": beggars known as *léperos* and described by Calderón de la Barca as "moving bundles of rags." Poinsett noted the "filthy" mud-brick slums behind grand avenues "lined with handsome stone buildings." He described the beggars as "Indians and Mestizos, lively and extremely civil, asking alms with great humility, and pouring out prayers and blessings with astonishing volubility."[38]

Arriving "direct from the United States to this country," Calderón de la Barca marveled at the Mexican contrast. She praised the northern republic's flourishing villages with churches, stores, and homes painted white or red. Put up in the hurry of prosperity, they would "never make fine ruins"—in contrast to the stone palaces and cathedrals of Mexico City. In the hyper-commercialized United States, she found "the past forgotten, the present all in all, and the future taking care of itself." By contrast in Mexico "everything reminds us of the past; of the conquering Spaniards who seemed to build for eternity. . . . It is the present that seems like a dream, a pale reflection of the past." Noting that the "hard-working, independent, and stiff-necked" North Americans coveted Mexico, she worried that, in the future, conquered Mexicans would find "their cathedral turned into a large meetinghouse and all painted white—the silver railing melted down, the silver transformed into dollars [and] the Virgin's pearls sold to the highest bidder."[39]

North Americans rejected republican solidarity with Mexico on cultural and racial grounds, denying common cause with a mixed-race people of Catholic faith. American leaders felt even greater antipathy toward Haiti, a Catholic nation formed from a French colony overthrown by rebelling slaves. Fearing that the Haitians would export their revolution to the American South, the United States refused to recognize Haiti.[40]

Haitians' triumph over slavery defined the new nation, whose flag adapted the French Tricolor but eliminated the white third. The constitution limited citizenship and land ownership to people of African descent (but honored a few trusted whites with fictive status as Blacks). Offering citizenship to any immigrant of African ancestry, Haiti welcomed escaped slaves from around the Caribbean. A Haitian president explained that his republic had a "sacred obligation to never recognize any slave on its territory," therefore "every individual that sets foot on Haitian soil is free." He invited all "children of Africa" to come to Haiti to enjoy freedom and citizenship. At nearby Jamaica, a British admiral warned against attacking Haiti because the people were "very tenacious of their liberty and proud of being free."[41]

Port-au-Prince served as Haiti's capital. Battered by earthquakes, hurricanes, and wars, the capital appeared reassembled from scraps of an older, grander city. Other than a few merchants' houses of brick, the residences were wooden, flimsy, and two-stories tall. Although better suited to resist earthquakes, the structures suffered from massive fires, which swept through the town in 1820, 1822, 1827, and 1843. The dirt streets gullied and became impassible in tropical rains. The city's premier building, the Palais du Gouvernement, former residence of the French governor, housed the president. Because Haitians feared another French invasion, the city had two forts to guard approaches from the interior and a battery of cannons to protect the harbor.[42]

Most white visitors mourned the lost colonial regime as "opulent," so they dwelled on signs of collapse and disrepair in Port-au-Prince. A champion of slavery dismissed the nation's leaders as "lunatics," their people as "absorbed in vice, living in sloth and sensuality, careless of everything," and Port-au-Prince as "only remarkable for ruins and every species of filth and uncleanliness." This critic did not consider the challenges of maintaining grand structures in a land of earthquakes, hurricanes, and tropical heat and humidity. Nor did he reflect on the difficulties of rebuilding a city and nation ravaged by war and imperiled by foreign invaders bent, like him, on reimposing slavery.[43]

Some visitors looked more closely to reach a balanced perspective. After lamenting the many burned and ruined plantations, the missionary John Candler praised "the freedom and physical happiness of those who were once slaves in this land, but who are oppressed no longer." The British consul, Charles Mackenzie, regretted that Port-au-Prince lacked comfort and elegance beyond the presidential palace, but the common people enjoyed ample food at reasonable prices. Mackenzie also marveled that the republic's leaders would "associate on terms of familiarity with the lowest member in the scale of society, without any feeling of degradation." No slave in Washington, D.C., could say the same of the leaders in the United States.[44]

Poor and militarized, Port-au-Prince was the most embattled of American capitals, but sympathetic visitors saw hope in the cheerful welcome and festive gatherings by Haitians proud of having defeated powerful enslavers. For all their troubles, Haitians benefited from freedom, for their numbers doubled between 1804 and 1824, in stark contrast to the era of slavery when deaths annually had exceeded births. Heavy imports of enslaved Africans had sustained the colonial population. While the free people were healthier, they produced smaller crops for export. To assert their freedom, most people raised subsistence crops on small farms rather than cultivate sugar cane as workers on big plantations. "They do not, and they will not work hard to please anybody," Candler noted.[45]

Port-au-Prince suffered more from war than any other capital in North America, but all of them experienced invasion and partial destruction: York in 1813, Washington in 1814, New Echota in 1832, and Mexico City in 1847–1848. Their scars revealed the dangers unleashed by the revolution that had created the United States. Citizens of that first American republic disliked British persistence in

Canada and rejected solidarity with Natives, Haitians, and Mexicans. The leaders of the United States feared their neighbors as havens for Indians and runaway slaves and potential sources of subversion.

But American citizens also feared one another as potential threats to their precious Union. In 1832, the elderly chief justice of the Supreme Court, John Marshall, reviewed the tangled history of his divided nation to conclude, "The Union has been preserved thus far by miracles. I fear they cannot continue." They did not, for nineteen years later, the Union collapsed in a civil war that took more than 800,000 lives. In that conflict, Americans confronted their greatest fear.[46]

"Le 1er, Juillet 1801, Toussaint L'Ouverture," engraving by Eugène Marie François Villain. While God approves from above, Touissaint L'Ouverture presents a constitution for the people of Saint-Domingue (now Haiti). Library of Congress 2004669332.

ONE ❧ CONSTITUTIONS

George Washington grew up in Virginia on the transatlantic and colonial margins of the British Empire. As the owner of fifty slaves and 10,000 acres, his father belonged to the gentry that governed Virginia. After the death of his older brother, Washington inherited the estate and secured even greater wealth by marrying Martha Custis, a widow. That fortune provided the foundation and connections on which ability could build influence and power in an unequal society. "Would Washington have ever been Commander of the Revolutionary Army or President of the United

States, if he had not married the rich widow of Mr. Custis?" John
Adams later mused.[1]

During the 1750s, Washington served as a colonial army officer
fighting the French and their Indian allies on Virginia's frontier. He
championed expansion westward beyond the Appalachian Mountains
into the Ohio and Mississippi Valleys, but Washington struggled to
overcome rivalries between the British colonies, each pursuing its
narrow interest at the expense of others. In 1756, Washington insisted
that there was "Nothing I more sincerely wish than a union of the
Colonys in this time of Eminent danger." He looked to the British to
coordinate the colonies and longed for a commission and command
in the British army.[2]

Washington never got that royal commission, and, during the
1760s, Britain alienated colonists by imposing taxes levied by Parliament, a legislature that did not and could not represent the colonists. As a speculator in frontier lands, Washington also resented
British efforts to restrict colonial expansion westward. He supported
the "Patriots" who emerged in every colony to resist British measures. Losing confidence in the British Empire, Washington saw a
new potential for an American union that could claim the West by
pursuing independence.[3]

In April 1775, war erupted between Patriots and Britons, who
got support from American Loyalists. A Continental Congress of
delegates from thirteen colonies took charge of the war effort and
appointed Washington to lead the Continental Army. A tall, strong
man with erect posture and great dignity, he looked the part of a

*Previous page, clockwise from top, left: "George Washington (1732–1799),"
engraving by J. Hinton, from the Universal Magazine, c. 1784.* Library of
Congress 2004668035. *"John Adams (1735–1826)," engraving by Cornelius
Tiebout, 1796.* Library of Congress 2014645329. *"Temple of Liberty," engraving, by
Jared W. Bell, 1834. This engraving insists that the preservation of American
liberty depends on perpetuating the Union.* Library of Congress 2008661765.

general. Washington had to manage an army of Virginians, Carolinians, Pennsylvanians, New Yorkers, and New Englanders, all deeply suspicious of one another and united only by dread of British taxes and troops. In private, Washington shared some of those prejudices, deriding New Englanders as "an exceeding[ly] dirty & nasty people." But in public he "hoped that all Distinctions of Colonies will be laid aside" in "the great and common cause in which we are all engaged."[4]

His troops were slow to get the message. During the winter of 1775–1776, Massachusetts soldiers taunted and hurled snowballs at Virginia riflemen until a thousand men erupted in a massive brawl. A soldier recalled "biting and gouging on the one part, and knockdown on the other with as much apparent fury as the most deadly enemy could create." In a rage, Washington rode up, dismounted, and "with an iron grip seized two tall, brawny, athletic, savage-looking riflemen by the throat, keeping them at arm's length, alternately shaking and talking to them." The brawlers broke and fled "at the top of their speed in all directions." Washington would make an American army if he had to choke every soldier in it.[5]

Washington confronted a contradiction: a revolution in the name of liberty demanded unity, sacrifice, and discipline, but most citizens defined liberty as the pursuit of individual gain. A divided and weak Congress could procure little material support for the army from fractious states and civilians who hoped that someone else would sacrifice to win the war for them. Enduring eight long, hard years of war, a few thousand common soldiers fought for a people largely indifferent to their hunger and rags.[6]

Far from united in support of independence, at least a fifth of the people remained loyal to Britain—and many more just wanted to be left alone on their farms. Loyalists cherished British rule as a source of prosperity and order, so they distrusted the Patriot leaders as reckless demagogues. The revolution became a brutal civil war, as Patriots and Loyalists fought to suppress one another and to pressure the wavering into taking a side.[7]

In addition to seeking independence, Patriots fought for a radical form of government: a republic where common men elected their leaders. Republicanism defied the monarchs and aristocrats who governed Britain and other European powers. Attacking the British colonial order as artificial and corrupt, Patriots promised an equal and open competition for property and office. Merit rather than connections would earn wealth and leadership in this new order. That promise appealed to artisans in towns and farmers in the country.[8]

But the political experiment was risky, for past republics had been unstable and short-lived, collapsing into anarchy until a military despot seized power to restore order. Washington warned his countrymen, "There is a natural and necessary progression from the extreme of Anarchy to the extreme of Tyranny, and . . . arbitrary power is most easily established on the ruins of Liberty abused to Licentiousness." Americans blamed failed republics on a "licentious" people lacking a quality known as "virtue": a purposeful self-restraint that promoted the common good. But most Americans fell short. Washington complained that "notwithstanding all the public virtue which is ascribed to these people, there is no nation under the Sun" that "pay[s] greater adoration to money than they do."[9]

Washington concluded that the Union needed a stronger government with the coercive "energy" to compel people to pay taxes and fight their enemies. Washington regretted the weak confederation that the Patriots had formed to unite their states during the war. Lacking common bonds as Americans, most people identified with their particular state and distrusted outsiders. Carolinians resented Virginians almost as much as New Yorkers despised New Englanders. In 1777, a disgusted congressman assured a friend: "Rely on it, our Confederacy is not founded on Brotherly Love."[10]

Not until November 1777, more than a year after declaring independence, did Congress agree on "Articles of Confederation and Perpetual Union"—and it took nearly four more years to persuade all of the states to ratify that constitution. Patriots wanted a confederation just strong enough to wage war and persuade France to make an alliance against Britain. By keeping peace among their states, they also hoped to prevent the sort of bloody wars that had roiled a divided Europe. Only by forming a union could states define their boundaries and preserve authority within those bounds. Lacking a common sense of nationality, Americans needed a union to manage their differences and distrust.[11]

But Patriots also meant to keep Congress too weak to interfere in the domestic policies of the member states. Having fought against Britain's centralizing power, few wanted to create a consolidated nation. While the pressures of war pushed states together, the dread of central power kept pulling them apart. The smaller states—New Jersey, Delaware, Rhode Island, and New Hampshire—feared domination by the larger ones, including Massachusetts, New York, and Virginia. Under the Articles, the states conceded only a few, limited powers to Congress: to wage war, conduct diplomacy, and arbitrate disputes between them. To satisfy small states, each delegation cast a single vote, so little Rhode Island had as much weight as vast Virginia. On the major issues of war and peace, only a supermajority of nine states (out of thirteen) could commit the confederacy.[12]

The Articles built an alliance of states rather than a cohesive nation. John Adams characterized Congress as a "diplomatic assembly" of ambassadors from thirteen sovereign states. Congress was *not* a national legislature that could frame laws and impose them on the states or citizens. Able only to request, Congress relied on state legislatures to adopt and execute essential laws, such as those to recruit soldiers. Congress also lacked the powers, long exercised by the British Crown over colonies, to regulate trade or veto state laws. "We have no coercive or legislative Authority," declared a North Carolina congressman, who added "that the states alone had Power to act coercively against their Citizens."[13]

In early 1781, the confederation verged on collapse as the Continental Army suffered from mutinies by unpaid, starving, and ragged soldiers. New enlistments dwindled while desertions soared. Washington's army shrank to just 3,500 men in the spring. Respect for Congress dissolved into mockery, suspicion, and contempt. With help from a French fleet and army, Washington rescued the tottering country by trapping a British army at Yorktown in Virginia, compelling its surrender in October. British support for the war collapsed, leading to a peace treaty completed in 1783 that recognized American independence within generous boundaries that stretched westward to the Mississippi.[14]

Some congressmen wanted to create a stronger national government before peace dissolved the army. Led by Gouverneur Morris, his cousin Robert Morris, and Alexander Hamilton, these congressmen sought to rally the troops to pressure the states to grant Congress the power to tax people. Then Congress could pay soldiers and pension officers. But the scheme horrified Washington as it would "open the flood Gates of Civil discord" and "deluge our rising Empire in Blood." He would show virtue by defending civilian rule. In March 1783, Washington persuaded his officers to stand down. Hamilton expressed dismay: "I confess could force prevail I should almost wish to see it employed. I have an indifferent opinion of the honesty of this country, and ill-forebodings as to its future system."[15]

Congress discharged the troops without paying them and, in December, Washington resigned his command and returned to civilian life. Only twenty congressmen attended that resignation because just seven states sent delegations to the increasingly irrelevant Congress. In a "solemn and affecting spectacle," Washington projected a dignified and selfless devotion to the republican cause: a precious rarity among his squabbling countrymen. By surrendering power, Washington rejected the example of Julius Caesar, a military commander who had betrayed the ancient Roman republic. Thomas Jefferson exulted that Washington had "prevented this revolution from being closed, as most others have been, by a subversion of that liberty it was intended to establish."[16]

Refugees

During the war, thousands of enslaved people had fled to seek freedom by helping the British fight the war, for most Blacks regarded Britons as truer champions of liberty. At war's end, Patriots demanded that the British restore runaway slaves to their masters, who included Washington and Jefferson. But the departing British commander in North America, Sir Guy Carleton, considered the runaways as free and no longer anyone's property. Withdrawn to the Bahamas or Nova Scotia, the former slaves obtained freedom but not land, which kept them poor, so most moved on to Sierra Leone, a new British colony in western Africa.[17]

During 1783 and 1784, 60,000 Loyalists fled as refugees to British colonies: the Bahamas, Quebec, Nova Scotia, or its offshoot, New Brunswick. The imperial government provided free land, seed grain, tools, and provisions during their first two years on the land. In the northern colonies, common families received 100 to 300 acres, enough for a farm, while officers and officials got up to 5,000 acres.[18]

British colonial officials sought to cast their empire as morally superior to the nearby American republic, which suffered from economic depression and political turmoil during the 1780s. Quebec's new governor, Lord Dorchester (formerly Sir Guy Carleton), insisted that Americans of the republic "should on all occasions perceive how much they are fallen, and the loyalists find, upon every comparison, strong reasons to congratulate themselves upon having persevered in their duty."[19]

But the Loyalist influx increased political strife in Quebec, where the governor and his council governed without an elected assembly. Lacking any experience with an assembly, the Francophone peasants, known as *habitants*, accepted political exclusion so long as the colony did not tax them or interfere with the Catholic Church. On the governing council, British officials sided with the Francophone landlords, known as *seigneurs*, to form a "French Party" that opposed reform as the slippery slope to an American-style revolution. They insisted that a largely Francophone and Catholic colony could best resist subversion by American republicanism.[20]

The French Party faced opposition from a "British Party" composed of Protestant and Anglophone tradesmen and merchants, who clustered in the towns of Montreal and Quebec City. Only 2,000 before the war, their number grew during the 1780s, with the influx of 8,000 Loyalist refugees. The British Party sought to Anglicize the colony by making English the official language; introducing the English common law; adopting freehold land tenures; and securing an elected assembly. But they wanted only Anglophone Protestants to vote and hold office. In Quebec, a British minority resented that imperial officials favored the French majority.[21]

The turmoil in Quebec dismayed imperial officials in London, who imposed a top-down compromise designed by Lord Grenville. In 1791, Parliament adopted Grenville's Canada Constitutional Act, which divided Quebec into two new provinces: "Upper Canada" along the Great Lakes and "Lower Canada" in the lower St. Lawrence Valley including Montreal and Quebec City. The division was cultural as well as geographic, for Francophones predominated in Lower Canada while Anglophone Loyalists prevailed in Upper Canada.[22]

The Canada Constitutional Act reflected the lessons of the revolution as understood by Britons and Loyalists who rejected republicanism. To avert popular discontent, Parliament vowed never again to tax the colonists for a revenue. Indeed, taxes were lower in Canada than in the United States, where the new leaders had to raise more money to pay heavy war debts. In a rich irony, discontented Americans could reduce their burden by moving to Canada to resume their allegiance as British subjects. In 1800 a newcomer explained why he had left the republican Union: "We fought seven years to get rid of taxation, and now we are taxed more than ever!"[23]

By providing each colony with an assembly elected by landowners, Grenville sought "a juster & more effectual security against the growth of a republican or independent spirit, than any which could be derived from a Government more arbitrary in its form or principles." British leaders defined the assembly as a royal favor, rather than as a popular right, and as the last, not the first, step toward a more representative government. The assembly had to share power with a "legislative council" of colonial notables, who served in the upper house of the legislature. Nominated by the governor and appointed by the Crown, council members served for life.[24]

Both houses of the legislature faced constraint by a powerful governor, who served at the Crown's pay and pleasure. He could summon, suspend, or dissolve a legislative session. The governor appointed the Speaker of the legislative council and could veto any Speaker chosen by the assembly as well as any bill, and the governor's veto was complete, without any provision for an override. Nor could legislators review executive measures or expenditures. To become law, an assembly initiative had to win assent by the legislative council, governor, and imperial bureaucracy in London, where the Crown had up to two years to kill a colonial law.[25]

Parliament designed the Canadian governments to avoid popular discontent *and* to discourage popular participation. On the one hand, the British promoted a content and inert public by minimizing taxes and providing an assembly. On the other hand, the imperial rulers also restricted electoral power to prevent demagogues from fomenting unrest. Lord Thurlow explained that the British "have given them more civil liberty, without political liberty." In sum, the British worked to deny the colonists both the civil motives and the political means for agitation.[26]

The contrast between the Canadian mixed constitution and American republicanism reveals the double difference made by the revolution. American state constitutions made elections more frequent, important, and accessible. Where a colonial voter could elect only assemblymen, the postwar American citizen chose his governor, lieutenant governor, and state senators as well as assembly representatives. Republican logic maximized the popular sovereignty that the British mixed constitution sought to contain. During the 1780s, however, it was far from clear that the republican model would outlast the Brit-

ish counterrevolutionary alternative in North America. The balance
of power would hinge on which regime could control the vast and
fertile land south of the Great Lakes and west of the Appalachian
Mountains.[27]

Pivot

By drawing a new border through the Great Lakes, the Paris peace
treaty of 1783 gave up key British forts, including Detroit and Niagara, to the Union. Cast on the American side of the border, Native
peoples felt betrayed by the treaty made by their British allies. A
Creek chief wondered whether the king meant "to sell his friends as
slaves, or only give our lands to his and our enemies?" Natives wished
to live as free people between, rather than be divided by, the American Union and the British Empire.[28]

Native pressure persuaded Quebec's governor to hang on to the
forts in defiance of the peace treaty. The home government endorsed
that retention because the Americans had violated the treaty by
blocking British merchants from collecting prewar debts and preventing Loyalists from reclaiming confiscated properties. By keeping
the posts and cultivating Indian allies, the British also prepared for the
collapse of the weak United States, a collapse that seemed imminent
during the 1780s.[29]

During the summer of 1783, chiefs from thirty-five Indian nations
of the Great Lakes and Ohio Valley met to form a confederation. They
vowed to resist settler expansion westward beyond the Ohio River.
Rejecting American efforts to divide and conquer, the chiefs denied
that any single Indian nation could cede land without common consent. Americans dreaded the new Indian confederacy as a threat to
the expansion deemed essential to the survival of their own union.[30]

The American confederation claimed the land north and west of
the Ohio River. To attract settlers and sell land, Congress forsook the
unpopular British precedent of keeping dependent colonies. Instead,
Congress formed temporary territories that eventually would enter

the Union as new states on a par with the original thirteen. A series of Northwest Ordinances created a process for surveying townships and lots on a grid plan for sale to land speculators and settlers. The ordinances also established a territorial government with an appointed governor, secretary, and three judges. Once a territory had 60,000 free inhabitants, they could draft a republican state constitution and apply to Congress for admission to the Union.[31]

But settlers defied the federal government as impotent. Pressing across the Ohio River, squatters staked claims, built cabins, cleared land, planted corn, fought Indians, and threatened to create their own republic. A bold squatter nailed a notice to a tree: "I do certify that all mankind, agreeable to every constitution formed in America, have an undoubted right to pass into every vacant country, and to form their constitution." Federal troops burned a few cabins and warned off the squatters, but they returned in larger numbers once the soldiers moved on. A congressional leader, John Jay, worried, "Shall we not fill the Wilderness with white Savages, and will they not become more formidable to us than the tawny ones who now inhabit it?"[32]

Federal weakness emboldened adventurers to try to create their own countries in the vast and fertile country west of the Appalachians. Seeking to make money by selling land titles to settlers, adventurers recruited ambitious men by appointing them as judges and militia officers. Such posts paid fees and salaries and generated the honors coveted by competitive Americans eager for distinction. The adventurers' model was Vermont, where the brothers Ethan and Ira Allen had created a republic by breaking away from New York during the 1770s.[33]

In the Tennessee settlements, adventurers created the state of Franklin by seceding from North Carolina in 1784. Leading settlers resented that North Carolina had stinted them in patronage and large land grants. To secure settler support, the adventurers founded a judicial system to register land claims and resolve disputes, and they organized a militia to fight Indians who resisted the intrusion on their land.[34]

The Franklinites sought congressional recognition of their new state by admission to the Union on a par with the old states. During the 1780s, however, congressmen balked at recognizing Vermont or Franklin for fear of setting a precedent that would inspire more bids to divvy up old states. For example, Virginia's leaders wanted to stop Kentucky from seceding. Jefferson worried that "our several states will crumble to atoms by the spirit of establishing every little canton into a separate state." The original thirteen states managed the Union as their club to preserve boundaries and revenues by frustrating secessionist movements.[35]

Denied recognition by Congress, the Franklin project faltered. During the late 1780s, North Carolina's leaders won back many leading settlers with land grants and patronage appointments. In 1788, Franklin's governor, John Sevier, sought to bolster settler support by attacking and burning Cherokee villages and massacring chiefs who had surrendered. But that brutality provoked Cherokee revenge raids that Sevier could not repel, and that failure increased defections to North Carolina's rule, completing the collapse of Franklin.[36]

In the federal domain north and west of the Ohio River, Congress sought to block the emergence of another Vermont or Franklin. To do so, Congress had to impress settlers by dispossessing Indians, but the United States lacked the money to raise enough troops for the job. So settlers conducted their own brutal war that destroyed Native villages and cabins, butchering men, women, and children. A Virginian described the Ohio Valley settlements as "theatres of violence, rapine & villainy." Unable to control settlers or defeat Indians, the federal government appeared irrelevant in the West.[37]

Settlement beyond the Appalachian Mountains threatened to alienate settlers from the American Union. Westerners could best get their crops to market by water, either via the Great Lakes and the St. Lawrence River to British Quebec or southwestward down the Ohio and Mississippi Rivers to Spanish New Orleans. Worried that economic interest would entice settlers out of the United States and into an association with the British or Spanish empires, a congressman regarded "every emigrant to that country from the Atlantic states as forever lost to the Confederacy."[38]

To promote western secession, the British and Spanish sent secret agents into the new settlements, where they found local leaders seeking contingency plans for the anticipated collapse of the United States. Washington worried, "The Western settlers . . . stand as it were upon a pivot—the touch of a feather would turn them any way." Thanks to their trade "with the Spaniards on their right & rear, or the British on their left, they will become a distinct people from us" with "different interests, & instead of adding strength to the Union, may in case of a[n American] rupture with either of those powers, be a formidable & dangerous neighbor."[39]

Some eastern leaders wanted to block western settlement because so many common people fled westward to evade debts and the heavy taxes that states had imposed to finance the costs of war. Eastern creditors complained, and legislators worried that the exodus increased the tax burden on people who stayed behind—which then drove even more families to flee across the mountains. And easterners feared that the settlers would secede to form governments that could menace the eastern confederation. Regarding settlers as "fit instruments ready to be laid hold of by [our] Enemies," a congressman insisted that, if the settlements were "not under the general Controul, the sooner exterminated the better."[40]

But the confederation was too weak to stem the swelling tide of western settlement. Addressing easterners, a Kentucky settler demanded, "Do you think to prevent the emigration from a barren Country loaded with Taxes and impoverished with debts to the most luxurious and fertile Soil in the world?" Despite an Indian war, the western population grew three times faster than did that of the eastern states during the 1780s.[41]

That western growth also alarmed the Spanish governors of Louisiana and Florida. Louisiana's Baron de Carondelet, warned his superiors: "This vast and restless population, driving the Indian tribes continually before them and upon us, is endeavoring to gain all the

vast continent occupied by the Indians between the Ohio and Mississippi Rivers, the Gulf of Mexico, and the Appalachian Mountains." A
governor of Florida feared the settlers as "distinguished from savages
only in their color, language, and the superiority of their depraved
cunning and untrustworthiness." Spanish officials worried that hostile settlers would sweep across the Mississippi River and Great Plains
to take New Mexico and eventually Mexico, the silver-rich core
of the Spanish Empire. A colonial governor insisted that America's
"needy adventurers" believed that they "need only scratch the soil in
the Spanish American dominions to find fistfuls of gold and silver"
and would commit "whatever lawless act, however crazy or extreme,
to realize their nonsensical dreams."[42]

The immense British and Spanish frontier provinces were vulnerable because so thinly populated by colonists. Sprawled along the
entire western side of the Mississippi River, Louisiana claimed about
828,000 square miles but had only 20,000 colonists in 1782, and Florida had merely 4,000. In 1790, Upper Canada had just 14,000 colonists
in settlements scattered along 1,500 miles of waterways. In Florida,
Louisiana, and Upper Canada, colonists lived in small pockets surrounded by Native peoples.[43]

To keep American settlers away, the British and Spanish cultivated alliances with Indians by bestowing presents of guns and
ammunition. The Spanish relied on a mixed-blood chief, Alexander McGillivray, the son of a Creek woman, Sehoy Marchand, and
a Scottish merchant and Loyalist, Lachlan McGillivray (based in
South Carolina). Well educated in Charleston and dressed in gentility, Alexander McGillivray ran two plantations with 60 slaves and
300 cattle. He assured the Creeks that he "was a mestizo and yet
at the same time Indian like them." Understanding imperial rivalries and dreading American expansion, he worked to sustain Creek
autonomy. McGillivray assured a Louisiana governor, "The Crown
of Spain will Gain & Secure a powerful barrier in these parts against
the ambitious and encroaching Americans." Deriding the United
States as too weak to survive, McGillivray predicted that the kings

of Spain, Britain, and France "must settle the matter by dividing America between them."[44]

In 1784, Spain tried to slow settler expansion by closing New Orleans to American trade via the Mississippi. Imperial officials reasoned that fewer settlers would move west if they could not prosper by shipping their flour, hemp, corn, pork, and lumber downriver to reach the global market at New Orleans. A barely literate Kentuckian warned that, without access to that port, "our Weston Cuntery is nothing." But closure risked infuriating settlers, who might descend the Mississippi in armed force to seize New Orleans. A rabble-rouser insisted, "The Americans are amphibious animals. They cannot be confined to the land alone. Tillage and commerce are their elements. . . . Both they will have, or perish." With only 400 regular soldiers to defend Louisiana in 1787, Spanish officials had to proceed carefully.[45]

To reduce that danger, Spanish agents offered a carrot as well as a stick. They would reopen that trade if westerners seceded from the United States to accept a dependent association with the Spanish Empire. By granting a few special licenses to trade at New Orleans, the Spanish tried to buy the "interest" of western leaders. The chief Spanish client was James Wilkinson, an American general who settled in Kentucky, where he prospered as a politician and merchant dealing in tobacco. Visiting New Orleans, Wilkinson offered allegiance to Spain in return for a license to trade and an annual pension. To hasten secession, he advised Spain "to assert every Power & every Art" to "increase the animosity of the Eastern and Western People of America."[46]

Fluid and conditional loyalties prevailed in the West among a restless people ever moving and bargaining. Having fought for America's independence, Wilkinson felt "at Liberty, after having contended for Her happiness, to seek for my own." Baron de Carondelet barely trusted people "accustomed to changing their domicile just as they do a shirt." Another Louisiana governor agreed: "The sanguine Spirit of an American leads Him to interpret every doubtful Measure to His own advantage." Westerners' self-interest trumped attachment to the United States, a weak confederation with dim prospects during the 1780s.[47]

Colonial officials also enticed Americans to move across the border to become Spanish subjects in Louisiana or Florida. In return for large grants of free land (240 to 800 acres per person) and access to the New Orleans market, the new subjects swore allegiance to Spain and pledged to defend Louisiana against any invader. By recruiting some Americans as subjects, the Spanish meant to build a militia to repel raids or invasion from the other side of the border. But attracting Americans contradicted Spain's efforts to sustain Native alliances by keeping settlers away. McGillivray warned the Spanish: "filling up your country with those accursed republicans is like placing a common thief as a guard on your door and giving him the key."[48]

During the 1780s and early 1790s, about 20,000 Americans settled in Louisiana as Spanish subjects. Some, including Daniel Boone, located near St. Louis, but many more moved to the Natchez District, on the lower Mississippi, where the Spanish Crown subsidized tobacco cultivation. "May God keep us Spanish," wrote one grateful newcomer.[49]

The British also recruited American settlers to strengthen Upper Canada. The colony's first governor, John Graves Simcoe, promised at least 200 acres of land per family in return for small fees and an oath of allegiance. Between 1793 and 1796, Simcoe attracted about 12,000 newcomers called the Late Loyalists.[50]

During the 1780s, the United States lacked any evident "Manifest Destiny" to dominate the West. Military defeats by an Indian confederacy frustrated the frontier land sales that the Union desperately needed for revenue and credibility. American weakness emboldened British and Spanish governors, who retained border forts, intrigued with Indian chiefs and leading settlers, and manipulated access to external markets. British Canada and Spanish Louisiana offered alternative polities that enticed western settlers to forsake the United States. Would the Mississippi watershed ultimately belong to an expansive republic or to European empires allied to Native peoples?

The empires and Indians were the best bet, for the American confederacy was imploding.[51]

Ashes

The long, hard war of the revolution had devastated the American economy and inflicted widespread misery by destroying farms, plantations, and towns while uprooting thousands of refugees. British warships captured 1,100 merchant ships, disrupting the export trade essential to prosperity. Economic historians find a 30 percent decline in national income between 1774 and 1790: "America's greatest income slump ever," and an "economic disaster."[52]

Patriot leaders hoped that independence would restore and enhance prosperity through free trade with the entire world. Instead, Americans suffered from postwar British trade restrictions and found that the Spanish and French also discouraged free trade to favor their own colonies. In a world of mercantile empires, Americans were left on the outside looking in. During the mid-1780s, a trade depression depleted the money supply, deprived artisans of work and farmers of markets, and soured relations between impoverished debtors and impatient creditors.[53]

Congress could not challenge the British terms of trade for want of a navy or the authority to coordinate the trade policies of all thirteen states. By 1785, the bankrupt Congress had sold off the last of its warships and reduced its army to just 300 men. Weak and diffuse, the confederacy had become a diplomatic joke in Europe. Spain's ambassador reported that America was "almost without Government, without a Treasury, or means of obtaining money, and torn between hope and fear of whether or not their Confederation can be consolidated." Britain's Lord Sheffield declared that the United States "should not be, for a long time, either to be feared or regarded as a nation."[54]

Giving up hope, many congressmen stayed home, often depriving Congress of a quorum, while state governments adopted clashing trade regulations and bickered over their borders. Most states stopped

paying contributions to Congress, starving the Confederation of
operating funds and the money to pay interest on a massive war debt.
A North Carolina delegate sadly concluded "that the Confederated
compact is no more than a rope of sand, and if a more efficient Government is not obtained, a dissolution of the Union must take place."[55]

That dissolution seemed imminent in 1786, when the American
minister of foreign affairs, John Jay, negotiated with the Spanish
ambassador, Don Diego María de Gardoqui. For a period of twenty-
five years, Jay agreed to barter away navigation rights on the Mississippi River for Spanish commercial concessions in overseas trade.
By opening Spanish ports to American flour and fish, those concessions would benefit farmers and merchants in the northeast, where Jay
lived. Mired in an economic depression, northeastern leaders saw a
Spanish deal as their salvation.[56]

But Jay's proposal outraged southern leaders, who had speculated
in western lands that would lose value without trade access to New
Orleans. Charging northern leaders with a power grab meant to
weaken them, southern leaders warned that westerners would secede
and southerners would join them, dissolving the Confederation. Virginia's governor, Patrick Henry, vowed that he "would rather part with
the confederation than relinquish the navigation of the Mississippi."[57]

In turn, northern leaders accused southerners of grasping for
greater power by keeping the Northeast mired in depression. Some
northern leaders contemplated seceding to create their own union.
That prospect unhinged Virginia's James Monroe, who regarded
Pennsylvania as the key state in the balance of power: "If a dismemberment takes place that State must not be added to the eastern
scale. It were as well to use force to prevent it as to defend ourselves
afterwards." It had come to that: dueling threats of secession and
civil war.[58]

A corrupt bargain in land helped to postpone the crisis of the
Union. In 1787, Congress sold 3 million acres at the mouths of the
Muskingum and Miami Rivers on the northwest side of the Ohio
River. The price of 9 cents per acre was less than a tenth of what

Congress previously had set as the minimum price. In fact, Congress sold the land for political rather than financial reasons. The buyers belonged to two cartels of influential northerners. Former champions of Jay's deal and restrictions on western settlement, the buyers suddenly became "interested" in trans-Appalachian development. In January 1788, a Virginia congressman marveled, "I think little is to be feared from the Project for ceding the Navigation of the Mississippi to Spain; almost a total change of Sentiment upon that Subject has taken place. The Opposition has acquired great Strength from the Sales of Western Territory; many Inhabitants of the Eastern States of great Influence & powerful Connections have become Adventurers in that Country & are now engaged in forming Settlements at Muskingum, Miamia, &c."[59]

Violent protests by indebted farmers also helped to reunite southern and northern leaders. To evade high taxes and crushing debts, farmers in western and central Massachusetts sought to "regulate" their state government. In 1786 in Massachusetts, hundreds gathered with clubs and firearms to block the county courts from meeting, which prevented lawsuits from foreclosing on farms and livestock. Conservatives blamed a local leader, Daniel Shays, and misnamed the regulation as "Shays's Rebellion." In coastal counties, the state raised an army that marched west to attack and scatter the regulators. But the regulation had shocked conservatives throughout the Union as a threat to private property and social order. They noted smaller-scale regulations in rural pockets from New Hampshire to South Carolina as farmers blocked courthouse sessions and foreclosure sales. A leading Pennsylvanian declared, "The flames of internal insurrection were ready to burst out in every quarter . . . and from one end to the other of the continent; we walked in ashes concealing fire beneath our feet."[60]

Convention

Northern and southern leaders agreed that a collapse of the Union would invite bloody wars between jealous states, which would then invite manipulation, invasion, and domination by foreign empires. Washington feared "becoming the Sport of European politics, which may play one State against another." Benjamin Franklin warned: "Our States are on the point of separation, only to meet hereafter for the purpose of cutting one another's throats."[61]

Reformers longed for a stronger union that could bind the states together in a "peace pact." Otherwise, Jay warned, "Every state would be a little nation, jealous of its neighbors, and anxious to strengthen itself by foreign alliances, against its former friends" in other states. He feared that the Union would split "into three or four independent and probably discordant republics or confederacies, one inclining to Britain, another to France, and a third to Spain, and perhaps played off against each other by the three" empires in perpetual, destructive wars like those that tormented Europe. A dread of internal division bred a fear of foreign manipulation—and both drove the push for a new federal constitution.[62]

A stronger union also could restrain trouble within the states. The republican promise of equal opportunity invited common men to seek democratic reforms in their states or to mount regulations to block unpopular laws. A wealthy Philadelphian complained, "They call it democracy—a mobocracy in my opinion would be more proper. All our laws breathe the spirit of town meetings and porter shops." Conservatives with old money resented men of new wealth with crude manners but political aspirations. Preaching deference, a gentleman insisted that most men should "be content with the station God has assigned them, and not turn politicians when their maker intended them for farmers." Elites insisted that the proper leader needed wealth, higher education, genteel manners, and solidarity with other rich men.[63]

Conservatives became disgusted when many state legislatures adopted debtor relief measures to benefit common farmers at the expense of their creditors. Those measures included issuing inflationary paper money, reducing or delaying taxes, or allowing payment in farm produce rather than scarce cash. Creditors accused states and voters of bad faith and injustice, for relief measures depreciated the value of private property. Conservatives had lost confidence in state governments as too responsive to public opinion, as "too democratic."[64]

Nationalists hoped to kill two political birds with one stone by ditching the ineffectual Articles of Confederation and writing a new federal constitution. While rescuing the federal government from impotence and irrelevance, they would also subordinate the state governments that had become too strong and too democratic: too prone to favor debtors at the expense of creditors. Hamilton attributed the new nationalism to "most men of property in the several states who wish [for] a government of the union able to protect them against domestic violence and the depredations which the democratic spirit is apt to make on property." Contrary to popular mythology, most of the founders did not intend to create a democracy. Instead, they designed a national republic to restrain state democracies, which they blamed for many of the Union's woes during the 1780s. By limiting state power, nationalists hoped to save republican government from a descent into democratic anarchy or a switch to monarchy.[65]

To replace the Articles of Confederation with a national constitution, delegates gathered at a convention in Philadelphia during the summer of 1787. James Madison of Virginia proposed a plan that favored the largest and most populous states, which alarmed the delegates from small states. For nearly a month, the two sides deadlocked with both threatening to bolt and doom the convention. Backing away from the brink in July, the delegates narrowly agreed to a compromise that granted an equal vote to every state in the Senate while allowing the big states more seats in the House of Representatives.[66]

The heated debates over representation exposed a second, even more dangerous, fault line between northern and southern states. Slaves comprised less than 4 percent of the northern population, compared to 40 percent in the South. Determined to protect their property rights in humans, southern delegates worried about entering a more powerful union with northerners critical of slavery. Southerners wanted a union strong enough to defend their states against slave rebellion and foreign invasion but too weak to tax or emancipate slaves.[67]

Some northern delegates outraged southerners by arguing that only free citizens should count in allocating seats in the House of Representatives. By excluding slaves, that proposal would reduce the South's relative weight in the Union. After angry debates, the delegates compromised by mandating that three-fifths of the enslaved people would count in allocating congressional seats and presidential electors to the states. In a second compromise, delegates kept the slave trade open for another twenty years. Third, the delegates agreed to a fugitive slave clause that required northern courts, juries, and sheriffs to force interstate runaways back into southern bondage. A South Carolina delegate later boasted to his constituents, "We have obtained a right to recover our slaves in whatever part of America they may take refuge, which is a right we had not before."[68]

By adopting the "three-fifths clause," prolonging slave importation, and providing a fugitive slave clause, the Federal Constitution defended slavery as the price of a stronger union. When the proposed constitution became public, a Rhode Island clergyman asked, "How does it appear in the sight of Heaven, that *these states*, who have been fighting for liberty . . . cannot agree in any political constitution unless it indulge and authorize them to enslave their fellowmen!" But he reluctantly accepted the new constitution as the only way to avert a "state of anarchy, and probably of civil war." His generation merely bought time, for eventually the United States would divide in a bloody civil war fought over the westward expansion of slavery.[69]

Wrapping up their business in September 1787, the delegates created a powerful president who could, with advice and consent from the Senate, conclude treaties and appoint executive officials and federal judges. The chief executive also had a veto that could only be overridden by two-thirds votes of both houses. A set of compromises, the new constitution had some features to disappoint most of the delegates. Washington thought it merely "the best that could be obtained at this time."[70]

The "Federalist" proponents of a national constitution created a useful fiction: that they served a united and sovereign American people. Hence the Federal Constitution begins with "We the People" rather than "We the States." In fact, few people thought and acted as Americans in 1787. Instead, they were Virginians, New Englanders, Carolinians, New Yorkers, and Pennsylvanians. All primarily shared a distrust of one another. Hamilton warned that only the new constitution could save America from "splitting . . . into an infinity of little, jealous, clashing, tumultuous commonwealths, the wretched nurseries of unceasing discord." Mutual suspicion forced them together to frame a constitution to keep the peace: both between the states and within them, where creditors battled with debtors and slaves might revolt. Federalists asserted an American people as an act of faith, hoping to generate a self-fulfilling prophecy for the future. An American national identity emerged later, slowly, painfully, and partially.[71]

The new constitution needed ratification by nine states to go into operation, but the Federalists faced fierce opposition. Their "Anti-Federalist" opponents warned that the new constitution would centralize power in the hands of an aloof aristocracy. Congress would have fewer members than any state legislature but would rule over thirteen states and a vast western territory. The proposed president also held veto and appointive powers greater than any state governor. Contrary to republican principles, which favored annual elections, representatives would serve for two years, the president for four, and senators for six. Anti-Federalists regarded the large districts, long terms, powerful executive and senate, and distant government as designed for distant elitists to tax and exploit common people with impunity. Because the constitution created a government with greater power than Britain had ever exercised over the colonists, Anti-Federalists charged that the Federalists reversed the revolution by undermining liberty.[72]

A nationalizing constitution alarmed most citizens, who were common farmers with limited educations, parochial perspectives, and suspicions of central power. But the Federalists were better organized for conducting the Union's first political campaign. They rallied most of the wealthy Americans who could best afford to finance that campaign. Lawyers, merchants, speculators, and newspaper publishers welcomed a new government that could protect private property from populist regulators and democratic state legislatures. Creditors also anticipated that a stronger federal regime could fund the public debts generated by the war. As congressmen, constitutional delegates, or Continental officers, Federalists had worked with one another across state lines, so they could better coordinate an interstate campaign than could the dispersed and disconnected Anti-Federalists. Ratification triumphed in mid-1788.[73]

New, controversial, and often ambiguous, the Federal Constitution took shape under the administration of President George Washington, starting in 1789. The Union seemed poised either for future greatness or sudden collapse. Although endowed with immense potential for economic and demographic growth, the United States remained a weak country in a dangerous world of powerful empires. Despite the new constitution, sectional tensions threatened to compound the external danger. The Union seemed like a finely tuned mechanism that all too easily could unravel if one region became too powerful. At the first meeting of Congress, Madison feared "contentions first between federal & antifederal parties, and then between Northern & Southern parties."[74]

To mollify Anti-Federalist voters, Madison pushed to amend the Federal Constitution with guarantees for civil liberties, subsequently known as the Bill of Rights. Approved by Congress and the president in October 1789, ten of Madison's amendments secured the necessary approval from three-quarters of the states by the end of 1791. Protecting individuals against federal abuses, the Bill of Rights did not restrict the states or powerful individuals from abridging civil liberties.[75]

The Bill of Rights left untouched the slavery suffered by a fifth of Americans. In February 1790, Congress rejected petitions from Pennsylvanians seeking a gradual plan to extend liberty "without distinction of colour, to all descriptions of people" and thereby remove "this Inconsistency from the Character of the American People." Most northern congressmen dared not risk the fragile Union by offending southern politicians. Almost every congressman endorsed Madison's resolution "that Congress have no authority to interfere in the emancipation of slaves, or in the treatment of them."76

Instead of freeing slaves, Congress strengthened slavery by adopting the Fugitive Slave Act of 1793. The law denied trial by jury or the protections of habeas corpus to accused runaways. Tacitly permitting kidnappings, so long as the victims were Black, the law empowered bounty hunters who profited by finding and seizing runaways in northern states. Free Blacks protested, but the House refused to receive their petitions. A Georgia congressman bluntly explained, " 'We the people' does not mean them." A maverick congressman, George Thacher of Massachusetts, protested that slavery was "a cancer of immense magnitude that would some time destroy the body politic." But Thacher warned in vain. To retain southern allegiance, the Union had to protect slavery.77

Land

To realize the potential of their new Union, Americans needed to gain control of the West, where the country could create its future through expansion. During the 1790s, the West lay nearby, just across the Appalachian Mountains. The Union had to push back Indians and control settlers or risk losing that vast and fertile region to a rival empire or a secession movement.78

The Indians of the upper Ohio Valley were a mix of Shawnees, Delawares, Mingos, Wyandots, Miamis, and Piankashaws. These Natives were not unchanging primitives clinging to some ancient life of subsistence, for they drank alcohol, wore manufactured cloth, wielded iron hoes and steel axes, and used guns for hunting and war. Enmeshed in the transatlantic market, they procured manufactured goods in exchange for animal pelts taken by hunters. Native dwellings resembled the log cabins of their settler rivals. Natives also acquired horses, pigs, cows, and poultry. The valley's Indians spoke a smattering of English and French and shared spiritual ideas with Christian missionaries. Although adapted to the intruding culture, Natives clung to their distinctive identities and homelands. Despite the partial convergence of frontier cultures, settlers exaggerated differences to justify dispossessing Indians as supposed savages.[79]

But the governing Federalists distrusted most western settlers as ignorant, violent, and indolent—and in need of federal control. The new territorial governor, Arthur St. Clair, sought to teach them "that the Government of the Union was not a mere shadow." Then "their progeny would grow up in habits of Obedience and Respect . . . and the Countless multitudes which will be produced in that vast Region would become the Nerves and Sinews of the Union." By restraining settlers, Federalists sought to convert the West from the Union's greatest threat into its primary asset.[80]

Federalist land policy favored speculators over settlers by mandating a minimum price of $2 per acre, a minimum purchase of 640 acres, and full payment down. Unable to meet such terms, common settlers instead had to buy their 160-acre farms on credit from, and at a markup paid to, wealthy land speculators. Federalists reasoned that a high land price would compel settlers to work harder to raise money, thereby improving their moral characters. Federalists also expected that speculators would become community leaders who could command deference from their common neighbors.[81]

Federal officials wanted to regulate the pace at which Indians receded and settlement advanced by compelling settlers to live in compact and orderly communities led by gentlemen. A slower expansion would buy time for Natives gradually to adapt to the "civilization" dictated by Americans. To promote that adaptation, the federal government bestowed farm tools and domesticated livestock on chiefs. But federal paternalism irritated settlers, who wanted to disperse and grab more Indian land. They welcomed federal power only when deployed against Natives.[82]

That federal power struggled to defeat the Indian confederacy in the Ohio Valley. In 1791, warriors surprised an American army camp, commanded by St. Clair, inflicting a catastrophic defeat that killed 630 soldiers. The victors stuffed the mouths of dead troops with dirt to mock their fatal lust for Indian land. Native victories discredited the government and halted the sale and settlement of land in the federal territory, depriving the Union of desperately needed revenue. Meanwhile, western warfare consumed nearly five-sixths of the federal budget. Staggered by the high cost of defeat, the federal government suspended military operations in 1792 to seek a diplomatic solution. Adopting British colonial precedents, the administration treated chiefs with diplomatic respect and hoped to define a boundary line with forts to separate settlers from Natives. By offering $16,150 in presents, the Federalists sought to buy land and peace.[83]

When the Indians refused to make any land-cession deal, Washington launched a new invasion in 1794. Commanded by Anthony Wayne, federal troops defeated the Indians at Fallen Timbers and destroyed their villages and vast cornfields in the nearby Maumee Valley. Demoralized by the loss of homes and crops, the Indians also resented that British troops had holed up in a nearby fort rather than come to their assistance. Without a reliable British ally, the Indian confederacy dissolved as the distinct nations made separate deals, conceding the southern two-thirds of Ohio to the United States in the Treaty of Greenville of August 1795. American leaders had shattered the parallel effort by Indians to build their own confederation.[84]

The British also backed down from a confrontation with the United States. Embroiled in a massive new European war, the British could ill afford another conflict across the Atlantic. In the Jay Treaty of 1794, the British surrendered the border forts along the southern shores of the Great Lakes to the United States, which at last realized the boundary promised by the Treaty of Paris in 1783.[85]

The European war also persuaded the Spanish to reconcile with the Americans. Fearing a British attack, the Spanish bought American neutrality with generous terms in the Treaty of San Lorenzo concluded in October 1795. Accepting the American version of their border as the 31st parallel, the Spanish abandoned their borderland forts and Indian allies. The Spanish also opened up the Mississippi River to duty-free American trade. With that treaty, the Spanish sacrificed a Native buffer zone.[86]

Disgusted Spanish colonial officials insisted that the treaty cast Indian allies "in the mouth of the wolf" and undermined the security of Louisiana and Mexico. Governor Carondelet tried to sabotage his government's treaty by delaying the surrender of border forts while reviving his intrigues to promote secession by Kentucky and Tennessee. His lieutenant, Manuel Gayoso de Lemos, explained that the Treaty of San Lorenzo would collapse if they could cripple the United States: "Spain made a treaty with the Union, but if this Union is dissolved, one of the contracting parties exists no longer and the other is absolved from her engagements." But the settlers of Natchez rallied to the Americans, so Gayoso belatedly turned over the forts in March 1798. An American official felt astonished by Gayoso's new affection: "We met and saluted in the Spanish manner by kissing! . . . Men's kissing I think a most abominable custom."[87]

The Jay Treaty, the Treaty of Greenville, and the Treaty of San Lorenzo combined to secure an American edge in the West, a vast region that previously had defied federal control. Thanks to these diplomatic triumphs, the Union gained grudging respect from western settlers. As the Indians' resistance receded, western settlement accelerated. In 1805, a traveler noted, "The woods are full of new settlers. Axes were resounding and the trees literally were falling about us as we passed." By 1800, half a million Americans lived west of the Appalachian Mountains, three times as many as in 1790.[88]

Principles

As president, Washington assembled talented men in his cabinet, but to his dismay, the secretary of state, Jefferson, and secretary of the treasury, Hamilton, bickered and undermined one another. Although drawn to radical, new ideas crafted by French philosophers, Jefferson relied on his wealth as a Virginia planter who owned nearly 200 people. Charming and versatile, Jefferson avoided overt disagreements but worked cleverly behind the scenes to promote his views and ruin his enemies. Verbose and confrontational, Hamilton provided a pointed contrast. Born into obscurity in the West Indies, he won rich patrons through conspicuous brilliance. Settling in New York City, he prospered as a lawyer and championed the interests of wealthy men. Jefferson favored a diffuse and consensual union of equal states, while Hamilton meant to build a powerful, centralizing empire like that of Britain.[89]

To establish national credit, Hamilton wanted the Union to assume the states' wartime debts, increasing the federal total to $76 million. He calculated that the annual interest payments of $5 million literally would "interest" public creditors in supporting the new constitutional union; and those creditors were wealthy people whose support seemed essential to Hamilton. Federal customs duties, excise taxes, and western land sales could generate the revenue to pay that interest and finance the government's annual operations. To manage those funds, Hamilton persuaded Congress to create a national bank modeled on the powerful Bank of England. To diversify and accelerate economic development, he promoted a new industrial sector to complement the Union's agricultural base. With this complex program, Hamilton enhanced federal power as a collector of taxes and dispenser of payments.[90]

Hamilton's program outraged many southern congressmen, who feared that the new taxes would, at their region's expense, enrich northern merchants who held so much of the federal debt. To break the deadlock in Congress, Jefferson and Madison brokered a compromise with Hamilton. In return for moving the Union's capital southward to a new city, Washington, D.C., Madison and Jefferson rounded up southern votes for Hamilton's fiscal program. But they soon regretted that deal and organized a political party of fellow "Republicans" to resist the Federalist administration of Washington and Hamilton.[91]

Federalists and Republicans clashed over the degree of democracy needed to sustain republican government. Preaching deference, Federalists insisted that stability required government by an elite secure in the public esteem. Common people should favor gentlemen of superior education, wealth, and status, and those elected officials should enjoy immunity from "licentious" criticism. Every stable society, Federalists believed, accepted inequality. "There must be," a Federalist preached, "rulers and subjects, masters and servants, rich and poor."[92]

Republicans accused the Federalists of betraying the egalitarian legacy of the revolution by centralizing power and increasing taxes. Indeed, Republicans charged their rivals with seeking to impoverish and subdue common people, thereby subverting the republic in favor of monarchy and aristocracy. Republicans promised instead to create a liberal society in which an impartial government would secure equal opportunities for common men by refusing any superior privileges for elites. Republicans claimed that equal rights would reward the industrious poor rather than perpetuate the idle rich. Without the allegedly artificial distortions of an elitist government, society would naturally and properly promote equality. Freed from parasitical Federalist rulers, common people could enjoy, as one Republican put it, "that happy mediocrity of condition" essential for a true republic to endure.[93]

White supremacy limited the Republican vision of democracy and equality. While seeking equality for white men, most Republicans promoted subordination for Black and Native peoples. Because Federalists emphasized class gradations, they could treat Indians and African Americans as inferior but worthy objects of elite paternalism. In response, Republicans accused Federalists of undermining white men by coddling Natives and Black people.[94]

Where Federalists wanted national consolidation, Republicans favored a decentralized union that reserved most power to the states, which they considered more democratic. Republicans insisted that dispersing power would frustrate the crypto-aristocrats who would dominate a national government. In response, Federalists denounced the Republican vision as dangerously naïve and anarchic.[95]

Both sides disdained political parties as selfish and divisive threats to the common interest of a true republic. Paradoxically, that dread of parties drove each group to organize and practice an especially bitter partisanship meant to discredit the other. Claiming exclusively to speak for the American people, each party cast rivals as insidious conspirators bent on destroying freedom and union. Both parties believed that free government hung in the balance, which lent desperation to their struggle. The Union polarized between two angry parties, each denying the legitimacy of the other. Jefferson declared, "The republicans are the *nation*; their opponents are but a faction." Federalists said the same of their foes.[96]

Political partisanship became so shrill because the stakes seemed so high. Federalists and Republicans knew that all previous republics in European history had been unstable, short-lived, and overthrown from within. The attorney general, Edmund Randolph, feared that partisanship would ignite a civil war: "It is a fact, well known, that the parties in the U.S. are highly inflamed against each other. . . . As soon as the sword is drawn, nothing will be able to restrain them."[97]

In 1794 that civil war seemed imminent in the backcountry from Pennsylvania south to Georgia, where farmers resisted Hamilton's excise tax on alcohol. That tax bore especially hard on western farmers, who lacked cash and distilled much of their grain into whiskey, which could better bear the cost of overland transportation to distant markets in the East. Country people wanted the government exclusively to rely on the revenue from import duties collected at the seaports. Likening their resistance to the Patriot opposition to Parliament's taxes, backcountry protestors refused to pay and abused any neighbors who broke ranks by helping the federal tax collectors. Reviving the tradition of regulation of government by armed populists, the resistance resembled the so-called Shays's Rebellion of the mid-1780s in New England.[98]

Federalists insisted that "busy and restless sons of anarchy" were bringing "us back to those scenes of humiliation and distress from which the new Constitution has so wonderfully extricated us." To denigrate their opponents, Federalists labeled the resistance "the Whiskey Rebellion," an insult that has stuck in histories. In August 1794, Washington called 15,000 state militiamen into federal service and sent them into western Pennsylvania to suppress the tax resistance. The president deemed this massive force essential because "we had given no testimony to the world of being able or willing to support our government and laws." Standing down, the regulators stayed home rather than confront overwhelming force. Federal troops arrested twenty supposed rebels, whom they hauled back to Philadelphia for trial.[99]

Blaming the rural turmoil on local clubs of radicals known as the Democratic-Republican Societies, Federalists denounced "self-created societies" as a threat to public respect for elected officials. If such societies triumphed, Washington warned, "We may bid adieu to all government in this Country, except mob, or Club government." Unable to compete with Washington's popularity, the Democratic-Republican Societies dissolved.[100]

During the mid-1790s, Federalist policies produced peace, prosperity, and popularity. Recovering impressively from the depression of the 1780s, the economy boomed during the 1790s as Hamilton's financial program stabilized the currency and restored investor confidence. The federal assumption of state debts enabled the states to cut their taxes in half. After 1793, when war erupted in Europe, American shippers reaped enhanced trade as neutral carriers. Merchants paid higher wages, had more ships built, and erected grander homes. Wages for skilled artisans in the seaports doubled between 1790 and 1796. Farmers also got higher prices for their produce. In 1795, a Boston newspaper exulted, "The affairs of Europe . . . rain riches upon us; and it is as much as we can do to find dishes to catch the golden shower." Voters rewarded the Federalists, who controlled Congress through the 1790s. In 1792, Washington won a unanimous reelection, and John Adams succeeded him, by a narrow margin, in the election of 1796. But the Federalists would overplay their hand at the end of the decade, when American politics became entangled in the French Revolution.[101]

Erupting in 1789, the new revolution overthrew monarchy and aristocracy in France, substituting a republic. At first, almost all Americans welcomed the revolutionary creation of a sister republic by their wartime allies. But the French Revolution became more controversial in 1792–1793, when radicals known as Jacobins seized power and executed the king, queen, and thousands of other opponents. The radical turn provoked war with the European monarchies, including Britain. As the French counterattacked and conquered their Dutch, Swiss, and Italian neighbors, Federalists soured on the new revolution. Already wary of democracy, they derided the French Revolution as promoting anarchy and despotism. Federalists began celebrating Britain as a domain of regulated and rational liberty, a reassuring bastion of stable government, and the source of profitable commerce.[102]

Because Republicans continued to celebrate and defend the French Revolution, Federalists dreaded that their rivals meant to copy the terror tactics of the French Jacobins. Cultivating a xenophobic American patriotism, Federalists cast Republicans as traitors in league with "foreign disorganizers." Federalists claimed that only the United States could sustain a stable republic—and only so long as they kept European ideas and radicals away.[103]

As the French and British escalated their naval warfare, both powers pressured the United States for assistance. To sway Americans, the British counted on the value of their trade and the might of their navy. The French countered with appeals to republican solidarity against monarchs and to American gratitude for their military help during the American Revolution. The Washington administration opted for neutrality because the indebted United States could ill afford a new conflict with either European power.[104]

That neutrality policy irritated the French, who began seizing American merchant ships trading with the British in 1797. To even discuss the controversy, French diplomats demanded bribes from American emissaries sent to Paris by the new president, Adams. The seizures and indignities outraged American popular opinion, which the Federalists exploited to prepare for war, enlarging the army and navy and raising taxes. Adams sent warships to attack French shipping in the West Indies.[105]

War alarmed the South lest an enemy rouse a slave revolt. In 1798, Washington warned that if the French invaded "there can be no doubt of their arming the Negro[e]s against us." The American consul in New Orleans, Daniel Clark, reported a wild rumor that France would send "1,500 armed black troops . . . to disseminate the Doctrine of emancipation" in the South. Clark added a divine warning, "Until Slavery is done away among the human Species, God will not be reconciled with us."[106]

In Congress, Federalists rammed through alien laws meant to discourage immigration. They disliked newcomers because most came from Ireland and voted Republican in America. Adopting a nativist position, Federalists derided most newcomers as ignorant, poor, violent, and brutish. A congressman insisted, "The time is now come when it will be proper to declare that nothing but birth shall entitle a man to citizenship in this country." Congress empowered the president to expel any alien deemed "dangerous to the peace and safety of the United States." Congress also increased the probationary period for naturalization to fourteen years from the previous five.[107]

Federalists moved to silence Republican newspapers and orators. In 1798, Congress passed a Sedition Act to criminalize criticism of federal leaders if a jury deemed the accusations "false, scandalous, and malicious." But proving the truth of a subjective opinion was difficult when critics faced partisan juries. Culprits risked up to two years in prison and $2,000 in fines.[108]

Republicans denounced the Alien and Sedition Acts as further proof that the Federalists were crypto-aristocrats subverting free speech and republicanism. Rural people put up liberty poles to protest Federalist measures, likening them to British tyranny. In November 1798, the Kentucky state legislature adopted provocative resolutions written by Jefferson, who insisted that the states had created the Union. Therefore, any state legislature could determine the constitutionality of federal laws and nullify their execution within a state's bounds. Virginia adopted similar resolutions drafted by Madison. Detecting "a regular conspiracy to overturn the government," Hamilton advised Adams to send federal troops southward to "put Virginia to the Test of resistance." But the president rejected that dangerous advice.[109]

Both parties looked to the election of 1800 to discredit their rivals, so the campaign rhetoric became especially dire and bloody. Depicting Jefferson as a dangerous atheist and Jacobin, a Federalist warned that, under a Republican administration, "murder, robbery, rape, adultery, and incest will be openly taught and practiced, the air will be rent with the cries of distress; the soil will be soaked with blood, the nation black with crimes." A Republican countered by denouncing Adams as a would-be king and "one of the most egregious fools on the continent."[110]

Republicans won by exploiting the unpopularity of increased federal taxes and Sedition Act prosecutions. In the fall, they captured both houses of Congress and appeared to have elected Jefferson as president and Aaron Burr as vice president. But Jefferson and Burr had deadlocked in Electoral College votes that, per the Federal Constitution, did not then distinguish between votes for the offices of president and vice president. The tie cast the decision into the House of Representatives, where each state could cast one equal vote, which meant that Jefferson needed to capture at least nine of the sixteen delegations.[111]

In early 1801, Federalists in Congress favored Burr, a handsome, charming, clever, and indebted opportunist open to making a deal.

For a suspenseful week, congressmen could reach no resolution, so Federalists and Republicans muttered about preparing for civil war. Working behind the scenes, Hamilton lobbied for Jefferson as the lesser of two great evils. In mid-February, the deadlock broke in Jefferson's favor. A relieved congressman noted that, had the Federalists stolen the presidency from Jefferson, "what other result would follow but civil war?" In that event, "his head would not have remained on his shoulders for twenty-four hours afterward."[112]

Sobered by the constitutional crisis over the election, Congress crafted the Twelfth Amendment. Ratified by the states, the amendment obliged each member of the Electoral College to cast one vote for president and the other for vice president. Thereafter, the president and vice president would almost certainly belong to the same party. Where the Constitution writers of 1787 had sought to preclude partisan divisions, the Twelfth Amendment assumed their inevitability. Pushed out of the Republican Party, Burr ran for governor of New York with Federalist support. Losing that election, he blamed Hamilton and shot him dead in a duel in July 1804. By winning the duel, Burr lost his popularity and damned his political fortunes.[113]

Victorious Republicans claimed to have defended a republican union imperiled by Federalist aristocrats. Jefferson insisted that the federal government should heed public opinion and tolerate free speech. Congress killed the Sedition Act, while Jefferson pardoned those convicted under that law. To reward their immigrant voters, Republicans reduced the period of naturalization to five years from the punitive fourteen years mandated by the Federalists in 1798. A democratic sensibility had prevailed over deference in the election of 1800.[114]

Jefferson prioritized reducing taxes and the national debt. By cutting the army, navy, and diplomatic corps, Republicans could abolish the unpopular excise and land taxes. Jefferson also tried to pay down the national debt that Hamilton had designed for perpetuity. During their twelve years in power, Federalists had increased that debt from

$76 million to $83 million; during his eight years as president, Jefferson reduced it to $57 million.[115]

Republicans insisted that a limited federal government committed to civil liberties and equal rights for white men would inspire a passionate support that no monarchy could match. Jefferson claimed that the diffuse United States had the "strongest Government on earth," precisely because its lack of coercive power won popular devotion. Rejecting the "energy" favored by Federalists, he reasoned that militiamen would rush to defend a country that demanded so little of them. But Jefferson could always make loopholes to expand government when it served his purposes.[116]

Jefferson described his election as "the revolution of 1800," which he claimed was "as real a revolution in the principles of our government as that of 1776 was in its form." Rejecting Hamilton's vision of a consolidated nation, Jeffersonian Republicans favored a strict construction of the Constitution to limit the federal government in favor of the states. The Republicans also championed the rights and interests of common white men while accepting their prejudices against Blacks and Indians. Voters rewarded Jefferson with a landslide reelection in 1804, when Republicans also increased their majorities in the House and Senate. Federalists would never recover executive or legislative power in the federal government.[117]

But Federalism endured in the Supreme Court. In 1801, Jefferson ascended to the presidency shortly after John Marshall became chief justice as a last-minute appointment by the outgoing president, Adams. As a Continental Army captain, Marshall had become a nationalist who disdained the states'-rights philosophy of the Republicans. Although a fellow Virginian, Marshall considered Jefferson "unfit . . . for the chief magistracy" because he would "sap the fundamental principles of the government." Jefferson feared becoming entrapped by Marshall's quick mind and rigorous logic. The new president assured another judge, "So great is his sophistry [that] you must never give him an affirmative answer, or you will be forced to grant his conclusions. Why, if he were to ask me whether it were day-light or not, I'd reply, 'Sir, I don't know, I can't tell.' "[118]

Given Republican control of Congress and the presidency, Marshall proceeded carefully and patiently, cultivating unanimity on the court. He arranged for all the judges to room and board together during their annual sessions in Washington, D.C. In those close quarters and over many bottles of Madeira, Marshall's amiable manners, keen wit, and sharp mind swayed his colleagues. A popular story held that the justices belatedly discovered that their boarding house permitted them to drink only in wet weather—when it seemed essential for good health. Marshall asked a colleague to look out the window for rain clouds on the horizon. Alas, he reported a clear, sunny sky. But Marshall quickly noted, "Our jurisdiction extends over so large a territory that . . . it must be raining somewhere." He uncorked the Madeira bottle. By 1819, Republican presidents had appointed most of the Supreme Court justices, but they had come around to Marshall's Madeira and Federalist philosophy, to Jefferson's dismay.[119]

Marshall bolstered the authority of the Supreme Court as a coequal branch with Congress and the presidency. By upholding the doctrine that the Federal Constitution emanated from a sovereign American people, Marshall refuted the Jeffersonian insistence that it was a compact by sovereign states. In *McCulloch v. Maryland* (1819), the Marshall court defended the federal Bank of the United States against a Maryland tax levied to protect state-chartered banks. By broadly interpreting the Federal Constitution's "necessary and proper" clause, Marshall vindicated the national bank and rejected the Maryland tax. Outraged by that ruling, Jefferson accused Marshall of "working like gravity, without intermission . . . to press us at last into one consolidated mass."[120]

The Marshall court promoted a national market in which interstate investment and commerce benefited from federal laws that trumped state intervention. The court also insisted that business corporations were private properties that could neither be revoked nor diminished by legislative action. Jefferson raged that this legal doctrine subordinated democratic legislatures to the dictates of a previous generation. During the nineteenth century, corporations proliferated to become the country's dominant form of business enterprise, supplanting partnerships and sole proprietorships.[121]

Jefferson was president for eight years, while Marshall served as chief justice for thirty-four years thanks to a life tenure provided by the Federal Constitution. He participated in more than a thousand decisions, writing over half, giving Marshall an impact comparable to Jefferson's during a pivotal generation in developing the Union. Echoes of their clashing principles have ebbed and flowed in competition ever since, informing constitutional and political disputes to our own time.[122]

Rebellions

Jefferson was especially indebted to southern voters and legislators, for he won 82 percent of the electoral votes in the South compared to only 27 percent in the North. Although Federalists had not challenged slavery, many southerners worried about the future uses of federal power if the nation subordinated their states. Attentive to those who had elected him, President Jefferson refused to meddle with slavery, reasoning "that no more good must be attempted than the nation can bear." In 1802, Jefferson's postmaster general, Gideon Granger, fired the free Blacks employed in his department because, he alleged, their free movement could promote slave revolts. That dread had increased during the 1790s thanks to a massive slave revolt at Saint-Domingue in the French West Indies.[123]

Saint-Domingue was the richest colony in the Caribbean, but that wealth benefited French planters rather than the enslaved people who produced the sugar. About the size of Maryland, Saint-Domingue occupied the western third of the island of Hispaniola. Because of brutal work conditions and tropical diseases, slave deaths exceeded births in the colony. Every year, planters imported thousands of Africans to replace the corpses, so most of the colony's people were Africans by birth. Many enslaved men were former soldiers, captured after lost battles in Kongo and sold to European traders. These newcomers knew how to organize and fight when opportunity appeared.[124]

Their chance came when the French Revolution produced divisions among the white and mixed-race minorities of Saint-Domingue. The revolutionary ideals of liberty, equality, and fraternity were particularly subversive in the highly unequal, racially divided, and despotic regimes of Caribbean colonies. In August 1791, enslaved Africans rebelled by killing overseers and masters and torching the buildings and cane fields of a thousand plantations. In 1792, France's revolutionary regime sent 6,000 troops to restore order in Saint-Domingue. To win support from free people of color, the commanders offered them legal equality, but that concession outraged most of the white colonists, who rejected the revolution. Desperate French commanders then promised freedom to slave rebels who would provide armed assistance. During the summer of 1793, Black troops enabled the revolutionaries to triumph in Saint-Domingue.[125]

In early 1794, the revolutionary regime in Paris emancipated the slaves in the French West Indies without offering any compensation for masters. The French also granted equal citizenship to the emancipated. They even allowed Black representatives to serve in the national legislature, something that American Patriots never did. At war with Britain, the French took these measures to rally Black men to defend the French West Indies and promote slave revolts in the British West Indies.[126]

Rather than embrace the Saint-Domingue rebels as fellow revolutionaries, Americans denounced them as Black brutes and terrorists "unworthy of liberty." In reporting the violence in Saint-Domingue, American writers dwelled in lurid detail on atrocities committed by Blacks while skipping over the greater brutalities committed by their white oppressors. Although Americans had declared revolution a universal right for the oppressed, they shuddered when enslaved people claimed that right. In 1794 a South Carolina legislator warned colleagues to desist from declaring that "equality is the natural condition of man," lest they produce the "ruin of the country, by giving liberty to the slaves, and the desolating [of] the land with fire and sword in the struggles between master and slave."[127]

In 1800, the southern nightmare nearly became real in Jefferson's Virginia. An enslaved blacksmith named Gabriel secretly organized a revolt in and around the state capital, Richmond. "We have as much right to fight for our liberty as any men," declared Jack Ditcher, one of Gabriel's lieutenants. The rebels planned to burn riverside warehouses as a distraction and then rush into the heart of town to grab Governor James Monroe, seize weapons from the state arsenal, and plunder the state treasury. The rebels hoped then to negotiate for their freedom.[128]

On the appointed night, August 30, a violent thunderstorm lashed Richmond with sheets of rain, washing away many bridges. Blocked by swollen streams and rivers, few rebels could make it to their rendezvous point. The confusion spread alarm among those in on the secret. To save themselves, a few fearful slaves revealed the plot to their masters, who alerted militia officers. Called into service, militiamen patrolled the roads and arrested suspects.[129]

Trials commenced on September 11, and executions began the next day. Gabriel died in front of a crowd on October 10, when a noose snapped his neck. By December 1, twenty-seven men had paid with their lives for failing at revolution. They met death with a defiant resolve that alarmed a watching master, John Randolph: "The accused have exhibited a spirit, which, if it becomes general, must deluge the Southern country in blood. They manifested a sense of their rights, and contempt of danger, and a thirst for revenge which portend the most unhappy consequences."[130]

Citing Saint-Domingue, Americans feared that new slaves from Africa were especially prone to revolt. As president, Jefferson promoted one major reform of slavery: a ban on importing more Africans as slaves. Passed by Congress in March 1807, the ban became effective January 1, 1808: the first year when the Federal Constitution permitted such a prohibition. The overwhelming vote, 113 to 5, in the House of Representatives attested to broad support in the South as well as the North. Most southern leaders reasoned that natural increase by the current slave population sufficed for expanding the plantation economy westward. The ban signaled no commitment to abolish slavery or to meddle with the booming interstate trade in slaves. Indeed, by eliminating the competition from foreign importers, Virginians and Marylanders could sell more slaves to farmers and planters in the West and Lower South.[131]

The official ban on importing slaves reduced, but did not eliminate, the influx of Africans. Between 1807 and 1862, another 25,000 Africans became slaves in the United States. Importers brought them to Spanish Cuba, just ninety miles from the southern coast of America; from there it was easy to smuggle slaves to Alabama, Florida, or Georgia.[132]

Pirates

While enslaving Black people, Americans felt outraged by the slavery of white men by the Barbary States of North Africa. Located on the southern shore of the Mediterranean Sea, the Muslim states of Algiers, Tunis, and Tripoli (Libya) raided the ships and coasts of Christian states in Europe, taking captives for enslavement or ransom. These raids were means to a bigger end: inducing Europeans to pay tribute to protect their trade and people.[133]

Lacking a navy during the 1780s, American merchant ships in the Mediterranean offered easy pickings for Barbary pirates. The plight of captive sailors inspired a spate of popular books and plays about darker-skinned Muslims enslaving and abusing white Americans. That mistreatment led some Americans to question slavery at home as hypocrisy. A Philadelphia writer confessed: "For this practice of buying and selling slaves, we are not entitled to charge the Algerines with any exclusive degree of barbarity. The Christians of Europe and

America carry on this commerce a hundred times more extensively than the Algerines."[134]

In 1794, Congress funded construction of six warships to afford the United States some clout in negotiating with the Barbary States. But war in the distant Mediterranean would be expensive and tricky. The alternative was to pay tribute and ransom as most European powers did to preserve their profitable trade. Presidents Washington and Adams agreed that it was more cost effective to pay rather than fight the Barbary States.[135]

By 1800, the United States annually paid $1,250,000 to Barbary States: a fifth of the federal government's budget. The Americans also disavowed any holy war against Islam, assuring Tripoli's rulers in 1797 that "the Government of the United States of America is not, in any sense, founded on the Christian religion."[136]

In early 1801, the new ruler of Tripoli, Yusuf Karamanli, declared war when the United States refused to increase its tribute. A distant conflict confronted Jefferson with a dilemma. On the one hand, he wanted to cut the American navy to help reduce taxes and the national debt. On the other hand, Jefferson despised paying tribute to pirates and hoped to save money by deploying "an armed force . . . for suppressing their insolencies." Jefferson also promoted a world order premised on free trade, so he opposed any commercial interference, whether British or Barbary.[137]

In 1802, Jefferson anticipated later presidential games by declining to seek a congressional declaration of war. Instead, he sent warships to the Mediterranean as an armed force of "observation." Of course, they clashed with Tripolitan vessels. That enabled Jefferson to seek congressional funding for a war—still without a formal declaration. Rather than fight all of the Barbary States, Jefferson kept up tribute payments to the strongest, Algiers and Tunis, while attacking Tripoli.[138]

Like most American presidents launching a foreign war, Jefferson expected a quick, easy, and cheap victory. Instead, he reaped a long, frustrating, and expensive conflict. Unable to match the firepower of the largest American warships, known as frigates, Tripolitans relied on smaller, faster vessels better suited for hit-and-run raids on merchant ships in the shallower waters of the Mediterranean. Rather than venture out to fight the American frigates, Tripolitans dared them to attack their heavily fortified port bristling with cannons. For two years, the American squadron accomplished little but sail around off the port while Tripolitan corsairs slipped around the ineffective blockade. Requiring $500,000 during the first year, the American naval force cost twice what Karamanli had demanded in tribute. In the second year, an expanded squadron nearly doubled the cost to $900,000.[139]

Then catastrophe struck. In October 1803, an American captain sailed the frigate *Philadelphia* too close to shore, where it ran aground. Tripolitan gunboats swarmed around the helpless ship to compel the captain to surrender. In addition to capturing 300 sailors as hostages, the Tripolitans seized the frigate by pulling it off the rocks and into their harbor.[140]

To make the best of that bad situation, the American naval commander, Edward Preble, hatched a daring operation conducted by his most able lieutenant, Stephen Decatur, Jr. In February 1804, on a small vessel with a select crew, Decatur sailed into the harbor at night to board and burn the *Philadelphia*, while defying cannon fire from the shore batteries. The coup won Decatur promotion to captain: the youngest in the navy at age twenty-five. But the war effort did not look good when the navy's greatest accomplishment was burning one of its own frigates. Demanding $1.5 million in 1804, the conflict cost ever more American money and lives.[141]

A breakthrough came by land thanks to a former army officer and diplomat, William Eaton. In Egypt, Eaton recruited 500 mercenaries, supplemented by 8 American marines, to invade Tripoli from the east. He sought to topple Yusuf Karamanli in favor of his alienated brother Hamet, who promised to make peace on American terms. In the spring of 1805, with support from three American warships,

Eaton's force crossed six hundred miles of desert to seize the coastal town of Derna, as a precursor to marching west to attack Tripoli.[142]

But Preble had retired from command, replaced by Samuel Barron, who decided to cash in on Eaton's little victory rather than prolong the war. In June 1805, Yusuf Karamanli accepted $60,000 in ransom for his American captives, including the captain and crew of the *Philadelphia*. Karamanli also agreed to forsake further tribute or future attacks on American shipping. In return, Americans called off their blockade and terminated support for Hamet, who had to flee back into exile in Egypt, while Derna reverted to his brother's rule.[143]

Returning to the United States, Eaton felt embittered by the hasty treaty that aborted his mission and betrayed Hamet. Soured on Jefferson and his countrymen for tolerating slavery at home, Eaton wrote, "Barbary is hell. So, alas, is all America south of Pennsylvania; for oppression, and slavery, and misery are there." In 1790, the United States had 697,624 enslaved Blacks compared to about 10,000 enslaved whites in the Barbary States.[144]

Union

Against long odds, and with immense trouble, diverse and fractious colonies had won independence and formed a union of thirteen states. That union seemed essential to free, republican government on a continental scale. In an inaugural address of the next generation, Andrew Jackson declared, "Without union our independence and liberty would never have been achieved; without union they never can be maintained." The passion for union fed on a mythic history that cast the founders as united in principles and goals during the revolutionary generation. Recover that spirit, orators insisted, and the Union will endure. Otherwise, they warned, the continent would be deluged in blood.[145]

But leading Americans differed over the meaning of union, clashing over how much power the federal government needed. Federalists like Hamilton, Marshall, and Washington sought a truly national government, with the power to control states and compel people to follow federal laws. But Jefferson and Madison worried that central power would alienate states into breaking the Union. They treated union as a state of mind sustained by affective ties between people across state lines. Madison explained that union depended on "the people of America" being "knit together as they are by so many cords of affection." Any effort to force a resistant state or region to obey the federal majority risked dissolving those cords.[146]

Most American leaders accepted that preserving slavery was the price of union. They also agreed that the Union needed to expand westward, to claim Native lands for American settlers and thereby push the British and Spanish farther away. Most Americans favored, in the words of an Ohio newspaper editor, "a union of common American blood . . . of white men committed to the furtherance of Anglo-Saxon civilization." That definition regarded Blacks and Indians as perpetual outsiders. But radical reformers emerged during the 1830s to press for a more inclusive republic, one that treated Blacks as equal citizens and protected Indian nations. Although despised by most Americans, these reformers doubted that the Union could endure if entangled in slavery and violence.[147]

The shared passion for union as an ideal combined with clashing definitions of that union to produce acrimony. In 1833 a visiting Briton marveled that "the seeds of discord are plentifully scattered throughout the Union" and yet Americans agreed that disunion would produce disaster, precisely because of their differences. Mutual distrust was the bond of union.[148]

Clockwise from top, left: "Thomas Jefferson (1743–1826)," engraving by Charles Balthazar Julien Févret de Saint-Mémin, 1805. Library of Congress 97503644. *"John Marshall (1755–1835)," engraving by Charles Balthazar Julien Févret de Saint-Mémin, 1808.* Library of Congress 00650588. *"The Burning of the Frigate the* Philadelphia *in the Harbor of Tripoli," engraving by John B. Guerrazzi, 1805.* Library of Congress 2006691576 (LC-USZ62-59).

TWO 🔖 EMPIRES

I n 1788, when George Washington became the first American
president, Sacagawea was born far to the west. The daughter of
a Shoshone chief, she grew up at the headwaters of the Missouri
River in the northern Rocky Mountains. Although unfamiliar with
the distant Americans of the Atlantic coast, Shoshones knew of British
traders operating from Hudson Bay, far to the northeast, and French
traders based at St. Louis in the Spanish colony of Louisiana. Unable
to reach those traders, Shoshones felt their impact indirectly and violently. Armed with trade guns and mounted on horses, warriors from

points to the east raided the poorly armed Shoshones to take captives. In 1800, Hidatsa raiders ravaged a Shoshone encampment, killing four men and four women and taking away nine children, including twelve-year-old Sacagawea.[1]

The raiders took her eastward to their village on the middle Missouri River in the heart of the continent, within present-day North Dakota. The Hidatsas and their Arikara and Mandan neighbors lived in villages of earthen lodges surrounded by stockades set beside broad and fertile riverside fields, where women cultivated corn, beans, and squash. The earth-lodge villagers also ventured onto the surrounding Great Plains to hunt bison (buffaloes) that roamed in immense herds. The Hidatsas, Arikaras, and Mandans had their own powerful enemies: the numerous and aggressive Lakota. Expanding westward from the Mississippi Valley, close to French traders, the Lakota had even more guns that they deployed to seize bison-hunting territory, horses, and captives from the earth-lodge peoples.[2]

Seeking better access to firearms, the Hidatsas sold Sacagawea to a Francophone trader based in their villages: Touissant Charbonneau. She became a commodity in an emerging market driven by profit and served by violence. In 1804, President Jefferson sent an expedition far up the Missouri River to investigate the Native world. That expedition would come to depend on Sacagawea, who knew many things that Americans still had to discover. The earth-lodge peoples would welcome Americans as potential allies and suppliers of arms, who could improve the odds of resisting the Lakota. But the new allies would prove even more dangerous than old enemies.[3]

Opposite, clockwise from top left: "Aaron Burr (1756–1836)," engraving by G. Parker after a John Vanderlyn painting, 1836. Library of Congress 206681406. *"James Wilkinson (1757–1825)," engraving by Charles Balthazar Julien Févret de Saint-Mémin, 1808.* Library of Congress 2007676899. *"Captain Lewis Shooting an Indian," engraving by Patrick Gass, 1810.* Library of Congress 2001699660.

Empire of Liberty

Americans created a distinctive empire, where settlers had political clout. Noting that frontier folk "will settle the lands in spite of everybody," Jefferson considered it "necessary to give way to the torrent." He understood the lesson that had eluded the British and later the Federalists: that an empire in America could only hope to *appear* strong by helping settlers, who wanted cheap and fertile land taken as quickly as possible from Natives. Federal leaders needed to ride, rather than resist, the settler tide heading west.[4]

Jefferson promoted an "Empire of Liberty," which favored white men at the expense of Indians. By pushing westward, to create thousands of new farms, settlers could promote a relative equality among white men that Jefferson considered essential to sustain a republic. But the American population doubled every twenty-two years. To reproduce a society of many small farmers and republican government, the United States needed to take twice as much land from Indians in every passing generation.[5]

The Jefferson administration made it easier for settlers to buy public lands taken from Indians. The government reduced the minimum tract offered for sale from 640 acres to a more affordable 160 acres and sold land on a credit of four years, seeking just 5 percent ($16) as a down payment. Jefferson also put Ohio on the fast track to statehood, which it achieved in 1803 and became a political bastion for Republicans. The more democratic land policy increased the pace of settlement. In 1800, Ohio had just 45,365 settlers, but that increased fivefold to 230,760 by 1810.[6]

Jefferson regarded Natives as the racial equals but cultural inferiors of white people. He wanted Indians to intermarry with settlers and adopt their gender roles, private property, and agricultural methods. Then they could dissolve their tribal governments and forsake Native identities to become absorbed as individuals into American society, thereby denying the British and Spanish of Native allies. Meeting with chiefs, Jefferson insisted, "I repeat that we will never do an unjust act towards you. On the contrary we wish you to live in peace, to increase in numbers, to learn to labor as we do." Jefferson reasoned that, by forsaking their traditional mix of hunting, gathering, and horticulture, Natives would need less land, freeing up more territory for federal sale to settlers. When Indians resisted land cessions and cultural obliteration, however, Jefferson declared, "We have only to shut our hand to crush them."[7]

Jefferson directed territorial governors to "press on the Indians, as steadily and strenuously as they can bear, the extension of our purchases." The president advised governors to advance trade goods on credit to induce Indians to cede more lands to pay those debts. When most Indians balked, territorial officials found a few pliable chiefs in each Native nation to make the desired cessions. During Jefferson's administration, territorial governors procured 200,000 square miles for a mere penny or two per acre in thirty disputed treaties.[8]

Jefferson also thought that Americans eventually would obtain the Spanish colonies of Florida and Louisiana. "Those countries cannot be in better hands," Jefferson wrote in 1786. Considered weak and declining, the Spanish seemed the ideal short-term trustees for America's future lands. Jefferson believed that, as settlers pressed into those territories, the Spanish would surrender them to the United States. He only feared that Spain might prove "too feeble to hold them till our population can be sufficiently advanced to gain it from them piece by piece."[9]

In 1791, Jefferson advised President Washington to welcome the Spanish policy of enticing American settlers into Louisiana and Florida: "I wish a hundred thousand of our inhabitants would accept the invitation. It will be the means of delivering to us peaceably, what may otherwise cost us a war." Playing a clever game, Jefferson encouraged Washington to "complain of this seduction of our inhabitants just enough to make them believe we think it [a] very wise policy for them, and confirm them in it."[10]

That dream of eventually robbing the Spanish turned into a nightmare in 1801, when Americans learned that the world's most powerful and aggressive empire—France—was taking Louisiana from the Spanish. Newly become president, Jefferson considered this news "very ominous to us." In 1799 an especially able and ruthless general, Napoleon Bonaparte, had seized power in a coup that substituted his dictatorship for the troubled republic of the French Revolution. In October 1800, Napoleon compelled the Spanish to restore Louisiana to French rule. He sought Louisiana to provision the sugar plantations of Saint-Domingue, which had passed into the hands of rebels who were former slaves.[11]

In 1802, Napoleon sent an army of 16,000 troops across the Atlantic to restore French rule and slavery to Saint-Domingue and then to occupy Louisiana. The French commander, Victor-Emmanuel Leclerc, had married Napoleon's sister. After defeating and arresting Saint-Domingue's ruling Black general, Toussaint Louverture, Leclerc shipped him to France, where he died of cold and hunger in a wretched prison high up in the frigid Alps. In Saint-Domingue, the invaders tried to crush lingering resistance through terror, massacring thousands of Black men, women, and children.[12]

After victory in Saint-Domingue, the French seemed poised to take armed possession of Louisiana, and that threatened the United States. As the seaport near the mouth of the Mississippi, New Orleans controlled the trade brought downstream by the vast network of rivers at the heart of the continent. Barred by the Appalachian Mountains from easy access to eastern markets, western farmers depended on floating their bulky crops down to New Orleans. If the Union failed to provide settlers with access to overseas markets for their wheat, flour, cattle, and lumber, they might rebel and secede. Although Napoleon had not yet shown his hand in Louisiana, Americans expected the worst: that he would shut down American trade via the Mississippi in order to pressure western settlers to break with the Union and join his empire. A Virginia Republican noted the "intimate connection between the free Navigation of the Mississippi and the existence of a Union with the Western country."[13]

Americans worried that their Union was vulnerable to division by a wily enemy. A Virginia politician noted the powerful "differences in interest between eastern and western America" that induced settlers to "watch the movements of the General Government with a Jealous eye." He described westerners as "like a large combustible mass. They want only a Spark to set them on fire. They will have the uninterrupted use of that river either by treaty or by the sword." The American consul in New Orleans agreed that most western people were "indifferent about their Country" and "would find their Interest in seceding from the General Government."[14]

New Orleans was the key to holding the West. Jefferson noted, "There is on the globe one single spot, the possessor of which is our natural & habitual enemy. It is New Orleans, through which the produce of three-eighths of our territory must pass to market, and from its fertility [the West] will ere long yield more than half of our whole produce and contain more than half of our inhabitants." Without control over New Orleans, he concluded, "we cannot exist."[15]

American leaders also feared that war with France would inflame the Union's other two great internal threats: Indians and rebelling slaves. Despite Napoleon's bid to restore slavery in Saint-Domingue, James Madison worried that American slaves instead would credit the French for liberating their Caribbean slaves during the early 1790s, at the radical peak of the French Revolution. Madison noted "the inquietude which would be excited in the Southern States, whose numerous slaves have been taught to regard the French as the patrons of their cause." He dreaded that enslaved people would exploit the chaos of war to rebel and demand their own freedom.[16]

Americans also expected the French to rally Indian allies to strike at the United States. Natives nurtured a romantic nostalgia for the French of the colonial era as generous and benevolent, as the antithesis of the rude and grabby Americans. Indiana's governor warned, "The happiness they enjoyed from their intercourse with the French is their perpetual theme. It is their golden age." An old chief asked the governor, "Why do you not make us happy as our Fathers the French did[?] They never took from us our lands, . . . but now if a poor Indian attempts to take a little bark from a tree to cover him from the rain, up comes a white man and threatens to shoot him, claiming the tree as his own." That mystique plus generous gifts of firearms would enable French agents to build a formidable alliance of Native peoples. In moments of crisis, Americans obsessed about the fault lines within their Union.[17]

In 1802, Federalists urged a military strike to seize New Orleans as, in Hamilton's words, "the key of the Western Country" and "essential to the permanency of the Union." But Jefferson worried that war would serve the Federalist agenda of consolidating national power through a large military, increased taxes, and a perpetual national debt. He dreaded armed conflict with France as "7 years of war, the loss of 100,000 lives, an hundred millions of additional debt, many hundred millions worth of produce & property lost for want of market." By seeking a diplomatic solution, Jefferson defended his vision of a limited federal government, with a small military, shrinking debt, and low taxes.[18]

But how could the United States pressure the French without military force? Jefferson's solution was characteristically theatrical. By threatening to ally with the British, Jefferson hoped to scare the French into selling New Orleans. To present that bluff, Jefferson sent James Monroe to join the American minister to France, Robert R. Livingston, in negotiating with the French. But what if Napoleon called Jefferson's bluff? Then the president risked inviting British forces into Louisiana, and Jefferson dreaded them as even worse neighbors than the French.[19]

Jefferson wanted Napoleon to sell New Orleans and throw in Florida, although that still belonged to Spain. But the president did *not* seek to buy the entire Louisiana Territory, which stretched along the western bank of the Mississippi River. Jefferson rejected adding territory beyond the Mississippi as "almost as great a misfortune as a contraction of it on this side." The pressing issue was to reassure American settlers by restoring their access to overseas markets—and thereby secure the shaky Union. Obtaining New Orleans would suffice, and Jefferson wanted to keep the cost low, so he hoped to pay no more than $6 million for just enough land to solve the immediate problem.[20]

Jefferson's bluff did not impress Napoleon, but the Americans got a lucky break thanks to people whom they despised: the Black rebels of Saint-Domingue. The French occupation unraveled when yellow fever and guerrilla resistance killed most of the invaders, including General Leclerc. Facing a resumed war in Europe and a depleted treasury, Napoleon could not afford to send more troops to die in the tropics, so he withdrew his shattered force from Saint-Domingue.[21]

Then Napoleon decided to sell Louisiana before the British could seize that colony in a renewed war. "Damn sugar, damn coffee, damn colonies," Napoleon muttered. In April 1803, he surprised the American diplomats by offering all of Louisiana for $15 million. Livingston and Monroe tried to persuade the French to accept half that amount for just New Orleans and, perhaps, West Florida. But Napoleon insisted that the Americans must take the whole colony and pay his full price.[22]

Monroe and Livingston consented because, they reasoned, "The Bond of our Union will be strengthened." Writing home to Jefferson and Madison, the diplomats adopted a defensive tone to justify taking all of Louisiana: "Perhaps the best course will be to keep it for many years vacant." This tone seems incredible in retrospect, given the bargain price and immense potential value of that vast territory.[23]

Jefferson welcomed the deal because it saved the Union from civil war, "which was to burst in a tornado, and the public are unapprised how near this catastrophe was." He also cherished the vast new territory because it pushed European powers away from the Indians and slaves within the United States. In 1803, Jefferson assured Andrew Jackson (then a Tennessee militia general), "The acquisition of Louisiana is of immense importance to our future tranquility insomuch as it removes the intrigues of foreign nations to a distance from which they can no longer produce disturbance between the Indians & us." But that security always proved temporary, for as settlers entered the new land, the distance between them and the rival empires shrank, renewing the danger of foreign military aid to Indians and rebelling slaves.[24]

The American purchase outraged the Spanish because Napoleon had promised never to alienate Louisiana to another power. The Spanish had hoped that French Louisiana would persist as a buffer zone to keep Americans far away from Mexico, Spain's most precious colony. But Jefferson defied the Spanish protests because Spain was too weak to add the United States to its enemies.[25]

The purchase compromised Jefferson's strict construction of the Federal Constitution, which did not explicitly authorize the purchase of foreign territory. He had long condemned the Federalists for loosely constructing the Constitution to justify expanding federal power. But the Louisiana deal was too good to pass up, as it secured New Orleans. Jefferson wanted a constitutional amendment to allow the purchase, but there was no time for ratification because Napoleon required American acceptance within six months. Rather than dither, Jefferson advised his fellow Republicans: "It will be well to say as little as possible on the Constitutional difficulty & that Congress should act on it without talking." In October, the Senate overwhelmingly ratified the treaty. On behalf of the national interest, Jefferson had wrestled with his conscience and won.[26]

Jefferson fought a second winning bout with that conscience by turning against the rebels in Saint-Domingue although their victories had helped deliver Louisiana to the United States. In 1804, they declared full independence from France, naming the new country "Haiti." The reigning general, Jean-Jacques Dessalines, was a dictator who ordered a massacre of white civilians, killing at least 3,000. That atrocity became the prism through which most Americans, particularly southerners, viewed Haiti.[27]

Rather than welcome Haiti as a sister republic, Jefferson and Congress sought to quarantine and undermine the new nation as a moral contagion. They saw Haiti as a den of Black terrorists who set an ominous precedent that American slaves might follow. An American senator considered it dangerous to "cherish the black population of St. Domingo whilst we have a similar population in our Southern States." In 1806, Jefferson and Congress placed an embargo on trade with Haiti and rejected diplomatic recognition. Both measures undercut the Haitian economy. Then white Americans pointed to the poverty of Haiti as supposed proof that Blacks could never govern their own nation.[28]

Children

In March 1804, American officials and troops completed the transfer of Louisiana by occupying St. Louis. In disgust, an outgoing French official declared, "The Devil may take it all." But what was it all? In theory, the purchase reached north and west across the Great Plains to the Rocky Mountains. Later measured as 827,000 square miles, the purchase nearly doubled the size of the United States, but no one could be sure in 1804 because Euro-Americans had not explored the western margins, and fiercely independent Native peoples occupied the land. Settlers held only a narrow strip along the Mississippi River and the lower Missouri River.[29]

In claiming the territory, Jefferson consulted neither the region's Indian majority nor the colonial minority (primarily French-speakers). While the Natives meant to remain independent, the leading colonists welcomed joining the United States, provided they became equal citizens with local self-government. Given their numbers (at least 50,000), the inhabitants warranted a territorial government with an appointed governor but an elected assembly. The treaty terms also obligated the United States promptly to treat the Louisianans as citizens.[30]

But Jefferson and most congressmen distrusted Louisianans as too alien and ignorant for immediate and full incorporation into the Union. A congressman derided them as a "Gallo-Hispano-Indian omnium gatherum of savages and adventurers." Jefferson insisted that French culture and Spanish rule had failed to prepare the inhabitants for republicanism: "Our new fellow citizens are yet as incapable of self-government as children." In March 1804, Congress organized the purchase as two territories: downriver "Orleans," around New Orleans, where most of the colonists lived, and upriver "Louisiana," where a vast Native land surrounded a few riverside settlements. Lacking elected assemblies, the new territories were ruled by new-comers appointed by Jefferson to serve as governors, councils, and judges. Alas, Jefferson made poor choices. To govern Orleans, Jefferson named William C. C. Claiborne, although he could speak neither French nor Spanish. To administer Louisiana, Jefferson relied on James Wilkinson, despite his notoriety for corruption.[31]

Louisianans complained that American republicanism in practice was "a sort of Hocus-Pocus, tending to worst[en] their condition." In November 1804, leading Francophones from New Orleans visited Washington, D.C., to protest the authoritarian territorial government, but neither Jefferson nor Congress took them seriously. Although the president had declared self-government a universal human right, he reserved his Empire of Liberty for Anglophone Americans. In 1805, Congress partially relented by allowing Orleans a territorial legislature and a track to statehood, which it received in 1812 as "Louisiana," while the upriver territory became "Missouri."[32]

While resolving the French threat at New Orleans, the Louisiana Purchase threatened to make the United States too big to succeed. A congressman denounced the western mass of the purchase as "a great waste, a wilderness unpeopled with any being except wolves and wandering Indians." But leading Americans also worried that the vast domain would attract too many settlers and spawn new states hostile to the Union. A Federalist warned, "Admit this western world into the union, & you destroy . . . the whole weight & importance of the eastern states in the *scale* of politics." The Union had a tenuous balance that would collapse if it grew too much in one direction. Hamilton feared that settling the vast purchase would lead to "the dismemberment of a large portion of our country, or a dissolution of the Government." Federalists preferred to cluster Americans so that they could closely interact to trade, build sociability, and enforce order. A Connecticut newspaper dreaded that expansion beyond the Mississippi would generate "neighboring nations for the destruction of each other."[33]

Even Jefferson worried about settlers dispersing in the vast new territory, but he had a plan. To create an immense reservation for Indians on the west bank of the Mississippi, Jefferson proposed to withdraw all the settlers from upper Louisiana, relocating them east of the river. Then he would push westward the Natives who then lived east of the Mississippi. Jefferson wanted fully to settle the lands east of the great river before allowing Americans to proceed further west. He expected that process of infill to take fifty years. During that interim, Jefferson believed that Indians could assimilate to American "civilization." On paper and in theory, it seemed neat and almost sensible.[34]

But Jefferson's scheme did not fit the complexity of frontier life. Few eastern Indians wanted to fight western Natives for land, and the settlers of upper Louisiana clung to their farms and villages. In addition, Americans were already flocking to settle west of the Mississippi. Senator Rufus King (of New York) scoffed: "Nothing but a cordon of troops will restrain our people from going over the River and settling themselves down upon the western bank." Dependent on elections, American leaders were not about to evict so many citizens from their land claims, so Congress tabled Jefferson's scheme, and the federal government began selling land in the region to newcomers.[35]

American rule introduced a more repressive racial order premised on a harder distinction between white freedom and Black slavery. In 1804, Louisiana had about 25,000 enslaved people and 2,000 free Blacks. The former Spanish and Catholic regime had mandated paternalistic policies meant to protect enslaved people from abusive masters. Because Spanish law allowed slaves to work on their own account for part of the week to make enough money to buy their freedom, Spanish America had many more free Blacks than did the southern United States. In 1789, Spanish authorities introduced a new code of laws that mandated minimum standards for feeding and clothing the enslaved. Although poorly enforced, the code infuriated Louisiana's masters, who claimed that any diminution of their power emboldened insolence, resistance, and rebellion by Blacks.[36]

Congress initially tried to reduce the danger of slave rebellion by suspending the importation of slaves into the new territories—unless they belonged to and came with American settlers. But Congress lifted the ban in 1805 after local planters howled with outrage and threatened secession. For the next three years, imported slaves poured in to meet the voracious demand from expanding sugar plantations. While welcoming slaves, the territory rejected free Black immigrants as a supposed menace.[37]

In 1806, the territorial legislature adopted a harsh new slave code to eliminate Spanish paternalism, discourage manumissions, and deprive the enslaved of their traditional rights to own property and buy and sell goods. The code barred any government regulation of the master's power: "The condition of a slave being merely a passive one, his subordination to his master . . . is not susceptible of any modification or restriction." Planters embraced the more complete white supremacy promoted by American rule.[38]

Territorial legislators also overrode the Spanish and French tradition of treating free Blacks as an intermediate caste with many civil rights. To depress them into a status closer to the enslaved, the new code mandated: "Free people of color ought never to insult or strike white people, nor presume to conceive themselves equal to the white[s]." Imprisonment awaited a free Black who spoke disrespectfully to whites or failed "to yield to them in every occasion." Any white man, no matter how low in status, could lord it over every free Black, no matter how prosperous. The legislators also demobilized the free Black militia that had been so important to the colony's defense and to social aspirations by men of color.[39]

As Americans tightened white supremacy in Louisiana, some slaves fled across the nearby borders with Spanish Tejas (Texas) and Florida. Irritated by the Louisiana Purchase, the Spanish welcomed runaways as a way to weaken the neighboring American regime. Dread of that enticement led Jefferson to inflate the Louisiana Purchase by claiming that it included Tejas and West Florida. Thereby he sought to push the Spanish farther away from American plantations. But by expanding their land claims, the United States compounded Spanish irritation and prolonged borderland tensions. Jefferson posted half of the American army in and around New Orleans to watch for Spanish invasion, slave revolt, and internal disaffection.[40]

Adventure

In the borderland between Tennessee and the Gulf of Mexico, American and Spanish claims overlapped with several Native peoples. None were strong enough to dominate a vast and fertile land of immense commercial potential. The region attracted adventurers with grand schemes far beyond their limited means. They tried to create real power through reflecting illusions. With wild claims of command over Indians and settlers, adventurers tried to impress foreign powers and thereby procure financial and military support. Then that patronage could sway borderlands people to join the speculative adventure in nation building. The most daring adventurer, William Augustus Bowles, proposed the "Muskogee Nation": a hybrid polity of Creeks, Seminoles, and settlers. To dazzle outsiders, Bowles vowed to create European-style institutions for Muskogee: newspaper and university, army and navy, and court system.[41]

Bowles exploited the upheaval wrought by the American Revolution. In 1777, at the age of fourteen, he ran away from home in Maryland to enlist in a Loyalist regiment, winning a commission as a junior officer. Sent to help defend Pensacola in Florida, Bowles deserted after quarreling with a superior. Finding haven among the Creeks, Bowles charmed his hosts and learned their ways and words. Tall, strong, and handsome, Bowles made a striking impression enhanced by extreme self-confidence. A Spanish official later called Bowles a "daring rascally rogue," but Governor Carondelet grudgingly praised Bowles as "an extraordinary young man" and "a lively and resolute spirit." Shifting as interest dictated, Bowles could pose and dress as an adopted Indian chief or a polished gentleman. Despite opposing American interests in the West, Bowles cultivated a federal official: "Altho' we may differ in politics, yet as Gentlemen we may associate, and be friends."[42]

Visiting Britain in 1790, Bowles posed as "Ambassador from the United Nations of Creeks and Cherokees, to the Court of London." Wearing Creek attire topped by a feathered turban, he sought British money and munitions to drive the Spanish from Louisiana and then push southwest to seize silver-rich Mexico. Bowles promised a magic trick: to unite two rival Indian nations, Creeks and Cherokees, with 6,000 of their usual foes, the American settlers. If the British would not invest in his scheme, Bowles threatened to conquer Canada.[43]

Neither fantasy nor bluster impressed Britain's skeptical rulers, so Bowles sailed to Florida in 1791 with only a dozen volunteers in a small schooner. Denying his failure in London, Bowles claimed to hold a British royal commission as "Director General" of the Creeks. What he lacked in resources, Bowles made up for in imagination.[44]

Landing on the Gulf Coast, Bowles challenged the Creek leadership of Alexander McGillivray, the son of a Native woman and a Scots trader. Weary of his Spanish patrons as ineffectual, McGillivray sought federal help against the Creeks' primary enemy, the State of Georgia, which so aggressively seized Native lands. Visiting federal leaders in 1790, McGillivray concluded the Treaty of New York, which restored some Creek lands taken by Georgia and provided $1,500 in annual presents to the Creeks. Secretly, the Washington administration also commissioned McGillivray as a general with a salary of $1,200. Rumors of his American pay induced the Spanish to raise their annual pension for McGillivray to $3,500 in 1792. By playing one side off against another, McGillivray became the richest man of the borderlands, but power among the Upper Creeks troubled many Lower Creeks, who welcomed Bowles as an alternative spokesman.[45]

Bowles sought to supplant McGillivray as the primary broker of trade goods in the Creek country. McGillivray held a secret interest in Panton, Leslie & Company, a British firm with a Spanish contract to trade with Indians from posts in West Florida. In early 1792, Bowles disrupted that supply chain by seizing and plundering one of the firm's posts, giving away loot to buy support among the Lower Creeks and their Seminole kin. Outraged by the coup, McGillivray denounced Bowles as a "mad desperado." To deal with Bowles, a Spanish officer pretended to recognize the Muskogee Nation. Such recognition appealed to Bowles's vanity, so he boarded a Spanish ship for negotiations. Instead, the commander carried him off to New Orleans as a prisoner. Ever resourceful, Bowles sought to turn defeat into victory by charming the Spanish governor of Louisiana, pitching the Muskogee Nation as the best way to rally Indians against the United States. Instead, his captors sent Bowles off to a series of Spanish prisons: first Havana, then Cádiz, followed by Manila.[46]

In 1797, Bowles escaped in West Africa during a voyage meant to take him to Cádiz. Undaunted by his ordeal, Bowles procured another schooner and a few armed volunteers to return to the Gulf Coast in 1799. It helped him that McGillivray had died in 1793, leaving a leadership vacuum that Bowles meant to fill. With charisma and some trade goods, he rallied 400 Lower Creeks and Seminoles to seize a small Spanish post at San Marcos in Florida in May 1800. He also created a Muscogee Navy run by Bahamian freebooters who attacked Spanish merchant ships.[47]

But Bowles had overplayed his hand, stirring up too much trouble for Americans and Spanish in the borderland. Many Creeks also soured on an adventurer who broke so many promises. In 1803, Americans and Creeks lured Bowles to a meeting and seized and surrendered him to the Spanish. Too late, he realized, "This country is hard . . . not like [a story of] Arabian nights," for "men don't go to sleep on a dunghill and wake up in an Imperial Bed in a Palace." Instead, he awoke in a Spanish dungeon.[48]

In the end, Bowles's biracial Muskogee Nation appalled the neighboring powers that he had needed to impress. Even the British, his supposed mentors, let Bowles crash and burn. Euro-American empires and republics treated Natives as backward allies or dependents, the better to manipulate them in war or dispossess them in treaties. By asserting control over frontier expansion and its rewards, the Union pursued power at the expense of Indians. American leaders would not welcome an Indian republic planted in the way of their westward expansion. British officials also disdained a "Muskogee Nation" that empowered Natives. In 1801, Governor John Halkett of the Bahamas disavowed Bowles's "piebald government . . . propped up by issuing mock commissions and holding sham courts" to empower "white American, British, and Spanish outlaws." The whole point of an American empire or republic was to make property and power by dominating Natives—rather than sharing the rewards with them. McGillivray had noted that in American eyes, "Indians are only fit to be subdued and our country divided among a people who are white."[49]

Conspiracy

In December 1805, Bowles died in Havana's grim Morro prison at the age of forty-two, as syphilis and hunger ravaged his body. Meanwhile, two powerful Americans launched a new adventure to build power and wealth in the vast West, where federal control remained weak despite the recent Louisiana Purchase. General James Wilkinson commanded the federal army in the West. Possessed of some charm but little ability save for intrigue, Wilkinson deceived almost everyone, including the Spanish, who kept him on their payroll as a double agent. Despite rumors of this treason, Jefferson retained Wilkinson in command of the American army on the sensitive and contested border with the Spanish Empire.[50]

Vice President Aaron Burr joined Wilkinson in a mysterious western game of geopolitics. After losing the presidency to Jefferson in 1801 and killing Hamilton in a duel in 1804, Burr had bleak political prospects in the East, so he looked westward for a new opportunity. During the winter of 1804–1805, he met Wilkinson at the national capital, where they hatched a conspiracy. At a minimum, Burr would rally armed volunteers along the Ohio River to descend in boats to New Orleans for an invasion of Tejas (Texas) and silver-rich Mexico. That would violate American neutrality law, but adventurers often did so. Wilkinson encouraged Burr because the scheme enabled the general to demand more money from the Spanish for his information. Tensions with Spain were good for Wilkinson's business of deceiving both sides.[51]

Gifted at improvisation, Burr tried out shifting scenarios with different people to see what they might do for him. Sometimes Burr claimed that he also would promote western secession from the United States to add to Mexico in a new empire based at New Orleans. So Burr told Anthony Merry, the British ambassador who had grown disgusted with Jefferson and the United States. Merry informed his home government that Burr requested British naval support "to effect a Separation of the Western Part of the United States from that which lies between the Atlantic and the Mountains." Maybe Burr spoke in earnest, but he probably just played Merry to secure warships for an attack on Mexico. The British, however, did not take the bait, leaving Burr to pursue his western ambitions without foreign support.[52]

During the spring and summer of 1805, Burr visited Ohio, Kentucky, and Tennessee to woo western leaders. The proposed attack on the Spanish Empire appealed to many, including Senators James Adair of Kentucky and Andrew Jackson of Tennessee, who provided boats, provisions, and advice about potential officers. By conquering Mexico and New Mexico, Jackson hoped to secure "a permanent barrier against the inroads and attacks of foreign powers on our interior." He believed that American insecurity required dominating the rest of the continent.[53]

Writing to Jefferson in January 1806, the federal district attorney for Kentucky, Joseph Daveiss, warned that Burr and Wilkinson were plotting "To cause a revolt of the Spanish provinces, and a severance of all these western states and territories from the union to coalesce & form one government." Daveiss told Jefferson to beware of the West's leading men at the national capital: "Depend on it, you have traitors around you to give the alarm in time to their friends." But Jefferson responded indifferently, answering only one of seven anxious letters from Daveiss, whom the president distrusted as a Federalist married to a sister of Chief Justice John Marshall.[54]

During the summer of 1806, Burr rallied a few dozen supporters to descend the Ohio and Mississippi Rivers bound for New Orleans to rendezvous with Wilkinson. Burr expected to attack Tejas in the fall, so Wilkinson shifted American troops closer to the border and sent a subordinate, Zebulon Pike, with a scouting party across the Great Plains to probe the defenses of New Mexico. As a cover story, Pike posed as an explorer, but Spanish troops arrested and held him captive until June 1807.[55]

Rather than imperil his lucrative ties with Spain, Wilkinson betrayed Burr at the last minute. Making a truce with the Spanish commander in Tejas, Wilkinson withdrew his troops from the border, aborting the confrontation needed to initiate Burr's plan. In October 1806, the general also wrote a fateful and fanciful letter to Jefferson, reporting that Burr was leading a traitorous conspiracy involving thousands of armed men to promote western secession. In fact, Burr had only about sixty active supporters in his riverboats. Declaring martial law in New Orleans, Wilkinson jailed Burr's friends and anyone who criticized the general's arbitrary rule. To motivate planters to find and capture Burr, Wilkinson spread the rumor that Burr meant to rally slaves to revolt and kill their masters. Taking Wilkinson at his word, Jefferson denounced Burr and ordered his arrest. To avoid assassination by Wilkinson, Burr fled eastward disguised as a common farmer, complete with a fake beard.[56]

In February 1807, federal troops captured Burr and took him to Richmond, Virginia, for trial. Eager to convict and execute Burr, Jefferson spent nearly $100,000 to gather information and witnesses.

But the prosecution faced three great obstacles: the high standard of proof for treason under the Federal Constitution, a skeptical judge, and a slippery lead witness.[57]

To prove treason required at least two witnesses to an "overt act of war" against the United States. But Burr had never attacked anyone. The prosecution charged that a muster by sixty supporters on an island in the Ohio River sufficed as an act of war. But Burr had not been there at the time. His attorney mocked, "What kind of invisible army must this have been, when in the course of three months not an individual could be found to testify to its existence." The presiding judge, Chief Justice Marshall, suspected the president of playing fast and loose with facts to secure a political conviction.[58]

The prosecution relied on devious testimony by Wilkinson and a letter written in cipher allegedly by Burr in July 1806. At the trial, a witness recalled the pompous Wilkinson "swelling like a turkey cock" while Burr coolly displayed "a slight expression of contempt." Under cross-examination, Wilkinson admitted to doctoring the letter, which had seemed suspiciously explicit for an operator as sly as Burr. Indeed, an indiscreet associate had written the original, unsigned letter. After Wilkinson stepped down, the foreman of the grand jury, John Randolph, declared, "Wilkinson is the only man I ever saw who was from the bark to the very core a villain." The lead prosecutor declared that his faith in the general was "shaken, if not destroyed."[59]

On August 31, 1807, Marshall informed the grand jury that the prosecution lacked enough evidence to indict Burr: "Treason may be machinated in secret, but it can be perpetrated only in the open day and in the eye of the world." A day later, the jury found a verdict of not guilty. After a second trial of Burr for violating the Neutrality Act, Burr won another acquittal and went free. Jefferson seethed, blaming Marshall as an arch-Federalist allegedly involved in Burr's massive conspiracy. Wilkinson remained the American commander of the western army and a Spanish double agent. The retention of "this viper" infuriated Jackson, who lost confidence in Jefferson's judgment.[60]

The Burr controversy attested to the western instability of the Union. Leading men, including a former vice president and two United States senators, had schemed to invade a foreign land and perhaps to unravel their own country. In the Burr crisis of 1806, the new Francophone citizens of Louisiana proved more loyal to the United States than some long-standing and higher-status Americans.[61]

In the grip of his fancies, Jefferson speculated that it did not much matter whether westerners stayed tied to the United States, so long as they nurtured a compatible, republican form of government. "Whether we remain in one confederacy, or form into Atlantic and Mississippi confederacies, I believe not very important to the happiness of either part. Those of the western confederacy will be as much our children & descendants as those of the Eastern." But in practice, Jefferson blocked his rival, Aaron Burr, from creating a distinct Empire of Liberty in the West.[62]

Pacific

In 1804, while the Burr conspiracy developed in the Mississippi Valley, Jefferson sent an expedition westward from St. Louis in search of a route through the Rocky Mountains to the Pacific Ocean. He entrusted this sensitive mission to his confidential secretary, Captain Meriwether Lewis, and his fellow Virginian, Captain William Clark. While they would pass through a dimly understood mid-continent, the expedition sought to reach a Pacific coast already explored and contested by Spain, Russia, and Britain—and long occupied by a complex array of Native nations.[63]

During the eighteenth century, Russian, French, and British naval expeditions probed the Pacific in defiance of Spanish claims to control that vast ocean. Although commanded by naval officers, and worked by common sailors, the Pacific voyages also included artists, astronomers, cartographers, and naturalists to study and depict the waters, skies, soils, plants, animals, weather, and peoples of distant islands and coasts. The empires claimed to serve science, which they cast as a universal ideal betrayed by the secretive Spanish.[64]

Driven by the intellectual movement known as the Enlightenment, eighteenth-century science was a new mix of ideology and methodology. Educated Europeans sought to collect and organize information about everything on earth, which fed a sense of imperial mastery. The explorers also sought to identify marketable commodities for commercial exploitation and to learn how best to pacify distant peoples as imperial subjects. Europeans claimed that science endowed them with the right to govern peoples deemed primitive. By publishing their findings in learned and international journals, empires competed for prestige and to claim distant places. This intellectual game punished the Spanish for keeping secret their Pacific discoveries.[65]

The Russians broke into the Pacific from fur-trade posts on Siberia's Kamchatka Peninsula. In 1729 and 1741, Vitus Bering, a Danish mariner in the Russian service, commanded two voyages that discovered the strait, later named for him, separating Siberia from North America and the Aleutian Islands, a chain extending westward from Alaska. The voyagers returned with hundreds of sea otter pelts that netted high prices and keen interest from merchants in Kamchatka engaged in trade with China. Russians referred to sea otters as "soft gold."[66]

Well-armed traders, known as *promyshlenniki*, followed Bering's lead into the Aleutian Islands. With brutal violence, they forced Aleut peoples to become market hunters. After exterminating sea otters in the Aleutians, the *promyshlenniki* extended their operations eastward to the islands and coasts of southern Alaska. During the 1780s at Kodiak Island and Sitka, a merchant cartel established the first permanent Russian settlements in North America. In 1799 the Russian government awarded a monopoly over the region to that cartel as the Russian-American Company. Relying primarily on Native laborers and hunters, the Russians had only 400 colonists in Alaska in 1800.[67]

But there were more than enough Russians to alarm the Spanish. During the 1760s, exaggerated reports persuaded Spanish colonial officials that the Russians were about to extend their operations
southward to California and on to Mexico. To preempt that supposed
Russian move, the Spanish belatedly settled California. Unable to
attract many colonists to the distant region, officials instead sought
to convert Indians into Hispanics by indoctrination at missions run
by Franciscan priests. By 1784, California had four presidios, nine
missions, and 900 Hispanic colonists stretched thin along a 500-mile-
long coast from San Francisco to San Diego.[68]

During the late 1760s, the British joined the race to explore the
Pacific. They feared falling behind their imperial rivals in the search
for new trade and colonies in that corner of the globe. Imperial competition coupled with Enlightenment science to drive British exploration just as anxieties about the Russians had pushed the Spanish to
occupy California.[69]

The British entrusted Pacific exploration to Captain James Cook,
a talented navigator and cartographer who crisscrossed the South
Pacific during the late 1760s and early 1770s. Defining people, shores,
and islands in maps, charts, and journals of unprecedented detail and
precision, Cook set the scientific protocols emulated by subsequent
explorers seeking equal credit for their empires.[70]

During his third voyage, 1776–1779, Cook probed the North Pacific,
visiting the Pacific Northwest in 1778. The region's Natives had adapted
to the mild and rainy climate abounding in timber, fish, sea otters, seals,
and whales. Well fed by fishing and marine hunting, the rain-coast
Natives had developed a large population. Although divided into at least
six language groups and hundreds of villages, the peoples shared elaborate ceremonies, a detailed art in wood carving, and complex social hierarchies led by powerful chiefs. Rival chiefs raided far and wide for slaves
and prestige, but they also traded along the coast and up the major rivers
with Indians of the mountainous interior.[71]

After leaving the rain coast, Cook and his men sailed to the Hawaiian Islands, a mid-oceanic and subtropical range of volcanic peaks

colonized by Polynesians. In February 1779, Cook died in a battle
provoked by his bungled attempt to seize Hawaiians accused of stealing iron tools and a small boat. Cook's successor sailed away to China
and then eastward across the Indian Ocean, around southern Africa,
and north up the Atlantic to England.[72]

In 1784, publication of Cook's journals caused a sensation in
Europe by revealing the potential profits of trading metal tools and
weapons for sea otter pelts on the rain coast. Mariners could take
the pelts to China to procure porcelain, tea, spices, and silks for
sale back in Europe. British merchants sent twenty-six ships laden
with trade goods to the rain coast between 1785 and 1790. Starting in 1788, American merchant ships also visited that region. In
1792, Captain Robert Gray found the mouth of the greatest river on
that coast, a river that he named the Columbia: a discovery founda-
tional to American claims to the region. Once the rare experience of
government-sponsored explorers, circumnavigation became a commercial commonplace during the late 1780s.[73]

The British and American ships on the rain coast alarmed Spanish
officials, who suspected a new threat to precious Mexico. In 1789,
a Spanish naval expedition visited Nootka, the primary village for
the sea otter trade. The commander seized four British ships, arresting their captains and crews as trespassers on Spanish territory. In
1790, when Britain's rulers threatened war, the Spanish backed down,
releasing the ships, cargoes, and prisoners. The Spanish also conceded
the right of other nations, including the United States, to trade with
Indians of the rain coast. In 1795, the Spanish abandoned their new
fort at Nootka, to the delight of the Moachats, who demolished the
buildings to harvest nails and hinges to make into tools and weapons.[74]

Natives believed that they had discovered the intruding mariners,
who seemed remarkable for body hair, bad manners, and alluring
metals. Dwelling at the mouth of the Columbia, Clatsops remembered the first sighting of a sailing ship by a woman walking along
the beach. At first she thought, "It is a monster!" As it came closer,
she noted, "Then a bear came out of it . . . but his face was that of a

human being." Boarding the ship, other Clatsops saw boxes of iron, copper, and brass. Then they set fire to the vessel, and "it burned just like fat." Salvaging the metals and two "bears" for slaves, the Clatsops prospered by trading with Indians of the interior, swapping a single nail for a deer hide. Symbolic rather than literal, the memory dwelled on the Natives' ability to master the intruders and possess their metals.[75]

Savvy customers and negotiators, rain-coast Indians frustrated mariners bent on cheating them. A captain lamented, "We were, more or less, the dupes of their cunning." Invoking phrenology, another American cited their "bump of avariciousness being very prominent." But those bumps were at least as common among mariners.[76]

Maquinna of the Moachats was an especially shrewd and demanding chief. A sea captain marveled, "He asks for anything he pleases. . . . He asks for wine and sherry, coffee upon finishing if there is any, and chocolate in the mornings." Polite when treated well, Maquinna became deadly when crossed. In March 1803, a reckless American captain gave Maquinna a defective gun and insulted him when the chief complained. The next day, Maquinna led several canoes filled with men out to the ship, the *Boston*, apparently to trade. Instead, they overwhelmed and killed all but two of the crew: a blacksmith and sail-maker useful to the Moachats as slaves. The many dead included the captain.[77]

In the global sea otter trade, Hawaii offered a key transit point where vessels could stop for repairs and a resupply of water, wood, and provisions. This busy crossroads of trans-Pacific trade became a hothouse of cross-cultural encounters. By working as sailors on foreign ships, Hawaiians discovered China, Europe, and the United States. Others became laborers at trading posts on the rain coast. Meanwhile, some Europeans and Americans joined Hawaiian society. They included military advisors who helped chiefs fight for local supremacy with new firearms. By 1810, Chief Kamehameha of Hawaii won the arms race with cannons and a British-built warship, uniting the islands as his kingdom.[78]

Mackenzie

On his last voyage, Captain Cook had found a large inlet—now named for him—on the coast of Alaska. Cook speculated that the inlet received a large river that flowed westward from the continental interior. Perhaps an overland probe from the east could find that waterway and descend it to the Pacific, establishing a trade route across North America and on to the riches of China. This speculation intrigued Montreal's Scottish fur traders, who had expanded their trade westward into the Manitoba country in the heart of the continent. Indulging in wishful thinking, they claimed that the Rocky Mountains were nearby, low, and narrow—a scant obstacle to exploring westward in search of a navigable river, called "Oregan," that allegedly flowed into Cook's outlet.[79]

During the late 1780s, a young trader named Alexander Mackenzie identified the Oregan with the Deh-Cho River, the outlet for the Great Slave Lake. During the summer of 1789, Mackenzie descended the Deh-Cho with a few Indian guides and French-Canadian boatmen in birch-bark canoes. But, instead of flowing westward into the Pacific, that river turned northward to the Arctic Ocean, so Mackenzie renamed it the "River of Disappointment." He might not be pleased that maps now call it the Mackenzie River. The 1,120-mile journey did establish Mackenzie's diplomatic and logistical abilities to probe deep into territory possessed by Natives with good reason to suspect the motives of intruders.[80]

During the spring and summer of 1793, Mackenzie tried again by heading west. His small party ascended the Peace River into the Rocky Mountains, which proved far higher, wider, and more difficult than imagined. But Indians had long traversed the mountains that seemed so mysterious and daunting to Mackenzie. He eventually found his way after noticing British-made metal goods among the Natives. Where, he asked, had they obtained them? They replied: from traders to the west. In Mackenzie's words, he "pursue[d] that chain of connexion by which these people obtain their ironwork."[81]

Breaking through the mountains, he descended the Bella Coola River to the Pacific, where Mackenzie enacted the Enlightenment's ceremonies of possession. He recorded ethnographic, botanical, faunal, and geologic information in a journal and employed a bulky chronometer and sextant to calculate and record his geoposition. Finally, he painted on a large rock: "Alexander Mackenzie, from Canada, by land, the twenty-second of July, one thousand seven hundred and ninety-three." His strange equipment and painting alarmed the local Bella Bella people as a menacing sorcery: not a bad guess given how much they would suffer from Euro-Americans who followed Mackenzie's lead. Noting their anger, Mackenzie hastened down the coast, where he traded metals for sea otter pelts to help prove that he had reached the Pacific. Where European trade goods had led Mackenzie over an Indian trail to the coast, a Native trade good proved his Pacific arrival to Europeans.[82]

With measurements, notes, and pelts, Mackenzie could return to Montreal and travel across the Atlantic to London in search of official credit for his exploration. In 1801, he published a book to document his travels and pitch his commercial and imperial plans. Mackenzie proposed that the British Empire build and garrison forts on the rain coast to secure Indian allies—and thereby control the region's sea-otter trade with China. Otherwise, he warned, the pushy Americans would do so.[83]

For his exploits, Mackenzie won a knighthood, but imperial officials could not commit to his grand project. War with France had drained the coffers of empire, and the proposal crossed powerful interests. The Hudson's Bay Company wanted to control the fur trade in western Canada, and the East India Company asserted a monopoly over the China trade. The harrowing difficulties of his journey also undermined the proposal, for Mackenzie's route was impractical for moving bulky goods. His grand scheme sank in direct and inverse proportion to his renown as an explorer.[84]

Mackenzie's most eager—but horrified—reader was the American president, Thomas Jefferson. Ever suspicious of the British, Jefferson felt certain that they would embrace Mackenzie's scheme to occupy the rain coast just to spite the United States. In fact, British officials had more important interests to tend in Europe and India. The empire was far less monolithic and united than Jefferson imagined. A bundle of often clashing interests—including the East India Company and Hudson's Bay Company, the British Empire had no consistent plan to restrict the Americans.[85]

But as with the Spanish overreacting to the Russians, or the British to the French, Americans acted on their fears to justify expansion as defensive. Although insisting on his scientific sincerity, Jefferson distrusted that professed by foreigners. In 1783, he had warned, "I find they have subscribed a very large sum of money in England for exploring the country from the Mississippi to California. They pretend it is only to promote knolege. I am afraid they have thoughts of colonizing into that quarter."[86]

During the 1780s and 1790s, Jefferson dreamed of sponsoring an American overland probe to the Pacific. He procured every available book on that ocean, including Captain Cook's journals. In 1802, Jefferson bought Mackenzie's book describing his expedition and promoting a military occupation of the rain coast.[87]

In 1803, Jefferson gave a copy of the book to his protégé, Meriwether Lewis, who would co-lead the American attempt to reach the Pacific by land. That expedition also carried a map made in Philadelphia derived from British prototypes based on information gathered by Cook and Mackenzie. Thanks to the British maps and journals, Lewis and his collaborator, William Clark, had a good understanding of their Pacific destination. They just needed to find their way there from the upper Missouri River, where traders had visited the Mandan villages for over sixty years.[88]

Given his strict construction of the Federal Constitution, Jefferson doubted that Congress had the authority to fund scientific exploration, so he pitched the expedition as meant to promote trade with Indians. But the president feared that a commercial purpose would alarm Spanish officials into blocking the expedition. So, he told them that the journey was purely scientific and no reason for their alarm. The Spanish ambassador, Carlos Martinez de Yrujo, urged Jefferson to desist, but the president assured Congress that the Spanish regarded the proposed journey as "a matter of indifference" because "a literary pursuit, which it is in the habit of permitting within its dominions." Jefferson had mastered the political art of telling shifting tales suited to what others wanted to hear. But Yrujo could see that Jefferson meant "to discover the way by which the Americans may someday extend their population and their influence up to the coasts of the South Sea."[89]

Emulating the methods of Cook and Mackenzie, Lewis and Clark were to make frequent and precise celestial measurements to fix the latitude and longitude of places and keep a detailed journal to describe flora, fauna, soil, and climate. Jefferson also sought ethnographic information to assist American officials, traders, and missionaries in managing Native peoples. Recognizing that mercantile voyages to the rain coast had become routine, Jefferson authorized the explorers to hitchhike home on a ship if the overland return seemed too dangerous. His instructions presumed a Pacific coast already well understood and routinely visited by sea.[90]

If less than an unprecedented push into the unknown, the expedition had to overcome a late start in the geopolitics of science. If endowed with the insights of predecessors, Lewis and Clark also faced the challenges of winning American access to a contested corner of the globe. By building on what others had learned, Lewis and Clark helped to secure a Pacific footing for the United States against formidable competitors. But first the expedition had to cross two-thirds of the continent held by the diverse Indians of the Great Plains and Rocky Mountains.[91]

Great Plains

Two thousand miles long by four hundred miles wide, the Great Plains are a windswept and arid grassland bounded by the Rocky

Mountains on the west and the more humid prairies and forests of the Mississippi Valley to the east. The region seemed like an endless ocean of grass. After four days of traveling without spotting a tree, the sight of a few in a valley led an Irish traveler to marvel: "By Jesus! We're in sight of land again!" The grass sustained vast herds of bison: immense, shaggy, grazing beasts that provided meat and warm robes to hunters.[92]

During the early eighteenth century, Plains peoples first acquired horses by trading with or stealing from Spanish New Mexico to the southwest. On horseback, they could cover far more ground in less time to find and overtake herds of bison. By killing more bison, the Great Plains peoples became better fed, clothed, and housed. Enriched by meaty protein, they raised the tallest children on the continent, taller even than the relatively well-fed people of the United States. A Crow woman later recalled, "Ah, I came into a happy world. There was always fat meat, glad singing, and much dancing in our villages."[93]

But that happiness did not last. The alluring combination of horses and bison drew more Native nations to relocate onto the Great Plains. Coming from either the Rocky Mountains to the west or the Mississippi Valley to the east, the newcomers included Osages, Comanches, Cheyennes, Arapahos, Blackfeet, and Lakotas (known to their foes as the Sioux). They competed with one another and with the earth-lodge peoples over access to horses and bison. A Cheyenne tradition insisted that their supreme being had provided a warning: "If you have horses everything will be changed for you forever. . . . You will have to have fights with other tribes, who will want your pasture land or the places where you hunt." He concluded, "Think before you decide."[94]

Escalating warfare took a heavy toll. Many young men died competing for honor and status by displaying courage in combat. Because women outnumbered men, the most successful chiefs accumulated several wives as markers of their high status. They also acquired large horse herds. As trade in buffalo hides expanded, the women had to work harder, feeding and tending horses, scraping and tanning more hides, drying meat, and making pemmican: a combination of dried meat and berries that provided portable meals. Targeted by raids, women especially suffered from warfare. And the horse-centered way of life was environmentally unstable, as Natives killed too many buffalo and depleted the grasslands by acquiring too many horses.[95]

The wars became more deadly as Natives procured arms and ammunition from traders who ventured up the Missouri River from St. Louis or from British posts to the north in Canada. By combining guns and horses, some Natives preyed on more distant Indian nations that fell behind in the arms race. The strong became stronger by taking horses, women, and children and hunting territory from their defeated rivals. No primeval land of scant change, the Great Plains was a vast, dynamic zone of shifting peoples, adopting new ways of life and adapting tribal identities.[96]

The swirling movement of peoples onto the Great Plains set off shock waves that hit colonists as well as Natives. Moving southeastward out of the Rocky Mountains, Comanches obtained firearms and horses. Then they drove out, killed, or captured peoples known to outsiders as Apaches. Fleeing westward into New Mexico or southward into Texas, the Apaches raided Hispanic ranches and missions and Pueblo villages. In 1777, New Mexico's governor reported that Apache attacks had reduced his province "to the most deplorable state and greatest poverty." In 1786, a new governor drew the Comanches into an alliance by offering generous presents of guns and ammunition. In return, their warriors helped Hispanics attack Apaches, capturing hundreds for sale as slaves to distant Cuba. The bloody alliance reduced Apache pressure on New Mexico, which began to revive.[97]

Far to the north, the Mandans and other earth-lodge villagers initially held their own because they outnumbered the newcomers, primarily Lakotas from the Mississippi Valley. During the late 1770s, however, an epidemic of smallpox altered the balance of power. The traders who brought guns unknowingly carried microscopic pathogens in their bodies and on their breath. The densely settled earth-lodge villages were especially vulnerable to smallpox, a deadly crowd disease. [98]

After losing so many defenders to disease, the smaller villages succumbed to attacks. Of the Lakotas, a French trader remarked, "Their very name causes terror, they having so often ravaged and carried off the wives and children of the [A]ricaras." The survivors crowded into fewer, larger, and heavily fortified towns. From thirty-two villages in 1770, Arikaras shrank into just two towns by 1785. But that crowding increased their vulnerability to epidemics.[99]

While Comanches controlled the southern plains and Lakotas dominated the north, Osages prevailed between them on the middle plains. Originally from the Mississippi Valley, they moved southwestward to claim the region between the Arkansas and Missouri Rivers during the mid-eighteenth century. Well armed with trade guns, Osages drove Caddos and Wichitas southward into Texas and raided the weak Spanish posts and settlements along the Arkansas River.[100]

Jefferson recognized that Indians dominated the Great Plains. Referring to Osages and Lakotas, Jefferson concluded "with these two powerful nations we must stand well, because in their quarter we are miserably weak." Jefferson wanted Lewis and Clark to contact and study Native peoples of the Great Plains, making allies where possible. The explorers carried dozens of American flags and scores of silver medals, bearing Jefferson's image, to give to helpful chiefs as symbols of their good favor with the United States.[101]

Lewis and Clark

During the spring of 1804, Lewis and Clark led forty men in boats up the Missouri River. Although well armed, the expedition suffered from the want of any women. In the Native world, their absence in an intruding party signaled hostile intent. And the explorers entered a war zone dominated by Lakotas, who attacked and plundered traders ascending from St. Louis to trade with the earth-lodge peoples.

Writing of the Lakotas, Jefferson assured Lewis, "On that nation, we wish more particularly to make a friendly impression, because of their immense power." But Lewis and Clark relied on bluster and displays of weaponry, stinting on presents. Confrontations became heated with insults and threats that kept the expeditionaries on edge as they ascended the river. Clark called the Lakotas "the vilest miscreants of the savage race, and must ever remain the pirates of the Missouri."[102]

In the early fall, the explorers found a warmer welcome upon reaching the Hidatsa and Mandan villages on the upper Missouri. The villagers hailed the Americans as potential allies who could provide the firearms needed to resist their enemies. Irritated by Lakota harassment, Lewis and Clark warmed to the Mandans: "We were ready to protect them and kill those who would not listen to our Good talk." Plunging into the complicated geopolitics of the Great Plains, Americans began choosing enemies and friends.[103]

Building a fort, the explorers hunkered down near the primary Mandan village for a long, cold winter of blizzards. On sunny days, they did a brisk business selling or repairing weapons, primarily metal hatchets. The sojourners also pursued their female hosts. A chief asked an American, "Why is it that your people are so fond of our women[?] One might suppose they had never seen any before."[104]

In their greatest coup, Lewis and Clark hired a resident trader, Toussaint Charbonneau, to accompany them westward. They valued Charbonneau primarily for his sixteen-year-old wife, Sacagawea. Because her Shoshone people lived in the Rocky Mountains near the headwaters of the Missouri River, she offered the language and local knowledge to solve the greatest geographic challenge facing the expedition. And Sacagawea provided the female presence that the expedition had lacked in its first, dangerous season. "The sight of this Indian woman," Clark explained, persuaded Natives "of our friendly intentions, as no woman ever accompanies a war party of Indians in this quarter." Bearing her newborn in a cradleboard strapped to her back, Sacagawea was "a token of peace."[105]

During the spring and summer of 1805, Lewis and Clark slowly ascended the Missouri River, struggling against the powerful current in search of the Shoshone homeland in the mountains. In late summer, time became of the essence, for the explorers dreaded becoming entrapped by an early snow in the Rockies. If snowbound, they could starve to death. Lewis and Clark needed Shoshone guides to show the way through the mountains and provide horses to haul their equipment. But grim experience with raiders made the Shoshone skittish about any armed group coming from the east. Lacking firepower, they hid in the mountains to wait for intruders to tire and depart.[106]

In August, the expedition had a great stroke of luck as Lewis and Clark stumbled upon a Shoshone band led by Sacagawea's older brother, Cameahwait. Brother and sister broke into a joyous dance upon their surprise reunion five years after she seemed lost forever. In return for generous presents and the promise of future trade, the Shoshone provided guides and horses. Cameahwait explained, "If we had guns, we could then live in the country of the buffaloe and eat as our enemies do and not be compelled to hide ourselves in these mountains and live on roots and berries as the bear do."[107]

Crossing the continental divide, the expedition reached the Snake River, which flowed westward into the Columbia. Building boats, the explorers descended to their destination: the river's mouth on the Pacific coast. Erecting a fort, they wintered uneasily among the Clatsops. Used to pork and beef, the Americans grumbled about having to eat, day after day, the world's finest salmon. In the spring of 1806, they retraced their route up the Columbia and Snake Rivers and across the Rocky Mountains to the Missouri River, which they descended rapidly, thanks to the downstream flow, reaching St. Louis in September.[108]

The Lewis and Clark expedition receives acclaim for losing only one member, a sergeant who died of a burst appendix early in the journey. We pay too little attention to the two Blackfeet Indians killed by the explorers on their return journey in July 1806. Upset at the American alliance with the Shoshones, the Blackfeet tried to steal horses and guns from the expedition but suffered casualties in the ensuing firefight. By taking some Indians as allies, Lewis and Clark made enemies of others. The West's more beleaguered peoples rallied to the Americans as potential game-changers. Interpreting them as "friendly" Indians, the explorers were quick to share their enemies as undeserving "hostiles." Those included the powerful Lakotas and Blackfeet.[109]

Mountain Men

Following the Captain Cook model, Lewis and Clark returned with eight volumes of journals, detailing their observations of flora, fauna, Indians, and geography. Clark conceded that their new knowledge depended on Native sources rather than the explorers' discovery: "Our information is altogether from Indians collected at different times." Arranged by Jefferson, publication staked an enhanced American claim to their route and its rain-coast destination. Although Lewis and Clark had failed to find a commercially viable route through the Rockies to the Pacific, the expedition did reveal the rivers and streams deep within the continent that fur traders and trappers could exploit. In 1821 a trader noted, "By the journey of Captains Lewis and Clark across the Rocky Mountains to the Pacific Ocean the whole of that western region is now laid open."[110]

In 1811, New York's leading fur merchant, John Jacob Astor, founded "Astoria," a trading post at the mouth of the Columbia River near the winter encampment of Lewis and Clark. After landing Astor's men, the mariner Jonathan Thorn sailed north in the *Tonquin* to trade with the Moachats at Nootka on Vancouver Island. Overreacting to a misunderstanding, Thorn insulted them, so they returned in war canoes to attack and capture the *Tonquin*, killing Thorn. A dying sailor ignited the gunpowder store on board, blowing up the ship and at least a hundred Natives.[111]

In the short term, the Astorians had to adapt to a Native world. Avoiding Thorn's mistake, the post's chief trader, Duncan McDougall, wisely married Ilche, the daughter of a Chinook chief, by paying a dowry of fifteen guns and fifteen blankets. Increased trade and improved security led Astoria's chief clerk to report that "everything went on well owing to Mr. McDougall's marriage." No deferential American wife, Ilche claimed joint leadership at Astoria, so another trader called her "haughty and imperious." By dint of her marriage, the post belonged to the Chinook as well as to Astor.[112]

A British fur-trade cartel, the North West Company, also claimed the region and resented Astoria as an intrusion. In 1813, with the help of a British warship, the North Westers intimidated Astor's men into selling the trading post to them for a bargain price. Tearing down Astoria, the victors located their operation up the Columbia River at Fort Vancouver, near the juncture of the Willamette River.[112]

Other American fur trappers ventured up the Missouri River into the Rocky Mountains. Known as mountain men, these trappers included several veterans of the Lewis and Clark expedition exploiting their new knowledge of Indians and beaver-rich streams. In 1808, the former expeditionary John Colter led a trapping venture up the Missouri and Yellowstone Rivers to the boiling hot springs and geysers of a region named "Colter's Hell," now Yellowstone National Park.[113]

Fur traders wanted trappers willing to go into the mountains to seek beavers during the winter, when the pelts were thickest and, so, most valuable. On most frontiers, traders relied on Native hunters, but along the Rocky Mountains the local Indians wisely shifted to lower elevations for the winter, rather than risk becoming snowbound to starve or freeze to death. When spring returned, people in the mountains also risked falling prey to hungry grizzly bears awaking from hibernation. For want of willing Indian hunters, traders recruited more reckless people—young white men—to trap in the mountains.[114]

During the 1820s, William H. Ashley, an elegant Virginian who moved to Missouri, dominated the fur trade on the upper Missouri watershed. In theory, his mountain men were "free trappers," unlike the hired servants of the North West Company or Hudson's

Bay Company in Canada and Oregon. But Ashley exploited them through a system of debt peonage. Recruiting poor but able-bodied young men in St. Louis, he advanced their traps, guns, ammunition, and provisions on credit, payable during the next summer in beaver pelts. To facilitate that exchange, Ashley brought a caravan of packhorses and wagons to the foothills for an annual rendezvous in the early summer. Laden with alcohol on the way out, the wagons returned heaping with beaver pelts. At the rendezvous, Ashley had a monopoly of whiskey and a captive market of thirsty men rendered stir-crazy by months of isolation in bitter cold.[115]

During the late 1820s and early 1830s, the rendezvous attracted a thousand trappers to what a witness described as "one continued scene of drunkenness, gambling, and brawling and fighting, as long as the money and the credit of the trappers last." But that was not long. After a week of debauchery, most mountain men returned to the Rockies with hangovers and increased debt to trap for another winter.[116]

Mountain men needed Native wives for companionship, protection, and help. Native kin often saved a trapper's life by fending off enemies. Native women also knew the lay of the land and how to prepare beaver pelts for market and buffalo meat for eating. If without Indian wives, trappers often succumbed to hunger, cold, bears, or raids by Blackfeet and Arikaras.[117]

Despite the dangers and hardships, survivors clung to the mountain life as better than the tedium of working a midwestern farm. The trapping business attracted plenty of tough and contentious men addicted to alcohol and lying. They included Mike Fink, who quarreled with another mountain man and conned him into a contest of shooting cups of whiskey off one another's heads from a distance of sixty yards. Fink shot first, putting a bullet between the eyes of his dim rival. But an outraged witness promptly shot Fink in the heart.[118]

The most sober and frugal of mountain men was Jedediah Strong Smith, who became one of Ashley's first hunters in 1822. A year later, Smith barely survived a grizzly bear that tore off an ear and much of his scalp. The trapper had a friend stitch both back to his head. In

1824, Smith learned from Indian guides about the South Pass through the Rockies (in present-day Wyoming), to find and cross the arid Great Basin to reach California. Smith then turned north, venturing into Oregon, where one of his men tried to rape a Native woman, provoking an attack that killed nineteen trappers, leaving only three survivors, including Smith. His luck ran out in 1831, when he died in a firefight with Comanches on the southern Great Plains. During a peripatetic life, Smith discovered and revealed the dimensions of the West for Americans.[119]

By finding a cross-country trail to California, Smith initiated a transcontinental trade in horses with Native peoples of California's Central Valley: Mariposas, Miwoks, Moquelumnes, and Yumas. They stole livestock from Hispanic missions and ranchos along the Pacific coast. Those thefts surged once the valley Indians could broker horses to American traders, who took the animals east across the continent to sell to farmers and ranchers in Arkansas and Missouri.[120]

The fur trade ultimately brought more death than opportunity to western Indians. In June 1837, a steamboat of the American Fur Company arrived at the Mandan villages. Some of the crew and passengers had smallpox, and the vessel's operators failed to quarantine them, so the scourge raced through the Native peoples who had flocked in to trade. Most died, reducing the Mandans to 300 survivors.[121]

The fur trade also devastated wild animals, who suffered from the "tragedy of the Commons," the plight of a valuable resource taken by people pursuing immediate profit. Unlike a cow on a farm, no one owned a living beaver on a mountain stream. Unlike in a regulated commons, no collective group limited what one person could take. So, no one had a vested interest in breeding and preserving any fur-bearing animals. The beaver only became one man's valuable commodity when he killed it. Competing with hundreds of other trappers, he sought to kill as many as possible to make money. The trapper assumed that the local supply was doomed, sooner or later, so he might as well kill as many as possible as fast as he could. That loss was greatest on the northwestern slope of the Rockies, where the

Hudson's Bay Company worked to keep out the Americans by systematically trapping all the fur animals in a broad buffer zone along the Snake River.[122]

Ashley sold his company at the peak of the market in 1826, when abundant supply met great demand because eastern and European gentlemen prized beaver hats. But within ten years, the fur trade began to collapse as overhunting depleted beavers, inflating the price of their pelts. As that supply became unreliable and more expensive, hat manufacturers shifted to silk, deflating demand for furs. In 1840, traders held the last rendezvous with the mountain men.[123]

In legend, mountain men were loners who escaped into the wilderness, forsaking the capitalist society of their nation. In fact, they expanded that society until it discarded them after they overhunted their commodity and fashions shifted. In the process, they had brought greater afflictions into Native encampments: diminished wildlife and increased alcohol and disease. By helping the mountain men, Natives became enveloped by a market economy that sought profits without accounting for the human and environmental costs. The men at the top reaped the spoils. Astor shifted his capital into real estate, primarily in New York City, where he became the wealthiest man in America. Ashley grew richer by investing in Missouri lands, and he served three terms in Congress.[124]

Fur traders and trappers served as the shock troops of American expansion and environmental transformation. Behind them came farmers by the thousands to dispossess Indians and consolidate the American hold on the land. That westward surge built the United States as the federal government sold public lands and organized new territories, which later became states. In 1790, fewer than 100,000 Americans lived west of the Appalachian Mountains; by 1840 that number had grown to 7,000,000, more than 40 percent of the nation's population. From no states west of the mountains in 1790, the total grew to eleven by 1840, and three of them, carved out of the Louisiana Purchase, lay beyond the Mississippi.[125]

Endings

During the Lewis and Clark expedition, Clark's enslaved body servant, York, served ably as a hunter, teamster, and boatman. During the journey, the officers treated York as on a par with the white soldiers, even allowing him to vote on a key decision. Returning to St. Louis in 1806, York reverted to slavery over his protests that Clark had promised to free him for exemplary service. Clark complained, "He has got Such a notion about freedom and his emence Services, that I do not expect he will be of much Service to me again." In 1808, Clark punished his slaves as malingerers: "I have been obliged [to] whip almost all my people, and they are now beginning to think that it is best to do better and not Cry hard when I am compelled to use the whip. They have been troublesome but are not all so now." Clark considered York especially "insolent and Sulky. I gave him a Severe trouncing the other Day and he has much mended Sence." Then Clark rented York "to a Severe master [so] he would See the difference and do better." At least that temporary master lived near York's wife in Louisville, Kentucky. Alas, upon arrival there, York learned that her own master had taken that wife far away to Natchez, depriving York of his great consolation in a hard life.[126]

About 1816, Clark belatedly freed York, who worked as a teamster in Louisville. Sixteen-years later, Clark told a self-serving story of York preferring Clark's mastery over freedom. Unable to prosper, York allegedly sold his horses but "was cheated" and became a day laborer who "fared ill. 'Damn this freedom,' said York, 'I have never had a happy day since I got it.' He determined to go back to his old master—set off for St. Louis, but was taken with the cholera in Tennessee & died." Part of the story rings true: whites did abuse and cheat free Blacks with legal impunity. But it is implausible that York died in a desperate bid to get back to his old master, for Tennessee was not on the way from Kentucky to St. Louis. Instead, York was bound south to Natchez on the road to his lost wife.[127]

At the end of the Lewis and Clark expedition, Sacagawea returned with Charbonneau to the Hidatsa villages on the upper Missouri. He pursued the slave trade in Indian captives: the business that had wrenched his wife away from the Shoshone. Lewis dismissed Charbonneau as "a man of no particular merit" and "useful as an interpreter only," but he collected $500 for nineteen months of service, while the more essential Sacagawea got only a few presents. The difference reflected the assumption that a woman belonged to her husband.[128]

Sacagawea's story ultimately splits into two versions. According to American documents, she died of typhoid fever in December 1812, at the age of twenty-four, at Fort Manuel, a fur trading post. The resident clerk thought her "a good and the best Woman in the fort." Her seven-year-old son Jean Baptiste and year-old daughter Lisette Charbonneau became the wards of William Clark, who had grown fond of the boy during the expedition and nicknamed him Pomp. He later became a mountain man, gold miner, and a hunting guide for European aristocrats visiting the vanishing West.[129]

But another version of Sacagawea endured in the oral history of the Shoshones. In this account, she left Charbonneau and returned home to her people, dying on their Wind River Reservation in 1884. In this version, we find Native endurance and adaptation to traumatic changes. Historians struggle to tell a history that balances the resourcefulness of Indians and the power of Americans to conquer the continent. By having two Sacagaweas in the end, we can tell both stories.[130]

Top: "Hunting the Buffaloe," engraving by John T. Bowen, 1837. Library of Congress 2013645331. *Bottom: "In Crowds the Ladies Ran, All Wish'd to See & Touch the Tawny Man," engraving by William Satchwell Leney after a drawing by Elkanah Tisdale, 1807. The visit of a native chief to Philadelphia appears in the foreground, while a group of boys taunt a monkey in the background.* Library of Congress 2014649334.

THREE ❧ WARS

A ndrew Jackson made a vivid impression on Thomas Jefferson. In 1797 at the age of thirty, Jackson represented Tennessee in the United States Senate. Tall, thin, with red hair, keen blue eyes, and perfect posture, he commanded attention. But Jefferson mainly recalled Jackson's temper: "His passions are terrible. . . . He could never speak on account of the rashness of his feelings. I have seen him attempt it repeatedly, and as often choke with rage." Jefferson considered Jackson "a dangerous man" who might try to become a dictator. A master of self-control, Jefferson thought that quality essential to lead a republic, but he dreaded that the citizens might welcome a strongman who defied restraint by law.[1]

Jackson grew up in a violent place and time: the Waxhaws region of the South Carolina backcountry during the American Revolution, when Patriots waged a brutal civil war against Indians, Loyalists, and Britons. Taken prisoner as a boy of fourteen, Jackson enraged a British officer by refusing to clean his boots: a demeaning task ordinarily imposed on enslaved Blacks. Swinging his sword, the officer slashed the boy across the forehead, leaving a lifelong scar. Jackson told this story as the essence of his being: a white man who would accept neither restraint nor insult. As a young man, he learned to express, rather than restrain, his passions and to vindicate violence as just revenge.[2]

Although sometimes choked by rage, Jackson had a keen intellect that was quick to detect and seize opportunities. By 1788, he had begun to practice law in the boomtown of Nashville in fast-settling Tennessee, where his profits bought a plantation, the Hermitage, and 150 slaves. A hard master, Jackson raged against any who dared to defy him. He offered $50 in reward for a recaptured runaway, Tom Gid, "and ten dollars extra for every hundred lashes a person will give to the amount of three hundred." Pursuing his self-interest, Jackson initially lacked strong ties with the new United States, which seemed distant, weak, and temporary. To trade with Louisiana and obtain land at Natchez, Jackson swore allegiance to the Spanish Empire in July 1789.[3]

Jackson despised anyone who got in his way, including judges and legislators. In 1812, Silas Dinsmore, a federal official, enforced a law that required documents of ownership for any master bringing slaves into Mississippi Territory. As an investor in the slave trade to Nat-

Opposite from top left: "Andrew Jackson (1767–1845)," lithograph by an unknown artist, 1815. Library of Congress 2012645404. *"Rachel Donelson Jackson (1767–1828)," engraving by Francis Kearny, 1829.* Library of Congress 90710120. *"Dreadful Fracas atween the Gineral and the Bentons at Nashvil," cartoon by an unknown artist, 1834.* Library of Congress 2005683542.

chez, Jackson felt both threatened in his business and insulted in his manhood by this regulation. Confronting Dinsmore, Jackson displayed pistols and declared, "These are General Jackson's passports." Later, when the official again tried to enforce the law, Jackson sputtered, "*My God!* Is it come to this? Are we *freemen, or are we slaves?*" A white man who did not control his slaves might as well be one in Jackson's view. And a man proved his freedom through violence against anyone who restrained him, so Jackson threatened to destroy "Silas Dinsmore in the flames of his agency house." To spare Dinsmore from that fiery fate, the federal government sacked him and so appeased Jackson, a rising star in Tennessee politics.[4]

A patriarch needed a wife to manage the household, particularly during his long absences to attend courts, buy land, pursue runaway slaves, rage at officials, or fight Indians. At twenty-one, Jackson fell for Rachel Donelson Robards, although she was already married. Rachel felt drawn to Jackson as more charismatic, ambitious, and able than her feckless husband, Lewis Robards. In 1789, Rachel and Andrew went to Natchez, then in Spanish territory, to live together, flaunting their adultery to complete the public rupture of her marriage. Robards sought and obtained a divorce, citing his wife's infidelity. Then Andrew and Rachel could legally marry in 1794.[5]

The couple settled into devoted domesticity as each performed a gender and class role to perfection. Jackson provided while Rachel managed. To refute slanders against her early morality, she developed a conspicuous Christian piety and persuaded Jackson to attend church. Rachel personified his perceived duty: to defend white women and children against Indians, Britons, and slanderers.[6]

In Jackson's version of Christianity, he never turned the other cheek. In May 1806, an ambitious young lawyer, Charles Dickinson, quarreled with Jackson over a horse race. Then Dickinson signed his death sentence by profaning the "sacred name" of Rachel. Jackson demanded a duel despite Dickinson's fame as quick with a pistol. Rather than compete with that speed, Jackson opted to let his rival shoot first. Then, if Jackson survived, he could take his time to make Dickinson squirm before shooting with calm and deadly accuracy. Dickinson's bullet penetrated Jackson's chest, breaking two ribs. While gushing blood, Jackson took precise aim and shot Dickinson dead. "I should have hit him, if he had shot me through the brain," Jackson asserted. He endured pain for life because doctors dared not remove a bullet so close to his heart.[7]

Ambitious men in the South often fought duels or brawls to defend their honor after feeling insulted by another. Even the best of friends could fall out suddenly. An aspiring young lawyer, Thomas Hart Benton, had been Jackson's protégé, but they quarreled in 1813 when Benton's brother Jesse dared to duel with another favorite of Jackson's. Wielding a whip, Jackson attacked Thomas in a Nashville hotel, bellowing, "Now you d[amne]d rascal, I am going to punish you." Whipping a white man insulted him as on a par with an enslaved person. Stepping in to defend his brother, Jesse fired a pistol, shattering Jackson's shoulder. Dreading Jackson's "thirst for vengeance," Thomas worried, "I am in the middle of hell and see no alternative but to kill or be killed; for I will not crouch to Jackson." The brothers fled to Missouri, where Thomas became a United States senator.[8]

Far from discrediting Jackson, violent words and deeds made him popular in Tennessee, where he won elections as congressman, senator, state judge, and major general in command of the state militia. Southern voters favored elite men provided they also had a popular touch and a flair for defending their honor. Jackson displayed modest origins as well as current wealth by keeping his original log cabin beside his new mansion. Americans celebrated the rich man who seemed to rise from humbler origins through hard work. Possessing plenty of their own resentments, common white men adopted Jackson as their great avenging champion.[9]

Jackson insisted that a proper man had to defend white women and children by destroying the greatest supposed threat to them: Indians. Jackson declared his bloody motto as "An Eye for an Eye, Toothe for Toothe, and Scalp for Scalp." His vengeful style thrilled southern men who dreaded Indians on the frontier and slave revolts on their plantations. By promoting aggressive expansion, Jackson vowed to punish the nation's enemies and push the survivors farther away. Fears of internal enemies interacting with external foes bred the American dream of boundlessness as security.[10]

Hangman

The wildest geopolitical schemes seemed plausible at the end of the eighteenth century, during a generation of revolutions. Patriots created the first independent republic in the Americas by rebelling against and defeating the mighty British Empire. A few years later, French revolutionaries destroyed their monarchy and aristocracy. Then an obscure Corsican, Napoleon Bonaparte, rose through the ranks to lead the French to repeated victories over the combined might of Europe's monarchies. Seizing power in France, Napoleon led the most powerful empire in European history. But rebel slaves in Saint-Domingue rejected French rule and defied Napoleon to create the first republic run by Blacks. No kingdom or colony seemed safe from a sudden, dramatic rupture that rewarded obscure men with great ambitions.[11]

In Canada, British officials worried that French agents would promote a rebellion by the French Canadians of Lower Canada (now Quebec). In November 1796, a British warship intercepted an American merchant ship 200 miles south of Ireland. Bound west from Holland, the misnamed *Olive Branch* carried two dozen cannons and 20,000 muskets with bayonets. The ship's manifest claimed that the weapons belonged to a clever Vermont politician, Ira Allen, who shipped them to arm the militia of his state. In fact, the French provided the arms for Allen to smuggle across Vermont's northern border to arm rebels in Canada. If that rebellion succeeded, Allen wanted Vermont to secede from the United States to join Canada in forming a new republic called United Columbia. By exploiting the turbulent uncertainty of the age of revolutions, Allen sought to make his own nation at the expense of both the United States and the British Empire. Instead, in December 1797, a British court confiscated the *Olive Branch* and her cargo. Allen escaped to France, where the authorities jailed him for fleecing them. Released in 1800, he sailed for the United States, a bankrupt man.[12]

At least Ira Allen was alive, which could not be said for David McLane, who died for his misplaced faith in United Columbia. A militia major and merchant from Rhode Island, McLane was tall, handsome, restless, and naïve. In the spring of 1796, McLane fled from his creditors to become a French agent in Canada, posing as a horse trader and timber speculator. Few believed his guise, and he lost more credibility by proposing a harebrained scheme to drug the British garrison at Quebec with opium. He also could speak little French: no small liability in an agent sent to rally Francophones for rebellion. And his mission was pointless, for the French canceled their invasion plans after the loss of the *Olive Branch*. In May 1797, British officials arrested McLane. Tried and convicted of treason, he hung from a gallows just beyond Quebec's stone walls. In the United States, the Federalist administration of John Adams disavowed McLane in order to maintain good relations with the British.[13]

The Federalists lost power in 1801, when Thomas Jefferson became president. Noting Jefferson's praise for the French Revolution, British officials worried that he would export a republican revolution to their Canadian colonies. In Upper Canada, an American emigrant, Asa Danforth, Jr., did try to rally support for a republican revolt. He had some vague encouragement from Aaron Burr, who liked to fish in troubled waters and could inspire ambitious young men to take reckless risks. But the scheme fizzled in 1802, and Danforth fled back across the border to New York, where he landed in a debtor's prison. In the end, Danforth found the commercial republic as remorseless as the security-obsessed empire.[14]

An Upper Canadian official aptly characterized Danforth's plot as "a tissue of Absurdity & Improbability." It lacked both of the elements needed for success: strong local support and an American invasion force. And Burr had no money and little power to contribute after his foiled bid to steal the presidency from Jefferson in 1801. At the peak of the plot, Jefferson was undermining Burr's political base in New York rather than seeking to expand it into Canada. Far from the reckless radical of his British reputation, Jefferson wanted to reduce federal taxes and the national debt rather than provoke an expensive war with the British in 1802. Five years later, an American invasion became more plausible.[15]

Embargo

Britain's rulers insisted that no one who was born a subject could renounce that identity and its duties, which ended only with death. No emigration, not even a legal process of naturalization, could alienate a British subject, who remained obligated to serve his king in time of war. Indeed, a subject committed treason if he fought against the sovereign of the kingdom of his birth. For the British, the "natural-born subject" meant anyone from anywhere in the empire, including Ireland and Canada.[16]

British officers insisted upon their right and duty to stop and board the ships of any nation to retrieve runaway subjects for impressment into naval service. The British desperately needed sailors for the hundreds of warships fighting a massive, global war against the French Empire led by Napoleon. But sailors dreaded service on a British warship as harsh, dangerous, hungry, and underpaid servitude. To evade impressment at home, thousands of British sailors flocked to the United States to seek the better conditions offered by American merchants. Profiting as neutral carriers in a world at war, American merchants paid premium wages to attract the sailors of other nations. By 1807 at least 9,000 British subjects (most of them Irish) worked on American merchant ships.[17]

Crisis loomed as the British Empire and the American Union competed for a limited pool of sailors in a world at war. British naval captains intercepted American merchant ships to impress any supposed British subjects in their crews. Defining American citizens narrowly and British subjects broadly, naval captains simply took the best sailors. Between 1803 and 1807, the British impressed 10,000 Americans, some citizens by birth but most by naturalization. To defend the practice,

British leaders insisted that they helped the entire world by fighting the despotic Napoleon, so they expected Americans to cooperate. Blockading French-held seaports, British officers also stopped and confiscated American ships suspected of trading with the enemy. As the world's dominant naval power, the British claimed the right to enforce their version of international law on the high seas.[18]

The American notion of the voluntary citizen clashed with the British insistence on the perpetual subject. By enforcing their maritime power, Britons threatened to reduce American commerce and sailors to a quasi-colonial dependence. Republicans defended American sovereignty by asserting the rights to trade freely with the world and to create citizens by naturalization.[19]

On June 22, 1807, off the coast of Virginia, a British warship, the frigate *Leopard*, intercepted the American frigate *Chesapeake*. The British captain meant to search the American ship for deserters from the Royal Navy. When the American captain refused to cooperate, the *Leopard* unleashed a devastating broadside at close range, killing three and wounding eighteen. The *Chesapeake*'s captain surrendered, and a British boarding party seized four sailors before releasing the frigate to return to port for repairs. All four had served in the Royal Navy, but only one was British by birth. The other three were Americans. After a court martial, the captors hanged the Briton and imprisoned the other three sailors. The episode sent a pointed warning: that American warships offered no safe haven for British deserters.[20]

The British attack on the *Chesapeake* outraged American newspapers, town meetings, and congressmen. Angry resolutions demanded war, but the nation was ill prepared. In addition to shrinking the navy, Jefferson had reduced the army to only 3,000 men: too few to defend a land frontier of 10,000 miles and a coastline at least twice that long. Seeking to cut taxes and the national debt, the president balked at the expense of rebuilding the military.[21]

But the crisis obliged Jefferson to do *something*, so he opted for a commercial war through a measure known as "the Embargo." Jefferson reasoned that the British needed American exports of food more than Americans needed Britain's manufactured goods. By starving British factory workers, Jefferson hoped to promote strikes and riots that would compel British leaders to accept the American position on neutral rights in wartime. In December 1807, Congress passed an Embargo Act that barred exports and imports and forced American merchant ships to stay in port.[22]

Jefferson overestimated the British dependence on American commerce, and he underestimated American reliance on overseas trade. Britons found alternative sources of food and a new market for their exports in Latin America. Meanwhile, the American economy withered, idling thousands of sailors, laborers, and artisans. The price of imported consumer goods soared while employers cut wages in half. Farmers could not export their produce, so the domestic market became glutted with grain. In New York, the price of wheat fell from $2 per bushel before the embargo to 75 cents a year later.[23]

In September 1808, a starving Bostonian wrote to Jefferson: "I can't get no work by working about on the worves, for you have destroy'd all our Commerce & all the ships lie rotting in our harbours." He added, "You are one of the greatest tirants in the whole world, you are wurs than Bonaparte a grate deel. I wish you could feal as bad as I feal with 6 Children round you crying for vittles." The man had a small house, but "I cant eat my house," so he threatened to raise $400, "if I have to work on my hands & [k]nees for it," to hire four assassins "to shoot you if you don't take off the embargo."[24]

Jefferson and Madison insisted that the embargo would inspire Americans to demonstrate virtue by sacrificing self-interest and consumerism for the common good. Instead, smuggling surged along the Canadian border, where merchants swapped American farm produce for British manufactures. Embarrassed by that defiance, Jefferson doubled down on his surprising expansion of federal power by calling out thousands of militiamen to patrol the borders, leading to deadly firefights with smugglers. The frustrated secretary of the treasury, Albert Gallatin, complained, "I had rather encounter war itself than to display our impotence to enforce our laws."[25]

The unpopular embargo revived the Federalist Party in the North-east, the region most dependent on maritime commerce. Federalists insisted that Jefferson's supposed cure was far worse than the British disease of meddling with ships and sailors. Despite British interference, transatlantic trade had been profitable, but merchants reaped only losses when Jefferson locked up their vessels. Disgusted by both Jefferson and Napoleon, Federalists celebrated Britain as the world's champion of true liberty against French despotism and Republican hypocrisy.[26]

Federalists charged that Jefferson's southern-dominated party designed the embargo to impoverish and weaken the New England states "and on their ruin to erect the riches and glory of another part of the nation." Promoting regional loyalty, northeastern Feder-alists denounced Virginians as domineering parasites: "Beings suck-led by slaves, pampered in indolence, and effeminate by indulgence! Can New-England, rich in intellect, and knowledge, and wealth . . . support this forever?" Federalists warned that slaveholders sought to dominate and figuratively enslave New Englanders. The *Salem Gazette* claimed that Yankees faced "one horrible alternative, Civil War or Slavery." Instead of uniting the country, the embargo exposed sectional tensions within the weak Union and debunked Jefferson and Madison's hope that mutual affection could produce consensual bonds between the states.[27]

In the election of 1808, the Federalists doubled their seats in Con-gress, almost entirely from districts in the North. Rather than risk future elections on defending an unpopular law, the Republicans in Congress terminated the Embargo in March 1809. After commercial war failed, Republicans had to prepare for real war if the British clung to impressment and blockade.[28]

Eclipse

Republicans also blamed the British for Indian resistance to Ameri-can expansion in the West. By providing arms and ammunition, the British cultivated Indian allies to help them defend Canada against an

American invasion. Michigan's territorial governor, William Hull, concluded, "The British cannot hold Upper Canada without the assistance of the Indians," but the "Indians cannot conduct a war without the assistance of a civilized nation." While the British regarded their Indian alliance as a defensive measure to counter republican aggression, Americans saw that alliance as a provocation because they claimed Natives as properly their dependents.[29]

Indians resented land cession treaties imposed by the territorial governor of Indiana, William Henry Harrison. Relentless and resourceful, Harrison made deals with older chiefs representing smaller tribes or minorities within larger nations. Most of the Indians, especially young warriors, rallied to the defiant leadership of two Shawnee brothers, Tenskwatawa, a religious prophet, and Tecumseh, a charismatic war chief. Rejecting Harrison's treaties as illegitimate, the brothers vowed armed resistance and gathered supporters at Prophetstown, in the Wabash Valley of northern Indiana.[30]

Tecumseh and Tenskwatawa sought to rebuild the Indian confederacy of the 1780s by uniting many Native nations to resist American expansion. Harrison warned his superiors that Tecumseh was "one of those uncommon geniuses, which spring up occasionally to produce revolution and overturn the established order of things. . . . He has been in constant motion. You see him today on the Wabash and in a short time you hear of him on the shores of Lake Erie or Michigan, or on the banks of the Mississippi, and wherever he goes, he makes an impression favorable to his purpose." Tecumseh also crossed into Canada to consult with British officers and secure weapons.[31]

While Harrison respected Tecumseh, the governor dismissed Tenkswatawa as a religious fraud. Thinking himself clever, Harrison tried to discredit the prophet by urging Indians to "demand of him some proofs at least of his being the messenger of the Deity. . . . If he is really a prophet, ask of him to cause the sun to stand still—the moon to alter its course—or the dead to rise from their graves. If he does these things, you may then believe that he has been sent by

God." Harrison did not realize that astronomers had predicted a total eclipse of the sun for June 16, 1806. From an almanac, Tenkswatawa could predict the impending eclipse and, so, gained greater credibility and fame as a divine messenger.[32]

Foiled in prophecy, Harrison tried war. In November 1811, exploiting Tecumseh's absence on a diplomatic mission, the governor menaced Prophetstown with 1,200 troops, provoking an attack by warriors on his encampment at Tippecanoe Creek. Despite suffering heavy casualties, Harrison repulsed the attack, and fleeing Indians burned Prophetstown. Rather than pursue them, Harrison retreated to his base at Vincennes.[33]

Republicans endorsed Harrison's claims that Tippecanoe was a great and glorious victory over bloodthirsty savages instigated and armed by the British. Andrew Jackson worked himself up into a rage over the American casualties: *"The blood of our murdered Countrymen must be revenged. That banditti, ought to be swept from the face of the earth"* along with the "secret agents of great Britain." Unwilling to recognize Indian initiative (or British caution), American leaders regarded Natives as pawns in an insidious British plot to ravage frontier settlements. Republican journalists recycled the canard that British agents paid bounties to Indians for scalps taken from American heads. As the savages of American nightmares, Indians evoked a hatred that could best rally white men for a war on the British. Such a war would target Canada to cut off the munitions used by Indians to resist American expansion.[34]

Republican congressmen and journalists treated maritime and frontier grievances as mutual threats. They denounced British impressment as enslaving "freeborn Americans . . . by the dealers in the flesh and blood of white men." A mariner complained that impressed sailors "were stripped, tied up, and most cruelly and disgracefully whipped like a negro slave. Can anything be . . . more humiliating to the feelings of men born and brought up as we all are?" Republicans linked the scars of naval flogging with Indian scalping as twin cuts of British brutality. They exhorted American men to defend their sailors, women, and children from bloody violation by Britons and Indians.[35]

In November 1811, Madison urged Congress to prepare the nation for war against Britain. He had support from the Speaker of the House, Henry Clay. From the frontier state of Kentucky, Clay longed to conquer Canada and "extinguish the torch that lights up savage warfare." He led a group of relatively young and bellicose Republican congressmen known as War Hawks, who wanted to prove themselves to be worthy heirs of the revolutionary fathers. War Hawks hoped that war would purify the American character, which they feared had been softened by a long indulgence in commerce.[36]

Despite the nation's military weakness, Republicans had to declare war or lose credibility: "The honor of the nation and that of the party are bound up together and both will be sacrificed if war be not declared." Republicans feared that inaction would discredit republican government as too weak to defend the nation, and that their failure would doom liberty by inviting the Federalists to resume power. Madison later explained that "he knew the unprepared state of the country, but he esteemed it necessary to throw forward the flag of the country, sure that the people would press forward and defend it." Republicans hoped that early victories would make the war popular and buy time to build up the army.[37]

In June 1812, Congress and Madison declared war in a partisan vote, with every Federalist opposed and 81 percent of the Republicans in favor. Federalist opposition prevailed in the Northeast, while Republicans rallied support for the war in the Middle Atlantic, southern, and western states. By declaring war, Republicans sought to dishonor and marginalize Federalists as British dupes and American traitors.[38]

In the first fighting of the war, Republican mobs struck Federalists in Baltimore rather than Britons in Canada. On June 22, rioters tore down the printing office of the city's leading Federalist newspaper. The defiant publisher fortified a new office and rallied armed Federalists to defend it. On July 27, hundreds of Republicans stoned the building, smashing windows and shutters. The defenders opened fire, killing a rioter and wounding several others. City officials arrested the Federalists but promised to protect them. Instead, the mob broke open the jail to beat the prisoners while watching women cried "Kill the Tories!" One Federalist died and eleven suffered crippling injuries. At a subsequent trial, jurors acquitted the rioters.[39]

Most of the Republican press defended the riot and verdict, which further alienated Federalists. Refusing to help the war effort, they discouraged army enlistments and loans to the government. A few spied for the British, and many more smuggled supplies to them. Federalists hoped to regain power by discrediting the Republicans with military defeats. Rather than uniting Americans, the new war divided them more bitterly than ever.[40]

War

In 1812, the United States had only 5 substantial warships, known as frigates, while the Royal Navy had over 500 warships, including 102 ships-of-the-line larger than anything in the American navy. Building a proper navy was expensive, and Republicans wanted to keep taxes low by waging war on the cheap. Because an army cost less, Republicans pinned their strategy on invading Canada.[41]

But that Canadian strategy exposed contradictions in Republican goals as well as fractures in their political coalition. Most Republicans sought to conquer Canada only temporarily: to obtain a bargaining chip that they would restore to the British in a peace treaty in return for maritime concessions. Western Republicans, however, wanted to keep Canada to disrupt the British alliance with Indians. Although uncertain what to do with Canada, Americans invaded anyway, and counted on Canadians to welcome them as liberators. Congressman John Harper insisted, "They must revere the principles of our Revolution and Government, they must sigh for an affiliation with the great American family." But why would Canadians risk their necks to help invaders who might later return them to British rule?[42]

Republicans expected an easy victory. Surely, they reasoned, 7.7 million Americans could overwhelm the 300,000 British subjects in Canada. In August 1812, Jefferson declared that "the acquisition of Canada, this year, as far as the neighborhood of Quebec, will be a mere matter of marching" and would culminate in "the final expulsion of England from the American continent."[43]

In Lower Canada, Francophone *habitants* distrusted American invaders even more than their British occupiers, who had protected the Catholic Church. *Habitants* noted that most Americans were Protestants vocal in their prejudices against Catholics. In June 1812, some militiamen rioted when a false rumor insisted that the British would draft them to serve in the regular army and send some far away to the West Indies. Acting quickly, the governor general, Sir George Prévost, discredited the rumors and suppressed the riots with a savvy balance of resolve and restraint. Reassured that they would only serve near home, the French Canadians fought against the American invaders.[44]

In Upper Canada, most of the inhabitants were Americans by birth, but few would support the invaders. About a third of the people were true Loyalists: refugees from the American Revolution and their children. A British military surgeon, lodged with a farm family of "good, kind, simple people," who recalled relatives "shot before their own doors, or hanged on the apple trees of their own orchards." He concluded, "I found their hatred to the Americans was deep rooted and hearty." Loyalists would fight against Republican invaders and for a colony that gave them free land.[45]

Two-thirds of the Upper Canadians were Late Loyalists: American settlers who arrived after 1790. Drawn across the border by low taxes and cheap land, they took little interest in politics. Busy with their families and farms, they just wanted to be left alone. An observer noted that it was "of no consequence to them who governs if they have good land, light taxes & can raise a plenty of wheat." They would accept American forces if they came in overpowering numbers quickly to oust the British, but all bets were off if the invaders faltered.[46]

A charismatic and able general, Isaac Brock, governed Upper Canada. He understood the importance of Native warriors in defending a heavily forested and thinly settled colony. Deft at guerrilla warfare, they intimidated poorly trained American invaders. Indians also could pressure Canadian militiamen to do their duty. Those militiamen provided logistical support and garrisoned forts, while British regulars and Indians bore the brunt of fighting Americans in field and forest.[47]

Although Americans had declared the war, the British hit first by surprising the American garrison at Michilimackinac, the key post on the upper Great Lakes. That July victory impressed the Indians, who rallied to the British in hopes of destroying the American forts and settlements intruded into the Native homelands north and west of the Ohio River.[48]

In August, Brock attacked Detroit, where he confronted the elderly American commander, William Hull, who had more men: 2,500 to Brock's 1,925. But Hull was a pessimist who squabbled with subordinates and distrusted his own troops. Fearful of an Indian massacre if he resisted, Hull surrendered without firing a shot. The victory swung most Upper Canadians off of the political fence and into support for Brock's defense of their colony. Meanwhile, Americans felt humiliated and betrayed by Hull's shocking surrender.[49]

After Hull's debacle, President Madison needed a victory to restore American morale. But his best hope lay on the Niagara Front where the commander, Stephen Van Rensselaer, was a Federalist who disliked his Republican soldiers as much as they distrusted him. In October 1812, Van Rensselaer sent troops across the Niagara River to attack and capture Queenston Heights. Brock quickly counterattacked. Shot in the chest, he crumpled and died, but his men prevailed, killing or capturing 1,100 invaders. Many more Americans refused to cross the river from terror of Indians and a suspicion that Van Rensselaer was sending them on a suicide mission. After the defeat, Van Rensselaer resigned, and no other Federalist would hold a major command in this Republican war.[50]

Trying invasion again in 1813, Americans briefly occupied York, the capital of Upper Canada, looting the town and burning the parliament buildings. In September on Lake Erie, an American naval flotilla destroyed a British squadron, enabling an army led by William Henry Harrison to reclaim Detroit. In October, Harrison's men pursued and defeated Britons and Indians, killing Tecumseh. But to the east, Americans suffered defeats on the Niagara front and along the St. Lawrence River. The war became more destructive as both sides plundered and burned farms and villages, bringing misery to civilians.[51]

The American war effort suffered from inept commanders. Few officers had training or aptitude. "Our army is full of men fresh from lawyers' shops and counting rooms," Congressman Peter B. Porter lamented. In 1812, a veteran officer, Winfield Scott, regarded most of his new peers as "imbeciles and ignoramuses." Lacking self-discipline, these new officers struggled to train their enlisted men. Too many officers proved better at shooting one another in duels than at fighting the British. One officer lamented "that our little army is torn to pieces by dissentions & broils which disgrace it."[52]

Hampered by too many bad officers, the army also lacked enough good soldiers. Patriotism did not suffice to fill the ranks, and Congress offered paltry financial incentives to enlist: a $16 bonus and $5 a month in pay. When a farm laborer could earn $10 per month, why get shot at for half that amount? Congress did promise 160 acres of frontier land to each recruit, but poor men preferred more money. One "wished [that] every member of Congress had 160 acres of land stuffed up his [ass]." Congress also mandated five years of service, too long for most American men. Proud of their freedom, they disliked submitting to a military discipline that resembled bondage. Porter insisted that his constituents would "not become slaves to the Army for five years."[53]

Racial prejudice hampered an American army that desperately needed more troops. Despite insufficient enlistment by white men, the government barred Black men from serving in the army. That restriction disgusted the secretary of war, who came from New York: "We must get over this nonsense . . . if we mean to be what we ought to be." But southern Republicans, including the president, opposed arming Black men, even free Blacks, as the slippery slope to slave revolts.[54]

Forbidden to fight for the republic, southern slaves regarded the British as liberators. Around Chesapeake Bay and along the coast of Georgia, British naval commanders recruited 600 runaways as "Colonial Marines" by offering freedom, a $20 bounty, and postwar land in a Crown colony. Cherishing the chance to fight against their masters and help free more enslaved people, the Colonial Marines became reliable and determined fighters along the American coast. A British admiral praised them as "a most efficient and useful Corps now above 400 strong, which is constantly and actively employed with us here and giving daily proofs of its gallantry and grateful attachment to us."[55]

For want of enough regular soldiers, the Madison administration had to call thousands of state militiamen into federal service for a few months at a time. Untrained and reluctant, militiamen provided little return for the high cost of supplying and arming them. Many refused to cross into Canada, citing constitutional scruples. If forced into combat, they often threw down their arms and ran away in fear.[56]

In 1814, Congress recruited more white men as regulars by raising a private's monthly pay to $8 a month, the land bounty to 320 acres, and the cash bounty to $124. But it was too little too late because British reinforcements had begun to flow into the fight in North America after toppling Napoleon in Europe. Those reinforcements enabled the British to turn the tables against the Americans by launching four offensives. One force, based in Montreal, swept up Lake Champlain to assault the American naval base at Plattsburgh, New York. A second expedition occupied eastern Maine. A third penetrated Chesapeake Bay to attack Washington, D.C. The fourth headed by sea to seize New Orleans. If all four succeeded, the Union faced ruin.[57]

In 1814, Americans fought better on the defensive than they had while invading Canada. They did suffer a humiliating defeat in August, when the British swept into the federal capital and burned its public buildings, including the White House and Capitol. In September, however, Americans repelled the British attack on Baltimore, a victory that inspired Francis Scott Key to write "The Star-Spangled Banner," which would become the nation's anthem. Later that month, an American squadron crushed the British flotilla on Lake Champlain, saving Plattsburgh. Americans also won a few victories on the Niagara front, but withdrew in the fall with nothing to show for the latest bloodshed. At year's end, the fate of the primary British attack, on New Orleans, remained in suspense.[58]

Meanwhile, the federal government faced collapse. In New England, Federalists toyed with seceding because they despised the administration and its mismanaged war. They also resented domination by Virginia, the land of Jefferson, Madison, and slavery. An angry Federalist vowed, "New England will never submit to be a colony of Virginia." Dread of domination by another state or region kept the Union uneasy and tentative, as politicians eyed one another warily while muttering threats of secession. The governor of Massachusetts covertly contacted the British commander in Nova Scotia to seek military protection if the New England states seceded.[59]

In the fall, Federalist delegates convened in Hartford, Connecticut, to discuss disunion. Cautious men, they settled for half measures, proposing that the New England states assume their own defense and keep their federal tax payments. They also demanded seven constitutional amendments meant to reduce the rights of immigrants and the power of Virginia. The demands simply bought time. Expecting inevitable rejection by the Republican administration and Congress, the delegates vowed to meet again in June 1815 to reconsider secession.[60]

In December 1814, the secretary of the treasury reported that taxes could generate only a quarter of the revenue needed to fight for another year. Only loans could bridge that gap, but investors had lost confidence in the administration as the war seemed futile and endless. The country lacked hard money because American smugglers had exported so much to buy British manufactured goods. The banking system verged on collapse because, in 1811, the Republicans had killed Alexander Hamilton's national bank. Without stable banks, the federal government struggled to pay and supply troops. Unpaid for more than a year, the troops at Detroit threatened to mutiny. And without money, the government could not recruit more troops for another campaign. A disgusted officer insisted that a miracle "can alone save this Government & this Nation from disunion & disgrace." The nation needed that miracle at New Orleans.[61]

Patriots

While invading Canada, Americans also fought to the south and west against Indians and Britons. In 1812, southern Republicans feared that annexing Canada would strengthen the North with new states, thereby weakening the South in the Union's precarious balance of regional power. In May 1812, a Delaware congressman reported, "No proposition could have been more frightful to the southern men, and it seems they had never thought of what they were to do with Canada before, in case they conquered the country." The Union seemed too fragile to expand in only one direction.[62]

Georgians wanted to balance the conquest of Canada by seizing the rest of Florida from Spain. East and West Florida were weak colonies, with only 13,000 colonists, most clustered around the small port towns of St. Augustine, on the Atlantic coast, and Pensacola and Mobile on the Gulf. By contrast, 250,000 Americans lived in Georgia and another 260,000 in Tennessee. The Florida hinterland belonged to Seminole Indians and maroons: former slaves escaped from American plantations to become sharecroppers raising crops for their Native landlords. "They dress and live pretty much like the Indians, each having a gun, and hunting a portion of his time," a Georgian reported. Southerners dreaded such a nearby refuge as an enticement for their slaves to plot deadly rebellions and mass escapes.[63]

In January 1811, about 200 enslaved men did revolt along the east bank of the Mississippi in Louisiana. They burned five sugar plantations before they were suppressed by state militia aided by federal troops. The victors killed about 100 rebels in battle and executions, displaying their severed heads on posts beside the roads to intimidate the region's surviving slaves. "They look like crows sitting on long poles," a naval officer remarked. Although the rebels acted without British or Spanish support, southerners believed otherwise.[64]

Southern leaders longed to oust the Spanish from Florida and replace Native and maroon villages with plantations owned by white men and worked by enslaved people. Jackson wrote, "I hope the government will permit us to traverse the Southern coast and aid in planting the American eagles on the ramparts of Mobile, Pensacola and Fort St. Augustine. . . . British influence must be destroyed, or we will have the whole Southern tribe of Indians to fight and [slave] insurrections to quell in all the Southern states."[65]

The Madison administration had already begun to subvert and annex Florida. In 1810, the administration encouraged settlers in westernmost Florida to rebel against Spanish rule. Primarily American settlers living around Baton Rouge, the rebels envied the more rapid economic development and stricter slave code of Louisiana. In September, they seized the Spanish fort at Baton Rouge, killing the commander and another soldier before arresting and deposing the local governor. Led by wealthy planters, the rebels declared independence as the republic of West Florida.[66]

In October 1810, Madison sent federal troops to occupy the area, which Congress annexed to Louisiana. Denying that he had encouraged the rebels, Madison claimed that the troops went in to restore order. He had developed a model to facilitate further expansion: American settlers would rebel against a colonial power, establish a free republic, and create disorder that the United States could exploit to seize control. This model fostered aggression cloaked by claims of honoring international law.[67]

In retaliation, the Spanish ambassador to the United States, Luis de Onís, sought to disrupt an American Union that seemed flimsy and weak, with an army of only "six thousand despicable men" and a navy "for the most part disarmed." He proposed that Spain ally with Great

Britain to promote secession by disaffected New Englanders to divide the United States "into two or three republics . . . in a state of perfect nullity." Only the New England "republic of the north" would thrive, while the rest of the shattered United States "would perish from poverty and quarrels among themselves."[68]

Spain's leaders were too preoccupied by war in Europe to act on Onís's North American scheme. But Madison took it seriously, obtaining a copy of the letter and submitting it to Congress. In January 1811, Congress authorized the president to seize the rest of Florida as a defensive measure. In this way, geopolitical fantasy reverberated, persuading both Americans and their rivals that the imperiled Union needed expansion to survive.[69]

To subvert East Florida, Madison employed a special agent: General George Mathews, a veteran of the Revolutionary War and a former governor of Georgia. He followed the West Florida playbook by urging East Floridians "to gather and declare independency, and call across the river for protection, to afford him a pretext for acting, and he would immediately support them with a sufficient strength."[70]

Many of Florida's planters had come from Georgia and South Carolina, drawn by generous Spanish land grants during the 1780s. But they dreaded the powerful Seminoles and the safe haven that they offered for runaway slaves. The Americans in Florida also disliked paternalistic Spanish laws that protected slaves from abuse. In 1810, a leading rebel, William Dell resented his prosecution for whipping a slave until he broke free, ran to a river and drowned. Dell declared, "If he was in the United States, he would not care if [the slave] did drown." Restive planters longed to impose the American racial regime in Florida to dispossess Indians, restore runaways to slavery, and empower masters to do as they pleased.[71]

In March 1812, Mathews launched the "Patriot War" by leading 250 armed volunteers from Georgia across the border to seize the Spanish post at Fernandina Island (now Amelia Island). Joined by about 100 rebels from within the colony, the Patriots marched south to attack St. Augustine while American naval gunboats blockaded that port. But St. Augustine was well fortified and garrisoned by free Black militiamen reinforced by 270 free Black soldiers from Cuba. Florida's governor explained that the militiamen were runaways from Georgia who "will be loyal and will defend themselves to the death in order not to return to their former slavery." A Patriot officer conceded that, for the Spanish, the "negroes . . . are their best soldiers." Their freedom depended on defeating American invaders.[72]

The Spanish also won support from Indians and maroons with the help of a clever slave named Tony Proctor, who spoke the Seminole language. Patriots had captured Proctor and forced him to serve as their translator on a visit to the main Seminole village at Alachua, where Mathews sought assistance from the chiefs. Translating Mathews's speech at a public council, Proctor snuck in his own warning that the Americans meant to dispossess and enslave the Seminoles and maroons. Ignorant of the Seminole language, Mathews was none the wiser, and the chiefs played along by pretending to need more time for their decision. Meanwhile, Proctor escaped to the Spanish, and the governor rewarded him with freedom. Then Seminoles and maroons attacked rebel plantations and ravaged the Patriot supply line from Georgia to the army besieging St. Augustine. In September, their attacks turned the Patriot retreat into a rout, driving the invaders back to Fernandina.[73]

Calling the Florida invasion a "tragi-comedy," an embarrassed Madison sacked Mathews for striking prematurely, before the United States could provide some legal cover by declaring war on Britain. General John Floyd was not fooled by the scapegoating of Mathews: "All the sin of direct invasion rests on the shoulders of the Government . . . against a weak, defenseless, unoffending neighbor." To replace Mathews as special agent, the president appointed Georgia's governor, David B. Mitchell, who worked to revive the invasion.[74]

By relying on Blacks and Indians to defend Florida, the Spanish outraged southerners. Mitchell reported that victories by maroons and Black militiamen inspired a surge of slave escapes: "Most of our male negroes on the Sea Board are restless and make many attempts to get off to [St.] Augustine," and "many have succeeded." Mitchell denounced East Florida as a menacing "refuge of fugitive slaves; and from thence emissaries . . . will be detached to bring about a revolt of the black population of the United States." Writing to the Senate, Madison charged that the Spanish had "armed & excited different Tribes of Savages to a merciless war ag[ain]st the U.S." and used "troops of a character & colour well calculated to [promote] revolt" by southern slaves. Treating Black troops as war criminals, Patriots executed those that they captured and threatened to do the same to Spanish officers who served with them. Patriots killed some free Black civilians simply for being free.[75]

In December 1812, Madison urged the Senate to annex East Florida, but northern senators balked. William Hunter of Rhode Island opposed acquiring Florida's "wide waste of sands, its dismal swamps, [and] its mixed mongrel population." Where Madison deployed racial fear to push for expansion, Hunter employed that same fear to justify keeping people out of the Union. He also derided the invasion as immoral: "It is a wicked war; it is robbery" and "an artificial, concerted, contrived, petty, patched-up miserable treason, paid for by our money, fomented by our people." Albert Gallatin warned the administration that its "Southern" scheme of taking Florida "disgust[ed] every man north of Washington." The Senate narrowly rejected annexing East Florida.[76]

Despite the Senate's rebuke, Madison delayed withdrawing troops from East Florida. In February 1813, southern volunteers destroyed the Seminole villages around Alachua. After that show of force, the administration withdrew its regular troops from Fernandina, compelling the remaining rebels to retreat into Georgia in May 1813. A year later, some tried to revive the fight, but they suffered a bloody defeat that ended the rebellion. The Patriot War left a wasteland of burned plantations and dislocated people. Freebooters from Georgia exploited the chaos by raiding into Florida to seize Blacks, free and slave, for sale in the United States.[77]

New Orleans

While withdrawing from East Florida, the Madison administration seized more of West Florida. In April 1813, General James Wilkinson led 600 federal troops from Louisiana to overwhelm the 70 Spanish soldiers defending Mobile. This seizure added the Gulf Coast of Alabama and Mississippi to the United States. Transferring Wilkinson to the northern front, the administration made Andrew Jackson the American commander in the Southeast.[78]

In 1813–1814, Jackson confronted an uprising by a traditionalist faction of Creeks, known as the Red Sticks, who despised Americans as land thieves. Inspired by Tecumseh and their own prophets, the Red Sticks attacked Native collaborators and American settlers in Alabama. In August 1813, they overwhelmed Fort Mims, killing 250 men, women, and children. In early 1814, Jackson counterattacked by leading an army from Tennessee deep into Creek country. In March, his troops and some Native allies crushed and massacred the Red Sticks at Tohopeka, a village on a horseshoe-shaped bend in the Tallapoosa River. Most of the 600 Creek fatalities were women and children. To make an accurate count, Jackson had his men cut off the nose of each corpse and bring them to him.[79]

Addressing his troops, Jackson exulted, "The fiends of the Tallapoosa will no longer murder our women & children, or disturb the quiet of our borders." He added, "How lamentable it is that the path to peace should lead through blood & over the carcasses of the slain!! But it is in the dispensations of that providence which inflicts partial evil, to produce general good." By general good, he meant a landscape "of elegant mansions, and extensive rich & productive farms" belonging to the masters of slaves. Some Creeks had helped Jackson's army, but he punished them as well as the Red Sticks in a peace treaty that he dictated at Fort Jackson in August 1814. At gun point, Jackson secured a cession of 23 million acres: more than half of the Creek domain and more land than the federal government had instructed Jackson to seek. By trapping Creeks within a zone of ceded land for

American settlement, Jackson sought "to destroy the[ir] communication with our enemies everywhere."[80]

Relentless in his enmity, Jackson pursued the 2,000 Red Sticks who had fled south to join their Seminole kin in Florida, where they got supplies and support from the Royal Navy. Acting without authorization from his own government, Jackson violated Spanish neutrality by seizing Pensacola in November 1814. After dispersing the British, Spanish, and their allies, Jackson withdrew westward to defend New Orleans, the key to controlling the Mississippi watershed.[81]

With a British attack looming in December, Jackson needed more men to defend the city, so he welcomed 600 free Black volunteers. By fighting for their country, free Blacks hoped to earn greater respect and secure more rights. When planters protested military service by people of color, Jackson replied, "They must be either for, or against us—distrust them, and you make them your enemies."[82]

Jackson also drafted thousands of enslaved men from their masters, who received pay for their labor. Serving with shovels rather than arms, slaves did the hard and dirty work of digging trenches, erecting breastworks, and moving supplies and cannons through swamps and across rivers during the cold, driving rains of December. An officer explained that enslaved workers "ease[d] the labour of the soldiery and preserve[d] their health and activity for more important service." By placing thousands of enslaved men under military supervision, Jackson also discouraged them from escaping to the British. But some did flee. A British officer found a young runaway named George, wearing a spiked iron collar imposed by his master as a punishment. Moved by George's plight, the officer had a blacksmith remove the painful collar, which the officer sarcastically called an "ingenious symbol of a land of liberty."[83]

On January 8 near New Orleans, the British attacked Jackson's strong position, suffering 1,500 casualties compared to a mere 71 for the dug-in defenders. The one-sided victory thrilled Americans, who felt relieved after suffering so many discouraging defeats in Canada. A North Carolina congressman claimed that the battle proved that "a free republic is capable of self-preservation, and of standing the shock of war." By celebrating Jackson as freedom's champion, the congressman overlooked the thousands of enslaved men who dug trenches and lugged cannons at New Orleans. In April, a witness described Jackson's triumphant travel through the South: "He is everywhere hailed as the savior of the Country. . . . He has been feasted, caressed, & I may say idolized. They look upon him as a strange prodigy; & women, children, & old men line the road to look at him as they would at the Elephant."[84]

Most Americans overlooked Jackson's abuses of power at New Orleans. Long after the British had sailed away, Jackson clung to martial law and kept militiamen in service, refusing them permission to go home. Defying protests from the governor, legislature, and judges, Jackson insisted that he needed complete control over a city allegedly infested with spies and traitors. Bristling at any criticism, he censored the local newspaper and exiled or jailed critics, including two judges accused by Jackson of "aiding, abetting, and exciting mutiny within my camp." In March 1815, Jackson relented, lifting martial law, releasing his prisoners, discharging the militia, and paying a $1,000 fine for contempt of court. Daunted by Jackson's immense popularity, the Madison administration dared not discipline its victorious but rogue general.[85]

News of Jackson's great victory reached the national capital in early February, at the same time that Americans learned of a peace treaty negotiated in late December at Ghent in Belgium. Anticipating a new war in Europe, the British wanted to withdraw their troops in America, so they offered generous terms. By restoring the prewar boundaries with Canada, the British relinquished their conquests in northern Michigan and eastern Maine. The treaty said nothing about the maritime issues—blockade and impressment—that had provoked the war. Unable to settle them, the negotiators preferred to make a hasty deal before their nations had to prepare for another expensive campaign in the spring. Learning of the treaty, Americans felt giddy with relief as they celebrated with banquets, parades, fireworks, illuminations, toasts, and ringing bells. A New Englander noted, "Our Town was frantic with joy at the news of Peace. It has come just in season to save our Country from destruction."[86]

The coincidental news of peace at Ghent and victory at New Orleans enabled Republicans to spin the war as an American triumph. Forgetting their many northern defeats, Americans dwelled instead on their late victories at Baltimore and New Orleans. Having failed to wrest any maritime concessions from the British, Republicans redefined national survival as victory. James Monroe assured Congress that "our Union has gained strength, our troops honor, and the nation character, by the contest." Although treaty had preceded battle, Americans liked to believe that victory at New Orleans had forced the British to sue for peace.[87]

In a third February coincidence, Federalist emissaries from the Hartford Convention reached Washington to present their constitutional demands only to find the capital celebrating peace and victory. Unlucky in their timing, the delegates were mocked by Republicans as defeatists and traitors. Ignored by president and Congress, the emissaries went home in a disgrace inflicted by the unanticipated events at New Orleans and Ghent. Thereafter, the Hartford Convention became a synonym for treason, hurled at Federalists during every election. Most voters preferred the comforting myth of a glorious war confirmed by an honorable peace, so the Federalists crumbled at the polls, even in New England. In 1816, the Republican candidate, Monroe, easily won the presidency, and the Federalists lost a third of their seats in Congress. They lost half of the rest two years later. A Republican exulted, "Never was there a more glorious opportunity for the Republican Party to place themselves permanently in power."[88]

Nationalism

In May 1815, a few months after making peace with Britain, the Madison administration sent Commodore Stephen Decatur with a squadron of warships to the Mediterranean to punish the Algerines for resuming their predation on American merchant vessels. Winning two naval battles, Decatur compelled the Algerines to make peace on American terms. The other Barbary States quickly made similar deals. That naval and diplomatic triumph consolidated a new mood of national pride back home.[89]

Madison sought to strengthen the federal government so that it could better manage future conflicts. He exploited the postwar burst of patriotism to press Congress for reforms, particularly the creation of a new Bank of the United States to replace Hamilton's original that had expired in 1811. The president also favored high tariffs on imported manufactures to protect new American industries from foreign competition. And he supported an ambitious federal program of internal improvements—roads, harbor dredging, and canals—meant to unite the country, promote economic development, and accelerate western settlement. In 1816, Congress supported Madison's new policies.[90]

By adopting a nationalist program, Madison stole from the Federalists and completed their marginalization. As Republicans became the Union's only party, however, they divided into factions that pivoted on leading men who jockeyed for the presidency. Ideological conflict also roiled the party thanks to diehard "Old Republicans" from the South, who clung to the states'-rights and small federal government orthodoxy of the past. They warned that nationalism would centralize power to the detriment of regions, states, and individual rights: a nightmare that they called "consolidation." Old Republicans also regarded any expansion of national authority as a potential threat to slavery.[91]

The Old Republicans' greatest orator was the eccentric and acerbic John Randolph, who invested patriotism in his state: "When I speak of my country I mean the commonwealth of Virginia." Tall, lean, and effeminate, he compensated with a keen mind and fierce but witty diatribes. Defiant of restraint, he carried a horsewhip and brought hunting hounds into the halls of Congress in violation of the rules. To sustain his fiery speeches, which lasted for several hours, he drank freely from a bottle of brandy held by an accompanying slave. Randolph lacerated Clay, Madison, and Monroe for betraying the true, old faith and imperiling southern interests by pandering to northern commercial men. Randolph blasted the tariff as a tax that bore "on poor men, and on slaveholders." And if Congressmen claimed enough power to fund internal improvements, he warned, "They may emancipate every slave in the United States."[92]

In 1816, the Old Republicans reaped a windfall when most congressmen voted to raise their pay, providing an easy issue for opponents to exploit during the fall election. Two-thirds of congressmen lost their seats. Their defeats spooked President Madison, who retreated to a more conventional Republican position by vetoing an ambitious new internal improvements bill, citing constitutional qualms that he had lacked a year before. Issued on his last day in office, Madison's veto strengthened the Old Republicans and defined the ideological battle lines of national politics for the next generation.[93]

Article Nine

A popular myth dismisses the Battle of New Orleans as insignificant because it came after the war allegedly ended at Ghent in late December. In fact, the war persisted until February 17, when the United States government ratified the treaty. It is also misleading to see the Battle of New Orleans as just some coda at the end of the War of 1812. Instead, the battle fell in the middle of a longer war that erupted in 1810 and persisted until 1819, primarily on America's southwestern frontier. In addition to the so-called War of 1812, that bigger and longer conflict included the American invasions of West Florida in 1810 and 1813, Harrison's attack on Prophetstown in 1811, the Creek War of 1813–1814, and invasions of Florida in 1814, 1816, and 1818. Historians usually—but mistakenly—treat these conflicts as discrete and minor episodes rather than as parts of a bigger conflict. Adding them up reveals a sustained, and ultimately successful, American push to dominate their frontier. That push served a defensive imperialism meant to prevent external foes from aiding internal enemies: slaves and Indians.[94]

Seen in the middle of a longer conflict—"the War of the 1810s"—the Battle of New Orleans assumes immense strategic and political significance. By emboldening Americans and chastening Britons, that one-sided battle helped the United States to turn an ambiguous peace treaty to great advantage. Sobered by defeat, the British would recede from helping Indians after the war, while Americans accelerated their dispossession of Native peoples and destruction of maroon havens.[95]

At Ghent, British diplomats had tried to secure an independent Indian country south of the Great Lakes. During the summer and fall of 1814, that insistence stalled the negotiations, for American diplomats would never accept a British protectorate over a permanent Indian homeland. A British negotiator remarked, "I had, till I came here, no idea of the fixed determination which prevails in the breast of every American to extirpate the Indians and appropriate their territory." To conclude the treaty, the British had to renounce their proposed Indian buffer zone. Instead, they settled for a vague article (the ninth) restoring their Native allies "to all the rights, privileges, and territories which they enjoyed in the year 1811." American negotiators accepted that clause because it would do nothing to protect Indians in the future. A British official later noted that Americans could fulfill Article Nine by allowing the Indians "to return to their former Situation for a week or a month" before dispossessing them.[96]

Americans won the peace by exploiting the ambiguity of Article Nine. A territorial governor insisted, "This is the time to expel the British entirely from the Indian country." During the summer of 1815, American officers convened treaty councils to make peace with Indian chiefs. Although Americans adhered to the letter of Article Nine by demanding no new land cessions, the negotiators pressured the Indians to ratify disputed cessions made before the war. To intimidate chiefs, American officers threatened to unleash "Merciless Jackson . . . as the Instrument of Vengeance" on Natives who refused American terms. Treaty commissioners also announced plans to construct new forts deep within Indian country: on the upper Mississippi River and northern Great Lakes. By demonstrating American domination, the new forts denied that Indians remained sovereign peoples living on their own territory between Canada and the United States.[97]

A new federal law also banned Canadian-based traders from dealing with Indians within the American border. By asserting an American trade monopoly within the border, the United States tried to exclude British influence from Indian country. Delighted by the land cessions, trade law, and forts, the territorial governor of Michigan, Lewis Cass, exulted, "A very few years more will present an iron frontier which [will] laugh to scorn the combined efforts of British & Indians."[98]

Resenting the new forts, Indian chiefs appealed for military support from their British allies in nearby Upper Canada. British officers sympathized with the Natives, but the home government wanted peace in North America to preserve Britain's profitable export trade in manufactures to the United States. With the military debacle at New Orleans seared in their memories, British leaders also balked at any renewed war deep within North America. In 1816, the imperial government directed its officers in Canada to stand down and advise the chiefs to accept American domination.[99]

The ultimate meaning of the Treaty of Ghent became what Americans could get away with and what Britons could live with. During the War of 1812, Americans had failed to conquer Canada, but that had always been a means to another end: rupturing the British alliance with Native peoples living within the United States. After the peace treaty, Americans achieved that end by enforcing a harder border, intruding forts within Indian country, and disrupting British trade with Natives. By securing the northern border, Americans could build their Union through western expansion.

The southern exploitation of Article Nine was even more brazen thanks to Jackson. In 1815, the Madison administration conceded that the treaty obligated the United States to restore to the Creeks the 23 million acres taken by Jackson's treaty in 1814. But Jackson argued with masterful sophistry that the Creek War was distinct from the War of 1812. Therefore, the United States need not return the cession that he had extorted. Rather than confront the formidable Jackson, the administration belatedly embraced his interpretation. The government also could not stop the settlers, who poured into the Creek cession. From just 9,000 in 1810, Alabama's population surged to 144,000 by 1820. No federal government was about to evict so many citizens from their new farms. A territorial official warned Madison, "How can a jury be found . . . to convict a man of *intrusion*,—where every man is an intruder?"[100]

Despite the official peace, Jackson resumed attacking maroons and Seminoles in Florida. At the end of the War of 1812, the British government had instructed a Royal Marine officer, Major Edward Nicolls, to turn his fort on the Apalachicola River over to the Spanish. But Nicolls sympathized with the maroons, so he entrusted that base to them instead. On a bluff beside the river, about fifteen miles above its mouth, the fort mounted eight cannons and one howitzer. Claiming the status of British subjects, the three hundred maroons continued to fly the Union Jack over their fort. Southerners denounced the "Negro Fort" as a great menace that attracted runaways and sent out raiding parties against plantations in Georgia and Alabama. On August 27, 1816, American gunboats ascended the river and opened fire. A cannon shot penetrated the main powder magazine, which erupted in a massive explosion, destroying the fort and killing most of the defenders. Survivors fled deeper into Florida to join the Seminoles. Other refugees escaped to the Bahamas, a British colony off the Atlantic coast.[101]

In 1818, Jackson invaded Florida with 3,000 men "to chastise a savage foe . . . combined with a lawless band of Negro brigands." After burning Seminole towns and seizing the Spanish posts at Pensacola and St. Marks, Jackson executed captives, including an elderly British trader, Alexander Arbuthnot, and a former Royal Marine officer, Robert Ambrister. Although both were independent operators, Jackson treated them as British covert agents, traitors to the white race, "unprincipled villains," and "unchristian wretches." Jackson also lured two Seminole chiefs into negotiating only to have them lynched. He claimed to have taken the "Just Vengeance of heaven" on "the exciters of the Indian war, and horrid massacre of our innocent women & children on the Southern frontier."[102]

The federal government officially regretted the invasion and executions but refused to censure or remove Jackson. Indeed, the general became even more popular by smiting Britons for aiding Indians and runaway slaves. The British government protested the executions but did nothing more, balking at a renewed war with the Americans as bad for business.[103]

The secretary of state, John Quincy Adams, endorsed Jackson's actions rather than "encounter the shock of his popularity." Indeed, Adams exploited Jackson's rampage to pressure the Spanish diplomat, Luis de Onís, to cede Florida to the United States. Unable to defend that colony, the Spanish sold it for $5 million in February 1819. At that time, the Americans renounced their shaky claim to Texas, while Spain conceded any right to the Oregon country, thereby strengthening the American claim to that region. In 1821, federal troops took possession of Florida, with Jackson as the first territorial governor.[104]

The Adams-Onís Treaty capped the War of the 1810s, in which the United States won more territory and power to the south and west than to the north. In bending the Treaty of Ghent to serve American expansion, the United States pursued contrasting northern and southern border policies. Unable to conquer Canada, Americans reluctantly accepted their northern border. Indeed, starting in 1815, they hardened that boundary to pin down Indians and separate them from British agents, traders, and soldiers. At the same time to the south, Americans exerted their superior power by erasing their border with Spanish Florida, creating a chaos that culminated in the Spanish cession of 1819.[105]

Borders

In Canada, the British worked to consolidate their border with the United States through reformed immigration policies. They renounced John Graves Simcoe's vision of Upper Canada as a haven for discontented Americans and a vehicle for disrupting the United States. During the 1790s as governor, Simcoe had enticed American emigrants to become subjects. But subsequent colonial officials distrusted the Late Loyalists and accused many of helping American invaders during the War of 1812.[106]

In fact, most of the Late Loyalists had become proud Canadian subjects of the Crown during the war as they became alienated from Americans who plundered and burned. After soldiers looted his home, a Late Loyalist expressed "a thorough detestation of the Americans & felt strongly the blessings of British protection." After the war, the border more clearly separated recent enemies committed to rival forms of government: American republicanism and the British mixed constitution.[107]

But British officials insisted that they needed more reliable subjects in Upper Canada, so they discouraged migration from the United States and subsidized immigrants from the British Isles. Until 1820, every emigrating British family received free passage, farm tools, six months of rations, and 100 acres of land. The aid started a chain migration, as early arrivals wrote home to encourage kin and friends to follow. Between 1815 and 1842, the colony attracted 159,000 British emigrants but only 32,000 from the United States. The American-born share of the population fell from 60 percent in 1812 to 7 percent in 1842, as the colony became more British in people, culture, and politics.[108]

In Upper Canada, hardline Loyalists—known as "Tories"—exploited the postwar reaction against all things American. The leading Tories were John Strachan, an Anglican bishop, and his former student, John Beverley Robinson, who became the colony's attorney general. Forming an oligarchy known as the Family Compact, Strachan, Robinson, and their friends dominated the assembly, legislative and executive councils, and district magistracies. Behaving like a tight-knit family, they helped each other acquire lands, offices, and contracts—and to punish their critics. Championing elite rule, the Tories insisted that human inequality reflected "the universal order of nature, from the Divinity, downwards, to the . . . meanest insects." They denounced any dissent as a crypto-republicanism that invited anarchy and another invasion by looting Americans.[109]

In fact, their critics were moderate reformers, who celebrated British rule but envied the more rapid economic growth on the American side of the border. Compared to the dynamic United States, Upper Canada seemed a sleepy, rural backwater kept undeveloped by a suspicious and selfish little cabal.[110]

In 1817, Robert Gourlay arrived from Scotland to rally opposition to the Family Compact. Thirty-nine years old, Gourlay was a restless activist who had tried to improve conditions for Britain's rural poor. Getting nowhere at home, he immigrated to Upper Canada, where he gathered and published economic data meant to nudge the government toward more liberal trade and immigration policies. When the Tories balked, Gourlay organized local meetings to petition the Crown for "a radical change of system in the government of Upper Canada." This agitation outraged the Tories, who distrusted civil society: any private groups, outside of government, that tried to mobilize public opinion. Charging Gourlay with sedition, the colonial government arrested and expelled him in August 1819.[111]

During the late 1820s and early 1830s, elections became increasingly contested and heated as a reform movement pushed for legislative control over the colonial executive. The royal governor, Sir Francis Bond Head, supported the Tories and miscast the contest as a "moral war . . . between those who were for British institutions, against those who were for soiling the empire by the introduction of democracy." By rallying most of the immigrant vote, and violently intimidating reform voters, the Tories captured two-thirds of the assembly seats in 1836. Vindictive in victory, Head dismissed from office anyone who favored reform. The defeated reform candidates included William Lyon Mackenzie, a fiery journalist from Scotland who denounced the election as fraudulent and the new assembly as illegitimate. Favoring violent resistance, Mackenzie saw an opportunity in late 1837, when the British withdrew most of their troops from Upper Canada to suppress a revolt in Lower Canada.[112]

Louis-Joseph Papineau led the Lower Canadian reformers of the Parti Patriote. Like their Upper Canadian counterparts, the Patriotes became frustrated and radicalized by the corruption and inflexibility of their colony's executive government. Denied reform within the constitution, the Patriotes prepared to declare independence, so the government tried to arrest the leading radicals. Refusing to go quietly, they organized an armed resistance that won an initial victory over loyalist troops at Saint-Denis in November 1837, but Papineau lost his nerve and fled to the United States. A month later, government troops defeated and scattered the armed Patriotes at Saint-Eustache. When they rallied at Beauharnois in November 1838, the government won a second crushing victory. The victors executed a few rebels and sent fifty-eight more to the penal colony on Tasmania in the distant Pacific. Suspending the elected assembly, a British governor and an appointed council ruled Lower Canada for the next three years.[113]

In December 1837, at the peak of the Lower Canada rebellion, Mackenzie made his own move in Upper Canada. At Montgomery's Tavern on the main road north of Toronto, he rallied 500 supporters to march on the capital. Lacking guns, most marchers carried pikes, pitchforks, or clubs. Intercepted and attacked by well-armed Tory militiamen, the protestors broke and fled after suffering three dead. In the spring of 1838, the government hanged two reformers as traitors, but Mackenzie escaped across the Niagara River to western New York.[114]

To revive his rebellion, Mackenzie recruited Americans to invade and revolutionize Upper Canada. By promising each volunteer $100 in silver and 300 acres, he enlisted a few hundred Americans, primarily men thrown out of work by the great depression of 1837.

From Vermont to Michigan, they organized secret societies, known as Hunters' Lodges, to prepare for invading Upper Canada. Rather than seeking to expand the United States, the Hunters wanted to create an independent republic committed to greater economic equality. They hoped that a radical Canadian republic would set an example to inspire true reform in the United States.[115]

Mackenzie's cause got a publicity boost in December 1837, when Canadian Tories burned the *Caroline*, an American steamboat used to ferry Hunters across the Niagara River for raids. The Tory attack killed an American on board, which produced outrage in American newspapers. That support dwindled when the Hunters bungled their raids into Upper Canada during 1838. Never mustering more than 400 men for a raid, the Hunters crossed the Detroit, Niagara, and St. Lawrence Rivers to loot and burn, but they were routed by larger numbers of loyal militiamen. After the victors executed twenty raiders and shipped seventy-eight to Tasmania, Governor Head exulted, "The struggle on the continent between Monarchy and Democracy has been a problem which Upper Canada has just solved."[116]

Mackenzie never got the support that he had expected from the federal government. Most of the Union's leaders, including the president, wanted to avoid war with the British Empire. They also distrusted Mackenzie as a hothead who exaggerated his support in Canada. The president sent 2,000 troops to the border under the command of General Winfield Scott to suppress the Hunters. During the War of 1812, Scott had helped to invade Upper Canada, but in 1838 he protected that colony from American raiders. In 1839, the federal government arrested Mackenzie for violating American neutrality. Convicted, he served eleven months in prison, where he felt betrayed by Americans.[117]

By jailing instead of aiding Mackenzie, federal leaders conceded that they could coexist with the British as their Canadian neighbors. Congressmen and journalists often rhetorically attacked Britain and her colonial rule over Canada. The bombast surged during border disputes, but federal leaders always compromised to avoid a new war.

By casting British rule as unnatural, Americans implicitly justified inaction, for they counted on nature to deliver Canada up to the United States in due time. Even the greatest publicist of expansion, journalist John L. O'Sullivan, argued for American patience because he assumed that British rule in Canada inevitably and peacefully would collapse. American inaction and compromise assured Canada's persistence in the British Empire.[118]

In 1839, a border dispute erupted over conflicting claims to valuable timberlands in the Aroostook region of northern Maine. Maine and New Brunswick mobilized their militias, while newspapers bellowed for war, but the "Aroostook War" claimed only one fatality: a Mainer who died from a stray bullet fired by a celebrating soldier on his side. The sole confrontation with the enemy came in a borderland bar where Maine and New Brunswick militiamen drank together until one offered a toast to Maine. A brawl erupted that bloodied noses and broke one arm.[119]

Both Union and Empire had too much to lose from a new war, for each was the other's leading trading partner. American entrepreneurs and states also relied on investment capital from Britain. A British investment agent in the United States noted, "England, in a war with this country, her largest debtor, the consumer of her manufactures, has all to lose and nothing to gain." Similar sentiments prevailed among American exporters of farm produce and borrowers of British funds.[120]

In 1842 in Washington, D.C., the American secretary of state, Daniel Webster, and a British diplomat, Lord Ashburton, negotiated a compromise treaty that awarded 7,000 square miles of disputed territory to Maine and 5,000 to New Brunswick. As a corporate lawyer, Webster favored peace as best for business, and he worked well with his former client, Lord Ashburton, who owned a banking firm. To deflate war fever and promote his deal, Webster planted editorials in leading newspapers, which he paid for with State Department funds. Forsaking their usual truculent tone, American senators quickly ratified the Webster-Ashburton Treaty to keep the northern peace.[121]

Durham

Citing the Hunter raids, Tories tried to repress all Upper Canadian reformers as pro-American traitors. In fact, most were moderates who favored neither republicanism nor American annexation. Simply seeking a more responsive and transparent colonial government, the moderates cursed Mackenzie for his reckless folly as well as the Tories for their repression.[122]

The political rancor and violence appalled the British government as evidence of something fundamentally wrong in the two Canadas. In late 1838, the British sent a special high commissioner, Lord Durham, to investigate the troubles and propose solutions. After five months touring Canada, Durham developed a sympathy for the moderate reformers of Upper Canada but an animus against the Francophone radicals of Lower Canada. Durham blamed the Upper Canada revolt on provocations by an entrenched, stubborn, and irresponsible Tory elite. But in Lower Canada, he insisted that excessive Francophone pride was equally to blame for a failure to compromise on both sides.

Returning to Britain, Durham published a report that proposed two fundamental measures. First, he promoted "responsible government," which meant legislative control over the executive government. Second, he proposed a union of Lower and Upper Canada. But the two measures were in tension. While responsible government offered greater autonomy, the proposed union would subordinate French Canadians within a larger Anglophone polity. In that union, Britain would still handle foreign and military affairs and appoint the executive and judicial officers, but they would have to answer to an elected Canadian legislature, just as a British cabinet depended on Parliament.[123]

Believing in the superiority of British culture and institutions, Durham rejected the former policy of tolerating French traditions, language, and religion in Lower Canada. He saw a Canadian union as the way to prod French Canadians to abandon their culture and language in favor of British ways and words. A supporter described "the main end" as "keeping Lower Canada quiet now, & making it English as speedily as possible."[124]

In 1841, the British government opted for union without responsible government: for controlling the French Canadians over providing more autonomy. An appointed governor general represented the crown and possessed a complete power to veto any bill or to refer it to his superiors in London for final judgment. In Lower Canada, the new arrangement pleased only the Anglophone merchants of Montreal. In Upper Canada, the Tories felt betrayed. "Lord Durham has thrown a firebrand amongst the People," one complained. Upper Canadian reformers supported the new union in the belief that it would promote economic development and provide greater strength for defense against any future American aggression. They also hoped that their cooperation would induce the British eventually to embrace responsible government in Canada. Their support for the new union led the Tories to become the opposition, inverting their fetish for complete loyalty to the home government.[125]

The new Canadian union included 1.1 million people and stretched for 2,000 miles from the mouth of the St. Lawrence River, on the east, to the head of Lake Superior, on the west. In a land of new and muddy roads, most people and their goods moved by boat along the St. Lawrence waterways, which connected the Atlantic Ocean to the Great Lakes. Francophones were nearly half of the population, but their proportion declined annually as more immigrants poured in on ships from Britain to settle new farms around the Great Lakes. More rural than the United States, Canada had only a few small cities. The largest, Montreal, had just 40,000 inhabitants. The union of 1841 did not include New Brunswick, Nova Scotia, and Prince Edward Island, which remained distinct British colonies.[126]

In 1842, the leading French-Canadian politician, Louis Lafontaine, allied with the primary Upper Canadian reformer, Robert Baldwin, to form a legislative majority that pressed for responsible government. The reformers benefited from a philosophical shift in the imperial government in favor of liberal principles. In 1847, a new governor,

Lord Elgin (son of the man who took the Elgin marbles from the Acropolis in Greece), arrived with permission to accept responsible government. He chose his cabinet entirely from the reformers, and Lafontaine became Canada's prime minister.[127]

But Lafontaine faced a new challenge from his old mentor, Papineau. Pardoned and returned from exile, Papineau agitated against the union and in favor of an independent republic for Quebec. To defeat that challenge, Lafontaine sought to demonstrate the benefits of the union government for French Canadians by securing compensation for property destroyed by Loyalist forces in suppressing the rebellion of 1837–1838. The Tory opposition howled that compensation would reward traitors, but Elgin favored Lafontaine's bill, which passed in April 1849. In Montreal, angry Tories burned Lafontaine's new house and stormed the parliament building, smashing furniture and setting the building ablaze. With a truly Canadian devotion to order, the Speaker kept to his chair in the burning building until a motion to adjourn had passed. The rioters also harassed Elgin, but he clung to the principle of responsible government, and the British Parliament endorsed his decision.[128]

But Britain hurt Canada's economy by adopting a free trade policy that benefited British consumers. Unable to compete with American farmers and loggers, Canadians needed the protected market of Britain for their exports of lumber, fish, wheat, and flour. Free trade shrank the British demand for Canadian products, generating a recession in Canada. That recession inspired a surprising new movement pushed by Montreal's Anglophones, who sought to escape from both free trade and Francophone politicians by seeking annexation by the United States. Elgin marveled, "whether merchants be bankrupt, stocks depreciated, roads bad, or seasons unfavourable—annexation is invoked as the remedy for all ills, imaginary or real."[129]

During the summer and fall of 1849, annexationists filled meeting halls and newspaper columns in Montreal, but their agitation faltered elsewhere in Canada. Most Canadian leaders disdained the United States as chaotic, corrupt, and hypocritical in keeping slaves while boasting of freedom. A newspaper declared, "Ere we annex ourselves to a slave-holding Republic, we'll go down with the British flag—the *true* emblem of *true* liberty—flying at the mast-head." Most Canadians wanted to sustain a distinctive society within the British Empire and outside the United States. In 1850, an economic recovery deflated the brief boom for annexation.[130]

Most Americans also saw little to gain from annexing Canada. As Britain loosened its control, and ceased to treat Indians as allies, Americans no longer had any reason to fear Canada. And with slaveholders dominating American foreign policy, they were not about to add any free states to the north, as that would weaken their power within the Union. On both sides of the border, most people agreed that the two polities could coexist and trade to mutual advantage.[131]

Tilt

The War of 1812 often seems inconsequential, as a stalemate that changed no border. In fact, that conflict fell within a longer and bigger War of the 1810s, which shifted the geopolitics of North America. Embattled and imperiled at the start of that decade, Americans secured continental predominance by 1819, as the Spanish forsook Florida while the British retreated behind the Canadian border. Both empires abandoned Indian allies, who lost their crucial suppliers of modern weaponry. Thereafter, Indians could slow but not stop American domination. Secretary of war John C. Calhoun said of Indians: "our views of their interest, and not their own, ought to govern them."[132]

But it also mattered that the Americans settled for hardening their northern border while expanding southwestward across the continent. Anglophobia persisted in American politics, but expansionists focused their overt attacks on weaker peoples—Indians, maroons, and Mexicans—cast as supposed British proxies. That shift irritated Yankees who wondered why federal leaders compromised boundary issues with Canada while expanding the nation to the south and west. As that tilt obtained vast new lands suitable for plantation slavery, Americans bitterly debated the future of their Union.[133]

Top: "A Correct View of the Battle near the City of New Orleans on the eighth of January 1815," engraving by Francisco Scacki, 1815. In the center foreground, the British general Edward Pakenham suffers a mortal wound. Library of Congress 2006677463. *Bottom: "Destruction of the American Steamboat Caroline," print by an unknown artist, 1900. This represents the burning by Canadian Loyalists of a vessel supplying rebels on the Niagara River. Here the flaming and drifting* Caroline *plunges over Niagara Falls.* Library of Congress 2016817282.

FOUR ⚭ RACE

Born a Wolof in the Senegal region of West Africa in 1793, Anna Madgigine Jai was captured in war in 1805 and taken by a trader to Cuba, where Zephaniah Kingsley, Jr., purchased her in 1806. The son of a South Carolina Loyalist, Kingsley became a ship captain and slave trader. Sailing around the Caribbean and across the Atlantic, he saw the diverse slave regimes of West African kingdoms and European colonies. In 1803, Kingsley moved to Spanish East Florida and bought four plantations beside the St. Johns River, where his enslaved people raised oranges and grew cotton.[1]

In late 1806, Kingsley married thirteen-year-old Anna "by her native African customs" and not, he added, "according to the forms of Christian usage." He described her as "a fine, tall figure, black as jet, but very handsome." He had concluded that Africans "were superior to us, physically and morally. They are more healthy, have more graceful forms, softer skins, and sweeter voices." Adopting African polygamy, Kingsley took two other wives, but Anna remained his favorite and business partner. Kingsley hired tutors to teach music, dancing, modern languages, and polite literature to his mixed-race children.[2]

During Zephaniah's frequent sea voyages, Anna managed their complex household and plantation with an air of command, having grown up in a chief's family. "She was very capable, and could carry on all the affairs of the plantation in my absence, as well as I could myself," Zephaniah noted. In 1811, he freed Anna and their three children. Obtaining a nearby farm on another Spanish grant, Anna worked it with twelve slaves of her own. While race mattered to officials in Spanish Florida, class carried more weight, so Anna enjoyed legal rights denied to free Blacks in the United States.[3]

Applying African and Spanish concepts to his practice of mastery, Kingsley deployed the task system, in which a laborer could stop working after completing that day's assignment. This contrasted with the despised gang system of American plantations, where an overseer compelled slaves to labor long days under close and painful supervision. Kingsley's slaves also enjoyed Saturday afternoons and all of Sunday as their own. In that time, they could fish and hunt,

Opposite, from top: "Kingsley Plantation, Slave Quarters (perspective view looking southeast)," photo by Paul A. Davidson, 1934. During the 1820s, Zephaniah Kingsley erected thirty-two slave houses built of tabby stone. The building in the foreground has been reconstructed while those in the rear remain in ruins. Kingsley arrayed the houses in a semicircular arc. Historic American Buildings Survey (Library of Congress).

tend gardens, and make crafts for sale. With the proceeds, they could buy their freedom, which Kingsley set at half the market price. As he expected, these incentives encouraged his slaves to work harder with less friction. Defending marriages, Kingsley avoided disrupting family units and "encouraged as much as possible dancing, merriment, and [fancy] dress" on Saturdays and Sundays. Rather than employ a white overseer, Kingsley empowered and later freed a Black manager. While favoring slavery as the best labor system for a hot climate, Kingsley rejected the American obsession with white supremacy, for he trusted and freed Black people who helped him prosper. Kingsley promoted his "patriarchal or co-operative" version of slavery as less brutal to slaves and less dangerous for masters. Kingsley claimed that his slaves "love me like a father," but of course many were his children.[4]

In 1811–1812, Anna and Zephaniah suffered in the Patriot War, the American-sponsored rebellion in East Florida. Raiders from both sides destroyed the Kingsleys' buildings, took many slaves, and butchered their livestock. Kingsley played a double game by overtly helping the rebels while covertly feeding information to the Spanish governor at St. Augustine. Anna was more consistent as a Spanish Loyalist who dreaded the rebels as looters and slave hunters. A colonial officer praised her as a "heroine" with "great enthusiasm concerning the Spaniards and extreme aversion to the rebels."[5]

After the war, Kingsley expanded his holdings to 32,000 acres worked by more than 200 slaves. He relocated his main plantation to an island near the mouth of the St. Johns River, where Anna lived in her own house, which fit with the Wolof practice that each wife and her children had a distinct home near that of the patriarch. The semicircular arrangement of tabby-stone slave quarters also resembled a Wolof village—and diverged from the rectilinear pattern favored in the American South.[6]

In 1821, Americans acquired Florida and threatened to impose the starker slave regime of the United States. At first, Kingsley hoped to influence the new order as a member of the territorial council. He wanted to preserve slavery but insisted that masters should act with moderation and within limits defined by the old laws of the Spanish colony. Those laws had punished planters who murdered slaves or disrupted their marriages and families.[7]

Kingsley also favored the Spanish policy of promoting manumissions to build a middle caste of free Blacks invested in preserving the social order. "We must have slaves to cultivate our lands and free colored people are a necessary consequence of having slaves," he reasoned. The Spanish approach rewarded able and enterprising enslaved people who worked hard to buy their freedom and that of their family—rather than plot trouble and rebellion. "The door of liberty is open to every slave who can find the means of purchasing himself," Kingsley explained. Once freed, Blacks provided a militia to defend the property system that benefited them. In Spanish Florida, they had the same rights as common whites, save for the chance to hold political office. They could own land, bear arms, serve on juries, and testify against white people in trials. Kingsley urged American newcomers to make "a considerable sacrifice of local prejudice to the shrine of self-interest" by preserving the Spanish system.[8]

Instead, the territorial government wrote prejudice into the legal code. The councilors virtually outlawed manumissions by requiring a master to pay a $200 penalty for everyone emancipated, and ordered every freed person to leave Florida within thirty days or face sale back into slavery. Any free Black who moved into Florida also risked enslavement if he or she could not pay a $500 penalty. New laws barred people of color from giving legal testimony, possessing guns, or serving on juries and enforced on them a curfew and special poll tax. The legislators prohibited interracial marriage and barred inheritances by mixed-race children. Any white man who married a colored woman faced a $1,000 fine and lost his civil rights. Southern Americans favored a simpler, two-caste system: free whites and enslaved Blacks without free Blacks as mediators. In 1824, Robert Brown, a Black entrepreneur in St. Augustine, protested the higher poll tax assessed against his people: "They would have us pay for the degradation that has been laid on us."[9]

Despising the new racial regime, Kingsley told his children that the "inequitable laws of this territory" degraded his genteel children below uneducated whites and denied them "that protection and justice [due] in every civilized society to every human being." No one, he insisted, should persecute free people "for being a shade darker than our selves."[10]

In response, the territorial governor, William P. Duval, derided Kingsley as a learned and genteel fraud who "cherishes in his bosom his *ebony wife*." Most Americans regarded any open love for a Black woman as discrediting a white man in public life. Both Congress and the president ignored the petitions from Kingsley and other long-resident planters who protested the new laws.[11]

A free thinker, Kingsley dismissed key notions cherished by most white Americans. He derided their racist stereotypes of Blacks and insistence that all whites were superior; their naïve belief that mass colonization could remove millions of Blacks from America to Africa; and the democratic cult of public opinion as just and wise. He denounced a democracy where leaders would "consult popularity rather than policy and their own good sense." Of Blacks, he said, "They are now equally virtuous, moral, and less corrupted than the ordinary class of laboring whites." Kingsley even vindicated the slave rebels of Haiti as courageous, resourceful, and less brutal than their white opponents. He named two sons, born during the 1830s, Micanopy and Osceola, after Seminole chiefs who resisted American expansion in Florida.[12]

Visiting the North, Kingsley attended antislavery meetings. Abolitionists hardly knew what to make of a learned man who despised racism but defended slavery if well managed. When abolitionist and women's rights activist Lydia Maria Child challenged his slaveholding, Kingsley replied, "All we can do in this world is to balance evils. I want to do great things . . . and in order to do them, I must have money."[13]

When the Haitian president, Jean-Pierre Boyer, offered special incentives for colored Americans to emigrate, Kingsley visited that republic. In the name of his oldest son, Kingsley bought 35,000 acres on the island's north shore, where he settled Anna and his other two wives and most of their sons during the late 1830s. They relocated and freed 53 slaves, who worked as sharecroppers with the option to buy homesteads after nine years. But Kingsley always hedged his many bets, keeping plantations with over 80 slaves back in Florida as the financial foundation for his diverse domains.[14]

Kingsley praised Haiti as a "land of liberty and equal rights, where the conditions of society are governed by some law less absurd than that of color." He ridiculed America's "pseudo republicans" for treating Haitians as inferior, when they could read "daily accounts of mobs and persecution of color" in the United States. Kingsley felt "ashamed to receive such kindness and hospitality" from Haitians, a people whom Americans excluded from a reputable inn or stagecoach. Reflecting on a full life, he confessed, "The more I've seen of the world, the less I understand it. It's a queer place; that's a fact."[15]

Sections

Prior to the American Revolution, slavery was legal, profitable, and accepted in every British colony. As a complex movement, the revolution generated proslavery as well as antislavery arguments. Antislavery reformers insisted on freedom as inalienable, but conservatives regarded private property rights as essential to liberty. Crediting white men with courage in defeating British "slavery," Patriots derided their slaves as cowards who had failed to fight for and win their own freedom. This derision overlooked the many slaves who did fight during the revolution—and the tortures and executions that Patriots inflicted on slaves who rebelled. By denouncing slavery as degrading, republicanism could deny that the enslaved had the virtue to deserve freedom. Whites especially cherished their own freedom because they denied it to the enslaved. Thomas Jefferson noted that southerners were "zealous for their own liberties, but trampling on those of others."[16]

Because the Union lacked constitutional jurisdiction over slavery in the states, antislavery reformers had to act through state governments. Abolition was possible in the North, where less than 5 percent of the voters owned slaves. Between 1780 and 1810, most northern states gradually emancipated their slaves through laws designed to soften the blow for masters and taxpayers. In 1780, Pennsylvania's law freed no slaves then alive, merely those born after the law passed and only once they turned twenty-eight years old. The gradual emancipation laws sought to free northern states of slavery, rather than to ensure freedom for the enslaved. To save taxpayers from compensating masters for their lost property, the laws obliged young slaves to pay for eventual freedom by working without compensation into their mid-twenties. The process unfolded very slowly in most states. Pennsylvania still had some elderly slaves in 1847, when the state finally and fully abolished the system.[17]

Northern racism intensified as the free Black population grew. A French visitor, Alexis de Tocqueville, noted, "The prejudice of race appears to be stronger in the states that have abolished slavery than in those where it still exists." Another traveler reported that northern Blacks were "subjected to the most grinding and humiliating of all slaveries—that of universal and unconquerable prejudice." This traveler horrified white people by shaking hands with Black men.[18]

In public gatherings, whites enforced subordination on Blacks. It was rarely safe for them to attend Independence Day celebrations. When some tried in Philadelphia, whites attacked them for "defiling the government." Few Blacks could vote or serve on juries, and none held political office. In the few states that permitted them to vote, they usually dared not try for fear of white mobs. Free Blacks also remained vulnerable to kidnappers who hauled them south for sale as slaves.[19]

Denied access to public education and better-paying jobs, most Blacks worked as stevedores, sailors, barbers, bootblacks, domestic servants, and laundresses. A young man despaired, "Shall I be a mechanic? No one will employ me; white boys won't work with me. Shall I be a merchant? No one will have me in his office; white clerks won't associate with me. Drudgery and servitude, then, are my prospective portion." Kept down, most free Blacks lived from day to day on pittances and without real estate or long-term security. Discrimination forced them to cluster together in the least desirable neighborhoods and to avoid crowds of white people as sources of violence. A dentist, Joseph Willson, complained, "The exceedingly illiberal, unjust, and oppressive prejudices of the great mass of the white community" are "enough to crush—effectually crush and keep down—any people."[20]

Despite discrimination, a small, middle class did develop as some artisans and shopkeepers prospered. Black activists created their own institutions, including churches, schools, and Masonic lodges, to provide community bonds and some social security. Black associations organized petitions and protests against racial discrimination and formed vigilance committees to defend their community against kidnappers and to help runaways from the South.[21]

While slavery shrank in the North, the system expanded in the South, where 90 percent of American slaves lived. Southern masters deemed slavery essential because they could never rely on free whites for the hard, dirty work of plantations. "You can't drive 'em like you can a nigger," a master explained. Southerners also preferred slavery to living among free Blacks, deeming them more dangerous than slaves. No southern state legislature adopted emancipation.[22]

Three states in the Upper South—Delaware, Maryland, and Virginia—did liberalize the legal process of "manumission" by which a master could free slaves by a will or deed. Manumissions modestly increased the free Black population in Virginia from 2,000 in 1782 (1 percent of all Blacks) to 20,000 (7 percent) in 1810. Maryland's free Black population grew from 4 percent of Blacks in 1755 to 20 percent in 1810.[23]

The growing numbers of free Blacks alarmed Virginia's legislators, who in 1806 made further manumissions difficult and rare. Masters demonized free Blacks as allegedly lazy, larcenous, and rebellious—as setting wretched examples to the enslaved. By dreading the freed as active subversives, southerners contradicted the stereotype of Blacks as sluggish loungers. But whether seen as lazy, thieving, or scheming, free Blacks were cast as proof that emancipation menaced whites.[24]

Southerners restricted the rights of free Blacks, who could not vote, serve on juries, or join the militia, and could only own a gun with permission from a county court. The freed also had to register with the court and obtain a certificate to display to any suspicious magistrate or slave patroller. No colored person could testify against a white who cheated or struck him or her.[25]

The great majority of southern Blacks remained enslaved, and their conditions worsened with the increased mobility of white people after the revolution. In the older states along the Atlantic coast, declining soil fertility and a growing population pushed outmigration. Exploiting territories newly taken from Indians, thousands of white families moved south and west in search of bigger farms with better land to raise cotton. A minor crop during the colonial era, cotton became profitable and widespread in the Lower South after the invention in 1793 of Eli Whitney's cotton gin: a machine to separate valuable fibers from their husks. The gin was fifty times more efficient than handwork.[26]

Requiring a growing season of at least 200 frostless days, cotton could thrive in the Lower South but not farther north. Cotton planters benefited from a booming export market as textile factories multiplied in Britain, France, and the American Northeast. From South Carolina and Georgia along the Atlantic coast, cotton cultivation spread westward into Alabama, Mississippi, Louisiana, Arkansas, and eventually Texas. In 1818 an Alabaman reported that the "price they receive for one year's crop will pay for the price of the land." Requiring relatively little capital to commence production, cotton cultivation drew thousands of common whites to the frontier, where they hoped to rise into the planter class. Great planters also moved west to enhance their estates.[27]

As they expanded their fields and crops, planters scrambled to buy more slaves from the Upper South, so prices rose. In 1803 a male field hand sold for about $600 in South Carolina compared to $400 in Virginia: a $200 difference enticing to Virginia sellers and Carolina slave traders. In Alabama, a traveler saw an arriving coffle of "the poor creatures . . . arranged two abreast, secured by a long chain that passes down between them, and in this manner are driven forward; all prospect of escape being cut off by the loaded rifles on either hand." Between 1790 and 1860, in one of the largest forced migrations in world history, slave traders and migrants herded over a million slaves from Virginia and Maryland to expand southern society to the Mississippi River and beyond. Hauled from Maryland to Columbia, South Carolina, Charles Ball recalled his auction during the Fourth of July while drunken whites sang and shouted "in honor of free government and the rights of man."[28]

That migration disrupted enslaved families and their communities, as forced migrants had to forsake wives, husbands, parents, and children left behind. Francis Fedric remembered "the heart-rending scenes" when his master prepared to move west to Kentucky: "Men and women [were] down on their knees begging to be purchased to go with their wives or husbands . . . children crying and imploring not to have their parents sent away from them; but all their beseeching and tears were of no avail." Interstate sales and planter migration ruptured at least a quarter and perhaps half of the first marriages for the enslaved.[29]

Dislocated slaves bore the harshest labor of clearing and cultivating new farms, usually in summer climes even hotter than they had endured in Virginia or Maryland. In Alabama, a newcomer reported that planters drove their slaves to clear land every night until midnight and then rousted them to begin cutting again an hour before dawn. He described the nearby town as "thronged with people on Sunday, talking about cotton and niggers."[30]

By driving slaves to work harder and faster, masters steadily increased cotton production. Cultivation demanded long hours of hard work through a long growing season. Planting in the spring led to weeding under the hot summer sun and culminated at summer's end in harvest. Picking cotton bloodied hands with the sharp edges of husks around the fibers. A planter who moved to Mississippi calculated that, thanks to close supervision and ready flogging, "my negroes [do] twice as much here as negroes generally do in N[orth] C[arolina]." But if a slave met a work quota today, the overseer would expect more tomorrow—with failure punished by the whip. In 1805, masters accepted 50 pounds of cotton as a good day's picking; by 1830 they demanded 130 pounds. For every pound short of quota, a slave received one stroke with the lash. A former slave recalled, "When the price [of cotton] rises in the English market, the poor slaves immediately feel the effects, for they are harder driven, and the whip is kept more constantly going." Cotton planters achieved an unprecedented rate of work by tightly supervising and often punishing their enslaved workers.[31]

Producing staple crops for export, masters borrowed to secure land and slaves, so they had to turn a profit to pay the interest—or face bankruptcy. "All despise poverty and seem to worship wealth," a southern magazine noted. A South Carolina master explained that he deserved the slave's earnings "because I bought him; and in return for this I give him maintenance, and make a handsome profit besides." Another planter justified his exploitation of slaves: "A gentleman has the right to make the most of this life, when he can't calculate on anything better than roasting in the next."[32]

Buying labor and deploying it as capital, cotton planters were the consummate American capitalists. They worked hard to exploit their property, making sophisticated measurements of inputs and outputs, even collecting data linking slave productivity to the number of lashes inflicted. Tracking the interdependence of crop and bondage, planters calculated that a slave was worth exactly 10,000 times the prevailing price of cotton per pound. So when cotton sold for 7 cents a pound, a field hand had a value of $700. Southern leaders worked to keep that human capital as liquid as possible for sale, movement, and inheritance. So they defeated proposed state laws to legalize slave marriages and protect families from disruption by sales. No ancient holdover, American slavery was thoroughly modern and brutally efficient at exploiting labor.[33]

In boom times of high cotton prices, planters felt flush with opportunity and impending riches. But planters could not feel secure for long. By investing everything in cotton cultivation, they became vulnerable to storms, drought, and crop-infesting bugs and worms. Planters also plunged into a capitalist market prone to sudden and deep busts that alternated with the exhilarating booms. In bad times, planters tried to work their slaves even harder lest creditors foreclose on them.[34]

To get ahead, ambitious common men hired out as overseers on the plantations of gentlemen. Working long hours to supervise restive slaves, the overseer relied on a cowhide whip. Planters complained that their overseers were negligent, dishonest, and brutal. But masters sent contradictory messages by ordering overseers to maximize the crop by driving the slaves hard—but not to whip too much and increase running away.[35]

The cotton frontier developed a culture of violence, with murder rates by whites on whites in central Georgia forty-five times higher than in New England. A highly competitive society, the cotton frontier bred frustration and anger among those who failed to prosper. Prickly men, they resented any insult as dishonoring. So they fought and killed one another to prove that they were white men and not slaves, who had to endure insults and blows. A South Carolina judge explained, "To submit to a blow would be degrading to a freeman" but "not degrading to a slave" nor "to a woman," for they were already dishonored. In North Carolina, a congressman castrated two men he accused of sleeping with his wife. After he served a brief jail term, voters honored him with a seat in the state legislature. In Alabama, William Lowndes Yancey won a congressional election after killing an unarmed man by pistol-whipping, shooting, and stabbing with a sword for good measure.[36]

Slavery

Three-quarters of southern enslaved people worked in the fields, while the rest served as artisans or domestics who prepared meals, cleaned homes and dishes, tended children, and groomed horses. House slaves got better food and clothing but paid for them in closer supervision by masters who demanded submissive performance. A former house slave, Lewis Garrard Clarke, recalled, "We were constantly exposed to the whims and passions of every member of the family; from the least to the greatest, their anger was wreaked upon us." Save in the short days of winter, enslaved people worked long hours for six days a week, with a respite on Sunday and sometimes on Saturday afternoon.[37]

To maximize profits by cutting costs, masters provided the minimal diet, clothing, and shelter needed to keep slaves working. A South Carolinian explained, "A full belly quells dissension & rebellion, but too full a one breeds inordinate laziness." Enslaved people usually had enough cornmeal and pork to eat, but that monotonous diet could lead to pellagra, a debilitating nutritional disorder. A family generally had a wooden cabin, about sixteen-by-eighteen feet with a sleeping loft overhead. Clothing consisted of bad shoes and coarse cloth bought from northern mills.[38]

Any defiance infuriated self-righteous masters as ingratitude. Even the most "benevolent" of masters could brutally punish those who denied his moral superiority. Charles Ball described the "back of the unhappy Maryland slave" as commonly "seamed with scars from his neck to his hips." Masters also readily sold slaves to punish resistance. A former slave, William Johnson, recalled, "master used to say that if we didn't suit him he would put us in his pocket quick— meaning that he would sell us."[39]

Enslaved people suffered most from sales that disrupted their families. A woman declared: "Selling is worse than flogging. My husband was sold six years ago. My heart has bled ever since, and is not well yet. I have been flogged many times, since he was torn from me, but my back has healed in time." A Virginian noted the horror of slaves facing sale: "The sentence of banishment strikes them like the message of death. I have myself heard, with shuddering, their wild and frantic shrieks."[40]

Southern masters routinely assigned Black women to menial work in the fields. A former slave, Williamson Pease, recalled, "Women who do outdoor work are used as bad as men." But planters also valued enslaved women as mothers who produced children for future work and sale. Thomas Jefferson deemed "a woman who brings a child every two years as more profitable than the best man on the farm. What she produces is an addition to capital, while his labor disappears in mere consumption." At slave auctions, buyers invasively examined women as potential breeders. An enslaved man recalled, "They felt all over the woman folks."[41]

By law, a white man could rape a slave but never marry her. Indeed, social pressure demonized any white man who treated a Black woman as his wife. By claiming to have killed the Indian leader Tecumseh in battle, Richard M. Johnson of Kentucky thrived as a politician—until rivals called attention to his informal marriage to a mixed-race slave, Julia Chinn, who ran their plantation during his absences to attend Congress. "She was a source of inexhaustible happiness and comfort to me," Johnson recalled. Thanks to a school sustained at Johnson's plantation, their light-skinned daughters, Adaline and Imogene, acquired good educations and fine manners. A local farm boy saw them at a party hosted by Johnson: "They Ware Dressed as fine as money Could Dress them & to one that Did not [k]no[w], they ware as white as anny of the Laydes thare."[42]

Political critics denounced Johnson for treating mixed-race people as equal to whites. A Kentucky newspaper editor was "shocked and outraged by the marriage of a mulatto daughter of Col. Johnson to a white man, if a man, who will so far degrade himself, who will make himself an object of scorn and detestation to every person who has the least regard for decency, can be considered a white man." Another editor preferred the discretion of Thomas Jefferson in hiding his long liaison with the enslaved Sally Hemings: "Like other men, the author of the Declaration of Independence had his faults, but he was at least, careful never to insult the feelings of the community with an ostentatious exhibition of them." Although this editor kept his own Black mistress on the sly, he claimed to occupy the high

"An Affecting Scene in Kentucky," engraving by Henry R. Robinson, 1836. Produced during the election of 1836, this engraving attacks Richard M. Johnson for his common-law marriage to the enslaved Julia Chinn and his attempt to introduce their two daughters into white society. Library of Congress 208661287.

moral ground, declaring that Johnson's "chief sin against society" was that "he scorns all secrecy, all concealment, all disguise." During the late 1830s, vicious criticism of his "mongrel daughters" and "mulatto bastards" ruined Johnson's bid to become president.[43]

Few white men married a slave, but many preyed upon enslaved women. Frederick Douglass recalled, "My father was a white man." As a child, he saw that presumed father (his master) brutally whip Douglass's fifteen-year-old aunt Hester, until blood dripped onto the floor. He did so to punish Hester for rejecting his advances. Given the power imbalance, few women could resist a persistent master. Mary Boykin Chesnut of South Carolina complained, "Like the patriarchs of old, our men live all in one house with their wives and concubines, and the mulattoes one sees in every family exactly resemble the white children." White wives looked the other way to sustain marriages. Chesnut marveled, "Any lady is ready to tell [you] who is the father of all the mulatto children in everybody's household but their own. Those she seems to think drop from the clouds."[44]

James Henry Hammond of South Carolina preached marital fidelity and morality among his slaves by having adulterers flogged. But Hammond kept two enslaved mistresses: a mother and her daughter, the latter only twelve when her abuse began. Hammond instructed his white son and heir never to sell "any of my children or possible children" because, he reasoned, "Slavery *in the family* will be their happiest earthly condition."[45]

Harriet Jacobs escaped from her abusive master by hiding for seven years in the attic of her free grandmother. Jacobs referred to masters as "fiends who bear the shape of men." Some attractive young women of lighter complexions were sold in the "fancy trade" to become prostitutes or concubines for wealthy men, particularly in New Orleans and Charleston. Of a young Black woman, Jacobs noted, "If God has bestowed beauty upon her, it will prove her greatest curse." Enslaved men were also victims, forced to stand aside as masters abused their wives and daughters.[46]

While unequal in power, whites and Blacks lived in close proximity and interacted with a daily intimacy that surprised visitors used to stricter segregation in the North. That proximity misled owners into thinking that they understood their slaves—and that the enslaved cherished their masters. "We learned to say 'Yes Sir!' And scrape and bow, and to do exactly just what we was told to do, make no difference if we wanted to or not," Robert Falls recalled. But owners could never achieve the domination of their dreams, for enslaved people led dual lives that they kept half hidden. They cherished stolen moments, when they could slip away to visit friends, hunt, and tend a garden. Sitting around a fire at night, they shared songs and told stories rich in supernatural spirits, talking animals, and moral lessons. Animal trickster tales taught subtle defiance by featuring small but clever creatures deceiving stronger but dimmer ones.[47]

At night and on Sundays, enslaved people moved through the woods between plantations to visit friends, spouses, and children. Traveling risked running afoul of slave patrols sponsored by county governments to stop and beat slaves roaming without written passes from a master. But in the South's forested landscape of dispersed farms, enslaved people found places to hide. While brutal, slave patrollers were also negligent, often lounging in taverns rather than watching the roads. And enslaved people better knew the paths through the woods.[48]

By day, enslaved people suffered from the master's power, but they became almost free at night, when master and overseer retreated to their families and homes. A master complained that slaves took "uncurbed liberty at night, [for] night is their day." They rambled to hunt and fish, attend dances, and steal food and alcohol for hidden barbecues. A former slave, Abraham Chambers, recalled the parties: "Some clap and some play de fiddle, and man, dey danced most all night." By acting as if free by night, they avoided a full submission to the slavery of their days.[49]

Enslaved people sustained an "invisible church" of Black preachers, who covertly assembled believers in a barn or the woods. A former slave recalled rejecting the services promoted by his master: "Dat ole white preacher jest was telling us slaves to be good to our marsters. We ain't keer'd a bit 'bout dat stuff he was telling us 'cause we wanted to sing, pray, and serve God in our own way." That way meant shouts, songs, jumps, and an emphasis on how Moses had led Hebrew slaves to freedom. Christianity helped enslaved people endure the torments of this world and imagine a better life.[50]

Black Christianity coexisted with traditional African beliefs and practices, often called magic. To recover lost goods, stray lovers, and sick children, enslaved people turned to conjurors, who doubled as folk doctors savvy about plants and roots with medicinal properties. While Christianity prepared people for the afterlife, folk magic provided small advantages in this world.[51]

Most enslaved people enjoyed a weeklong vacation over Christmas and New Year's. Josiah Henson recalled his youth in Maryland: "Slavery did its best to make me wretched, but, along with memories of miry cabins, frosted feet, weary toil under the blazing sun, curses and blows, there flock in others, of jolly Christmas times, dancing before old massa's door for the first drink of egg-nog, [and] extra meat at holiday times." Frederick Douglass noted that holidays served as "safety-valves, to carry off the explosive elements." Without those interludes, "the rigors of bondage would have become too severe for endurance." In a perverse synergy, the release offered by nights, Sundays, and Christmas helped slaves to endure and so helped slavery to persist.[52]

Resistance

Although masters obsessed about the danger of slave revolts, such rebellions were few and local. Enslaved people balked at fighting whites, who were better armed and organized for military conflict. Collective revolt was more difficult in the American South, where half the people were white, than in the West Indies, where enslaved Blacks comprised over 90 percent of the population. To succeed, rebels had to recruit many people—but growing numbers increased the risk that someone would reveal secret plans.[53]

Rather than rebel, enslaved people resisted through acts of deception by individuals or small groups. "Is not cunning always the natural consequence of tyranny?" asked former slave Francis Fedric. Henry Bibb added that "the only weapon of self-defence that I could use successfully was that of deception." Enslaved people slowed their work, pretended to misunderstand orders, faked sickness, broke tools, stole food, got drunk, burned down buildings, slipped poison into white people's food and drink, and ran away. Clever slaves exploited the masters' stereotype of them as lazy and stupid. Josiah Henson knew Dinah to be as "clear witted, as sharp and cunning as a fox." But she faked idiocy to evade work and punishment. When assigned a distasteful chore, "She would scream out 'I won't; that's a lie—catch me if you can' and then she would take to her heels and run away."[54]

Night provided a cover for trickery. Henson recalled his "midnight-visits to apple-orchards, broiling stray chickens, and first-rate tricks to dodge work." Taking revenge on a stingy master named Riley, Henson remembered "driving a pig or a sheep a mile or two into the woods to slaughter for the good of those whom Riley was starving. I felt good, moral, heroic." The clever young man who killed, hid, and shared a hog became the hero of his slave quarters. Slaves justified theft with a labor theory of value: they took a small part of what they had earned by hard labor extorted from them. A Virginian reported that they said, "Massa, as we work and raise all, we ought to consume all. . . . Massa does not work; therefore he has not [an] equal right; overseer does not work; he has no right to eat as we do."[55]

Enslaved people also resisted by running away. Most fugitives were unmarried boys and young men: the slaves in the greatest danger of sale and able to endure the hardships of escaping pursuers with dogs. Advertisements posted by masters dwelled on the skills and intelligence of runaways, for a disproportionate number had plied trades that revealed the roads and waterways to the wider world: boatmen, carriage drivers, house slaves, and artisans.[56]

Fewer women fled because children slowed flight, and mothers could not bear to leave them behind. A grandmother told Linda Brent to stay put: "Stand by your own children, and suffer with them till death. Nobody respects a mother who forsakes her children; and if you leave them, you will never have a happy moment." James Curry reported that his mother had twice tried to escape before marrying, but thereafter, "Having young children soon, it tied her to slavery." The families that consoled and nurtured enslaved people also helped masters pin them down. Women who did run usually did so after dislocation by a recent sale; they sought to get back to family in their former neighborhood.[57]

Some runaways fled to seek a northern state, but long-distance flight was especially risky. A refugee ran through a gauntlet of slave patrols, suspicious whites, and slave catchers with bloodhounds. Catchers could whip or kill any fugitive with impunity; and masters usually sold recaptured runaways to the dreaded Lower South. Most refugees left the Upper South, which offered a shorter run to the North. Fleeing from Georgia, Charles Ball revealed the long odds facing a fugitive from the Lower South. Four years before, he had come south in chains from Maryland, but he had memorized landmarks and roads. Ball began his flight in August, when he could count on finding ripe corn in the fields for sustenance. Avoiding roads because well patrolled, he waded through swamps and found paths in the woods, navigating by stars at night and swimming across rivers and streams. After seven months, Ball reached Maryland only to run into a slave patrol that wounded him with buckshot before beating, binding, and casting him into jail.[58]

A northern state offered only a limited freedom, for most white people disliked Blacks and might help slave catchers. Thanks to bounty hunters and federal fugitive slave laws, runaways could find no security within the United States. "When I arrived in the city of New York," Moses Roper recalled, "I thought I was free; but learned I was not." Escaping from Virginia to Ohio, John Malvin noted, "I found every door closed against the colored man except the jail and penitentiaries, the doors of which were thrown wide open to receive them." Lewis Garrard Clarke did not feel safe until he reached Canada: "There was no 'free state' in America, all were *slave* states—bound to slavery, and the slave could have no asylum in any of them."[59]

For greater safety, fugitives moved on to Canada, where the British refused to extradite former slaves to the United States. Britons and Canadians liked to claim moral superiority over the slaveholding republic, cast as a domain of hypocrites. In 1837, Joseph Taper with wife and son escaped from Virginia to Pennsylvania. But they had to flee again when the local newspaper ran a runaway notice posted by his master and a notorious bounty hunter appeared in the neighborhood. In 1839, Taper and family reached Canada, where he prospered as a farmer. A year later, he contrasted Canadian freedom and American slavery in a letter to his former master:

> Since I have been in the Queen's dominions, I have been well contented. Yes, well contented for Sure, [where] man is as God intended he should be. That is, all are born free & equal. This is a wholesome law, not like the Southern laws, which puts man made in the image of God on [a] level with brutes. . . . My wife and self are sitting by a good comfortable fire happy, knowing that here are none to molest [us] or make [us] afraid. God save Queen Victoria.

He exhorted masters to beware of the Christian "day of Judgment" and "repent of this evil, & let the oppressed go free."[60]

Crediting the British Crown for their haven, the refugees were "extravagantly loyal." Indeed, they distrusted Canadian reformers who pushed for a more popular government because it reminded Blacks of the American democracy that had kept them enslaved. A British official welcomed their enlistment to fight the 1837 rebellion by reformers: "The Natural hatred of the coloured people to the Americans would be a guarantee for their fidelity."[61]

In the northern United States, an informal network of sympathizers, later known as the "Underground Railroad," provided hiding places and sustenance for fugitives. Most of the "conductors" were free

Blacks, but white abolitionists, especially Quakers, also contributed. After escaping from slavery in Maryland, Harriet Tubman returned thirteen times to help seventy people escape to freedom. That state offered an unprecedented reward of $12,000 for her capture, but no one could ever collect. During the 1840s, about a thousand runaways a year made it to the North (and often on to Canada).[62]

That seemed like a scant loss for a system that held 3 million people in bondage in 1850, but the fugitives had an impact far beyond their numbers. They were enough to outrage masters, who demanded more northern help in retrieving them. And that southern pressure became an irritant that soured northern moderates on supporting slavery. Runaways also challenged the system by publishing searing accounts of their sufferings, which contradicted proslavery propaganda. Their eloquence also undermined the vicious stereotype of Blacks as insensitive fools.[63]

Many more runaways hid in the woods or a swamp within a few miles of their plantation. In Florida, Tom Wilson explained, "I felt safer among the alligators than among the white men." Hiding by day in huts or caves, these "outliers" ventured out at night to gather roots, nuts, and berries, to hunt for small game, and to steal chickens and pigs from their former masters. Outliers also got food slipped to them by friends and relatives who had stayed behind. Runaways usually hid nearby, an overseer reported, "because they did not like to go where they could not sometimes get back and see their families." When life in hiding became too cold and hungry, they could return to their masters, often after negotiating some small concession.[64]

Some outliers became "maroons" by forming long-lasting refugee communities hidden deep within forests and swamps. A former slave recalled that those "niggers was too smart fo' white folks to git ketched." Stealing firearms, some groups became strong enough to defy slave hunters. During the 1840s in Halifax County, North Carolina, maroons stole seventy-five hogs from a farmer who doubled as a slave catcher. They then offered to leave his farm alone if he would call off his dogs.[65]

An especially large and enduring maroon community lay in the

Great Dismal Swamp of 2,000 square miles along the Virginia–North Carolina border. During the 1830s, the swamp hosted several hundred people, living in hovels on small islets. Some of them hired out for wages with logging companies willing to evade the law to obtain cheap and good workers. Others cut shingles to sell. But many stayed hidden, subsisting by raising sweet potatoes and hunting raccoons and opossums. A former resident reported, "Dar is families growed up in. . . . Dismal Swamp dat never seed a white man, an' would be skeered most to def to see one."[66]

In 1811, James Hubbard became fed up with working as an enslaved nail-maker for Thomas Jefferson at Monticello. With forged papers, Hubbard escaped to pass as free in Lexington, a market town about seventy miles away. Unaware of where Hubbard had gone, Jefferson sold him on spec to a carpenter, Reuben Perry, for $300—and another $200 if found. Perry advertised a reward for Hubbard's capture, describing him as twenty-seven years old, six feet tall, with "stout limbs and strong made, of daring demeanor, bold and harsh features, dark complexion, apt to drink freely."[67]

To earn the extra $200 from Perry, Jefferson hired a slave hunter who found, caught, and returned Hubbard to Monticello. "I had him severely flogged in the presence of his old companions, and committed to jail, where he now awaits your arrival," Jefferson informed Perry. Jefferson considered Hubbard too defiant to remain in Virginia: "He will never again serve any man as a slave. The minute he is out of jail and his irons [are] off, he will be off himself." Jefferson urged Perry "to sell him out of state." Because Hubbard had a monetary value in a market economy (even as a distressed asset), he had no chance of equality and the pursuit of happiness despite the "self-evident truths" expressed in the Declaration of Independence.[68]

Slaves knew that the so-called "good masters," like Jefferson, belonged to a brutal system that treated Black people as property. Of supposed paternalists, a former slave declared, "They are not masters of the system. The system is master of them." A traveler asked a slave if her mistress treated her well. "Yes," she answered, "but I could take better care of myself." In old age, Amy Chapman told an interviewer: "I kin tell you things about slavery times dat would make yo' blood bile, but dey's too terrible. I jus' tries to forgit." Delia Garlic was more succinct: "Dem days was hell."[69]

Colonization

While slavery divided the country, racism united most whites, North and South. James Madison lamented, "We have seen the mere distinction of colour made . . . a ground of the most oppressive dominion every exercised by man over man." But he thought the prejudice too deep to change, so Madison wanted to remove "from our country the calamity of its black population." Northern Blacks remained second-class citizens, denied the vote in most states, limited to menial occupations, and segregated in schools, public accommodation, and transportation. Northern whites might dislike slavery in principle, but they did not want southern Blacks moving north in practice. By denigrating Blacks, northerners and southerners found a common ground that helped them cooperate in politics.[70]

In December 1816 in Washington, D.C., leading politicians organized the American Colonization Society (ACS) to promote deporting Blacks to Africa as colonists. Drawn from the North and the Upper South and both political parties, the organizers included Henry Clay, Francis Scott Key, James Madison, John Marshall, John Randolph, John Tyler, and Bushrod Washington (a Supreme Court justice and nephew of the late president George Washington). Even Andrew Jackson joined for a while. The "colonizationists" insisted that Blacks were a divisive presence that kept the nation from fulfilling its republican potential. Determined to whiten America, colonizationists rejected the alternative of retaining African Americans in a multiracial republic of equal citizens. Randolph declared that both races could never "occupy the same territory, under one government, but in the relation of master and vassal." He claimed that colonization would "secure the property of every master in the United States" by ridding the nation of free Blacks.[71]

The society insisted that Blacks could never escape from poverty and degradation in America because of entrenched white prejudice. Only in their own homeland could former slaves thrive and demonstrate their true worth by spreading Protestant Christianity in Africa. Unlike proslavery men, colonizers deemed Blacks capable and deserving of freedom—but insisted that they had to leave America to realize their potential. Andrew Judson spoke more frankly than most colonizationists: "The colored people can never rise from their menial condition in our country," and "they ought not to be permitted to rise here."[72]

Francis Scott Key displayed the contradictions of a colonizationist. A wealthy lawyer in Washington, D.C., he owned a Maryland plantation worked by enslaved people. While considering slavery to be incompatible with republicanism, Key regarded Blacks as inferiors who could not coexist in freedom among whites. He defined free Blacks as "the greatest evil that afflicts a community." Key freed seven of his slaves, but kept eight as unworthy of freedom. "I am still a slaveholder and could not, without the greatest inhumanity, be otherwise," Key rationalized, for he considered it "immoral to free them and expect them to flourish" in America. As a lawyer, he represented some slaves, whom he considered unusually "worthy," in suits against abusive owners, but Key also prosecuted abolitionists for sedition and helping slaves escape to freedom.[73]

Most colonizationists hoped that an African colony would reduce slavery by encouraging more masters to manumit. Such a haven became essential as southern states required manumitted Blacks to leave, while most northern states barred them from moving in. But the society's southern members continued to own, buy, and sell slaves. In 1821, the president of the ACS, Bushrod Washington, sold fifty-four slaves away to the Lower South, for he wanted money more than his conscience needed moral consistency. A witness to their coffle passing southward saw "unhappy wretches," including "husbands [who] had been torn from wives and children, and many relatives left behind."[74]

During the 1820s, eight northern states urged the federal government to apply the revenue from western land sales to buy thousands of slaves and send them to Africa. But no slave state endorsed this proposal, save for little Delaware. Opposition was almost universal in the Lower South, where planters dreaded colonization as the slippery slope to an emancipation mandated by the federal government. In 1827, Georgia's legislature condemned colonization as "wild, fanatical, and destructive" as well as "ruinous to the prosperity, importance, and political strength of the southern states." The legislators feared that colonization might free the Upper South of slavery, rendering the Lower South a weak, minority region in a Union hostile to slavery.[75]

On behalf of the American Colonization Society, President James Monroe secured federal aid to found a West African colony named Liberia, where American naval officers bought land at gunpoint from resistant chiefs. To honor the president, the colonizers named their capital Monrovia. The federal government subsidized the shipment of free Blacks there, and added captives liberated from illegal slave ships. The federal involvement horrified southern conservatives, such as Randolph, who renounced the ACS during the 1820s.[76]

The colonization movement also stalled because few free Blacks would go to a distant and alien continent. Most were third- or fourth-generation Americans who preferred to tough it out in America rather than take a dangerous leap to a colony where deadly malaria prevailed. Madison noted that his slaves had a "horror of going to Liberia." The 12,000 emigrants sent by the ACS fell far short of America's surging enslaved population, which doubled between 1820 and 1850, an increase of 1.5 million.[77]

In January 1817 in Philadelphia, 3,000 free Blacks met in a church to consider colonization. The owner of a sail-making firm, James Forten, moderated the meeting, which loudly rejected colonization as an "unmerited stigma . . . cast upon the reputation of free people of color." Forten noted, "Every heart seemed to feel that it was a *life and death question."* Having invested blood, sweat, and tears in America, free Blacks claimed the nation as their own. They also refused to forsake "the slave population of this country; they are brethren by the ties of consanguinity, of suffering and of wrong." Free Blacks would stay to fight for "the entire abolition of slavery in the United States."[78]

Some free Blacks did want to escape from the United States, but they preferred emigration to Haiti, which had Black leaders, rather than to Liberia, where the ACS prevailed. African Americans celebrated Haitians for vindicating their race with a courageous struggle for freedom. A Boston activist, David Walker, praised Haiti as "the glory of the blacks and terror of tyrants."[79]

In 1807, Haiti had been divided by two rival generals: Henri Christophe in the north and Alexandre Pétion to the south. Christophe's troops forced peasants to work on plantations raising coffee and sugar for export, generating a revenue that enriched his regime. That money sustained a large army and public schools. An Anglophile who hated the French, Christophe hoped to make English the leading language in his kingdom. To the south, Pétion led the Republic of Haiti, but he ruled as a president-for-life. Pétion became more popular than Christophe by redistributing plantation land in small parcels for free peasants. By raising subsistence crops instead of sugar and coffee, they depleted the export economy, rendering Pétion's republic poorer than Christophe's monarchy.[80]

Haiti's leaders dreaded another invasion, which France threatened to mobilize in 1814. French proponents spoke of a genocidal campaign to kill most Haitians followed by a massive importation of enslaved Africans to restore a plantation economy. To avert that threat, Christophe sought diplomatic recognition by other European monarchs. Emulating their grand style, he built a massive palace, Sans Souci, and rode about in gilded coaches imported from London. Christophe also formed an aristocracy of eighty-seven barons, counts, and dukes drawn from his army's officers.[81]

Christophe had 20,000 laborers build Citadel La Ferrière, a massive fortress 130 feet tall, on a 2,600-foot-high mountain overlooking Cap-Haïtien and the Atlantic. Bristling with 200 cannons behind thick stone walls, the Citadel took fifteen years to complete. The strongest fortification in the New World, the Citadel had cisterns and storehouses to sustain 5,000 defenders for a year. Christophe built the fortress as a refuge should French invaders drive him from his palace below. Where Sans Souci expressed Christophe's hopes of European acceptance, the Citadel displayed his fears.[82]

In 1820, the Citadel failed to stop a rebellion by Christophe's people, enraged at his coercive labor policies. Facing defeat and suffering from a stroke, Christophe shot himself, legend says with a silver bullet, and was buried in his Citadel. Meanwhile, Pétion had died, passing southern power to his protégé, Jean-Pierre Boyer, another veteran general of the Haitian struggle for independence. Exploiting Christophe's death, Boyer marched north to reunite Haiti.[83]

In 1822, Boyer's troops conquered the adjoining Spanish colony of Santo Domingo to block support there for a French invasion of Haiti. After abolishing slavery there, he recruited loyal settlers by appealing to free Blacks in the United States, promising them a "land of true liberty." Boyer offered financial subsidies, tools, provisions, and small farms to emigrating families. Between 1820 and 1860, about 13,000 American Blacks moved to Haiti, more than the 12,000 sent by the ACS to Liberia.[84]

To avert invasion, Boyer sought diplomatic recognition by European powers. In 1825, when a French fleet menaced the republic, he agreed to pay a staggering indemnity of 150 million francs in return for French acceptance of Haitian independence. Meant to compensate France's former slaveholders, that crushing debt pushed Boyer to squeeze more revenue out of his people by increasing exports. To do so, he reinstituted a form of coerced labor on plantations producing sugar and coffee. This provoked hardships and turmoil, to the dismay of many American immigrants, who also struggled to adapt to a new language and the Catholic faith. About a third of them returned to the United States.[85]

Illinois

As an expanding country, the shape and fate of the Union emerged in the West through settlement. The extent of freedom depended on whether slavery could colonize the western territories that would become states. In the Northwest Ordinance of 1787, the federal government organized territorial government in the region north and west of the Ohio River. The ordinance prohibited slavery there, but many of the settlers came from the South and brought along their slaves. To accommodate them, territorial officials created a loophole. Masters could keep Black "indentured servants" provided that servitude was "voluntary." A proponent insisted that the settlers had "the indisputable right to permit blacks voluntarily to indenture themselves." But a ninety-nine-year indenture imposed on illiterate people was hardly voluntary, and Blacks could not protest their contracts because they could not legally testify against whites. In 1818, when Illinois applied to become a state, Congress mandated that its new constitution had to ban slavery, but that constitution preserved indentured labor. In 1820, Illinois had 450 free Blacks and 917 Blacks held in de facto slavery.[86]

In 1824, proslavery men sought to entrench and expand servitude by pushing for a convention to rewrite the state's constitution. They sought to attract wealthy southern planters and thereby boost an economy still reeling from the depression of 1819. A convention advocate told state legislators: "Look at those trains of wagons with their splendid teams, their carriages and their gangs of negroes. They are going over to fill up Missouri, and make it rich, while our State will stand still and dwindle, because you won't let them keep their slaves here."[87]

The "conventionists" posed as populists defending the right of common voters to write a new constitution that would eliminate alleged elitism. They appealed to "white folks," a group placed above Blacks in race but below a distrusted white elite, known as "big folks," in class. Poorly educated farmers resented the paternalism of the federal government that had imposed restrictions on servitude. Many common whites worried that they would lose the value of their racial superiority if Blacks also became free in their midst. Populists wanted the color line firmed up by keeping Blacks in servitude.[88]

As governor, Edward Coles fought against a new constitution that might permit slavery. Born a master in an elite family in Virginia, Coles had renounced slavery as a college student. In 1814 he urged his hero Thomas Jefferson to lead a public crusade for emancipation in Virginia. Rebuffed by Jefferson, Coles despaired of redeeming his native state. In 1819, he moved to Illinois, acquired 9,000 acres, freed twenty slaves, and provided each family with a new farm of 160 acres. Three years later, Coles won election as the state's governor, but he did not appeal to many "white folks." Wealthy, college-educated, with refined manners and fancy clothes, Coles violated the savvy advice that an Illinois politician should "shake hands with everybody, and wear an old coat, with at least one good hole in it."[89]

Antislavery men worked to claim the populist mantle by casting the convention advocates as wealthy slaveholders keen to grab power. An anticonventionist warned, "The planters are great men, and will ride about, mighty grand, with their umbrellas over their head." The Coles party also played the race card by noting that slavery would bring many more Black people into Illinois.[90]

The campaign became heated and violent, as each side accused the other of betraying republicanism. A mysterious fire burned the state capitol in Vandalia, a mob harassed Coles, and thirteen men died in political violence. A resident reported, "families and neighborhoods were so divided and furious and bitter against one another, that it seemed a regular civil war." Ultimately, in a referendum on August 2, 1824, the citizens rejected holding a convention by a vote of 6,640 to 4,972. While preventing an expansion of slavery in Illinois, the vote did not free any of the Blacks already held in servitude. That emancipation waited until the 1840s, when the state supreme court finally struck down the indenture system. But even then, Illinois retained discriminatory laws against free Blacks.[91]

Coles's victory did keep Illinois from developing a full-blown slave society, and thereby tipping the Union's tenuous balance of power in favor of the South. The 1824 referendum demonstrated that an antislavery program could succeed by appealing to the racial prejudice and class resentments of common white men. The conventionists anticipated Jacksonian Democrats by defining a populism premised on white supremacy. The anticonventionists evolved into Whigs and later Republicans, who cast slavery as a threat to the equality and freedom of white men.[92]

Diffusion

Southern leaders wanted no restriction on the westward movement and sale of enslaved people. In older states, planters believed that they had too many slaves for their own safety and more than their farms and plantations demanded. But rather than free "surplus" slaves, masters preferred to sell or move west with them. This relocation supposedly "diffused" the danger of revolt by alleviating the crowded concentration of enslaved people in old states. Proponents also insisted that "diffusion" benefited slaves by moving them to the western land of milk and honey, where they could be better fed, clothed, and housed. Some southerners even argued that diffusion could lead to emancipation once slaves became small minorities spread evenly across a vast country. "An uncontrouled dispersion of the slaves now within the U.S. was not only best for the nation, but most favorable for the slaves," concluded Madison.[93]

Southerners in Congress got a shock on February 13, 1819, when James Tallmadge, Jr., of New York proposed amendments to a bill to admit Missouri as a new state in the Union. Tallmadge wanted to require Missouri to ban further slave imports and adopt a gradual emancipation law. Most northern congressmen, Republicans as well as Federalists, supported Tallmadge, for they believed that slavery contradicted and threatened free government. Jonathan Roberts of Pennsylvania insisted that slave states were "marred as if the finger of Lucifer had been drawn over them." Tallmadge would preserve the West for free white settlers, who alone could sustain a true republic. In effect, he sought to extend the Illinois regime of restriction westward into Missouri to freeze out slavery.[94]

Tallmadge and other "restrictionists" rejected diffusion as a fraud. John Sergeant of Pennsylvania demanded, "Has any one seriously considered the scope of this doctrine? It leads directly to the establishment of slavery throughout the world." Rather than leading to emancipation, expansion swelled the western demand for slaves, inflating their value in the older, eastern states. If diffused, slaveholding would dominate the Union.[95]

In response, southerners denied that Congress had any constitutional authority to impose restrictions on a new state. They regarded the Federal Constitution as a sectional compromise that had mollified the South by preserving the political equality of every state in the Union. They saw restriction as a power play by a northern majority to confine and subordinate the South. The North could command the nation's future by claiming the West for its own people and institutions, while the restricted South became a claustrophobic corner of poverty and weakness in the Union. Counting on diffusion to release the pressure of Black population growth, southerners accused restrictionists of exposing them to a Haitian-style revolution. John Tyler of Virginia predicted that restriction would intensify the "dark cloud" of slavery "over a particular portion of this land until its horrors shall burst."[96]

Southerners threatened disunion and civil war if restriction prevailed. Thomas Cobb of Georgia warned northerners that they were "kindling a fire which . . . could only be extinguished in blood!" The southern threats irritated northern congressmen, who retorted that they were ready to fight. Each side then accused the other of imperiling the Union. Neither wanted secession, but both regarded the Union as too vulnerable to survive any major shift in regional power. Nathaniel Macon of North Carolina anticipated "near relations plunging the bayonet into each other."[97]

In February 1820, alarmed moderates crafted a compromise to save the Union. Maine (previously part of Massachusetts) became a free state, while Missouri joined without any restriction on slavery. The compromise preserved the balance of power in the Senate of eleven free and eleven slave states. Congress also imposed a line west of Missouri to the Pacific at 36° 30′ latitude, barring slavery to the north, where most of the remaining federal territory then lay. While southerners got Missouri, they faced more free states entering the Union later.[98]

Political leaders feared that the compromise bought only a little time for a tenuous Union. Henry Clay predicted "that within five years from this time, the Union would be divided into three distinct confederacies" one northeastern, one southern, and one western." John Quincy Adams regarded the compromise as a sop to slavery, "the great and foul stain upon the North American Union" that inevitably would provoke a "calamitous and desolating" civil war. But Adams kept this sobering thought to the privacy of his diary, for he hoped to become president of a Union held together by compromise.[99]

Jefferson blasted the compromise as violating the proper equality of states within a consensual Union. In the regional division drawn across the West, he saw looming disaster: "A geographical line, coinciding with a marked principle, moral and political, once conceived and held up to the angry passions of men, will never be obliterated; and every new irritation will mark it deeper and deeper." He predicted that a civil war would "burst on us as a tornado, sooner or later." Jefferson insisted that restriction betrayed the revolution: "I regret that I am now to die in the belief that the useless sacrifice of themselves, by the generation of '76 to acquire self-government and happiness to their country, is to be thrown away by the unwise and unworthy passions of their sons." By blaming the trouble entirely on Yankees, whom he cast as power-mad frauds, Jefferson failed to practice the mutual love of his ideal Union.[100]

Southerners supported the Union when it served their interests, as it usually did, for the South enjoyed a political clout disproportionate to the region's declining share of the nation's citizens. That power derived from the Federal Constitution's three-fifths clause and the greater cohesion of southern congressmen when compared to their northern counterparts. Southern leaders cherished a robust national government when it enforced the fugitive slave law in northern states and pushed expansion southwestward into Florida, Texas, and beyond. Southerners cheered when the Union acted aggressively against Britons, Indians, and maroons. But southern leaders scuttled back to a states'-rights position at the slightest hint that northerners might deploy federal power to limit slavery.[101]

By loudly threatening secession, southerners could intimidate most northern congressmen. If that did not work, some southerners resorted to personal insults and menace. As debates became tense, they displayed pistols and bowie knives in Congress. When a northerner denounced slavery, a southern congressman felt insulted and demanded a duel, which had a silencing effect. Claiming superior honor, southern leaders disdained Yankees as crass and cowardly for evading duels by citing religious qualms. In 1838, a new congressman, Joshua Giddings of Ohio, lamented, "We have no Northern man who dares boldly and fearlessly declare his abhorrence of slavery and the slave-trade." But Giddings refused "to remain silent and witness my country's disgrace." By speaking his mind, Giddings outraged southerners and reaped seven physical assaults, one with a bowie knife, in Congress.[102]

Blood

Free Black sailors on northern ships carried word of the congressional debates over slavery to southern ports. The news animated the leaders of Black Methodist churches in Charleston, South Carolina, where the leading free Black was Denmark Vesey, a prosperous carpenter in his fifties. Born in Africa, Vesey had lived in the West Indies before his master brought him to Charleston. In 1799, Vesey bought a winning lottery ticket and used the proceeds to buy his freedom for $600.

But his former master enraged Vesey by refusing to let him buy freedom for his wife and children. In his version of the Missouri debates,
Vesey insisted that Congress had freed all slaves in America but that
masters had repressed news of that order in South Carolina. Inspired
by the Haitian Revolution, he plotted a revolt.[103]

In the spring of 1822, city officials got wind of the plot. Some
minor participants confessed under torture, but the leaders, including Vesey, stayed silent. In July and August, officials hanged him and
thirty-four other suspects. South Carolina's governor marveled that
they "met their fate with the heroic fortitude of Martyrs." But mobs
of white men attacked their widows when they appeared in the street
wearing mourning. The city leaders shut down and demolished the
church where Vesey had worshiped. They also established a permanent armed guard of 150 men to patrol the streets from a fortified
headquarters known as the Citadel.[104]

In 1822, South Carolina's leaders adopted rigorous laws to penalize
every free Black man, assessing an annual tax of $50 and requiring
a white "guardian" to vouch for his character. Violators would be
whipped and sold into slavery. To block aspirations to gentility, the
authorities prosecuted free Blacks who wore fine clothing in public.
Another law required every free Black sailor or passenger on a visiting
ship to stay in a filthy jail until his vessel was ready to sail. South Carolinians likened the law to the procedures for quarantining newcomers suspected of bearing a deadly disease. An attorney explained, "In
South Carolina, we think the presence of a free negro, fresh from the
lectures of an Abolition Society [as] equally dangerous." Seven other
southern states adopted similar laws.[105]

In August 1831, the great southern nightmare erupted in South-
ampton County, Virginia, where a messianic preacher, Nat Turner,
led a midnight assault to slaughter sixty white people, steal their guns,
and rally more enslaved people. Beginning with six men, Turner's
force grew to sixty, but they were still too few, their cohesion too
weak, and they lacked training with firearms, so the rebels succumbed

to militia counterattacks. Enraged victors killed many who surrendered, and, in the chaotic aftermath, spooked Virginians murdered at least another forty slaves, who had never been part of the plot. Saved for a trial, Turner died on the gallows, one of twenty-three legally executed. The victors turned his skin into purses and his bones into trophies. A mob also tarred and feathered an English visitor overheard to say that slaves deserved freedom.[106]

In January 1832, the revolt shocked Virginia's legislators into considering a proposal for gradual emancipation and colonization introduced by Thomas Jefferson Randolph, a grandson of the former president. Randolph sought to whiten Virginia rather than free slaves. His plan would apply only to those born after July 3, 1840. Becoming state property, the children would be worked for Virginia's profit until adulthood and then the state would sell them farther south or ship them to Africa. Randolph expected the process to take nearly a century.[107]

After a lively debate, Virginia's legislators rejected any plan, no matter how slow, to abolish slavery. The majority wanted no further discussion of the troubling issue because they considered slavery essential to their society, economy, and culture. John Thompson Brown urged fellow legislators to put up and shut up about slavery, which he deemed "our lot, our destiny—and whether, in truth, it be right or wrong—whether it be a blessing or a curse, the moment has never yet been, when it was possible to free ourselves from it." A college president, Thomas R. Dew, agreed, "It is in truth the slave labour in Virginia which gives value to her soil and habitations, take away this and you pull down the atlas that upholds the whole system." Blaming Turner's revolt on outside agitators, legislators made it illegal for a Black to preach or for anyone to teach a slave to read and write. The other southern states followed suit.[108]

Abolition

In the North, an abolition movement emerged among free Blacks and spread to sympathetic whites. Disgusted by slavery as a great moral evil, abolitionists rejected the colonization movement as tepid and futile. Instead, they wanted immediate emancipation without compensating slave owners and for freed Blacks to remain in the United States as equal citizens. Abolitionists regarded "slavery as founded in wickedness, and tears, and blood, and as sustained by avarice and crime," so "it ought immediately to be overthrown." Modeling an inclusive Christian fellowship, white abolitionists welcomed Blacks into their societies and urged citizens to empathize with them as brethren whose sufferings affected everyone.[109]

Born free but Black in North Carolina, David Walker had moved to Charleston, where he attended church with Denmark Vesey. When authorities executed Vesey and destroyed the church, Walker fled to Boston, where he opened a shop that mended and sold clothes. A voracious reader and fiery writer, he published, in 1829, *David Walker's Appeal*, a passionate denunciation of slavery and the moral evasions by white Americans. Rejecting colonization, Walker declared, "America is more our country, than it is the whites," for enslaved labor had built the country and the tears and blood of Blacks had poured onto its soil.[110]

Walker justified violence to seize freedom. "Had you not rather be killed," he asked, "than to be a slave to a tyrant, who takes the life of your mother, wife, and dear little children?" Walker warned slave owners, "Your DESTRUCTION *is at hand.*" Refuting their insistence that emancipation would lead to a race war by vengeful free Blacks, Walker insisted that true safety lay in extending freedom and equality to all people: "Treat us like men, and there is no danger but we will all live in peace and happiness together. For we are not like you, hard-hearted, unmerciful, and unforgiving." Georgia imposed the death penalty on anyone who circulated Walker's book. Within a year, he died of tuberculosis, but his words lived on, for Black sailors carried copies of Walker's book to southern seaports. "What a happy country this will be," Walker had written, "if the whites will listen."[111]

In Boston in 1831, a year after Walker died, a white journalist, William Lloyd Garrison, launched *The Liberator*, a weekly newspaper promoting abolition and racial equality. Born into poverty and raised in pious Christianity, Garrison empathized with exploited people. Moved by reading Walker's *Appeal*, Garrison abandoned his support for colonization and challenged Americans to renounce racism. Insisting that "moderation against sin is an absurdity," Garrison vowed, "I will be as harsh as truth, and as uncompromising as justice. . . . I will not equivocate. I will not excuse. I will not retreat a single inch AND I WILL BE HEARD." Unlike Walker, Garrison was a pacifist who opposed slave insurrections, but southerners refused to believe him. Georgia offered a $5,000 reward to entice kidnappers to seize and haul Garrison south for trial and execution.[112]

In 1832, Garrison helped organize the New England Anti-Slavery Society, which grew into a national network financed by pious businessmen and driven by the activism of African Americans, Quakers, and devout women. By 1838, the national society had nearly 250,000 members spread throughout the North. Abolitionists recruited new members with lecture tours and drives to flood Congress with anti-slavery petitions.[113]

Their greatest orator was Frederick Douglass, the former Frederick Bailey. Born into slavery in Maryland in 1818, Bailey taught himself to read and write from newspapers and old spelling books, for he considered literacy "the pathway from slavery to freedom." His master caught him trying to escape and assigned Bailey to a professional slave breaker, Edward Covey, who imposed severe work and daily whippings. When Bailey fought back and beat Covey, the master relented and sent the young man to Baltimore to work as a shipwright. In 1838, disguised as a free sailor, Bailey escaped on a train to Philadelphia. To evade slave hunters, he moved to Massachusetts and changed his last name.[114]

Douglass's insights and eloquence commanded rapt attention from large audiences. Elizabeth Cady Stanton recalled, "He stood there like an African prince, majestic in his wrath, as with wit, satire, and indignation" he recounted his sufferings as a slave. In 1845, Douglass published a vivid and moving autobiography, but that increased his exposure to slave hunters, so donors purchased his freedom by paying his owner in 1847. Moving to Rochester, New York, Douglass launched a newspaper, the *North Star*, to promote abolition and women's rights, with the motto, "Right is of no Sex—Truth is of no Color—God is the Father of us all, and we are all Brethren." Grateful to female activists, Douglass declared, "The Cause of the slave has been peculiarly women's cause."[115]

Born a slave in rural New York in 1797, Isabella Baumfree worked at a tavern and slept in a dank cellar. Sold at age ten, she suffered separation from her mother. A devout Christian, Isabella prayed to God to reform her abusive new masters. After suffering several whippings, she modified her prayer, "God, maybe you can't do it. Kill them." That also did not work.[116]

In 1826, she was the mother of four children, but her master sold one, five-year-old Peter, away to Alabama. Distraught, Isabella confronted her mistress, who retorted, "A fine fuss to make about a little nigger! Why, haven't you as many of 'em left as you can see to?" Selling a slave out of state defied New York law, so Isabella appealed to a judge, who ordered the boy retrieved. Peter returned covered with sores and scars. In 1827, the state freed the last of New York's enslaved people, including Isabella, who renamed herself Sojourner Truth: a devout traveler preaching the truth about God and freedom. Although illiterate, she dictated her memoirs, which became a bestseller. Tall and strong, she confronted hecklers who insisted that she was a man. Once, in exasperation, she bared her breasts, shaming the skeptics.[117]

Radical abolitionists soured on the Federal Constitution for protecting slavery. A former slave, William Grimes, wrote with biting sarcasm, "If it were not for the stripes on my back which were made while I was a slave, I would in my will, leave my skin a legacy to the government, desiring that it might be taken off and made into parchment and then bind the Constitution of glorious happy and free America." Garrison denounced the Constitution as "a Covenant with Death and an Agreement with Hell" and publicly burned a copy. Noting southern threats to secede, Douglass declared: "I welcome the bolt whether it come from Heaven or from Hell that shall sever this Union." Radicals angered most Americans, who revered the Federal Constitution and the Union.[118]

Although a minority among northerners, abolitionists terrified southern leaders, who insisted that any public criticism of slavery could ignite a bloody slave revolt. John C. Calhoun of South Carolina assured the Senate that slavery was "indispensable to the peace and happiness of both" races: "It cannot be subverted without drenching the country in blood." Worried for the cherished Union, John Tyler blasted female abolitionists as "the instrument[s] of destroying our political paradise."[119]

Southerners dreaded the ties of northern abolitionists with their counterparts in Britain. In 1833, British abolitionists persuaded Parliament to emancipate the 750,000 slaves of the British West Indies. Douglass exulted that West Indian emancipation "made the name of England known and loved in every slave cabin from the Potomac to the Rio Grande." That notion chilled southern masters. A South Carolinian accused Britons of "abolish[ing] slavery in the West Indies, for the sake of encouraging a negro revolt in the Southern States, and thus, revenging yourselves on America." To discredit American abolitionists, southerners accused them of undermining the Union to help the British regain domination over the United States. Senator Robert Walker of Mississippi denounced abolitionists as "Americans in name, but Englishmen in feelings and principles."[120]

Southern leaders cast the British as hypocrites who liberated unworthy slaves while oppressing the white people of Ireland and exploiting the factory workers of England. Southern ideologues claimed that their slaves fared better than did poor Britons. Addressing British leaders, James Henry Hammond of South Carolina demanded, "Relieve them. Emancipate them. Raise them from the condition of brutes, to the level of human beings—of American slaves at least."[121]

Proslavery

In response to abolitionist criticism, southern leaders forsook the older view of slavery as a "necessary evil." Hammond assured Congress that slavery "is no evil" but "the greatest of all the great blessings which a kind Providence has bestowed upon our glorious region." Hammond drew on a shift away from eighteenth-century intellectuals, who had treated racial difference as only skin-deep and the consequence of culture and environment. By the 1830s, that enlightenment faded in America, giving way to a new pseudoscience that insisted on fixed racial distinctions defined by a biology that cast Blacks as inferiors allegedly closer to apes than to white men.[122]

Southern leaders renounced the notion of human equality, even if endorsed by Jefferson. John Randolph assured Congress "that all men are born free and equal—I can never assent to, for the best of all reasons, because it is not true." He deemed it "a most pernicious falsehood, even though I find it in the Declaration of Independence." A Louisiana master was even blunter in declaring that men might be born equal but "niggers and monkeys *aint*." Champions of slavery cast themselves as true men, tough-minded about a harsh world of inequalities. They derided abolitionists as weaklings dominated by women, who promoted a "whining, canting, sickly kind of humanity" distasteful to true masculinity.[123]

Proslavery ideologues asserted that every society needed a lowest class to endure menial labor for bare subsistence, and they regarded Blacks as best suited for that degraded role, thereby sparing white men. A South Carolina judge declared, "It is the order of nature and of God that the being of superior faculties and knowledge . . . should control and dispose of those who are inferior." Stereotyping Africans as brutal, lusty, and heathen cannibals, southerners insisted that American slavery converted them into happy, docile, grateful, and Christian laborers.[124]

Racists dwelled on the supposed misery, insanity, indolence, and criminality of free Blacks. An Alabama senator charged that they "prefer to revel in the brothel, until imprisoned in a jail or penitentiary." Proslavery writers insisted that abolitionists seduced the happy slave "to steal him from an indulgent and provident master; to carry him to a cold, strange, and uncongenial country, and there leave him . . . to starve, freeze, and die, in glorious freedom."[125]

While proclaiming the happiness of slaves, masters confronted a different reality on their plantations. Fifty-three slaves escaped from Hammond's plantation between 1831 and 1855. Imposing collective punishment, Hammond reduced food and increased work for those who stayed behind. Still he was "astonished and shocked to find" that his slaves had learned "most of what the abolitionists are doing." In private, he characterized running a plantation as "like a war without the glory."[126]

Southern leaders held a contradictory view of Blacks. While insisting that slaves were content, masters warned that they could erupt into rebellion if agitated by outsiders. One southerner likened slavery to "a huge deadly serpent, which is kept down by the strain of every nerve and muscle," but "someday or other it will burst the weight that binds it and take a fearful retribution." Another master predicted, "If the negroes were free, the whites would soon be slaves, or their throats would be cut." To avert race war, southerners demanded white solidarity in defending slavery.[127]

As abolitionism emerged in the North, it vanished in the South. Criticism by outsiders bred a prickly defiance called regional pride. At the start of the nineteenth century, some southern religious denominations had criticized slavery, but they reconsidered during the 1820s and

1830s as proslavery became the badge of regional loyalty. Southerners broke ties with northern churches in their denominations rather than accept any criticism of slavery. South Carolina's leading Presbyterian noted, "Slavery is implicated in every fiber of southern society."[128]

Defending slavery as divinely ordained, white evangelicals told Blacks to submit to lifelong servitude and obey their master's every command. "The great God above has made you for the benefit of the Whiteman, who is your law maker and law giver," a minister stated. An escaped slave recalled another white man preach "dat niggers had no more soul than dogs, and dey couldn't go to heaven any more than could a dog."[129]

Southern churches rejected the northern Protestant emphasis on improving society through moral reform and political action. Holding a darker view of human society, southern evangelicals saw people as depraved by sin and redeemed only as individuals. Most southerners distrusted any social reform movement as guilty by association with abolitionism. Embracing conservatism, southern men derided the North as a hotbed of an irrational radicalism that threatened the foundations of social order. A South Carolina planter boasted that the South was conservative and "the enemy of innovation and change."[130]

Voters

Although slavery enriched the largest slaveholders, it limited overall economic development within the South. Only the richest families lived in the white-columned mansions of legend. Most planters had land and slaves but dwelled in log cabins with chimneys of sticks and clay and few glass windows. They were too busy to acquire fancy furniture or put up white picket fences around yards of flowers and grass. Investing in land and slaves, they had little money left for cultivating the appearances of prosperity and sensibility that mattered much more in the North. "They think only of making money, and their houses are hardly fit to live in," a newcomer said of Alabama's planters.[131]

Thoroughly rural, the South had fewer schools, libraries, cities, canals, and good roads per square mile or per capita than did the North. Rates of illiteracy ran far higher among white people. Slavery kept the Black third of the population in poverty, reducing the consumer market as an engine for development. Southern capital flowed into plantations, leaving little to develop industries. A Mississippian recalled, "A plantation well stocked with hands is the *ne plus ultra* of every man's ambition who resides at the south," for "nothing less [would do] than a broad plantation waving with the snow white cotton bolls."[132]

In 1860, the per capita income of white southerners was $103, compared to $141 in the North. Most of the difference came from the South's much larger number of poor whites, who pulled down the average. The plain folk varied from the near-subsistence farmers called "crackers" and "rednecks" to the substantial "yeomen farmers," who produced surplus crops and bought or rented a few slaves. The average slaveholder owned between five and ten slaves, and only about 5 percent of southern white families had more than twenty slaves. Although farmers might own or rent a few slaves, they too worked in the fields, for want of the means to hire an overseer. While large plantations claimed the most fertile lands along the rivers, smaller farms prevailed on the pine-covered hills.[133]

One British visitor found in the South "the most unbridled democracy, and an earnest defense of the institution of slavery." Most southern whites saw no contradiction. Their social standing had two hinges, one between the free and the enslaved, and the other among the free between those who owned slaves and those who did not. That simple equation enabled free whites to claim solidarity and for farmers to elect planters as leaders.[134]

Over time, southern slaveholding became concentrated in fewer hands: 36 percent of white families owned slaves in 1830, but only 26 percent did so in 1860. Although social mobility into the slaveholder class diminished, yeomen farmers clung to dreams of making that leap. "The non-slaveholder knows," a southern journalist wrote, "that as soon as his savings will admit, he can become a slaveholder, and thus relieve his wife from the necessities of the kitchen and the laundry and his children from the labors of the field." Possessing slaves marked success and status. "A man's merit in this country is estimated according to the number of Negroes he works in the field," a planter explained.[135]

Southern leaders argued that slavery guaranteed the freedom and dignity of all white men. The *Richmond Enquirer* asserted, "Freedom is not possible without slavery." Abel P. Upshur of Virginia said of the common white man: "However poor, or ignorant or miserable he may be, he has yet the consoling consciousness that there is a still lower condition to which he can never be reduced." A slave society gave poor whites the cheap thrill of belonging to a supposed master race that could bully Black people with legal impunity.[136]

By repelling abolitionists, southern leaders claimed to defend the autonomy of common white men as landowners and family patriarchs. Small farmers and great planters mutually defended a society organized as independent households, each a petty monarchy in command of dependents: women, children, and slaves. Asserting that abolitionism menaced the "God-given distinctions of sex and race," farmers united with planters to defend the rights of property and patriarchs.[137]

By embracing racial inequality, common men accepted the class inequality that empowered great planters to govern their states. Three-quarters of legislators in the Lower South and two-thirds in the Upper South owned slaves as did almost every southern governor and senator. Voters favored politicians who vowed to protect the South against meddling abolitionists, northern politicians, and British imperialists. Every candidate sought to outdo his rival in defending slavery, and it became political suicide to criticize the system.[138]

In 1849, Kentucky tested the support of plain folk for slavery in an election for a convention to redraft the state's constitution. For a southern state, Kentucky had relatively few enslaved people, less than a fifth of the population, so antislavery men hoped to use the convention to mandate gradual emancipation. Cassius Marcellus Clay led the antislavery cause in Kentucky. Although Clay did not much like Black people, he believed that Kentucky would prosper better through gradual emancipation. Seeking "the complete independence and liberty of my own [people], the white Anglo-Saxon race of America," Clay did not favor political rights or social equality for freed Blacks.[139]

Polemical and confrontational, Clay infuriated proslavery men, but tangling with him was risky. A big, powerful, relentless man, Clay knew how to use a bowie knife. In 1843, an assassin hired by proslavery men fired at Clay but merely wounded him. Clay leapt on his assailant and gouged out an eye and sliced off an ear before others could intervene. In 1845, he began publishing an antislavery newspaper, the *True American*, in Lexington. Expecting attack, he fortified a brick office, mounted two small cannons, and mined it with gunpowder to blow up if attackers overwhelmed him. Twelve hundred enraged men met and unanimously resolved to destroy his "abolition paper" at the peril of "his blood, or our own, or both, or of all [whom] he may bring, of bond or free, to aid his murderous hand." Bedridden at home with typhoid fever, Clay could not defend his office, so his foes pounced, seizing and shipping his press out of state. Clay resumed publication across the Ohio River in Ohio.[140]

In 1849, proslavery men threatened to kill antislavery candidates for Kentucky's constitutional convention—and did shoot and kill at least one. In a crowded courthouse, a defiant Clay marched to the podium and pulled from his satchel a copy of the Federal Constitution and a Bible, announcing that both supported his free speech. "And for those who regard neither the laws of God or man, I have this argument." Clay placed two pistols and a bowie knife on the table. He completed that speech, but three proslavery brothers, the Turners, attacked him with clubs and knives at another event. One stabbed Clay in the side and a second pressed a pistol to his head, but it misfired three times. Clay then gutted one Turner with a knife, killing him. To everyone's surprise, Clay recovered from his many wounds. The dead Turner became a martyr, proslavery men said, "in the great cause of white supremacy."[141]

Proslavery candidates argued that slavery "tends to exalt the free population" and warned that freeing slaves would compel poor whites to work as "menials and cooks and scullions in the kitchens of more wealthy neighbors." Proslavery men also denounced antislavery candidates as race mixers eager to wed "some dark-skinned Dulcinea" and "rear an interesting family of little *kinkey-heads*."[142]

Impressed by that reasoning, Kentucky voters defeated every antislavery candidate save two. The winning delegates collectively owned nearly 3,000 slaves. One winner declared that slavery had created "the most enlightened, the richest, and the most cultivated people upon the face of God Almighty's earth. Slavery is not an evil, and I want rather more of it." The new constitution did just that, declaring property rights superior to all other rights. The new constitution saddened Abraham Lincoln, a Kentuckian by birth who had moved to Illinois, where he developed antislavery convictions. In 1849, Lincoln despaired for a "peaceful extinction of slavery" in Kentucky or, indeed, anywhere in the South: "The Autocrat of all the Russias will resign his crown, and proclaim his subjects free republicans sooner than will our American masters voluntarily give up their slaves."[143]

Contrary to the wishful thinking of many Patriots, slavery did not wither away after the American Revolution. Instead, it became more profitable and entrenched as the South expanded westward. From 698,000 in 1790, the number of enslaved people soared to nearly 4 million by 1860, when they comprised a third of the South's population (half in the Lower South). In 1860, the monetary value of enslaved people exceeded that of all the nation's banks, factories, and railroads combined. Masters would never part with so much valuable human property without a fight.[144]

Cotton cultivation drove the soaring value of slaves. Cotton became king in the American economy as exports surged from 3,000 bales in

1790 to 178,000 in 1810 and 4 million by 1860 (each bale contained
about 400 pounds). By 1840 cotton accounted for over half of the
value of all American exports, and the United States produced more
cotton than the rest of the world. No mere backwater, the South was
the powerful half of a nation committed to Black slavery as well as
white freedom.[145]

Southerners enjoyed clout in politics and diplomacy because of
cotton's economic might. Britain and France (and the northeastern United States) needed cotton to sustain their most valuable
industrial sector: textiles. If America abolished slavery, southerners
warned that 3 million British workers would starve in unemployment. Emancipation would also ruin the massive investments by
British capitalists in southern banks and plantations—almost always
secured by mortgages on slaves. Southern leaders also counted on
support from industrialists in the North, where a Massachusetts senator noted the "unhallowed alliance between the lords of the lash
and the lords of the loom." In exchange for cotton, northern factories produced the shoes and rough clothing worn by slaves. In addition, New England shippers carried slaves along the southern coast
and exported cotton to Britain. An Alabaman noted that abolition
in the South "would cause convulsions in all the governments of the
civilized world."[146]

Voyage

In August 1845, Frederick Douglass crossed the Atlantic to escape
from slave hunters and seek British support for abolition in the United
States. He boarded a steamship, *Cambria*, bound for Liverpool, but
the captain denied Douglass a proper cabin because it "would give
offense to the majority of American passengers." Instead, Douglass
settled into steerage. Among the diverse passengers, he found a mix of
doctors, lawyers, soldiers, sailors, artisans, and even a lion-tamer. The
voyagers included Hispanics, Britons, and Americans, "the meander-
ing Jew, the Whig and the Democrat, the white and the black." He

added, "There were slaveholders from Cuba and slaveholders from Georgia. We had antislavery singing and pro-slavery grumbling."[147]

Because copies of his celebrated *Narrative* circulated on board, Douglass attracted curiosity, and the captain invited him to address the passengers. This outraged proslavery travelers who "got up a mob—a real American, republican, democratic, Christian mob" to shout down and rough up Douglass. A Georgian yelled, "I wish I had him in Savannah! We would use him up!" To shame them, Douglass read aloud the slave codes from southern states. Infuriated, the mob rushed forward to try to hurl him overboard: "They were ashamed to have American laws read before an English audience." Supporters defended Douglass, and the captain silenced the "mobocrats" by threatening to put them in irons. They did not want to experience even a small and brief taste of slavery. Douglass concluded with wry irony that the episode was "enough to make a slave ashamed of the country that enslaved him."[148]

The clash on board the *Cambria* reflected the conflicts over slavery corroding the Union at home. Both proud of, and anxious for, their republic, Americans dreaded criticism, especially when shared with the British. Many Americans would resort to collective violence as a form of popular sovereignty. Most did not know what to do about the slavery that divided their society, so they thought it best to silence those who offered harsh truths and painful solutions.

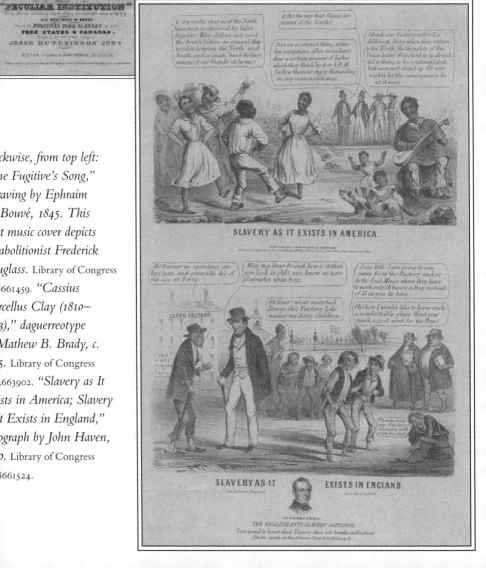

Clockwise, from top left: "The Fugitive's Song," engraving by Ephraim Bouvé, 1845. This sheet music cover depicts abolitionist Frederick Douglass. Library of Congress 3661459. "Cassius Marcellus Clay (1810–1903)," daguerreotype by Mathew B. Brady, c. 1845. Library of Congress 4663902. "Slavery as It Exists in America; Slavery as It Exists in England," lithograph by John Haven, 1850. Library of Congress 3661524.

FIVE ❧ DEMOCRACY

In 1835, Joice Heth was the "Greatest Natural and National Curiosity in the World." So said her owner and promoter, P. T. Barnum. Heth was a national wonder as George Washington's former nanny, who attended his birth and guided his childhood before he "led our heroic fathers on to glory, to victory, and freedom." While Washington defended American freedom, Heth remained enslaved.[1]

Heth seemed a natural curiosity thanks to a supposed age of 161 years. She looked the part: blind, toothless, weighing only forty-six pounds, and paralyzed in every limb but her right arm, with long nails that resembled talons. Barnum thought she might "as well have been called a thousand years old as any age." But Heth was lucid and articulate, spinning remarkably detailed stories about "dear little George" and singing her favorite hymns. But she also cursed if denied tobacco or whiskey. No mere display, Heth was a performer, interacting with customers who peppered her with questions. If challenged, she became eloquent with indignation. In return for working up to fourteen hours a day, six days a week, she got three square meals, some whiskey, tobacco, and a bed.[2]

Heth created the act as a slave in Kentucky, for her master's father had emigrated from Virginia, where he had known Washington. She listened carefully to tales of the great man and they helped her reinvent herself to prolong her life. Few slaves survived into old age after suffering a paralytic stroke and losing sight, but Heth regenerated her market value by performing as Washington's nanny. Her master then could sell Heth to a Yankee. Heth said that she wanted to die in a free state, and so she did, just not as a free person. A late career of illusion improved on grim reality for Heth.[3]

As a boy in Connecticut, Barnum became a shopkeeper's clerk. He later remembered, "The customers cheated us in the fabrics" and "we cheated the customers with our goods. Each party expected to be cheated." Barnum concluded, "We must believe little that we saw, and less that we heard." This became his code. From dabbling in journalism and politics and watching preachers with a skeptical eye, Barnum realized: "Humbug is an astonishingly wide-spread phenomenon—in fact almost universal." Why not, he asked, make a living by selling humbug to eager Americans? In 1834, he moved to New York City

Opposite, from left: "Phineas T. Barnum (1810–1891)," photograph by unknown, 1855. Library of Congress 2017896468. *"Sojourner Truth (1797–1883)," photograph by unknown, 1864.* Library of Congress 98501256. *"The Celebrated Negro Melodies, as sung for the Virginia Minstrels," music cover lithographed by W. Thayer, 1843.* Library of Congress 2016647558.

and shifted into show business to profit from the gaps between American beliefs and reality.[4]

Offering more than mere humbug, Barnum served up controversy. He understood Americans' fascination with the fantastic—and pride in their keen scrutiny and ability to detect any fraud, as nobody's fools. Because credulity and suspicion danced together in American minds, Barnum invited them to question as well as to believe Heth's story. He displayed alleged historical documents, including her bill of sale in 1727 to the Washington family, but Barnum also planted doubting stories in the press. One claimed that Heth was, in fact, an automaton constructed of rubber, whalebone, and metal springs with a ventriloquized voice. People then paid for another visit to see if they could detect the con. Carefully cultivated and renewed, controversy sold tickets.[5]

Barnum later boasted of turning a "worthless" old slave into a gold mine. He even claimed to have pulled out all her teeth to make her look plausibly ancient. That such a claim won him credit rather than horror with readers reveals a lot about him and them during the 1840s. Old, female, and Black, she had three strikes against her in the eyes of most white people, who felt that Barnum could do what he wanted with her body to make money.[6]

Netting $1,500 a week for Barnum, Heth more than repaid the $1,000 it cost him to buy her. Barnum owned Heth for eight months—until she died in February 1836. He then kept her working, by arranging a public autopsy as a pay-per-view. For fifty cents each (twice what it had cost to see her alive), over a thousand customers gathered to watch a surgeon slice into Heth. The doctor concluded that she could not be a day over eighty. Barnum made the most of this publicity, casting himself as conned by Heth and her former owner. "I believed the documents in her possession as much as I believe the declaration of independence," Barnum declared in a revealing comparison. But he also planted another story in a newspaper: that the doctor had autopsied the wrong woman's body, and that the real Heth was alive and well in retirement in Connecticut.[7]

Heth launched Barnum's career as the greatest showman of the century. His autobiography became second only to the Bible in American readership during Barnum's lifetime. In 1842 in New York City, he opened Barnum's American Museum, a five-story building packed with 150,000 objects and performers: "industrious fleas," odd plants, shells, clever animals, wax figures, dioramas, and dwarves, giants, and "freaks." They included "Snow White Negroes from Brazil," the "North Carolina Fat Boy" (a seven-year-old who weighed two hundred pounds), and a stuffed Fiji Mermaid that seemed to be half-woman and half-fish. In fact, she was sewn together from the top half of a monkey and the tail of a fish. Barnum claimed to offer an antidote to the "severe and drudging practicalness" and "sordid love of acquisition" of American life, but he measured his own success in money made by tricking people.[8]

Americans mourned Heth's death as the loss of a precious connection to George Washington and the origins of their republic. Her lifetime spanned an age of transformations that both dazzled and daunted Americans. Her obituary noted that since Washington's birth "we have fought our battles of independence, established our government, and peopled our country with twelve millions of freemen." In Heth's youth, people traveled by foot or on horses but "now, with the speed of the wind, steam propels us over land and water, and balloons transport us through the air!" The economic and technological changes seemed marvelous, but Americans worried that they might lose the great but tenuous achievement of the revolutionary generation: the republican Union.[9]

Patriotism

Free Americans took pride in their prospering republic that had rejected rule by a king and aristocracy of inherited power. Compared to Europeans, free Americans enjoyed greater equality in property and rights. A French visitor noted the modest gap between voters and leaders because almost everyone worked: "Their generals distill brandy, their colonels keep taverns, and their statesmen feed pigs."[10]

At festive Fourth of July celebrations, Americans cherished the revolution and challenged the young to defend the republican government. The "Glorious Fourth" featured public readings of the Declaration of Independence, firing cannons, parades of town fathers and militiamen, orators preaching patriotism, bands playing anthems, great banquets, lots of firecrackers, and even more alcohol. "The Americans may have great reason to be proud of this day," a visiting Briton noted, "but why do they get so confoundedly drunk?"[11]

Newspapers, politicians, and orators praised fellow Americans as "the greatest people under the canopy of heaven" and expected confirmation from European visitors. A Briton reported that Americans had "a restless and insatiable appetite for praise, which defied all restraint of reason or common sense." Another traveler thought that they practiced "the self-deception of believing that they really are that which they only wish to be."[12]

So it infuriated Americans when they read British travel accounts that mocked the republic as a land of impertinent, slovenly, drunken braggarts, cheats, and brawlers who beat their wives and slaves while spitting tobacco. With grim fascination, visitors dwelled on southern louts who grew their thumbnails long to gouge out eyes in no-holds-barred fights. A traveler "saw more than one man who wanted an eye, and ascertained that I was now in the region of 'gouging.'" Genteel Britons knew plenty of vulgar people at home; but it rankled them to find that sort empowered as citizens in America.[13]

Travelers divided over whether the republican experiment offered inspiration or warning to Europe. Visiting conservatives wanted to preserve the status quo at home, so they delighted in discrediting the American republic. In 1807 a Briton concluded, "The excess of the democratic ferment in this people is conspicuously evinced by the dregs having got up to the top." But reform-minded visitors mourned that, in the words of the British writer Harriet Martineau, "the civili-

zation and the morals of the Americans fall far below their own principles." Reformers hoped that criticism would motivate Americans
to do better, and thereby vindicate republicanism for the benefit of
the watching world. But even sympathetic criticism ignited the com-
bative patriotism of hypersensitive Americans, who derided Britain
as a tyranny run by aristocrats exploiting the degraded, vice-ridden
workers of an industrial hellscape.[14]

As a substitute for king and aristocracy, Americans invested sovereignty in "public opinion," so they felt free to speak alike, for they
dreaded falling on the unpopular side of an issue. The French visitor,
Alexis de Tocqueville, detected a "tyranny of the majority." Anxious
over their competitive individualism, people longed to hold the same
opinions as others. An American assured Tocqueville, "This is a free
country, sir! Every man may do or think what he pleases, only he
must not let other people know it."[15]

After 1815, politics became more democratic as most states wrote
or rewrote their constitutions to eliminate property requirements to
vote, enfranchising every white man, or at least those who paid any
tax. The nation's most influential editor, Thomas Ritchie of the *Richmond Enquirer*, regretted the change: "The Republic has degenerated
into a Democracy."[16]

Democratization flowed within limits of gender and race. Women
remained excluded from voting and office-holding. No slave could be
a citizen, and most states barred free Blacks from voting. Indeed, their
participation in politics shrank as it expanded for poor white men, for
the same states that dropped class restrictions enhanced racial exclusion. Free Blacks lost the vote in Connecticut, Maryland, New Jersey,
New York, North Carolina, Pennsylvania, Rhode Island, and Tennessee between 1806 and 1838. In New York, Black men could only
vote if they met a property requirement recently lifted from whites.
In 1826, only 16 of the 12,500 Black men in New York City qualified
to vote. And every new state, except Maine, barred Blacks from voting. Between 1840 and 1870, northern states held nineteen referen-

dums on enhancing the political rights of Blacks, but only two passed, and the rest lost by an average margin of five-to-one. For want of civil rights, free Blacks became scapegoats villainized by politicians pandering to the prejudice of whites. An abolitionist lamented candidates' "attacking the unpopular and defenceless colored man. . . . We dislike them because we are unjust to them."[17]

In his inaugural address of 1817, President James Monroe, a slaveholder, extolled the republic as perfect. "And if we look to the condition of individuals, what a proud spectacle does it exhibit! On whom has oppression fallen in any quarter of our Union? Who has been deprived of any right of person or property?" At that time, 1.5 million Americans (15 percent of the total) suffered from enslavement. But Monroe and most citizens regarded Blacks as outsiders, irrelevant to the calculus of happy citizens.[18]

Alas, those citizens were not all that happy. Fear and boasting alternated for Americans, who tried to soothe anxiety with bombast. Voters cherished freedom as the autonomy of every white man from control by anyone else. But that liberty seemed imperiled by power—by the drive of leading men to dominate others. Supposed threats came from many directions: crypto-aristocrats subverting from within; foreign monarchies menacing from without; Indians on the frontier; rebels on plantations; banks with power over the currency; and grasping politicians from a rival party or region. Candidates treated elections as epic struggles to defend liberty from power—and thereby save the republican Union.[19]

To win elections in a democratic republic, politicians had to mingle freely with common white men at taverns, militia musters, and courthouses. Rising men of new money did better than those with inherited estates, who seemed too elitist. By the 1830s, two leading parties, Democrats and Whigs, competed for power by claiming to defend liberty. Democrats championed a libertarian and egalitarian individualism suspicious of government as in service to wealthy elites. Favoring power dispersed to localities and states, Democrats

wanted the federal government only to deliver the mail, recover runaway slaves, and fight Indians, Britons, and Mexicans. Whigs sought
a more activist government to accelerate economic development and
promote moral reform. Democrats proved better at cultivating a populist style, so they prevailed at most elections. Between 1829 and 1860,
they elected two-thirds of the congressmen and three-fifths of the
senators. During those thirty-two years, Democrats controlled the
House for twenty-four years and the Senate for twenty-eight. They
also won six of the eight presidential contests.[20]

A man pledged his honor to stand by a fellow Democrat (or Whig)
in electoral and legislative contests. Parties organized festive parades
that involved thousands, culminating with free food and drink at
barbecues. Ambitious and able young men could rise by serving on
committees that organized events, turned out the vote, and battled
with the rival party. Victory won patronage jobs with pay and honor.
Almost every newspaper affiliated with a party to provide readers
with ideas and talking points in support of a slate of candidates. The
best editors doubled as campaign managers, who reaped the spoils of
victory: at least as a postmaster but perhaps in a president's cabinet or
a diplomatic position.[21]

Elections were masculine, competitive, drunken, and often violent. With partisans plying supporters with free alcohol, emotions
surged, leading to clashes with fists, sticks, knives, and even guns to
control polling places. In Philadelphia, a rowdy recalled that once
the parties had assembled their forces, "Then a rush would be made
for possession of the polls and the best fighters would get possession." Victors could drive away rival voters or seize and destroy
ballot boxes. A conservative lamented, "A resort to brute force has
now become familiar and expected. . . . The demon of democracy is abroad and triumphant and will drive us to the devil before
long." He missed an earlier era, when a smaller and more deferential electorate had favored elites of inherited wealth and high social
standing.[22]

Transport

By the 1820s, the nation stretched from the Great Lakes to the Gulf of Mexico and from the Atlantic to the Rocky Mountains. Americans worried that the nation was growing too fast and becoming too vast to hang together. Living farther apart in more distinctive regions, they seemed apt to divide into several contentious nations. In 1817, John C. Calhoun warned Congress, "No country enjoying free- dom, ever occupied anything like as great an extent of country as this Republic." Calhoun exhorted, "We are under the most imperious obligations to counteract every tendency to disunion. Let us, then, bind the republic together with a perfect system of roads and canals." Otherwise, he feared, "We will divide, and in its consequences will follow misery and despotism." Calhoun expressed the consensus that only union could preserve free government in America by averting civil wars and foreign interference.[23]

Prior to 1815, the federal and state governments improved roads by chartering turnpike companies, which cleared out stumps and rocks, built bridges, and upgraded surfaces with a bed of gravel and small stones known as macadam. But turnpikes only marginally increased the pace of movement, which depended on horses and rarely exceeded eight miles an hour. Beyond the turnpikes, most roads remained muddy, rutty, traps that wrecked many wagons.[24]

New steamboats had a greater impact, beginning in 1807 on the Hudson River. Drawing little water, the flat-bottomed steamboat was the perfect technology for a nation blessed with so many long, wide, navigable rivers, particularly in the vast watershed of the Mis- sissippi River, which stretched for 2,000 miles from the Appalachians on the east to the Rocky Mountains on the west and from Minnesota on the north to the Gulf of Mexico to the south. Some 536 steam- boats traversed that river in 1840, up from the 17 of 1817. A steamboat could ascend the Mississippi and Ohio Rivers from New Orleans to Louisville, a distance of 1,350 miles, in just eight days—a journey that before had taken three months of back-breaking rowing against a powerful current. Steamboats also lowered travel costs to about 2 cents per mile versus 23 cents a mile on a stagecoach.[25]

But steamboats were risky: hastily built, unregulated by government, and prone to explode. Between 1825 and 1830, 42 steamboats blew up, killing 273 people. A New Yorker, Philip Hone, declared: "We have become the most careless, reckless, headlong people on the face of the earth. 'Go ahead' is our maxim and pass-word; and we do go ahead with a vengeance, regardless of consequences and indifferent about the value of human life. What are a few hundred persons, more or less?"[26]

To connect rivers and lakes over hilly terrain, states built canals, which could raise and lower boats through sets of locks. In 1817, the New York state legislature funded construction of the Erie Canal to link the Great Lakes with the Hudson River and, via the Hudson, with New York City. Completed in 1825, the canal ran 363 miles, fifteen times longer than the biggest previous canal in America. Requiring eighty-three locks to mount an elevation of 675 feet, the Erie Canal was the most complex construction project in America or Europe to that date. Americans boasted that the great canal vindicated a republic by demonstrating their ingenuity.[27]

The Erie Canal cut freight rates to a tenth of their former level, multiplying the goods that could bear transport to distant markets. By bringing more western produce to market, the canal doubled the shipping out of New York City, which became the Union's premier city and seaport. A magnet for immigrants from both the hinterland and Europe, New York City quadrupled in population after 1820 to reach half a million by 1850.[28]

Addressing a pervasive anxiety, New York's governor, DeWitt Clinton, promised that the Erie Canal would "avert this awful calamity" of "a dissolution of the Union" by drawing people together through "the golden ties of commerce and the adamantine chains of interest." That canal did build ties between Northeast and Midwest, but their emerging economic and political bonds made southerners feel marginalized and more uneasy within the Union.[29]

Pennsylvania sought to compete with New York by building a long-distance canal to link the Ohio and Delaware Rivers. But construction had to traverse a 2,300-foot elevation that defied canal technology, so the project nearly bankrupted the state. That Pennsylvania canal quickly became outmoded by the development of a superior technology for overland travel: the railroad.[30]

The first American railroad, the Baltimore & Ohio, began construction in 1828. By 1840, the nation had 450 locomotives operating on 3,200 miles of track. In 1806, when the politician Henry Clay first traveled from Kentucky to Washington, D.C., the journey took three weeks over muddy roads on a horse. Forty years later, he made the trip in just four days on a train. Railroads hastened the pace and increased the predictability of travel, but the new technology also made life louder and smokier.[31]

Seaports in different states competed to construct railroads to capture hinterland commerce at the expense of rivals. Building with different gauges (width) of track, competing railroads frustrated efforts to link all into a national system: an apt symbol of the weak Union. And the steam engines of early railroads were as unregulated and prone to crash or explode as steamboats.[32]

The New England painter and inventor Samuel F. B. Morse (1791–1872) developed a telegraph that, for the first time, enabled messages to travel hundreds of miles almost instantaneously. On May 24, 1844, Morse assembled many national leaders in the chambers of the United States Supreme Court to watch him send the first electromagnetic message over a metal wire strung along poles to his assistant forty miles away in Baltimore. Within six years, the United States had 10,000 miles of telegraph wire, stretching westward to Chicago and south to New Orleans. Thanks to the telegraph, distant merchants instantly learned of market conditions and prices throughout the network: information that increased efficiency and lowered transaction costs.[33]

Motion

Improved transportation enabled Americans to move farther and more often, shifting into and out of new communities of diverse strangers. In town after town, the federal census revealed that only about half of the heads of household remained there just ten years later; some had died, but most had moved. In 1826 in Rochester, New York, a city of 5,000 people, 100 moved out per day and 110 replaced them. Dreaming of making money and gaining security, families shifted westward to create new farms on the frontier. An observer complained that they were lured by "marvelous tales of fortune made in a day." Commercial towns seemed to spring up overnight at crossroads or river junctions as speculators sought to cash in on the surge of settlers. At Buffalo during the late 1820s, a British visitor noted, "All the buildings have the appearance of having been run up in a hurry, though everything has an air of great pretension."[34]

The roads and rivers became crowded with professional itinerants, especially peddlers bringing consumer goods to new homesteads. Bored with a farm boy's life in Vermont, James Guild left home in 1821. Acquiring a trunk filled with combs, needles, buttons, thread, and beads, Guild headed west to Ohio and south to South Carolina. He supplemented peddling by repairing pots and spoons. Later he toured with a bison for exhibition, before learning how to paint portraits. Adaptable, versatile, and mobile, Guild personified American possibilities.[35]

Everything seemed uncertain and unstable among a people in perpetual motion and competition. In 1836, Henry Watson moved from New England to Alabama and noted: "If a man is away six months & returns, he must expect to find himself among strangers. . . . The whole of these new states are in the same moveable state. Their restlessness brought them here, and the same cause carries them on." Watson noted that transience strained social bonds: "No man knows when he gets acquainted whether he will ever know him long enough to make it worth his while to cultivate his friendship."[36]

Visitors marveled at the busy haste of free Americans, moving hither and yon to make money. A satirist declared that Americans would skin fleas if they could sell the hides. An English traveler declared, "every bee in the hive is actively employed in search of . . . money; neither art, science, learning, nor pleasure can seduce them from its pursuit." A Frenchman noted, "Here, all is circulation, motion, and boiling agitation." Another visitor concluded, "An American is born, lives, and dies twice as fast as any other human creature."[37]

Americans dreaded losing in the competition of economic life. An immigrant marveled, "How they rush around, these Americans, afraid they will die before they can finish what they have begun. And so they do die, worn out." From cradle to grave, they told one another that every individual had to make his own way in a competitive economy that allegedly rewarded skill and hard work with riches while punishing indolence and stupidity with poverty. But the boom-and-bust cycle of capitalism ruined many a hardworking American.[38]

As movement disrupted traditional communities defined by residence, people sought to create alternatives organized by voluntary affiliation. They formed societies to disseminate Bibles, cultivate world peace, promote vegetarianism, convert overseas heathens, reform prisons and asylums, and improve penmanship. In Cincinnati, a newspaper editor found fifty reform groups active and concluded, "The truth is we are *society mad*."[39]

Some people tried to merge reform societies with new utopian communities meant to transform human nature and purify social interaction. Such new places would re-create communities of residence as places of voluntary commitment. In New England, the philosopher Ralph Waldo Emerson mused, "We are all a little wild here with numberless projects of social reform, not a reading man but has a draft of a new community in his waistcoat pocket." With select membership and rational rules, the founders hoped to transcend tradition and inequality. In their own controlled community, reformers sought a moral perfection impossible in the wider society, but they also hoped to set an example for outsiders to emulate and thereby transform the world.[40]

In 1825, at New Harmony, Indiana, a wealthy industrialist from Scotland, Robert Owen, founded a utopian community dedicated to collective property and cooperative work. Owen explained: "I am come to this country to introduce an entire new system of society; to change it from an ignorant, selfish system to an enlightened social system which shall gradually unite all interests into one." Utopias appealed to Americans who longed to stabilize their contentious, ever-moving individualism.[41]

But New Harmony crumbled into acrimony within two years. Unable to shed the social conditioning of their upbringing, the members clashed over distributing the fruits of their labor. Women wondered why they still had to do all the cooking, housework, and child care in the new utopia. And the community's lofty goals bred frustration when results faltered. The fluidity and experimentalism of American life helped to generate utopian communities—and then pulled them apart from within.[42]

To cope with the uncertainties of new homes and neighbors, ambitious men joined the Freemasons, a secret society that promoted bonds of trust between members. Thriving in new commercial towns, the lodges attracted prosperous farmers, artisans, and shopkeepers. As democracy challenged the traditional power of inherited wealth and status, Freemasonry promised an alternative way to distinguish aspiring men from the common mass. Membership allegedly certified superior talent, sensibility, liberality, and virtue. But for inclusion to remain special, the brethren had to exclude most of their neighbors as too rustic and crass.[43]

As a self-selected community of insiders, the Freemasonic lodge weakened the bonds of community beyond its membership. Their secret rites, passwords, signs, and handshakes secured by oaths also

contradicted the transparency demanded by republicanism. As brethren, Freemasons favored one another in social, political, and business
transactions. Posing as the natural elites of their communities, they
appeared in public to stage processions and supervise ceremonies to
lay cornerstones for big buildings. Their mutual support, elitism, and
displays of leadership aroused jealousy and suspicion among outsiders,
who felt disadvantaged.[44]

The excluded longed to know what went on within the lodges,
and William Morgan promised to tell them. A stonemason in upstate
New York, Morgan joined a lodge in a small village, but, when he
moved to a larger town, Batavia, the members rejected him. Insulted,
Morgan sought revenge by announcing in a local newspaper that he
would publish an exposé of Freemasonry. Outraged Freemasons tried
to burn down the local print shop and harassed the printer and Morgan with petty legal charges. In September 1826, they jailed Morgan
for a $2 debt, and then several men spirited him away in a carriage.
In vain, Morgan, bellowed "Murder! Murder!" In October 1827, a
bloated and disfigured body washed up on the banks of the Niagara River. Morgan's wife and dentist identified the corpse as the
missing man.[45]

Outraged citizens accused Freemasons of abduction and murder.
Morgan's book published and became a best-seller thanks to the furor
over his fate. Grand juries indicted and prosecutors tried several Freemasons for Morgan's demise, but judges and jurors convicted only
one, the county sheriff, who got a thirty-month sentence. Freema-
son witnesses refused to testify, citing their oaths of secrecy. Public
outrage grew at the apparent complicity of prominent Freemasons in
covering up the crime.[46]

In 1828, an "Anti-Masonic" political movement rallied voters who
believed that Freemasons had corrupted politics, compromised justice, and rigged business in their favor. Anti-Masonic newspapers and
candidates vowed to save the republic by purging Freemasons from
public office. The furor led thousands to quit the order, and hundreds

of lodges closed. By lowering the profile of Freemasonry, that decline reduced the political traction of Anti-Masonry. By 1840, most of its leaders and voters shifted into the Whig Party, which shared their drive to improve public morality.[47]

Mothers

Dislocation from family and friends bore especially hard on women whose ambitious husbands had moved them away from home. Newly arrived in Tennessee, a woman wrote home to relatives in Virginia: "I feel almost friendless. The intimacy of dear and loved relatives have been broken by the bitter pill of separation. . . . I feel exceedingly desolate and lonely." After migrating to Alabama, a wife despaired to hear her husband talk of moving yet again to supposedly better land farther west: "I expect to spend the remainder of my days in moving about from place to place. . . . You have no idea how tired I am of hearing about moving." She sarcastically wished that her husband would simply move all the way to California at once "because I think he would be obliged to stop then, for he could go no farther."[48]

By the prevailing law of coverture, a husband controlled the family's property, and his wife had no legal standing to own land, enter contracts, or bring lawsuits. The culture justified that male power by defining men and women as radically different in nature. Bold and assertive men allegedly contrasted with women cast as more pious, benevolent, retiring, and chaste. Therefore, a man and woman comprised two halves of their fulfillment as a united, marital being. A magazine insisted, "Man shines abroad—woman at home. Man talks to convince—woman to persuade and please. Man has a rugged heart—woman a soft and tender one. Man prevents misery—woman relieves it." But the two halves were unequal, with men superior by law. Within the home, the patient and nurturing wife was supposed to moderate and regenerate her husband for the public realm of strife, work, and politics.[49]

Americans believed that no republic could survive unless the citizens possessed virtue: a selfless devotion to the public good. Reformers insisted that sons could best learn republican virtue from their mothers. A leading champion of this "republican motherhood," Judith Sargent Murray, claimed that God had "assigned [to them] the care of making the first impressions on the infant minds of the whole human race, a trust of more importance than the government of provinces, and the marshalling of armies." Women could not govern, but they could shape the men who did. This conviction promoted reverence for women in their domestic role, but that then increased the pressure on them to stay at home.[50]

To prepare young women to become republican wives and mothers, reformers expanded private schooling for women during the early nineteenth century. New academies attracted the daughters of wealthy and middle-class families who could afford the tuition. The schools trained articulate young women, who often felt frustrated by the social expectation that they marry and resume domesticity. In 1848 a New York woman longed to become a doctor and attain the "true ennoblement of woman, the full harmonious development of her unknown nature, and the consequent redemption of the whole human race." She believed that women had equal intellectual ability and a superior empathy that could uplift humanity if allowed equal education and opportunity.[51]

Middle-class women found a public opening by joining benevolent societies that pressed for social reforms and delivered charity to poor people. Wrapped in Christian purpose, these organizations claimed to pursue moral rather than political causes. Insisting that women exceeded men in piety and morality, benevolent reformers sought to heal the social damage wrought by male selfishness. But for propriety, most society women avoided public speaking to mixed groups, relying on men to deliver their speeches and chair meetings.[52]

Beneath that veneer of male supervision, benevolent women displayed a capacity for business. They raised funds, organized and led volunteer staffs, and delivered social services neglected by local and state governments. Then they petitioned and lobbied those governments to do better. To preserve the legitimacy of this work as "domestic," women got little or no pay for their benevolence; but that also meant that men left them alone to manage their societies and funds. The New England reformer Lydia Maria Child exulted, "Those who urged women to become missionaries and form tract societies have changed the household utensil to a living energetic being."[53]

By becoming abolitionists, the most daring women concluded that the restrictions of gender mirrored those of race. The South Carolinian Angelina Grimké noted, "The investigation of the rights of the slave has led me to a better understanding of my own." Her sister Sarah added, "All I ask [of] our brethren is that they will take their heels from our necks and permit us to stand upright on that ground which God designed us to occupy." Antislavery women challenged the taboo against women addressing or leading public groups that included men. When told to stick to domesticity, a female abolition society retorted, "Have women no country—no interest staked in public [good]—no liabilities in common-peril—no partnership in the nation's guilt and shame?" Sarah Douglass (not related to Frederick) declared, "We abolitionist Women are turning the world upside down."[54]

William Lloyd Garrison regarded freedom for Blacks and equality for women as two sides of the same coin. He recognized that women's energy and talents sustained the antislavery movement. Maria Weston Chapman coedited his newspaper, *The Liberator*, and managed finances and correspondence for the American Anti-Slavery Society. So Garrison defended public speaking and social leadership by women.[55]

But female activists alarmed the abolitionist financier Lewis Tappan, who called Chapman "a talented woman with the disposition of a fiend." In 1840, Tappan broke with Garrison when the society appointed Abby Kelley Foster to an important committee. Citing women's "more delicate physical organization," Tappan rejected "the right of my fair countrywomen to interfere with public affairs." Focusing on abolition alone, Tappan opposed the pursuit of women's rights as a provocative distraction that would alienate many potential supporters. Activists coped with endless debate over the proper balance between purity and pragmatism within their societies.[56]

Frances Wright (1795–1852) provoked controversy by embracing every form of radicalism. An immigrant from Scotland to New York City, Wright coedited a newspaper, the *Free Enquirer*, to promote antislavery, atheism, birth control, civil rights for women, free western land for farmers, universal public education, unions, and a political party for workers. Wright's pugnacious style reflected her radical views and thereby doubly offended conventional people. Tall, strong, forceful, with short, fiery red hair, Wright mixed freely with men and always spoke her mind. A young Walt Whitman revered Wright as "sweeter, nobler, grander—multiplied by twenty than all who traduced her." But she had many critics, including cautious reformers, who blanched at her defiance of gender norms and conventional morality. Catharine Beecher denounced Wright: "There she stands, with brazen front and brawny arms, attacking . . . all that is venerable and sacred in religion, all that is safe and wise in law, [and] all that is pure and lovely in domestic virtue." For conservative and moderate critics "Fanny Wrightism" became a short-hand dismissal for every form of radicalism.[57]

A daughter of wealth, Elizabeth Cady Stanton (1815–1902) graduated from the Troy Female Seminary in 1833 only to find that custom and law closed every profession to her, save marriage and motherhood. Marrying Henry Stanton, she felt trapped by domesticity and depressed by life in the village of Seneca Falls in western New York. Stanton longed to liberate women from a society that tended "to destroy her confidence in her own powers, to lessen her self-respect, and to make her willing to lead a dependent and abject life." Stanton published an invitation for a women's rights convention to meet in the local church in July 1848. To her pleasant surprise, 300 people, two-thirds of them women, showed up; the attendees included the celebrated abolitionist Frederick Douglass.[58]

The feminist reformers adopted Stanton's "Declaration of Sentiments" modeled on Jefferson's Declaration of Independence. The new Declaration called for equal property and civil rights for women, including the vote. By pressing for political rights, Stanton abandoned the premise of benevolent reform: that domesticity sustained a superior female morality that politics would corrupt. Critics charged that a politically active woman forgot "the delicacy and reserve of her sex."[59]

In 1848, most newspapers either ridiculed the Seneca Falls convention as a "Petticoat Revolution," or denounced it as "the most shocking and unnatural incident ever recorded in the history of womanity." One newspaper mocked the delegates as "aged spinsters, who have been crossed in love." Pursuing equal civil rights for women would take a very long time in America.[60]

Faith

Protestant churches offered the primary communities for Americans seeking order in their transient lives. Most of the thirteen original states had sustained religious establishments that favored a single denomination with tax support. But such establishments contradicted the individual choice championed by the republican revolution. So the states gradually abolished them, culminating in Massachusetts in 1833. Protestants divided into many denominations. Rather than seeking a full separation of church and state, the contending churches wanted public support for a Protestant moral order, including Bible readings in the schools and Sabbaths free from distraction. Pious folk just wanted no single denomination to benefit from an establishment.[61]

The demise of religious establishments increased the competition between rival denominations for members. The old, established churches—Episcopal, Presbyterian, and Congregational—relied on college graduates for ministers, but they were expensive and slow to educate. So traditional churches struggled to keep pace with the growing population expanding westward into hundreds of new settlements. Evangelical churches—Baptists and Methodists—offered many cheaper, itinerant preachers to fill the vacuum. Their preachers lacked social graces, family connections, and formal education. A Kentucky evangelist, Peter Cartwright (1785–1873), confessed that Methodist preachers "could not, many of us, conjugate a verb or parse a sentence and [we] murdered the king's English almost every lick."[62]

Evangelicals promoted an emotional, physical mode of worship that appealed to common people skeptical of college learning. In the summer, Methodists convened thousands for "camp meetings," weeklong gatherings for outdoor worship led by several preachers. Continuing late into the night by the light of fires, the bellowing preachers and mass singing and shouting generated surges of emotion. Losing control of tongues and bodies, overwrought people spoke gibberish while running, jumping, and barking like dogs. Cartwright recalled that many were "seized with a convulsive jerking all over, . . . and the more they resisted against it, the more they jerked."[63]

Evangelical churches grew faster than the population, but traditional churches fell behind. From 150 congregations in 1770, Baptists grew to 858 in 1790, becoming America's largest denomination. Methodists expanded from 20 congregations in 1770 to 712 in 1790. By comparison, Episcopalians suffered from disestablishment, shrinking from 356 congregations in 1770 to just 170 in 1790.[64]

The thriving evangelical churches began to attract more prosperous members, and that trend had a moderating effect. Rather than mock education and fear wealth, evangelical leaders began to solicit contributions to found seminaries. After 1810, these seminaries trained a new generation of moderate ministers who discouraged emotional and mystical outbursts among the laity. But that moderation invited competition from newer and wilder sects: Adventists, Disciples of Christ, Shakers, Freewill Baptists, Republican Methodists, and New

Israelites. By claiming divine sanction through visions and prophe-
cies, newer groups appealed to poor people who felt forsaken by the
newly respectable Methodists and Baptists. American evangelicalism
was powerful, diverse, and volatile—ever evolving on both the moderate and radical wings as some preachers pursued respectability and
others defied it.[65]

In 1774, an English Quaker, Ann Lee (1736–1784), migrated to
the United States, settling near Albany, New York. Where Jesus had
been the Son of God, Lee posed as the Daughter, completing the gender unity of the divine. Her followers became known as Shakers for
their ecstatic dance of spiritual worship. Committed to gender equality, they divided leadership between women and men, who lived in
separate dorms. Shakers dissolved nuclear family relations in favor
of celibacy, so they had to make converts to survive and grow as a
group. Their tight sense of community and divine mission attracted
4,000 adherents living in nineteen villages stretching from Maine to
Kentucky. Most of the converts were women, seeking an escape from
patriarchal family life.[66]

Protestant theology adapted to the country's more democratic culture. During the colonial era, almost all Protestant churches sustained
Calvinist doctrines, which emphasized inherent human depravity
and utter dependence on divine grace for salvation. During the early
nineteenth century, the competition for believers led most denominations instead to emphasize the free will of every person to seek
salvation.[67]

A former lawyer turned Presbyterian evangelical, Charles Grandison Finney (1792–1875) perfected the new psychology of converting
sinners. Touring widely, Finney carefully staged revivals to maximize
attendance and impact. Charismatic and shrewd, Finney spoke in a
fervent, spontaneous, folksy style. His revivals featured "the anxious
bench" in the front row, where he placed people who seemed sufficiently repentant to convert once under sufficient emotional pressure
from his piercing gaze and penetrating voice. Finney's preaching provoked sobs, groans, cries, and shrieks as people begged God to save

them. In 1830, Finney enjoyed his greatest triumph in Rochester, New York, where he doubled church membership in six months. A fellow Presbyterian hailed that surge as "the greatest work of God and the greatest revival of religion that the world has ever seen."[68]

In religious revivals and broader social changes, many Americans saw signs of an imminent "Millennium," when Christ would return to reign for a thousand years of peace and justice. To hasten the onset of that happy age, devout people felt an urgency to reform social ills, provide Bibles for all, and send missions to convert foreign heathens. "The great aim of the Christian Church . . . is not only to renew the individual man, but also to reform human society," a minister explained.[69]

In upstate New York, a farmer and Baptist preacher, William Miller, interpreted scripture as predicting the return of Christ in 1844—a disciple later specified October 22, 1844. Through print and preaching, Miller attracted thousands of followers who quit jobs or neglected farms to prepare for the rapture. Although Christ failed to show, the Millerites organized a new denomination, the Seventh-Day Adventists. After Miller died in 1849, the Adventists found an inspirational new leader in Ellen Gould Harmon White, a religious visionary from Maine.[70]

During the early nineteenth century, the United States developed a unique religious culture in which many competing denominations increased the overall popularity of Protestant Christianity. About two-thirds of Americans regularly attended church, more than in Europe, where church establishments still prevailed. American denominations and missionary societies flooded the nation with devotional tracts: 6 million in 1830, when the nation also had more than 600 religious newspapers. The number of clergymen grew from about 1,800 in 1775 to nearly 40,000 by 1845. Exceeding the growth in population, that expansion raised the ministerial presence from 1 per 1,500 people in 1775 to 1 per 500 in 1845.[71]

Most Americans regarded republicanism and Protestantism as intertwined, for both preached individual choice and encouraged voluntary association. And both denounced monarchy. A Methodist preacher loudly prayed, "O lord have mercy on the sovereigns of Europe—convert their souls—give them short lives and happy deaths—take them to heaven—and let us have no more of them." Tocqueville noted, "The Americans combine the notions of Christianity and of liberty so intimately in their minds that it is impossible to make them conceive of the one without the other."[72]

Temperance

A republic invested sovereign responsibility in a broad citizenry of white men. But while Americans were making a republic, they became drunker than ever. By 1830 the annual consumption of hard liquor reached four gallons per capita—which included women and children. Given that men drank most of all, their annual consumption exceeded six gallons per person, a doubling of the 1790 level (and three times consumption today in the United States). For want of good wine and a taste for beer, most Americans drank hard cider or distilled liquors, particularly whiskey, which was abundant and cheap thanks to robust crops of grain. A traveler thought the Americans "certainly not so sober as the French or Germans, but perhaps about on a level with the Irish."[73]

In 1829, a federal official calculated that three-quarters of the nation's laborers drank daily at least 4 ounces of the hard stuff. Both army and navy relied on a daily alcohol ration to recruit and retain hard-drinking men. Although George Washington owned a whiskey distillery, he thought alcohol was "the ruin of half the workmen in this Country. . . . An aching head and trembling limbs, which are the inevitable effects of drinking disincline the hands from work, hence begins sloth."[74]

Gentlemen drank too. An American recalled, "There were drunken lawyers, drunken doctors, drunken members of Congress.

Drunkards of all classes." Gentlemen just indulged more expensive tastes with brandy or Madeira wine. A traveler noted that "the American stage coach stops every five miles to water the horses, and *brandy the gentlemen!*" A colleague recalled that Chief Justice John Marshall had been "brought up upon Federalism and Madeira, and he [was] not the man to outgrow his early prejudices." During the 1790s, the governor of New York hosted a dinner where 120 gentlemen downed 135 bottles of Madeira, 60 bottles of beer, 36 bottles of port, and 30 bowls of rum punch.[75]

Americans drank at weddings, christenings, funerals, cornhuskings, barbeques, horse races, public hangings, the Fourth of July, and even camp meetings. Any election included drinking. To win elections to become militia officers, ambitious men treated the rank and file to free drinks. An aspiring colonel assured his men, "I can't make a speech, but what I lack in brains I will try and make up in rum." Political office also required generous treating of voters. A Kentucky politician declared that "the way to men's hearts is *down their throats.*" Treating demonstrated that a candidate was generous and accessible, and not an aristocrat who might subvert the republic.[76]

Material conditions and dietary customs also bred heavy drinking. Whiskey seemed safer to consume than the brackish, muddy water found in much of the country. For lack of municipal sewage and water systems, waste infested rivers and the ground water for wells. Americans also thought that cold water was unhealthy, even deadly, if consumed on a hot day. When asked what he thought about the local water, an American replied, "It's very good for navigation." People believed that alcohol helped them digest massive meals heavy with salted and fried meat, especially pork. Americans ate more meat than any other people on the planet and did so at a dizzying rate. "As soon as food is set on the table," a traveler marveled, "they fall upon it like wolves on an unguarded herd." An Irish traveler noted that "Americans 'go ahead' too fast to enjoy the blessings of sound sleep and good digestion."[77]

Rapid change also promoted anxieties that drove Americans to drink. With so many people on the move, they felt like strangers and sought to take the edge off by sharing a drink—or they drank alone to cope with loneliness. Told that every individual rose or fell on merit, people blamed themselves for falling short—or felt belea-guered by enemies. And sharing a drink manifested the republican equality of free men, so they derided a teetotaler as "a cold-blooded and uncongenial wretch."[78]

While offering short-term sedation, heavy drinking compounded the woes of sots and their families. Drunks destroyed their livers and minds, abused wives, children, and enslaved people, and mired fam-ilies in debt and poverty by neglecting work. Drinking also lowered the inhibitions and compounded the anger of rowdies and rioters, who often ruled the city streets.[79]

In 1826, devout Protestants and capitalist entrepreneurs orga-nized the American Temperance Society, which grew to 2,200 local branches and 170,000 members within five years. Protestant ministers began to preach that no good Christian should drink a drop of alcohol, and profit-minded employers wanted sober workers. The temperance society promoted speaking tours by reformed alcoholics and celeb-rity preachers, urging members to sign a written pledge to abstain from all alcohol. Temperance advocates published antidrinking tracts, including the 1836 best-seller, *Deacon Giles's Distillery*, where demons distilled liquor into barrels labeled Death, Murder, Poverty, and Delir-ium Tremens. New temperance clubs, hotels, and steamboats enabled teetotalers to drink water and avoid drunken company. Temperance contributed to a larger cultural shift in favor of self-discipline, moral-ity, frugality, and piety. Displaying these qualities became essential to earn trust, credit, and social acceptance for middle-class people—and for workers who aspired to rise into that class.[80]

Temperance became the most popular of America's many reform movements, for other reformers agreed that their cause would benefit from sobriety. Abolitionists believed that slaveholders would emanci-pate once they sobered up. Women assumed that men would become less abusive and more receptive to reform if they stopped drinking. Temperance advocates succeeded in cutting per capita drinking in half between 1830 and 1840. When persuasion failed, the advocates turned to state or municipal governments for coercion, securing laws banning the local sale of alcohol. But they confronted clever retailers and defiant drinkers. In 1838, when Massachusetts passed a law against selling liquor, an enterprising dealer painted stripes on a pig and advertised that, for 6 cents, a person could see this wonder and receive a free shot of whiskey. Soon striped pigs multiplied in bars throughout the state.[81]

Culture

American culture became more democratic as middle-class people grew more refined, narrowing the gap in lifestyle between them and the wealthy. Prosperous tradesmen, shopkeepers, and farmers read more, adopted polished manners, and wore nicer clothes. Teacups and saucers, carpets, clocks, portraits, and looking glasses proliferated in their homes as they entertained more visitors. Watching closely, they measured one another for signs of refinement or vulgarity. A dread of scorn compelled attention to every detail of appearance and behavior.[82]

This middle-class gentility expanded beyond the cities into hundreds of country towns, where prosperous families could obtain urban goods and notions of respectability. Prosperous farmers painted their barns and homes, hired a local artist to depict the family, donned finer clothes on Sunday, and rode to church in new carriages. Churches banned dogs, provided cushions in the pews, and installed stoves to make winter services bearable; the faithful stopped chewing and spitting tobacco during worship. This middle-class gentility abounded in the northern states, but proved scarcer in the West and scarcest of all in the South, where most rural folk preserved a plain style of life.[83]

While softening the boundary between the wealthy and middle classes, the new gentility drew a harder line between the respectable above and the poor below, derided as coarse and vulgar. Middle-class folk blamed poverty on bad taste and slack morals. In theory, poor people could prosper by improving their manners, reading uplifting books, and acquiring a few genteel goods. In fact, the poor struggled just to get by from one day to the next. Laborers were often unemployed or underemployed, while many small farmers eked out a bare living from hard work.[84]

Because republics depended on a broad electorate, reformers promoted public education to improve the minds and morals of citizens. Otherwise, reformers worried, the republic would collapse as demagogues or aristocrats seized power by exploiting an ignorant public. James Madison warned that a "popular government, without popular information . . . is but a Prologue to a Farce or a Tragedy; or, perhaps both." But most citizens preferred lower taxes, and many farmers and artisans wanted to keep their children at work. So, in most states, legislators rejected systems of public education until the 1820s and 1830s, and then only adopted them in northern states. Rather than wait on taxpayers, ambitious people formed voluntary associations to support schools and libraries, debating clubs and lyceums through subscriptions and tuition.[85]

Self-education prevailed as at least three-quarters of Americans in 1800 could read: one of the highest rates in the world. Newspapers and books multiplied as printing presses spread beyond the seaports into the countryside. The 100 newspapers of 1790 became nearly 400 by 1810. An expanding federal postal system spread letters and publications across the nation. The 69 post offices of 1788 mushroomed to 903 in 1800. By 1830, the postal department employed 8,700 people, three-fourths of all federal employers. The United States had the most extensive and intensive postal network in the world, with 74 post offices per 100,000 inhabitants compared to 4 in France and 17 in Britain. And federal policy subsidized the mailing of newspapers, delivering 16 million copies a year by 1830.[86]

During the 1830s, print became even cheaper and more abundant with the adoption of new steam presses twenty-five times faster than the old hand presses of Benjamin Franklin's day. Steam presses cut the cost of a newspaper to just a penny, a sixth of the former cost. The "penny press" featured crime, scandal, adventure, and oddities. A publisher noted that Americans preferred to read "the details of a brutal murder, or the testimony of a divorce case, or the trial of a divine for improprieties of conduct, [rather] than the same amount of words poured forth by the genius of the noblest author of our times."[87]

The market rewarded sensation rather than brilliance. John Marshall's ponderous and expensive multivolume biography of Washington sold few copies, for readers preferred Mason Locke Weems's brief, cheap, melodramatic, and fanciful version of Washington, who could not lie about chopping down his neighbor's cherry tree. Americans read few books and many newspapers, rich in political bombast and ads for runaway slaves. Cultural mediocrity was, most Americans believed, the worthy price paid for a republic of equal rights for white men.[88]

In the theater, melodramas prevailed, with titles that included *The Cannibals or Massacre Island, A Tale of Blood,* and *The Monk! The Mask! The Murder!* A newspaper noted, "We live in times of such intense excitement, that the public taste is in a measure perverted. . . . It is of no importance how extravagant and unnatural a dramatick spectacle may be; the more so the better." Exciting audience participation, melodramas and minstrel shows discouraged a taste for high-brow theater. In New York City, an actor performing as Hamlet on stage heard the audience yell out that he should stop reciting Shakespeare and instead sing a popular song, "Possum up a Gum Tree."[89]

That song came from a new genre, the minstrel show: free-form comedies where white performers in rags and blackface pretended to play music, sing, and talk like Black people. By imitating and distorting the songs and stories of African Americans, white performers constructed American popular culture. Minstrel shows caricatured Blacks with wide eyes, gaping mouths, protruding lips, woolly hair, clumsy feet, and fractured English. The Virginia Minstrels promised an evening of "oddities, peculiarities, eccentricities, and comicalities of that Sable Genus of Humanity." Minstrels created the character of Jim Crow, an old slave who combined a shuffling walk with sudden hops while singing nonsense songs. They also developed Zip Coon, an over-the-top Black dandy in the city. Ridiculing abolition as "bobolushun," performers treated slavery as amusing, natural, and right.[90]

British critics mocked the low quality of American arts. In 1820 a critic demanded, "Who reads an American book? Or goes to an American play or looks at an American picture or statue?" Caught between the pedestrian tastes of most Americans and the mockery of British critics, ambitious writers longed to create a distinctive, national literature. In 1832, a college president sought books and plays "such as Americans may be proud of, and such as British criticism may no longer ridicule or annihilate." But writers and artists struggled to produce imaginative works in a nation obsessed with practicality.[91]

During the 1820s, Washington Irving (1783–1859) and James Fenimore Cooper (1789–1851) went halfway by adapting American characters and scenes to the style of English novels. Born into prestige and wealth, Cooper and Irving felt uneasy with rapid changes that made society more materialistic and democratic. Irving crafted nostalgic stories of bygone rural life in the Hudson Valley. Cooper initially wrote frontier adventures featuring noble scouts and Indians who would fade away to permit an orderly civilization to improve the land. When American society instead became more fractious and grasping, Cooper devoted his later novels to denouncing a "country with no principles, but party, no God, but money, and this too with very little sentiment, taste, breeding, or knowledge." Few Americans would buy such novels.[92]

A more inventive writer, Edgar Allan Poe (1809–1849), explored the darker, secretive recesses of the individual mind. Reading the popular press, he found follies and murders to elaborate into macabre tales of insanity, sadism, and gloom. Favoring an evocative tone that involved the reader's imagination, Poe avoided the preachy moralism and literal description of conventional American writing.[93]

Genteel and well educated, Poe disdained egalitarian notions: "The queerest idea conceivable" is that "all men are born free and equal." He concluded, "Democracy is a very admirable form of government—for dogs." Poe warned that democracy would culminate in rule by a "usurping tyrant" known as the "Mob": "insolent, rapacious, filthy . . . with the heart of an hyena and the brains of a peacock." That Mob killed Poe in October 1849, when he arrived in Baltimore during a typically raucous election. He could not resist the alcohol pressed on him by rival partisans bidding for a vote that he could not give. Poe drank himself into a stupor that led to hallucinations and death.[94]

The nation's most influential philosophical writer, Ralph Waldo Emerson (1803–1882) wanted to create a distinctive culture derived from common people and freed from British airs. But he did not necessarily like what Americans had made so far: "'Tis a wild democracy; the riot of mediocrities and dishonesties and fudges." Emerson later added, "*Manifest Destiny, Democracy, Freedom*, fine names for an ugly thing." Witty, charming, and accessible, he became a popular and well-paid lecturer and essayist. Emerson welcomed reforms but balked at joining any organization. "I was born a seeing eye, and not a helping hand," he explained.[95]

Emerson's protégé, Henry David Thoreau (1817–1862), grew up in the same Massachusetts town, Concord, as the son of a pencil manufacturer. Thoreau joined Emerson in leading a philosophical movement known as Transcendentalism. These thinkers cultivated the individual's power to transcend conventional life by rejecting consumerism, the market, and government. Through simple, frugal living, and wide reading, an American could become truly free at last. Thoreau preached, "It is hard to have a southern overseer; it is worse to have a northern one; but worst of all when you are the slave-driver of yourself."[96]

Another New England Transcendentalist, Margaret Fuller (1810–1850), led an even more daring life by seeking equality with men.

Fuller edited an experimental literary magazine, *The Dial,* which published much of Thoreau's early work. In her own essays, she urged Americans to open every profession to women: "Let them be sea-captains, if they will." She went to Europe to cover the revolutions of 1848, becoming the first American woman to work as an overseas correspondent.[97]

In 1850, after marrying an Italian revolutionary and having a child, Fuller sailed home to America, but the ship ran aground and broke up in a storm off Long Island. Fuller, husband, and son drowned. She was forty years old. Scavengers stole most of the goods and papers that floated ashore. With money borrowed from Emerson, Thoreau traveled to Long Island to search, in vain, for her body and last book manuscript, but the only remains that washed ashore were a few shark-gnawed bones. Margaret Fuller had died for want of a better (and perhaps female) sea captain.[98]

Her adventurous feminism did not sit well with her more conservative peers. Writing to a sister, Sophia Hawthorne denounced Fuller: "I am really glad she died. There is a vein of coarseness in her nature, not feminine. I hate reform-women as a class do not you? I think it is designed by GOD that woman should always spiritually wear a veil, & not a coat & hat."[99]

Fine art also reflected the American ambivalence that celebrated material progress but worried that it generated vulgarity, greed, crime, madness, and mob violence. During the mid-1830s, Thomas Cole (1801–1848) produced an epic set of five paintings called *The Course of Empire.* Each depicted a social stage beginning with the lush nature of hunter and pastoral states, reaching a climax in the lavish, Roman architecture of a powerful empire before collapsing as mobs riot and smash, leaving ruined desolation in a reviving nature. Cole also painted lovely landscapes that were vanishing as Americans pursued economic development "with a wantonness and barbarism scarcely credible in a civilized nation." They "desecrated by what is called improvement. . . . Nature's beauty without substituting that of Art."[100]

Cole's doubts did not afflict the grandest artist of the early republic, John Banvard (1815–1891) of Kentucky, who created "the largest
painting in the world!" During the 1840s, Banvard traveled the length
of the Mississippi River, making sketches. Returning to his Louisville studio, he created an oil painting on canvas made from southern
cotton by Lowell mill girls. Twelve feet high, it grew to half a mile
in length. On a special stage, Banvard narrated as he had it unfurled
slowly to reveal scenes of steamboats, raft men, Indians, and farmers.
Wildly popular, the display earned him enough money to build a
palace modeled on England's Windsor Castle and meant to exceed in
grandeur Barnum's mansion on the other side of Long Island Sound.
None of the massive painting now survives, attesting to the ephem-
eral nature of American culture, just as Cole had warned.[101]

Workers

The transportation revolution promoted a more integrated national
market as goods moved more quickly and cheaply over long distances. That integration fed regional specialization as people developed their comparative advantages in local resources. So, the fertile
Midwest shipped bumper crops of grain, pork, and beef eastward to
feed the growing populations of cities. Unable to compete with those
midwestern farms, the farmers of New England began to specialize
in garden crops and dairy production to serve the nearby cities. An
abundant supply of cheap food enabled town and city folk to make
their living in workshops and factories.[102]

The market integration encouraged enterprise by local mechanics
and inventors, who tinkered with everything from guns and clocks
to ploughs and looms. Most of these tinkering entrepreneurs operated
out of the commercial villages of rural New England and the Middle
Atlantic states, where they tapped into the waterpower of scores of
small dams. "Anything new is quickly introduced here. . . . There is
no clinging to old ways," a German visitor remarked.[103]

These entrepreneurs developed new modes of organizing labor. In the "putting-out system," New England merchants provided raw materials to rural households, where women and children made brooms, chairs, shoes, and straw and palm-leaf hats. In 1837 in Massachusetts, families produced 3.3 million palm-leaf hats. From their modest pay, they bought consumer goods from the merchants' stores. The merchants then sold the handicrafts to far-flung markets.[104]

The nation's first small factories emerged in New England villages. The immigrant Samuel Slater brought English textile know-how to Rhode Island during the 1790s. Because New England had the nation's highest population density, it had a comparative advantage for manufacturing, which needed cheap labor to compete with British imports. Slater and his emulators primarily employed women and children because their labor was cheapest of all. For seventy hours of labor per week, a woman got $2.00 and a child a tenth of that. Republican thinkers felt reassured that such women's husbands remained independent farmers. Dreading the British model of industrial society, Americans wanted to avoid creating a working class of men dependent on low wages for the rest of their short and hungry lives.[105]

In Massachusetts, Francis Cabot Lowell developed larger textile factories that united spinning and weaving in the same building. During the 1820s, Lowell's heirs and associates built immense factories along the Merrimack River at a place named after Lowell. By 1844 the Lowell mills annually produced 100 million yards of cloth using an eighth of the cotton grown in the United States. The large, tall red-brick factories had white cupolas at the top, creating an appearance of urban beauty and order that astonished British visitors used to grimier mill towns. Relying on waterpower, Lowell did not generate the soot and smoke of coal-powered factories.[106]

The "Lowell System" employed young, single women drawn from rural towns. They lodged in company boardinghouses supervised by pious matrons, who took the "mill girls" to mandatory church services every Sunday. These moralizing measures reassured rustic parents who sent daughters off to work in Lowell. After working and saving for a few years, the mill girls expected to return home to marry a farmer. During the 1820s, they received relatively good pay, $2.50 per week, but half went to cover their room and board. And the workdays were twelve to fourteen hours long, in hot, humid rooms of clattering machines. Cotton fibers filled the air, leading to lung diseases.[107]

The distinctive Lowell labor system proved short-lived. During the 1830s, employers cut wages, provoking massive strikes in 1834 and 1836. During the 1840s, the millowners shifted their work force to Irish immigrants, who were hungry enough to work cheap. In 1836 only 4 percent of Lowell's workers were foreign-born men; by 1860 that rose to 62 percent. America was developing an industrial working class derived primarily from immigrants.[108]

Most Americans still lived on farms and plantations in the countryside, but the manufacturing sector was growing faster than agriculture. By 1840, 17 percent of American men worked in manufacturing. That percentage rose even higher in the Northeast, reaching 40 percent of men in Massachusetts. Because laborers had to walk to work, industrialization concentrated people, promoting urbanization.[109]

Manufacturing workplaces became more crowded and complex, with hierarchies of command and obedience. Industrialization increased employers' power over the workers' time. Employers relied on clocks linked to bells to ring the hours for starting and finishing work—and they docked the pay of, or fired, workers who arrived late or left early. In the old days, masters had provided alcohol to help apprentices and journeymen get through their workday. In the new work regimes, owners provided no alcohol and banned workers from bringing in their own bottles. And no level of government offered any protection for workers' rights or conditions, leaving those to the power of the employer. In 1832, the average manufacturing workday exceeded eleven hours.[110]

Commercialization broke down the work process into smaller steps, each assigned to different workers, and often linked to machines setting a brisk pace that humans had to follow. This "deskilling" of the work process increased productivity and lowered labor costs. Industrial laborers became human cogs, each doing a small part, none mastering the whole process of making the product. For example, some shoe workers cut soles, and others cut out uppers, and still others stitched them up. Because almost anyone quickly could learn a limited skill, the pool of available, cheap labor expanded and included women and children. Producing more shoes faster at lower cost and with more standardized results, this process generated profits for employers— but it ruined traditional artisans, who crafted entire shoes. Some artisans adapted and prospered as employers of deskilled employees, but most lost their independence to become wage workers. In Boston, half of the journeymen carpenters of 1790 could become masters with their own shops. By 1825 that proportion slipped to just 11 percent.[111]

An urban garment trade expanded to exploit cheap female labor by applying the new work processes. Employers had tailors cut out garment pieces and then delivered them to poor women to stitch together in garrets and cellars. Paid per garment completed, they became known as "sweated" labor because the women had to work so hard and fast to satisfy employers. At 7 cents a shirt, a woman could earn no more than $1 per week—less than half the wages for a male laborer. A dollar barely covered the rent, leaving little to feed children. Dispersed from one another, the women could not combine to form a union. Plus, ships brought in more immigrant laborers who needed work. To make ends meet, women sent children out to work at odd jobs, scavenge in the streets, or steal food from vendors' carts. In New York City, reformers noted, "It has been alleged that if people are honest and industrious they may always make some decent living in this happy Land, . . . but what can a bereaved widow do, with 5 or 6 little children, destitute of every means of support but what her own hands can furnish" which "does not amount to more than

25 cents a day?" Younger women could supplement their earnings as sex-workers, but that was a dangerous business.[112]

While self-employed artisans declined, a new middle class emerged to manage railroads, stores, insurance firms, banks, and factories. Although employees rather than owners, the clerks and bookkeepers, agents, salesmen, and superintendents relied on salaries or commissions and identified with their employers rather than with the wage workers beneath them in prestige and income. Wearing shirts with white collars, the new middle class felt superior to the blue-collar workers who got grease rather than ink on their hands. The class distinction also had an ethnic dimension as the prized new jobs usually went to American-born men, who shared that background with the owners of their firms.[113]

Before 1820, apprentices and journeymen usually lodged with their employers, sharing their meals and alcohol. Thereafter, such a merger of home and work persisted in rural America, but in towns and cities that combination dissolved. At day's end, employers wanted to retire to a domestic retreat far from the racket and smoke of work—and far from their workers, who seemed louder and grubbier. A Philadelphian noted that apprentices "after a hard day's work were turned loose upon the street at night by their masters or bosses."[114]

Distinct neighborhoods segregated by class emerged. Most housing for workers was flimsy, filthy, and prone to collapse or burn. For want of municipal regulation, landlords hastily built cheap tenements crammed into back alleys with poor access to fresh air, sunlight, and water. A Philadelphian reported: "Whites and blacks, old and young, rumsellers and their customers, were packed together there, amid noxious smells, rags and filth, as thick and foul as insects in a decaying carcass." These rough neighborhoods also hosted gambling dens, dance halls, cheap brothels, cockfighting pits, and many bars. The drunken, raucous disorder appalled respectable, middle-class people, who intervened through moral reform societies that delivered pious tracts. Prosperous folk were much less inclined to tax themselves to improve water, sanitation, and housing for the poor.[115]

As artisans saw their conditions deteriorate, they resented the growing wealth of the capitalists who owned banks, stores, and factories. By the 1840s in the major cities, the richest 5 percent of free men owned 70 percent of the taxable property. The term "millionaire" first came into use during the 1840s. While newspapers extolled the self-made man who became rich, most of the wealth derived from inheritance and from owning urban real estate as population surged.[116]

Workers worried that inequality threatened their social mobility and the survival of a republic that traditionally relied on an electorate of independent men who owned a farm or shop. The economic dependence of wage laborers seemed antithetical to republicanism. While politicians insisted that America was becoming more democratic, workers felt deprived of their dignity as republican citizens, for they saw a grim future of lifelong labor for low wages in harsh conditions. They blamed this decline on "an unequal and very excessive accumulation of wealth and power into the hands of a few."[117]

Workers held "producerist" views that credited labor for creating all value in goods. That labor theory of value discredited capitalists as parasites living off the hard work of employees. In 1830, a workingman's newspaper noted, "There appears to exist two distinct classes, the rich and the poor; the oppressor and the oppressed; those who live by their own labor, and they that live by the labor of others." Capital seemed an insidious power created out of exploited labor and then deployed to keep workers in poverty and subordination.[118]

Growing up in poverty in Connecticut, Thomas Skidmore (1790-1832) became an itinerant worker and radical thinker. In 1829, Skidmore published *The Rights of Man to Property!* which demanded a redistribution of wealth from the rich to the poor. In New York City, he helped organize a political party for workers to seek control of the state legislature and rewrite the state constitution to enfranchise all men and women. Then he expected to abolish the inheritance of wealth, confiscate large properties, and operate banks and manufactories as public enterprises with shares distributed to every adult—women as well as men, Black and white. Skidmore concluded, "No Wealth, no Want."[119]

After some initial, local success in 1829, the New York City Working Men's Party collapsed from internal divisions a year later. Most of the voters joined the Democrats, who had secured a few, modest reforms, including new state laws enabling workers to obtain liens for back pay and abolishing imprisonment for debt. In 1832, Skidmore died of cholera at the age of forty-two.[120]

Politics frustrated workingmen because of a paradox: as the system became more overtly democratic, allowing more common men to vote, elected legislatures lost power to the unelected judiciary. Commercialization and industrialization raised many new issues involving property, and those issues primarily fell to courts, rather than legislatures, to decide. The courts favored economic development by private interests as promoting the general welfare. Conservatives exalted the law as a transcendent ideal that provided perfect justice if freed from political interference. A Massachusetts judge warned that, if property became the legislative "spoil of the multitude, [it] would annihilate property, and involve society in a common ruin."[121]

Judges defined the market as a private realm where every individual had equal rights. Therefore, politicians should not meddle with individuals freely contracting to buy and sell goods and labor. Ideology held that competition was fair and rewarded merit so long as no one tried to game the system through combinations, which threatened "the sacred right of property." In 1836 a New York judge declared, "Every American knows, or ought to know, that he has no better friend than the laws, and that he needs no artificial combination for his protection." That judge denounced unions as the un-American spawn of immigrant agitators.[122]

Urban workers formed unions to seek better pay and conditions and shorter hours, with a ten-hour day as the primary goal. Only through solidarity could they hope to match the economic power of their employers. In Massachusetts, an association of workingmen asserted "our right and our duty to combine to protect our rights and interests, and keep ourselves from being ground down into slavery."[123]

The unions suffered from self-imposed limitations. The skilled craft workers had greater leverage, but they balked at sharing it with the more numerous unskilled laborers. Unions also excluded Blacks and women, treating them as enemies best driven from the better jobs to shrink the labor pool and increase the bargaining power of white men. Unions aspired to bolster patriarchal families, where the man could earn a "family wage" sufficient to support a wife and children at home. But many women had to work for want of a husband, or a reliable one.[124]

When the economy boomed, strikes by unions scored some wins, especially if many crafts federated for a general strike across an entire city. Labor federations emerged in a dozen cities, and they formed a National Trades' Union in 1834 as "security against the entire degradation of the whole mass of the working men in the United States." In 1835, a strike by Philadelphia's federation led employers to accept a ten-hour workday. But the great depression of 1837 threw so many men out of work that employers could draw on a huge pool of desperation. To break strikes, employers brought in substitute workers, derided as "scabs" by unionists. Then the bosses imposed wage cuts and hour increases.[125]

Capitalists and judges insisted that a worker should simply quit his job if dissatisfied, but few laborers could afford to do so. In Massachusetts, workers explained, "We are poor men; men obliged to labor for our daily bread; dependent on those who choose to employ us, and compelled by the invincible law of hunger to accept the wages they offer. They hold us then at their mercy, and make us work solely for their profit." And if workers did quit, "There are enough more ready to take our place."[126]

Employers sued unions as illegal conspiracies against free enterprise. In the first American labor conspiracy case, involving Philadelphia shoemakers in 1806, a state court ruled that any union was illegal. After 1820, however, state courts took a more nuanced line, accepting that workers could unite to negotiate their pay and terms of employment—but added that they could do nothing to pressure any-one to join their association. This new line claimed to protect other workers rather than employers. In 1836, a Philadelphia newspaper explained that "to annoy, harass, perplex or molest" nonunion labor-ers and "prevent them from working" was not a "conspiracy, against their employers" but a "trespass against the other journeymen." This argument cast union pressure as menacing individual freedom, but workers saw such rulings as threats to their liberty. New York labor-ers protested: "The Freemen of the North are now on a level with the slaves of the South! With no other privileges than laboring that drones may fatten on your life-blood!"[127]

Mobocracy

The United States population surged from almost 4 million in 1790 to over 17 million by 1840. Most of the growth came from natu-ral increase, but immigration also increased, primarily from Ireland, where British mismanagement exacerbated a blight that devastated the potato harvests during the 1840s. "God sent the blight, but the British sent the famine," the Irish said. A million people starved to death. To seek a better life, thousands crowded into sailing ships bound across the Atlantic. From 100,000 in 1847, Irish migration to the United States more than doubled to 221,000 in 1851.[128]

Most of the Irish immigrants were Catholics, who confronted cultural dominance by Protestants in the United States. They also clashed with American-born workers, who resented the newcom-ers as unwanted competition who allegedly would subvert republi-can government out of slavish loyalty to their monarch, the Pope. "The bloody hand of the Pope has stretched forth to our destruc-tion," nativists warned. In August 1834 in Charlestown, Massachusetts, Protestants attacked and burned an Ursuline convent, driving out the nuns, while firemen stood by and watched. A decade later, a nativist mob invaded an Irish neighborhood in Philadelphia to burn two Catholic churches, a convent, and many homes.[129]

To oppose nativism, Irish Catholics joined the nation's dominant political party, the Democrats, who supported their opposition to Protestant prayers and Bible readings in the public schools. Democrats also defended the right of immigrants to drink alcohol, resisting the temperance pressure favored by Whigs. In addition to promoting an anti-British foreign policy that delighted Irish Americans, Democrats provided opportunities for ambitious immigrants to run for political office.[130]

Democrats promoted the equality of white men and their superiority over other races. A politician accepted "to an equality with me, sir, the white man,—my blood and race, whether he be a Saxon of England or Celt of Ireland, but I do not admit as my equals either the red man of America, or the yellow man of Asia, or the black man of Africa." Democrats defended southern slavery as the price of preserving the Union. And without that Union, they argued, the states could not confront the mighty British, the exploiters of Ireland.[131]

Race had to trump class for poor immigrants to rise in America's competitive society. Arriving as impoverished laborers, they shared neighborhoods and competed for jobs with free Blacks, which generated frictions. The Irish also sought to refute nativist taunts that likened them to Blacks, including cartoons depicting "Paddy" as a swarthy ape. Asserting their whiteness, Irish Americans reviled Blacks and abolitionists as threats to the Union—and as allies of the hated British. The abolitionist Frederick Douglass rued, "The Irish, who, at home, readily sympathize with the oppressed everywhere, are instantly taught when they step upon our soil to hate and despise the Negro."[132]

Irish street gangs fought to repel nativists and abuse Black people. Gangs adopted fearsome names: Rats, Stingers, Skinners, Flayers,

Bleeders, Blood Tubs, Garroters, Hyenas, and Deathfetchers. In Philadelphia, one gang apparently did not get the concept, calling themselves the Dock Street Philosophers. More aptly named, the Killers
became the most notorious of the city's gangs. A Philadelphian said,
"They were 'just the boys' to sack a Theatre or burn a Church." In
addition to routine street crime, gangs often became "Blackbirders,"
who kidnapped Black children for sale to the South.[133]

Free Blacks and Irish immigrants mixed and clashed in Moyamensing, a Philadelphia neighborhood. An Irish American explained that
his neighbors had "imbibed the idea that the Blacks, not being citizens, have no right to stay in the city, and that if they can drive them
out of the city, they will have their places, and have enough work
to do." In August 1834, Blacks frequented a carousel known as the
"Flying Horses," so white rioters smashed it to pieces and then looted
and burned two Black churches and thirty-seven houses, while beating many African Americans and killing two. A newspaper reported,
"The mob exhibited more than fiendish brutality, beating and muti-
lating some of the old, confiding and unoffending blacks, with a
savageness surpassing anything we could have believed men capable of."[134]

In August 1842 in Moyamensing, African Americans staged a
parade to promote temperance and celebrate emancipation in the
British West Indies. The marchers carried a banner displaying a slave
breaking his chains with a rising sun in the background. That banner offended Irish immigrants, who claimed that it depicted the fiery
destruction of whites. And they hated temperance as much as they
despised Blacks. So a thousand persons plundered African Americans'
homes, burned a meeting hall and a church, and beat several Blacks,
while the rest fled. An Irish woman directed the rioters to attack
a home "that I want to have mobbed—there's some negroes living
there, who are living just like white folks."[135]

Almost every American city suffered from race riots in which
white majorities punished Blacks who displayed prosperity or defi-

ance. In Providence, Rhode Island, in October 1824, when some African Americans refused to step aside for whites on the sidewalk, a mob invaded the Black neighborhood to destroy twenty houses. For three days in August 1829, hundreds of white men invaded "Bucktown," the Black district of Cincinnati, to loot and destroy the homes of 1,200 people, most of whom fled to safety in Canada. When Blacks rebuilt Bucktown, whites invaded again in August 1841, this time bringing a cannon to clear the streets before destroying homes and a church.[136]

Mobs of all sorts multiplied in America between 1820 and 1850, affecting countryside as well cities, native-born as well as immigrants, white and Black people. In four months of 1835, newspapers reported 109 riots, so the *Richmond Whig* characterized the American political system as a "Mobocracy" rather than a democracy. On May 3, 1847, a Philadelphia newspaper reported as noteworthy: "no rioting yesterday."[137]

Police forces were small and ineffectual, so mobs ruled the streets unless a governor called in the state militia. In 1833, Philadelphia had only one patrolman for every 3,352 inhabitants, while London had one per 434. Hired to protect middle-class interests, policemen rarely ventured into the more dangerous working-class neighborhoods. As political appointees, they sided with local leaders against unpopular minorities. By excluding Blacks from the police and militia, whites kept them vulnerable to mobs. Few whites faced arrest for rioting; fewer still were convicted by juries, and pardons released almost everyone convicted.[138]

In New York City during the 1820s and 1830s, working-class toughs, known as Bowery Boys, meant to police the theater in favor of American nationalism and social equality. Many were Irish immigrants who claimed American patriotism as their own. They favored American actors with a bombastic style over their restrained competitors coming over from Britain to make money. As favorites of Whig cosmopolitans, the Britons earned extra animus from the democratic Boys.[139]

A reckless British actor, William Charles Macready, publicly denounced the Bowery Boys as ignorant fools. On May 7, 1849, they took their revenge by attending Macready's next performance, in *Macbeth*, at the Astor Place Opera House. The leading American actor, Edwin Forrest, bought tickets for the Boys, so that they could pelt Macready with insults, rotten eggs, potatoes, and chairs. Three days later, Macready tried again, while militiamen defended the opera house. But handbills had spread through the city asking, "Working Men, shall Americans or English Rule in this City?" A mob of 20,000 surrounded the opera house, howling "Burn the damned den of the Aristocracy" while smashing the windows with paving stones. A rioter yelled, "America rules England to-night, by Jesus." Militiamen fired into the crowd, killing twenty-two and wounding forty-eight more. Suspending the play, Macready left America never to return.[140]

Small differences could suffice for a riot. In Hagerstown, Maryland in 1834, Irish canal workers from County Cork fought against those from County Longford, killing dozens before federal troops restored order. In 1847, when a steamboat from Baltimore arrived at Annapolis, young men from the rival cities attacked one another with stones, which escalated to gunfire. When the Annapolis men hauled out two cannons, the Baltimore steamer hastily departed.[141]

Cities allowed ethnic neighborhoods to organize volunteer fire companies that competed in racing to flames, with honor going to the first to arrive, who then mocked the laggards. If two or more companies reached a fire, brawls broke out over priority, while buildings burned. In Philadelphia, two fire companies, one named for Franklin and the other for Washington, waged an epic feud. To get extra muscle, both formed alliances with ethnic gangs, including the notorious Killers, who liked Washington better than Franklin. In December 1842, the Washingtons set a false alarm that drew the Franklins into an ambush by several hundred foes. Driven off, the Franklins lost their prized and well-decorated horse-drawn engine to desecration by the Washingtons. A day later, 400 Franklins took revenge by storming the rivals' fire house to destroy their engine.[142]

Riots affected the countryside as well as the cities. In the upper Hudson and Delaware Valleys of New York, thousands of farmers held about 1.8 million acres by leases from wealthy landlords who had suspect land titles dating to the colonial era and based on feudal law. In 1839, the landlords tried to evict renters in arrears, but about 10,000 families organized an armed resistance. Disguised as Indians with calico masks, antirenters intercepted sheriffs and forced them to burn their writs of eviction and then to buy drinks for the rioters. To enforce solidarity, antirenters pulled down the houses of farmers who supported landlords. In 1845, after antirenters killed a persistent deputy sheriff, the state cracked down and arrested dozens of suspects. Despite considerable electoral clout, the antirent block could not budge legislators and governors into challenging the state courts that defended the rights of property. The antirent movement collapsed. Some farmers moved away and others bought their land from landlords.[143]

Often ambitious men formed "vigilance committees" to gain an aura of legalism for their riots. Impatient with judges and juries as slow and ineffectual, vigilance committees enforced their own moral code on people defined as deviants. Vigilantes destroyed offending taverns, gambling halls, or brothels, and tarred and feathered, whipped, and sometimes hanged the managers and patrons. Claiming to represent "the people," vigilantes meant to "deal with these villains according to their just desserts."[144]

The young lawyer and politician Abraham Lincoln dreaded "the worse than savage mobs" and "the increasing disregard for law which pervades the country; the growing disposition to substitute the wild and furious passions in lieu of the sober judgement of courts." A Philadelphian warned that the United States would "be destroyed by the eruption of the dark masses of ignorance and brutality which lie beneath it, like the fires of a volcano."[145]

Nauvoo

During the 1820s in upstate New York, Joseph Smith, Jr., the son of a poor farmer, became an adept at a folk magic that helped him seek buried treasures. Those magical practices led him to experience visions of angels. One guided him to a buried set of gold plates inscribed with hieroglyphs. By entering a trance, Smith translated the text into English, which he published as the *Book of Mormon* in 1830. This scripture told of ancient, lost tribes of Israel migrating to North America to build a civilization later crushed by the ancestors of Indians. Smith's followers considered themselves "Latter-Day Saints," but outsiders called them "Mormons."[146]

The newfound scripture, and Smith's continuing revelations, addressed the religious dilemmas of American Protestants. Mormonism appealed to people who felt confused by the contentious competition between rival denominations. They recoiled, Smith noted, from "scene[s] of great confusion and bad feelings . . . priest contending against priest, and convert against convert." With visions and a new scripture, Smith offered an appealing certitude to pious seekers troubled by theological disputes. One convert, Brigham Young, explained, "I wanted to know the truth that I might not be fooled." Mormons believed that Smith restored Christianity to its original purity, but other denominations denounced Smith as a fraud and his new faith as a heresy.[147]

By gathering in distinct communities, Mormons sought to build a utopia led by Smith as their prophet and president. In addition to escaping denominational diversity, Mormons rejected the contention of democratic politics by following the dictates of a council led by Smith. They also opposed the consumption of alcohol, tobacco, and coffee that bonded so many American men together. Calling themselves "Saints," they labeled outsiders as "gentiles," a term that conveyed mistrust and contempt. Seeking mutual affirmation, and greater safety, Mormons gathered in Kirtland, Ohio, in 1831.[148]

To accommodate growing numbers, Smith sought more land in Missouri. In 1838, Smith led the migration westward, but their clannish economy and block voting angered other Missourians, who also distrusted a people who refused to keep slaves. An anti-Mormon meeting declared that "as non-slaveholders, and opposed to slavery," Mormons were unwanted "in this peculiar period, when abolitionism has reared its deformed and haggard visage in our land." Hostile vigilantes looted and burned homes and tarred and feathered or whipped Mormons to drive them out. Fighting back, Mormons organized their own militia to assault and burn out their hostile neighbors. Those foes appealed to the state's governor, who outlawed the Mormons and called out the state militia to fulfill this order: "The Mormons must be treated as enemies, and must be exterminated or driven from the State." Missourians killed about 40 Mormons, while the rest abandoned their farms and fled to Illinois.[149]

In 1839, with support from the Illinois state government, Mormons founded the city of Nauvoo on the Mississippi River. The city's charter empowered them to organize their own government, including a well-armed militia, the Nauvoo Legion. Smith served as mayor, recorder of deeds, chief judge of the municipal court, and commander of the Legion. Smith called his system "theo-democracy" and announced plans to run for president of the United States. The city's population grew to 15,000, making Nauvoo the largest community in Illinois—and the most formidable utopian community in America. A New York City editor visited and marveled at the "industry and energy" that he thought "may revolutionize the whole earth one of these days."[150]

The Mormons' growing numbers, authoritarian government, distinctive ways, block voting, and clannishness alarmed their Illinois neighbors. In June 1844, that alarm became outrage when dissident Mormons revealed that Smith and his inner circle had introduced the practice of polygamy. They claimed to restore the proper patriarchy of the Old Testament, but polygamy offended the mainstream sensibility in nineteenth-century America. To smite the Mormon critics of polygamy, Smith had their newspaper destroyed.[151]

In surrounding towns, angry gentiles concluded that the Mormon theocracy subverted core American values of private property, political competition, and marital monogamy. In armed force, these critics rallied to storm Nauvoo. To avert a bloodbath, the state's governor ordered Smith and his brother Hyrum arrested and jailed in nearby Carthage. But, on June 27, 1844, a lynch mob broke into the jail and assassinated the brothers. In early 1845, the state legislature revoked the Nauvoo city charter and ordered the Mormons disarmed. Hostile militiamen burned outlying farms owned by Mormons and fired cannons at their temple in Nauvoo.[152]

Mormons crafted a distinctive culture and sought to live apart from other Americans. By withdrawing, they aroused the special fury and tyranny of the majority. In 1845, Mormons prepared to leave Nauvoo and migrate beyond the United States into the Great Basin on the west side of the Rocky Mountains. "Far from Gentiles and oppression," Mormons meant to found a utopian nation freed from pressures to conform to the American majority. Instead, Mormons demanded conformity within their ranks to a dissident version of America.[153]

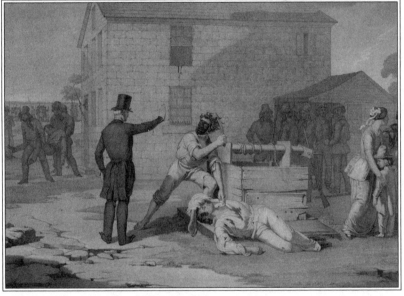

Clockwise from top left: "Elizabeth Cady Stanton (1815–1902), with her sons Daniel and Henry," photograph by unknown, 1848. Library of Congress 2006683458. *"Margaret Fuller (1810–1850)," engraving by unknown, 1840.* Library of Congress 2002712183. *"Martyrdom of Joseph and Hyrum Smith in Carthage Jail, June 27, 1844," lithograph by Charles G. Crehen, 1851. In this lithograph sympathetic to Mormons, rioters carry away Hyrum Smith's corpse in the background, while a well-dressed angel halts the mutilation of Joseph Smith, Jr., in the foreground.* Library of Congress 96508302.

SIX ❧ MONSTERS

Starting in 1811, Henry Clay of Kentucky became the leading congressman of the next forty years. Clay's charisma compensated for a homely but amiable face and lank, rambling gait. He fought duels, flirted shamelessly, drank heavily, told wry jokes, and played cards and the fiddle. A prim lady commiserated with Clay's wife, Lucretia: "Isn't it a pity that he gambles so much?" Lucretia replied, "I don't know, he usually wins." Henry Clay attracted throngs to hear and see his animated speeches. An admirer recalled, "Mr. Clay's voice has prodigious power, compass, and richness. . . .

He is aware of its seduction, and exerts it with great effect." Save for
Andrew Jackson, almost everyone liked Clay, even John C. Calhoun,
a rival who concluded, "I wouldn't speak to him, but, by God! I love
him."[1]

Although his style was southern, Clay championed a political economy that appealed to Yankees. Unlike the Old Republicans, Clay
favored a robust national government that could accelerate economic
development. Regarding industry and agriculture as synergetic,
rather than competitors, Clay urged an "American System" that promoted both. That system featured a national bank, high tariffs to protect industries, and federal funding for internal improvements—river
and harbor enhancements, and new turnpikes, bridges, and canals.
In Clay's American System, farmers would feed a growing domestic
market of urban manufacturers, who made the tools and clothing
needed by those farmers. By linking regions through long-distance
commerce, Clay hoped to dissolve the tensions that threatened the
Union: "to make us really and truly one family—one community in
interest and in feeling."[2]

Devoted to the American Colonization Society, Clay defended the
eroding middle position in politics on the divisive issue of slavery.
Fifty enslaved people worked his Ashland plantation near Lexington,
but Clay disliked slavery in principle. Hostile to abolitionism as too
radical, he favored gradually ridding America of both slavery and
Black people.[3]

During the early 1820s, Calhoun shared Clay's nationalism but not
his qualms about slavery. The great political theorist of South Caro-

*Opposite, clockwise from top left: "John C. Calhoun (1782–1850)," engraving
by A. L. Dick, 1830.* Library of Congress 91705240. *"Henry Clay (1777–1852),"
engraving by Peter Maverick after a painting by Charles Bird King, 1822.*
Library of Congress 2013645296. *"Francis Scott Key (1780–1843)," engraving by an
unknown artist, n.d.* LC 2004672074 (LC-USZ62-53017). *"Osceola (1804–1838),"
engraving by George Catlin, 1838.* LC 96508305 (LC-DIG-pga-00467).

lina, Calhoun championed liberty but only for white men. Harder-working than Clay, Calhoun was less likable. Legalistic, learned, and humorless, Calhoun lacked imagination beyond political theory. A joke insisted that he had tried to compose a poem but could not get past his first word, "Whereas." Clay described Calhoun as "careworn, with furrowed brow, haggard and intensely gazing." Tall and gaunt with bushy eyebrows and a square jaw that rarely smiled, he struck an observer as a "cast-iron man, who looks as if he had never been born."[4]

Andrew Jackson also claimed nationalism as his mandate for seeking federal power, but he expressed a nationalism defined by emotion rather than policies. Jackson posed as the paragon of integrity, candor, and courage, unwilling to trim his opinions or actions to satisfy or serve anyone else: "I have an opinion of my own on all subjects, and when that opinion is formed, I persue it *publickly*, regardless of who goes with me. . . . I please myself by doing that which I believe to be right." So he had never "engaged in a political combination of any kind—or for any purpose." Jackson appealed to masculine pride: "We are the free born sons of America; the citizens of the only republic now existing in the world; and the only people on earth who possess rights, liberties, and property which they dare to call their own." But he warned that Americans' freedom had insidious enemies: Britons, Indians, and rebel slaves. Jackson had a special talent for making liberty and power seem visceral and in conflict.[5]

Although Jackson acquired wealth in land and slaves, he kept the common touch, including blunt writing that overrode spelling, grammar, and nuance. He cast his political campaigns as crusades to protect common men from elitists and their special interests. His enemies unwittingly contributed to his popularity by mocking the general's manners and words as vulgar.[6]

Bargains

In the presidential race of 1824, Clay, Calhoun, and Jackson faced competition from the secretary of the treasury, William H. Crawford of Georgia, and the secretary of state, John Quincy Adams of Massachusetts. Recognizing Jackson's superior popularity sooner than the other rivals, Calhoun dropped out of the presidential race to seek the vice presidency on a ticket with Jackson. In September 1823, Jackson also got a lucky break when his chief competitor for the southern vote, Crawford, suffered a stroke that slurred his speech and dimmed his vision.[7]

In the election, Jackson won a plurality, rather than a majority, of the popular and Electoral College vote. In the crucial Electoral College tally, Jackson had 99 votes to 84 for Adams, 41 for Crawford, and 37 for Clay. With his primary support in the South, Jackson benefited from the Federal Constitution's three-fifths clause. Without it, Adams would have led in the Electoral College by 83 to 77 votes. Jackson was the candidate of slavery as well as democracy.[8]

Because no candidate had captured a majority, the Federal Constitution stipulated that the House of Representatives would choose among the top three vote-getters. In lobbying congressmen, Adams had the advantage over Jackson of greater familiarity as a Washington insider. Jackson's militarism and violence also unnerved legislators. Clay worried that the general would become a dictator and lead the nation onto "the fatal road which has conducted every other republic to ruin." Favoring Adams as sounder in policy and more stable in personality, Clay helped him win the presidency on February 9, 1825. In return, Adams made Clay secretary of state, the primary cabinet position for seeking the presidency.[9]

Although a Jackson intermediary had offered the same deal to Clay and been rebuffed, the general seethed with self-righteous fury: "So you see, the *Judas* of the West has closed the contract and will receive the thirty pieces of silver. His end will be the same." In the Bible, Judas hanged himself in remorse over betraying Jesus. Jackson's newspapers also howled with outrage, and local protests burned 153 effigies of Clay. In the long run, Adams and Clay helped Jackson pose as the champion of a people betrayed by a "corrupt bargain" among political insiders.[10]

In December 1825, Adams announced an ambitious nationalist program. Rejecting the Old Republican antithesis between liberty and power, the president declared, "Liberty is power." He sought federal funding for roads, canals, harbors, a national university, and even an astronomical observatory. Although he got neither university nor observatory, Adams persuaded Congress to spend as much on internal improvements in four years as had been funded during the preceding twenty-four years.[11]

Frosty and reserved, Adams lacked the popular touch. He disliked the many seekers of office and favor who called on him at the White House: "They crawl upon one like a nest of spiders." A young congressman noted, "His manners are so distant and anti-republican and his nature so austere" that close acquaintance cost him "all the friends whom at a distance his political reputation has acquired." In 1826, his foes won control of Congress and proceeded to demonize and block everything that Adams proposed. "The best actions of my life make me nothing but enemies," he reflected. Adams's nationalism provoked most southerners to rally around Jackson. They included Vice President Calhoun, who embraced states' rights with the fervor of a convert.[12]

Jackson also benefited from electoral management by Martin Van Buren of New York. A son of innkeepers, Van Buren was short, dapper in dress, polite, charming, and clever. Enjoying politics as a game of maneuvers and tricks, he favored only principles that helped him win the next election, earning the nickname "the Little Magician." Rejecting the Adams fantasy of nonpartisanship, Van Buren insisted, "We must always have party distinctions." A senator allegedly tried to pin Van Buren down by asking if the sun rose in the East. He replied, "Well I have often heard it to be the case but have never risen early enough to know." Van Buren delighted in telling this story to glory in his own cleverness. In body and temperament, he contrasted with the tall and fiery Jackson, but Van Buren was his perfect political partner. Jackson could play the blunt and uncompromising

Patriot above politics because he had the master manipulator working for him behind the show. Another politician marveled, "Van Buren glides along as smoothly as oil and as silently as a cat."[13]

Adopting the name "Democrats," Van Buren's party linked ambitious editors, operatives, and bankers throughout the Union to practice partisanship with a professionalism that overwhelmed Adams and his disorganized supporters. To support Jackson in the election of 1828, Van Buren revived Jefferson's coalition of "the planters of the South and the plain Republicans of the north." Van Buren did so by silencing the northern "clamour ag[ains]t Southern Influence and African Slavery" aroused by the Missouri controversy in 1819–1820. Democrats cultivated common white voters by endorsing their dislike of Blacks, moral reformers, and learned elitists. Democrats warned that liberating Blacks and giving them civil rights would devalue the freedom and citizenship of white men. A British visitor noted, "The more democratic the papers are in their general politics, the more indignant are they at all attempts to make their coloured brethren as free as themselves."[14]

Adams's supporters denounced Jackson as "a wild man" too crude and violent to respect laws and the Federal Constitution. Their newspapers listed Jackson's many duels, brawls, and executed militiamen— all thoughtfully accompanied with images of coffins. The critics did not count his Indian victims, for newspapers lacked enough column space, and most Americans wanted more dead Indians. A Jackson campaign ditty countered that the election was "Between J.Q. Adams who can write, and Andy Jackson who can fight." A savvy newspaperman concluded that the moralistic Adams imagined "man *as he should be*," while the Jackson campaign "appealed to him *as he is*."[15]

Most voters preferred the man who could fight. In the fall of 1828, Jackson captured 56 percent of the popular vote and 68 percent of the Electoral College. While Adams commanded New England and half of the Midwest, Jackson took the other half, swept the South, and captured Pennsylvania and New York: the two key states for his triumph. Democrats also won control of Congress. The heated campaign produced an unprecedented turnout: a million voters. Indeed, Jackson captured three times as many votes as all the candidates combined in 1824. But Jackson's victory was no pure triumph for democracy: he got 73 percent of the popular vote in the slave states but only 50 percent in the free states.[16]

Although only sixty-one in 1828, Jackson suffered from old dueling wounds, advancing rheumatism, clogged lungs, lost teeth, and chronic dysentery. After years of smoking, his coughing fits produced, in Jackson's words, "great quantities of slime." Never serene, he became more irritable from severe pain and quack treatments. His rage grew as Adams supporters dredged up and published old slanders about the adulterous origins of his marriage to Rachel Donelson. Uneasy in high society, the plain Rachel felt depressed at the prospect of becoming the first lady. "I assure you," she told a friend, "I had rather be a doorkeeper in the house of God than to live in that palace at Washington." God answered her prayers. In late December 1828, between Jackson's election and inauguration, Rachel died of heart failure. Shaken by his loss, Jackson blamed her death on the campaign slanders by his political enemies, especially Henry Clay. There would be hell for them to pay.[17]

Jackson had campaigned against special interests that misused access to government to further enrich themselves, but his political lieutenants coveted the federal patronage. Firing half of the presidential appointees, which was then unprecedented, Jackson claimed that he cleansed the government of corruption, but his appointees fell short of his promises. The new customs collector of New York City, Samuel Swartwout, managed to steal over a million dollars before fleeing the country. Jackson's patronage policy became known as the "spoils system" because a supporter had declared, "To the victor belonged the spoils."[18]

Parlors

Only men served in government, but their wives and daughters could exercise influence by managing the social settings that drew politicians together. After the War of 1812, Washington developed a lively social scene of daytime visits for tea and evening balls, dinner parties, and theater performances. By making and accepting social visits, elite women created bonds that built trust between their husbands. A leading Washington socialite, Margaret Bayard Smith, calculated that in three weeks she received 197 visitors.[19]

Social networks counteracted the impersonal rigidity demanded by pure republicanism, which mandated that every politician act as a defiant individual defending liberty by refusing to cooperate with power. But no government could function if everyone stuck to that impossible ideal, for politicians needed to make deals to win elections and secure legislation. In parlors and dining rooms, wives and mothers convened politicians to make connections, build trust, and gather gossip. Slight, sickly, shy, and brainy, James Madison benefited from his charming, festive, and fashionable wife, Dolly Madison, who wore a feathered turban at parties. A British diplomat thought she acted and looked "every inch a queen." The somber John Quincy Adams also relied on his gracious and talented wife, Louisa Catherine Adams, who convened parties, where she sang and played piano and harp. She once invited over five hundred guests, including almost every member of Congress.[20]

The influence of elite women grew in association with the "restrained manhood" of husbands who practiced self-discipline and sought moral improvement in society. Such men promoted schools, churches, and reform societies. Treating wives with respect, they avoided gambling, drinking, and profanity. In politics most gravitated toward the Whigs, and in foreign policy they favored overseas trade, persuasive diplomacy, and religious missions rather than war. Most restrained men were middle-class Protestants, who were especially numerous in the Northeast.[21]

But more American men practiced "martial manhood," which demanded self-assertion rather than self-discipline. Martial men displayed their prowess at drinking, gambling, and fighting. They meant to protect their wives as dependents within patriarchal households. At the national level, they favored aggressive expansion at the expense of Indians, enslaved people, and Britons. Drawn from southern planters, common farmers, and working-class immigrants, these men felt at home in the Democratic Party—and irritated by the moralizing Whigs.[22]

As the most martial of men, Jackson disdained parlor politics as aristocratic and contrary to the plain simplicity and perfect rectitude of his idealized republic. Mourning the loss of his beloved wife, Jackson blamed her death on scandalmongering that originated in social gossip. Nor could he tolerate female participation in politics, no matter how indirect.[23]

At the start of his term, Jackson faced a crisis over Margaret O'Neale Timberlake Eaton, the new bride of his friend and secretary of war, John Eaton. A tavern keeper's daughter, Margaret grew up in Washington and, at age sixteen, had married a naval officer, John Timberlake. During his long absences, she took several lovers, including Eaton, who boarded at her family's tavern. In April 1828, Timberlake committed suicide, apparently in misery over her affairs. Nine months later, she married Eaton, who then tried to introduce her into the capital's high society. A scandalized insider marveled, "Eaton has just married his mistress, and the mistress of eleven doz[en] others!" Brash, talkative, voluptuous, and assertive, Margaret did not conform to genteel expectations.[24]

By refusing to socialize with the couple, political wives upheld their moral power to regulate respectability by excluding the undeserving. They would neither call on Margaret nor accept her invitations. If they found her at a party, they snubbed her with the silent treatment or stormed out to make a scene, drawing their husbands away with them. The so-called "Peggy Eaton affair" threatened to derail the new administration as John Eaton kept busy challenging his wife's male critics to duels. The challenged included the secretary of the treasury and the pastor of the city's Presbyterian church. A friend warned Jackson about Margaret: "She will do more to injure your peace and your administration than one Hundred Henry Clays."[25]

As a senator during the early 1820s, Jackson had lodged with Margaret and her family. Seeing nothing untoward then, he refused to believe anyone else's testimony to the contrary. On the eve of his inauguration, some Washington insiders called on the president-elect to warn him that naming Eaton to the cabinet would lead to a social crisis. Jackson fumed: "I had not come here by the people's will to make a Cabinet for the fashionable ladies, but for the benefit of my country."[26]

Jackson saw Eaton's detractors as snobs, and he felt contempt for any man who followed his wife's lead in social life. The president equated Margaret with his late wife as fellow sufferers from malign slander. Margaret recalled, "He did not like or dislike people; he loved them or hated them." Loving Margaret as a surrogate daughter, Jackson assembled his cabinet and two clergymen in September 1829, when he announced, "She is as chaste as a virgin!" Clay mocked, "Age cannot wither nor time stale her infinite virginity."[27]

An old-fashioned patriarch, Jackson expected to control his cabinet members and for them to command their wives. If the president vouched for the Eatons, then everyone in his administration would have to fall into line and welcome them into high society. This included his nephew and secretary, Andrew Jackson Donelson, and the nephew's wife, Emily, who was the president's official hostess. When they refused to invite Margaret to the White House, Jackson exiled them to Tennessee.[28]

The controversy alienated Jackson from Vice President Calhoun, who stood by his imperious wife, Floride Bonneau Calhoun, who rallied elite women against Margaret. Calhoun praised their social boycott as a "great victory . . . in favor of the morals of our country, by the high-minded independence and virtue of the ladies of Washington." The president's fury grew when Van Buren dug up dirt on Calhoun and fed it to Jackson, who learned that, in cabinet meetings during 1818, Calhoun had denounced the general's invasion of Florida. "The plot is unmasked," Jackson declared.[29]

By exploiting the Eaton scandal, Van Buren supplanted Calhoun as Jackson's favored successor. A widower, Van Buren had no wife to snub the Eatons. By calling on them to show support, Van Buren impressed the president, who praised him as "a pure republican" laboring "to promote the best interests of his country," while Calhoun was driven "by selfish ambition" and "had secretly employed all his talents in intrigue and deception . . . to disgrace my administration." In fact, Calhoun was no match for Van Buren in the arts of intrigue and ambition.[30]

Van Buren resolved the crisis by persuading Jackson to compel his entire cabinet to resign in April 1831. That removed both the Eatons and their critics from the center of the social whirl. A New York newspaper marveled, "Well, indeed, may Mr. Van Buren be called 'The Great Magician' for *he raises his wand, and the whole Cabinet disappears.*" Jackson honored Van Buren with a prestigious diplomatic appointment and arranged for Eaton to become governor of Florida. Calhoun's allies in the old cabinet got nothing. By ousting the Eatons from high society, elite women won a battle; but Jackson won the war, gaining command of his cabinet and marginalizing Calhoun.[31]

Nullification

Forsaking his presidential hopes, Calhoun sought to renew his support in South Carolina by attacking the federal tariff of 1828, which southerners called the "tariff of abominations." Designed by Van Buren to advance Jackson's electoral prospects in the industrializing Middle Atlantic states, that law had raised an already protective tariff by 40 percent. By increasing the cost of imported manufactures, primarily from Britain, a high tariff protected new American industries, but John Randolph mocked the law as designed to promote the manufacture of a president. South Carolinians howled that the increased tariff reduced the income of cotton plantations by about 20 percent.[32]

Calhoun revived the concept of state nullification first broached by Thomas Jefferson in the Kentucky Resolves of 1798. Calhoun insisted that the Federal Constitution was a compact among sovereign states to protect the interests of every state: "Ours was a federal Constitution—the states were its constituents, not the people." He argued that a protective tariff violated the Constitution by allowing a national majority to oppress a minority section: "An unchecked majority is a despotism." Calhoun claimed that an offended state could "interpose" between its citizens and the federal government by holding a special convention to nullify within its borders any federal law deemed unjust and unconstitutional.[33]

Although Jackson favored states' rights, he claimed to embody majority rule, so the president despised nullification and Calhoun. For once, Jackson agreed with the nationalist Daniel Webster of Massachusetts. Defining a democratic nationalism, Webster linked majority rule, individual liberty, and the Union of the states: "Liberty *and* Union, now and forever, one and inseparable."[34]

In 1832, Jackson signed a new tariff law that lowered many duties, but South Carolina refused to compromise, rejecting any protective tariff. In November, the state held a special convention that nullified the tariff laws of 1828 and 1832. The nullification ordinance also threatened secession if the federal government tried to collect customs duties in South Carolina. The legislature organized and armed 25,000 volunteers to defend the state's freemen from becoming the "slaves of wool-weavers and spindle-hurlers" of the North. A defiant nullifier declared, "The man who has owned slaves can never be made a slave" because of his "free spirit that has arisen from his habits of command."[35]

Jackson took nullification as a personal affront. On December 10, 1832, his proclamation denounced nullifiers for acting "in direct violation of their duty as citizens of the United States." In his second inaugural address, delivered on March 4, 1833, Jackson warned Americans that nullification and secession would compel their sons to become "soldiers to deluge with blood the fields they now till in peace. . . . The loss of liberty of all good government, of peace, plenty and happiness, must inevitably follow a dissolution of the Union."[36]

The president vowed to collect tariffs with military force and to punish resistance as treason: "I will hang the first man of them I can get my hands on to the first tree I can find." Thomas Hart Benton, warned a South Carolina senator, "I tell you, Hayne, when Jackson begins to talk about hanging, they can begin to look out for the ropes!" Congress backed Jackson by passing a "Force Bill" that authorized sending troops to uphold federal laws in South Carolina. The president reinforced the two federal forts in Charleston harbor and sent two warships to protect them.[37]

South Carolina counted on support from the other southern states, but they held back, satisfied with the tariff cuts of 1832. Nor did they relish confronting Jackson, who was popular in their states for fighting and expelling Indians. In 1833, the legislatures of eight southern states condemned nullification as unconstitutional. They recognized that the Union defended, rather than threatened, slavery. Robert J. Walker of Mississippi warned that nullification would lead to a civil war "and upon the ruins of this now happy Union might arise the darkest despotism that ever crushed the liberties of mankind." Although opposed to nullification, the other southern states balked at using armed force against South Carolina.[38]

In 1833, Clay sought to avert civil war by brokering another tariff law to lower some rates while promising an even greater cut in nine years. Calhoun supported the new law, which provided sufficient cover for South Carolinians to recede from confrontation. The state's

convention met again in March to declare victory, repeal its nullification of federal tariff laws, and then, in a final gesture of defiance,
nullify the Force Bill, although that law had become moot.[39]

The nullification crisis revealed a polarization over interpreting
the Federal Constitution. Most northerners vowed to fight for their
constitutional theory of a permanent and paramount Union. That
theory troubled southerners, who claimed a theoretical right for any
state to secede if mistreated by the national majority. A South Carolinian declared, "Nullification has done its work. It has prepared the
minds of men for a separation of the States." Jackson expected that
South Carolina eventually would "blow up a storm on the subject of
the slavery question" and "destroy the Union."[40]

Terror-Death

Jackson's defense of majority rule pleasantly surprised many northerners, but most southerners understood that on every issue save nullification, the president defended slavery and states' rights. In 1833,
the abolitionist Lydia Maria Child denounced the apparent resolution of the nullification crisis as hollow. She insisted that the political
posturing and compromising kept 15 percent of Americans in slavery: a "third party, which is never heard or noticed, except for purposes of oppression." She argued that to avert civil war, the Union
had to abolish slavery: "Who does not see that the American people
are walking over a subterranean fire, the flames of which are fed by
slavery?"[41]

Jackson, however, sought to preserve the Union by helping South
Carolina suppress abolitionists and harass free Blacks. In 1822, in the
wake of the Denmark Vesey plot, the state had ordered the jailing of
all free Blacks on arriving merchant ships for the duration of their
visit. This Negro Seaman Act violated the Federal Constitution,
which required every state to afford equal rights to visiting citizens
from every other state. The act also struck at the interest of northern

merchants, who employed Black sailors as cheap and reliable. In 1825, President Adams had appealed to South Carolina to repeal its law, but the state legislators refused to budge. When Jackson came to power, his attorney general, Roger B. Taney of Maryland, vindicated South Carolina by asserting that no Black man could ever be a citizen of the United States: "The African race in the United States, even when free, are everywhere a degraded class, and exercise no political influence. . . . They were not looked upon as citizens by the contracting parties who formed the Constitution." In vain, northerners pointed out that their states had, indeed, recognized free Blacks as citizens during the revolution. In 1836, Jackson rewarded Taney by appointing him chief justice of the Supreme Court, replacing the recently deceased John Marshall.[42]

Southern leaders overreacted to abolitionists from a dread that any agitation could provoke a massive slave revolt that would destroy their lives and way of life. A Mississippi newspaper denounced abolitionists as "fiend-like fanatics" stirring up "the infuriated slave to fire his master's dwelling, and glory in the ruin of families perishing in the flames." Insistently repeated, this lurid fantasy of murderous Black brutes became a southern conviction.[43]

As the price of continued union, southerners demanded northern silence on slavery. In 1836, Mississippi governor John Quitman insisted, "The morality, the expediency, and the duration of the institution of slavery are questions, which belong exclusively to ourselves." Boasting that his valet John would never leave, even if offered "a thousand freedoms" by abolitionists, Quitman took him north on a vacation trip to Rhode Island, where John escaped.[44]

James Henry Hammond of South Carolina wanted northern states to extradite abolitionists to the South for trial and execution: "These men can be silenced in but one way, *Terror-death*. . . . This is the *only remedy. This alone can save the Union.*" When northern states balked at extraditing their citizens to the gallows, southerners urged northern Democrats to organize "a little more mob discipline" to disrupt abolitionist meetings and smash their newspapers.[45]

Northern leaders of "property and standing" did denounce abolitionists for allegedly promoting "insurrection and anarchy, and ultimately, a disseverment of our prosperous Union." A Pennsylvania congressman declared, "The Union I hold to be of more value than the freedom of all the negroes that have ever lived in it." The defenders of slavery and Union insisted that, by including women and Blacks in their groups, abolitionists threatened forms of inequality needed to maintain social order. Opponents luridly accused abolitionists of promoting interracial marriage and mixed-race offspring.[46]

During the 1830s, northern mobs attacked abolitionist meetings and African-American neighborhoods. In New York City in 1834, white rioters tore down sixty structures including six churches. "Throughout the night the screams of tortured Negroes could be heard," a witness reported. In Connecticut in September 1834, a mob destroyed a boarding school for Black girls run by the Quaker teacher Prudence Crandall. In the peak year, 1835, racists mounted forty-six riots, including one in Boston, where a mob nearly lynched William Lloyd Garrison.[47]

One night in August 1835, a young enslaved man, Arthur Bowen, attended a secret antislavery meeting with other African Americans in Washington, D.C. Drinking on his return home, Bowen grew more resentful of his owner, Anna Thornton. She was the widow of William Thornton, the architect who designed the Capitol and the probable father of the mixed-race Bowen. That paternity apparently highlighted the arbitrary nature of slavery for the young man. Confronting the widow with an axe in his hand, Bowen shouted, "I've got just as much right to freedom as you!" His mother intervened to push Bowen away, and a few days later he surrendered to the police. Defiant, Bowen told them, "We *ought* to be free, and we *will* be free. And if we are not, there is going to be such confusion and bloodshed as to astonish the world." He was a prophet. Unfortunately, that August, the city had many angry white men with time on their hands, for hundreds of mechanics at the Navy Yard were on strike. Hating Black workers as cheap competition for jobs, the strikers tried to break open the jail to lynch Bowen, but marines drove them off.[48]

Washington's district attorney was Francis Scott Key, who had written the "Star-Spangled Banner," an anthem with a verse denigrating runaway slaves who helped the British during the War of 1812. Blaming abolitionists for agitating Bowen, Key arrested a newcomer from Connecticut, a doctor named Reuben Crandall (the brother of Prudence), who had a trunk full of antislavery newspapers and pamphlets. Key charged Crandall with trying "to excite sedition and insurrection among the slaves." The Navy Yard mechanics returned to the jail in hopes of hanging Crandall, or at least cutting off his ears, but again left empty-handed when confronted by city militia.[49]

A mob of 400 men moved on to attack Beverly Snow, the free Black owner of a popular oyster house, charging him with insulting white women. The real provocations were that Snow had married one and had prospered, owning more property, and dressing better, than the white mechanics. "Snow will certainly be torn to pieces by the mechanics if he be caught," a resident noted. He escaped by hiding in a sewer, but the rioters trashed his business and home, three schools for African Americans, a church, a brothel, and the homes of prosperous Black activists. The riot became known as the August "Snow-Storm."[50]

The drunken rioters acted with impunity so long as they limited their attacks to Black people. When they began to menace the homes of wealthy whites, including Key, the city government called out the militia. The city refused to compensate the riot's victims and passed an ordinance barring African Americans from assembling after dark. President Jackson met with the leading rioters and vowed "to promote their happiness" by cracking down on free Blacks who violated restrictions on their lives.[51]

In 1836, Key prosecuted Bowen and Crandall. A jury convicted

Bowen of attempted murder, but the president let Anna Thornton sell him far away to Florida, where the territorial governor, John Eaton, brokered the transaction. At Crandall's trial, Key upheld "the right of the whole slaveholding community to self-protection" against the "friends of human rights and [racial] amalgamation." The jury acquitted Crandall for want of evidence that he had circulated antislavery writings to Black people. But he left jail a broken man, dying two years later of tuberculosis contracted during his eight months of confinement.[52]

In the wake of riots and trials, Washington whites increased their legal restrictions on free Blacks, enforcing a curfew on them at night and refusing them licenses to run shops. "If they wish to live here, let them become subordinates and laborers, as nature has designed," a newspaper insisted. Snow fled north to Toronto, where he prospered as a restauranteur in a city without slavery. He helped found the Upper Canada Anti-Slavery Society, which assisted fugitives from the United States.[53]

In 1836 in St. Louis, a mob broke into the city jail to seize a Black man suspected of killing a white. Chained to a large tree by the mob, the African American burned to death. A judge aptly named Luke E. Lawless exonerated the lynch mob and encouraged them next to destroy an antislavery newspaper edited by the Reverend Elijah Lovejoy. That editor fled across the Mississippi to Alton, Illinois, but another mob smashed the new press and shot Lovejoy in 1837.[54]

In 1838 in Philadelphia, rioters attacked Pennsylvania Hall, newly built by abolitionists for their meetings. The rioters felt offended by an antislavery convention that mingled both genders and races as equals, which one newspaper denounced as "an open violation of *common decency*—the association of *black and white*—male and female." Another newspaper said that abolitionists provoked bystanders by walking "Whites and blacks, arm-in-arm" through the streets. Handbills were passed around the city to rally angry citizens to defend "the right of property and the preservation of the

Constitution" by breaking up the convention. Smashing windows and breaking down the door, rioters drove out the abolitionists and torched the building. White firemen assembled to protect adjoining buildings but let the Hall burn to the ground, while 30,000 people watched and cheered.[55]

Gags

In 1835, abolitionists sent a mass mailing to Charleston, South Carolina, but the city's federal postmaster locked up the tracts to enforce a state law against circulating antislavery works. Then a mob broke into the post office to seize the tracts for burning before a hooting crowd of 2,000. Although Jackson disliked that mob action, he denounced abolitionists for "exciting the negroes to insurrection and to massacre," so he concluded that they should "atone for this wicked attempt with their lives." He insisted that "peace within our borders . . . depends on the maintenance of good faith of those compromises of the constitution upon which the Union is founded." He directed all southern post offices to intercept and impound the "unconstitutional and wicked" publications of abolitionists.[56]

Southern leaders also sought to suppress petitions in favor of abolition submitted to Congress, lest they become part of the public record and reach enslaved people to provoke a race war. Calhoun concluded, "Abolition and Union cannot coexist." In 1836, Congress adopted a "gag rule" that tabled every petition broaching the issue of slavery, thereby precluding discussion. This alone, Van Buren argued, could restore "the harmony of our happy Union."[57]

Defending their right to petition, outraged abolitionists submitted more petitions signed by additional thousands: 414,000, including 201,000 women, during the session of 1837–1838. Female petitioners outraged conservatives, who saw a double threat to social order by questioning gender as well as racial constraints. Congressional critics mocked the signers as "old grannies and a parcel of boarding-school misses," who acted like men rather than "attend to knitting their own hose and darning their stockings." The critics ridiculed male abolitionists as "imbecile, timid men," dominated by assertive women.[58]

The gag rule enraged John Quincy Adams, the former president who now represented Massachusetts in Congress. Adams marveled, "Slavery and democracy . . . would seem to be incompatible with each other. And yet at this time, the democracy of the country is supported chiefly, if not entirely by slavery." He championed the right of every American, Black and white, female and male, to petition Congress for redress. By reframing the issue in terms of free speech, Adams put southerners on the defensive.[59]

A master of legislative procedures and debate, Adams alarmed southern leaders, who called him "the acutest, the astutest, the archest enemy of Southern slavery that ever existed." After Adams humiliated Thomas Marshall of Kentucky in congressional debate, Marshall confided: "I wish I were dead. I do. I would rather die a thousand deaths than again to encounter that old man."[60]

As a lawyer Adams helped defend fifty-three enslaved Africans who had seized control of their slave ship, the Spanish schooner *Amistad*, sailing along the coast of Cuba in 1839. Led by Cinqué, they had killed the captain and tried to sail back to Africa. Instead, they landed on the coast of Long Island, New York. President Van Buren had them arrested and charged with murder, mutiny, and piracy, but abolitionists financed their defense. In 1840, the federal district court in Connecticut ruled in favor of the Africans, but the Van Buren administration appealed to the Supreme Court, where Adams argued for the Africans' "natural right to liberty." In 1841 the court freed them for return to Africa, but only thirty-five had survived their imprisonment.[61]

The gag rule, the dignity of the *Amistad* defendants, and violence against abolitionists soured many northerners against slavery. An abolitionist explained: "Instead of putting us down, they put us and our principles up before the world—just where we wanted to be."

Another claimed that violence did more than "a thousand lecturers to convince the sober and disinterested, that slavery is a crime." The 200 antislavery societies of 1835 multiplied to 1,000 by 1837.[62]

Most northerners wanted to leave slavery alone in the South, but they felt insulted by southern efforts to silence them. They concluded that southerners meant "to crucify the freedom of the free, in order to secure the continued slavery of the slave." A northern newspaper noted that "the actual slavery of one portion of a people must eventually lead to the virtual slavery of the other." Critics derided northern Democrats who supported the gag rule and antiabolitionist violence as "doughfaces," as "northern men with southern principles." Put on the defensive, most northern Democrats joined Adams and the Whigs to defeat the gag rule in 1844. By overreacting to abolitionists, who had been weak, southerners provoked a broad northern reaction far more dangerous to southern political power in the Union.[63]

Bank War

Between 1815 and 1830, the American economy grew at an unprecedented rate with help from a boom in new banks created by the states. In 1790, the United States had only three commercial banks; by 1835 that rose to 584. In the absence of federal paper money, printed banknotes provided an expanding money supply that improved on barter or book accounting to facilitate transactions.[64]

But the reckless management of many banks undercut the value of their notes. Insecure in the value of their wages or pay for their crops, workers and farmers distrusted banknotes, suspecting wealthy bankers of manipulating the currency with the help of political friends. Bankers became intertwined with politicians who could grant or withhold incorporation, often in exchange for shares or loans granted to helpful leaders. Barely regulated by state governments, banks often loaned out more in notes than their assets could sustain. All then came crashing down when the economy went bust in a depression, leaving farmers and artisans with worthless notes. They then could lose their livestock, shops, and farms to lawsuits and foreclosure.[65]

The federal Bank of the United States (BUS) could provide some regulatory stability. Chartered in 1816 for a twenty-year term, the federal bank was a private-public partnership in which the government held a fifth of its stock and appointed a fifth of the directors. The rest belonged to wealthy investors, primarily from northeastern cities. Based in Philadelphia, the BUS possessed branches in many states and had a capital that dwarfed that of state banks. By offering loans to businessmen throughout the country, the federal bank promoted economic development. In payments for those loans, the BUS received many state banknotes. The BUS regulated state banks by demanding payment in specie on notes from institutions deemed reckless. If they failed to pay, state banks could collapse, weeding out the weakest institutions. In effect, the BUS could expand or contract the nation's money supply to either boost a lagging economy or restrain one overheated by inflation. While valuable to the economy as a whole, this regulatory power could ruin the investors in weak banks and the holders of their notes.[66]

During the depression of 1819, when many businesses and state banks failed, critics blamed the BUS: "The bank was saved, but the people were ruined." Missouri senator Thomas Hart Benton added, "All the flourishing cities of the West are mortgaged to this money power. . . . They are in the jaws of the monster! A lump of butter in the mouth of a dog! One gulp, one swallow, and all is gone!"[67]

Critics derided the president of the federal bank, Nicholas Biddle of Philadelphia, as a wealthy, well-educated elitist. A graduate of Princeton at age fifteen and the editor of a literary magazine, Biddle patronized the fine arts and hosted genteel dinner parties. At a time when few Americans other than sailors went overseas, he had toured London, Paris, and Greece. Flaunting his brilliance, Biddle lacked common sense in politics, making him a tempting villain for Andrew Jackson, who dreaded "the Monster Bank."[68]

Believing in Old Republicanism rather than modern econom-
ics, Jackson despised any government investment in, or regulation
of, commerce as "corrupt" for playing favorites. He vetoed bills for
federal funding of internal improvements if he thought the money
would benefit his foes, especially Clay. Yet Jackson approved other
internal improvement bills that favored his own supporters. Thrilled
by the president's stirring rhetoric, most voters did not much care
about his inconsistencies and pettiness. A congressman protested one
veto until he heard from his district and concluded that Jackson knew
"his constituents better than he himself had known them."[69]

But Clay thought that he knew best of all. Preparing to run against
Jackson for the presidency in 1832, Clay sought to make the BUS the
central issue. Although the bank's federal charter would not expire
until 1836, Clay persuaded Biddle to apply for a new charter in January 1832. Six months later, Congress approved renewal. An outraged
Jackson told his secretary of state, "The bank, Mr. Van Buren, is trying to kill me, *but I will kill it*."[70]

A week later, Jackson vetoed the recharter bill and blasted the BUS
as an unconstitutional "concentration of power in the hands of a few
men irresponsible to the people." Playing to popular Anglophobia,
Jackson implied that British investors controlled the BUS and manipulated the economy to subvert American independence. Jackson
exaggerated the number of British investors and ignored their exclusion from the institution's governance. Ultimately, Jackson played the
class card: "The rich and powerful too often bend the acts of government to their selfish purposes" at the expense of "the humble members of society—the farmers, mechanics, and laborers—who have
neither the time nor the means of securing like favors." By crushing
the monstrous bank, Jackson promised to make the economy fair at
last. American politicians thrive by claiming to defend democracy
against a conspiracy of elitists.[71]

Jackson's veto message shocked Biddle as "a manifesto of anarchy" expressing "all the fury of a chained panther biting the bars

of his cage." But Jackson chose his enemies carefully, targeting the BUS rather than all bankers. Indeed, his crusade won support from wealthy men who had invested in state banks that would benefit from destroying their primary competitor and regulator. These included New York's Wall Street bankers, who sought to replace Philadelphia as the nation's financial center.[72]

As Clay had hoped, the presidential election of 1832 became a referendum on Jackson's domineering style, especially his Bank veto. Clay's Whig supporters denounced Jackson as "King Andrew the First," a ruthless tyrant who trampled on constitutional precedents to become a dictator. Relishing that fight, Democrats reprinted the Bank veto message as their entire party platform. Both parties cast the other as a dire threat to republicanism. In the end, most voters chose Jackson as their champion to save the republic. He won 54 percent of the popular vote and 219 Electoral College votes compared to just 49 for Clay. In the South, 88 percent of the voters favored Jackson.[73]

A sore winner, Jackson punished his enemies, especially Biddle, who had subsidized Clay's failed campaign. Without seeking congressional approval, Jackson pulled federal deposits from the BUS, allegedly to prevent it from "destroy[ing] the vote of the people lately given at the ballot box." To complete that withdrawal, Jackson had to fire two successive secretaries of the treasury who protested his violation of laws requiring the government to deposit its funds in the BUS. In September 1833, Jackson appointed the pliable Roger Taney to the treasury, and he pulled the funds and placed them in state institutions run by Democrats. They included a Baltimore bank in which Taney invested and served as legal counsel. While claiming to fight corruption manifested by the BUS, Jackson opened up a new font of patronage for the Democrats in the so-called "pet banks." Biddle seethed: "This worthy President thinks that because he has scalped Indians and imprisoned Judges he is to have his way with the Bank."[74]

By eliminating regulation by the BUS and empowering "pet banks," Jackson unwittingly flooded the economy with state banknotes that fueled a speculative boom with inflated money. Too late, Jackson regretted "the paper system & gambling menace that pervades our land & must if not checked ruin our country & our liberty." His solution of requiring payment in gold or silver for federal lands reversed the economy into deflation in 1837. Other than the symbolic thrill of smiting the elitist Biddle, common men reaped no benefit from the Bank War. Instead, state bankers and Democratic insiders reaped windfall profits and wrenched the economy between inflation and deflation.[75]

An immigrant house painter, Richard Lawrence, blamed his unemployment on Jackson's destruction of the federal bank. On January 30, 1835, Lawrence became the first person to try to assassinate an American president. Surprising Jackson at an exit from the Capitol, Lawrence fired a pistol, but the gunpowder fizzled because of the damp day. A bystander tackled Lawrence, while Jackson waved his heavy cane and bellowed, "Let me get him!"[76]

Interrogated by the district attorney, Francis Scott Key, Lawrence insisted that he was the rightful heir to the British throne and that Jackson had murdered his royal father. In April, Key secured Lawrence's incarceration in a mental asylum, where he spent his last twenty-six years. That verdict dismayed Jackson, who considered Lawrence as rational as he was. Surely, Jackson thought, the trigger man served a conspiracy of political enemies led by a Mississippi senator, George Poindexter. The Senate investigated and cleared Poindexter, but Mississippi's legislators retired him from the Senate to show gratitude to Jackson for his help in getting rid of their Indians.[77]

Indian Removal

Jackson sought to expel Indians and sell their lands as rapidly and cheaply as possible to afford every white "citizen of enterprise the opportunity of securing an independent freehold." Democrats meant to disperse white men across the expanding country as landowners free from domination by an employer or landlord. Senator Benton asserted, "The public lands belong to the People, and not to the federal government." Benton accused Whigs of discouraging cheap western land in order to please eastern industrialists, who wanted to retain a large pool of cheap laborers. He thundered that Whigs wanted to keep "the vast and magnificent valley of the Mississippi for the haunts of beasts and savages."[78]

Democrats insisted that broad land ownership sustained relative equality—without which free government would collapse. They dreaded that industrial and urban growth would concentrate wealth in the hands of a few men while poverty spread among their many dependent employees crowded into urban ghettoes. Democrats insisted that western land should offer a "safety valve" to release social tensions in the East before they exploded into class warfare. Democrats reasoned that even workers who stayed home benefited from a westward migration that reduced the number of urban laborers and thereby pushed up wages for the rest. An Illinois congressman warned that if the government slowed western settlement, "white slavery will be substituted for black. . . . Wherever corporations rule, the great mass of the people are enslaved." Lacking empathy for enslaved Blacks, Democrats wanted to avert dependence for white men.[79]

Whigs preferred to slow western expansion because they favored concentrating people and capital for economic development—rather than dispersing both in many new settlements. A leading Whig claimed, "The creation of capital is retarded rather than accelerated by the diffusion of a thin population over a great surface of soil." To slow western settlement, Whigs favored higher prices for public lands. That policy also promised to increase the federal revenue for Whigs to fund roads, canals, and railroads meant to increase commerce and unite Americans. During the 1830s, however, the Democratic vision prevailed, mandating cheap land, which increased the pressure of settlement on Indian lands.[80]

Jackson longed to remove all eastern Indians westward beyond the Mississippi and "extinguish the Indian title to all lands lying within the states composing our federal union." He regarded Native domains as intrusions within the American Union and as lingering security threats that the British and runaway slaves could activate. Yet, he also rejected proposals by some Indians to "seek their own country beyond the limits of the United States" as he wanted "to keep our Indians within our own limits." Beyond American bounds, Jackson feared, Indians could renew their armed resistance by allying with a foreign power. He meant to confine Indians on shrinking reservations deep within the country, where their sovereignty would dissolve. In his view, American security required isolating Indians from foreign influence, terminating Native nations, and absorbing the survivors "in the mass of our population."[81]

Jackson cast Natives as barbarians hostile to civilization. He insisted that no sensible person "would prefer a country covered with forests and ranged by a few thousand savages" over a Union "occupied by more than 12,000,000 happy people and filled with all the blessings of liberty, civilization, and religion." Jackson underestimated Native cultures and overestimated the happiness of Americans. He claimed that in the West "wandering savages" could "pursue happiness in their own way and under their own rude institutions."[82]

Long before Jackson's presidency, the federal government had pressured Natives to make treaties that ceded land in return for initial presents followed by small annual payments. Indian reservations soared in land value as they became enveloped by settlements. Settlers and land speculators then called on the federal government to remove all Indians living east of the Mississippi. In principle, removal was supposed to be voluntary, but the government coerced Natives by declining to protect them from invading settlers. A critic of removal explained that Indians reluctantly sold what "would otherwise be taken by force."[83]

To escape encroaching settlers, some Indians did move west, but most clung to their homelands by making the most of the plows, livestock, spinning wheels, and forges that the federal government provided to promote the American way of life. In the southeast, Cherokees, Chickasaws, Choctaws, Creeks, and Seminoles developed farms and plantations with livestock and enslaved people. These Natives built mills and roads and embraced literacy and Christianity with the help of Protestant missionaries. Cherokees even created a syllabary for their language and published a newspaper.[84]

While adopting selected aspects of American culture, Indians intended to remain sovereign nations allied to, rather than erased by, the United States. Indians adapted as nations so that they would not have to assimilate as individuals submerged within American society. Cherokees, Choctaws, and Creeks replaced their dispersed village and clan chiefs with central governments on the American model. The new regimes made collective laws and established police forces and courts to punish crimes, including the treason of selling land to Americans. The Native nations expected Americans to honor their treaties by protecting Indian lands. Cherokees reminded federal officials "that the Cherokees are not foreigners, but original inhabitants of America."[85]

Indians' adaptations made them more persistent, undercutting the self-serving prophecy of Americans that Natives were doomed to extinction. Calhoun noted, "The great difficulty arises from the progress of the Cherokees in civilization. They are now, within the limits of Georgia, about fifteen thousand, and . . . all cultivators, with a representative government, judicial courts, Lancaster schools, and permanent property." For Calhoun this was a "great difficulty" because it made them harder to move. But southern leaders insisted that only a few mixed-race chiefs made the improvements while most Indians remained savages who wasted fertile land.[86]

In 1830, Native nations still held a tenth of Georgia, a sixth of Alabama, and half of Florida and Mississippi. As Indians improved their farms, those lands became even more alluring to white men who wanted to expand their cotton plantations. Although Native nations practiced slavery, southern whites distrusted any alternative polity within their bounds as an invitation to runaways—and they worried that a safe haven for fugitives would entice all slaves to rebel. A Georgia newspaper warned that if "our savage neighbors may be allowed to abide in our bosom, our slaves may be filched from us."[87]

In February 1825, state and federal officials persuaded eight Creek chiefs, led by William McIntosh, to cede all of their nation's lands in western Georgia. For this cession, the United States paid $200,000 to the Creeks and $25,000 to McIntosh. Most of the Creeks disavowed the treaty as corrupt and made without their consent. They executed McIntosh and two other signers as traitors. The Creeks also appealed to the Adams administration, which invalidated the state treaty. Georgia's governor, George Troup, threatened Adams with civil war if federal troops enforced his decision as "the unblushing allies of the savages whose cause you have adopted."[88]

Backing down, Adams pressured the Creeks to make a new treaty that reserved 3 million acres for them and modestly increased their payment to $217,000. But Georgia refused to compromise, clinging to the original treaty by sending settlers and surveyors to seize the contested territory. That defiance exposed the impotence of the federal government. The secretary of war, James Barbour, concluded that Natives "see that our professions are insincere, that our promises are broken, that the happiness of the Indian is a cheap sacrifice to the acquisition of new lands."[89]

In 1827, Georgians moved to dispossess the Cherokees of 5.2 million acres by asserting legal jurisdiction over their lands and dissolving their government. Georgians claimed that they acted to control "barbarous and savage tribes." Denied sovereignty, Natives were merely Georgia's "tenants at her will," who could be evicted at any time. In 1830, the state barred Cherokees from holding meetings or entering into contracts with anyone. Alabama and Mississippi fol-

lowed Georgia's lead to dissolve Indian governments and land holdings. These states even forbade Indians from hunting, fishing, or
trapping.[90]

Because southern state laws barred Indians from testifying against
any white man, it became open season for settlers to rob Indians of
their cattle, horses, slaves, and farms—sometimes killing Natives who
resisted. In Alabama, a squatter exhorted his friends: "Now is the
time, or never! Hurrah boys! Here goes it! Let's steal all we can." A
popular song in Georgia declared:

All I want in this creation
Is a pretty little wife and a big plantation
Away up yonder in the Cherokee nation

In a common swindle, a white man forged a promissory note made
out to him and allegedly signed by an Indian—who could not deny
it in court. Then the forger would get a court order to take livestock,
slaves, or land to satisfy the debt. The state had its own swindle:
Georgia held a lottery and raffled off lands in the Cherokee Nation.
In 1830, the discovery of gold in Cherokee country drew in a horde
of intruders who brought slaves to work their mines. When Cherokees got in the way, the invaders beat them, burned their homes, and
raped their women.[91]

Jackson won the presidency with almost unanimous support from
the voters of Alabama, Georgia, and Mississippi. They expected him
to remove their Indians, and Jackson made that cause the imperative
priority of his administration. Publicly, Jackson told Indians to move
beyond the Mississippi "or submit to the laws" of the southern states.
Privately, he conceded "that the Indians could not possibly live under
the laws of the state." Jackson's policy spread misery among Indians,
but he concluded: "I feel conscious of having done my duty to my
red children." If they stayed and suffered, Jackson declared, "It will be
attributable to their want of duty to themselves, not to me."[92]

Natives found champions among Protestant clergymen and laity from the Northeast. These friends organized protest meetings and petitions to Congress, and produced newspaper essays and pamphlets to defend aboriginal rights. The friends noted the inconsistency of uprooting people who had followed the government's advice to embrace civilization. One petition denounced removal as "cruel, unjust, and disgraceful to our Government." Another warned that forced removal would betray the nation's founding ideals, and "the only free gov[ernmen]t on earth" would be "converted into a Despotism of the most frightful character." The petitioners included thousands of pious women. "We are unwilling that the church, the schools, and the domestic altar should be thrown down before the avaricious god of power," declared women from Maine.[93]

To counter moral criticism of removal, Jackson claimed that he would save the Indians by removing them to the West, where the federal government could "exercise a parental control over their interests and possibly perpetuate their race." A few reformers supported his position. They included the superintendent of Indian affairs, Thomas McKenney, and a Baptist preacher, Isaac McCoy, who insisted that Natives faced extermination unless removed far beyond settlers and their alcohol. These reformers claimed that only a few mixed-blood chiefs opposed removal while the silent majority of Indians longed to escape misery by heading west.[94]

Southerners wanted to oust Indians without dithering about morality. Georgia governor Wilson Lumpkin derided the opponents as "Northern fanatics, male and female . . . protesting against the removal of the poor, dear Indians." Southerners accused northern opponents of seeking to enhance their region's relative power by blocking southern development. The removers also charged Yankees with hypocrisy, for their ancestors had driven out or killed most of New England's Indians. Southern leaders also detected a threat to slavery if federal treaties transcended state laws. A southerner warned:

"If the general government has a right to make treaties with the Indians living within the states because they are red, it has an equal right to make treaties with the negroes because they are black."[95]

In May 1830, Congress approved Jackson's Indian Removal bill to fund the expulsion of eastern Indians. The bill passed easily in the Senate but more narrowly in the House, where slave-state congressmen gave overwhelming support, 61 to 15, while northerners opposed, 41 to 82. To smite his pious critics, Jackson pulled federal funding for their mission schools and purged the Bureau of Indian Affairs, replacing veteran agents with cronies. The sacked officials included McKenney, who had helped Jackson pass the removal bill but then had developed moral qualms about it.[96]

To pressure Indians to make "voluntary" treaties of removal, Jackson had treaty commissioners warn Natives that persistence would "entail destruction upon their race" by federal troops and state militia in support of squatters. In violation of past treaties, Jackson withheld annuity payments to Indian nations until they agreed to move. If they still refused, Jackson threatened to "leave the poor deluded Creeks & Cherokees to their fate, and their annihilation." In sum, Indians faced a "voluntary choice" between destruction and exile. In September 1830, Choctaws cracked under the pressure and ceded all of their homeland in Mississippi. Removing a year later, the migrants suffered from winter weather and the failure of federal officials to provide clothing or enough food. Of the 14,000 expelled Choctaws, 2,500 died in the move. "These white folks," a Choctaw declared, were "monsters."[97]

To pressure the Cherokees, Georgia enforced its prejudicial laws and barred them from exercising any legal jurisdiction. The state convicted George Tassel for murdering a fellow Cherokee, and then brazenly executed him in defiance of a stay ordered by Chief Justice Marshall of the Supreme Court. The execution occurred on Christmas Eve.[98]

Georgia also outlawed missionaries who persisted in Cherokee country. When eleven refused to leave, the state convicted and sentenced them to four years in prison at hard labor. Nine then accepted state pardons that compelled them to depart, but two appealed to the U.S. Supreme Court. In March 1832, Marshall ruled that federal treaties protected Indian nations from state laws designed to harass them. He added, "If the judicial power fall short of giving effect to the laws of the Union, the existence of the federal government is at an end."[99]

Legend has it that Jackson undercut the decision by refusing to enforce it; that legend is politically true but legally false. Jackson did disdain the decision, but the court did not and could not command federal intervention in this narrowly defined case. The ruling merely directed Georgia to release the two missionaries. Instead, the defiant governor kept them in prison for seventeen months until they accepted pardons on the state's terms in 1833.[100]

Under increasing pressure, the Cherokees split into two factions. A minority led by John Ridge and Elias Boudinot accepted removal as the only way out of a deteriorating situation. In the Treaty of New Echota (December 1835), Boudinot and Ridge sacrificed the Cherokee domain in Georgia in return for $5 million and land in future Oklahoma. While the treaty party headed west, most Cherokees denounced the deal as illegitimate and stayed put until forced out by American troops in 1838. Wrenched from their homes with only the clothes on their backs, Cherokees suffered from malnutrition, exposure, disease, and brutality during a forced march in winter. Meanwhile, squatters looted and burned Cherokee homes. Known as the Trail of Tears, this searing experience killed at least 4,000 of the 18,000 Cherokees rounded up. A veteran soldier recalled, "The Cherokee removal was the cruelest work I ever knew."[101]

In Alabama, the Creeks suffered even worse. An 1832 removal treaty with the federal government gave them the option to stay behind on allotted farms, but speculators and settlers used violence and fraud to drive them out. When the federal government failed to protect the Indians, they attacked the intruders. Then 10,000 federal troops and Alabama militiamen rounded up and evicted all the Creeks, killing many and raping others. Seeking to remove Indians on the cheap, the government contracted out provisions for the journey to the lowest bidders. To maximize profits, the bidders cheated both government and Indians by delivering too little food and of rotten quality. At least a quarter of the Creeks died. But an Alabama settler claimed that Indian expulsion was "redemption from a land of Barbarians to a land of civilization."[102]

While expelling Seminoles from Florida, southerners planned to enslave the Black runaways who had joined them. Slave traders accompanied American troops to profit from captured Black Seminoles. General Thomas Jesup explained, "This . . . is a negro, not an Indian war."[103]

Although only about 5,500 in number, the Seminoles put up fierce resistance by setting ambushes and then hiding in the cypress swamps of southern and central Florida. In 1835, Seminoles wiped out 100 soldiers led by Major Francis Dade. Frustrated American commanders brought in thirty-three bloodhounds from Cuba to "tear to pieces all the red devils they can catch." But Americans struggled to get their bearings in a watery region that an officer described as "one vast forest castle, surrounded by moats." Many frustrated officers resigned from the army, and hundreds of disgusted soldiers and militiamen deserted or died of malaria and dysentery.[104]

To break the stalemate, General Jesup invited Seminole chiefs to meet for negotiations under a white flag, but then he seized and sent them off in irons to a military prison. Jesup's duplicity contradicted Americans' claims of moral superiority over Indians, whom they cast as treacherous savages. The deceived chiefs included their primary leader, Osceola, who languished and died in the dungeon at Fort Moultrie in South Carolina. An army surgeon severed and embalmed Osceola's head for sale to a showman who displayed a "cabinet of heads."[105]

The remaining Seminoles fought on under the leadership of Coacoochee, who escaped from Jesup's military prison with the help of Blacks working there. In early 1838, Jesup urged his superiors to let the Seminoles remain in the swampy Everglades of southern Florida—a region that no settler coveted. Five hundred Seminoles agreed to a truce and camped near Jesup's army to await an answer from the government. In reply, the secretary of war assured Jesup that national honor required fighting to kill or remove every Seminole in Florida. The general promptly surrounded and seized the encamped Seminoles, who had made the mistake of trusting his word.[106]

The prolonged war cost 1,500 American lives and at least $30 million, but eventually the richer and more populous Union wore down the Seminoles, who could not replace their losses. As Seminole villages and crops went up in flames, growing numbers of Native children starved and died. An army surgeon called them "haggard, shriveled devils" and "ugly little nudities." By capturing and deporting westward women and children, the army demoralized warriors, who lost their primary reason for fighting. The war killed a quarter of the Seminoles, while American losses were a tiny fraction in a national population of 13 million. By August 1842, when the army declared victory, Americans had removed most of the Seminoles, but a few hundred outlasted their foes by hiding in the Everglades.[107]

Jesup had promised to protect the freedom of the Black Seminoles who surrendered and accepted removal. In 1848, however, the U.S. attorney general, disavowed Jesup's pledge of freedom and ordered federal troops to seize the Black Seminoles in the West. Many escaped to Mexico, which welcomed them by providing land, provisions, arms, and tools. In return, they defended the Mexican borderland against Comanche raiders and repelled Texans trying to force them into slavery. No Americans fought harder for freedom than the Black Seminoles.[108]

Bad Axe

The United States also tried to remove Indians from New York and the Midwest: Haudenosaunees, Ojibwas, Wyandots, Shawnees, Delawares, Miamis, Pottawatomies, Ho-Chunks, Kickapoos, Sauks, and Mesquakies. Most balked and reminded federal officials of past promises to protect their reservations.[109]

The Sauk and Mesquakie (or Fox) resented their forced removal across the Mississippi River to Iowa, where they suffered from attacks by their long-time enemies, the Dakotas. In 1832, Black Hawk, led 1,600 Sauk and Mesquakie back to their old homes along the Rock River in northern Illinois and southern Wisconsin. Moving as families, they did not expect to fight, but the governor of Illinois sent militia to attack them. Old William Clark, of Lewis and Clark fame, had made the fraudulent treaty that had dispossessed the Sauk and Mesquakie. In 1832, he denounced them as "faithless and treacherous" and urged a "War of *Extermination*."[110]

Americans jumped to their usual conclusion that insidious British agents had set the Indians on a murderous mission. In fact, British officials refused Black Hawk's request for military help, and he began to withdraw back to Iowa, but the militia attacked anyway—and suffered defeat. Secretary of War Lewis Cass then sent in federal troops with a commander who vowed that Black Hawk's band would be "crushed as a piece of dirt." In August 1832, soldiers trapped the starving and fleeing Indians at the juncture of the Bad Axe River with the Mississippi, massacring hundreds of men, women, and children. Dakotas killed many who made it across the big river.[111]

The 150 survivors included Black Hawk, who became a federal prisoner consigned by Jackson's order to a dungeon, where a British visitor said that the sight of the "shriveled looking old man . . . in this hot prison-house full of people made my heart ache." In 1838, death brought him no relief, for whites stole the corpse for display in an Iowa museum, which burned in 1855.[112]

Cass cited the Black Hawk War to justify ousting the other Indian nations from the Midwest, although they had kept the peace. In 1833, federal officials compelled Ho-Chunks, Kickapoos, and Pottawatomies to make treaties forsaking their homelands. Troops hunted down Natives who tried to stay behind, while hunger and disease took a toll on those who moved. In 1840 a Chicago booster celebrated: "The miserable race of men have been superseded by a population distinguished for its intelligence and enterprise."[113]

Margaret Fuller had her doubts. In 1843, Fuller left New England to visit settlements in the Rock River Valley, the former home of the Sauk and Mesquakie: "It is only five years since the poor Indians have been dispossessed of this region of sumptuous loveliness, such as can hardly be paralleled in this world. No wonder they poured out their blood freely before they would go." Settlers found many signs of the Indian imprint on the land: arrowheads and pottery in the soil, caches for storing food, wooden troughs for pounding corn, tomahawk blazes on trees, "the body of an Indian woman, in a canoe, elevated on high poles, with all her ornaments on," and "an ancient Indian village, with its regularly arranged mounds. As usual, they had chosen with the finest taste." These Natives belied the American notion that Indians were savages who made no impact on the land.[114]

One day, Fuller's settler host looked up to see "a tall Indian standing at gaze on the knoll. . . . The Indian saw him, gave a wild, snorting sound of indignation and pain, and strode away." Fuller thought, "I scarcely see how they can forbear to shoot the white man where he stands." And she marveled when her host added, "They cannot be prevented from straggling back here to their old haunts. I wish they could. They ought not to [be] permitted to drive away *our* game." His sense of possession was complete.[115]

By 1842, after a decade of coercive treaties, the federal government had removed 100,000 Indians and secured 100 million acres of eastern land in exchange for 32 million western acres and $68 million. During the late 1830s, the federal government spent two-fifths of its annual budget on killing or removing Indians. But the Union profited by reselling the eastern lands for $80 million. U.S. senators claimed victory over Indians: "They are on the *outside* of us, and in a place which will ever remain an *outside*." In fact, American settlers would soon follow to surround and dispossess them again.[116]

Some Natives eluded expulsion by taking refuge in mountains or swamps. In northern Michigan, most of the Odawa and Ojibwa stayed put because settlers considered their lands too cold for agriculture. Elsewhere dispossession proved thorough as invading settlers dug up Indian graves and burial mounds to steal jewelry, artifacts, and bones. Dentists harvested teeth for replacing those decayed in the jaws of whites. A scientist, Josiah Nott, collected Creek skulls to measure in support of his crackpot theories of Indian racial inferiority. Natives were right to fear losing the graves of their ancestors.[117]

Jackson led a massive and unprecedented display of federal power by helping states, land speculators, and settlers to dispossess Indians. Federal officials could deploy troops against Indians but not to control settlers. Treaties extorted land in return for federal promises to protect the new Native reservations, but when squatters soon followed, officials made another treaty to take more land with new promises, inevitably broken. Alexis de Tocqueville characterized the United States as "the most grasping nation on the globe," and he marveled at the dispossession of Indians within legal forms: "It is impossible to destroy men with more respect for the laws of humanity."[118]

Aboriginia

Jackson claimed that "the philanthropist will rejoice that the remnant of that ill-fated race has been at length placed beyond the reach of injury and oppression, and that the paternal care of the General Government will hereafter watch over them and protect them." In fact, the woes of removed Indians persisted in the West, where they suffered from bitter internal divisions generated by removal. The Creek factions coped by separating to live fifty miles apart, but the Cherokees turned to violence, killing the leaders of the party that had signed the removal treaty, John Ridge and Elias Boudinot, as traitors. "I have signed my death warrant," Ridge had said when he endorsed the treaty. The factions exchanged killings until 1846, when they made an uneasy peace.[119]

Americans dumped the removed Indians in the future states of Oklahoma and Kansas on the eastern margins of the Great Plains, a region considered too arid and treeless for agricultural settlement. In 1820, an army officer, Stephen H. Long, probed the southern plains and named the place the "Great American Desert." Arriving poor, sick, and dispirited, the refugees had to build new homes in a difficult environment. Pottawatomies complained that their new land was "too poor for snakes to live upon. Our men are not accustomed to the Prairie. They have always lived in the woods."[120]

The region's longer-resident Indians resented the intrusion by thousands of newcomers. Both sets of Natives competed for limited supplies of timber, water, alluvial soil, and game—especially bison. That competition led to deadly warfare between Native nations. A Dakota chief complained that Americans worked "to push us into the Jaws of our enemies." By setting Indians against one another, Americans won the West. Then settlers followed to push the removed Indians still farther west. Removal was a recurring nightmare.[121]

In 1834, the Baptist preacher Isaac McCoy proposed a pan-Indian government for a territory named Aboriginia. Despite Indian distrust of the scheme, McCoy lobbied Congress to create a federal territory with McCoy as the governor assisted by a council of twenty-four elected chiefs. Under his plan, Natives could send a nonvoting delegate to Congress. In time, Aboriginia could evolve into a state admitted into the Union on an equal standing with other states.[122]

Congress rejected the bill because few congressmen wanted to empower any Indians. McCoy had helped the Jacksonians achieve removal, but then they abandoned him. During the 1850s, the United States took most of Aboriginia to create the Kansas and Nebraska Territories, where rival bands of northern and southern settlers fought over the expansion of slavery.[123]

Manitoulin

During the War of 1812, British officials valued Indians as military allies to help defend Canada against American invasion. To preserve their prowess as warriors, Britons left Native cultures alone and treated chiefs with diplomatic respect, including the bestowal of annual presents of goods and munitions. After the war, however, imperial officials sought to reduce expenditures by discarding the Natives as allies. One official insisted that presents "encouraged their natural indolence and improvidence; kept them a distinct people; fostered their natural pride and consequent aversion to labour and created an undue feeling of dependence upon the crown." Colonial officials also wanted to take Native land to accommodate an influx of immigrants seeking farms. From 750,000 in 1821, Canada's settler population surged to 2,300,000 in 1850.[124]

In Upper Canada, Britain's Indian policy began to converge with the American version. Between 1815 and 1824, the colonial government secured nearly 7.4 million acres in one-sided land cession treaties. Officials meant to restrict Indians (known in Canada as "First Nations") to enclaves known as "reserves," akin to American reservations. On those reserves, missionaries and officials promoted Christianity and European ways, including agriculture with private property lines and domestic livestock. In 1821, a visiting American official, Jedidiah Morse, met with the governor, who applauded federal Indian policies and sought "to co-operate with us . . . for the accomplishment of the great and common object in view, the complete civilization of the Indians."[125]

First Nations, however, resented the new push for an assimilation that would strip them of their language, traditions, and band identity and leadership. An Ojibwa chief protested the effort as meant "to break them in pieces." Natives regarded annual presents from the Crown as earned by them for defending the colony against invaders and for sharing their land, fish, and game with colonists.[126]

On the reserves, Protestant missionaries set up "model villages" that featured a chapel, parsonage, school, grist and sawmill, black-smith shop, framed or log homes with stone or brick chimneys, barns, gardens, and orchards. But few Indians could satisfy missionaries who demanded sweeping cultural changes. And the reserves attracted traders plying a cheap alcohol that fueled demoralization and vio-lence. So critics insisted that the villages taught alcoholic vice rather than civilized virtues.[127]

During the late 1830s, Sir Francis Bond Head, the governor of Upper Canada, concluded, "The greatest kindness we can perform towards these simple-minded people is to remove and fortify them as much as possible from all communication with Whites." Accusing Indians of "impeding the progress of civilization in Upper Canada," Head pushed to relocate and consolidate many Native bands on Man-itoulin, a large island on the northeast side of Lake Huron. Following American precedent, the governor pressured Natives by warning that he could not protect them from invading squatters. An Ojibwa band noted that "their Great Father was determined to have their land— [and] that they were poor and weak and must submit." As invading settlers depleted fish and game, Natives needed Crown protection and presents more than ever, so they reluctantly parted with more land to satisfy officials.[128]

The relocated Natives struggled to cultivate crops on rocky and infertile Manitoulin. An Ojibwa complained that the island's fields primarily produced "large rocks and small stones." A visiting offi-cial described the islanders as "poverty-stricken creatures, wretchedly clad in rags and skins."[129]

In 1838, outraged Methodist missionaries sent their prized Native student, Peter Jones, to London to lobby imperial officials against Head's removal policy. The colonial government did restore a few small, village tracts and relented on pressuring Natives to relocate to Manitoulin. But the British failed to provide secure land tenure for the Native reserves. During the 1850s, the colony sold most of the island to settlers. Upper Canada's government promised Natives a share in the revenues from those sales, but white officials embezzled the funds.[130]

The Canadian version of Indian removal played out with some striking parallels to the American example: government collusion with invading settlers; traders promoting alcohol abuse; officials who despaired of civilizing Natives; conniving techniques to coerce Indians to sell land; missionaries defending Natives provided they became Christian; and resourceful Indians who persisted by adapting to the newcomers.

But there were also differences. Compared to the United States, Indian removal was less thorough, relentless, and deadly in Canada during the 1830s. Upper Canada lacked the long, bloody history of settler wars that had generated so much fear and hatred of Natives in the United States. Canada also did not have the democracy for white men that, in the Union, demanded removal and tolerated brutality toward Indians. North of the border, the British Crown retained executive power and gloried in a paternalism that provided a tad more restraint in managing Natives. By avoiding the bloody excesses of U.S. Indian policy, British officials claimed a cherished moral superiority over Americans. Compared to their southern neighbors, Crown officials usually understood that there were more cost-effective ways to dispossess Indians than by killing them. If Canada's Indian peoples lost their lands almost as fast as in the United States, they lost far fewer lives in massacres and forced marches. While not a pretty picture, Indian relations in Canada compared favorably to the American horrors.[131]

Hell-Carnival

During the 1830s, Jackson's removal policy generated a speculative boom in federal land sales, bank expansion, monetary inflation, and easy credit. In 1833, the United States sold a million acres of public land in Mississippi, twice as much as in any other state. Two years later, land sales there tripled to 3 million acres. In 1840, Mississippi produced 200 million pounds of cotton: a quarter of the entire American crop. That boom derived from the combination of Jackson's prosettler land policy, Indian removal, and the gutting of banking regulation with the demise of the Bank of the United States.[132]

In Mississippi, ambitious men could buy land and slaves on credit and pay for them out of the soaring profits made by raising and selling cotton. A newly arrived farmer wrote home to relatives in North Carolina, "I like this country better than any country I have ever yet seen for making money." But easy money and frontier conditions attracted plenty of swindlers, counterfeiters, horse thieves, and slave traders. Strangers thrown together to compete for land and slaves made for an unstable society of mutual distrust, rampant gambling, and frequent violence. Schools and churches were few in a state that a visitor characterized as "one vast cotton field." Another newcomer described Mississippi as a "hell-carnival," where "avarice and hope joined partnership."[133]

The carnival depended on slaves brought in to replace the Choctaws, recently driven out of the state. During the 1830s, the Black population of Mississippi tripled to become 52 percent of the state's total. A visitor explained that the planters sought "to sell cotton in order to buy negroes—to make more cotton to buy more negroes, *ad infinitum*." As the number of enslaved people soared, a planter worried that "we will one day have our throats cut in this country."[134]

After helping a gang that stole slaves and horses, Virgil Stewart testified against the ringleader, John Murrell, securing his conviction in Tennessee. To exploit his new fame, Stewart published a lurid pamphlet, *The Western Land Pirate*. It claimed that Murrell had recruited hundreds of poor white men and enslaved people into a secret society that would kill masters and then plunder banks and plantations. The leading plotters allegedly told enslaved people "that they are entitled to their freedom as much as their masters, and that all of the wealth of the country is the proceeds of black people's labor." The supposed plot fed into the pervasive anxieties of the strangers drawn into the Mississippi boom. Dependent on poor whites to control Blacks, planters dreaded any hint of a cross-racial alliance by the downtrodden.[135]

Traveling through central Mississippi, Stewart peddled his pamphlet, which caused a sensation. In June 1835, his warnings prompted white folks to claim that they had overheard slaves plotting rebellion. Alarm filled in the details as brutal interrogators seized suspects and fed them leading questions framed by Stewart's fantasy: that many white people were behind the plot. That fantasy also reinforced planters' conceit that their slaves were, in fact, content until misled by conniving white men. To put a stop to their torment, interrogated Blacks confirmed names suggested by their torturers.[136]

Thinly legitimated as vigilance committees, mobs grabbed suspects, Black and white, for brutal whippings, which led to confessions that in turn expanded the terror of an impending revolt. The vigilantes sought out and hung Black preachers, cutting off and impaling their heads as a public warning to others. Any white man who tried to protect an accused slave from a brutal interrogation became a suspect and often died on the spot. Misled by interrogators, many suspects sought to save their lives by confessing, only to face a brutal execution. A young man named Hunter had the misfortune to leave Tennessee for central Mississippi in early July. Seeking work as a teacher, he asked a lot of questions and was seen talking to slaves. Seized, stripped naked and tied to posts, he suffered a whipping that reached a nearly deadly 500 lashes before he would confess. But rather than keep their promise to free him, the vigilantes hanged Hunter. Cutting off his head, they cast it into the road for hogs to eat.[137]

Some leading planters worked up the courage to denounce the deadly violence as anarchy based on lies. When this criticism led to firefights, the state's leaders belatedly restored the rule of law, but no one was punished for lynching men without trial. To whitewash the crisis, the authorities blamed agitation by shadowy abolitionists for stirring up the slaves. This story enabled planters to deny that they had provoked the plot by inflicting misery on enslaved people. Declaring slavery "a blessing both to master and slave," public meetings demanded that all ministers preach in favor of slavery or get out of the state. Rather than shaking bondage, the scare consolidated it in Mississippi.[138]

In 1837, a depression ripped through the nation. Crop prices and wages plunged, state banks failed, and thousands lost jobs. Foreign capital shifts triggered the depression, but a financial system destabilized by Jackson's Bank War worsened the impact within the United States. The depression hit Mississippi harder than any other state. Seeking scapegoats, the state's governor, Alexander McNutt, blamed British creditors for conspiring to "mortgage our cotton fields and make serfs of our children." McNutt wanted Mississippi to have enslaved Black people rather than white serfs. But the panic ruined many smaller planters, consolidating the power of elite planters in the state. In the end, the Jacksonian version of democracy helped to make Americans more unequal.[139]

Top: *"Destruction by Fire of Pennsylvania Hall, the New Building of the Abolition Society," 1838 print by John T. Bowen.* Library of Congress 2014645336. Bottom: *"New Method of Assorting the Mail, as Practised by Southern slaveholders, or Attack on the Post Office, Charleston, S.C.," print by unknown, 1835.* Library of Congress 2008661779.

B orn in 1795, James K. Polk grew up in North Carolina and attended the state university, graduating first in his class. Slight and sickly, Polk compensated with relentless hard work. Moving to Tennessee, he studied law, speculated in land, and acquired plantations, where Polk employed brutal overseers, for he believed that flogging improved morale: "A slave dreads the punishment of stripes . . . and that description of punishment has, besides, a beneficial effect upon his fellow-slaves." Polk's plantations had an especially high rate of infant mortality and adult efforts to escape.[1]

In 1824, Polk won a seat in congress despite lacking charisma or humor, but his drive impressed Andrew Jackson, who became Polk's patron. He also married well. Growing up in a slave-owning family of devout Presbyterians, Sarah Childress Polk persuaded James to swear off dancing, drinking, and card-playing. Their tepid parties were rescued by her flair for fancy dress, fine manners, and charming conversation. Even his enemies liked her. Well educated and clever, Sarah knew how to play the dutiful, deferential wife in public, but in private she became James's primary political advisor. By overtly deferring to her man, Sarah cultivated hidden power. Savvy politicians cultivated her influence to sway her dour, secretive, and stubborn husband. Another political wife thought that "perhaps Mr. and Mrs. Polk together will make a very good President."[2]

Sarah reinforced James's commitment to white supremacy as God's will. One day, they looked out the window of their mansion at enslaved workers in the garden, and she said: "The writers of the Declaration of Independence were mistaken when they affirmed that all men are created equal." She added, "There are those men toiling in the heat of the sun, while you are writing, and I am sitting here fanning myself . . . surrounded with every comfort." Rather than see this difference as arbitrary and unjust, Sarah concluded, "We were created for these [different] places." The Polks believed in the power of white men over people of color as divine will.[3]

A pioneering chicken hawk in politics, Polk lacked military experience but demanded war early and often against Indians, Britons, and Mexicans. In 1821, Mexico had won independence by fighting

Opposite, clockwise from top left: "James Knox Polk (1795–1849),"
daguerreotype by Mathew B. Brady, 1849. Library of Congress 2004664042.
"Sarah Childress Polk (1803–1891)," lithograph by N. Currier, 1846. Library of
Congress 96525379. *"A new rule in Algebra. . . . The three Mexican prisoners,"*
print by Edward Jones, 1846. This American cartoon mocks Mexican prisoners
who lost legs from amputation after a battle. Library of Congress 2003689269.

against Spain, but Polk rejected any solidarity with Mexicans as fellow republicans. Instead, he dwelled on their alleged inferiority to justify American expansion.[4]

Ploughing the Sea

At the end of the eighteenth century, Spain claimed a vast empire in South America and the southwestern third of North America. In 1800, Spanish America had 17 million people, but only a fifth of them enjoyed the higher status of white people, with the rest divided among Indians, Africans, or the mixed-race peoples known as *mestizos*. The Spanish subdivided colonial whites into the American-born majority, known as *criollos* (creoles), and a small minority (about 150,000) of the Spanish-born, known as *peninsulares*. Favored by the Crown, the *peninsulares* lorded it over *criollos*, and both exploited the colored majority.[5]

Resenting the *peninsulares*, some *criollos* sought greater power by pursuing independence from Spain. Looking north, they envied the more dynamic economic growth of the United States, which they attributed to independence, republicanism, and free trade. "Good God, What a contrast to the Spanish System!" wrote Francisco de Miranda, an ambitious Venezuelan who regarded the American Revolution as "the infallible preliminary to our own."[6]

Charming, idealistic, and romantic, Miranda longed to liberate and unify Spanish America with a British-style parliament and a constitutional monarch. During the war of the American Revolution, he had served as an officer in Spanish royal forces posted in Florida and the Caribbean. After the war, he visited New York City and befriended Alexander Hamilton before going to France to participate in the more radical revolution there. As a moderate, Miranda narrowly escaped the guillotine, so he advised a compatriot in Venezuela, "Two great examples lie before our eyes, the American and French revolutions. Let us discreetly imitate the first. Let us carefully avoid the disastrous effects of the second."[7]

In 1806, Miranda returned to Venezuela to promote revolution with the help of British money and 200 volunteers raised in the United States. But he botched his landing and found little local support for his republican revolution. Abandoning the effort after just eleven days, Miranda sailed away into exile, while most of his volunteers died in Spanish dungeons.[8]

In 1806, most *criollos* feared that revolution would disrupt their control over the darker-skinned majority of menial laborers and peasants. *Criollos* dreaded the precedents set by the bloody, disruptive French Revolution of the 1790s and its offshoot in Saint-Domingue, where slave rebels had killed masters and destroyed plantations. A *criollo* leader, Simón Bolívar, noted: "A great volcano lies at our feet. Who shall restrain the oppressed classes? Slavery will break its yoke, each shade of complexion will seek mastery." *Criollos* supported royal rule so long as it sustained their privileged position.[9]

In 1808, however, the French destabilized the Spanish Empire by invading Spain to replace the king with one of Napoleon's brothers. That collapse of traditional authority created political uncertainty throughout Spanish America. In response, *criollos* sought a controlled revolution that would preserve and, indeed, enhance their power by displacing the *peninsulares*. Bolívar noted, "Americans by birth and Europeans by law, we find ourselves engaged in a dual conflict, disputing with the Natives . . . and at the same time struggling to maintain ourselves in the country of our birth against the opposition of the [Spanish] invaders. Thus our position is most extraordinary and complicated."[10]

In 1810–1811, revolutions rippled across South America, from the Rio de la Plata (Argentina) through the Andes and northward to Venezuela and New Granada (Colombia). Miranda resurfaced but again proved erratic and ineffective. Falling into Spanish hands, he died in prison in 1816. In Venezuela and New Granada, the revolution's leadership passed to his younger compatriot, Bolívar, whose family owned haciendas and plantations worked by hundreds of slaves. But he had acquired an open and idealistic mind from higher education and travel in Europe. Short, slight, and brown in complexion, he had piercing black eyes and an intense charisma that commanded attention.[11]

In the name of freedom, Bolívar became authoritarian, adopting ruthless measures meant "to liberate peoples who are ignorant of the value of their rights." Bolívar cultivated support from the colored masses to obtain enough soldiers to defeat the royalists. Considering it "madness that a revolution for liberty should try to maintain slavery," Bolívar freed his own slaves and those who ran away from other masters to join his forces. To arm them, he secured military aid from the Black republic of Haiti.[12]

In 1821, Bolívar crushed the royalists in Venezuela and New Granada, but he struggled to define a new social order in a region devastated by a decade of civil war between plundering and murderous armies. Slavery persisted for many Blacks until 1854, for Bolívar could free only those who had fought for him. Free Blacks and *mestizos* gained legal equality, but most remained impoverished in a hierarchical society dominated by *criollo* landlords. Bolívar sadly concluded that the white elite, "although they speak of liberty and constitutions, they want these only for themselves, not for the people, whom they wish to see continue under their oppression. . . . In spite of all their liberalism, they prefer to regard the lower classes as their perpetual serfs." He died of tuberculosis in December 1830 at the age of forty-seven. A month before, Bolívar had despaired, "He who serves a revolution ploughs the sea."[13]

Mexico

The Latin American struggle for independence proved especially prolonged and bloody in Mexico, where stark racial and class differences made any upheaval terrifying to privileged whites. Spain also gave priority to fighting to keep Mexico, which abounded in rich mines that produced two-thirds of the silver extracted in the Americas— and a third of the empire's revenue.[14]

In addition to mines, Mexico's elite relied on haciendas: large landed estates worked by peasants known as *campesinos*. Most were

Indians who lived in huts, rags, and close to starvation. Because haciendas monopolized the best lands, Mexico had relatively few middle-class farmers, the class that predominated in the United States. A Mexican bishop noted, "The maldistribution of land has been one of the principal causes of the people's misery." Another bishop declared that Mexico was divided between "those who have nothing and those who have everything. . . . There are no gradations or mean." Growing numbers of desperate people turned to banditry in the countryside. Others sought work by flocking into Mexico City, the biggest city in the Americas with 130,000 inhabitants.[15]

After the downfall of Spain's monarchy in 1808, *criollos* and *peninsulares* jockeyed to dominate the viceregal government in Mexico City. The governing viceroy appealed for white solidarity lest they all reap a popular uprising: "We must stay united if we wish to be dominant." In late 1808, however, *peninsulares* staged a coup and sent the viceroy back to Spain. The victors ran a repressive regime that outraged *criollos*, who, in desperation, solicited support from the poor masses for a revolution. For this, they needed the help of a popular and radical priest, Miguel Hidalgo y Costilla.[16]

Hidalgo served a parish in the Bajío region of central Mexico. Middle-aged and balding, he had a dark complexion, lively green eyes, two illegitimate children, intellectual curiosity, and wide reading. Empathizing with the *campesinos* of his parish, Hidalgo denounced colonial elites as greedy parasites: "Their God is money." Promoting a liberation theology, he favored a social revolution to take land from the rich for redistribution to the poor. He also wanted to abolish slavery and the tribute exacted from Indians. In 1810, Hidalgo encouraged his followers to make pikes and swords for armed revolt.[17]

When the governing junto arrested or scattered his *criollo* sponsors, Hidalgo had to mobilize and lead a revolution on his own. Thousands of angry *campesinos* rallied to his call for a revolution in the name of the toppled king and Mexico's premier saint, the Virgin of Guadalupe. They passionately believed that she communicated daily with Hidalgo to inspire a holy crusade that would purify Mexico of impiety and exploitation. Terrified by this radical uprising, Mexico's bishops and archbishops denounced Hidalgo as a heretic who challenged the divinely ordained hierarchy of society.[18]

Rage at generations of humiliation led the rebels to massacre captured whites and loot their mansions and mines. The bloodshed shocked many *criollos*, including a young Lucas Alamán, who dreaded the "monstrous union of religion with assassination and plunder." As the revolutionary force multiplied and spread, Hidalgo felt swept along in a ferocious movement beyond his control.[19]

On the outskirts of Mexico City, a smaller but better-armed and better-trained royalist force confronted Hidalgo's 80,000 followers, most wielding only spears, machetes, stones, and clubs. Routed in battle, Hidalgo retreated. A year later, as his support dissipated, he fled northward but fell into an ambush that led to his capture, trial, and execution. The commander of the firing squad recalled that Hidalgo died as he "stared straight at us with those beautiful eyes." Royalists displayed his head in a metal cage in Guanajuato, the city where his revolt had begun. The victors executed hundreds of other rebels.[20]

In 1812, another radical priest, a *mestizo* named José María Morelos y Pavón, revived the radical revolution in central Mexico. Morelos had studied theology with Hidalgo before becoming a parish priest. Like his mentor, Morelos sympathized with the poor and sired illegitimate children. He too vowed to purge *peninsulares*, abolish slavery and racial inequality, and redistribute land to "narrow the gap between wealth and poverty." Morelos insisted "that the children of the peasant and the sweeper should have the same education as the children of the rich." Unlike Hidalgo, Morelos promoted a republic rather than a restored monarchy. Calm, brave, honest, devout, and funny, Morelos built a small but well-disciplined force adept at guerrilla warfare.[21]

Morelos's radicalism repelled most *criollos*, who supported repression by a brutal but competent new viceroy sent from Spain to govern Mexico. In 1814, the royalist cause also got a boost from Napoleon's downfall, which restored the Bourbon monarchy in Spain. A year later, royalists captured, tried, and executed Morelos. Although

Alamán supported the royalists, he admired Morelos's ability and integrity: "The most impressive man produced by the revolution in New Spain fell pierced by four bullets."[22]

For five years, conservative *criollos* ran Mexico on behalf of the Crown and the Catholic Church. In 1821, however, a liberal *junta* seized power in Spain and tried to limit the power and property of Church and aristocracy. Suddenly, conservative *criollos* preferred independence for Mexico. To win some popular support, they promised civic equality for all, discarding the old racial discriminations, but they refused to redistribute property. *Criollos* rallied to the leadership of Agustín de Iturbide, a wealthy and handsome landlord, conservative Catholic, and ruthless officer, who had fought against Hidalgo and Morelos by massacring prisoners and civilians. Most of the royalist army deserted to join Iturbide, who captured Mexico City in September 1821. A year later, he became Agustín I, "constitutional emperor of the Mexican empire." From afar, the republican Bolívar mocked Iturbide as "emperor by the grace of God and of bayonets."[23]

Iturbide did not reign for long. Arrogant and stubborn, he irritated and then dismissed Congress. Then he alienated an ambitious, twenty-eight-year-old officer, Antonio López de Santa Anna, who revolted at Veracruz in December 1822. Flamboyant, energetic, ruthless, insincere, and greedy, Santa Anna possessed an alluring but dangerous charisma. His hero was the egotistical Napoleon rather than the self-disciplined Washington. Bolívar despised Santa Anna as "the most perverse of mortals." By promising a republic, Santa Anna built an army that soon dominated the country. In despair, Iturbide abdicated in March 1823. A year later, he tried a comeback but was captured and shot.[24]

The triumphant republicans divided between conservatives and liberals. The son of a mine owner, Lucas Alamán developed a great dread of anarchy after enduring a decade of revolution and civil wars. During the 1820s, he led conservatives, who sought a centralized, hierarchical, and Catholic society that preserved inequality of wealth as essential to social stability. They opposed liberals, who favored a federal system to disperse power among Mexico's nineteen states. Led by Lorenzo de Zavala, liberals sought to weaken the Church, land-lords, and the army by promoting social mobility through individual competition. They expected free enterprise to reward merit and hard work, gradually softening Mexican inequality. In a compromise, the constitution of 1824 created a federal system of strong states while preserving the power and wealth of the Church and army. The nation had a bicameral congress and a weak president.[25]

The old colonial regime had divided subjects into castes with dis-tinctive laws, rights, and privileges, but republican Mexico officially treated every citizen as an individual with equal standing. Civic equal-ity, however, seemed hollow where property was so unequally distrib-uted. Indeed, the republic worsened the plight of the lower orders, who no longer could appeal to the Crown as a counterweight to the elites. For want of land reform, *campesinos* remained laborers or tenants bound to their landlords. A critic noted, "I hear people say that there are no Indians any more, that we are all Mexicans. . . . This sounds like a brave illusion to me." Indeed, as theoretical citizens compelled to com-pete as individuals, Indians lost the legal protection of their corporate status under the old regime. This loss led to the confiscation and sale of their communal lands—especially on the northern frontier.[26]

Casting California's missions as backward and repressive, the repub-lic dissolved them during the late 1820s and early 1830s. Wealthy men bought the mission lands for transformation into *ranchos*. In theory, sec-ularization liberated the Indian residents. In fact, they lost their com-munity and became impoverished and indebted laborers on *ranchos*.[27]

In northern California, Mariano Guadalupe Vallejo commanded the local military and reigned over Rancho Petaluma: 66,000 fer-tile acres carved out of a former mission. To work the land, Vallejo obtained 700 Native servants, many of them former mission Indians. His troops captured other Indians by raiding villages in the nearby hills. Vallejo's younger brother Salvador remembered, "They tilled our soil, pastured our cattle, sheared our sheep, cut our lumber, built our houses, paddled our boats, made tiles for our houses, ground our grain, killed our cattle, dressed their hides for market, and made our unburned bricks." Indians also cared for "our children and made every one of our meals." Salvador romanticized the relationship: "We loved them and they loved us. . . . The Indians knew that our superior education gave us a right to command and rule over them." But they received no pay, only some clothing, food, and crude housing— and any ingratitude reaped severe punishment.[28]

Dissolving the missions also enriched John August Sutter, a Swiss opportunist who had abandoned his wife and debts to move to America. Heading west, Sutter charmed the local governor (who was Vallejo's uncle) into granting him 48,400 acres at the juncture of the American and Sacramento Rivers. With Indian laborers, Sutter erected a fortified compound built of adobe bricks. A gracious and generous host to visiting Euro-Americans, Sutter became a terror to the local Natives thanks to his private army of 200 men, primarily recruited from former trappers and sailors.[29]

By seizing the fertile valleys for his horses and cattle, Sutter deprived Miwok and Nisenan peoples of land for hunting and gathering. Some Natives made the best of a bad situation by becoming his farm hands. Others raided Sutter's herds for food, but his mounted troops destroyed their villages and took hundreds of captives. Sutter had them whipped until they accepted his mastery, and he executed runaways as examples for the rest. At the entrance to Sutter's Fort, a Swiss visitor saw "the long, black hair and skull of an Indian dangling from one of the gateposts."[30]

By 1848, Sutter employed a thousand dependent Indians. He served them a thin porridge poured into hollowed-out tree trunks, where they ate with their bare hands until driven off to labor in his shops, orchards, and wheat fields. Two weeks of hard work earned a shirt or a pair of pants. Sutter sold Indian children as slaves to pay off his creditors, and he kept a few young women as a captive harem.[31]

While Sutter and Vallejo prospered on the northern frontier, Mexico suffered from a decayed economy and ravaged infrastructure. A decade of civil war had devastated cities, mines, and haciendas, and killed 600,000 people, about a tenth of the population. Mines produced merely a quarter of their 1809 yield, and agriculture generated only half of its former produce. Mexican manufacturers could not compete with the cheaper and better-quality goods imported from Britain. While gaining political independence from Spain, Mexico became an economic dependency of the British Empire, which provided the credit that prevented national bankruptcy. In return, Britons gained political leverage and favored trade access.[32]

Independence also exposed Mexico to increased raiding by northern Indians seeking captives and horses. During the 1810s, most of the frontier garrisons withdrew southward to fight in the civil wars of independence. Thereafter, the republic could afford neither to restore the garrisons nor revive the colonial policy of buying peace from the Indians with generous presents and diplomatic respect. Exploiting the porous defenses, Apaches and Comanches traveled eight hundred miles south from the Great Plains and New Mexico to strike at ranches and villages in northern and even central Mexico. They killed men and took women and children as captives for adoption or sale in other Mexican provinces, especially New Mexico. During the 1830s and 1840s, the raiders created a wasteland of ravaged and abandoned farms and ranches.[33]

Although no longer a colony, Mexico was not yet a cohesive nation. Most of its 7 million people lived in hundreds of small villages dispersed across 3 million square miles and often separated by broad deserts or tall mountain ranges. Divided by prejudices and inequality, the people lacked a common identity. State governments commanded more support than did the distant and weak federal regime.[34]

Mexico also suffered from political instability. Between 1822 and 1847, Mexico endured fifty coups, often led by Santa Anna, who became president eleven times. An eager and hyperactive conspirator but inept and impatient administrator, Santa Anna offered no consistent program to address his country's woes. Bored by governing, he often resigned the presidency only to seek excitement by seizing power again. In 1829, Santa Anna renewed his popularity by crushing a Spanish bid to reconquer Mexico. He promoted a dangerous belief that only a strongman could enable Mexico to transcend weakness and poverty to become a powerful and prosperous nation.[35]

Doctrine

People of the United States had mixed feelings about the revolutions sweeping across Latin America. In newspaper columns, congressional speeches, and Fourth of July toasts, they celebrated Hispanic revolutionaries as fellow republicans rejecting European monarchs and empires. In these festive moments, Spanish-American revolutions seemed to emulate and validate the American Revolution. At the same time, many Americans dismissed Hispanics as culturally and racially backward—and unfit for self-government. North Americans increasingly believed that their Protestant faith, entrepreneurial commerce, British legal and constitutional heritage, and white skins uniquely qualified them to sustain a republic. John Adams declared, "The People of South America are the most ignorant, the most bigoted, [and] the most Superstitious of all the Roman Catholicks in Christendom." He equated their new republics with creating "Democracies among the Beasts, Birds, or Fishes."[36]

In 1807, Bolívar had visited the United States and praised her republican institutions and commercial prosperity as models for Latin America. But he also distrusted American republicanism as a cloak for aggression. The United States, he predicted, was "destined by Providence to plague America with miseries in the name of Liberty." To preserve and enhance their own Union, North Americans preyed on their southern and western neighbors.[37]

But territorial expansion risked rupturing the Union that kept peace between the states. While pushing away external danger, expansion might ignite fractures within the United States. If the nation expanded too much in one direction, it would empower part of the Union at the expense of the rest, arousing alarm. During the War of 1812, southerners had demanded Florida to counterbalance the anticipated conquest of Canada to the north. The northern conquest failed, but the United States did pressure Spain into selling Florida in 1819. President Monroe took the deal but worried that expanding southward would antagonize northerners by diminishing their relative clout in the Union. He explained to Jefferson that expansion raised "difficulties, of an internal nature, which menace the union itself." American leaders struggled to maintain a balance of power between rival regions in a tenuous union.[38]

Monroe delayed recognizing the new, breakaway republics in Latin America to avoid antagonizing Spain during the negotiations to acquire Florida. Having completed that transfer in 1821, the administration recognized the new nations a year later. By then, the United States lagged behind the British Empire in competing for influence and trade in Latin America. In 1830, British trade with Latin America was double that of the United States. The British foreign minister, George Canning, slyly noted, "Spanish America is free; and if we do not mismanage our affairs . . . she is English."[39]

In 1823, however, Canning noted a new threat from Europe's reactionary monarchies—Russia, France, Austria, and Prussia—that had formed a "Holy Alliance" to send troops to overthrow Spain's liberal government and restore an absolutist monarchy. British leaders feared that the Holy Alliance would next intervene in Latin America to rebuild the Spanish Empire by suppressing the republics. Canning approached the American ambassador in London to propose mutually warning the Holy Allies to stay out of the Americas. Although the British had far more global power, sustained by the world's premier navy, Canning flattered the Americans by inviting them to become equal partners in a joint statement. But he underestimated the lingering American resentments of Britain.[40]

American leaders feared any partnership with the British as, in fact, an insidious bid to dominate them. Still dependent on British consumer goods and investment capital, Americans worried, in Henry Clay's words, that their states were "sort of independent colonies of England—politically free, commercially slaves." Hence, American leaders felt compelled to assert their diplomatic independence with a shrill defiance. Angling to succeed Monroe as president, John Quincy Adams favored a unilateral American statement as more popular with America's Anglophobic voters.[41]

In December 1823, the president sent to Congress a long message that included three paragraphs subsequently known as the "Monroe Doctrine." He declared that no European power could intervene against a sovereign nation in the western hemisphere. The statement did not specify what the United States would or could do if the Holy Alliance did intervene. In fact, the Holy Allies never intended to meddle in the Americas from a healthy respect for Britain's Royal Navy.[42]

During the twentieth century, the Monroe Doctrine would help the United States to claim hemispheric supremacy as a superpower. In 1823, however, the Union was far weaker at home and abroad—and that weakness drove the creation of the Monroe Doctrine. Adams worried that the British secretly meant to compromise with the Holy Alliance to divvy up the Spanish colonies: "Then what would be our situation—England holding Cuba, France Mexico" and "Russia might take California." Then those powers might place "different portions of the Union in conflict with each other, and thereby endanger the Union." During the recent crisis over Missouri's admission as a slave state, angry congressmen had threatened secession and civil war. To preserve the Union, Monroe sought to keep all European powers, including Britain, as far from American shores as possible. "There never was a period since the establishment of our Revolution," declared Monroe's message, when "there was greater necessity . . . for patriotism and union." The Monroe Doctrine began as a defensive act meant to hold the states together.[43]

In early 1825, Adams did succeed Monroe as president, but most southerners did not trust a politician from New England. He ignited their alarm by proposing to send official delegates to a special Congress at Panama. Planned by Bolívar, the Panama Congress would assemble representatives from every nation in the hemisphere to discuss mutual security and trade. As Adams's secretary of state, Henry Clay welcomed the congress as an opportunity to counteract British influence in the new nations, but many Americans balked at any alliance as entangling. Jockeying to discredit and replace Adams as president, Andrew Jackson thundered, "The moment we engage in confederations, or alliances with any nation, we may from that time date the downfall of our republic."[44]

During the winter of 1825–1826, Jackson's ally Martin Van Buren opposed the Panama Congress to rally southern support for Jackson's new party, the Democrats, who championed white supremacy. Denouncing Latin American nations for extending citizenship to colored people, Democrats warned that the special congress would promote the abolition of slavery throughout the hemisphere. Thomas Hart Benton of Missouri opposed dealing with nations that had "black Generals in their armies and mulatto Senators in their Congresses! . . . I would not debate whether my slave is my property." John Randolph of Virginia insisted that no white American could sit in a congress with a "motley mixture" of "the native African, . . . the mixed breeds, the Indians, and the half breeds." A listener said that Randolph "conjured up black and hideous phantoms, with flat noses, thick lips, and frizzy hair, and then tilted at them, with desperate and relentless fury." Benton and Randolph insisted that only white men could conduct a proper republic.[45]

Opponents claimed that the Panama Congress somehow would compel the United States to recognize Haiti and welcome her diplomats—thereby igniting a massive slave revolt within the United States. Benton insisted that the "peace of eleven States in this Union will not permit the fruits of a successful negro insurrection to be exhibited among them. It will not permit black consuls and ambassadors . . . to parade through our country, and to give their fellow blacks in the United States, proof in hand of the honors which await them, for a like successful effort on their part." John Floyd of Virginia denounced the Panama Congress as "this moon-struck project, which threatens . . . the whole of our Southern frontier." If America's slaves did revolt, alarmists predicted that the mixed-race armies of South America would march north to help them.[46]

To increase foreign trade, most northerners supported sending a delegation, so an angry debate roiled Congress. A member described "a perfect Scene of Confusion" with "the Chairman crying out Order, Order, Order" while congressmen ranted about "hurly burly, helter skelter, Negro states and yankies." In late March 1826, Congress narrowly approved sending delegates, but the long debate delayed them from arriving until the Panama Congress had adjourned after accomplishing nothing. The controversy helped Van Buren rally the new Democratic Party behind Andrew Jackson as the white man's champion.[47]

Cuba

To protect and promote slavery, southerners took control of American foreign and military policy. Prior to the Civil War, two-thirds of the presidents and secretaries of state and four-fifths of the secretaries of war and the navy came from the South. Proslavery men seethed when any Yankee held a key position. In 1841, Abel Upshur of Virginia denounced the retention of Edward Everett of Massachusetts as ambassador to Britain: "The present condition of the country imperiously requires that a southern man & a slaveholder should represent us at that court. And yet a Boston man is appointed, half schoolmaster, half priest, and whole abolitionist." In fact, Everett was a moderate on slavery and a rare northerner with a high diplomatic post—until supplanted by a Maryland slaveholder at Upshur's request.[48]

Southerners insisted that slavery promoted greater economic growth by enabling masters to compel concerted labor to improve farms and plantations. An Alabama congressman praised "the immense superiority of a system of associated slave labor over free individual labor." Pointing to Brazil and Cuba, southerners claimed that slave societies grew faster than republics that had "gone through a farce of abolishing slavery."[49]

Subscribing to a domino theory, southern leaders felt threatened by the prospect of Brazil or Cuba abolishing slavery. If the South became an isolated society clinging to slavery, southerners feared increased pressure from northern abolitionists, foreign powers, and slave rebels. By defending Spanish rule in Cuba and the monarchy of Brazil, southern politicians abandoned republican scruples against foreign-held colonies and kings. Defending slavery took priority over expanding republicanism.[50]

Southern leaders felt locked in a hemispheric struggle against the British Empire as "the center and source of antislavery fanaticism." A South Carolina congressman declared, "Our systems are at issue and the contest will be for mastery of the world. One or the other must go down or yield." That struggle seemed more urgent during the 1830s, when the British emancipated their slaves in the West Indies. Fearing that Britain sought "to form around our southern shores a cordon of free negroes," southerners dreaded "the coils of an Anaconda from which there was no escape but in death."[51]

Southern leaders bristled when British officials freed slaves from American shipwrecks on the shores of Bermuda and the Bahamas: island colonies near the United States. Rather than serve as slave catchers for Americans, imperial officials refused to extradite runaways and castaways. An American diplomat, Andrew Stevenson of Virginia, denounced the British "distinction in principle between property in persons and property in things."[52]

Southern leaders worried that their enslaved people would mutiny to steal vessels for flight to British colonies. That fear became real in November 1841, when 135 enslaved people seized the brig *Creole* bound from Virginia to New Orleans. Their leaders included the aptly named Madison Washington, who had escaped from Virginia to Canada but had returned to try to liberate his wife, only to suffer seizure and renewed slavery. Killing one of the crew, the mutineers took the vessel to the Bahamas, where British officials freed them. Southerners raged that this decision threatened their lives by inviting slave revolts in America.[53]

Florida's masters complained that their slaves stole boats to sail across the hundred-mile passage to the Bahamas. By 1840 about 6,000 American slaves had found haven there to prosper as sponge divers and wreckers of stranded vessels. Claiming that British naval officers enticed and helped runaways, John C. Calhoun accused Britain of assisting "the coulored races of all hues . . . against the white" to foment "a war between races of the most deadly and desolating character."[54]

Although American law barred importing slaves from overseas, federal leaders refused to cooperate with the British naval efforts to suppress that trade on the coast of Africa. This refusal had broad American support, for northerners as well as southerners recalled that the British had impressed American sailors and interfered with neutral merchant ships during the Napoleonic wars. But proslavery men especially distrusted Britain as the great ideological adversary in the contest between free and slave labor. In December 1841, Britain induced most of Europe's other powers to cooperate in naval enforcement of a global ban on the slave trade, but American diplomats persuaded France to drop out of that agreement, which they cast as a scam to advance British naval and commercial domination.[55]

While waging a diplomatic struggle against British antislavery, southerners hoped to avoid a shooting war. They wanted no disruption in trade with Britain, the primary market for their cotton. Respecting the might of the British fleet, they also feared attacks on their commerce and seaports. Worst of all, the British might land "raven-colored troopers" from the West Indies to promote a Haitian-style rebellion by American slaves. These fears made southerners wary of occasional northern efforts to confront the British over the boundary with Canada.[56]

If war did come, southern leaders hoped to keep British invaders far away by fighting instead on the high seas. During the 1840s, some states'-rights politicians became avid promoters of a robust federal investment in a bigger navy. The converts included Abel P. Upshur. Appointed secretary of the navy in 1841, Upshur pushed for a larger and more modern fleet of steam-powered warships mounting heavier cannons. Recalling the British raids along the southern coast during the War of 1812, Upshur insisted that a bigger American navy could prevent British "incursions, aiming at revolution" by arousing "hostile elements of our social system against one another," which was southern code for slave rebellion. Adams marveled at the sudden conversion of states'-rights politicians into proponents of naval expansion, which he said "comes reeking hot from the furnace of slavery."[57]

Southerners wanted to deploy the navy to protect slavery in Cuba from alleged British interference. During the Latin American revolutions, conservative *criollos* had kept Cuba in the Spanish Empire. As revolution destroyed sugar plantations in Haiti, Cuba's planters expanded their operations to fill the supply gap in the market. They imported more enslaved Africans and built steam-powered mills to make Cuba the world's top sugar producer. Many Americans invested in Cuba as planters or as merchants importing slaves and exporting sugar and coffee. Cuba became second only to Britain as an American trade partner, producing 60 percent of the sugar and 40 percent of the coffee imported into the United States. While generating profits for planters and merchants, sugar work drove slaves to early graves. "Sugar is made with blood," Cubans said.[58]

Southerners wanted to annex Cuba for the United States, but they could live with it as a Spanish colony that preserved slavery. They just could not abide the prospect of Britain pressuring Spain to abolish slavery in Cuba—or that a slave revolt there would create a larger and closer version of Haiti that could export revolution to the United States. John Randolph warned that the South could "be invaded from Cuba in rowboats." Blocking Bolívar's promotion of a republican revolution in Cuba, Americans defended the colony of a European monarchy—quite contrary to the Monroe Doctrine.[59]

In 1843, the United States sent a naval squadron to Havana to counteract a rumored slave revolt allegedly promoted by British agents. A revolt did break out in one province, but the British had nothing to do with it. Brutally suppressing the rebels, Spanish authorities executed hundreds—and whipped thousands more, rendering 1844 "the Year of the Lash" in Cuba. The American consul in Havana, Robert

Blair Campbell of South Carolina, applauded repression: "No punishment can be too severe for the intermeddling fanatic who attempts
to arm the slave against the master." Campbell boasted that he had
"no sickly sensibility on the subject of slavery."[60]

Texas

Southerners also coveted Tejas (Texas), the northeastern region of
the Mexican state of Coahuila y Tejas. During the 1810s, brutal civil
wars had cut the population in half owing to combat, executions,
dislocation, and disease. In 1820, the region had only 2,500 Hispanics,
outnumbered by 3,000 American squatters and 40,000 Natives. But
Mexicans cherished Tejas as a fertile land of immense agricultural
and commercial potential. By developing that potential they hoped
to rescue their republic from poverty and debt. In Tejas, both Americans and Mexicans saw the key to continental power, but only one
republic could enjoy the prize.[61]

Unable to keep American settlers out of Tejas, Mexican officials
tried to convert them into Mexican citizens. An official sought "honest, hard-working people, regardless of what country they come
from . . . even hell itself." In 1825, Coahuila y Tejas adopted a colonization law that welcomed newcomers who would adopt the Catholic faith and embrace Mexican citizenship. Exempt from taxes for
six years, the settlers could bring in tools and implements duty-free.
The newcomers were called Extranjeros to distinguish them from the
Hispanic Tejanos.[62]

The Coahuila y Tejas government awarded vast land grants to
speculators known as *empresarios*, who received a bonus of 22,000 acres
for every 100 settler families introduced to Tejas. Seventeen of the
twenty-four *empresario* contracts went to Americans, who recruited
their countrymen as settlers. The old scoundrel James Wilkinson
sought to recoup his bankrupt estate by seeking an *empresario* contract. After three futile years in Mexico City, he died there of gout
and poverty in 1825.[63]

The premier *empresario* was Stephen F. Austin, a lawyer from Missouri, whose late father had secured a vast land grant along the Brazos, Colorado, and San Bernard Rivers, with Galveston as its port. Never marrying, Austin claimed that Tejas was his bride, and he regarded settlers as his children: "I look upon them as one great family under my care." He ran his own plantation worked by slaves and offered especially large farms at low prices: for just $60, a settler received 960 acres plus another 100 acres for each child and 80 acres for each slave. By comparison, the United States government charged $100 for a farm of just 80 acres, with no bonus for children and slaves. Ruined by the depression of 1819, many American debtors moved to Tejas to raise cotton and cattle, exploiting the rich soil, long growing season, and access to coastal trade.[64]

The settlers insisted that they needed slaves. Austin explained that in Tejas, "Nothing is wanted but money, and negros are necessary to make it," so settlers sought "negroes to make cotton to *buy more* negroes." Because lands were so cheap, the common Texan could afford to buy slaves. A Mexican official noted that "their entire fortunes consists of the ownership of their Slaves." Without them, another conceded, "her inhabitants would be nothing." Antislavery in principle but proslavery in practice, Austin considered the system essential to develop Tejas in the short term but ultimately dangerous to white people. He dreaded slave revolts but concluded, "It is in vain to tell a North American that the white population will be destroyed some fifty or eighty years hence by the negroes, and that his daughters will be violated and Butchered by them." So Austin kept his qualms private while he recruited slaveholders to settle Tejas.[65]

A dutiful *empresario*, Austin learned Spanish, and promoted Catholicism and loyalty to Mexico. That loyalty received a test in late 1826 from a rebellion in East Texas. The rebels rallied to the reckless leadership of Haden and Benjamin Edwards, brothers and former *empresarios* sacked by the government for violating their contracts. To recover their lands and seize more, the brothers organized a popular rebellion by claiming to defend slavery against Mexican interference. They also won support from some Cherokees who had come westward to settle in northeast Tejas. Shortly before Christmas, the squatters and Cherokees arrested Mexican officials and declared independence as the "Republic of Fredonia." The rebels reserved the southern two-thirds of Tejas for "White People" and the northern third for "Red People." Fredonia exemplified a common phenomenon on American frontiers: opportunists creating their own polity with the power to make land grants to buy support.[66]

In early 1827, Austin rallied loyal settlers to help Mexican troops suppress the rebellion. Appealing to settler prejudices, Austin denounced the Fredonians for making an "Unnatural and bloody alliance with Indians." The Edwards brothers and other defeated rebels fled across the border to Louisiana, while the Cherokees executed their chief who had supported Fredonia. The loyal majority of Extranjeros seemed to vindicate the *empresario* system as a safe means for developing Tejas.[67]

But Extranjero numbers grew rapidly, reaching 12,000 in 1829 to outnumber the region's Tejanos by three-to-one. That growth alarmed Mexican officials when they concluded that most of the settlers defied Mexico's laws and constitution. Exporting their cotton and cattle across the American border, settlers developed Texas as an economic satellite of the United States with only a tenuous political tie to Mexico. Noting the methods used to subvert and obtain Florida, the Mexican politician Lucas Alamán lamented, "Where others send invading armies," the North Americans "send their colonists."[68]

In 1828, an investigative commission, headed by General Manuel de Mier y Terán, visited Texas and found a growing population hostile to Mexican laws. Terán bristled at their brutal treatment of enslaved people: "They pull their teeth, they set dogs upon them to tear them apart, and the mildest of them will whip the slaves until they are flayed." Cherishing Tejas as a potential engine for enriching Mexico, Terán worried that its loss would sentence his nation to "a precarious existence at the cost of many humiliations." He concluded that anyone who "does not oppose the loss of Tejas is an execrable traitor who ought to be punished with every kind of death."[69]

In September 1829, the Mexican president outlawed slavery by executive decree. Because slavery was rare in the heart of the nation, the ban was easy to announce there. The ban also played well with nationalists who claimed moral superiority over their northern neighbors. A Mexican legislator declared, "It is not conceivable that a free Republic should subject some of its children to slavery. Let us leave such contradictions to the United States of North America."[70]

But the ban outraged Extranjeros, who insisted that they needed "the robust and almost tireless labor of this race of human species called blacks." Although Mexico delayed enforcing the decree in distant Tejas, some slaves fled south, deeper into Mexico, to become free. The Extranjeros also worried that news of the Mexican law would depress further immigration by southerners, who wanted security for their human property, and without continued settlement, economic development would stagnate in Tejas.[71]

In April 1830, the federal government of Mexico sought tighter control in Tejas by banning further immigration from the United States and the introduction of new slaves. Austin characterized the new law as meant "to keep out turbulent and bad men, vagabonds, and Slaves." But he insisted that the region could not prosper without more bad men bringing in slaves: "Texas *must be* a slave country." His neighbors would tolerate no antislavery sentiments: "To say anything to them as to the justice of slavery, or its demoralizing effects on society, is only to draw down ridicule." To evade the new law, Extranjeros resorted to a legal fiction that their Black laborers were leased rather than owned. For example, in 1833 an enslaved woman named Clarissa had to sign a notarized contract "renouncing and disclaiming all her right and claim to personal liberty for & during the term of ninety-nine years."[72]

Having only 200 soldiers in Tejas, Mexico's leaders could not control the settlers. Austin dismissed any effort "to dam out the North Americans" as like "trying to stop the Mississippi with a dam of straw." Indeed, Extranjeros more than doubled in Tejas during the four years after 1830. General Mier y Terán lamented, "There is no physical force that can stop the entrance of the *norteamericanos,* who are exclusive owners of the coast and the border of Tejas." In despair, Terán put on his dress uniform before plunging a sword through his heart on July 3, 1832.[73]

In early 1834, Santa Anna staged another coup and this time ruled as a conservative centralizer who abolished state governments and jailed his critics. Although Extranjeros had long disliked subordination within Coahuila y Tejas, they expected far worse from a centralized dictatorship in distant Mexico City. In 1835, Extranjeros and Tejanos united in a rebellion that initially sought to restore federalism and demand statehood for their region within Mexico. Similar uprisings by federalists arose in several Mexican states, including Yucatán and Zacatecas. On a lobbying trip to Mexico City, Austin was seized and jailed for eighteen months, charged with sedition for advocating statehood for Tejas.[74]

Austin's arrest and absence weakened the cause of moderation in Tejas, where populist firebrands promoted revolutionary independence. The new leaders included William Barret Travis, an ambitious young lawyer, who had fled from his creditors and a failed marriage in Alabama. By promoting an independent republic called Texas, Travis sought to make "a splendid fortune." In 1836, the firebrands met in convention to declare independence. The new republic attracted ambitious southerners, including a humorous former congressman from Tennessee, David Crockett. After losing his bid for reelection, Crockett told his constituents that "they might go to hell, and I would go to Texas." Alarmed by rumors that Santa Anna would promote slave revolts in the United States, southern volunteers joined the fight in Texas.[75]

Despite their Tejano supporters, Texans defined their struggle in racial terms, deriding Mexicans as a mongrel race who would liberate enslaved people. The Texan military commander, Sam Houston, appealed for recruits by playing the race card: "The last drop of our blood would flow before we would bow under the yoke of these half Indians." Convinced that white freedom depended on Black slavery,

Texans asserted that Mexicans meant "to give liberty to our slaves, and to make slaves of ourselves."[76]

Santa Anna did promise freedom to enslaved people who ran away to join his army, and he cast Mexico as the true land of freedom: "Shall we permit those wretches to moan in chains any longer in a country whose laws protect the liberty of man without distinction of cast or color?" In Brazoria, masters reported that enslaved people "were on the tip-toe of expectation, and rejoicing that the Mexicans were coming to make them free!"[77]

In early 1836, Santa Anna invaded Tejas with 6,000 men, but they were untrained conscripts led by many officers in gaudy uniforms: a fitting army for a showman generalissimo. In March, the troops captured and butchered small Texan garrisons at Goliad and the Alamo, the latter a former mission in San Antonio where Crockett and Travis died. Pressing on into East Texas in April, Santa Anna blundered into an ambush at San Jacinto, where Sam Houston routed the Mexicans, killing 630 (many of them after surrendering), and capturing another 700, including the dictator.[78]

To save himself from lynching, Santa Anna signed a treaty conceding independence to Texas within extraordinary borders that included all lands as far south and west as the Rio Grande—far beyond the region's former limit on the Nueces River. The new boundary secured for Texas the eastern half of New Mexico, including the capital of Santa Fe, but Mexico's Congress rejected the treaty as extorted from a captive. For the next seven years, Mexicans and Texans exchanged bloody raids, but both republics were too poor and disorganized to defeat the other, producing a stalemate.[79]

The first president of Texas, Houston, had served as an American congressman and Tennessee governor until a failed marriage led to his nervous breakdown. He fled to live among the Cherokees of northeast Texas, where he drank himself nearly to oblivion. The Texas Revolution provided a chance to sober up and resume his political career in a new republic.[80]

The victorious Texans consolidated their racial order. Suppressing slave rebellion in the Brazos valley, Texans hanged several and "whipd nearly to death" another one hundred. The republic's constitution legalized slavery and outlawed freeing any enslaved people. Legislators opposed the "infusion of dissatisfaction and disobedience into the brain of the honest and contented slave by vagabond free negroes." So they ordered free Blacks to get out or risk sale as slaves. A free Black rancher, Greenbury Logan, was no vagabond. Petitioning to remain, Logan complained, "Every privilege dear to a free man is taken away," but the government ordered him to leave. The new constitution made Texas the most proslavery regime in North America.[81]

Independence, cheap land, and the enhanced security of slavery attracted a surge of southerners to develop more cotton plantations. The depression of 1837 contributed by pushing more farmers to flee from their debts by moving across the border into Texas. During the decade after 1836, the new republic's population more than doubled, reaching 125,000, of whom 27,000 were enslaved.[82]

Although most Tejanos had supported the revolution, they became second-class citizens under the new regime. Denouncing them as "the friends of our enemies," vigilantes drove Tejanos from farms and ranches and destroyed several villages. The mayor of San Antonio, Juan N. Seguín, reported that "the scum of [American] society" treated Tejanos "worse than brutes" on "the pretext that they were Mexican." In fact, their "only crime was that they owned large tracts of land and desirable property." Thugs did much of the dirty work for land speculators who bought up lands for a song from intimidated Tejanos. Early in the process, a frank speculator wrote that San Antonio's Tejanos were "not sufficiently scared to make an advantageous sale of their lands." He advised sending a couple of hundred armed men to persuade them. Despite his military service for Texan independence, Seguín felt like "a foreigner in my native land." Texans accused him of treason, and vigilantes threatened his life. In 1842, Seguín and his family fled to Mexico, where he joined the army.[83]

Indians also suffered from Texan independence. In northeast Texas, Cherokees held land grants from the government of Mexico, but land speculators coveted their fertile fields for cotton plantations. Houston tried to protect his Cherokee friends, but he retired from the presidency in 1838. His replacement, Mirabeau Lamar, came from Georgia, where he had helped to dispossess and remove Cherokees. Lamar sought to do the same in Texas. Denouncing Cherokees as "wild cannibals of the woods" with "the ferocity of tigers and hyenas," he vowed "an exterminating war" to produce "their total extinction" unless they left Texas immediately.[84]

In 1839, when Cherokees resisted, state troops defeated and slaughtered many. Their aged chief Duwali died wielding a sword given to him by Houston. The victors took Duwali's scalp and sent it to Houston to mock his attempts to protect the Cherokees. State troops burned Cherokee villages and drove the survivors northward beyond the republic. A land speculator exulted, "The Land Mania is great. . . . We have whipped off the Cherokees."[85]

Lamar also sent volunteers, known as Texas Rangers, to seek out and destroy Comanche villages, killing more women and children than men. In retaliation, Comanches raided Texan settlements to burn farms and take captives. In March 1840, Texan officials invited Comanche chiefs to meet them in San Antonio to negotiate a peace. To signal their good intentions, the Comanches brought along their families. But the Texan offer was a sham. Once the chiefs had entered the Council House, Texans seized them as hostages. When they resisted, Texans killed thirty-five Comanches, including five women. Plenty of Comanches remained on the western plains to take vengeance on settler families in Texas.[86]

Prolonged warfare with Mexicans and Comanches bankrupted Texas and discredited the republic's government. Failing to collect taxes or import duties, the government instead printed money, which fueled hyperinflation. A disgusted citizen denounced the Congress of Texas as "the most imbecile body that ever sat [in] judgment on the fate of a nation." For lack of funds, the government could not even deliver the mail, and had to eliminate its navy and reduce its army to just 600 men. The ramshackle new town of Houston served as the capital. Visitors from France derided the swampy, disease-ridden place as a "detested, self-polluted, isolated mud-hole of a city," comprised of "patched up shantees of rough boards" save for the log cabin that served as the president's residence and the barn that housed Congress. In 1838, two leading presidential candidates committed suicide in despair. In 1842, Houston's secretary confided, "We are in collapse, perfectly prostrate and powerless" and "worse than all, without confidence in ourselves." In 1844, the republic defaulted on its massive debt.[87]

Most Texans longed to lose the public debt and forsake independence by joining the United States. As an American state, they would gain military aid against Mexico and improved access to investment capital. But Presidents Jackson and Van Buren balked at annexing Texas for fear of dividing the Union along regional lines given northern opposition to adding slave territory.[88]

By bankrupting Texas, Lamar lost popularity, which enabled the political comeback of Houston, who resumed the republic's presidency in 1841. A Texan noted, "Old Sam. H[ouston], . . . is still unsteady, [and] intemperate, but drunk in a ditch is worth a thousand of Lamar." To secure American annexation, Houston played a clever game by flirting with British diplomats, pretending to seek an alliance.[89]

Britain's overly enthusiastic ambassador to Texas, Charles Elliot, believed that his empire's money could entice Texans to abolish slavery. Indeed, Elliot dreamed that a free Texas would block the westward expansion of American slavery and supplant the United States as the prime supplier of cotton to British mills. In fact, Britain's home government was too cautious to adopt Elliot's costly and risky plan; nor were Texans willing to forsake slavery for money. A French emissary assured his government, "Slavery is, as your Excellency knows, the foundation stone of Texian society."[90]

By flirting with the British, Houston meant to spook American leaders, particularly southerners, so that they would push to annex Texas. A Texas emissary in London, Ashbel Smith, assured Americans that Britain wanted to convert Texas into "a negro nation, a sort of Hayti on the continent" and "a refuge for fugitive slaves from the United States." Smith warned that preserving "Slavery in Texas is a question of life or death to the slave-holding states of the American Union." He easily persuaded Duff Green, a Marylander whom John Quincy Adams aptly called America's roving "ambassador of slavery." From London, Green reported that the British would incite "rebellion and servile war in the South, by purchasing and emancipating the slaves of Texas."[91]

Southern leaders took the bait laid out by Houston, Smith, and Green. Senator Robert Walker of Mississippi warned that Britain would create "a government of Zamboes and Mestizoes, of Africans and Mulattos on the borders of Louisiana and Arkansas . . . to unite with and instigate the people of their own colored race within our limits to deeds of bloodshed and massacre." A Texan diplomat in Washington exulted: "You would be amused to see their fear of England, and that is the secret of our success if we do succeed."[92]

Supposed British scheming unhinged Andrew Jackson, who insisted that the empire meant to form "an iron Hoop around the United States" that would cost "oceans of blood and millions of money to burst asunder." During the 1810s, Jackson had seized Florida to destroy a haven for runaways. Thirty years later, he exhorted the federal government to do the same with Texas. Otherwise, he predicted, "Our slaves in the great valley of the Mississippi" would become "worth nothing, because they would all run over to Texas and under British influence [be] liberated." Then, he predicted, Britain would rally "hordes of savages" and former slaves to spread "servile war" throughout the South. Seventy-seven years old and ailing, he added, "I am gasping for breath while using my pen." Jackson sacrificed his health to write because of the high stakes: "the perpetuation of our republican system, and . . . our glorious Union." In his mind, white freedom depended on saving slavery by annexing Texas.[93]

The alarmed southerners included John Tyler. Elected vice president in 1840, he became president in 1841 when William Henry Harrison died of pneumonia after just a month in office. Although elected

as a Whig, Tyler held the standard views of a states'-rights Democrat. He even complained that Washington, D.C., had too many businesses named "National," such as the "National Hotel" and "National
Oyster-House." President Tyler vetoed almost every bill passed by the
Whigs in Congress, including two efforts to charter a new national
bank. Renounced and shunned by Whigs, Tyler sought to win reelection in 1844 by appealing to southern Democrats, who wanted Texas.[94]

To lead the push for annexation, Tyler relied on his old friend
and new secretary of state, Abel P. Upshur, who had modernized the
navy. Upshur privately felt that the North had slandered the South
over slavery and should accept the annexation of Texas as atonement:
"The history of the world does not present an example of such insult,
contempt, and multiplied wrongs and outrages from one nation to
another as we have received and are daily receiving from our northern brethren!!"[95]

To broaden support for annexation, in 1844 Senator Walker published a pamphlet that appealed to northern racial anxieties and fan-
tasies. A former Pennsylvanian, Walker had moved to Mississippi to
acquire cotton plantations worked by slaves. He also invested in the
lands and public debt of Texas, gaining personal incentives for promoting annexation. Walker hated Mexicans because his brother had
settled in Texas, fought for independence, and died after a grim stint
as a prisoner-of-war.[96]

Walker's pamphlet warned that British emancipation in Texas
would unleash a race war to enflame the South and send thousands of
Black refugees fleeing to the North. Then, Walker assured Yankees,
their "poor-house[s] and the jail, the asylums of the deaf and dumb,
the blind, the idiot and insane would be filled to overflowing" with
"the millions of the Negro race whom wretchedness and crime would
drive to despair and madness." Yet, without any sense of contradiction, Walker also argued that these alleged defectives would dominate the northern labor market, leading to "starvation and misery . . .
among the white laboring population." Walker insisted that annexation of Texas would push slavery and Blacks westward to a safer dis-

tance: "It is clear that, as slavery advanced in Texas, it would recede from the states bordering on the free states of the North and West." He even argued that, once Texas had absorbed America's Blacks, they somehow would become free and then move into Mexico, leaving the United States entirely to the white race.[97]

Although contradictory and fanciful, Walker's arguments appealed to northern Democrats, who championed white supremacy but claimed to dislike slavery in principle. A Pennsylvania politician reported that Walker's pamphlet "on Texas flew like wild-fire through the whole country." An Indiana congressman concluded that annexation would effect "what modern abolitionism has retarded, the peaceful and gradual emancipation of slaves in Kentucky, Virginia, Maryland, Delaware, and then in other states. . . . If there be for the liberated African a path of deliverance and a place of refuge beyond, that path lies through Texas." Democrats also claimed that annexation would rescue Americans from containment by the British Empire. Casting annexation as a renewed "struggle for American independence," Pennsylvania congressman Charles Jared Ingersoll insisted, "The dominion of the whole American continent will . . . be at stake. Shall it rest in America, or in a small island on the coast of Europe?"[98]

By acquiring Texas, Democrats hoped to dominate the global supply of cotton needed by British textile factories. In 1840, Britain imported 592 million pounds of cotton, more than half of the global supply, and 82 percent of that cotton came from the United States. Democrats argued that, in the event of war, the United States could ruin the British economy by cutting off cotton exports, throwing millions of Britons out of work. Then, a Michigan congressman predicted, "starving millions would rise in infuriated masses and overwhelm their bloated aristocracy." Tyler promised that a "virtual monopoly of the cotton plant" had "more potential in the affairs of the world than millions of armed men." On the other hand, an independent Texas would become "a fatal rival" to the United States.[99]

Destinies

During the summer of 1845, a New York–based Democratic journalist, John L. O'Sullivan, coined a celebrated phrase: "manifest destiny." He justified annexing Texas and Oregon as "the fulfillment of our manifest destiny to overspread the continent" and thereby accommodate "our yearly multiplying millions." Although "manifest destiny" suggested a new confidence in American might, O'Sullivan invoked the phrase to justify the defensive imperialism so long nurtured by fearful Americans. He claimed that only expansion could repel British plans "of thwarting our policy and hampering our power, limiting our greatness and checking the fulfillment of our manifest destiny." Expansion still served to protect a vulnerable republic from a dreaded synergy between enemies at home and abroad.[100]

Expansionists claimed that Americans had built a uniquely moral empire based on the consent of citizens—in alleged contrast to European empires premised on violent conquest. O'Sullivan proclaimed, "No instance of aggrandizement or lust for territory has stained our annals. No nation has been despoiled by us, no country laid desolate, no people over run." He overlooked the American devastation of Upper Canada during the War of 1812 as well as Jackson's deadly forays into Florida. And Americans had killed and dispossessed plenty of Indians.[101]

After securing Texas, expansionists wanted to seize California from Mexico. During the 1830s, American mariners and fur traders had noted the region's prime harbors, fertile land, and alluring climate. They concluded that California was wasted on Mexicans and could enrich many Americans. In 1841, some Americans began to travel overland to settle in northern California, clustering in the Sonoma Valley, where they ignored the authority of Mexican officials. One official complained that "Americans were so contriving that someday they will build ladders to touch the sky, and once in the heavens, they will change the whole face of the universe and even the color of the stars." He saw the settlers as an entering wedge for American conquest.[102]

Expansionists worried that Mexico would sell California to Britain to pay down an immense national debt. Congressman Caleb Cushing of Massachusetts warned that the British meant to hold Oregon and seize Hawaii and California to gain "a complete belt of fortresses environing the globe, to the imminent future peril not only of our territorial possessions, but of all our vast commerce on the Pacific." Southern leaders dreaded that Britons planned on "planting her colored battalions in the Californias" to advance "all of their abolition doctrines."[103]

By preemptively seizing California, expansionists claimed that the United States could escape from peril into greatness. Shaken by the depression of 1837, Democrats blamed insufficient demand in Europe for American farm produce. They hoped that securing ports on the Pacific would open a vast Asian market for American crops. Then, a Louisiana congressman predicted, "Fifty years will not elapse ere the destinies of the human race will be in our hands." Expansionists oscillated wildly between dreading America's peril in the present and dreaming of global domination in the future.[104]

In fact, it was impossible for midwestern farmers to get their bulky crops to the West Coast. In between lay nearly two thousand miles of immense obstacles: Great Plains, Rocky Mountains, Great Basin, and Sierra Nevada. But expansionists insisted that building a transcontinental railroad could convert their fantasy into reality, which, one vowed, "would place us in a position to defy, and if we please, dictate to all the world." Technology and expansion could transmute the Union's vulnerability into impregnability, so expansionists argued. But private enterprise could not afford the enormous cost of building a transcontinental railroad. Such an enterprise demanded a massive federal subsidy of the sort that the governing Democrats dreaded. Having killed the "monster bank," Democrats were not about to create a "monster railroad"—although they needed one to fulfill their transcontinental ambitions.[105]

Whigs feared expansion as dividing and distracting Americans from economic development within their boundaries. Clay preached, "It is much more important that we unite, harmonize, and improve what we have than attempt to acquire more." Whigs also worried that expansion would imbalance the fragile Union by favoring one region at the expense of another. Reversing the Democrats' priorities, Whigs wanted an activist federal government at home but greater restraint in foreign policy.[106]

Peacemaker

On February 28, 1844, the nation's political elite gathered on a new warship, the steam-powered USS *Princeton*, a showpiece of Upshur's drive to improve the navy. The *Princeton* featured the world's largest naval gun, euphemistically named the "Peacemaker," although it was designed to devastate and kill. The passengers included President Tyler and most of his cabinet, as well as James Madison's elderly widow, Dolley, and the Mexican ambassador, Juan Almonte. As the *Princeton* steamed down the Potomac River past Mount Vernon, the captain fired Peacemaker to honor the first president, but the weapon exploded into deadly shards of iron, killing Upshur and eight others.[107]

To replace Upshur as secretary of state, Tyler appointed Calhoun, the nation's most articulate defender of southern interests. Rather than adopt a diplomatic tone befitting his new post, Calhoun overtly justified annexing Texas as a boon to southern power and slavery. In April 1844, the Senate rejected a treaty of annexation proposed by Calhoun and Tyler because of aversion to provoking a war with Mexico. Clay declared, "I regard all wars as great calamities . . . and honorable peace as the wisest and truest policy of this country." Many senators just did not like Calhoun and Tyler.[108]

Expansion became the key issue in the presidential race of 1844, when both parties rejected Tyler. The Whigs nominated Clay to run against the Democrat, James K. Polk, a younger man favored by Jackson. Confident of victory, Whigs underestimated the obscure Polk, dismissing him as "General Jackson's chief cook and bottle washer." In addition to annexing Texas, Polk vowed to take all of Oregon, which then meant the entire Pacific Northwest including British Columbia. That package would balance a territorial gain in the Southwest with one in the Northwest, a prospect that swayed enough northerners to win Polk a narrow margin in the popular vote and a landslide of 170 to 105 in the Electoral College. Congratulating Polk, Jackson exulted, "I thank my God that the Republic is safe." The old general died a few months later, when he explained that his greatest regret in life was that he "didn't shoot Henry Clay."[109]

In December 1844, the lame-duck president, Tyler, renewed his push to annex Texas but this time sought a simple resolution, which needed just a majority to pass in both houses, rather than a treaty that required a two-thirds vote in the Senate. Supported by Democrats, northern and southern, the bill passed, although by just two votes in the Senate. An outraged John Quincy Adams insisted that the legislative trick reduced the Federal Constitution to a "menstruous rag" and was "the heaviest calamity that ever befell myself and my country." But slave traders celebrated, as the price of enslaved people rose by 21 percent during the year after annexation.[110]

Taking office in March 1845, Polk was forty-nine years old: then the youngest man to become president. In his first great challenge, Polk had to deliver on his reckless campaign promise to take all of the Oregon Country even if that provoked war with the British Empire. Settlers had strengthened the American position in Oregon. During the early 1840s, 6,000 Americans crossed the continent to settle and farm in the fertile Willamette Valley south of the Columbia River, where they outnumbered the 750 British subjects in the region. A British agent warned, "The restless Americans are brooding over a thousand projects, for improving the navigation, building steam Boats, erecting machinery and other schemes that would excite a smile, if entertained by a less enterprising people." By clearing the land and killing Indians, the new settlers ruined the local fur trade, inducing the British company to shift operations northward to Vancouver Island. An imperial official noted that Americans' strength lay in "Settlers . . . not in their Armies and Navies."[111]

Because of the American numbers in the southern half of Oregon, the British were open to splitting the territory. But when Americans demanded the whole, Britons reinforced their garrisons in Canada and sent thirty warships to the Pacific. Neither side, however, wanted a war that would disrupt trade and investment. In June 1845, Polk agreed to a compromise that partitioned the Oregon region, with the United States securing everything south of the 49th parallel of latitude save for Vancouver Island, which the British kept as part of British Columbia. The Union acquired 450,000 square miles, including the future states of Oregon, Washington, and Idaho as well as western Montana and Wyoming. Although sensible, this compromise troubled northern Democrats for it was only half of what Polk had promised them.[112]

Polk recognized that the American military could deal with only one adversary, and Mexico was more tempting because it was far weaker than the British Empire. Plus, Polk wanted to take New Mexico and California more than he coveted all of Oregon. Expanding the Union's bounds would push Mexico farther away, denying a nearby haven for runaway slaves from Texas. Driven outward by anxiety over runaways and revolts, southern expansion kept leapfrogging across the continent.[113]

In early 1846, Polk sent 4,000 troops across the Nueces River into the contested borderland of South Texas. An American officer could see the president's ploy: "We have not one particle of right to be here. It looks as if the government sent a small force on purpose to bring on a war, so as to have a pretext for taking California." The operation went exactly as Polk hoped. In April 1846, the American commander, General Zachary Taylor, reported that Mexican soldiers had attacked one of his patrols in the contested zone, killing 11 men and capturing 69 more.[114]

Pouncing on the news, Polk demanded that Congress declare war: "After reiterated menaces, Mexico has passed the boundary of the United States, has invaded our territory and shed American blood upon the American soil. . . . War exists, and, notwithstanding all our efforts to avoid it, exists by the act of Mexico herself." While claiming only to defend American territory and troops, Polk vowed to conquer California "to defray the expense of the war which that power by her long continued wrongs and injuries had forced us to wage." We have a long tradition of presidents seeking to make Mexico pay for American ambitions.[115]

Most northern Whigs opposed the war as immoral and unwise. A New York congressman denounced the hypocritical "cant about 'manifest destiny,' a *divine mission*, a warrant from the Most High, to civilize, Christianize, and democratize our sister republic at the mouth of the cannon!" But most southern Whigs joined northern and southern Democrats to declare war. Only fourteen congressmen and two senators dared to vote against war, for the great majority feared accusations of abandoning American troops under attack. The Mexican secretary of state, Lucas Alamán, marveled that "the most unjust war [was] provoked by the ambition not of an absolute monarch but of a republic that claims to be at the forefront of nineteenth-century civilization."[116]

Breaking with other Democrats, Calhoun regretted the war because Polk had provoked the conflict and lied about it to Congress: "It sets the example, which will enable all future Presidents to bring about a state of things, in which Congress shall be forced . . . to declare war however opposed to its conviction of justice or expediency." Dismayed by popular enthusiasm for war, Calhoun lamented, "Our people have undergone a great change. Their inclination is for conquest and empire, regardless of their institutions and liberty." Although proslavery, Calhoun would not sacrifice his constitutional scruples to expand the system by military means.[117]

Most Americans thought that Calhoun overthought the issue, for they expected a brief and glorious war over racial inferiors: alleged "mongrels" descended from Blacks and Indians. Mexicans "are reptiles in the path of progressive democracy," declared a Democratic newspaper, and they "must either crawl or be crushed." Calling them "the devil's grandchildren," a Texan asserted, "Why, they're [al]most as black as niggers any way, and ten times as treacherous."[118]

Masculinity compounded racism, for Americans derided Mexicans as too effeminate to resist white men. A former American ambassador to Mexico insisted, "I do not think that the Mexican men have much more physical strength than our women." Religion completed the toxic mix as most Americans regarded their Protestantism as superior to Mexican Catholicism. Expansionists argued that effeminate and Papist "mongrels" did not deserve to keep any land that they could not defend.[119]

Invasion

The United States had great military advantages over Mexico. Richer, larger, and industrializing, the Union could raise more troops and supply them better. The 17 million free Americans more than doubled the 7.5 million Mexicans. Most of Mexico's land was too arid or mountainous for commercial agriculture, and Mexicans lacked navigable rivers to move their crops to market. By contrast, the United States possessed vast tracts of cultivatable land, more navigable rivers, and many superior ports. Americans also enjoyed a per capita income three times that of Mexicans.[120]

Economic superiority endowed American troops with greater firepower, particularly in artillery. Their mass-produced muskets had twice the effective range of the older models used by Mexicans. Naval supremacy enabled Americans to move troops and supplies over long distances to strike at Mexico. That navy also could blockade Mexican ports to intercept supplies and block the collection of the customs duties that the southern republic relied on for revenue.[121]

Devastated by Indian raiders, Mexico's frontier provinces could offer little resistance to American invasion. The leaders of Chihuahua lamented that a state "desolated for fifteen years by the savages,

drowned in the blood of the men and in the lamentations of the widows and orphans, [became] an ideal theater in which to showcase the
power of the United States."[122]

Unstable government also weakened Mexico. Ambitious and feud-
ing generals undermined and overthrew the federal government in
frequent coups. Deep ideological divisions put liberal federalists at
bitter cross-purposes with conservative centralizers. Deeply in debt
to foreign creditors, and unable to collect most taxes, the Mexican
government had to devote 87 percent of its revenue to paying interest,
leaving precious little to fight a powerful invader. Mexico struggled
to feed, clothe, arm, and pay its troops, so many of them deserted to
go home. An American journalist, Jane Swisshelm, denounced the
one-sided war as a "giant whipping a cripple."[123]

During the first year of the war, American confidence in a quick
and glorious victory attracted thousands of volunteers. Many were
Whigs who meant to prove their patriotism despite qualms about the
war. Clay felt both proud and anxious when his son went off to fight
in an "unhappy War . . . between two neighboring Republics!" Polk
worried that the Union's top two generals, Winfield Scott and Zachary Taylor, were Whigs, for Americans were prone to elect victorious
commanders to the presidency. Thomas Hart Benton slyly noted that
Polk wanted "a small war, just large enough to require a treaty of
peace and not large enough to make military reputations, dangerous
for the presidency."[124]

In the spring of 1846, if Taylor had not provoked war in Texas,
Polk expected John C. Frémont to do so in northern California.
Starting from Missouri, Frémont's troops traveled overland to Cali-
fornia, where they rallied the region's 800 American settlers to seize
and jail Mexican officials. Adopting the technique developed in West
Florida and Texas, the rebels declared a new nation, the "Bear Flag
Republic," named for a creature depicted on their banner (although
many observers thought it looked more like a pig). The Bear (or Pig)
Flag Republic lasted about a week before the rebels happily submit-

ted to American rule and put up the Stars and Stripes. Their Hispanic neighbors, known as Californios, were dubious but intimidated.[125]

In July, an American naval squadron, commanded by Robert Stockton, seized the coastal towns of Monterey and San Francisco. Stockton boasted, "My power is more than regal. The haughty Mexican Cavalier shakes hands with me with pleasure, and the beautiful women look to me with joy and gladness as their friend and benefactor." In fact, Californios resisted where they could: in southern California. In December 1846, however, American reinforcements arrived and, a month later, captured Los Angeles, completing the conquest of California. The region lay too far away over wretched roads for the impoverished Mexican government to defend without a navy.[126]

Mexico also lacked the resources to hold New Mexico, a frontier province of 65,000 inhabitants. With 2,100 men, General Stephen W. Kearny crossed the Great Plains to seize New Mexico in August 1846. The Mexican governor panicked and fled southward, abandoning the territory without a fight. He rode away at a remarkable rate given his description as "a mountain of fat." An American official assured New Mexicans that it was "far preferable to become an inconsiderable portion of a powerful Republic, than a considerable one of a nation constantly engaged in revolutions . . . and powerless to defend the citizens of this province from the thousands of hostile Indians who surround them."[127]

Kearny set up a provisional government led by Charles Bent. Merchants liked the new regime as good for business, but common Hispanics and Pueblo Indians resented abuse by American volunteers. The Pueblos also worried that the aggressive newcomers were Protestants who would take Indian lands and threaten their Catholic faith. Despite American promises, the loss of lives, captives, and livestock to Apache and Navajo raiders surged during the occupation, for the volunteers preferred drinking and brawling to chasing elusive Indians in the mountains. In January 1847, Pueblos and poor Hispanics rebelled at Taos, where they broke into Governor Bent's house to kill and scalp him. Spreading through northern New Mexico, the rebellion killed dozens of occupiers, but American troops counterattacked with superior firepower. Storming Taos, they killed 150 rebels in combat and hanged 16 prisoners.[128]

While Frémont, Stockton, and Kearny secured California and New Mexico, the primary American army advanced south from Texas under the command of General Taylor. Poorly educated and shabbily dressed, Taylor did not look like a general, but he kept his cool under fire and had the uncommon ability known as common sense. During the spring of 1846, Taylor crossed the Rio Grande and defeated Mexican forces to capture the port of Matamoros. Pushing deep into northern Mexico, Taylor stormed the fortified crossroads city of Monterrey. An Illinois newspaper exulted, "The prowess of our brave soldiers has made the perfidious Mexicans bite the dust. The serpent of the Mexican arms now writhes in death agony in the beak of the American eagle."[129]

Newspaper praise for Taylor irritated Polk, who dreaded a Whig becoming a war hero. To sideline Taylor's army, Polk transferred four-fifths of his troops, including almost all of his regulars, to join a new thrust against the port of Veracruz. Polk entrusted this invasion force to General Winfield Scott, another Whig but a flamboyant egotist who seemed less likely to appeal to voters. Polk left Taylor with a shrunken force primarily composed of volunteers. They were vulnerable to a Mexican counteroffensive led by a surprising new commander.[130]

Too clever by half, Polk sought to shorten the war by conspiring with a devious partner: General Santa Anna. In 1845, after bungling his latest presidency, Santa Anna had been exiled to Cuba by the Mexican Congress. In Mexico City, a mob celebrated his ouster by smashing Santa Anna's statues and destroying a cenotaph built to hold and honor the leg that he had lost in an earlier war. Dragging that leg through the streets, rioters chanted, "Death to the Cripple, Long Live Congress!"[131]

In 1846, Polk's emissaries offered to escort the rest of Santa Anna back to Mexico to seize power and then conclude a peace treaty dictated by the American president. In August, Santa Anna's vessel passed through the American naval blockade to land at Veracruz. Discontented by defeats in northern Mexico, the people rallied to Santa Anna as a potential savior, restoring him as president. But to keep power, he had to repel the Americans, so Santa Anna double-crossed Polk and took command of Mexican forces. In February 1847, Santa Anna led 20,000 men northward to attack Monterrey, defended by Taylor with only 5,000 troops left exposed by Polk's political game.[132]

Fortunately for Taylor, Santa Anna was a better politician than commander. Driving his army on a forced march across two hundred miles of harsh terrain in three weeks, he lost a quarter of his men to exhaustion, hunger, and desertion. Santa Anna still had an advantage of three-to-one in manpower, but his troops were weakened by their ordeal. Rather than let them rest for a few days, he attacked Taylor's strong position on the high ground at a pass known as Buena Vista. Once again, superior American artillery fire evened the numeric odds by decimating Mexican charges. After two days of combat, Santa Anna abruptly withdrew southward to Mexico City. Having lost 2,000 casualties and as many deserters, his army was in bad shape, but it had captured some cannons and flags from the Americans, sufficient trophies for Santa Anna to claim victory once he got home. For him, war was a form of show business.[133]

News of the victory against superior numbers multiplied Taylor's acclaim in American newspapers—to Polk's dismay. But Taylor still seethed at Polk for his insulting treatment. Indeed, the general regretted that a rumor of Polk's demise was false: "I would as soon have heard of his death . . . as that of any other individual in the whole Union."[134]

Rackensackers

By the spring of 1847, American troops had captured the targeted prizes of the war—New Mexico and California—but resistance stiffened as they probed deeper into Mexico. The vast, mountainous, and arid landscape provided havens for guerrillas who disrupted the invaders' long supply lines. Mexican anger also grew as they encountered Americans who treated them and their Catholic faith with contempt. A Mexican declared, "Their motto is deceit, . . . and their boasted liberty is the grossest despotism, iniquity, and insolence, disguised under the most consummate hypocrisy."[135]

A third of the American army consisted of well-trained regulars recruited from the laboring class, particularly immigrants. The other two-thirds were volunteers drawn from the middle class and enlisted for a single year. A largely volunteer army fit republican principles that disliked the expense and distrusted the allegiance of full-time, professional soldiers.[136]

Defiant young men proud of their liberty, volunteers were a handful to manage. Claiming superiority over regulars, volunteers wore distinctive uniforms, balked at training and discipline, treated orders as optional, drank and gambled on their many idle days, and brawled with units from other states. Reckless with firearms, they often shot one another, usually (but not always) by accident. Unlike regulars, volunteers refused to do hard labor, which they associated with slavery. A volunteer declared, "I came here to fight them Mexicans, and not to make a mule of myself to haul wagons."[137]

Volunteers treated Mexicans with contempt, calling the men "greasers" and the women "greaseritas." Americans distrusted the inhabitants as deceptive and dangerous. A volunteer declared, "They are in short a treacherous race and have hearts, the most of them, as Black as their skins." He vowed to "give them a taste of war in all its horrors, and see if that will bring them to a sense of their folly in contending with the United States." Volunteers felt disgusted when they looted churches and saw Jesus represented as brown or Black.[138]

Volunteers robbed and brutalized Mexican civilians. Elected by their men, the volunteer officers either looked the other way or led the brutality. General Taylor confronted one company: "You are all a G[o]d d[amne]d set of thieves and cowards; you never came here to fight but to rob and plunder, and will run at the first sight of the enemy." General Scott complained that the volunteers "have committed atrocities—horrors—in Mexico, sufficient to make Heaven weep, & every American, of Christian morals, blush for his country. Murder, robbery & rape of mothers & daughters, in the presence of the tied up males of the families, have been common all along the Rio Grande." A regular concluded, "The majority of the Volunteers sent here are a disgrace to the nation."[139]

The worst of the lot were Arkansas volunteers known as "Rackensackers" for their raping, plundering, and burning ways. On February 13, 1847, at the village of Agua Nueva, the Rackensackers took revenge for the death of a comrade by rounding up dozens of civilians and herding them into a cave for slaughter. An American witness recalled, "Women and children were clinging to the knees of the murderers and shrieking for mercy . . . nearly thirty Mexicans lay butchered on the floor, most of them scalped. Pools of blood filled the crevices and congealed in clots." He assured a St. Louis newspaper: "Let us no longer complain of Mexican barbarity. . . . *No act of inhuman cruelty, perpetrated by her most desperate robbers, can excel the work of yesterday committed by our soldiery.*" Their commander, Archibald Yell, refused to punish his men, and he had clout as a former congressman and one of Polk's best friends.[140]

Seeking revenge, mounted guerrillas ambushed supply wagons and stray American soldiers. Daring and clever, the guerrilla chieftains became heroes in a nation so bitterly disappointed by their generals. In the usual cycle of warfare, invaders denounced guerrilla tactics as so treacherous and barbaric that they could justly brutalize civilians suspected of helping the resistance. Each side assigned original sin to the other and regarded its own violence as retaliation meant to teach a lesson. The war killed 20,000 Mexican civilians, often as dislocated, starving refugees from violence.[141]

As the war dragged on, many American soldiers became disillusioned. A junior officer, Ulysses S. Grant, declared, "I do not think there was ever a more wicked war than that waged by the United States on Mexico." He mourned to see his "republic following the bad example of European monarchies." Thirteen thousand Americans died in the war, about 17 percent of the force. Most fell to diseases contracted in filthy military camps rather than in combat. A volunteer officer described his camp as "a graveyard, a very hell on earth." Soldiers' letters home dwelled on sicknesses, the searing heat of summer, and atrocities. Few volunteers would reenlist, and ragged, emaciated, and often disabled veterans returning home daunted new recruits.[142]

Desertion swelled, taking over 8 percent of the force. Runaway volunteers headed for home, while those from the regulars often joined the Mexicans. Half of the regulars were immigrants, primarily from Ireland and Germany. As Catholics, they resented insults from, and mistreatment by, their Protestant officers. They also seethed when volunteers desecrated and looted Mexican churches.[143]

Mexicans sent handbills into the American camps to encourage Catholics to desert and join them, offering generous pay and land grants. About 200 deserters formed a special unit, the San Patricios, named for the patron saint of Ireland. Commanded by John Reilly, a tall Irishman who deserted just before the war began, the San Patricios fought with an extra resolve because capture meant almost certain execution as traitors to the United States.[144]

At home, support for Polk's war ebbed in the North. Abolitionists were the earliest and fiercest critics of the conflict as an unjust push to expand slavery by attacking a weaker nation. During the prowar surge of 1846, abolitionists suffered abuse and attacks by volunteers bound for Mexico. But antiwar sentiment spread in the North as the war dragged on into 1847. The Massachusetts state legislature denounced a conflict "so wanton, unjust and unconstitutional" that it "must be regarded as a war against humanity." In Pittsburgh, Jane Swisshelm rebuked a returning volunteer for complicity in "the blood of women and children slain at their own altars, on their own hearthstones, that you might spread the glorious American institutions of women-whipping and baby-stealing." The brutal war seemed to corrode republican principles. An Ohio senator warned that "each chapter we write in Mexican blood, may close the volume of our history as a free people."[145]

Occupation

On March 9, 1847, 11,000 American troops commanded by Winfield Scott landed near Veracruz to besiege 4,000 Mexican troops within the city's old stone walls. In a hurry, Scott bombarded the city with heavy artillery, for he wanted to get his men into the healthier central highlands to escape the tropical diseases of the coast. Rather than batter the city walls, Scott had his artillery target civilian homes, churches, hospitals, and schools within. An American soldier heard the "heart-rending wail of the inhabitants that was awful, the women and children screaming with terror." During four days, Scott's artillery fired 463,000 pounds of shot and shell, wrecking homes and killing over 400 civilians before the Mexican general capitulated. The shattered city shocked a volunteer who told his countrymen through a newspaper that, if they saw the carnage, "you would all turn Quakers."[146]

With 12,000 men, Santa Anna tried to block Scott's army from advancing into the highlands, but Scott's troops burst through the Mexican lines at Cerro Gordo on April 18. Santa Anna abandoned his carriage bearing $18,000 in gold, a lunch of roast chicken, and his artificial leg. Many more wounded men lost their legs after this battle. A Mexican recalled the "continuous screeching of the saw, [and] the screams of the amputees."[147]

Retreating to Mexico City, Santa Anna entrenched 25,000 troops and declared himself dictator, dissolving his nation's congress. In mid-August, Scott's troops stormed the Mexican fortification at Churubusco, capturing 72 San Patricios. Setting an example for his watching army, Scott had 16 hanged and another 16 given fifty lashes and branded with the letter D for deserter. In September, Scott's army shattered the capital's last defenses at Molino del Rey and Chapultepec Castle, where he hanged 30 more captured San Patricios from the top of the walls. The invaders swept into Mexico City, while Santa Anna withdrew his battered army to the suburb of Guadalupe Hidalgo.[148]

The apparent triumph turned into chaos as volunteers raped, robbed, and killed civilians, while Mexicans hurled stones and shot at the occupiers, yelling "Death to the Americans." The rioters killed or wounded about 200 Americans but suffered at least 1,000 of their own dead. The invaders whipped or executed many of their captured tormentors and looted and tore down their homes. An officer worried that the free rein to abuse and destroy "corrupted our men most fearfully. Many of them were perfectly frantic with the lust of blood and plunder." A regular officer saw drunken volunteers kill "five or six innocent persons walking the streets, for no other reason than their own amusement."[149]

Scott also struggled to protect his long supply line, reaching back to Veracruz, from Mexican guerrillas, who tortured and executed prisoners. Having produced a bloody mess, the invaders needed to find a way out with a peace treaty in hand. For that they looked to Nicholas Trist, sent by the Polk administration to Scott's army to negotiate with Mexico's leaders.[150]

Clockwise from top left: "General D. Antonio López De Santa-Anna (1794–1876)," print by A. Hoffy, 1847. Library of Congress 2004669619. *"Duff Green (1791–1875)," photograph by Mathew B. Brady, c. 1860.* Library of Congress 2017894239. *"Battle of Monterrey, The Americans Forcing Their Way to the Main Plaza, Sept. 23, 1846," lithograph by N. Currier, 1846.* Library of Congress 90709071.

EIGHT ✤ SOIL

To impose a peace treaty on his terms, President Polk sent Nicholas P. Trist to Mexico. A Virginia Democrat, Trist had married one of Thomas Jefferson's granddaughters and served as his personal secretary and executor during the 1820s. Joining the state department in 1828, Trist impressed Andrew Jackson, who appointed him U.S. consul in Havana. Trist won a promotion by Polk to become the chief clerk in the State Department, second only to the secretary. Polk made few friends, and they did not include Trist, so they misunderstood one another. Where Polk wanted unquestioning loyalty, Trist freelanced by acting on his own strong opinions.[1]

When the war began in 1846, Polk hoped to conquer and annex the northern third of Mexico, including California and New Mexico. A year later, however, as American troops pressed deeper into Mexico, Polk sought another third of that country by demanding the provinces of Sonora, Chihuahua, Durango, and Baja California. His desired boundary became the 26th parallel rather than the Rio Grande.[2]

But white supremacy cut two ways. On the one hand, Americans felt justified in dispossessing people of color. On the other hand, Americans balked at absorbing many of them. An Indiana congressman declared, "I do not want any mixed races in our Union, nor men of any color except white, unless they be slaves." Expansionists countered that most Mexicans would not last long under American domination. A New York journalist dismissed the "inferior races" of Mexico as "imbecile[s]" who would "melt away at the approach of Anglo-Saxon energy and enterprise as snow before a southern sun."[3]

Upon reaching the army in May 1847, Trist saw the horrors of war and occupation, which he considered "a thing for every right-minded American to be ashamed of." Expressing sympathy for Mexicans in dispatches, Trist irritated Polk, who wanted even harsher peace terms after Winfield Scott captured Mexico City in September: perhaps

Opposite, clockwise from top left: "Nicholas Philip Trist (1800–1874)," photograph by Brady-Handy, 1855. Library of Congress 2017896497. *"Ellen Craft (1826–1891), Disguised to Escape from Slavery," reprinted from William Craft, Running a Thousand Miles for Freedom (1860).* Boston Public Library. *"Daniel Drayton (1802–1857)," engraving by unknown artist, 1855.* Library of Congress 2003681334. *"Mary Edmonson (1832–1853) and Emily Edmonson (1835–1895)," photograph by unknown artist, 1850. Two sisters who tried to escape on the* Pearl: *Mary on the left and Emily on the right.* Library of Congress 91789694.

even absorbing all of Mexico. Polk ordered Trist to abandon negotiations and return home immediately. The president wanted to fight
on until the Mexicans begged for peace and accepted his dictation.[4]

With Scott's support, Trist defied his orders to return home, per-
sisting instead in negotiations, which had become more productive
after November 1847, when a coup ousted and exiled Santa Anna.
The new president, Manuel de la Peña y Peña, wanted to restore peace
to his battered and bankrupt country. British creditors also pressured
Mexico to make peace, so that the nation could resume collecting the
customs revenues needed to pay interest on the national debt.[5]

Writing to Polk, Trist explained that prolonging the war posed
"incalculable danger to every good principle, moral as well as political, which is cherished among us." Trist meant to save both republics:
Mexico from dismemberment and the United States from militarism.
Outraged by Trist's letter, Polk insisted that the diplomat had "proved
himself a very base man. I was deceived by him."[6]

On February 2, 1848, at Guadalupe Hidalgo, Trist concluded a
treaty that struck a balance between the conflicting desires of American leaders: to maximize conquered territory but minimize brown
inhabitants. Trist proposed, and the Mexican government accepted,
a line running up the Rio Grande to El Paso and then west overland
to the Pacific. This boundary secured thinly settled New Mexico
(including Arizona) and California, leaving the more densely populated core to Mexico. For 525,000 square miles, the United States
would pay just $18 million, of which $3 million would settle shaky
claims by American citizens against Mexico.[7]

Learning of the deal on February 19, Polk felt tempted to shelve
the treaty and persist in war to complete Mexico's destruction, but he
recognized that most Americans were weary of the conflict. And the
treaty met the administration's original desires: Texas, New Mexico,
and California. So Polk submitted the treaty for the Senate to consider.[8]

But on that day, while denouncing Polk for making the war,
eighty-year-old John Quincy Adams collapsed in the House of Rep-

resentatives. He died two days later, and the government shut down to honor a former president. Adams had seen annexing Texas as "the turning-point of a revolution which transforms the North American Confederation into a conquering and war-like nation. . . . A military government, a large army, a costly navy, distant colonies, and associate islands in every sea, will follow of course in rapid succession." Adams was prescient.[9]

After the funeral, the Senate approved the treaty on March 10, and Polk ratified it. Then he fired Nicholas Trist as an "impudent and unqualified scoundrel" and withheld all his pay subsequent to his orders to return home. This punishment plunged Trist and his family into genteel poverty until 1870, when Congress belatedly paid the arrears.[10]

In fact, Trist's treaty had saved Polk's administration from a military quagmire in Mexico and political trouble at home. By 1848, most congressmen, including Democrats, despised Polk. An American diplomat felt "not the slightest confidence in his truth or sincerity or manliness." Frosty, arrogant, and self-righteous, Polk treated congressmen with condescension. Most avoided the austere White House receptions. "I had rather be whipped than go," declared one senator. Disliking both sobriety and Polk, Sam Houston considered the president "a victim of the use of water as a beverage."[11]

The Tyler and Polk administrations nearly doubled the size of the United States by adding 1.2 million square miles, including Texas and the future states of California, Nevada, Utah, Arizona, New Mexico, Oregon, Washington, Idaho, and parts of Colorado, Wyoming, and Montana. To add insult to Mexican injury, in January 1848 prospectors found gold in California; it became the richest mineral discovery in human history. That gold might have retired Mexico's national debt; instead, it further enriched the United States. Where loss embittered Mexicans, the gain in land and gold fed American triumphalism. The victors celebrated conquest as might making right. Sam Houston reasoned, "Mexicans are no better than Indians, and I see no reason why we should not . . . take their land." General William Worth agreed that Americans had "been land stealers from time immemorial, and why shouldn't they [be]?"[12]

But some Americans worried that the massive conquest would corrupt and subvert their republic. In 1850, the Census Bureau reported that the United States had grown to "nearly ten times as the whole of France and Great Britain combined" and was "of equal extent with the Roman Empire or that of Alexander." Neither of those ancient empires had promoted human freedom. Could free government persist on an imperial scale? Abraham Lincoln lamented that Polk had seduced Americans with "military glory—that attractive rainbow that rises in showers of blood—that serpent's eye that charms to destroy."[13]

Onto the new lands, diverse Americans projected clashing visions of alternative societies and futures for the United States. Southerners sought to replicate their plantation complex, while northerners meant to reserve the region for free, white farmers. And Mormons opposed both by creating a theocratic order designed to fend off American control. Those clashing visions threatened to divide the Union that so recently had seemed to enjoy a complete triumph.

Boundaries

The peace treaty with Mexico promised property rights and U.S. citizenship to the 85,000 Hispanic residents of the ceded lands. But vigilantes and squatters dispossessed Mexican Americans through legal tricks and brutal violence. Federal officials let state laws and local vigilantes trump the treaty, enabling American settlers to take land from Hispanics. Texas legally restricted land ownership to "whites" and rejected Mexicans from that category. California also deemed most people of Mexican descent too colored to qualify for citizenship.[14]

Mexican laws had defined the Pueblo people of New Mexico as citizens with property rights. After the conquest, however, Americans balked at treating Indians as equals and began to take their lands.

The territorial governor admired the Pueblos' adobe villages, large livestock herds, and broad, irrigated fields but still insisted that they did not belong in an American territory: "It is inevitable, that they must be slaves, . . . or an early removal to a better location for them and our own people must occur."[15]

In Texas, newcomers harassed and ousted thousands of Hispanics, accusing them of helping Mexico and harboring runaway slaves. A Catholic priest complained, "The Americans of the Texian frontiers are, for the most part, the very scum of society—bankrupts, escaped criminals, [and] old volunteers." In Laredo, Texas, José María Rodríguez suffered from "a movement to clean out the Mexicans. They would rant at public meetings and declare that this was an American country and the Mexicans ought to be run out."[16]

California lost its Hispanic majority thanks to a gold rush that attracted thousands of Americans. In January 1848, a foreman working for land baron John Sutter found gold flakes beside the American River in the foothills of the Sierra Nevada. In December, President Polk confirmed and publicized the discovery, setting off a mania among young men in the East eager to get rich by going to California. "Nothing but the introduction of lunatic asylums can effect a cure," remarked a naval officer in San Francisco. Arriving by sea in ships or overland in wagons, newcomers increased the nonnative population of California from 14,000 in 1848 to 223,000 by 1852. The best way to fill a distant land with Americans was to announce the discovery of gold.[17]

Men of limited means could hunt for gold in the early days, when a pick, pan, and shovel sufficed to sift the sands of mountain streams. After the free-for-all of 1849 and 1850, however, mining became more capital-intensive as some miners formed companies to divert streams with dams and flush gravel through wooden sluices. In hydraulic mining, companies blasted and dissolved gravelly hillsides with jets of water to get at the gold. Or they tunneled deep into bedrock, seeking the quartz veins that held gold. As capital costs mounted, the common miner had to become a wage laborer, leaving most of the profits to his employer.[18]

Even in the early days, most miners found more frustration than gold. Single, young men prevailed: a type prone to drink and lash out when frustrated. The lure of easy gold had attracted many men described by a critic as "all the misfits of a maladjusted world." One unusually orderly miner wrote to his parents, "You mentioned [to] me to keep away from Indians, but I should feel myself more safe with them than with a large portion that call themselves Americans for, in fact, they are not one smite better than the fiends of Hell."[19]

Although new to California, Americans denounced Hispanics as "outsiders" who did not deserve to join the gold rush. A miner reported of his peers: "It made them mad to think that a lot of 'greasers' were getting the benefit of it, so they organized a company and drove them away by threats and force." Vigilante committees posted notices around a mining district giving Hispanics one day to clear out or face lynching. State legislators helped by imposing a "Foreign Miners' Tax" that required a hefty $20 a month fee. The tax's author, Thomas Jefferson Green, declared that he could "maintain a better stomach at the killing of a Mexican than at the crushing of a body louse."[20]

Hispanics became the usual suspects whenever a horse or cow went missing. Anglo miners held quick trials and lynched Hispanic suspects. A vigilante explained, "To shoot those Greasers ain't the best way. Give 'em a fair jury trial, and rope 'em up with all the majesty of the law." To complete the job, vigilantes burned the camps of Hispanic miners.[21]

Miners also devastated Native peoples, pushing them out of their villages in the valleys. Starving in the hills, desperate Indians sought food by hunting the cattle and horses of the newcomers. That outraged the Americans as theft, so they marked Indians for destruction along with bears and wolves. Vigilantes hunted for Indian villages to massacre men and enslave women and children to work as ranch hands, domestic servants, and prostitutes. In 1850, the federal government tried to reduce the slaughter with treaties that moved Natives away from the mines to small reservations. But the new Californians wanted no Indian reservations, and their protests led the U.S. Senate to reject the treaties. The killing and enslaving went on in California.[22]

The federal government also failed to control the better-armed Apaches and Comanches of the Southwest. In the Treaty of Guadalupe Hidalgo, Americans had promised to suppress raids across the new border into Mexico. The territorial governor of New Mexico announced that the Natives "must restrain themselves within prescribed limits and cultivate the earth for an honest livelihood, or, be destroyed." That bombast soon proved hollow. In 1850, a defiant Apache told an American army captain, "We must steal from somebody; and if you will not permit us to rob the Mexicans, we must steal from you." A year later, Apaches made that point to an American commission sent to survey the new international border through the desert. Stealing horses and mules from the surveyors, Apaches rode away showing and slapping buttocks in contempt. Along the border, Americans could barely defend themselves, much less protect Mexico. In a new treaty made in 1854, the Gadsden Purchase, Mexico accepted that the United States could not and would not protect them from Indian raiders. For $10 million—a fraction of its property losses—Mexico absolved the Americans of responsibility and threw in another 29,670 square miles of borderland.[23]

Deseret

Despite the great military victory and peace treaty, the fate of the West remained uncertain, for the great distances created spaces for emigrants to fission off rather than remain within the United States. By moving west beyond the Rocky Mountains, Mormons meant to create their own society as an escape from the United States, where a mob had assassinated their prophet, Joseph Smith, Jr., in 1844.[24]

Their new prophet and president, Brigham Young (1801–1877),

was a master organizer. A former carpenter and house painter from upstate New York, Young had become the chief lieutenant of Smith at Nauvoo in Illinois. In late 1845, on the eve of the Mexican War, Young prepared the faithful to migrate beyond the United States into the Great Basin. They named their arid but promised land Deseret, which they insisted meant "honeybee": an apt metaphor for the industrious, orderly, and hierarchical ideals of Mormons.[25]

To secure federal support for the Mormon move, Young agreed to raise a battalion of 500 men to assist the American seizure of New Mexico and California. Polk tolerated the Mormon settlement of Deseret "to conciliate them, attach them to our country & prevent them from taking part against us." But Young never forgot persecution by Americans, declaring "that they should be damned for these things, & if they ever sent any men to interfere with us here, they shall have their throats cut & sent to hell."[26]

In 1847, Young led the move, settling in the valley of the Great Salt Lake. Likening the region to the Holy Land, Mormons equated that lake with the Dead Sea of Judea. The Great Basin lay reassuringly distant from the American settlements to the east. "There is no other place on earth that the Saints can now live without being molested," Young declared.[27]

Rather than found a democracy to exalt man, the Mormons built "the Kingdom of God on Earth." Through hard work and divine worship, they meant to impress Christ into returning to destroy the wicked and initiate a millennium of perfect justice, dissolving human governments including that of the United States. But to hedge that bet, Young revived the Nauvoo Legion to protect Deseret.[28]

Young ruled as the viceroy of Jesus Christ, assuring the Saints that "they need not ask any questions but just do as they were told." Young subdivided the region into nineteen communities, known as wards, initially of about one hundred families each. Every ward had a governing bishop appointed by Young. In addition to presiding at worship services, a bishop supervised local schools and group labor and looked after widows, orphans, the sick and aged. From every

Mormon, the local bishop collected a tithe—10 percent of his produce or income as well as a day's labor in every ten days—to fund the Church's operations and social welfare programs.[29]

Young planned everything carefully, including Salt Lake City's grid of broad streets and self-contained economy. "We do not intend to have any trade or commerce with the gentile world," Young announced. In Deseret, the church ran stores, mills, factories, a bank, and a life insurance company—and discouraged competition by outsiders. Based at Salt Lake City, the Church built a Temple and subsidized the emigration of thousands of new converts from Europe. The hierarchical organization of Mormon society contrasted with the individualism of Americans. In Deseret, the wealthiest 10 percent of Mormon men practiced polygamy as a duty of leadership. Brigham Young eventually had twenty-seven wives and fifty-six children. This distinctive marital practice defined Mormons as beyond, and in defiance of, the American mainstream.[30]

Mormons founded dozens of rural communities from Idaho to California during the next twenty years. Most lay beside streams flowing out of mountain canyons. Las Vegas had its unlikely beginnings as a Mormon mission to Paiute Indians. Devoted to farming, the satellite communities consisted of adobe houses and barns suited to a tree-scarce environment. Rather than scatter on many isolated farms—as Americans did—Mormons initially clustered in fortified compounds, each supervised by a bishop. Mormons visited their family allotments of land to work by day. Clustering enabled the faithful to watch over one another and enhanced their defense against Indians. Collective labor built irrigation dams and ditches, facilitating agriculture in an arid land that received only a dozen inches of rain a year. With their characteristic mix of piety and pragmatism, Mormons prayed for rain but built irrigation ditches.[31]

Citing the Book of Mormon, the Saints claimed a strained kinship with Indians, cast as the descendants of "Lamanites," a lost tribe of Israel. After coming to America, the Lamanites allegedly lapsed into savagery and became cursed with darker skins. Mormons claimed a special duty to convert and redeem them as allies "to overthrow all gentile governments of the American continent." Mormons promoted missions and intermarriage with Indians, so that their children could "become white and delightsome." Young thought it "manifestly more economical and less expensive, to feed and clothe, than to fight them."[32]

Mormons treated Indians with a coercive paternalism meant to "civilize" them. Seeking "dominion over them for their good," Young advised Saints that "you must not treat them as your equals. . . . If they are your equals, you cannot raise them up to you." Young denied that Indians owned the land: "The land is the Lord's. . . . And it is for us to take that course that is best to obtain what He has provided for our support upon the earth." Young expected the Mormons "to take possession of all good valleys," pushing Indians to the desert or mountainous margins. [33]

About 12,000 Natives lived in the Great Basin: Shoshones and Utes held the mountain valleys to the north and east while Paiutes dwelled in the desert to the west. Indians resented losing scarce timber, pasture, and water to the newcomers. When Utes stole horses, killed cattle, and harassed settlers, Mormon punitive expeditions destroyed Indian villages, killing men and taking women and children as captives for forced adoption. "Let it be peace with them or extermination," Young preached. In Indian policy, the Mormon difference from Americans was a matter of degree rather than kind and of tone rather than results.[34]

Keeping peace with all the Indians was complicated because Utes preyed on the weaker Paiutes, taking captives. As a bond of alliance, Utes expected Mormons to buy some captives. When Mormons refused to buy two girls presented to them at Salt Lake City, a chief felt insulted. Killing one girl, he hurled her body, a Mormon recalled, "towards us, telling us we had no hearts, or we would have bought it and saved its life." The Mormons purchased the other girl. Thereafter, Young encouraged Mormons "to buy up the Lamanite children, as fast as they could, and educate them and teach them the Gospel."[35]

Violent persecution had developed a defiant insularity among Mormons, who sought to avoid Americans. Young wanted statehood for Deseret, and claimed the entire Great Basin plus southern California for an outlet to the Pacific: about 210,000 square miles. He expected Deseret to operate "as a sovereign and Independent state" within a loose Union, but in 1850, Congress imposed territorial status as "Utah," and defined that territory as but half of Young's claim for Deseret. To mollify Mormons, the American president appointed Young as territorial governor and Indian superintendent. But Americans bristled upon learning that Young dictated election results, appointed only bishops as judges, and denied that gentiles could own land in Utah. When some federal officials arrived, Mormons ostracized and harassed them until they left. Young preached that he "would sooner have his throat cut than submit to any interference with his family by the ungodly Gentiles." Mormons could see what they despised in the gentiles passing westward bound for Oregon, where they created the ultimate settler society.[36]

Oregon

After 1800, Native peoples in the Northwest sought supernatural explanation for the accelerating changes brought by British and American fur traders and mariners bearing strange customs, trade goods, and deadly diseases. A prophet among the Spokane people insisted that the world was coming to an end. He urged Indians to seek spiritual help from the East: "Soon there will come from the rising sun a different kind of man from any you have yet seen, who will bring with them a book and will teach you everything, and after that the world will fall to pieces." This prophecy seemed confirmed when some Haudenosaunee from Canada came to the Columbia Plateau as employees of British fur-trading companies. Familiar with Catholicism, they identified the book as the Bible and taught a few prayers and Sabbath rituals, which spread among Natives long before any missionary arrived.[37]

In 1831, Natives of the Columbia Plateau sent a delegation eastward across the Rocky Mountains and down the Missouri River in search of the sacred book. Reaching St. Louis, the emissaries thrilled America's evangelical Christians, who longed to convert Indians as a key step to hasten the end of a sinful world and bring on Christ's millennial rule. But these Christians could not comprehend the chasm between them and the Indians, who sought new forms of supernatural power to augment their traditions—not a total new system of belief. By sending missionaries westward to Oregon, Americans would help the Native world fall to pieces.[38]

Oregon's first Protestant missionaries were Methodists, who wanted to create a Christian utopia beyond, rather than within, the United States. A Methodist emigrant declared, "Oregon is our adopted country and we have no longing desires for our former home." Repelled by the sins of Americans, these missionaries romanticized Indians as simple children that they could mold into ideal Christians. In 1834, led by Reverend Jason Lee, they hastened to Oregon with a sense of urgency, eager to convert Indians before their ruin by the vices of the fur trade. The Methodists built their mission, school, mills, and model farm beside the falls of the Willamette River. They sought to reclaim "these wandering savages" by teaching "the blessings of Christianity and civilized life." A similar fantasy of converting Indians into perfect Christians had guided previous missionaries, including Franciscans in New Spain, Jesuits in New France, and Puritans in New England. The fantasy played out no better in Oregon than anywhere else.[39]

Natives experimented with new words and ways but as additions rather than substitutes for their supernatural beliefs. Such hybridity appalled missionaries, who wanted a rapid and total change of thought and behavior. Methodists also struggled to communicate theology through the simplified version of Chinook used for trade in the region. A jargon used to swap salmon for deerskins proved inadequate for explaining the Christian trinity. So Methodists had to boil their sermons down to uninspiring fatuities: "Your heart no good. Bye-and-bye you die. Your heart good, you go to God. God make very good your heart. Quick speak to God." Initially, Indians welcomed missionaries as bearers of a new magic that might offer protection against disease. Instead the epidemics worsened, suggesting that the newcomers offered poison instead of protection. In 1836, Lee sadly informed his eastern overseers: "The truth is we have no evidence that we have been instrumental in the conversion of one soul." In 1844, a Methodist inspector sarcastically reported that Lee's only achievement was that some Indian children "had experienced religion here and died when in school and hopefully had gone to heaven."[40]

Frustrated by Indian persistence in traditional ways, Lee made a fateful decision: to recruit white families from America to cross the continent and settle in the Willamette Valley. He reasoned that farmers could offer proper examples of civilization for Indians to emulate. Turning land speculator, Lee claimed huge tracts of prime land for sale to newcomers. Having failed to convert Indians, Lee meant to profit from their dispossession.[41]

Missionaries had hoped to build a better society on a distant frontier by leaving the United States. When Indians failed to embrace the missionary's fantasy, Methodists invited Americans to follow them, drawing westward the way of life that they once had tried to escape. Their dream of a Christian utopia led them, step by step, into creating an Oregon for settlers with no place for Indians. Contrary to their initial plans, the Methodist mission became the entering wedge for an American occupation. In 1838, Lee signed a petition urging American annexation of Oregon as soon as possible.[42]

During the early 1840s, settlers poured into Oregon, coming overland in covered wagons. By 1845, the 6,000 Americans dominated the 2,000 Native and 750 mixed-race peoples of the Willamette Valley. The newcomers organized a provisional government to adjudicate disputes, allocate lands, levy taxes, pay bounties for killing wolves, and help drive away Indians.[43]

Unlike fur traders, who needed Indian help as guides and hunters, settlers treated Natives as repulsive nuisances best pushed out or killed. A leading settler explained, "We came, not to establish trade with the Indians, but to take and settle the country exclusively for ourselves." Another settler described the Oregon Natives as "gaunt and dirty Diggers, a sort of half human, half vegetable race, indolently plodding along the margin of the river." A missionary declared that divine Providence was killing off the Indians "to give place to a people more worthy of this beautiful and fertile country."[44]

Settlers' pigs and cattle rooted out the plants gathered by Native women for sustenance; and settler hunters competed for, and decimated, game in the forests. Hungry Indians became desperate enough to work for the newcomers, accepting food and clothing in exchange. Commercial operations commanded Native labor to harvest, process, and ship away thousands of barrels of oysters, clams, crabs, and salmon. Once taken in modest amounts for local subsistence, the region's fish and shellfish became commodities depleted to serve a voracious external market. Mining sluices and mills polluted streams and obstructed fish migration.[45]

Indians dreaded the environmental degradation as a spiritual assault. After helping an entrepreneur catch salmon, some Chinooks warned him that spirits of the dead wanted them to desist: "You are a white man, and don't understand what [the dead] say; but Indians know, and they told us not to catch any more salmon." That boss wanted no more employees who communicated with the dead.[46]

The Indian dead surged as newcomers poured in, bringing new diseases. In 1830, the Willamette Valley had 15,000 Natives—but only 2,000 by 1845. Touring the region, a Briton found many deserted villages where "flocks of famished dogs are howling about, while the dead bodies lie strewn in every direction on the sands of the river." Abandoned or depleted villages opened up broad new tracts for settlers to claim and farm.[47]

In addition to attracting Methodists, the St. Louis visit of prophetic emissaries enticed a Presbyterian couple, Narcissa and Marcus Whitman, to establish a mission at Wailatpu on the Columbia Plateau east of the Willamette River. With help from Cayuse Indians, the missionaries built cabins, sheds, and a chapel. But soon the Cayuses balked at the missionaries' uncompromising style that required forsaking their traditions. Narcissa dismissed them as "savages" stuck in "the thick darkness of heathenism." Disgusted by Indians coming into her house, Narcissa concluded, "We must clean after them, for we have come to elevate them and not to suffer ourselves to sink down to their standard."[48]

Frustrated in their mission, the Whitmans joined Jason Lee in recruiting American families to move to Oregon to displace Indians. Passing by Wailatpu on route to the Willamette Valley, the overlanders unwittingly introduced another round of diseases. In 1847, a measles epidemic killed scores of Cayuse children. Their parents blamed poisoning by the Whitmans because they had seen Marcus put out arsenic for wolves. In November, Cayuse men broke into the mission and used axes to kill the Whitmans and nine others, who died for bringing settlers to Oregon and misery to Indians.[49]

Vowing revenge, the settler government "declare[d] the territory of said Cayuse Indians forfeited by them, and justly subject to be occupied and held by American citizens, resident in Oregon." Unable and unwilling to discriminate, armed volunteers attacked and burned all Native villages, of diverse peoples, few of them Cayuse. In early 1850, the Cayuses ran out of ammunition, so they made peace by surrendering five leaders of the attack on the Whitmans. After a hasty trial in June, the settlers hanged the five in Oregon City. On the gallows, one of them named Tilokaikt declared, "Did not your missionaries tell us that Christ died to save his people? So we die, to save our people." A newspaperman reported, "They were hanged, greatly to the satisfaction of the ladies who had traveled so far to witness the spectacle."[50]

In August 1848, Congress organized Oregon as a federal territory. The settlers' new delegate to Congress, Samuel Thurston, secured the Oregon Donation Land Act of 1850. Far more generous than any previous territorial land legislation, the Donation Act provided very large farms—320 acres for a single man and 640 acres for a married couple—at no cost. Oregon's settlers also could stake and occupy claims without waiting for the government to extinguish Indian title with treaties. In effect, the Donation Act abolished Indian rights to any lands desired by settlers. An Oregon newspaper declared, "There is nothing more farcical and grossly wrong than to treat with such miserable specimens of humanity as the Indians of this valley, (no more competent to contract than the wolves of the prairies) for lands to which they have a nominal title."[51]

By 1860, armed settlers had reduced Natives in the Willamette Valley to just 500. The territorial government paid bounty hunters to seek out and capture (but more often to kill) Indians who tried to hide rather than relocate. For want of treaties with the Natives, the government arbitrarily located reservations on poor and distant lands on the arid plateau to the east, far from their cherished valley. Deeply invested in the homes and graves of their ancestors and other spiritualized places, Natives felt wrenched and disoriented by removal. After hungry Indians took some cabbages and potatoes, an unusually reflective settler added, "These Indians would tell me that I have stolen their lands."[52]

Determined to create a white man's republic, Oregon's settlers wanted neither enslaved nor free Blacks in the territory. In 1844, an emigrant explained why he left Missouri: "Unless a man keeps niggers (and I won't), he has no even chance; he cannot compete with the man that does. . . . I'm going to Oregon, where there'll be no slaves, and we'll all start even." Others came, a settler explained, "to escape the constant dread of a negro insurrection" in Missouri or Kentucky. A third newcomer noted that Oregonians "hated slavery, but a much larger number of them hated *free negroes* worse even than slaves." Most of the settlers came from the midwestern or southern states, where laws barred free Blacks from moving in.[53]

In 1843, Oregon's provisional government outlawed slavery and, a year later, denied citizenship to free Blacks. Barring Black people from testifying in court against any white person, the law allowed abusive whites to exploit and assault them with impunity. The provisional government even ordered free Blacks to get out within two years or face a whipping of thirty-nine lashes every six months. In 1845, the government repealed the whipping feature, but substituted sale into short-term servitude as the penalty for persistence. In 1850, the Oregon Donation Land Act restricted landholding to whites.[54]

The zeal to oust free Blacks was striking given that only about fifteen lived in the Willamette Valley in 1844 (and fifty-four in 1850). Most were former sailors who had jumped ship and found Native wives. Settlers warned that free Blacks would ally with Indians, providing insights and information that could stiffen Native resistance. The territory's leading politician, Samuel Thurston, claimed that Black exclusion was "a question of life and death to us in Oregon." Otherwise, Thurston warned, Blacks and Indians would merge "and a mixed race would ensue inimical to the whites, and the Indians being led on by the negro, who is better acquainted with the customs, language, and manners of the whites, than the Indian, these savages would become much more formidable" in "long and bloody wars."[55]

A few liberals defended the free Blacks in petitions to the legislature calling for repeal of the law: "They have proved themselves to be moral, industrious, and civil." But the legislature refused to budge. In 1857, the drafters of the state constitution submitted the Black exclusion law to the voters, who supported it by 8,640 to 1,081. Many free Blacks moved to British Columbia in Canada, which offered a more welcoming racial order. Indeed, the first provincial governor, James C. Douglas, was a mixed-race former fur trader from Oregon.[56]

Trails

The Great Plains became part of the overland route taken by about 300,000 Americans between 1840 and 1860 to reach California, Oregon, and Utah. Most of the emigrants came from the Midwest or upper South, with Ohio, Indiana, Illinois, Kentucky, and Missouri as the chief states of origin. Men made the decision to move, often to the irritation of women, who had to leave parents and friends behind while doing their traditional household labor under the grueling conditions of an overland journey.[57]

For mutual support, families formed convoys of covered wagons pulled by oxen. To keep order, the men framed rules and elected leaders. But most groups fractured in acrimony over key decisions along the way, breaking up into several smaller parties. Adults walked while children and the sick jostled along in the wagons. Underestimating the tough terrain and long distances, most emigrants started out with too much furniture, burdens that wore out the oxen pulling the wagons. Upon reaching the Rocky Mountains or Great Basin, emigrants had to discard much of their stuff, including the wagons if the oxen died of exhaustion. The trail became one long dump. If overlanders fell behind schedule, they risked becoming trapped by an early snowfall in the Sierra Nevada, the last, great range of mountains that loomed between the Great Basin and California. In 1846, this was the fate of the infamous Donner Party, whose members first killed and ate their Indian guides before consuming their own who died.[58]

Dismissing Indians as roaming savages, the overlanders felt justified in taking whatever they wanted along the way: water, pasture, timber, game, and Indian lives. Midwestern newspapers fed grim expectations by fomenting exaggerated tales of Indian atrocities and massacres inflicted on overlanders. In fact, the travelers did more damage to the Natives. Between 1840 and 1860, emigrants killed about 426 Indians, compared to the 362 whites who died at Native hands: less than 2 percent of overlanders.[59]

Emigrants chopped down and burned trees, and their livestock consumed the grass needed by Indian horses and bison herds. Hunting bison for sport, the overlanders left most of the carcasses behind to rot, outraging Indians who needed the meat and hides to subsist. While the travelers called them nomads, the Natives meant to stay while the emigrants just passed through, leaving degradation in their wake. Some Indians stopped wagon trains to demand tolls in the form of presents, especially tobacco, as partial compensation for the damage. But outraged migrants dismissed Natives as thieves preying on honest Americans helping themselves to nature's bounty.[60]

To push Indians away from the overland trail, federal leaders built and garrisoned forts along the route. But the small and underpaid army struggled to control the mobile warriors of the Great Plains. Intimately familiar with their landscape, mounted on lighter, faster horses, and skilled at fighting from horseback, warriors could ride and fight rings around new soldiers brought in from the East. A federal Indian agent described the Plains people as the "most numerous, the most formidable—the most warlike, the best armed, and best mounted savages . . . on the face of the Globe."[61]

During the 1830s, American leaders had treated the Great Plains as a permanent Indian country, where they could resettle eastern Natives forcibly removed from their homelands. After achieving that removal, however, Americans reconsidered their policy of leaving Indians alone on the Great Plains. During the 1840s, officials began trying to separate Indian nations onto distinct reservations arbitrarily imposed on the Great Plains. Federal agents hoped that such separation would keep Natives from fighting one another as well as from harassing overlanders. An Arkansas senator vowed that reservations would "civilize, educate, and Christianize" Plains Indians and thereby "save and preserve them from falling by the bloody hand of each other, and make them, as we have other tribes, . . . better images of their Creator."[62]

The most powerful Natives of the Great Plains balked at restriction within imaginary lines. A Lakota Chief told American officials: "These lands once belonged to the Kiowas and Crows, but we whipped these nations out of them, and in this we did what the white men do when they want the lands of Indians." The power of reservations to pin down and separate Natives remained merely aspirational for another generation. But the United States had declared its vision for destroying the independence of Indians on the Great Plains.[63]

Proviso

Much of the western land conquered from Mexico seemed too arid for plantation agriculture, but southerners still welcomed the conquest, for it pulled a vast territory within the United States, where the Federal Constitution mandated the return of runaway slaves. After 1848, runaways faced a far longer and more deadly gauntlet to reach a more distant Mexico. William Gilmore Simms of South Carolina exulted that "our Mexican conquests" would secure "the perpetuation of slavery for the next thousand years." An enslaved man in Louisiana, Solomon Northrup, the author of *Twelve Years a Slave*, noted that "news of victory" in Mexico produced "only sorrow and disappointment" in the slave cabins but "filled the great house with rejoicing."[64]

The victory reduced southerners' fear of Britain, which had failed to help Mexico during the war. Britain also adopted a free trade policy that delighted southern leaders. Reduced British tariffs lowered the cost of, and increased the British demand for, agricultural commodities imported from the South. As a result, the price paid for cotton nearly doubled between 1845 and 1847. The British example also gave Polk political leverage to lower American tariffs on the British manufactures imported by planters, reducing their costs. Britain reformed her trade policy for domestic political reasons, but southerners preferred to believe that Britons sought to mollify the United States because they depended on southern cotton and felt awed by American victories in Mexico. Duff Green concluded that Britain would "cease to annoy our domestic institutions," the southern euphemism for slavery. Southern leaders claimed victory in their cold war with Britain over the fate of slavery in the western hemisphere.[65]

The declining dread of British power bore ironic fruit because that external fear had pulled South and North together within a Union for mutual defense. The loss of the British bogeyman invited Americans of rival regions to become more suspicious of one another. Internal fractures widened in proportion to the diminished perception of foreign danger.

Sectional suspicions weakened the political parties that had held the Union together. Democrats shared a dislike for Black people but disagreed over whether slavery sufficed to control them. An Indiana congressman explained that his constituents hated three things: "abolitionism, free-niggerism, and slavery." How long could they support a party led by southerners who hated the first two but defended the third? This split among Democrats created an opening for a third party to emerge that could oppose all three things despised by most white men in Indiana and other northern states.[66]

The populist animus toward free Blacks appeared in Mercer County, Ohio, during the summer of 1846, when nearly 400 former slaves arrived from Virginia. They had belonged to John Randolph, who freed them in his will: a surprise given his fiery defense of slavery as a congressman. Because Virginia law required newly freed people to leave the state within one year or face renewed slavery, Randolph provided funds to move his former slaves to Ohio and buy each family a small farm. But Mercer County's white farmers wanted no African-American community in their midst. Taking up arms, they met the steamboat carrying the newcomers and forced them to leave. Losing their farms, the freedmen dispersed to work for paltry wages as menial laborers. Then white men pointed to them as supposed evidence that free Blacks could never thrive. The congressman for that district, William Sawyer, declared, "Most of the free negroes in the state of Ohio [are] the most despicable of all creatures."[67]

While content to preserve slavery in the South, many northerners wanted to stop the system from expanding westward. They worried that extending plantation slavery would prevent common farmers from obtaining lands in the conquered territory. In August 1846, shortly after the war began, Congressman David Wilmot of Pennsylvania proposed a "proviso" that would ban slavery from territory conquered from Mexico beyond Texas. Hitherto a dutiful Democrat, Wilmot had supported the war, so his proviso shocked his southern colleagues. They had counted on the conquest to expand their way of life, but the Wilmot Proviso threatened to turn that alluring region into a permanent barrier to slavery.[68]

Refuting accusations of abolitionism, Wilmot declared allegiance to white supremacy. Rather than acting from any "sympathy for the slave," he sought to reserve "a fair country, a rich inheritance, where the sons of toil, of my own race and own color, can live without the disgrace which association with negro slavery brings upon free labor." Confiding to a friend, Wilmot viscerally expressed his joint animus against Blacks and their masters: "By God, sir, men born and nursed by white women are not going to be ruled by men who were brought up on the milk of some damn Negro wench!"[69]

But Wilmot and his supporters also believed that slavery eventually would wither and die if it could not expand: "Slavery has within itself the seeds of its own dissolution." If confined, antislavery men reasoned, agriculture by slave labor would exhaust the soil, leading southerners to free themselves from slavery by shipping the freed Blacks off to Africa.[70]

Slaveholders agreed that slavery had to grow to survive, so they felt threatened and insulted by Wilmot's proviso. Southerners insisted that their equality within the Union entailed their right to take slaves anywhere in federal territory. An Alabama senator thundered that he would "never consent that territory, acquired by common blood and common treasure, shall be open and free for the citizens of one portion of the Union, with their property, while the citizens of another portion of the Union and their property are to be excluded from it."[71]

Southerners dreaded becoming confined with an increasing enslaved population in one corner of an otherwise growing nation. In their nightmare scenario, enslaved people and plantation lands would lose value while masters lost their lives to a slave revolt. A South Carolina newspaper warned that the Wilmot Proviso threatened to surround the South with "those who will continually excite our slaves to insubordination and revolt." Denying the sincerity of northern congressmen, southerners detected a raw power grab meant to subordinate and ruin their region. Southerners claimed to love the Union more than their foes, who forced them to consider disunion. After extolling his version of a consensual Union, Robert Toombs of Georgia declared that if a northern majority did "fix a national degradation upon half the states" then "I am for disunion."[72]

By responding with uncompromising anger, southern congressmen fueled northern suspicions that a "slave power conspiracy" manipulated the federal government to the detriment of common white people. Northern Democrats resented the lack of southern support for seizing all of the Oregon country in 1846. An Ohio congressman explained, "The South acted with so much apparent treachery on the Oregon matter, that the mass of the Democrats in the free states have lost all confidence in Southern Democrats."[73]

By dividing northern and southern Democrats, the proviso unraveled the work of Jackson and Van Buren in constructing a party across sectional lines to keep slavery out of national politics. In 1846, the Wilmot Proviso passed the house 83 to 64 on a sectional vote. Fifty-two of the fifty-six northern Democrats in the House voted for the proviso. But the South held serve in the Senate, where it commanded half the seats and had more support from northern Democrats.[74]

The Wilmot Proviso divided white nationalism into two camps: northern Free Soilers, who insisted that proximity to slavery degraded free labor, and southerners, who argued that slavery enabled white men to fulfill their ambitions. In 1848, Wilmot helped found a new "Free Soil Party" to run candidates on the platform: "Free Soil, Free Speech, Free Labor, and Free Men."[75]

Appealing primarily to former Democrats in the North, Free Soilers accused slaveholders of exploiting common white men and debasing their political rights. A Free Soiler declared, "The question is not, whether black men are to be made free, but whether we white men are to remain free." A popular writer, James Russell Lowell, crafted a folksy character, Hosea Biglow, to insist:

Wy it's jext ez clear ez figgers,
Clear ez one an' one makes two,
Chaps that make black slaves o' niggers
Want to make wite slaves o' you

Rebranding their key policy as "the white man's Proviso," Free Soilers appealed to voters anxious over their own prospects and liberty in a Union dominated by slaveholders.[76]

The division among Democrats dimmed the presidential prospects of Polk's favored successor, Lewis Cass of Michigan. One of five northern senators to vote against the Wilmot Proviso, Cass insisted that he refused to "cover the country with blood and conflagration to abolish slavery." Tall and wide, Cass had a talent for bellicose bombast and few principles to hinder his relentless ambition. Frederick Douglass's newspaper denounced Cass as "Gross in person—almost idiotic in visage . . . and ready and eager to stoop to the dirtiest work of the slave power."[77]

Whigs rallied around a war hero, Zachary Taylor, and they had the good political sense to highlight his military feats and obscure his policy positions. That was easy because Taylor had neither held elected office nor ever voted. As a Louisiana slaveholder, Taylor seemed vaguely reassuring to many southerners, but not enough to upset northern Whigs. In the fall election, Taylor triumphed. Polk felt dismayed to give up his office to a general whom he had tried to ruin during the war. Three months after leaving office, the depleted and haggard Polk died at the age of fifty-three, a victim of his own mania for work to expand the Union by any means.[78]

In the North, Free Soilers captured a tenth of the presidential vote for their candidate, but most voters stuck to entrenched party loyalties. A leading Free Soiler, George Julian, recalled that "the charge of abolitionism was flung at me everywhere. I was an 'amalgamationist' and a 'wooly head.' . . . It was a standing charge of the Whigs that I carried a lock of Frederick Douglass['s hair], to regale my senses with its aroma when I grew faint." In the political discourse of the 1840s, "amalgamation" meant favoring racial mixing through marriage and children: a favorite accusation hurled by demagogues against anyone who defended the rights of African Americans.[79]

Pearl

A ship captain from Massachusetts, Daniel Drayton, held racist views until he sailed to the Chesapeake and came into contact with enslaved people. Drayton learned that "they had the same desires, wishes, and hopes as myself" and suffered as he would from the sale of their children. In April 1848, Drayton tried to help seventy-two fugitives escape from the District of Columbia on his schooner, the *Pearl*. Most were house servants belonging to members of the political elite, including Dolley Madison, widow of a president. In 1814, when British troops approached Washington, the enslaved valet Paul Jennings had helped Dolley remove George Washington's portrait from the White House. Thirty-four years later, Jennings felt betrayed because she reneged on James Madison's deathbed promise to free him. Instead, she hired Jennings out to James Polk and pocketed the earnings. Jennings got a break when purchased by Senator Daniel Webster, who allowed him to buy his freedom in 1847. Jennings then helped other slaves seek freedom by escaping on the *Pearl*. But adverse winds stalled the schooner, and thirty armed men pursued in a steamboat. They overtook, boarded, and captured the becalmed schooner, taking it back to Washington. A captor asked one fugitive why she had left her allegedly good master. She replied, "I wanted liberty, wouldn't you sir?"[80]

Drayton landed in the capital's jail, while a white mob raged through the streets eager to hang him. Foiled by guards at the jail, the mob move on to smash the office of an antislavery newspaper. Dolley Madison and other masters sold most of the recovered slaves to traders, who sent them to the Lower South, far from their families and friends. A sympathetic Ohio congressman, Joshua R. Giddings, saw "wives bidding adieu to their husbands; mothers in an agony of despair" and "little boys and girls weeping." Abolitionists saved a few by purchase. Put on trial in July, Drayton and his chief lieutenant, Edward Sayres, confronted a celebrity prosecutor, Philip Barton Key, the son of Francis Scott Key and nephew of Chief Justice Roger B. Taney. Convicted, Drayton and Sayres remained in jail for four years because they could not pay their massive fines of $10,000 and $7,000. Confinement ruined Drayton's physical and mental health; he committed suicide in 1857.[81]

A day after the April 1848 arrests, the episode spilled into Congress, where southerners howled that their families were imperiled by abolitionists. A North Carolinian vowed to dissolve the Union with "pleasure and joy" if southerners remained "taunted by fanatics and hypocrites—if their wives and little ones were to be assassinated and destroyed by intermeddling men with hearts black as hell."[82]

In the Senate, John P. Hale of New Hampshire shifted discussion to the mob that had nearly lynched Drayton. Hale called for tougher laws against riots in the District: a proposal that baited southern senators. Defending the Democrats' version of popular sovereignty, John C. Calhoun charged that Hale meant "to repress the just indignation of our people from wreaking their vengeance upon the atrocious perpetrators of these crimes." A few days before the *Pearl* sailed, Senator Henry Foote of Mississippi had addressed a crowd to celebrate revolutions in Europe for challenging "the age of tyrants and of slavery." But Foote never intended that age to end for enslaved people in America. Denouncing Hale, Foote urged him to visit Mississippi to "grace one of the tallest trees in the forest, with a rope around his neck."[83]

Keeping his cool in reply, Hale politely invited Foote to visit New Hampshire, where he could safely express his views, finding free debate instead of a lynching. Hale added that southern senators had revealed yet again that slavery was "incompatible with the right of free speech" and "that even the sacred rights of life and property must bow down before it." Hale's savvy response put the onus on northern Democrats to disavow the extremism of their southern allies. Illinois senator Stephen A. Douglas warned that southern extremism was "the best means to manufacture abolitionism" in the North. Unrepentant, Calhoun denounced Douglas's caution as "at least as offensive" as Hale's provocation. Such adamancy would cost the South, as more northerners balked at sacrificing their political rights to mollify slaveholders.[84]

Fugitives

In California, most Americans came from northern states, and they opposed enslaved labor as affording masters an unfair advantage in culling gold flakes from streams and hillsides. In October 1849, California delegates adopted a state constitution that barred slavery, and they petitioned for admission to the Union. To the surprise of southern Whigs, President Taylor endorsed that admission. A nationalist from long years of military service, Taylor lacked the usual southern conviction that slavery had to expand to survive. He also thought that admitting California (and New Mexico) immediately without a territorial stage would make the Wilmot Proviso moot, breaking the stalemate that so agitated Congress.[85]

Outraged southerners charged the president with conceding the substance of the Wilmot Proviso, depriving them of sharing in the territory conquered from Mexico. They also dreaded that a new free state would tip the regional balance of power in the Senate against them. Having decisively lost the House of Representatives, they clung to balance in the Senate as essential to protect their region and its property. Most southern leaders wanted New Mexico as a slave territory and to split California, with the southern half reserved for slavery. These leaders included Taylor's son-in-law, Senator Jefferson Davis of Mississippi. Alarmed by renewed threats of secession and civil war, Henry Clay likened Congress to "twenty-odd furnaces in full blast in generating heat, and passion, and intemperance, and diffusing them throughout . . . this broad land."[86]

To contain the crisis, Clay proposed a compromise package of laws that would admit California as a free state, while New Mexico and Utah became territories that tacitly permitted slavery. He also wanted to settle the Texas–New Mexico boundary dispute in favor of New Mexico by paying $10 million to mollify Texas. In addition, Congress would ban the troubling spectacle of slave trading in the District of Columbia while allowing slaveholding to persist there. Finally, Congress would stiffen the federal fugitive slave law to compel northern officials to cooperate with slave hunters and prevent northern juries from obstructing them. Such a federal law would vitiate "personal liberty laws" passed by some northern states to protect free Blacks from kidnapping by requiring jury trials in fugitive cases.[87]

Most southern leaders rejected any compromise. Although dying and unable to speak in public, Calhoun had a fiery speech read for him by a colleague. Denouncing northern leaders as aggressors bent on subordinating and ruining the South, Calhoun demanded a constitutional amendment to protect slavery in every federal territory and thereby restore the South's "power . . . of protecting herself before the equilibrium between the two sections was destroyed."[88]

Offended by a senator speaking for compromise, Henry Foote drew a pistol, plunging the Senate into an uproar before cooler heads disarmed him. A Boston newspaper declared: "If one-half of our Congressmen would kill the other half, and then commit suicide . . . we think the country would gain by the operation." Most southerners even opposed a proposal by a Maryland senator to compensate masters who lost runaways to the North. Lower South leaders feared that proposal as the slippery slope to a federal emancipation program that would isolate their region by draining slaves from the Upper South, adding to the number of free states.[89]

In the spring of 1850, civil war seemed imminent as Clay's compromise legislation stalled in Congress. Texas prepared armed volunteers to seize the contested border region from New Mexico, while Taylor mobilized federal troops to fight them. Then at a July 4 picnic, the president ate too many cherries and iced milk. Falling ill, he died of gastroenteritis five days later. The new president, Millard Fillmore of New York, was a flexible politician who cooperated with Stephen A. Douglas, an ambitious Illinois senator, to pass separately the elements of Clay's package. Passage depended on congressmen from the Upper South, who feared that the alternative was disunion, which they regarded as a greater threat to slavery than compromise. Because most runaway slaves fled from the Upper South, that region's politicians welcomed the tougher Fugitive Slave Law.[90]

In the capital, relieved inhabitants erupted with singing, drinking, and parading to celebrate the Compromise of 1850. An onlooker declared it was "a night on which it was the duty of every patriot to get drunk." But the morning brought a fierce and lingering hangover, for the sectional division persisted. Salmon P. Chase of Ohio noted that "the question of slavery in the territories has been avoided. It has not been settled." The older cohort of leaders did not live long enough to witness the collapse of compromise; Calhoun died in 1850 followed by Clay and Webster in 1852.[91]

By dispensing with juries and empowering slave hunters, the Fugitive Slave Law became the flash point for division. The law established special federal commissioners to rule on cases where masters identified Blacks as runaways. To bias their rulings in favor of masters, the law awarded a commissioner $10 for every slave sent south and only $5 when he ruled in favor of freedom. Although southerners usually clamored for states' rights, they championed a law that empowered the federal government to override northern state laws. But, with equal consistency, Yankees championed state laws when they clashed with an immoral use of federal power.[92]

Abolitionists harassed and obstructed slave catchers, while helping runaways flee across the border to British Canada. Frederick Douglass declared, "The only way to make the Fugitive Slave Law a dead letter is to make half-a-dozen more dead kidnappers." In Christiana, Pennsylvania, free Blacks did kill a Maryland slaveholder who came to grab four of them as runaways. Three of the leaders fled from Christiana to Canada with help from Douglass along the way. "Civil War—The First Blow Struck," announced a Pennsylvania newspaper.

Fillmore sent federal troops to Christiana to arrest thirty Blacks and ten white supporters for treason. That inflated charge backfired, for jurors could see no evidence that the accused had waged war on the United States.[93]

The new Fugitive Slave Law only recovered about 300 runaways, but those recoveries generated outraged reporting and protest meetings that promoted abolitionist sentiment in the North. When slave hunters hauled away Black neighbors, northern whites got a new and clearer view of slavery, and of runaways' longing for freedom. By compelling northern whites to assist slave catchers or break the law and face the consequences, the law appeared to subordinate the North. "The South goes clear up to the Canada line," a Boston abolitionist thundered. But southerners felt just as outraged by northern evasions of the law. Claiming betrayal by tricky northerners defaulting on their constitutional commitments, southerners threatened disunion if the northern states failed to enforce the Fugitive Slave Law.[94]

Craft

In 1848 a slight and dapper gentleman traveled north from Georgia accompanied by an enslaved valet: a familiar traveling pair in the South. But this pair had secrets. Dressed in cravat, dress boots, and a top hat, the supposed gentleman was, in fact, a mixed-race woman, and as much a slave as her darker-skinned companion, who had married her. Light enough to pass for white, Ellen Craft was the daughter of an enslaved mother and her master. Although Georgia law recognized no marriages by enslaved people, she considered herself married to William, whose master had sold his mother, father, and siblings to pay debts while mortgaging William to secure a bank loan. Both Crafts knew the lives of humans treated as commodities. Starting their journey in Macon, Georgia, the Crafts traveled by boat and train for a thousand miles to reach Boston, where, at last, they could marry legally and make money by plying their trades as carpenter and seamstress.[95]

Becoming celebrated public speakers, the Crafts promoted abolition by recounting their troubles and travels. Their clever journey and transgression of gender and racial appearances mocked the southern insistence on a clear racial divide between enslaved people and their masters. Articulate and intelligent, the Crafts refuted the lies that enslaved people were stupid, docile, and content. Ellen's light complexion warned northerners that masters were "as ready to enslave the whitest and the fairest as any other, provided only a pretext be afforded."[96]

Published in newspapers, the Crafts' story reached Ellen's former owner, who hired two bounty hunters to track them down in Boston. Although people called Massachusetts a "free state," no runaway was fully free there so long as the Fugitive Slave Law compelled authorities and citizens to arrest runaways. Friends helped the Crafts make a second escape, this time to Nova Scotia. Moving on to Britain, they sought to evade, in William's words, the "claws of the American eagle." A Scottish newspaper praised them for highlighting "the enormous inconsistency and criminality of a professed land of liberty and Christianity holding 3 millions of intelligent and immortal beings in bondage."[97]

A Boston friend, the abolitionist Wendell Phillips, blamed their travails on a Federal Constitution that favored property rights over human rights. Phillips exulted, "Weightier than the Constitution, stronger than laws, is one Ellen Craft, to open the hearts of Northern Freemen" to the threat of slavery. "The best way we know of to express our sympathy and respect" for the Crafts, he concluded, was "to labor for the overthrow of [the] Union." Ralph Waldo Emerson agreed: "Nothing seems to me more bitterly futile than this bluster about the Union. . . . The Union is no longer desireable."[98]

Conquered land was corroding the Union as Emerson predicted during the war: "Mexico will poison us." To claim the American future created by western settlement, northerners proposed the Wilmot Proviso and formed the Free Soil Party. Those developments infuriated southern leaders, who demanded new concessions from the North, particularly the Fugitive Slave Law, deepening sectional tensions.[99]

Both sides resorted to gendered denunciations: sure signs of drawing stark lines that resisted compromise. Southern leaders blasted Free Soilers as purveyors of a "sickly morbid philanthropy" that displayed a "fawning feeling for blacks." Southerners coded empathy for slaves as irrational, sentimental, and feminine. In response, Free Soilers cast southern leaders as lacking the "stamp of manliness" by their sneaky intrigues to expand slavery. Antislavery men urged northerners to prove their masculinity by refusing to submit to southern demands.[100]

Furor over the conquered territories plunged the nation into a prolonged crisis that culminated in a destructive civil war just thirteen years after the Treaty of Guadalupe Hidalgo. The Mexican War had trained a talented cohort of young army officers, including Jefferson Davis, Ulysses S. Grant, Stonewall Jackson, Robert E. Lee, George Meade, and William Tecumseh Sherman. In the Civil War, they applied what they had learned in Mexico to lead Americans in killing one another. They fought over conflicting notions of their country, with most southerners claiming a right to secede, while northerners (and some southerners) defended the Union as perpetual. Grant connected that devastating new war with the unprovoked conquest of northern Mexico: "Nations, like individuals, are punished for their transgressions." During the Civil War, Grant fought to restore a Union plunged into a bloodbath that Americans had feared from the start of their shaky confederation in 1776.[101]

Top: "Scene in Uncle Sam's Senate, 17th April 1850," print by Edward Williams Clay, 1850. Mississippi senator Henry S. Foote pointing his pistol at Thomas Hart Benton of Missouri. To the right stand Henry Clay and Daniel Webster. Library of Congress 2008661528. *Bottom:* "Southern Ideas of Liberty," engraving by unknown artist, 1835. In this cartoon, a southern judge with an ass's ears and a whip in hand sits on bales of cotton while trampling on the Constitution. He condemns abolitionists to tarring and feathering and to the gallows in the background. Library of Congress 2008661271.

Clockwise from top left: "Dr. John McLoughlin (1784–1815)," print by unknown artist, 1905. Library of Congress 2016651069. *"A Kalapuya Man: A Native of Oregon," engraving by Alfred T. Agate, 1844.* Library of Congress 2001696060. *"Fort Vancouver," lithograph by Sarony, Major & Knapp, 1855.* Library of Congress 2011647869.

EPILOGUE

A large, powerfully built man with piercing blue eyes and a great shock of white hair, John McLoughlin came from Quebec, the son of an Irish-born farmer and a French-Canadian mother. After studying medicine in Montreal, McLoughlin joined an uncle in the North West Company, Canada's leading firm in the fur trade. Serving as a clerk and physician at a trading post on the north shore of Lake Superior, the young man married an Ojibwa woman. That marriage committed him to a life in the fur trade rather than returning to conventional society in the east. Another trader noted the folly of a colleague who took eastward a Native wife: "to join in anything like civilized society with her is out of the question." But on a fur trade frontier, an ambitious trader needed an Indian wife to teach him local ways and provide the protection of her kinship network. These customary relationships produced mixed children, who formed a Métis people with cultural ties to both the Native and trader worlds. After his first wife died in childbirth in 1809, McLoughlin married a Métis woman, Marguerite, three years later.[1]

In 1821, the North West Company merged with the rival Hudson's Bay Company (HBC), with the latter name covering the new conglomerate. Three years later the HBC sent McLoughlin to run its most distant operation, in the Oregon Country. He supervised completion of Fort Vancouver, a cluster of a dozen log buildings within a massive stockade of Douglas fir logs, twenty feet high. A hive of activity, the fort included a dining hall, kitchen, storehouses, barracks, gunpowder magazine, and shops for bakers, blacksmiths, carpenters, and brickmakers. Outside the walls stood a sawmill, flour mill, hospital, stables, barns, orchards, and 3,000 acres of farm fields to raise food for the workers. The operation employed chief traders to supervise satellite trading posts and forty clerks, young and literate Britons or Canadians serving an apprentice in the business. The work of artisans and boatmen belonged to hired *engagés*, a mix of Haudenosaunees, Hawaiians, French Canadians, and Métis, most of them illiterate. Sustaining them all required the work of Native and Métis women, who cleaned, prepared meals, tended to children, made clothes, and dried and packed furs.[2]

McLoughlin worked closely with the local Chinook and Salish peoples to obtain protection and tap into their wide-ranging trade connections with more-distant Natives. He encouraged his traders and hunters to marry Indian women, and he treated chiefs with respect. His daughter recalled, "He put men in chains who treated Indians badly. That is the way they kept peace with the Indians." He cherished peace as good for business, and initially there were 200 Indians for every white man in the region. But if Indians attacked or robbed his hunters, McLoughlin sent out punitive expeditions to kill men and burn a village, which he called "the severity necessary for [our] own safety & security."[3]

A commanding paternalist, McLoughlin did not operate a democracy at Fort Vancouver. While he employed diverse people, they occupied gradated rungs in a corporate hierarchy. Within that hierarchy, merit could triumph over prejudice. McLoughlin's chief lieutenant and best friend, James C. Douglas, was the son of a free colored woman from Barbados and a Scottish merchant. In 1839, a visitor, Thomas Farnham, saw McLoughlin at the head of the table "directing guests and gentlemen from neighboring posts to their places." Farnham noted "the velvet bedecked Indian wives of even the highest in command," including Marguerite McLoughlin. A visiting American naval officer found children "of all shades of colour, from the pure Indian to that of the white."[4]

Hoping to sustain this fur-trade world, McLoughlin did not pressure Natives to change their beliefs or give up their lands, but he could not stop a wave of American settlers during the 1840s. The newcomers asserted white supremacy in the name of democracy, discarding the racial mixing and overt hierarchy of McLoughlin's community. The new order disdained Métis people as "half-breeds" and a "mongrel race," deemed worse than Indians for blurring the racial line. In 1855, Oregon Territory revoked citizenship for Métis people, a decision reiterated by the state constitution of 1857. A settler recalled that once Americans became a majority, the older residents "who had Indian families were rather exiled in civilized society" and often "found it more agreeable to go . . . to their wives' people." That meant living on a shrinking reservation surrounded by hostile settlers. Defending the rights of his children, McLoughlin protested that "half-breeds" were "as peaceable, orderly, and Industrious as any settlers in the country."[5]

During the late 1830s and early 1840s, McLoughlin had defied his corporate superiors by assisting the settlers out of a sense of charity, for many needed lumber, seeds, tools, and provisions to survive. As the settler numbers surged into the thousands, McLoughlin's motives became more political. He hoped to protect his operation by cultivating American good will, but that did not work. Eastern newspapers and congressmen demonized the Hudson's Bay Company as a ruthless and alien corporation that allegedly paid Indians to attack the overland wagon trains. In fact, McLoughlin had restrained Indians from attacking the emigrants. In 1845, the HBC sacked McLoughlin and, a year later, abandoned Fort Vancouver because of the decline in the fur trade linked to the rise of American settlement in the nearby Willamette Valley. Unwilling to move, McLoughlin stayed behind to operate farms and mills at Oregon City, the former site of a Methodist mission.[6]

Reliant on his Métis wife, McLoughlin treated Marguerite with love and respect, but that treatment irritated newcomers with social pretensions. Newly arrived from New York, a snooty woman mocked his devotion to Marguerite: "Though his wife was a half breed of the

Ojibway nation, coarse, short, fat, and flabby, he treated her like a princess in public and in private. He was as loyal to her as if she was a daughter of the Queen Victoria." At dinner "she was assigned a place of honor," and "he would suffer no indignity or slight to her. . . . as she waddled beside him like one of another species." Claiming a monopoly on respectability, white women froze Métis women out of polite circles in settler Oregon.[7]

McLoughlin applied for American citizenship, but territorial leaders postponed considering it while they rushed to secure a federal law that barred aliens from owning land in Oregon. When the bill passed, the territory's delegate, Samuel Thurston, exulted over his "triumphant success. . . . I see the scattered bones of D[r.] M[c]Laughlin, the HB Company, and their actors." McLoughlin could not obtain citizenship until after territorial courts had helped rivals take his mills and most of his land. In 1857, he died a bitter man, declaring, "I might better have been shot forty years ago than to have lived here, and tried to build up a family and an estate in this government. I became a citizen of the United States in good faith. I planted all I had here, and the government has confiscated my property."[8]

Oregonians later rehabilitated McLoughlin as the heroic "Father of Oregon," erecting statues in his honor including one in the U.S. Capitol. They also turned McLoughlin's house in Oregon City into a shrine, but when his granddaughter Angeline McLoughlin, who identified as an Indian and lived on a reservation, tried to visit, docents refused her admittance, which they limited to white people.[9]

ACKNOWLEDGMENTS

I am grateful to Ari Kelman and Andrés Reséndez for reading chapters and offering research leads and many acts of friendship. Pablo Ortiz persists as an exceptional spiritual guide, and Chris Reynolds and Alessa John are the best of friends. Emily Albu remains the kindest and most generous of human beings. My sister Carole and brother-in-law Marty amply atone for supporting the Evil Baseball Empire by their love and generosity.

I am grateful to Christa Dierksheide, Max Edelson, Justene Hill Edwards, Will Hitchcock, Carrie Janney, and Liz Varon for being exemplary colleagues, and I thank Jim Ryan for leading the university in challenging times. Gary Gallagher continued to teach me about the nature of the Union and the finer points of playing pool, while Ed Ayers, Brian Balogh, Ted Lendon, and Elizabeth Meyer bolstered morale with their great company and devotion to the Aberdeen Barn.

I thank C. Joseph Genetin-Pilawa for sharing a draft of his forthcoming work on Indians in the national capital. The book benefited greatly from the insights and hospitality of Kathleen DuVal and Marty Smith. For unmatched expertise on pirates, I am grateful to the esteemed Kevin R. Convey. I derived invaluable computer assistance from Tim Dunne and Marc Langlais.

Andrew Wylie and his assistants provided exemplary literary representation. Throughout the writing and production of this book, I benefited from the sage and supportive guidance of a consummate editor, Steve Forman, and his hypercompetent assistant Lily Gellman of W. W. Norton.

I dedicate this book to the members of the Gerry Haines seminar, a weekly gathering for beer, wine, and sage solutions to all of the world's problems. The members include Gerry, Tico Braun, Dick Holway, Allen Lynch, Chuck McCurdy, Erik Midelfort, Thomas Noble, Duane Osheim, Brian and Karen Parshall, and Brad Reed. Special thanks to Chuck for inviting me and Erik for getting me home safely—and to Anne Midelfort for always doing the right things.

I also dedicate this book to the memory of Elizabeth "Wendy" Hazard, who had the biggest of hearts and liveliest of spirits. I wish she were still here to play tennis and hearts and fight the good fight for equality in our still-embattled republic.

NOTES

INTRODUCTION

1. Ash and Musgrove, *Chocolate City*, 17–18; Costanzo, *George Washington's Washington*, 13–28; Dickey, *Empire of Mud*, 1–2, 8, 11–20, 58–60, Joel Poinsett quoted on 18; Freeman, *Field of Blood*, 22–23.

2. Costanzo, *George Washington's Washington*, 50–52; Dickens, *American Notes*, 149, 152–55, 161–62, quotes on 154; Foster, *Jeffersonian America*, 7–9 ("live like bears"), 49–51, 104 ("Never"); C. M. Green, *Washington*, 38–39, 44–47, 49, 78 (Abbé Corea quoted: "born" and "emptied").

3. Balogh, *Government Out of Sight*, 112–13; Costanzo, *George Washington's Washington*, 62–63, 65–74, 105, 107–109; Dickey, *Empire of Mud*, 1–2, 12–14, Pierre L'Enfant quoted on 1 ("mere"); Foster, *Jeffersonian America*, 8–10; C. M. Green, *Washington*, 38–39; D. Upton, *Another City*, 186–90.

4. Ash and Musgrove, *Chocolate City*, 18, 35–38, Augustus B. Woodward quoted on 37 ("a collection"); Dickey, *Empire of Mud*, xv, 1–2, 14–15, 117–19, Oliver Wolcott quoted on 1 ("The people"); C. M. Green, *Washington*, 24–26, 31, 39–40.

5. Costanzo, *George Washington's Washington*, 50–52; Dickey, *Empire of Mud*, 23–24, 47–51; Salmon P. Chase quoted in K. Wood, "'One Woman So Dangerous,'" 251 ("three classes").

6. Costanzo, *George Washington's Washington*, 52–55; Dickey, *Empire of Mud*, 65–66, 130–31; Freeman, *Field of Blood*, 53–55; C. M. Green, *Washington*, 52–53, 109–10.

7. Dickens, *American Notes*, 157–58; Finkelman, "Slavery in the Shadow of Liberty," 3–5, Washington grand jury quoted on 4; Freeman, *Field of Blood*, 62, 68–72, 75–76, 132–34; C. M. Green, *Washington*, 53–55, 95–99; Ricks, "1848 *Pearl* Escape," 210–11.

8. Dickens, *American Notes*, 155–56; Freeman, *Field of Blood*, 25–26; Foster, *Jeffersonian America*, 13–14; Fryd, *Art and Empire*, 2–6, 60–61, 177; Viola, *Diplomats in Buckskins*, 138–39.

9. Saunt, *Unworthy Republic*, 100–102; Viola, *Diplomats in Buckskins*, 174–78, Kentucky congressman quoted on 178.

10. Foster, *Jeffersonian America*, 22–42; Saunt, *Unworthy Republic*, 116; Turner, *Red Men Calling*, 45–87, 93–94; Viola, *Diplomats in Buckskins*, 70–77, 90–99, 104–6, 113–33, 137–42, *Washington Daily Intelligencer* quoted on 127 ("dogged").

11. Freeman, *Field of Blood*, 24–25, 43–45, Benjamin Brown French quoted on 24 and 44.

12. Edling, "More Perfect Union," 390–91; Hendrickson, "Escaping Insecurity," 216–42; Hendrickson, "First Union," 40–42; Jensen, "Sovereign States," 226–28, Fisher Ames quoted on 228 ("Instead of feeling"); Rakove, *Beginnings of National Politics*, 142–43, 156–64, 178–79.

13. Balogh, *Government Out of Sight*, 264–65; Kersh, *Dreams of a More Perfect Union*, 101–3, Episcopal national convention quoted on 103.

14. Freeman, *Field of Blood*, 10–11.

15. Hendrickson, *Union, Nation, or Empire*, 132–39; Onuf, *Jefferson's Empire*, 12–17.

16. Kersh, *Dreams of a More Perfect Union*, 115–18; Onuf, "Prologue," 25–26; Shankman, "Toward a Social History of Federalism," 645–48.

17. Hietala, *Manifest Design*, 10–11, John B. Jones quoted on 25.

18. Hendrickson, "First Union," 40–42; Onuf, "Empire of Liberty," 198–99; Rakove, *Beginnings of National Politics*, 142–43, 156–64, 178–79.

19. Freeman, *Field of Blood*, 43–45, 59–62; Gallagher, *Union War*, 1–3; Hendrickson, "First Union," 37–39; Kersh, *Dreams of a More Perfect Union*, 5–10, 20–21; Varon, *Disunion*, 6–9, Henry Clay quoted on 7.

20. Kersh, *Dreams of a More Perfect Union*, 106–8, 126–28, 145–49, James K. Polk quoted on 127.

21. S. Banner, *How the Indians Lost Their Land*, 199–200; Ostler, *Surviving Genocide*, 206–8; Perdue and Green, *Columbia Guide*, 82–85; Saunt, *Unworthy Republic*, 12–14, 22–24.

22. H. T. Malone, "New Echota," 6–13, J. S. White quoted on 8 ("most fashionable"), Benjamin Gold quoted on 9 ("an interesting").

23. Craig, *Upper Canada*, 56–57; Firth, ed., *Town of York*, xxxi–xl; Levine, *Toronto*, 9–25, John Stuart quoted on 32 ("York"); Masters, *Rise of Toronto*, 3–4; O'Brien, *Speedy Justice*, 23–25.

24. Levine, *Toronto*, 24–27; Masters, *Rise of Toronto*, 4–6.

25. Firth, ed., *Town of York*, lxvii, 219–20, 236–42, John Bennett quoted on 242 ("just emerging"); Levine, *Toronto*, 25–26, 32–33; Masters, *Rise of Toronto*, 4–7.

26. Firth, ed., *Town of York*, 224, 221–22, 229–30, 236–42, Elizabeth Simcoe quoted on 222, Joseph Willcocks quoted on 237 ("The heat"); Levine, *Toronto*, 29–32; A. Taylor, *Divided Ground*, 330.

27. Firth, ed., *Town of York*, 56–57, 328–30, George Heriot quoted on 57; Hallowell, ed., *Oxford Companion to Canadian History*, 617; Masters, *Rise of Toronto*, 7, 34; Levine, *Toronto*, 28–29.

28. Levine, *Toronto*, 38–40; A. Taylor, *Civil War of 1812*, 214–17.

29. Dickens, *American Notes*, 270–71; Hallowell, ed., *Oxford Companion to Canadian History*, 617; Levine, *Toronto*, 41–43; Masters, *Rise of Toronto*, 8–12, 48–49.

30. Calderón de la Barca, *Life in Mexico*, 87–88, 116–17; Poinsett, *Notes on Mexico*, 45–46.

31. Calderón de la Barca, *Life in Mexico*, 102–5; Krauze, *Mexico*, 19–20; Poinsett, *Notes on Mexico*, 54.

32. Calderón de la Barca, *Life in Mexico*, 200; Poinsett, *Notes on Mexico*, 49–50.

33. Calderón de la Barca, *Life in Mexico*, 171; Humboldt, *Political Essay on the Kingdom of New Spain*, 73–79, quotation on 75 ("would appear"); Poinsett, *Notes on Mexico*, 48–49.

34. Calderón de la Barca, *Life in Mexico*, 88–89, 106–7, 117 ("large" and "anti-republican-looking," and "The utmost"), 127 ("extraordinary variety"), 137 ("display"), 179–80; Poinsett, *Notes on Mexico*, 86–87.

35. Humboldt, *Political Essay on the Kingdom of New Spain*, 73–79, quotation on 74 ("No city"); Lynch, *Spanish American Revolutions*, 296–99; Russell, *History of Mexico*, 113.

36. Calderón de la Barca, *Life in Mexico*, 105–6 ("immense"), 173 ("on a magnificent"); Krauze, *Mexico*, 19–20.

37. Avila and Tutino, "Becoming Mexico," 237–38; Van Young, *Other Rebellion*, 226–27.

38. Calderón de la Barca, *Life in Mexico*, 91–92; Humboldt, *Political Essay on the Kingdom of New Spain*, 73–74, 79–90, quote on 84 ("wretches"); Poinsett, *Notes on Mexico*, 46–49.

39. Calderón de la Barca, *Life in Mexico*, 431–33.

40. Girard, *Paradise Lost*, 55–56; Heinl and Heinl, *Written in Blood*, 119–30, 148–49.

41. Ferrer, "Haiti, Free Soil, and Antislavery," 42–48, 59–60, Jean-Pierre Boyer quoted on 59 ("children"); Gonzalez, "Defiant Haiti," 128–31, Boyer quoted on 131 ("sacred" and "every individual"), Admiral Sir Charles Rowley quoted on 131 ("very tenacious"); J. S. Scott, *Common Wind*, 209–10.

42. Candler, *Brief Notices of Hayti*, 69–81, 88–94; Dubois, *Haiti*, 5–6, 44–45; Franklin, *Present State of Hayti*, 272–76; Mackenzie, *Notes on Haiti*, 1–18; M. J. Smith, *Liberty, Fraternity, Exile*, 36–37.

43. Quotations from Franklin, *Present State of Hayti*, 274–77; Heinl and Heinl, *Written in Blood*, 165–70; M. J. Smith, *Liberty, Fraternity, Exile*, 36–37.

44. Candler, *Brief Notices of Hayti*, 15–40; Mackenzie, *Notes on Haiti*, 1–37, quotation from 28–29.

45. Candler, *Brief Notices of Hayti*, 27–28, 38–43, quotations from 38 ("They do not"), and 40 ("the freedom"); Dubois, *Haiti*, 6–7, 11–12; Geggus, "Haiti and the Abolitionists," 132–33; Gonzalez, "Defiant Haiti," 124–26.

46. Baker, *Affairs of Party*, 258; John Marshall quoted in Hendrickson, *Union, Nation, or Empire*, 164; Kersh, *Dreams of a More Perfect Union*, 106–8.

CHAPTER 1: CONSTITUTIONS

1. John Adams to John Taylor, June 9, 1814, Founders Online, National Archives (https://founders.archives.gov/documents/Adams/99-02-02-6301); Chernow, *Washington*, 15–28.

2. George Washington to Robert Hunter Morris, Apr. 9, 1756, in Boyd et al., eds., *Papers of George Washington, Colonial Series*, 2:345–47; Calloway, *Indian World*, 102–47.

3. Calloway, *Indian World*, 171–206; Chernow, *Washington*, 136–51.

4. George Washington, General Orders, July 4, 1775, and G. Washington to Lund Washington, Aug. 28, 1775, in Chase et al., eds., *Papers of George Washington, Revolutionary War Series*, 1:54–58 ("hoped"), 334–40 ("dirty").

5. Israel Trask quoted in Chernow, *Washington*, 198.

6. C. Cox, *Proper Sense of Honor*, 22–23, 50–54; Martin and Lender, *Respectable Army*, 128–30.

7. Chopra, *Choosing Sides*, 2–3; Potter, *Liberty We Seek*, 10–16, 153–57, 172–80; Shy, *People Armed and Numerous*, 163–79, 218–19.

8. Jan Lewis, *Pursuit of Happiness*, 48–50; G. Wood, *Radicalism*, 229–43.

9. George Washington to Joseph Reed, Feb. 10, 1776, in Chase et al., eds., *Papers of George Washington, Revolutionary War Series*, 3:286–91 ("notwithstanding"); Washington to the States, June 8, 1783 ("There is"), Founders Online, National Archives (https://founders.archives.gov/documents/Washington/99-01-02-11404).

10. John Harvie to Thomas Jefferson, Oct. 18, 1777, in Boyd et al., eds., *Papers of Thomas Jefferson*, 2:34–36.

11. Hendrickson, "First Union," 40–42; Rakove, *Beginnings of National Politics*, 142–43, 156–64, 178–79.

12. Edling, "Consolidating," 170–71; Gould, *Among the Powers*, 10–11; Hendrickson, "First Union," 36–39, 45; Irvin, *Clothed in Robes of Sovereignty*, 274–76; Rakove, *Beginnings of National Politics*, 148–76.

13. John Adams to Thomas Jefferson, Mar. 1, 1787, Founders Online, National Archives (http://founders.archives.gov/documents/Adams/99-02-02-0072); Hendrickson, "First Union," 37–42; Rakove, *Beginnings of National Politics*, 163–92, Thomas Burke quoted on 167 ("that the states").

14. O'Shaughnessy, *Men Who Lost America*, 280–88; Rakove, *Beginnings of National Politics*, 268–69, 273–74; Stinchcombe, *American Revolution and the French Alliance*, 133–34, 151–53.

15. Kohn, "Inside History," 196–215; George Washington, "Speech to the Officers of the Army," March 15, 1783, in Rhodehamel, ed., *George Washington Writings*, 496–500; Alexander Hamilton to Washington, Mar. 25, 1783, in Syrett, ed., *Papers of Alexander Hamilton*, 3:305–307 ("I confess").

16. Thomas Jefferson to George Washington, Apr. 16, 1784, in Boyd et al., eds., *Papers of Thomas Jefferson*, 7:105–10; John Adams to Benjamin Rush, June 21, 1811 ("solemn"), Founders Online, National Archives (http://founders.

archives.gov/documents/Adams/99-02-02-5649); J. P. Martin, ed., *Ordinary Courage*, 161–62; Rakove, *Beginnings of National Politics*, 334–36.

17. Chopra, *Choosing Sides*, 47–48, 168–71; Egerton, *Death or Liberty*, 202–6; Gilbert, *Black Patriots and Loyalists*, 177–78, 188–96, 213–14; Jasanoff, *Liberty's Exiles*, 80–81, 94–96; Pybus, *Epic Journeys*, 61–72.

18. Chopra, *Unnatural Rebellion*, 210–13; Jasanoff, *Liberty's Exiles*, 6, 10–11, 63–64, 85–86, 93–94, 159–61, 126–29, 137–50, 165–74, 229–31, 240–41; Moore, *Loyalists*, 148–54, 161–70, 183–223.

19. G. Craig, *Upper Canada*, 35–38; Jasanoff, *Liberty's Exiles*, 188, 218; Lord Dorchester to Lord Sydney, Oct. 14, 1788, MG 11, 51:203, Library and Archives Canada (Ottawa).

20. Neatby, *Quebec*, 87–141, 172, and 181–92; Lanctot, *Canada and the American Revolution*, 17–18.

21. Upton, *Loyal Whig*, 150, 167; Greenwood, *Legacies of Fear*, 8–9; Harlow, *Founding*, 2:725–26.

22. Greenwood, *Legacies of Fear*, 35–38; Milobar, "Conservative Ideology," 45, 61–63; Lord Grenville, "Discussion of Petitions and Counter Petitions Re Change of Government in Canada," and Grenville to Lord Dorchester, Oct. 20, 1789, in Shortt and Doughty, eds., *Documents*, 976, 987–88.

23. Harlow, *Founding*, 2:760–62; American quoted in Maude, *Visit to the Falls*, 60; Lord Grenville, "Discussion of Petitions and Counter Petitions Re Change of Government in Canada [1789]," and Lord Dorchester to Grenville, Feb. 8, 1790, in Shortt and Doughty, eds., *Documents*, 983–86, 1004.

24. G. Craig, *Upper Canada*, 17–19; Greenwood and Wright, "Parliamentary Privilege," 412–15; Lord Grenville, "Discussion of Petitions and Counter Petitions Re Change of Government in Canada [1789]," in Shortt and Doughty, eds., *Documents*, 984–86.

25. Greenwood, *Legacies of Fear*, 45; "Discussion of Petitions and Counter Petitions Re Change of Government in Canada [1789]," in Shortt and Doughty, eds., *Documents*, 977.

26. Lord Thurlow to W. W. Grenville, Sept. 10, 1789, in Cruikshank, ed., *Correspondence of Simcoe*, 1:4–5; Jasanoff, *Liberty's Exiles*, 13–14; Milobar, "Conservative Ideology," 64.

27. G. Wood, *Radicalism*, 287–305; Young, *Democratic Republicans*, 17–22. For the reactionary nature of the postwar empire, see Bayly, *Imperial Meridian*, 1–15; E. Gould, "American Independence," 107–41.

28. Calloway, *American Revolution in Indian Country*, 273–77; Calloway, *Crown and Calumet*, 7–9; Dowd, *Spirited Resistance*, 93–94; DuVal, *Independence Lost*, 236–38, Creek chief quoted on 238.

29. Allen, *His Majesty's Indian Allies*, 56–57; Ritcheson, *Aftermath of Revolution*, 4–6, 33–37, 59–69; J. L. Wright, *Britain and the American Frontier*, 20–26, 36, 42–43, 80–86.

30. R. Allen, *His Majesty's Indian Allies*, 56–57; Calloway, *Crown and Calumet*, 14; DuVal, *Independence Lost*, 253–55, 294–98; Furstenberg, "Significance,"

663; White, *Middle Ground*, 413–17, 433–43, 447–48; J. L. Wright, *Britain and the American Frontier*, 69–72.

31. Cayton, *Frontier Republic*, 13–32; Griffin, *America's Revolution*, 251–52; Hinderaker, *Elusive Empires*, 228–31, 242; Onuf, *Origins of the Federal Republic*, 42–46, 154–60, 170–71; Onuf, *Statehood and Union*, 42–43, 46–49, 53–55, 58–66; Van Cleve, *We Have Not a Government*, 139–40.

32. John Jay to Thomas Jefferson, Dec. 14, 1786, in Boyd et al., eds., *Papers of Thomas Jefferson*, 10:596–99; Cayton, *Frontier Republic*, 2–11; squatter notice quoted in Jensen, *New Nation*, 357; Hinderaker, *Elusive Empires*, 227–31, 238–40; Van Cleve, *We Have Not a Government*, 136–37, 144.

33. Gould, "Independence and Interdependence," 735–36; Narrett, *Adventurism and Empire*, 3, 228, 253; Onuf, "State-Making in Revolutionary America," 797–815.

34. Narrett, *Adventurism and Empire*, 132–33; Roney, "1776, Viewed from the West," 680–86.

35. Thomas Jefferson to Richard Henry Lee, July 12, 1785, in Boyd et al., eds., *Papers of Thomas Jefferson* 8:287; Duval, *Independence Lost*, 314–20; Roney, "1776, Viewed from the West," 686–88.

36. Roney, "1776, Viewed from the West," 688–90.

37. Van Cleve, *We Have Not a Government*, 134–39, 155, John Francis Mercer quoted on 139.

38. Furstenberg, "Significance," 659–65; Jensen, *New Nation*, 170–73, Rufus King quoted on 171–72 ("every emigrant").

39. George Washington to Henry Knox, Dec. 5, 1784, in Abbot et al., eds., *Papers of George Washington, Confederation Series*, 2:170–72 ("with the Spaniards"); James Lewis, *American Union*, 14–22; Washington to Benjamin Harrison, Oct. 10, 1784, in Rhodehamel, ed., *George Washington, Writings*, 559–67 ("pivot"); Van Cleve, *We Have Not a Government*, 141–42.

40. Van Cleve, *We Have Not a Government*, 138, 140–41, 146–48, Arthur St. Clair quoted on 147–48.

41. Aron, *American Confluence*, 71–73; Van Cleve, *We Have Not a Government*, 177–78, unnamed Kentuckian quoted on 178.

42. Barthelemi Tardiveau to Count de Aranda, July 17, 1792, Baron Carondelet to Aranda, c. 1793, in Houck, ed., *Spanish Regime*, 1:360, 2:13 ("This vast"); Narrett, *Adventurism and Empire*, 125–26, Vicente Manuel de Zéspedes quoted on 187 ("need only" and "whatever"); Van Cleve, *We Have Not a Government*, 134–35; Weber, *Spanish Frontier*, 272–80, Zéspedes quoted on 272 ("distinguished").

43. W. E. Foley, *Genesis of Missouri*, 98–107; Kastor, *Nation's Crucible*, 26–34; McCalla, *Planting the Province*, 15–17, 249; Narrett, *Adventurism and Empire*, 162–63; Weber, *Spanish Frontier*, 276–78.

44. Dowd, *Spirited Resistance*, 93–94; DuVal, *Independence Lost*, 239–40, 246–58, 310–12, Alexander McGillivray quoted on 253 ("America"); Narrett,

Adventurism and Empire, 119–20, 209–10; Saunt, *New Order of Things*, 67–72, 88–89, McGillivray quoted on 89 ("was a mestizo"); Van Cleve, *We Have Not a Government*, 148–50; Weber, *Spanish Frontier*, 278–84, McGillivray quoted on 282 ("Crown of Spain").

45. Narrett, *Adventurism and Empire*, 130–32, Thomas Green quoted on 130 ("Weston Cuntery"), and John Sullivan quoted on 131–32 ("The Americans"); Van Cleve, *We Have Not a Government*, 162–64.

46. DuVal, *Independence Lost*, 318–20; Faber, *Building the Land of Dreams*, 37–38; Narrett, *Adventurism and Empire*, 133, 137–39, 147, 155–58, 164-74, James Wilkinson quoted on 170.

47. Narrett, *Adventurism and Empire*, 137–39, 155, 169–74, 181–82, James Wilkinson quoted on 137, Baron Carondelet quoted on 155, and Esteban Rodríquez Miró quoted on 173 ("sanguine Spirit").

48. Alexander McGillivray quoted in DuVal, *Independence Lost*, 323; Narrett, *Adventurism and Empire*, 121–24; Weber, *Spanish Frontier*, 278–81.

49. DuVal, *Independence Lost*, 320–22; John Gordon quoted in Hilton, "Being and Becoming Spanish," 18 ("May God"); Narrett, *Adventurism and Empire*, 147–48, 162–63.

50. John Graves Simcoe to Evan Nepean, Dec. 3, 1789, Simcoe to Henry Dundas, Aug. 12, 1791, and Nov. 23, 1792, in Cruikshank, ed., *Correspondence of Simcoe*, 1:7–8, 50–51, 264.

51. DuVal, *Independence Lost*, 268–69; Narrett, *Adventurism and Empire*, 126–30, 186; A. Taylor, *Divided Ground*, 113–19; Van Cleve, *We Have Not a Government*, 35.

52. Kulikoff, "War in the Countryside," 217–24; Lindert and Williamson, "American Incomes," 725–65, quotations from 741 ("America's greatest"), 752 ("economic disaster").

53. McCusker and Menard, *Economy of British America*, 361–75; Van Cleve, *We Have Not a Government*, 4–5, 19–25, 36–47.

54. DuVal, *Independence Lost*, 333–34, Diego de Gardoqui quoted on 334 ("almost without"); Edling, *Revolution in Favor of Government*, 85–88, Lord Sheffield quoted on 87; E. Gould, *Among the Powers*, 113–21, 125–27; Van Cleve, *We Have Not a Government*, 102–29.

55. McCoy, "James Madison and Visions of American Nationality," 244–45; R. Morris, *Forging the Union*, 93–95, Timothy Bloodworth quoted on 243; Van Cleve, *We Have Not a Government*, 12–13.

56. Hendrickson, *Peace Pact*, 205–6; Rakove, *Beginnings of National Politics*, 349–51; Van Cleve, *We Have Not a Government*, 162–69.

57. McCoy, "James Madison and Visions of American Nationality," 227–45; Van Cleve, *Slaveholders' Union*, 111–12, 159–61, Patrick Henry quoted on 159; Van Cleve, *We Have Not a Government*, 167–80.

58. Van Cleve, *We Have Not a Government*, 162, 171–76, James Monroe quoted on 176.

59. Cayton, *Frontier Republic*, 13–32; Narrett, *Adventurism and Empire*, 127–28; Van Cleve, *We Have Not a Government*, 147, 169, John Brown quoted on 184–85.

60. Richards, *Shays's Rebellion*, 9–12, 16–42, 63–64, 77–79, 113–14; Szatmary, *Shays' Rebellion*, 58–130, James Wilson quoted on 130; Van Cleve, *We Have Not a Government*, 214–42.

61. George Washington to the States, June 8, 1783 ("becoming"), Founders Online, National Archives (https://founders.archives.gov/documents/Washington/99-01-02-11404); Benjamin Franklin, speech, Sept. 17, 1787, in James Madison, "Notes from the 1787 Philadelphia Convention," National Heritage Center for Constitutional Studies (www.constitution.org); Alexander Hamilton, "The Federalist No. 9," in Syrett, ed., *Papers of Alexander Hamilton*, 4:333–39; Hendrickson, "Escaping Insecurity," 219–20.

62. DuVal, *Independence Lost*, 319–20, John Jay quoted on 320 ("confederations"); Gould, *Among the Powers of the Earth*, 130–34; Hendrickson, *Peace Pact*, 203–7, 216–18; Kersh, *Dreams of a More Perfect Union*, 59–60; Jay quoted in Sexton, *Monroe Doctrine*, 27 ("every state").

63. Bouton, *Taming Democracy*, 31–58; Holton, *Unruly Americans*, 165–68, Connecticut writer quoted on 165 ("be content"); Van Cleve, *We Have Not a Government*, 26–28, Benjamin Rush quoted on 28 ("They call"); G. Wood, *Creation of the American Republic*, 475–83.

64. Jensen, *New Nation*, 178, 311–12, Edmund Randolph quoted on 312 ("too democratic"); Van Cleve, *We Have Not a Government*, 6–7; G. Wood, *Creation of the American Republic*, 393–408, 415–32.

65. Bouton, *Taming Democracy*, 172–77; Alexander Hamilton, "Conjectures About the New Constitution," Sept. 17–30, 1787, in Syrett, ed., *Papers of Alexander Hamilton*, 4:275–77; Kornblith and Murrin, "Making and Unmaking," 54–56; G. Wood, *Creation of the American Republic*, 463–75.

66. Beeman, *Plain, Honest Men*, 28–29, 170–89, 200–204, 218–25; Berkin, *Brilliant Solution*, 102–13; Hendrickson, *Peace Pact*, 223–25, 240; G. Wood, *Creation of the American Republic*, 505–18.

67. Beeman, *Plain, Honest Men*, 153–55; Van Cleve, *Slaveholders' Union*, 103–5, 113–14; Varon, *Disunion*, 22–24; Waldstreicher, *Slavery's Constitution*, 86.

68. Beeman, *Plain, Honest Men*, 206–15, 310–34; Finkelman, "Making a Covenant with Death," 217–24, Charles Cotesworth Pinckney quoted on 224; Hendrickson, *Peace Pact*, 226–39; Van Cleve, *Slaveholders' Union*, 41, 115–17; Waldstreicher, *Slavery's Constitution*, 3–19, 77–100.

69. Beeman, *Plain, Honest Men*, 330–36; Samuel Hopkins quoted in D. B. Davis, *Problem of Slavery in the Age of Revolution*, 299 ("state of anarchy"); Van Cleve, *Slaveholders' Union*, 19; Waldstreicher, *Slavery's Constitution*, 101–5; Hopkins quoted in Zilversmit, *First Emancipation*, 156 ("How does it").

70. Beeman, *Plain, Honest Men*, 240–55, 299–307; Berkin, *Brilliant Solution*, 116–48, 178; Rakove, *Revolutionaries*, 379–84, 414–15; George Washington

to Benjamin Harrison, Sept. 24, 1787, in Abbot et al., eds., *Papers of George Washington, Confederation Series*, 5:339–40.

71. Beeman, *Plain, Honest Men*, 380–81; Kersh, *Dreams of a More Perfect Union*, 60–61; Murrin, "Roof Without Walls," 341–48; Alexander Hamilton, "Federalist No. 8," in Syrett, ed., *Papers of Alexander Hamilton*, 4:326–32; G. Wood, *Creation of the American Republic*, 523–31, 562–64.

72. Beeman, *Plain, Honest Men*, 408–10; Kornblith & Murrin, "Making and Unmaking," 55–56.

73. Beeman, *Plain, Honest Men*, 370–74, 394, 410–11; Bouton, *Taming Democracy*, 172–73, 179–81; Main, *Anti-Federalists*, 192–93, 204, 252–54.

74. Hendrickson, "Escaping Insecurity," 221–25; James Madison to Edmund Randolph, Mar. 1, 1789, in Hutchinson et al., eds., *Papers of James Madison*, 11:453–54.

75. Cornell, *Other Founders*, 158–63; Ketcham, *James Madison*, 289–92; Maier, *Ratification*, 446–56, 459–64; Rakove, *Revolutionaries*, 393–95; G. Wood, *Empire of Liberty*, 55–62, 71–72.

76. Egerton, *Death or Liberty*, 253–54; Ketcham, *James Madison*, 315–16, Madison quoted on 316; Nash, *Race and Revolution*, 38–40, antislavery petition quoted on 40 ("without distinction"); Parkinson, "'Manifest Signs of Passion,'" 49–50, petition quoted on 50 ("Inconsistency").

77. Litwack, *North of Slavery*, 33–34, George Thacher quoted on 34; Nash, *Race and Revolution*, 77–79; Newman, *Freedom's Prophet*, 146–48, Georgia congressman quoted on 148; Richards, *Slave Power*, 71–72; Robinson, *Slavery in the Structure*, 285–90; Van Cleve, "Founding a Slaveholders' Union," 130–32.

78. Henry Knox report, Dec. 26, 1791, in Abbott et al., eds., *Papers of George Washington, Presidential Series*, 9:318.

79. Aron, *How the West was Lost*, 7–11, 35; Calloway, *American Revolution in Indian Country*, 162–64; Hinderaker, *Elusive Empires*, 67–71, 178–82; R. White, *Middle Ground*, 324–39.

80. Arthur St. Clair to George Washington, Aug. 1789, in C. Carter, ed., *Territorial Papers*, 2:212; Cayton, *Frontier Republic*, 12–50; Onuf, "Liberty, Development, and Union," 179–213.

81. Hinderaker, *Elusive Empires*, 253–54; Nichols, *Red Gentlemen*, 180–85.

82. Henry Knox, reports, June 15, 1789, and July 7, 1789, *American State Papers, Indian Affairs*, 1:12–14, 53–54; Horsman, "Indian Policy," 44–47.

83. Cayton, *Frontier Republic*, 12–32; D. Jones, *License for Empire*, 157–79; Nichols, *Red Gentlemen*, 81–84, 98–127, 139–40; M. Rohrbough, *Land Office Business*, 15.

84. R. White, *Middle Ground*, 467–68; J. L. Wright, *Britain and the American Frontier*, 95–97.

85. Nugent, *Habits of Empire*, 47, 53; R. White, *Middle Ground*, 474–75.

86. Din, "Spain's Immigration Policy," 266–67; Faber, *Building the Land of Dreams*, 39–40; W. E. Foley, *Genesis of Missouri*, 76–78; Stagg, *Borderlines*, 36–38; Weber, *Spanish Frontier*, 274–75, 289–90.

87. Narrett, *Adventurism and Empire*, 231–34, 241–47, Juan Ventura Morales quoted on 231 ("in the mouth"); Andrew Ellicott quoted on 247 ("We met"); Manuel Gayoso de Lemos to Daniel Clark, June 17, 1796 ("Spain made"), Edward Alexander Parsons Collection, Dolph Briscoe Center for American History, University of Texas, Austin. For this citation, my thanks to Jacob F. Lee of Penn State.

88. Balogh, *Government Out of Sight*, 197–98; Faber, *Building the Land of Dreams*, 40–42; Nichols, *Red Gentlemen*, 171–76; G. Wood, *Empire of Liberty*, 316–17, traveler quoted on 316.

89. Elkins and McKitrick, *Age of Federalism*, 95, 114–16; Ferling, *Leap in the Dark*, 315–18; Freeman, *Affairs of Honor*, 55–56, 160–61; G. Wood, *Empire of Liberty*, 89–94.

90. Balogh, *Government Out of Sight*, 101–3; Elkins and McKitrick, *Age of Federalism*, 114–23, 297–304; G. Wood, *Empire of Liberty*, 92–109.

91. Balogh, *Government Out of Sight*, 99–100; Thomas Jefferson to Thomas Paine, June 19, 1792, in Boyd et al., eds., *Papers of Thomas Jefferson*, 20:312–13; Elkins and McKitrick, *Age of Federalism*, 154–61; Freeman, *Affairs of Honor*, 14–15, 74–76; G. Wood, *Empire of Liberty*, 84–85, 139–44.

92. Jedidiah Morse quoted in J. Banner, *To the Hartford Convention*, 57 ("There must be"); Elkins and McKitrick, *Age of Federalism*, 19–29, 750–52; A. Taylor, "From Fathers to Friends," 465–91.

93. Appleby, *Capitalism*, 51–53, 70–78, 90–94; Shankman, *Crucible of American Democracy*, 3–8, *Philadelphia Aurora* quoted on 3 ("happy"); Zagarri, "American Revolution," 492–94.

94. Ben-Atar and Oberg, "Introduction," 9–11; Cotlar, *Tom Paine's America*, 65–67; Sidbury, "Thomas Jefferson," 199–201.

95. Onuf, *Jefferson's Empire*, 53–56, 83, 95.

96. J. R. Howe, "Republican Thought," 147–65; Jefferson to William Duane, Mar. 28, 1811, in Looney et al., eds., *Papers of Thomas Jefferson, Retirement Series*, 3:506–9.

97. Freeman, *Affairs of Honor*, 1–10; Edmund Randolph to George Washington, July 30, 1794, in Abbott et al., eds., *Papers of George Washington, Presidential Series*, 16:523–30.

98. Bouton, *Taming Democracy*, 224–26, 230–38; Slaughter, *Whiskey Rebellion*, 127–35, 164–69, 177–89; G. Wood, *Empire of Liberty*, 134–36.

99. Elkins and McKitrick, *Age of Federalism*, 463–65, 476–84; George Washington, address to Congress, Nov. 19, 1794, in Rhodehamel, ed., *George Washington, Writings*, 887–95; Slaughter, *Whiskey Rebellion*, 133–35, 203–20, *Gazette of the United States* quoted on 133–34.

100. George Washington to Daniel Morgan, Oct. 8, 1794, in Abbott et al., eds., *Papers of George Washington, Presidential Series*, 17:40; G. Wood, *Empire of Liberty*, 196–97, 203–4.

101. Elkins and McKitrick, *Age of Federalism*, 439–41, 443, 842–43, [Boston] *Columbian Centinel* quoted on 441; G. Wood, *Empire of Liberty*, 200–202.

102. Cotlar, *Thomas Paine's America*, 99; Elkins and McKitrick, *Age of Federalism*, 303–30; G. Wood, *Empire of Liberty*, 174–75, 176–80.

103. Cotlar, *Tom Paine's America*, 82–114, David Osgood quoted on 93; S. Newman, "Paine, Jefferson, and Revolutionary Radicalism," 79–81; G. Wood, *Empire of Liberty*, 177–79.

104. Cotlar, *Tom Paine's America*, 86–88; Elkins and McKitrick, *Age of Federalism*, 336–54; Ferling, *Leap in the Dark*, 359–61; A. White, *Encountering Revolution*, 106–7; G. Wood, *Empire of Liberty*, 182–85.

105. Cotlar, *Tom Paine's America*, 97–98; Ritcheson, *Aftermath*, 331–52.

106. Daniel Clark, Jr., quoted in Narrett, *Adventurism and Empire*, 250–51; George Washington to Alexander Hamilton, July 14, 1798, in Syrett, ed., *Papers of Alexander Hamilton*, 22:17–21.

107. Bradburn, *Citizenship Revolution*, 148–67, 224–34; Robert Goodloe Harper speech, June 19, 1798, *Annals of Congress*, 5th Congress, 2d Session, 1991–92 ("The time"); Kettner, *Development of American Citizenship*, 244–45.

108. Balogh, *Government Out of Sight*, 105–6; Elkins and McKitrick, *Age of Federalism*, 709–11; Pasley, "*Tyranny of Printers*," 118–25, 176–78; A. Taylor, "Alien and Sedition Acts," 66–68.

109. Balogh, *Government Out of Sight*, 106–7; Lurie, "Liberty Poles," 673–98; Read, *Power versus Liberty*, 144–47; Alexander Hamilton to Theodore Sedgwick, Feb. 2, 1799, in Syrett, ed., *Papers of Alexander Hamilton*, 22:452–54 ("regular conspiracy," "clever" and "put Virginia").

110. Ferling, *Leap in the Dark*, 458–68, James T. Callender quoted on 459 ("one of the most"); G. Wood, *Empire of Liberty*, 268–71, Theodore Dwight quoted on 586 ("murder").

111. Elkins and McKitrick, *Age of Federalism*, 741–50; Onuf, *Jefferson's Empire*, 82, 100–102.

112. Ackerman, *Failure of the Founding Fathers*, 97–99, 203–6, Samuel Smith quoted on 204; Pasley, "1800 as a Revolution," 122–23.

113. Ackerman, *Failure of the Founding Fathers*, 203–9; Elkins and McKitrick, *Age of Federalism*, 753–54; Simon, *What Kind of Nation*, 207–8.

114. Freeman and Neem, "Introduction," 1–2; Grabbe, "European Immigration," 197–202.

115. Balogh, *Government Out of Sight*, 113; Bradburn, *Citizenship Revolution*, 281–82; Onuf, *Jefferson's Empire*, 80–81, 85, 93; Pasley, "1800 as a Revolution," 122–25.

116. Thomas Jefferson, "First Inaugural Address," Mar. 4, 1801, in Boyd et al., *Papers of Thomas Jefferson*, 33:148–52; Hendrickson, *Peace Pact*, 258–59; Onuf, *Jefferson's Empire*, 1–14, 107–21.

117. Jefferson to Spencer Roane, Sept. 6, 1819, in Looney et al., eds., *Papers of Thomas Jefferson, Retirement Series*, 15:16; Pasley, "1800 as a Revolution," 121–47.

118. Balogh, *Government Out of Sight*, 251–52; John Marshall to Alexander Hamilton, Jan. 1, 1801, in H. A. Johnson et al., eds., *Papers of John Mar-*

shall, 6:46–47; Newmyer, *John Marshall*, 80–81; G. Wood, *Empire of Liberty*, 434–36, Thomas Jefferson quoted on 434.

119. Balogh, *Government Out of Sight*, 251–52; Newmyer, *John Marshall*, 148–52; John Marshall quoted in Rorabaugh, *Alcoholic Republic*, 103; Simon, *What Kind of Nation*, 152, 161.

120. Balogh, *Government Out of Sight*, 250–56; Newmyer, *Supreme Court Justice*, 125–27; Thomas Jefferson to Archibald Thweatt, Jan. 19, 1821, Founders Online, National Archives (http://founders.archives.gov/documents/Jefferson/98-01-02-1782); G. E. White, *Marshall Court*, 541–52.

121. Balogh, *Government Out of Sight*, 251, 257–60; Newmyer, *Supreme Court Justice*, 129–36; North et al., *Growth and Welfare*, 66–67; G. Wood, *Empire of Liberty*, 458–66.

122. Ackerman, *Failure of the Founding Fathers*, 149–51; Simon, *What Kind of Nation*, 148–49, 192–93.

123. John, *Spreading the News*, 140–41; Onuf, *Mind of Thomas Jefferson*, 252–55; Jefferson to Walter Jones, Mar. 31, 1801, in Boyd et al., eds., *Papers of Thomas Jefferson*, 33:506.

124. Dubois, *Haiti*, 19–23; Geggus, *Haitian Revolutionary Studies*, 5–6; J. S. Scott, *Common Wind*, 136–41.

125. Blackburn, *Overthrow of Colonial Slavery*, 195–200, 215–16; Dubois, *Colony of Citizens*, 112–14, 155–56; Geggus, *Haitian Revolutionary Studies*, 7–8, 11–14; J. S. Scott, *Common Wind*, 161–69.

126. Blackburn, *Overthrow of Colonial Slavery*, 224–26, 235–36; Dubois, *Colony of Citizens*, 156–57, 166–67, 204–5; Geggus, *Haitian Revolutionary Studies*, 15–16, 22.

127. Henry DeSaussure quoted in Egerton, *Death or Liberty*, 263–64 ("equality"); V. Brown, "Vapor of Dread," 195-96; Dubois, "Unworthy of Liberty?" 45–46, 50–51, quote on 46 ("unworthy"); Hickey, "America's Response," 361–79; A. White, *Encountering Revolution*, 2–5, 206–7.

128. Egerton, *Gabriel's Rebellion*, 20–53, 64–65, Jack Ditcher quoted on 40 ("as much right"); Mullin, *Flight and Rebellion*, 141, 156–57; Nicholls, *Whispers of Rebellion*, 25–29; Sidbury, *Ploughshares into Swords*, 6–7.

129. Egerton, *Gabriel's Rebellion*, 69–79; Nicholls, *Whispers of Rebellion*, 57–70.

130. Egerton, *Gabriel's Rebellion*, 83–112; Nicholls, *Whispers of Rebellion*, 72–92; John Randolph to Joseph H. Nicholson, Sept. 26, 1800, in W. C. Bruce, ed., *John Randolph*, 2:250.

131. Deyle, *Carry Me Back*, 24; Drescher, *Abolition*, 137; Fehrenbacher, *Slaveholding Republic*, 136–47.

132. Chambers, *No God but Gain*, 110–11, 123–29; Fehrenbacher, *Slaveholding Republic*, 144–46, 164.

133. Gilje, *Making of the American Republic*, 251–52; Lambert, *Barbary Wars*, 33–41, 58–59.

134. Furstenberg, "Beyond Freedom and Slavery," 1295–1330; Gilje, *Making of*

the American Republic, 254; Lambert, *Barbary Wars*, 37, 105–6, 118–20, Matthew Carey quoted on 37.

135. Cogliano, *Emperor of Liberty*, 148–49; Gilje, *Making of the American Republic*, 252–55; Lambert, *Barbary Wars*, 55–64, 77–80.

136. Cogliano, *Emperor of Liberty*, 149–50; Gilje, *Making of the American Republic*, 255–56; Lambert, *Barbary Wars*, 8–9, 81–100, 117–18; Treaty of Tripoli quoted in Lepore, *These Truths*, 200–201.

137. Thomas Jefferson to James Madison, Aug. 28, 1801, in Boyd et al., eds., *Papers of Thomas Jefferson*, 35:162–64; Cogliano, *Emperor of Liberty*, 170–71; Gilje, *Making of the American Republic*, 255–56; Lambert, *Barbary Wars*, 43, 84–85, 91–92, 103, 124–25, 145.

138. Cogliano, *Emperor of Liberty*, 150–54; Lambert, *Barbary Wars*, 124–32.

139. Cogliano, *Emperor of Liberty*, 157–59; Gilje, *Making of the American Republic*, 256–57; Lambert, *Barbary Wars*, 128, 133–40.

140. Gilje, *Making of the American Republic*, 257–58; Lambert, *Barbary Wars*, 140–41.

141. Cogliano, *Emperor of Liberty*, 160–61; Gilje, *Making of the American Republic*, 258–59; Lambert, *Barbary Wars*, 139–49.

142. Cogliano, *Emperor of Liberty*, 166–68; Gilje, *Making of the American Republic*, 259; Lambert, *Barbary Wars*, 149–53; G. Wood, *Empire of Liberty*, 638–39.

143. Cogliano, *Emperor of Liberty*, 168–70; Gilje, *Making of the American Republic*, 259–60; Lambert, *Barbary Wars*, 153–54, 177–78.

144. Lambert, *Barbary Wars*, 40, 157–69; William Eaton quoted in G. Wood, *Empire of Liberty*, 639.

145. Kersh, *Dreams of a More Perfect Union*, 5–6, 62–64, Andrew Jackson quoted on 6; Onuf, "Empire of Liberty," 196–97.

146. Balogh, *Government Out of Sight*, 90–94, 110–11, 115–16; Kersh, *Dreams of a More Perfect Union*, 9–10, 71–72, James Madison quoted on 72; Onuf, "Empire of Liberty," 195–96; Varon, *Disunion*, 25–27.

147. Kersh, *Dreams of a More Perfect Union*, 5–6, William Thomas quoted on 6 ("a union"); Onuf, "Empire of Liberty," 210–12; Varon, *Disunion*, 55–85.

148. Kersh, *Dreams of a More Perfect Union*, 20–21, 59, 104–5, Thomas Hamilton quoted on 104; Onuf, "Empire of Liberty," 212–13; Varon, *Disunion*, 87–124.

CHAPTER 2: EMPIRES

1. Calloway, *One Vast Winter Count*, 293–301; Fenn, *Encounters at the Heart of the World*, 213–15, 394n36; A. Isenberg, *Destruction of the Bison*, 42; Ronda, *Lewis and Clark*, 143–44, 256.

2. Calloway, *One Vast Winter Count*, 301–3; Fenn, *Encounters at the Heart of the World*, 213–14; Lamar, ed., *Reader's Encyclopedia of the American West*, 1055; E. West, *Way to the West*, 51-84.

3. Fenn, *Encounters at the Heart of the World*, 214–18.

4. Thomas Jefferson to Edmund Pendleton, Aug. 13, 1776, and Jefferson to Samuel Huntington, Feb. 9, 1780, in Boyd et al., eds., *Papers of Thomas Jefferson*, 1:491–94 ("will settle"), 3:286–89 ("necessary"); Griffin, *American Leviathan*, 134–35; Hinderaker, *Elusive Empires*, 185–87, 227–28.

5. Thomas Jefferson to George Rogers Clark, Dec. 25, 1780, and Jefferson, "First Inaugural Address, Mar. 4, 1801, in Boyd et al., eds., *Papers of Thomas Jefferson*, 4:237 ("Empire of Liberty"), and 33:148–52; DuVal, *Independence Lost*, 343–45; Onuf, "Imperialism and Nationalism," 21–40.

6. Balogh, *Government Out of Sight*, 180–81, 187–88; Cayton, "Radicals in the 'Western World,'" 83–89; Nichols, *Red Gentlemen*, 193–97, 201; Rohrbough, *Land Office Business*, 23–41.

7. Horsman, *Expansion*, 104–9; R. White, *Middle Ground*, 473–74; Thomas Jefferson to William Henry Harrison, Feb. 27, 1803, in Boyd et al., eds., *Papers of Thomas Jefferson*, 39:589–93 ("We have only"); Jefferson speech to Wyandot chiefs, Jan. 10, 1809 ("I repeat"), Founders Online, National Archives (http://founders.archives.gov/documents/Jefferson/99-01-02-9516).

8. Thomas Jefferson to William H. Harrison, Feb. 27, 1803, and Jefferson to William C. C. Claiborne, May 24, 1803, in Boyd et al., eds., *Papers of Thomas Jefferson*, 39:589–92, and 40:422–23 ("press on"); Nichols, *Red Gentlemen*, 193–97; R. White, *Middle Ground*, 473–74, 496–500.

9. Thomas Jefferson to Archibald Stuart, Jan. 25, 1786, in Boyd et al., eds., *Papers of Thomas Jefferson*, 9:217–19; Isenberg, *Fallen Founder*, 285; Narrett, *Adventurism and Empire*, 253.

10. Thomas Jefferson to George Washington, Apr. 2, 1791, in Boyd et al., eds., *Papers of Thomas Jefferson*, 20:95–98.

11. Thomas Jefferson to James Monroe, May 26, 1801, in Boyd et al., eds., *Papers of Thomas Jefferson*, 34:185-86; Dubois, *Haiti*, 35–36; Onuf, "Prologue," 25–26, 30.

12. D. B. Davis, *Problem of Slavery in the Age of Revolution*, 150–51; Dillon and Drexler, "Introduction," 7; Dubois, *Colony of Citizens*, 344–45, 366–73, 402–4; Geggus, *Haitian Revolutionary Studies*, 25–26.

13. James Madison to Charles Pinckney, Nov. 27, 1802, in Stagg et al., eds., *Papers of James Madison, Secretary of State Series*, 4:146; James Lewis, *American Union*, 24–26, David Holmes quoted on 25.

14. James Barbour to Madison, Dec. 9, 1802, and Daniel Clark to Madison, Apr. 27, 1803, in Stagg et al., eds., *Papers of James Madison, Secretary of State Series*, 4:183–84 ("like a large," and "watch"), and 551–57 ("indifferent"); James Lewis, *American Union*, 25–26.

15. Thomas Jefferson to Robert Livingston, Apr. 18, 1802, in Boyd et al., eds., *Papers of Thomas Jefferson*, 37:263–67; James Lewis, *Louisiana Purchase*, 43–44.

16. James Madison to Robert R. Livingston, Sept. 28, 1801, in Stagg et al., eds., *Papers of James Madison, Secretary of State Series*, 2:142–47.

17. William Henry Harrison to the Secretary of War, July 5, 1809, in Esarey, ed., *Messages and Letters*, 1:353–54.

18. Alexander Hamilton to Harrison Gray Otis, Jan. 26, 1799, and Hamilton to Charles Cotesworth Pinckney, Dec. 29, 1802, in Syrett, ed., *Papers of Alexander Hamilton*, 22:440–42 ("to secure" and "essential"), and 26:71–73; Thomas Jefferson to Hugh Williamson, Apr. 30, 1803, in Boyd et al., eds., *Papers of Thomas Jefferson*, 40:292–93.

19. Thomas Jefferson to Robert Livingston, Apr. 18, 1802, and Jefferson to Pierre Samuel Du Pont de Nemours, May 5, 1802, in Boyd et al., eds., *Papers of Thomas Jefferson*, 37:263–67, 418-19; James Lewis, *Louisiana Purchase*, 34–37, 47–48.

20. Thomas Jefferson to Pierre Samuel Du Pont de Nemours, May 5, 1802, in Boyd et al., eds., *Papers of Thomas Jefferson*, 37:418–19; James Madison to Robert R. Livingston and James Monroe, Mar. 2, 1803, in Stagg et al., eds, *Papers of James Madison, Secretary of State Series*, 4:364–79.

21. Dubois, "Haitian Revolution and the Sale of Louisiana," 93–94, 111–13; Geggus, *Haitian Revolutionary Studies*, 26-27; A. White, *Encountering Revolution*, 4.

22. Napoleon quoted in Dillon and Drexler, "Introduction," 7; James Lewis, *Louisiana Purchase*, 56–61.

23. James Monroe and Robert R. Livingston to James Madison, May 13, 1803, and Monroe to Madison, May 14, 1803, in Stagg et al., eds., *Papers of James Madison, Secretary of State Series*, 4:601–606 ("The Bond"), 610–15 ("Perhaps").

24. James Monroe and Robert R. Livingston to James Madison, May 13, 1803, in Stagg et al., eds., *Papers of James Madison, Secretary of State Series*, 4:601–6; Thomas Jefferson to Andrew Jackson, Sept. 19, 1803, and Jefferson to Joseph Priestley, Jan. 29, 1804, in Boyd et al., eds., *Papers of Thomas Jefferson*, 41:395, and 42:368–70 ("which was").

25. James Lewis, *Louisiana Purchase*, 58–59, 76–77; Nugent, *Habits of Empire*, 66–68; Stagg, *Borderlines*, 41–45.

26. Balogh, *Government Out of Sight*, 172–73; Thomas Jefferson to Albert Gallatin, Aug. 23, 1803, in Boyd et al., eds., *Papers of Thomas Jefferson*, 41:243–33; James Lewis, *Louisiana Purchase*, 69–73.

27. Dubois, *Haiti*, 15–16, 41–46, 151–52; Fick, "From Slave Colony to Black Nation," 157–58; Geggus, "Haiti and the Abolitionists," 113–14; Heinl and Heinl, *Written in Blood*, 119–25, 129–30.

28. Dillon and Drexler, "Introduction," 8–9, George Logan quoted on 9 ("cherish"); Gonzalez, "Defiant Haiti," 126–28; Matthewson, *Proslavery Foreign Policy*, 124–35, 143–46; Sinha, *Slave's Cause*, 54–55.

29. Aron, *American Confluence*, 107–13; Charles Dehault de Lassus quoted in Calloway, *One Vast Winter Count*, 395; Lee, *Masters of the Middle Waters*, 195–96; Nasatir, *Borderland in Retreat*, 49–50.

30. Hyde, *Empires, Nations, and Families*, 5–6; James Lewis, *Louisiana Purchase*, 81–83; Lachance, "Louisiana Purchase," 146–52.

31. Thomas Jefferson to DeWitt Clinton, Dec. 2, 1803, in Boyd et al., eds., *Papers of Thomas Jefferson*, 42:70–71; James Lewis, *Louisiana Purchase*, 81–84, Fisher Ames quoted on 81 ("Gallo"); Kastor, *Nation's Crucible*, 45–51, 56; Vernet, *Strangers on Their Native Soil*, 31–43, 52–53.

32. Edward D. Turner to William C. Claiborne, July 30, 1804, in Carter, ed., *Territorial Papers*, 9:272 ("sort of"); Kastor, *Nation's Crucible*, 57–61, 80; Vernet, *Strangers on Their Native Soil*, 59–96.

33. Balogh, *Government Out of Sight*, 168–69, William Plumer quoted on 169 ("Admit"); James Lewis, *American Union*, 28–29, Alexander Hamilton quoted on 29; James Lewis, *Louisiana Purchase*, 62–64, 79, *Connecticut Courant*, Aug. 24, 1803, quoted on 64; Fisher Ames quoted in R. White, "Louisiana Purchase," 38 ("great waste").

34. Thomas Jefferson to Horatio Gates, July 11, 1803, and Jefferson to John Breckinridge, Aug. 12, 1803, in Boyd et al., eds., *Papers of Thomas Jefferson*, 41:6–8, 184–86.

35. Rufus King to Christopher Gore, Sept. 6, 1803, in King, ed., *Life and Correspondence*, 4:303; Aron, *American Confluence*, 116–20.

36. Herschthal, "Slaves, Spaniards, and Subversion," 293–95; Lachance, "Louisiana Purchase," 155.

37. William C. C. Claiborne to Thomas Jefferson, Nov. 25, 1804, in Carter, ed., *Territorial Papers*, 9:340–41; Hammond, "'Uncontrollable Necessity,'" 146–47; Kastor, *Nation's Crucible*, 5–6, 29–30, 51, 81–83; James Lewis, *Louisiana Purchase*, 84–86; Vernet, *Strangers on Their Native Soil*, 43–60, 143–44.

38. Herschthal, "Slaves, Spaniards, and Subversion," 294, 298–305; Kastor, *Nation's Crucible*, 81–82, Code of 1806 quoted on 81.

39. Kastor, *Nation's Crucible*, 81–82, 91, Code of 1806 quoted on 82 ("Free people").

40. Natchitoches Inhabitants to Edward Turner, July 29, 1804, Louisiana Inhabitants to William C. C. Claiborne, Sept. 17, 1804, and Claiborne to Thomas Jefferson, Sept. 18, 1804, in Carter, ed., *Territorial Papers*, 9:273–74, 297, 298; Herschthal, "Slaves, Spaniards, and Subversion," 283, 289–92.

41. Narrett, *Adventurism and Empire*, 255, 259–60; Saunt, *New Order of Things*, 75–77; J. L. Wright, *William Augustus Bowles*, 120–21, 140–50.

42. Narrett, *Adventurism and Empire*, 211–13, 215–17, Bernardo del Campo quoted on 217 ("daring"), Baron Carondelet quoted on 223; Saunt, *New Order of Things*, 86–87; J. L. Wright, *William Augustus Bowles*, 1–18, Bowles quoted on 115–16 ("Altho").

43. Gould, "Independence and Interdependence," 738–40; Narrett, *Adventurism and Empire*, 211–13, 215–22, William Augustus Bowles quoted on 215; J. L. Wright, *William Augustus Bowles*, 19–54.

44. Gould, "Independence and Interdependence," 739–40; Narrett, *Adventurism and Empire*, 218–22; J. L. Wright, *William Augustus Bowles*, 55–70.

45. Dowd, *Spirited Resistance*, 101–2; DuVal, *Independence Lost*, 295–309; Nar-

rett, *Adventurism and Empire*, 218–22; Saunt, *New Order of Things*, 78–88; J. L. Wright, *William Augustus Bowles*, 29–35.

46. Narrett, *Adventurism and Empire*, 221–23, Alexander McGillivray quoted on 221; J. L. Wright, *William Augustus Bowles*, 59–94.

47. Narrett, *Adventurism and Empire*, 254–55; Saunt, *New Order of Things*, 79, 88–89; J. L. Wright, *William Augustus Bowles*, 95–141.

48. Narrett, *Adventurism and Empire*, 259–61; J. L. Wright, *William Augustus Bowles*, 142–71, Bowles quoted on 121.

49. Gould, "Independence and Interdependence," 748–52; Alexander McGillivray quoted in Saunt, *New Order of Things*, 84; John Halkett quoted in J. L. Wright, *William Augustus Bowles*, 156–57.

50. Hoffer, *Treason Trials*, 38–40; Isenberg, *Fallen Founder*, 285–90; Lewis, *Burr Conspiracy*, 177–78; Malone, *Jefferson and His Time*, 5:217–23; Narrett, *Adventurism and Empire*, 248–49.

51. Hoffer, *Treason Trials*, 37–38; Isenberg, *Fallen Founder*, 286–87; Orsi, *Citizen Explorer*, 88–90, 102–104, 162–67; Ronda, *Finding the West*, 77–78.

52. Hoffer, *Treason Trials*, 40–41, 191–92; Isenberg, *Fallen Founder*, 290–92, Anthony Merry quoted on 290; James Lewis, *Burr Conspiracy*, 106–8; Orsi, *Citizen Explorer*, 89–90.

53. Burstein, *Passions of Andrew Jackson*, 71–73; Hoffer, *Treason Trials*, 43–44; Opal, *Avenging the People*, 124–25, 127–28; Remini, *Andrew Jackson*, 1:145–49, Andrew Jackson quoted on 149.

54. Joseph H. Daveiss to Thomas Jefferson, Jan. 10, 1806 ("Depend"), Daveiss to Jefferson, July 14, 1806 ("To cause"), Founders Online, National Archives (https://founders.archives.gov/documents/Jefferson/99-01-02-2980, and 4028); Hoffer, *Treason Trials*, 49.

55. Hoffer, *Treason Trials*, 47–50; Kastor, *William Clark's World*, 110–11; Orsi, *Citizen Explorer*, 127–203.

56. James Wilkinson to Thomas Jefferson, Oct. 21, 26, and Nov. 12, 1806, Founders Online, National Archives (https://founders.archives.gov/documents/Jefferson/99-01-02-4459, 4476, and 4537); Isenberg, *Fallen Founder*, 313, 319–23; Herschthal, "Slaves, Spaniards, and Subversion," 301; Hoffer, *Treason Trials*, 50–57; Kennedy, *Cotton and Conquest*, 267; James Lewis, *Burr Conspiracy*, 272–90.

57. Hoffer, *Treason Trials*, 141–53; Isenberg, *Fallen Founder*, 323–29; James Lewis, *Burr Conspiracy*, 291–319.

58. Hoffer, *Treason Trials*, 82–83; Isenberg, *Fallen Founder*, 323–47, John Wickham quoted on 333–34 ("What kind"); James Lewis, *Burr Conspiracy*, 178–84; Remini, *Andrew Jackson*, 1:157–58.

59. Isenberg, *Fallen Founder*, 341–50, Washington Irving quoted on 348 ("swelling"), John Randolph quoted on 349; James Lewis, *Burr Conspiracy*, 181–82, 310–11; Malone, *Jefferson and His Time*, 5:332–36, George Hay quoted on 363 ("shaken").

60. Hoffer, *Treason Trial*, 159–71; Isenberg, *Fallen Founder*, 351–63, John Marshall quoted on 336; James Lewis, *Burr Conspiracy*, 418–24; Malone, *Jefferson and His Time*, 5:337–46, 363–68; Andrew Jackson to Daniel Smith, Nov. 28, 1807, in Moser et al., eds., *Papers of Andrew Jackson*, vol. 2:175–76.

61. Kastor, *Nation's Crucible*, 136–39.

62. Thomas Jefferson to Joseph Priestley, Jan. 29, 1804, in Boyd et al., eds., *Papers of Thomas Jefferson*, 42:368–70; Burstein, *Passions of Andrew Jackson*, 83-85; Nugent, *Habits of Empire*, 49.

63. Ronda, *Astoria and Empire*, 31.

64. Cook, *Flood Tide of Empire*, 1–20; Gough, *Distant Dominion*, 8–20, 51–52, 93; Engstrand, "Seekers of the 'Northern Mystery,'" 78–110; Mackay, *Wake of Cook*, 16–17; G. Williams, "The Pacific," 552–75.

65. Cook, *Flood Tide of Empire*, 79–84, 100; Drayton, *Nature's Government*, 41–49, 66–67, 92–93; Gascoigne, *Science in the Service of Empire*, 16–33; Weber, *Spanish Frontier*, 285–86.

66. Igler, *Great Ocean*, 105–6; Vinkovetsky, *Russian America*, 6–8. For "soft gold," see Whaley, *Oregon*, 22.

67. Goetzmann, *New Lands*, 103–4; Hyde, *Empires, Nations, and Families*, 124–26; Igler, *Great Ocean*, 36–37, 106–8; Ronda, *Astoria and Empire*, 65–66; Vinkovetsky, *Russian America*, 29–37.

68. Calloway, *One Vast Winter Count*, 396–98; Cook, *Flood Tide of Empire*, 51–54; Goetzmann, *New Lands*, 104–5; Gough, *Distant Dominion*, 93–94; Weber, *Spanish Frontier*, 236–65.

69. Drayton, *Nature's Government*, 68–69.

70. Gough, *Distant Dominion*, 21–24; Withey, *Voyages of Discovery*, 126–322.

71. Ames and Machner, *Peoples of the Northwest Coast*, 89–103; Calloway, *One Vast Winter Count*, 398–99, 401–2; Cook, *Flood Tide of Empire*, 87; Gough, *Distant Dominion*, 30–43; Whaley, *Oregon*, 34–37.

72. Gray, *Making of John Ledyard*, 43–68; G. Williams, "The Pacific," 552–75; Withey, *Voyages of Discovery*, 370–400.

73. Cook, *Flood Tide of Empire*, 87–88, 100–107, 111–19; Gough, *Distant Dominion*, 51–71, 100; Gray, *Making of John Ledyard*, 100–107; Mackay, *Wake of Cook*, 59; Weber, *Spanish Frontier*, 285–89; Whaley, *Oregon*, 6, 12, 20–21; Zilberstein, "Objects of Distant Exchange," 594–600.

74. Calloway, *One Vast Winter Count*, 405–6; Goetzmann, *New Lands*, 107–8; Gough, *Distant Dominion*, 100–115, 130–31; Mackay, *Wake of Cook*, 85–87; Whaley, *Oregon*, 22–23.

75. Clatsop tradition quoted in Whaley, *Oregon*, 3–4.

76. Calloway, *One Vast Winter Count*, 407–10, John Meares quoted on 407 ("We were"); John Frost quoted in Whaley, *Oregon*, 145 ("bump"); Zilberstein, "Objects of Distant Exchange," 607–13.

77. Calloway, *One Vast Winter Count*, 407–10, unnamed captain quoted on 410; Igler, *Great Ocean*, 86–89; Whaley, *Oregon*, 24; Zilberstein, "Objects of Distant Exchange," 592–614.

78. Dawes, *Shoal of Time*; Kuykendall, *Hawaiian Kingdom*.

79. Ronda, *Astoria and Empire*, 5–13.

80. Gough, *First Across the Continent*, 62, 67–103; Ronda, *Astoria and Empire*, 6–10, 15–18.

81. Gough, *First Across the Continent*, 105–28, Alexander Mackenzie quoted on 128.

82. Gough, *First Across the Continent*, 143–56, Alexander Mackenzie quoted on 154.

83. Gough, *First Across the Continent*, 170–86; Rich, *Fur Trade*, 185.

84. Gough, *First Across the Continent*, 170–85.

85. Onuf, *Jefferson's Empire*, 100; Tucker and Hendrickson, *Empire of Liberty*, 42–43, 62.

86. D. Jackson, *Jefferson and the Stony Mountains*, 42–43; Thomas Jefferson to George Rogers Clark, Dec. 4, 1783, in Boyd et al., eds., *Papers of Thomas Jefferson*, 6:371.

87. D. Jackson, *Thomas Jefferson and the Stony Mountains*, 92–95, 197; Moulton, ed., *Journals*, 2:1–3; Ronda, "Dreams and Discoveries," 149–50.

88. David McKeehan to Meriwether Lewis, Apr. 7, 1807, in D. Jackson, ed., *Letters*, 2:401–2; D. Jackson, *Jefferson and the Stony Mountains*, 129-34; R. White, "Louisiana Purchase," 54–55.

89. Carlos Martínez de Yrujo to Pedro Cevallos, Dec. 2, 1802, and Thomas Jefferson to Congress, Jan. 18, 1803, in D. Jackson, ed., *Letters*, 1:4 ("to discover"), 11–13.

90. Kastor, *William Clark's World*, 88–90; Thomas Jefferson to Meriwether Lewis, June 20, 1803, in D. Jackson, ed., *Letters*, vol. 1:61–66; Ronda, *Finding the West*, 23–26.

91. Ronda, *Astoria and Empire*, 31.

92. A. Isenberg, *Destruction of the Bison*, 13–30; E. West, *Way to the West*, 3–12; L. C. Easton quoted in E. West, *Essential West*, 48.

93. Calloway, *One Vast Winter Count*, 267–76, Pretty Shield quoted on 273 ("Ah"); A. Isenberg, *Destruction of the Bison*, 6–10, 33–37; E. West, *Way to the West*, 51–84.

94. Calloway, *One Vast Winter Count*, 280–312, Cheyenne tradition quoted on 307; A. Isenberg, *Destruction of the Bison*, 39–44; E. West, *Essential West*, 58–59.

95. Hine and Faragher, *American West*, 138–39; A. Isenberg, *Destruction of the Bison*, 10–12, 83–85, 91–92; Ostler, *Plains Sioux*, 28–30; E. West, *Essential West*, 64–66.

96. A. Isenberg, *Destruction of the Bison*, 47–53; Saunt, *West of the Revolution*, 124–68; Weber, *Spanish Frontier*, 214; E. West, *Essential West*, 60–61; R. White, "Louisiana Purchase," 38.

97. Calloway, *One Vast Winter Count*, 384–87; Hamalainen, *Comanche Empire*, 18–67; Saunt, *West of the Revolution*, 91–115; Weber, *Spanish Frontier*, 220–35, Pedro Fermín de Mendinueta quoted on 221–22.

98. Fenn, *Encounters*, 154–62; A. Isenberg, *Destruction of the Bison*, 53–57; Saunt, *West of the Revolution*, 148-68; R. White, "Winning of the West," 319–43.

99. Calloway, *One Vast Winter Count*, 419–21; Fenn, *Encounters*, 165–72; Saunt, *West of the Revolution*, 148–68, Jean-Baptiste Truteau, quoted on 155.

100. Aron, *American Confluence*, 22–26, 36–38, 88–91; DuVal, *Native Ground*, 103–27; Lee, *Masters of the Middle Waters*, 180–85; Saunt, *West of the Revolution*, 169–86.

101. Thomas Jefferson to Robert Smith, July 13, 1804, Founders Online, National Archives (http://founders.archives.gov/documents/Jefferson/99 -01-02-0067); Hine and Faragher, *American West*, 141–42.

102. Barr, *Peace Came in the Form of a Woman*, 1–15; Ostler, *Plains Sioux*, 19–21; Ronda, *Lewis and Clark*, 28–41, William Clark quoted on 40; Thomas Jefferson to Meriwether Lewis, Jan. 22, 1804, in Boyd et al., eds., *Papers of Thomas Jefferson*, 42:325–26.

103. Fenn, *Encounters at the Heart of the World*, 222–24; Hine and Faragher, *American West*, 140–41, William Clark quoted on 141; Ronda, *Lewis and Clark*, 67–112.

104. Fenn, *Encounters at the Heart of the World*, 221–25; Hine and Faragher, *American West*, 140–41; Arikara chief quoted in Ronda, *Lewis and Clark*, 64.

105. Fenn, *Encounters at the Heart of the World*, 216–17, 391n8; William Clark quoted in Hine and Faragher, *American West*, 137 ("The sight"); Lamar, ed., *Reader's Encyclopedia of the American West*, 191, 1055, includes Clark quote ("token").

106. Fenn, *Encounters at the Heart of the World*, 216; Ronda, *Lewis and Clark*, 135–54.

107. Calloway, *One Vast Winter Count*, 422; Lamar, ed., *Reader's Encyclopedia of the American West*, 1055; Cameahwait quoted in Ronda, *Finding the West*, xv–xvi; Ronda, *Lewis and Clark*, 257–58.

108. L. Morris, *Fate of the Corps*, 6–9; Ronda, *Lewis and Clark*, 155–251; Utley, *Life Wild and Perilous*, 7–9; Whaley, *Oregon*, 24–25.

109. Kastor, *William Clark's World*, 122–23; Miller, *Prophetic Worlds*, 47–49; L. Morris, *Fate of the Corps*, 1; Ronda, *Lewis and Clark*, 238–44, 253–54; Utley, *Life Wild and Perilous*, 7–10.

110. Hine and Faragher, *American West*, 141–43; Kastor, *William Clark's World*, 101–4, 121–22; Ronda, *Finding the West*, 29–30, 118–20, 125–27, William Clark quoted on 27, Peter Corney quoted on 125.

111. Hyde, *Empires, Nations, and Families*, 104–5; Jetté, *Hearth of the Crossed Races*, 21–23; Ronda, *Astoria and Empire*, 87–115, 196–203, 235–37; Utley, *Life Wild and Perilous*, 25–26, 29–30.

112. Whaley, *Oregon*, 40–43, Alfred Seton quoted on 41 ("every thing"), Alexander Henry quoted on 42 ("haughty").

113. Hine and Faragher, *American West*, 148–49; Hyde, *Empires, Nations, and Families*, 95, 105–6; Ronda, *Astoria and Empire*, 252–301; Utley, *Life Wild and Perilous*, 34–35; Whaley, *Oregon*, 63–66.

114. Goetzmann, *New Lands*, 132–33; Hine and Faragher, *American West*, 149–

50; Lee, *Masters of the Middle Waters*, 209–10; L. Morris, *Fate of the Corps*, 38–48; Utley, *Life Wild and Perilous*, 11–22.

115. Hyde, *Empires, Nations, and Families*, 61–63; Miller, *Prophetic Worlds*, 55–56.

116. A. Isenberg, *Destruction of the Bison*, 49–50; Lamar, ed., *Reader's Encyclopedia of the American West*, 58–59, 424–26; Utley, *Life Wild and Perilous*, 44–54, 78–82; R. White, *It's Your Misfortune*, 47–48.

117. Hine and Faragher, *American West*, 154; Lamar, ed., *Reader's Encyclopedia of the American West*, 424–26, George Ruxton quoted on 425; Utley, *Life Wild and Perilous*, 79–85, 133–44, 168–70.

118. Hyde, *Empires, Nations, and Families*, 63–64, 91–92; R. White, *It's Your Misfortune*, 46–47.

119. Hine and Faragher, *American West*, 150–52; Lamar, ed., *Reader's Encyclopedia of the American West*, 121–22; L. Morris, *Fate of the Corps*, 136–38; Utley, *Life Wild and Perilous*, 44–47, 57–58.

120. Goetzmann, *New Lands*, 140–46; Hyde, *Empires, Nations, and Families*, 114–15; Lamar, ed., *Reader's Encyclopedia of the American West*, 1121–22; Utley, *Life Wild and Perilous*, 40–42, 55–67, 83–102.

121. Hyde, *Empires, Nations, and Families*, 313–14.

122. Fenn, *Encounters*, 316–25; Hyde, *Empires, Nations, and Families*, 336–40.

123. Hardin, "Tragedy of the Commons," 1243–48; Lamar, ed., *Reader's Encyclopedia of the American West*, 426; Rich, *Fur Trade*, 272–74; Utley, *Life Wild and Perilous*, 74–77; Whaley, *Oregon*, 75–76.

124. Hine and Faragher, *American West*, 156–58.

125. Lamar, ed., *Reader's Encyclopedia of the American West*, 426; Utley, *Life Wild and Perilous*, 85, 100.

126. Hine and Faragher, *American West*, 159; Onuf, "Empire of Liberty," 209–10.

127. L. Morris, *Fate of the Corps*, 139–48, William Clark quoted on 141–42; Ronda, *Lewis and Clark*, 56, 59, 64, 81, 111, 175.

128. L. Morris, *Fate of the Corps*, 144–48, Washington Irving quoted on 144.

129. Meriwether Lewis quoted in Lamar, ed., *Reader's Encyclopedia of the American West*, 191, 1055; Ronda, *Lewis and Clark*, 258–59.

130. Fenn, *Encounters at the Heart of the World*, 264–66; Lamar, ed., *Reader's Encyclopedia of the American West*, 190–91, 1055; L. Morris, *Fate of the Corps*, 113–17, 134, John Luttig quoted on 115.

131. Fenn, *Encounters at the Heart of the World*, 266; L. Morris, *Fate of the Corps*, 210–13.

CHAPTER 3: WARS

1. Daniel Webster, "Memorandum of Mr. Jefferson's Conversations," in Hayes, ed., *Jefferson in His Own Time*, 95; Burstein, *Passions of Andrew Jackson*, 37–38; Remini, *Andrew Jackson*, 1:153–54.

2. F. Anderson and Cayton, *Dominion of War*, 210–11; Burstein, *Passions of*

Andrew Jackson, 7–9; Howe, *What Hath God Wrought*, 328–29; Opal, *Avenging the People*, 15–45.

3. F. Anderson and Cayton, *Dominion of War*, 211–13; Burstein, *Passions of Andrew Jackson*, 10–12, 225–26; Jackson quoted in Howe, *What Hath God Wrought*, 329; Opal, *Avenging the People*, 73–81, 121–22.

4. Burstein, *Passions of Andrew Jackson*, 67–68; Andrew Jackson to Willie Blount, Jan. 25, 1812, and Jackson to George Washington Campbell, Oct. 15, 1812, in Moser et al., eds., *Papers of Andrew Jackson*, 2:277–79, and 334–36 ("*My God*" and "Silas Dinsmore"); Opal, *Avenging the People*, 137–38, Jackson quoted on 137 ("These are"); Remini, *Andrew Jackson*, 1:162–64, 392–93.

5. F. Anderson and Cayton, *Dominion of War*, 213–15; Burstein, *Passions of Andrew Jackson*, 12–14; Howe, *What Hath God Wrought*, 277–78; Opal, *Avenging the People*, 81–84.

6. Howe, *What Hath God Wrought*, 329–30.

7. Burstein, *Passions of Andrew Jackson*, 56–61; Opal, *Avenging the People*, 125–27; Remini, *Andrew Jackson*, 1:136–43, Jackson quoted on 142.

8. Burstein, *Passions of Andrew Jackson*, 93–97; Opal, *Avenging the People*, 146–47; Remini, *Andrew Jackson*, 1:181–86, Andrew Jackson quoted on 184, Thomas Hart Benton quoted on 186.

9. F. Anderson and Cayton, *Dominion of War*, 217; Burstein, *Passions of Andrew Jackson*, 17–25.

10. Andrew Jackson to Mateo Gonzalez Manrique, Aug. 24, 1814, in Moser et al., eds., *Papers of Andrew Jackson*, 3:119–21; Opal, *Avenging the People*, 8–14.

11. Palmer, *Age of the Democratic Revolution*, 3–20.

12. Greenwood, *Legacies of Fear*, 83–84, 89–93, 101–9; Graffagnino, "Twenty Thousand Muskets!!!," 417–27; Wilbur, *Ira Allen*, 2:68, 141.

13. Greenwood, *Legacies of Fear*, 124–26, 139–53, 164–70; Wilbur, *Ira Allen*, 2:323–24; T. Pennoyer to Thomas Dunn, Aug. 25, 1797, in Manning, ed., *Diplomatic Correspondence*, 1:498–99.

14. Errington, *Lion*, 63; Gates, "Roads, Rivals, and Rebellion," 235–37; Greenwood, *Legacies of Fear*, 195; A. Taylor, "Northern Revolution of 1800?" 390–91, and 406n18.

15. Peter Russell to William Osgoode, July 22, 1802 ("a tissue"), F 46, reel MS-75/5, Archives of Ontario (Toronto); Gates, "Roads, Rivals, and Rebellion," 250–51; Perkins, *First Rapprochement*, 129–32.

16. Kettner, *American Citizenship*, 50–55; Zimmerman, *Impressment*, 21.

17. M. Lewis, *Social History of the Navy*, 92–101; Perkins, *Prologue to War*, 28–29, 86, 93–95; Tucker and Reuter, *Injured Honor*, 33, 47; Zimmerman, *Impressment*, 18, 23–24.

18. Gilje, *Liberty on the Waterfront*, 158; Gould, "Making of an Atlantic State System" 254–55; Horsman, *Causes of the War*, 30–39; Stagg, *Madison's War*, 18–19; Tucker and Reuter, *Injured Honor*, 34–49.

19. Horsman, *Causes of the War*, 30, 84–87; Kettner *American Citizenship*, 173;

Perkins, *Prologue to War*, 7–10, 24–30, 74–75, 192; Tucker and Reuter, *Injured Honor*, 52, 65, 72, 208.

20. Dye, *Fatal Cruise*, 48–50, 57–58, 66–70; Tucker and Reuter, *Injured Honor*, 1–14, 71–75.

21. Perkins, *Prologue to War*, 39–41, 50–51; Skelton, *American Profession*, 7–8.

22. Carp, "Jefferson's Embargo," 130–31; Perkins, *Prologue to War*, 148–56; Stagg, *Madison's War*, 20–22; Tucker and Reuter, *Injured Honor*, 126–27.

23. Balogh, *Government Out of Sight*, 174–75; Carp, "Jefferson's Embargo," 131–32; Perkins, *Prologue to War*, 26–30, 157–59, 166–70, 204–5; Tucker and Reuter, *Injured Honor*, 119–22.

24. Anonymous to Thomas Jefferson, Sept. 19, 1808, Founders Online, National Archives (https://founders.archives.gov/documents/Jefferson/99-01-02-8710).

25. Carp, "Jefferson's Embargo," 135–37; Albert Gallatin to James Madison, Sept. 9, 1808, Founders Online, National Archives (https://founders.archives.gov/documents/Madison/99-01-02-3509); J. M. Smith, *Borderland Smuggling*, 52–65; Tucker and Hendrickson, *Empire of Liberty*, 224–25.

26. Stagg, *Madison's War*, 22–28.

27. Carp, "Jefferson's Embargo," 133–39, *Newburyport Herald* quoted on 134 ("Beings"), Bostonians quoted on 135 ("on their ruin"), and *Salem Gazette* quoted on 139 ("horrible alternative").

28. Carp, "Jefferson's Embargo," 140–41; Thomas Jefferson to Joseph C. Cabell, Feb. 2, 1816, in Looney et al., eds., *Papers of Thomas Jefferson Retirement Series*, 9:435–39.

29. Allen, *His Majesty's Indian Allies*, 120–22; William Hull to William Eustis, Mar. 6, 1812, in E. A. Cruikshank, ed., *Documents Relating to the Invasion of Canada and the Surrender of Detroit, 1812* (Ottawa: Government Printing Bureau, 1912), 22.

30. Edmunds, *Shawnee Prophet*, 28–71; Horsman, *Expansion*, 109–14, 142–57; Lee, *Masters of the Middle Waters*, 200–202; Sugden, *Tecumseh*, 117–21; R. White, *Middle Ground*, 474, 496–16.

31. Bowes, *Land Too Good for Indians*, 32–34; Edmunds, *Shawnee Prophet*, 67–93; Sugden, *Tecumseh*, 203–15, William Henry Harrison quoted on 215.

32. Bowes, *Land Too Good for Indians*, 32; Sugden, *Tecumseh*, 124, 130–31, Harrison quoted on 124.

33. Bowes, *Land Too Good for Indians*, 33–34; Hickey, *War of 1812*, 25–26; Stagg, *Madison's War*, 184–88; Sugden, *Tecumseh*, 225–36.

34. Bowes, *Land Too Good for Indians*, 34–35; Horsman, *Expansion*, 154, 167; Andrew Jackson to William Henry Harrison, Nov. 28, 1811, in Moser et al., eds., *Papers of Andrew Jackson*, 2:270.

35. Richard M. Johnson, speech, Dec. 11, 1811, *Annals of Congress*, 12th Congress, 1st Session, 465; [Canandaigua, N.Y.] *Ontario Messenger*, Dec. 15, 1812 ("freeborn"); Stagg, *Madison's War*, 110–11; Waterhouse, ed., *Journal*, 78, 93, and 188 ("were stripped").

36. Hickey, *War of 1812*, 26–30; Henry Clay quoted in Horsman, *Causes of the*

War, 182; Perkins, *Prologue to War*, 249–67, 343–47; Stagg, *Madison's War*, 71–79; Watts, *Republic Reborn*, 263–74.

37. Roger Brown, *Republic in Peril*, 76–82; John Binns quoted in Hickey, *War of 1812*, 27 ("The honor"); James Madison quoted in Pratt, *Expansionists*, 155 ("he knew").

38. John C. Calhoun, "Report on the Causes and Reasons for War," June 3, 1812, in Meriwether, ed., *Papers of Calhoun*, 1:116; Perkins, *Prologue to War*, 403–15; Stagg, *Madison's War*, 110–14.

39. Gilje, *Rioting in America*, 60–63; Hickey, *War of 1812*, 56–69; Pasley, *"Tyranny of Printers,"* 241–47.

40. J. M. Banner, *To the Hartford Convention*, 306–14.

41. Perkins, *Prologue to War*, 360–66; Hickey, *War of 1812*, 34; Stagg, *Madison's War*, 88–90.

42. John A. Harper, speech, Jan. 4, 1812, *Annals of Congress*, 12th Congress, 1st Session, House, 652; Malcolmson, *Very Brilliant Affair*, 14–16; Stagg, *Madison's War*, 4–6.

43. Thomas Jefferson to William Duane, Aug. 4, 1812, in Looney et al., *Papers of Thomas Jefferson, Retirement Series*, 5:293–94; Stagg, ed., "Between Black Rock and a Hard Place," 418–19.

44. Greenwood, *Legacies of Fear*, 213–23; W. B. Turner, *British Generals*, 27–29.

45. Klinck and Ross, eds., *Tiger Dunlop's Upper Canada*, 14–16.

46. Gourlay, ed., *Statistical Account*, 1:204, 223, and 249 ("Politics"); M. Smith, *Geographical View*, 67–70; Erastus Granger to Henry Dearborn, Sept. 14, 1807 ("no consequence"), American Memory Series, Thomas Jefferson Papers, Image #408, Library of Congress.

47. R. Allen, *His Majesty's Indian Allies*, 123–30; Malcolmson, *Very Brilliant Affair*, 33–35.

48. Antal, *Wampum Denied*, 46–47; Malcomson, *Very Brilliant Affair*, 76.

49. Antal, *Wampum Denied*, 93–99; Crawford, ed., "Lydia Bacon's Journal," 70–71.

50. Malcomson, *Very Brilliant Affair*, 68–69, 82–83, 158–73, 183–94; Quimby, *U.S. Army*, 1:69–71; M. Smith, *Geographical View*, 91–92.

51. Antal, *Wampum Denied*, 162–71, 191–92, 254–67, 285–89, 316–20, 331–39; Malcomson, *Capital in Flames*, 41–80; Malcomson, *Lords of the Lake*, 135–46; Quimby, *U.S. Army*, 1:183–88, 241–46.

52. W. Scott, *Memoirs*, 30–36, quote on 36; Skelton, *American Profession*, 53–56; Peter B. Porter quoted in A. Taylor, *Civil War of 1812*, 321; Isaac A. Coles to David Campbell, July 4, 1813 ("our little army") Campbell Family Papers, box 2, Special Collections Library, Duke University.

53. J. H. Campbell quoted in Stagg, *Madison's War*, 162–63 ("wished"); Peter B. Porter, speech, Feb. 18, 1812 ("not become"), *Annals of Congress*, 12th Congress, 1st Session, 1058–69.

54. J. Foner, *Blacks and the Military*, 3–22; John Armstrong to William Duane,

July 15, 1814, in Duane, "Selections from the Duane Papers," 63 ("We must"); Stagg, "Enlisted Men," 628.

55. George Cockburn to Andrew Fitzherbert Evans, Dec. 12, 1814 ("most efficient"), Sir George Cockburn Papers, reel 6, Library of Congress; G. Smith, *Slaves' Gamble*, 102–13, 122–31; A. Taylor, *Internal Enemy*, 275–314.

56. Kutolowski and Kutolowski, "Commissions and Canvasses," 5–38.

57. Hickey, *War of 1812*, 76–77, 164–65; Stagg, *Madison's War*, 366–68.

58. Benn, *Iroquois in the War of 1812*, 165.

59. Kerber, *Federalists in Dissent*, 164; J. M. Banner, *To the Hartford Convention*, 307–8.

60. Buel, *America on the Brink*, 219–29; Hickey, *War of 1812*, 269–78.

61. Hickey, *War of 1812*, 221–25, 231, 241–51; Stagg, *Madison's War*, 426–27, 503; Anonymous to John E. Wool, July 4, 1814 ("can alone"), John E. Wool Papers, box 7, New York State Library.

62. Stagg, ed., "Between Black Rock and a Hard Place," 421–22; James A. Bayard to Andrew Bayard, May 2, 1812, in Donnan, ed., "Papers of James A. Bayard," 196–97 ("No Proposition"); Gideon Granger to John Todd, Dec. 26, 1811, Granger Papers, Library of Congress; Pratt, *Expansionists*, 146–47.

63. Cusick, *Other War of 1812*, 188–91, *Georgia Gazette* quoted on 47; Nugent, *Habits of Empire*, 94, 99–102, 111–12; Patrick, *Florida Fiasco*, 147–51, 183–84; G. Smith, *Slaves' Gamble*, 65–66.

64. Herschthal, "Slaves, Spaniards, and Subversion," 308–9; Kastor, *Nation's Crucible*, 127–31, Samuel Hambleton quoted on 130; Rasmussen, *American Uprising*, 1–3.

65. Andrew Jackson to William Claiborne, Jan. 5, 1813, in Moser et al., eds., *Papers of Andrew Jackson*, 2:352; Owsley and Smith, *Filibusters and Expansionists*, 66–71; A. Rothman, *Slave Country*, 121–22.

66. Cusick, *Other War of 1812*, 3–4; Herschthal, "Slaves, Spaniards, and Subversion," 307–8; Kastor, *Nation's Crucible*, 71–72, 124–27, 131–32; Patrick, *Florida Fiasco*, 10–12; Stagg, *Borderlines*, 59–86.

67. Nugent, *Habits of Empire*, 108.

68. Luis de Onís to the Captain General of Caracas, Feb. 2, 1810, in *American State Papers, Foreign Affairs*, 3:404.

69. F. Anderson and Cayton, *Dominion of War*, 212–13; Hietala, *Manifest Design*, 173–86, 191–92; Stagg, *Borderlines*, 89–91.

70. Cusick, *Other War of 1812*, 4–5; James Lewis, *American Union*, 38; Patrick, *Florida Fiasco*, 1–9; Stagg, *Borderlines*, 87–114, George Mathews quoted on 94.

71. Cusick, *Other War of 1812*, 4–5, 49–51, 150, 298–99, William Dell quoted on 49; Nugent, *Habits of Empire*, 111–14; Patrick, *Florida Fiasco*, 12–15, 53–69; G. Smith, *Slaves' Gamble*, 67–68.

72. Cusick, *Other War of 1812*, 49–51, 186–87, 205, Governor Quesada quoted

on 51; Patrick, *Florida Fiasco*, 83–113; G. Smith, *Slaves' Gamble*, 69–79, Daniel Newnan quoted on 79 ("negroes").

73. Cusick, *Other War of 1812*, 8–9, 191–92, 216–17, 232–35, 252–53, 309; Patrick, *Florida Fiasco*, 179–82; Shafer, *Zephaniah Kingsley, Jr.*, 126–27; G. Smith, *Slaves' Gamble*, 69–75.

74. James Madison to Thomas Jefferson, Apr. 24, 1812, in Stagg et al., eds., *Papers of James Madison, Presidential Series*, 4:345–47 ("tragi-comedy"); John Floyd quoted in Cusick, *Other War of 1812*, 9; Patrick, *Florida Fiasco*, 182–94; Porter, "Negroes and the East Florida Annexation Plot," 9–29.

75. Cusick, *Other War of 1812*, 6–7, 185–89, 236–37; Patrick, *Florida Fiasco*, 149–50, 248–53; Saunt, *New Order of Things*, 245; G. Smith, *Slaves' Gamble*, 69–75, David Mitchell quoted on 75; James Madison to Congress, Dec. 8, 1812, in Stagg et al., eds., *Papers of James Madison, Presidential Series*, 5:487–88.

76. Patrick, *Florida Fiasco*, 248–53, William Hunter quoted on 251 ("It is" and "an artificial"); Stagg, *Borderlines*, 127–33, William Hunter quoted on 130 ("wide waste"), Albert Gallatin quoted on 132; James Madison to Congress, Dec. 8, 1812, in Stagg et al., eds., *Papers of James Madison, Presidential Series*, 5:487–88.

77. Cusick, *Other War of 1812*, 206–8, 258–59; Patrick, *Florida Fiasco*, 225–36, 254–83; G. Smith, *Slaves' Gamble*, 79–81.

78. Nugent, *Habits of Empire*, 116–17; Stagg, *Borderlines*, 130–31.

79. Opal, *Avenging the People*, 147–55; Remini, *Andrew Jackson and His Indian Wars*, 74–79; A. Rothman, *Slave Country*, 126–36.

80. Andrew Jackson to the Tennessee Troops, Apr. 2, 1814, Jackson to Cherokee and Creek Indians, Aug. 5, 1814, and Jackson to Rachel Jackson, Aug. 23, 1814, in Moser et al., eds., *Papers of Andrew Jackson*, 3:57–58 ("The fiends"), 103–4 ("to destroy"), 117 ("elegant mansions").

81. Opal, *Avenging the People*, 158–59; Owsley and Smith, *Filibusters and Expansionists*, 95–97; Saunt, *New Order of Things*, 275–81; Watson, *Jackson's Sword*, 65–69.

82. Andrew Jackson to William C. C. Claiborne, Sept. 21, 1814, and Claiborne to Jackson, Oct. 17, 1814, in Moser et al., eds., *Papers of Andrew Jackson*, 3:144 ("They must be"), 165; Kastor, *Nation's Crucible*, 174; A. Rothman, *Slave Country*, 144–46; G. Smith, *Slaves' Gamble*, 162–63, 205.

83. A. Rothman, *Slave Country*, 147–51, Benson Earle Hill quoted on 147 ("ingenious") and Howell Tatum quoted on 150 ("ease[d] the labour"); G. Smith, *Slaves' Gamble*, 164–66, 169.

84. Hickey, *War of 1812*, 211–13; A. Rothman, *Slave Country*, 151–53, 160–62, Israel Pickens quoted on 161 ("a free republic"), John Reid quoted on 162 ("He is"); G. Smith, *Slaves' Gamble*, 167–70.

85. Burstein, *Passions of Andrew Jackson*, 117–18; Kastor, *Nation's Crucible*, 174–78; Remini, *Andrew Jackson*, 1:308–15, Jackson quoted on 310.

86. Jenkins, *Henry Goulburn*, 86–87; Hickey, *War of 1812*, 297–98; Leverett

Saltonstall to Nathaniel Saltonstall, Feb. 18, 1815, in Moody, ed., *Saltonstall Papers*, 2:569 ("Our Town").

87. James Monroe to the United States Senate, Feb. 22, 1815, in S. M. Hamilton, ed. *Writings of Monroe*, 5:321–22; Hickey, *War of 1812*, 308–9; Owsley and Smith, *Filibusters and Expansionists*, 141.

88. Buel, *America on the Brink*, 229–34; Hickey, *War of 1812*, 279–80, 307–9, Joseph Story quoted on 308; Perkins, *Castlereagh and Adams*, 175–76.

89. Gilje, *Making of the American Republic*, 300–303; Howe, *What Hath God Wrought*, 77–79.

90. Balogh, *Government Out of Sight*, 132–33, 202–3; Howe, *What Hath God Wrought*, 80–86; Larson, *Internal Improvements*, 63–64; Schoen, *Fragile Fabric*, 92–94.

91. Balogh, *Government Out of Sight*, 133–36, 144–45; Howe, *What Hath God Wrought*, 82–85, 89–90, 94–95, 221–22; Larson, *Internal Improvements*, 66–67.

92. John Randolph quoted in Balogh, *Government Out of Sight*, 144 ("may emancipate"); Burstein, *America's Jubilee*, 172–74; Howe, *What Hath God Wrought*, 82–85, 95, Randolph quoted on 85 ("on poor"); Reynolds, *Waking Giant*, 30–31, 58–59, Randolph quoted on 31 ("When I speak").

93. Balogh, *Government Out of Sight*, 133–34; Larson, *Internal Improvements*, 64–65, 67–69.

94. Stagg, *Borderlines in Borderlands*, 140–41, 153; Watson, *Jackson's Sword*, 96–104.

95. Hickey, *War of 1812*, 279–80, 308–9; Owsley and Smith, *Filibusters and Expansionists*, 141.

96. Henry Goulburn quoted in Jenkins, *Henry Goulburn*, 86 ("I had"); Perkins, *Castlereagh and Adams*, 85–90, 99–109, 128 (Edward Cooke quoted: "to return"); Watson, *Jackson's Sword*, 69–70.

97. Allen, *His Majesty's Indian Allies*, 169; Calloway, "End of an Era," 5; Prucha, *Sword of the Republic*, 120–23; Robert McDouall to Frederick P. Robinson, Sept. 22, 1815, in Michigan Pioneer Historical Society, *Michigan Historical Collections*, 16:284 ("Merciless").

98. Allen, *His Majesty's Indian Allies*, 169–70; Lewis Cass quoted in Calloway, "End of an Era," 9–10; Prucha, *Sword of the Republic*, 126–28, 136–37.

99. Calloway, "End of an Era," 17; Clavin, *Battle of Negro Fort*, 71–72; A. Taylor, *Civil War of 1812*, 429–30.

100. Dupre, *Alabama's Frontiers*, 245–51; James Lewis, *American Union*, 58–59, 76–77, 81–85; Harry Toulmin to James Madison, Jan. 20, 1816 ("How can"), Founders Online, National Archives (https://founders.archives.gov/documents/Madison/99-01-02-4891); Watson, *Jackson's Sword*, 71–72.

101. Clavin, *Battle of Negro Fort*, 47–74, 103–28; Millett, *Maroons of Prospect Bluff*, 97–126, 214–30; Winsboro and Knetch, "Florida Slaves," 55–56.

102. Andrew Jackson to John C. Calhoun, May 5, 1818, and A. Jackson to Rachel Jackson, June 2, 1818, in Moser et al., eds., *Papers of Andrew Jackson*,

4:199 ("unprincipled villains," and "unchristian wretches"), 212–13 ("Just Vengeance"); Jackson quoted in Hahn, *Nation Without Borders*, 28–29 ("to chastise"); Opal, *Avenging the People*, 162–64.

103. Haynes, *Unfinished Revolution*, 205–6; Opal, *Avenging the People*, 165–71; Owsley and Smith, *Filibusters and Expansionists*, 141–63; Watson, *Jackson's Sword*, 141–63.

104. Hines and Faragher, *American West*, 182–83; Howe, *What Hath God Wrought*, 103–11; Nugent, *Habits of Empire*, 125–27; John Quincy Adams quoted in Opal, *Avenging the People*, 165 ("encounter").

105. Cusick, *Other War of 1812*, 304–5; James Lewis, *American Union*, 78–79; Shafer, *Zephaniah Kingsley, Jr.*, 150–55; Watson, *Jackson's Sword*, 63–64.

106. Romney, "Reinventing Upper Canada," 78–79.

107. William Forsyth quoted in Barrett, *Journal*, 42–43 ("a thorough"); Craig, *Upper Canada*, 85; Errington, *Lion*, 89–92; Howison, *Sketches*, 77; Mills, *Idea of Loyalty*, 27–31.

108. Craig, *Upper Canada*, 88, 125–30; Howison, *Sketches*, 61–64; J. K. Johnson, *Becoming Prominent*, 113; Klinck and Ross, eds., *Tiger Dunlop's Upper Canada*, 105–6.

109. Craig, *Upper Canada*, 108–11, *Upper Canada Gazette* quoted on 111 ("universal order"); Dunham, *Political Unrest*, 41–45; Errington, *Lion*, 92–93, 107–8, 166; J. K. Johnson, *Becoming Prominent*, 76–77, 116, 129–31; Mills, *Idea of Loyalty*, 25–31; Strachan, *Sermon Preached at York*, 16–17, 34, and 36.

110. Howison, *Sketches*, 79–81, 115; McNairn, *Capacity to Judge*, 29–32; Mills, *Idea of Loyalty*, 40–42, 48.

111. Dunham, *Political Unrest*, 47–59; Errington, *Lion*, 109–10; Howison, *Sketches*, 79–81; Wilton, *Popular Politics*, 27–32; Robert Gourlay quoted in S. F. Wise, "Robert Fleming Gourlay," *Dictionary of Canadian Biography*, 9:332–35.

112. Craig, *Upper Canada*, 228–44; Levine, *Toronto*, 46–47, 53–54; Mills, *Idea of Loyalty*, 106–7; Romney, "From the Types Riot," 139–40; Sir Francis Bond Head quoted in Wilton, *Popular Politics*, 179.

113. Careless, *Union of the Canadas*, 7; Greer, "1837–38," 12–16; Michel de Lorimier, "Chevalier de Lorimier," John B. Thompson, "Wolford Nelson," and Fernand Ouellet, "Louis-Joseph Papineau," *Dictionary of Canadian Biography*, vols. 7, 9, and 10 (www.biographi.ca/en).

114. Craig, *Upper Canada*, 245–55; Greer, "1837–38," 14–15; Levine, *Toronto*, 54–58; Mills, *Idea of Loyalty*, 104–8; Read and Stagg, eds., *Rebellion of 1837*, xi–lvii, xc; Wilton, *Popular Politics*, 189–90.

115. Greer, "1837–38," 15; Richards, "Americans, the Patriot War, and Upper Canada," 93–119.

116. Craig, *Upper Canada*, 249–59; Mills, *Idea of Loyalty*, 108–10, Sir Francis Bond Head quoted on 108; Read and Stagg, eds., *Rebellion of 1837*, lxxviii–xcii; R. C. Stuart, *United States Expansionism*, 126–38.

117. Jones and Rakestraw, *Prologue to Manifest Destiny*, 34–40; Richards, "Amer-

icans, the Patriot War, and Upper Canada," 104; R. C. Stuart, *United States Expansionism*, 127–37.

118. Harvey, "John L. O'Sullivan's 'Canadian Moment,'" 209–34; Jones and Rakestraw, *Prologue to Manifest Destiny*, 23–24; R. C. Stuart, *United States Expansionism*, 94–96, 128–34, 259–61.

119. Jones and Rakestraw, *Prologue to Manifest Destiny*, 8–17; Sexton, *Debtor Diplomacy*, 30–31.

120. Carroll, *Good and Wise Measure*, 305–6; Haynes, *Unfinished Revolution*, 221–22; Sexton, *Debtor Diplomacy*, 30–31, August Belmont quoted on 31.

121. Jones and Rakestraw, *Prologue to Manifest Destiny*, 17–20, 97–149; Karp, *Vast Southern Empire*, 51–52; Sexton, *Debtor Diplomacy*, 32–37.

122. Bothwell, *Penguin History of Canada*, 182–83; Wilton, *Popular Politics*, 190,

123. Careless, *Union of the Canadas*, 3–4; Craig, *Upper Canada*, 252–76; Greer, "1837–38," 16–17; G. Martin, *Britain and the Origins*, 13; Wilton, *Popular Politics*, 194–220.

124. Careless, *Union of the Canadas*, 1–4; G. Martin, *Britain and the Origins*, 85–86, Charles Buller quoted on 86.

125. Careless, *Union of the Canadas*, 3–19; Palmer, "Popular Radicalism," 427–28; Wilton, *Popular Politics*, 194–95, 218, Sir George Arthur quoted on 194.

126. Careless, *Union of the Canadas*, 20–32.

127. Careless, *Union of the Canadas*, 58–70.

128. Careless, *Union of the Canadas*, 115–26; G. Martin, *Britain and the Origins*, 91; Wilton, *Popular Politics*, 218–19.

129. Careless, *Union of the Canadas*, 15–17, 109–12, 127–28, Lord Elgin quoted on 128; Greenberg, "Practicability of Annexing Canada," 281; Wise and Brown, *Canada Views the United States*, 44–46.

130. Careless, *Union of the Canadas*, 128–31; Wise and Brown, *Canada Views the United States*, 49–73, Fredericton *Headquarters*, quoted on 71; Wilton, *Popular Politics*, 233–34.

131. Greenberg, "Practicability of Annexing Canada," 279–80.

132. Herschthal, "Slaves, Spaniards, and Subversion," 310–11; Perdue and Green, *Columbia Guide*, 80–81, John C. Calhoun quoted on 81.

133. Haynes, *Unfinished Revolution*, 211–21; A. Taylor, *Civil War of 1812*, 455–58.

CHAPTER 4: RACE

1. Horton and Horton, *Slavery*, 72; Patrick, *Florida Fiasco*, 48; Schafer, *Anna Madgigine Jai Kingsley*, 4–24; Shafer, *Zephaniah Kingsley, Jr.*, 94–100.

2. Horton and Horton, *Slavery*, 85–86; Shafer, *Zephaniah Kingsley*, 194–95; Zephaniah Kingsley, Jr., "Last Will and Testament," in Stowell, ed., *Balancing Evils Judiciously*, 120 ("by her native" and "forms of"); Kingsley quoted in Lydia Maria Child, "Letter from New York," in Stowell, ed., *Balancing Evils Judiciously*, 109 ("superior" and "a fine").

3. Schafer, *Anna Madgigine Jai Kingsley*, 24–26; Shafer, *Zephaniah Kingsley*,

192–93; Zephaniah Kingsley, Jr., quoted in Lydia Maria Child, "Letter from New York," in Stowell, ed., *Balancing Evils Judiciously*, 109 ("She was").

4. Horton and Horton, *Slavery*, 72; Schafer, *Anna Madgigine Jai Kingsley*, 27–34; Shafer, *Zephaniah Kingsley*, 101–14, 173–76, 181–82, 186–90; Kingsley quoted in Stowell, ed., *Balancing Evils*, 17 ("love me") and 69 ("encouraged"). For task and gang systems, see also Camp, *Closer to Freedom*, 27–28.

5. Cusick, *Other War of 1812*, 161–62, 219–20, 246, 287; Patrick, *Florida Fiasco*, 101, 186, 231, 261, 302–303; Schafer, *Anna Madgigine Jai Kingsley*, 35–44, José Antonio Moreno quoted on 43 ("heroine"); Shafer, *Zephaniah Kingsley*, 121–35.

6. Horton and Horton, *Slavery*, 86; Schafer, *Anna Madgigine Jai Kingsley*, 45–61; Shafer, *Zephaniah Kingsley*, 156–72, 191–94.

7. Cusick, *Other War of 1812*, 48–49; Horton and Horton, *Slavery*, 95–96; Zephaniah Kingsley, "Address to the Legislative Council of Florida," in Stowell, *Balancing Evils*, 26–35.

8. Shafer, *Zephaniah Kingsley*, 177–78, Kingsley quoted on 181 ("The door"); Stowell, *Balancing Evils Judiciously*, 1–2, Kingsley quoted on 2 ("considerable"); Kingsley, "Address to the Legislative Council of Florida," in Stowell, *Balancing Evils Judiciously*, 26–35, quotation on 35 ("We must have").

9. Schafer, *Anna Madgigine Jai Kingsley*, 61–64; Shafer, *Zephaniah Kingsley*, 178–80, Robert Brown quoted on 180 ("They would have us").

10. Schafer, *Zephaniah Kingsley, Jr.*, 180–84, 200–201; Kingsley, "Address to the Legislative Council," "A Treatise on the Patriarchal, or Co-operative System of Society," and "Last Will and Testament," in Stowell, ed., *Balancing Evils Judiciously*, 33 ("for being"), 64–65, and 120 ("inequitable").

11. Schafer, *Anna Madgigine Jai Kingsley*, 61–64; William P. Duval quoted in Schafer, *Zephaniah Kingsley, Jr.*, 197 ("cherishes"); Kingsley, "Memorial to Congress by Citizens of the Territory of Florida," in Stowell, ed., *Balancing Evils Judiciously*, 82–85.

12. Shafer, *Zephaniah Kingsley, Jr.*, 199, 206–7; Kingsley, "Address to the Legislative Council," "Treatise on the Patriarchal, or Co-operative System of Society," and "Last Will and Testament," in Stowell, ed., *Balancing Evils Judiciously*, 32–34, 40 ("They are now"), 62, 65–66 ("consult").

13. Shafer, *Zephaniah Kingsley*, 207–8; Lydia Maria Child, "Letter from New York," in Stowell, ed., *Balancing Evils Judiciously*, 107–15, Zephaniah Kingsley, Jr., quoted on 110 ("I have thought").

14. Schafer, *Anna Madgigine Jai Kingsley*, 65–69; Shafer, *Zephaniah Kingsley*, 208–29; Stowell, ed., *Balancing Evils Judiciously*, 19–21.

15. Zephania Kingsley, Jr., quoted in Stowell, ed., *Balancing Evils Judiciously*, 112 ("The more"); Kingsley, "Letters on Haiti," and "Last Will and Testament," in Stowell, ed., *Balancing Evils Judiciously*, 89–90 ("pseudo republicans" and "daily accounts"), 120 ("land of liberty").

16. Furstenberg, "Beyond Freedom and Slavery," 1295–1330; Robert Parkin-

son, "Manifest Signs of Passion," 59–65; Van Cleve, *Slaveholders' Union*, 42–45; Thomas Jefferson to Marquis de Chastellux, Sept. 2, 1785, in Boyd et al., eds., *Papers of Thomas Jefferson*, 8:467–70.

17. Blackburn, *Overthrow of Colonial Slavery*, 117–18, 272–74; Egerton, *Death or Liberty*, 93–101; Hahn, *Political Worlds*, 7–8; Nash and Soderlund, *Freedom by Degrees*, 103–6, 167–68; Van Cleve, *Slaveholders' Union*, 59–62, 66–68, 74–75, 89–90; Waldstreicher, *Slavery's Constitution*, 50, 60–61.

18. Baker, *Affairs of Party*, 231–37; Thomas Hamilton quoted in Hietala, *Manifest Design*, 12 ("subjected"); Litwack, *North of Slavery*, 64–77, 94–96, Alexis de Tocqueville quoted on 65 ("The prejudice").

19. Baker, *Affairs of Party*, 243–46, Philadelphians quoted on 246 ("defiling"); Hahn, *Political Worlds*, 35–36; Melish, *Disowning Slavery*, 84–162; Roediger, *Wages of Whiteness*, 35–36.

20. Berlin, *Many Thousands Gone*, 239–48; Joseph Willson quoted in Bushman, *Refinement of America*, 440 ("exceedingly illiberal"); J. Jones, *Dreadful Deceit*, 101–2; Litwack, *North of Slavery*, 153–59, young black man quoted on 154 ("Shall I be"); Nash and Soderlund, *Freedom by Degrees*, 167–93.

21. Hahn, *Political Worlds*, 36–38; Horton and Horton, *Slavery*, 89; J. Jones, *Dreadful Deceit*, 103–4; W. Jordan, *White over Black*, 422–26; Nash, *Race and Revolution*, 65–79; Newman, *Freedom's Prophet*, 1–19, 54–77; Newman, *Transformation*, 86–95; S. White, *Somewhat More Independent*, 144–45, 194–206.

22. Berlin, *Many Thousands Gone*, 263–64, 279–80; Frey, *Water from the Rock*, 217–18; Oakes, *Ruling Race*, 134–35, master quoted on 135 ("You can't"); A. Rothman, *Slave Country*, 2–3.

23. Dunn, "Black Society," 61–63; Nash, *Race and Revolution*, 17–19; Van Cleve, *Slaveholders' Union*, 93–96; Wolf, *Race and Liberty*, xi–xii, 6, 143.

24. W. Jordan, *White over Black*, 580–81; Morton, *Robert Carter*, 260–67.

25. L. K. Ford, *Deliver Us from Evil*, 68; Nicholls, "Passing Through This Troublesome World," 59–68.

26. Beckert, *Empire of Cotton*, 100–103; Faber, *Building the Land of Dreams*, 41–42; Frey, *Water from the Rock*, 214–22; Horton and Horton, *Slavery*, 69; Schoen, *Fragile Fabric*, 30–31, 41–46.

27. Beckert, *Empire of Cotton*, 107–8, 158; Berlin, *Many Thousands Gone*, 307–10; Dupre, *Alabama's Frontiers*, 263–66, John Hardie quoted on 266 ("price"); Horton and Horton, *Slavery*, 83–84; Lepler, *Many Panics*, 12–14; Oakes, *Ruling Race*, 73–76; Schoen, *Fragile Fabric*, 54–56.

28. Deyle, *Carry Me Back*, 16–21, 34–38; Dupre, *Alabama's Frontiers*, 259–61, William Tell Harris quoted on 259–60 ("poor creatures"); Horton and Horton, *Slavery*, 78–79, Charles Ball quoted on 79 ("in honor"); W. Johnson, *Soul by Soul*, 5–8; Kulikoff, "Uprooted Peoples," 149–51.

29. Dupre, *Alabama's Frontiers*, 258–59; Fedric, *Slave Life in Virginia and Kentucky*, ix; W. Johnson, *Soul by Soul*, 19–20; Kulikoff, *Tobacco and Slaves*, 429–30; Schermerhorn, *Business of Slavery*, 10–11.

30. Dunn, "Black Society," 59; settler quoted in Dupre, *Alabama's Frontiers*, 272–73 ("thronged").
31. Baptist, *Half Has Never Been Told*, 120–22, 133–40, A. K. Bartow quoted on 121 ("my negroes"); Beckert, *Empire of Cotton*, 110–11, 115–16, John Brown quoted on 110 ("When the price"); Beckert and Rockman, eds., *Slavery's Capitalism*, 72–73; W. Johnson, *Soul by Soul*, 191–93.
32. Oakes, *Ruling Race*, 120–28, southerner quoted on 121 ("A gentleman"), *Farmers' Register* quoted on 128 ("All despise"), South Carolina master quoted on 134 ("because").
33. Franklin and Schweninger, *Runaway Slaves*, 235; W. Johnson, *Soul by Soul*, 6; Kolchin, *American Slavery*, 172–79; Beckert and Rockman, eds., *Slavery's Capitalism*, 62–63; Schoen, *Fragile Fabric*, 3–4.
34. Oakes, *Ruling Race*, 123–26, 129–30.
35. Franklin and Schweninger, *Runaway Slaves*, 235–37; Kolchin, *American Slavery*, 100–104; Kulikoff, *Tobacco and Slaves*, 409–10; Oakes, *Ruling Race*, 174–75.
36. Ayers, *Vengeance and Justice*, 3–4, 10–11, 26; Glover, *Southern Sons*, 22–34, 45–46, 64; K. Greenberg, *Masters and Statesmen*, 23, 40–41; William Harper quoted in McCurry, *Masters of Small Worlds*, 219. For murder rates, see Baptist, *Half Has Never Been Told*, 219–20. For violent congressmen, see Freeman, *Field of Blood*, 70–71.
37. Camp, *Closer to Freedom*, 21–22, 43–44; Horton and Horton, *Slavery*, 122–23, Lewis Clarke quoted on 123; Kolchin, *American Slavery*, 104–10; D. G. White, *Ar'n't I a Woman*, 49–51.
38. Spann Hammond quoted in Faust, *James Henry Hammond*, 103; Oakes, *Ruling Race*, 110–11; Steward, *Twenty-Two Years a Slave*, 14; Walsh, "Work and Resistance," 98–105.
39. Camp, *Closer to Freedom*, 44–45; Steward, *Twenty-Two Years a Slave*, 14–17, 24; Ball, *Fifty Years in Chains*, 59; Franklin and Schweninger, *Runaway Slaves*, 243–52; W. Johnson, *Soul by Soul*, 19–20, 205–7, William Johnson quoted on 19; Kolchin, *American Slavery*, 126–27.
40. Unnamed enslaved woman quoted in Fedric, *Slave Life in Virginia*, 15 ("Selling is worse"); Gudmestad, *Troublesome Commerce*, 42–44; Horton and Horton, *Slavery*, 113–15; [G. Tucker], *Letters from Virginia*, 33 ("sentence"); D. G. White, *Ar'n't I a Woman*, 148–49.
41. Former slave quoted in D. B. Davis, *Problem of Slavery in the Age of Emancipation*, 12 ("They felt"); Horton and Horton, *Slavery*, 98–99, 105; Thomas Jefferson to John Wayles Eppes, June 30, 1820, Founders Online, National Archives (http://founders.archives.gov/documents/Jefferson/98-01-02-1352); D. G. White, *Ar'n't I a Woman*, 68–70, 99–103, Williamson Pease quoted on 120 ("Women")
42. Snyder, *Great Crossings*, 55–68; Townshend, *Lincoln and the Bluegrass*, 76–79, Ebenezer Stedman quoted on 77, Richard M. Johnson quoted on 79.
43. Snyder, *Great Crossings*, 201–9, 299–300, Lexington *Observer & Reporter*

quoted on 209 ("shocked"); Townshend, *Lincoln and the Bluegrass*, 76–79, Louisville *Journal* quoted on 78 ("Like other men" and "chief sin").

44. Blight, *Frederick Douglass*, 13–15; Camp, *Closer to Freedom*, 42–43; Frederick Douglass quoted in Delbanco, *War Before the War*, 40 ("My father"); Kolchin, *American Slavery*, 119–20, 123–25, Mary Boykin Chesnut quoted on 124 (" Like"); Snyder, *Great Crossings*, 53–54; D. G. White, *Ar'n't I a Woman*, 40–43, 51–52, Chesnut quoted on 40–41 ("Any lady")

45. Faust, *James Henry Hammond*, 85–88, Hammond quoted on 87 and 124.

46. Harriet Jacobs quoted in Horton and Horton, *Slavery*, 123 ("If God"); Kolchin, *American Slavery*, 119–20, 123–25, Jacobs quoted on 124 ("fiends"); D. G. White, *Ar'n't I a Woman*, 34–38, 78–79.

47. Baptist, *The Half Has Never Been Told*, 264–66, Robert Falls quoted on 265; Camp, *Closer to Freedom*, 1–2; Horton and Horton, *Slavery*, 107–8, 125; W. Johnson, *Soul by Soul*, 197; Kolchin, *American Slavery*, 133–34, 149–50, 154.

48. Camp, *Closer to Freedom*, 71–72; Diouf, *Slavery's Exiles*, 8–9; Hadden, *Slave Patrols*, 143–52.

49. A. Barr, *Black Texans*, 27; Camp, *Closer to Freedom*, 6–8, 60–61, 68–70; Kolchin, *American Slavery*, 149–50, Abraham Chambers quoted on 150; Sobel, *World They Made Together*, 33, 253n12; Steward, *Twenty-Two Years a Slave*, 30; [G. Tucker], *Letters from Virginia*, 79.

50. Baptist, *Half Has Never Been Told*, 200–203; Camp, *Closer to Freedom*, 45–46, 61; Kolchin, *American Slavery*, 143–44, Cornelius Garner quoted on 144 ("Dat ole").

51. Baptist, *Half Has Never Been Told*, 149; Heyrman, *Southern Cross*, 50–52; Kolchin, *American Slavery*, 146–48, 154–55; D. G. White, *Ar'n't I a Woman*, 134–36.

52. Frederick Douglass quoted in Aptheker, *American Negro Slave Revolts*, 64; Camp, *Closer to Freedom*, 65; Kolchin, *American Slavery*, 115–16, 118–19; Josiah Henson quoted in Lobb, ed., *Uncle Tom's Story*, 24–25; Grimes, *Life of William Grimes*, 39; Oakes, *Ruling Race*, 102.

53. P. Breen, *Land Shall be Deluged in Blood*, 7–8; Franklin and Schweninger, *Runaway Slaves*, 11–15; Horton and Horton, *Slavery*, 119–20; Oakes, *Slavery and Freedom*, 152–54.

54. Camp, *Closer to Freedom*, 2–4; Henry Bibb quoted in Delbanco, *War before the War*, 39; Fedric, *Slave Life in Virginia*, 17; Franklin and Schweninger, *Runaway Slaves*, 2–6; Horton and Horton, *Slavery*, 120–21; Josiah Henson quoted in Lobb, ed., *Uncle Tom's Story*, 116; Oakes, *Ruling Race*, 179–90; D. G. White, *Ar'n't I a Woman*, 79–85.

55. Ball, *Fifty Years in Chains*, ix, 298–99; Camp, *Closer to Freedom*, 69–70; Diouf, *Slavery's Exiles*, 107–8; Grimes, *Life of William Grimes*, 40; Josiah Henson quoted in Lobb, ed., *Uncle Tom's Story*, 24–25, 49; Richard Parkinson, *Tour in America*, 2:432 ("Massa"); D. G. White, *Ar'n't I a Woman*, 76–77.

56. Foner, *Gateway to Freedom*, 4–6; Franklin and Schweninger, *Runaway*

Slaves, 210–13, 224–28; W. Johnson, *Soul by Soul*, 31–32; Mullin, *Flight and Rebellion*, 89–91, 103.

57. Camp, *Closer to Freedom*, 36–38; Diouf, *Slavery's Exiles*, 72–73, 88–90, James Curry quoted on 89; Horton and Horton, *Slavery*, 129; D. G. White, *Ar'n't I a Woman*, 70–74, grandmother quoted on 74.

58. Horton and Horton, *Slavery*, 79–80, 105; Sinha, *Slave's Cause*, 422–23.

59. Delbanco, *War Before the War*, 30–35; Hahn, *Nation Without Borders*, 75–76, Moses Roper quoted on 75; Hahn, *Political Worlds of Slavery and Freedom*, 1–3, Lewis Garrard Clarke quoted on 2; Horton and Horton, *Slavery*, 89–90, John Malvin quoted on 90.

60. Franklin and Schweninger, *Runaway Slaves*, 293–294, Joseph Taper quoted on 294; Levine, *Toronto*, 79–83; Winks, *Blacks in Canada*, 168–74.

61. Winks, *Blacks in Canada*, 142–56, William Lyon Mackenzie quoted on 149 ("extravagantly loyal"), British official quoted on 151 ("Natural hatred").

62. Delbanco, *War Before the War*, 24–25; Horton and Horton, *Slavery*, 132–34, 137–38; Oertel, *Harriet Tubman*, 27–49; Sinha, *Slave's Cause*, 382–93, 438–39.

63. Camp, *Closer to Freedom*, 101–2; Delbanco, *War Before the War*, 36–37; Foner, *Gateway to Freedom*, 6–27; Schoen, *Fragile Fabric*, 173; Varon, *Disunion*, 99–100.

64. Camp, *Closer to Freedom*, 35–55; Diouf, *Slavery's Exiles*, 1–3, 9–12, 72–73, 80–84, 95–96, 106–21, overseer quoted on 73 ("because"), Tom Wilson quoted on 96; Fedric, *Slave Life*, 79–83; Franklin and Schweninger, *Runaway Slaves*, 100–109; Horton and Horton, *Slavery*, 127–29.

65. Cornelia Carney quoted in Camp, *Closer to Freedom*, 70; Franklin and Schweninger, *Runaway Slaves*, 27–28, 86–89; Oakes, *Ruling Race*, 181–82.

66. Diouf, *Slavery's Exiles*, 92–97, 209–29, Henry Clay Roome quoted in 218; Horton and Horton, *Slavery*, 92; Sidbury, *Ploughshares into Swords*, 24.

67. Thomas Jefferson, conveyance of James Hubbard, to Reuben Perry, Feb., n.d., 1811, Perry, advertisement for Hubbard, *Richmond Enquirer*, Apr. 12, 1811, in Looney et al., eds., *Papers of Thomas Jefferson, Retirement Series*, 3:411–13, 513n; Stanton, *"Those Who Labor,"* 145–49.

68. Gordon-Reed, *Hemingses of Monticello*, 443–44; Thomas Jefferson, to Reuben Perry, Apr. 16, 1812, in Looney et al., eds., *Papers of Thomas Jefferson, Retirement Series*, 4:620; Stanton, *"Those Who Labor,"* 150–52.

69. Amy Chapman and Delia Garlic quoted in Kolchin, *American Slavery*, 167; Oakes, *Ruling Race*, 183–84, James Pennington quoted on 183 ("They are not"), slave quoted on 184 ("Yes").

70. D. B. Davis, *Problem of Slavery in the Age of Emancipation*, 158–60; James Madison, "Popular Election of the First Branch of the Legislature," June 6, 1787, in Hutchinson et al., eds., *Papers of James Madison*, 10:32–34 ("We have seen"); Madison to Charles Sigourney, Sept. 25, 1828 ("calamity"), Founders Online, National Archives (https://founders.archives.gov/documents/Madison/99-02-02-1551).

71. John Randolph quoted in W. C. Bruce, *John Randolph*, 2:249 ("occupy"); Burin, *Slavery and the Peculiar Solution*, 13–14; Guyatt, *Bind Us Apart*, 267–68, Randolph quoted on 268 ("secure"); Horton and Horton, *Slavery*, 86–87; McCoy, *Last of the Fathers*, 281–82; Sinha, *Slave's Cause*, 163–64.

72. Burin, *Slavery and the Peculiar Solution*, 22–23; L. K. Ford, *Deliver Us from Evil*, 70–72; Guyatt, *Bind Us Apart*, 247–48, 263–64; Horton and Horton, *Slavery*, 91–92; Andrew Judson quoted in J. Jones, *Dreadful Deceit*, 140; Mason, *Slavery and Politics*, 112–13; Sinha, *Slave's Cause*, 164–66.

73. Ash and Musgrave, *Chocolate City*, 54–55, Francis Scott Key quoted on 55 ("I am" and "immoral," and "worthy"); Morley, *Snow-Storm in August*, 39–42, 58–61, Key quoted on 40 ("greatest evil").

74. Baptist, *Half Has Never Been Told*, 34–35, *Niles Register* quoted on 35; Egerton, *Charles Fenton Mercer*, 167–70; Gudmestad, *Troublesome Commerce*, 6–8; McCoy, *Last of the Fathers*, 281–82.

75. Burin, *Slavery and the Peculiar Solution*, 20–23; Guyatt, *Bind Us Apart*, 268–73; Howe, *What Hath God Wrought*, 264–65; Saunt, *Unworthy Republic*, 17–18, Georgia legislature quoted on 18.

76. Balogh, *Government Out of Sight*, 146–47; Burin, *Slavery and the Peculiar Solution*, 14–15, 141–42; D. B. Davis, *Problem of Slavery in the Age of Emancipation*, 111–18; L. K. Ford, *Deliver Us from Evil*, 304–19; Guyatt, *Bind Us Apart*, 272–75; McCoy, *Last of the Fathers*, 299–303; Rugemer, *Slave Law*, 285–86.

77. Burin, *Slavery and the Peculiar Solution*, 17, 24–25, 144–50; James Madison quoted in S. Dunn, *Dominion of Memories*, 50; Guyatt, *Bind Us Apart*, 326–27; Varon, *Disunion*, 49–50.

78. Guyatt, *Bind Us Apart*, 68–69, 279–80; Horton and Horton, *Slavery*, 88–91; H. Jackson, *American Radicals*, 13–20, James Forten quoted on 15; Newman, *Transformation of American Abolitionism*, 96–118; Sinha, *Slave's Cause*, 164–68, meeting quoted on 165.

79. D. B. Davis, *Problem of Slavery in the Age of Emancipation*, 45–52, 78–79, David Walker quoted on 79; Horton and Horton, *In Hope of Liberty*, 191–94; Sinha, *Slave's Cause*, 62–64, 168–70.

80. Dubois, *Haiti*, 52–61, 65–73; Fick, "From Slave Colony to Black Nation," 162–67; Geggus, "Haiti and the Abolitionists," 121–26; Girard, *Paradise Lost*, 60–62; Heinl and Heinl, *Written in Blood*, 133–45.

81. Candler, *Brief Notices of Hayti*, 29–31; Dubois, *Haiti*, 61–65, 76–84; Fick, "From Slave Colony to Black Nation," 160–62; Geggus, "Haiti and the Abolitionists," 117–23.

82. Dubois, *Haiti*, 53–54; Girard, *Paradise Lost*, 61–63; Heinl and Heinl, *Written in Blood*, 142.

83. Candler, *Brief Notices of Hayti*, 34–36; Dubois, *Haiti*, 84–88; Girard, *Paradise Lost*, 61–62; Heinl and Heinl, *Written in Blood*, 151–53; M. J. Smith, *Liberty, Fraternity, Exile*, 38–40.

84. Dubois, *Haiti*, 93–94; Ferrer, "Haiti, Free Soil, and Antislavery," 58–60;

Horton and Horton, *In Hope of Liberty*, 192–94; Wong, "In the Shadow of Haiti," 175–80, Boyer quoted on 177.

85. D. B. Davis, *Problem of Slavery in the Age of Emancipation*, 76–82; Dubois, *Haiti*, 7–8, 97–104; Heinl and Heinl, *Written in Blood*, 160–65; Horton and Horton, *In Hope of Liberty*, 194–96.

86. Finkelman, "Evading the Ordinance," 21–51; Simeone, *Democracy and Slavery*, 19–28, 97–98, *Republican Advocate* quoted on 19 ("indisputable right"); Sinha, *Slave's Cause*, 183.

87. Finkelman, "Evading the Ordinance," 48–49; Guasco, *Confronting Slavery*, 84–86, 113–14, 119–21, *Republican Advocate* quoted on 120; Simeone, *Democracy and Slavery*, 28–31.

88. Guasco, *Confronting Slavery*, 106–13, 121; Simeone, *Democracy and Slavery*, 4–8, 16–17.

89. Guasco, *Confronting Slavery*, 77–83, 91–96; Ketcham, "Dictates of Conscience," 53–62; Simeone, *Democracy and Slavery*, 4, 17–18, 99–101, George Flowers quoted on 100.

90. Guasco, *Confronting Slavery*, 106, 111–27, Morris Birkbeck quoted on 126; Simeone, *Democracy and Slavery*, 5–6, 137–38, 148–55.

91. Guasco, *Confronting Slavery*, 104–108, 115–16, 129–33, John Reynolds quoted on 108; Simeone, *Democracy and Slavery*, 30–31.

92. Guasco, *Confronting Slavery*, 131–33.

93. L. K. Ford, *Deliver Us from Evil*, 73–74; Gudmestad, *Troublesome Commerce*, 35–36; James Madison to James Monroe, Feb. 23, 1820, in David B. Mattern et al., eds., *Papers of James Madison, Retirement Series*, 2:16–18; McCoy, *Last of the Fathers*, 267–74; Varon, *Disunion*, 41–42.

94. Jonathan Roberts, speech in the U.S. Senate, Jan. 17, 1820 ("marred"), *Annals of Congress*, 16th Congress, 127; Hammond, *Slavery, Freedom, and Expansion*, 154–63; Mason, *Slavery and Politics*, 177; Rugemer, *Slave Law*, 251–52; Van Cleve, *Slaveholders' Union*, 10–11, 231–33; Varon, *Disunion*, 39–40.

95. John Sergeant quoted in Mason, *Slavery and Politics*, 180; Van Cleve, *Slaveholders' Union*, 235.

96. Freehling, *Road to Disunion*, 145–46, John Tyler quoted on 151; Mason, *Slavery and Politics*, 193–99, 203; Van Cleve, *Slaveholders' Union*, 229–34; Varon, *Disunion*, 41–45; Wolf, *Race and Liberty*, 175–78.

97. Baptist, *Half Has Never Been Told*, 154–56, Thomas Cobb quoted on 155; Freehling, *Road to Disunion*, 152–53; Varon, *Disunion*, 43–45, Nathaniel Macon quoted on 43.

98. Forbes, *Missouri Compromise*, 6, 94–96; Varon, *Disunion*, 46–47.

99. John Quincy Adams quoted in Reynolds, *Waking Giant*, 34; Henry Clay quoted in Sexton, *Monroe Doctrine*, 37.

100. Thomas Jefferson to John Holmes, Apr. 22, 1820 ("geographical line" and "I regret"), and Jefferson to James Breckinridge, Feb. 15, 1821 ("burst on

us"), Founders Online, National Archives (http://founders.archives.gov/documents/Jefferson/98-01-02-1234, and 1839).

101. Ericson, *Slavery in the American Republic*, 11–12; Forbes, *Missouri Compromise*, 8–9; Onuf, "Federalism, Republicanism, and the Origins of American Sectionalism," 33–37.

102. Freeman, *Field of Blood*, 53–55, 62, 68–72, 75–76, 132–34, Joshua Giddings quoted on 132 ("we have no"); Stewart, "Christian Statesmanship," 36–57, Giddings quoted on 44 ("remain silent").

103. Egerton, *He Shall Go Out Free*, 73–153; Horton and Horton, *Slavery*, 92–93; Rugemer, *Slave Law*, 255–61; J. S. Scott, *Common Wind*, 210–11; Varon, *Disunion*, 50–51. For a minimalist take on the revolt as concocted by alarmed masters to suppress black dissent, see Johnson, "Denmark Vesey," 915–76.

104. Egerton, *He Shall Go Out Free*, 154–214, 218–21; Rugemer, *Slave Law*, 261–65, James Hamilton quoted on 264; Sinha, *Slave's Cause*, 143.

105. Camp, *Closer to Freedom*, 104–105; Coleman, *Dangerous Subjects*, 31–32, Benjamin Hunt quoted on 32 ("In South Carolina"); Egerton, *He Shall Go Out Free*, 214–18; Horton and Horton, *Slavery*, 93–95; Schoen, *Fragile Fabric*, 117–19; Sinha, *Slave's Cause*, 196–97; Wong, "In the Shadow of Haiti," 164–67.

106. P. Breen, *Land Shall Be Deluged in Blood*, 9–16; Freehling, *Road to Disunion*, 178–81; K. Greenberg, ed., *Nat Turner*, 45–76; Haynes, *Unfinished Revolution*, 181; Horton and Horton, *Slavery*, 113–15; Schwarz, *Twice Condemned*, 255–59. Some accounts put the African-American deaths as high as 120, but Breen favors the lower figure of 40, while conceding that there could have been 60.

107. Baptist, *Half Has Never Been Told*, 209; Freehling, *Road to Disunion*, 181–85; Masur, "Nat Turner and Sectional Crisis," 154–59; Shade, *Democratizing the Old Dominion*, 195–99; Varon, *Disunion*, 78–81.

108. Freehling, *Road to Disunion*, 185–90; Masur, "Nat Turner and Sectional Crisis," 158–61, John Thompson Brown quoted on 158; Thomas R. Dew quoted in Oakes, *Slavery and Freedom*, 38; Schoen, *Fragile Fabric*, 147–48; Shade, *Democratizing the Old Dominion*, 199–203; Varon, *Disunion*, 81–84.

109. Varon, *Disunion*, 95–97, Robert B. Hall quoted on 96 ("Slavery").

110. Camp, *Closer to Freedom*, 102–3; Egerton, *He Shall Go Out Free*, 225–26; H. Jackson, *American Radicals*, 51–53, David Walker quoted on 52.

111. Hahn, *Nation Without Borders*, 47–48, David Walker quoted on 48 ("Treat us"); H. Jackson, *American Radicals*, 51–53, Walker quoted on 53 ("Had you" and "Your DESTRUCTION"); Sinha, *Slave's Cause*, 205–7; D. Walker, *David Walker's Appeal*, 73 ("What a happy"), and editor's introduction, xx–xxiii.

112. Burin, *Slavery and the Peculiar Solution*, 21–22; Howe, *What Hath God Wrought*, 425–26, William Lloyd Garrison quoted on 425 ("I will be"); H. Jackson, *American Radicals*, 54–60; Wilentz, *Rise of American Democracy*, 335–38, Garrison quoted on 336 ("moderation"); Varon, *Disunion*, 68–74.

113. Hietala, *Manifest Design*, 53–54; Horton and Horton, *Slavery*, 139–40; H. Jackson, *American Radicals*, 63–64; Wilentz, *Rise of American Democracy*, 403–5.

114. Blight, *Frederick Douglass*, 10–86; D. B. Davis, *Problem of Slavery in the Age of Emancipation*, 40–41, 226–31; Foner, *Gateway to Freedom*, 1–4; Horton and Horton, *Slavery*, 144–45.

115. Blight, *Frederick Douglass*, 87–173, 188–95; Horton and Horton, *Slavery*, 145–46, Elizabeth Cady Stanton quoted on 146; Lepore, *These Truths*, 248–50, Frederick Douglass's *North Star* quoted on 250; Douglass quoted in Howe, *What Hath God Wrought*, 653; Sinha, *Slave's Cause*, 425–28.

116. Horton and Horton, *Slavery*, 74–75, Isabella Baumfree quoted on 75; Howe, *What Hath God Wrought*, 50–51; Sinha, *Slave's Cause*, 433–34

117. Slave mistress quoted in Horton and Horton, *Slavery*, 76–77; Howe, *What Hath God Wrought*, 51; Sinha, *Slave's Cause*, 434.

118. Douglass quoted in Blight, *Frederick Douglass*, 185; Grimes, *Life of William Grimes*, 103; H. Jackson, *American Radicals*, 81–83, 192–94, William Lloyd Garrison quoted on 193.

119. Ginzberg, *Women and the Work of Benevolence*, 26; John C. Calhoun quoted in Kersh, *Dreams of a More Perfect Union*, 145; Richards, *Slave Power*, 128–29, John Tyler quoted on 129.

120. Hietala, *Manifest Design*, 18–20, Robert Walker quoted on 29; Oakes, *Ruling Race*, 137–38, South Carolinian quoted on 137; Rugemer, "Slave Law," 295–97, Frederick Douglass quoted on 303.

121. Haynes, *Unfinished Revolution*, 183–84; Schoen, *Fragile Fabric*, 161–62, 171–72, James Henry Hammond quoted on 172; Varon, *Disunion*, 52.

122. Hammond quoted in Faust, *James Henry Hammond*, 176–77; Hietala, *Manifest Design*, 171–72; Horsman, *Race and Manifest Destiny*, 139–57; Lepore, *These Truths*, 257–58.

123. Edwin C. Holland quoted in Egerton, *He Shall Go Out Free*, 209 ("whining"); John Randolph quoted in Kirk, *John Randolph*, 64; McCurry, *Masters of Small Worlds*, 212–14; Oakes, *Ruling Race*, 142–43, unnamed master quoted on 143 ("niggers"); Oakes, *Slavery and Freedom*, 114–15.

124. Delbanco, *War Before the War*, 39–40; Kolchin, *American Slavery*, 194–96; McCurry, *Masters of Small Worlds*, 229–31, William Harper quoted on 231; D. G. White, *Ar'n't I a Woman*, 57–58.

125. Delbanco, *War Before the War*, 37–40; *Raleigh Daily Register* quoted in Foner, *Gateway to Freedom*, 6 ("to steal him"); Hietala, *Manifest Design*, 29–31, 34–35, William L. Yancey quoted on 49 ("prefer"); Horsman, *Race and Manifest Destiny*, 273–74; Kersh, *Dreams of a More Perfect Union*, 118, 121–22.

126. Faust, *James Henry Hammond*, 94–105, Hammond quoted on 98 ("astonished" and "most of what"), and 105 ("like a war"); Franklin and Schweninger, *Runaway Slaves*, 292.

127. Horseman, *Race and Manifest Destiny*, 274; Jefferson, *Notes on the State of Virginia*, 151; Oakes, *Ruling Race*, 109–10, 132–33, Philip Gosse quoted on

110 ("a huge"), and John Mills quoted on 132 ("If"); Schoen, *Fragile Fabric*, 187; Townshend, *Lincoln and the Bluegrass*, 105–6.

128. Heyrman, *Southern Cross*, 223–24, 248–51; Kolchin, *American Slavery*, 185–86; McCurry, *Masters of Small Worlds*, 208–10, 226–27, James Henley Thornwell quoted on 210; Oakes, *Ruling Race*, 97–108.

129. Baptist, *Half Has Never Been Told*, 203–4, Isaac Johnson quoted on 204 ("The great God"); Robert Burns quoted in D. B. Davis, *Problem of Slavery in the Age of Emancipation*, 11 ("dat niggers").

130. Hahn, *Nation Without Borders*, 68–69; Kolchin, *American Slavery*, 187–89, Henry W. Ravenal quoted on 188; McCurry, *Masters of Small Worlds*, 210–12; Oakes, *Ruling Race*, 100–102; Quist, *Restless Visionaries*, 465–68; Tallant, *Evil Necessity*, 98–99.

131. Kolchin, *American Slavery*, 174–75; McCurry, *Masters of Small Worlds*, 27–30, 42–43, 72–74; Oakes, *Ruling Race*, 83–86, Henry Watson quoted on 86.

132. J. H. Ingraham quoted in Hermann, *Pursuit of a Dream*, 6–7; Kolchin, *American Slavery*, 174–79; Oakes, *Slavery and Freedom*, 37, 98–99, 102; Schoen, *Fragile Fabric*, 155–57.

133. Kolchin, *American Slavery*, 179–80; McCurry, *Masters of Small Worlds*, 43–48, 58–59; Oakes, *Ruling Race*, 38–40, 58–59, 65–67, 83–85; Oakes, *Slavery and Freedom*, 83–84.

134. McCurry, *Masters of Small Worlds*, 241–49; Oakes, *Ruling Race*, 138–47, James Silk Buckingham quoted on 147 ("the most"); Oakes, *Slavery and Freedom*, 37–38, 75–81; Schoen, *Fragile Fabric*, 5–6.

135. Kolchin, *American Slavery*, 179–81; McCurry, *Masters of Small Worlds*, 34–36, 53–55, 71–72; Oakes, *Ruling Race*, 123–24, John Mills quoted on 123 ("A man's merit"); Oakes, *Slavery and Freedom*, 94–95, J. D. B. DeBow quoted on 95 ("The non–slaveholder").

136. Abel P. Upshur quoted in Lepore, *These Truths*, 236; Oakes, *Ruling Race*, 40–41, 132–33, 141–44, *Richmond Enquirer* quoted on 141.

137. McCurry, *Masters of Small Worlds*, 60–61, 92–93, 116–17, 206–7, 221–25, Louisa Susanna Cheves McCord quoted on 223; Kolchin, *American Slavery*, 181–84.

138. Kolchin, *American Slavery*, 181–84; Oakes, *Ruling Race*, 143–44; Schoen, *Fragile Fabric*, 147–48.

139. Heidler and Heidler, *Henry Clay*, 448–49; Sinha, *Slave's Cause*, 487; Tallant, *Evil Necessity*, 94–97, 116–19, Cassius M. Clay quoted on 119; Townshend, *Lincoln and the Bluegrass*, 113–14.

140. Richardson, *Cassius Marcellus Clay*, 31–55; Tallant, *Evil Necessity*, 121–25; Townshend, *Lincoln and the Bluegrass*, 83–85, 102–19, public meeting resolutions quoted on 116.

141. Richardson, *Cassius Marcellus Clay*, 68–71; Tallant, *Evil Necessity*, 134–45; Townshend, *Lincoln and the Bluegrass*, 157–70, C. M. Clay quoted on 164–65, and proslavery man quoted on 170.

142. Heidler and Heidler, *Henry Clay*, 450–51; Richardson, *Cassius Marcellus*

Clay, 71; Tallant, *Evil Necessity*, 100, 145–50; Townshend, *Lincoln and the Bluegrass*, 167–68, Oliver Anderson quoted on 168.

143. Foner, *Fiery Trial*, 60–62, Abraham Lincoln quoted on 61; Sinha, *Slave's Cause*, 487; Tallant, *Evil Necessity*, 151–60, Elijah Nuttall quoted on 157 ("most enlightened").

144. Baptist, *Half Has Never Been Told*, 1–3, 20–27, 35–37; Foner, *Fiery Trial*, 16–17; Horton and Horton, *Slavery*, 71–72; A. Rothman, *Slave Country*, x–xi, 1–35; Schoen, *Fragile Fabric*, 161, 167–68.

145. Beckert, *Empire of Cotton*, 104–5, 119–21, 205–6; Schermerhorn, *Business of Slavery*, 7–8; Schoen, *Fragile Fabric*, 1–2.

146. Beckert, *Empire of Cotton*, 111–13; Beckert and Rockman, eds., *Slavery's Capitalism*, 181–82, 223–24, Charles Sumner quoted on 181 ("unhallowed"); John Winston quoted in Oakes, *Ruling Race*, 149 ("would cause"); Schermerhorn, *Business of Slavery*, 19–20.

147. Blight, *Frederick Douglass*, 140–41; D. B. Davis, *Problem of Slavery in the Age of Emancipation*, 291–93, Frederick Douglass quoted on 292–93.

148. Blight, *Frederick Douglass*, 141–42; Douglass quoted in D. B. Davis, *Problem of Slavery in the Age of Emancipation*, 293–94.

CHAPTER 5: DEMOCRACY

1. Harris, *Humbug*, 21–23; Reiss, *Showman and the Slave*, 1–2, P. T. Barnum quoted on 1 ("Greatest") and 34 ("led our").

2. Harris, *Humbug*, 20–22, Joice Heth quoted on 21; Reiss, *Showman and the Slave*, 18–20, 37–40, P. T. Barnum quoted on 19; Saxton, *P. T. Barnum*, 68–69.

3. Reiss, *Showman and the Slave*, 26, 212–24. While indebted to Reiss, the interpretation in this paragraph offers a more optimistic reading of Heth's initiative and partial success.

4. Harris, *Humbug*, 10–18, P. T. Barnum quoted on 12–13 ("The customers") and 17 ("We must"); Reiss, *Showman and the Slave*, 15–16; P. T. Barnum quoted in Reynolds, *Waking Giant*, 224 ("Humbug"); Pessen, *Jacksonian America*, 3; Saxton, *P. T. Barnum*, 33–35, 39–41.

5. Harris, *Humbug*, 22–23; Reiss, *Showman and the Slave*, 2, 29, 189–91; Saxton, *P. T. Barnum*, 69–70.

6. Reiss, *Showman and the Slave*, 3–4. Later in his career, Barnum became an antislavery politician, so he revised his autobiography to deny that he pulled out her teeth or abused her in any other way or made up her stories. See Saxton, *P. T. Barnum*, 72–74.

7. Harris, *Humbug*, 25–26; Reiss, *Showman and the Slave*, 2–3, 23–24, 189, P. T. Barnum quoted on 21; Saxton, *P. T. Barnum*, 71–73.

8. Harris, *Humbug*, 37–57; Reiss, *Showman and the Slave*, 3, 13–14, 184; Reynolds, *Waking Giant*, 224–25, 297–98; Saxton, *P. T. Barnum*, 2–3, 8–11, 33–34, 86–123, P. T. Barnum quoted on 11.

9. Reiss, *Showman and the Slave*, 52–54, *Family Magazine* quoted on 53.

10. C. Clark, *Social Change in America*, 79–80, traveler quoted on 79; Larson, *Market Revolution in America*, 13–14; G. Wood, *Empire of Liberty*, 5–6.

11. Burstein, *America's Jubilee*, 3–5, 29–30; Larkin, *Reshaping of Everyday Life*, 274–75, Frederick Marryat quoted on 275.

12. Haynes, *Unfinished Revolution*, 24–25, 36–37, 40–50, Edward Abdy quoted on 36 ("greatest people"); Kersh, *Dreams of a More Perfect Union*, 100; Rorabaugh, *Alcoholic Republic*, 174–75, Thomas Hamilton quoted on 175 ("a restless"), Henry Fearon quoted on 175 ("self-deception").

13. Gorn, "'Gouge and Bite,'" 18–43; Haynes, *Unfinished Revolution*, 25–28, 32–36; Larkin, *Reshaping of Everyday Life*, 290–91, Timothy Flint quoted on 291; Pessen, *Jacksonian America*, 8–14, 24–26.

14. Augustus Foster quoted in C. M. Green, *Washington*, 47 ("excess"); Haynes, *Unfinished Revolution*, 30–32, 36–37, 40–41; Howe, *What Hath God Wrought*, 308–9, Harriet Martineau quoted on 308.

15. Gilje, *Rioting in America*, 63–64; Kloppenberg, *Toward Democracy*, 613–14; Meyers, *Jacksonian Persuasion*, 33–56; Pessen, *Jacksonian America*, 17–18, Alexis de Tocqueville quoted on 17.

16. Baker, *Affairs of Party*, 243–44; Clark, *Social Change in America*, 111–14; Morley, *Snow-Storm in August*, 162–63, Thomas Ritchie quoted on 163; Wilentz, *Rise of American Democracy*, 183–202.

17. J. Jones, *Dreadful Deceit*, 100–101, 140–41, James Freeman Clarke quoted on 141; Kloppenberg, *Toward Democracy*, 637–38; Ryan, *Women in Public*, 22–27; Watson, *Liberty and Power*, 50–53.

18. Greenberg, *Wicked War*, 37; Howe, *What Hath God Wrought*, 92–93, James Monroe quoted on 92.

19. Baker, *Affairs of Party*, 258; Pessen, *Jacksonian America*, 31–32; Watson, *Liberty and Power*, 42–45.

20. Baker, *Affairs of Party*, 19–20, 130–31, 143–48; Balogh, *Government Out of Sight*, 147–48; Pessen, *Jacksonian America*, 23–24, 90–97; Watson, *Liberty and Power*, 33–35, 50–51, 185–86.

21. Baker, *Affairs of Party*, 22–24, 51–52, 117–18; Freeman, *Field of Blood*, 10–16; Hahn, *Nation Without Borders*, 63–64.

22. Feldberg, *Turbulent Era*, 55–61, Sidney George Fisher quoted on 57 ("A resort"); Gilje, *Rioting in America*, 66–67; Grimsted, *American Mobbing*, 200–203; Hahn, *Nation Without Borders*, 61–62; Ignatiev, *How the Irish Became White*, 160–61, William McMullen quoted on 160 ("Then").

23. Balogh, *Government Out of Sight*, 126–27, 204–5; Calhoun, "Speech on Internal Improvements," Feb. 4, 1817, in Meriwether, ed., *Papers of John C. Calhoun*, 1:398–406, quotations on 400–401.

24. Howe, *What Hath God Wrought*, 213–14; Larkin, *Reshaping of Everyday Life*, 211–19; Larson, *Market Revolution in America*, 24–25; Reynolds, *Waking Giant*, 12–13.

25. Feller, *Jacksonian Promise*, 22–25; Howe, *What Hath God Wrought*, 137–38,

214–15; Larson, *Market Revolution in America*, 31–32, 55; Rorabaugh, *Alcoholic Republic*, 83.

26. Howe, *What Hath God Wrought*, 214–15; Larkin, *Reshaping of Everyday Life*, 230–31; Philip Hone quoted in J. Rothman, *Flush Times and Fever Dreams*, iii.

27. Feller, *Jacksonian Promise*, 16–17; Howe, *What Hath God Wrought*, 117–18, 216–17; Larson, *Internal Improvement*, 75–78; Sheriff, *Artificial River*, 19–27.

28. Feller, *Jacksonian Promise*, 17–19; Howe, *What Hath God Wrought*, 118–20, 217–18; Kelly, "Gender and Class Formations," 102–3; Larson, *Market Revolution in America*, 51–52.

29. Balogh, *Government Out of Sight*, 127–28; DeWitt Clinton quoted in Reynolds, *Waking Giant*, 18.

30. Burstein, *America's Jubilee*, 122–25; Feller, *Jacksonian Promise*, 19–22; Larson, *Internal Improvement*, 78–87.

31. Howe, *What Hath God Wrought*, 562–64; Christopher Columbus Baldwin quoted in Larkin, *The Reshaping of Everyday Life*, 227–28.

32. Feller, *Jacksonian Promise*, 21–22; Howe, *What Hath God Wrought*, 563.

33. Howe, *What Hath God Wrought*, 1–4, 691–98; Larson, *Market Revolution in America*, 83; Lepore, *A Is for American*, 139–54.

34. Feller, *Jacksonian Promise*, 25–26, Frances Trollope quoted on 25 ("All the buildings"); P. Johnson, *Shopkeeper's Millennium*, 16–21; Oakes, *Ruling Race*, 77–89, *American Farmer* quoted on 89 ("marvelous tales"); Rorabaugh, *Alcoholic Republic*, 203–4.

35. Jaffee, "One of the Primitive Sort," 110; Larkin, *Reshaping of Everyday Life*, 208–10; Larson, *Market Revolution in America*, 90–91.

36. Faber, *Building the Land of Dreams*, 3–4; Oakes, *Ruling Race*, 78–80, Henry Watson quoted on 79.

37. Appleby, *Inheriting the Revolution*, 6–7, Michel Chevalier quoted on 7 ("Here"); traveler quoted in Rorabaugh, *Alcoholic Republic*, 203 ("An American"); Rothman, *Flush Times*, 2–4; Watson, *Liberty and Power*, 26–34, Frances Trollope quoted on 29 ("every bee").

38. Hietala, *Manifest Design*, 95–96; Larson, *Market Revolution in America*, 97, 137–38; Lebsock, *Free Women of Petersburg*, 9–11; Pessen, *Jacksonian America*, 77–80; Rorabaugh, *Alcoholic Republic*, 202–3, immigrant quoted on 203; Watson, *Liberty and Power*, 26–34.

39. Feller, *Jacksonian Promise*, 146–47, newspaper editor quoted on 146; Reynolds, *Waking Giant*, 175–76, Ralph Waldo Emerson quoted on 175; Ryan, *Womanhood in America*, 127–28.

40. Feller, *Jacksonian Promise*, 76–79; Howe, *What Hath God Wrought*, 292–93; Ralph Waldo Emerson quoted in Reynolds, *Waking Giant*, 157.

41. Feller, *Jacksonian Promise*, 77–78; Robert Owen quoted in Howe, *What Hath God Wrought*, 293–94.

42. Feller, *Jacksonian Promise*, 79–83; Reynolds, *Waking Giant*, 65–66.

43. Bullock, "Pure and Sublime System," 359–74; Bullock, "Revolutionary Transformation," 347–69.

44. Bullock, *Revolutionary Brotherhood*, 220–73; Kutolowski, "Freemasonry and Community," 543–61; Watson, *Liberty and Power*, 180–81; Wilentz, *Rise of American Democracy*, 274–76.

45. Bullock, *Revolutionary Brotherhood*, 277–79; Howe, *What Hath God Wrought*, 266–67, William Morgan quoted on 267; Wilentz, *Rise of American Democracy*, 272–73.

46. Bullock, *Revolutionary Brotherhood*, 280–307; Burstein, *America's Jubilee*, 291–92; P. Johnson, *Shopkeeper's Millennium*, 63–67.

47. Bullock, *Revolutionary Brotherhood*, 309–16; Goodman, *Towards a Christian Republic*, 3–33, 105–19, 234–45; P. Johnson, *Shopkeeper's Millennium*, 68–70; Watson, *Liberty and Power*, 181–85.

48. C. Clark, *Social Change in America*, 97; Oakes, *Ruling Race*, 87–88, Pauline Goode quoted on 87 ("I feel"), and Maria Lide quoted on 87–88 ("I expect" and "because").

49. Cott, *Bonds of Womanhood*, 63–100; *Ladies Museum* quoted in Feller, *Jacksonian Promise*, 147 ("Man shines"); Ginzberg, *Untidy Origins*, 30–32; Isenberg, *Sex and Citizenship*, 6–8; Lebsock, *Free Women of Petersburg*, 15–24; Jan Lewis, "Republican Wife," 689–713; Ryan, *Womanhood in America*, 113–18; Sievens, *Stray Wives*, 4–9, 12–13; Stanley, "Marriage, Property, and Class," 194–96.

50. Berkin, *Revolutionary Mothers*, 150–55; Cott, *Bonds of Womanhood*, 199–201; Kelly, "Gender and Class Formations," 110–12; Kerber, "'History Can Do It No Justice,'" 36–40; Norton, *Liberty's Daughters*, 238–55, Judith Sargent Murray quoted on 249; Zagarri, *Revolutionary Backlash*, 177.

51. Cott, *Bonds of Womanhood*, 101–25; Howe, *What Hath God Wrought*, 843–44, Elizabeth Blackwell quoted on 844; Lebsock, *Free Women of Petersburg*, 162–76; Ryan, *Womanhood in America*, 135–36.

52. Cott, *Bonds of Womanhood*, 149–54; Ginzberg, *Women and the Work of Benevolence*, 1–24; Ryan, *Cradle of the Middle Class*, 53–54, 111–23; Stansell, *City of Women*, xii–xiv, 21–22, 30–37, 74–75.

53. Cott, *Bonds of Womanhood*, 154–59; Ginzberg, *Women and the Work of Benevolence*, 36–49; Hewitt, "Religion, Reform, and Radicalism," 117–18; Lydia Maria Child quoted in Howe, *What Hath God Wrought*, 844–45; Kelly, "Gender and Class Formation," 110–11; Ryan, *Womanhood in America*, 150–53.

54. Howe, *What Hath God Wrought*, 651–653, Sarah Douglass quoted on 651, Angelina Grimké quoted on 845; H. Jackson, *American Radicals*, 79–83; Ryan, *Womanhood in America*, 130, 163–64, Philadelphia Female Antislavery Society quoted on 130, Sarah Grimké quoted on 163.

55. Ginzberg, *Women and the Work of Benevolence*, 63–65; H. Jackson, *American Radicals*, 79–83; Reynolds, *Waking Giant*, 375–76; Zaeske, "A Nest of Rattlesnakes," 99–100.

56. Ginzberg, *Women and the Work of Benevolence*, 34–35, 39–40, 64–68, Lewis Tappan quoted on 93; H. Jackson, *American Radicals*, 79–83; Ryan, *Womanhood in America*, 129–33; Varon, *Disunion*, 144–45.

57. Eckhardt, *Fanny Wright*, 168–206, Walt Whitman quoted on 3; Catharine Beecher quoted in Ginzberg, *Women and the Work of Benevolence*, 26; H. Jackson, *American Radicals*, 35–48.

58. Ginzberg, *Women and the Work of Benevolence*, 88–90; Howe, *What Hath God Wrought*, 837–38; H. Jackson, *American Radicals*, 143–47, Elizabeth Cady Stanton quoted on 147.

59. Ginzberg, *Women and the Work of Benevolence*, 85–86, 90–91, 97; H. Jackson, *American Radicals*, 145–47; Ryan, *Womanhood in America*, 129–33, *New York Commercial Advertiser* quoted on 131.

60. Greenberg, *Lady First*, xiv–xv, *Oneida Whig* quoted on xiv ("most shocking"); H. Jackson, *American Radicals*, 146–51, newspaper quoted on 146 ("aged spinsters"); Ryan, *Womanhood in America*, 164–65.

61. R. D. Brown, *Strength of a People*, 92–93, 98–99, 106–7, 146; Haselby, *Origins*, 28–34; Noll, *America's God*, 163–67, 173–74, 187–90, 203–4; G. Wood, *Empire of Liberty*, 576–86.

62. Haselby, *Origins*, 117–19, 128–29, 133–36; Noll, *America's God*, 169–70, 179–80, 187–88; Heyrman, *Southern Cross*, 61–64, 77–78; G. Wood, *Empire of Liberty*, 595–96, Peter Cartwright quoted on 596.

63. Larkin, *Reshaping of Everyday Life*, 278–81, Peter Cartwright quoted on 280; Noll, *History of Christianity in the United States*, 167, 221; Reynolds, *Waking Giant*, 129–31.

64. D. Andrews, *Methodists*, 76; Haselby, *Origins*, 120–21; Hatch, *Democratization of American Christianity*, 3–4; Noll, *America's God*, 165–70, 180–82, 196–97; G. Wood, *Empire of Liberty*, 578–81.

65. Frey, *Water from the Rock*, 251–56; Hatch, *Democratization of American Christianity*, 15–16; Heyrman, *Southern Cross*, 66–69, 156–58, 197–98; G. Wood, *Empire of Liberty*, 595–96, 608–16.

66. Howe, *What Hath God Wrought*, 297–98; Noll, *History of Christianity in the United States*, 185; Reynolds, *Waking Giant*, 158–61.

67. Appleby, *Inheriting the Revolution*, 187–88, 192, 201–4; Haselby, *Origins*, 1–4, 19–21; Hatch, *Democratization of American Christianity*, 6–7; Noll, *America's God*, 256–63.

68. Feller, *Jacksonian Promise*, 97–102, Lyman Beecher quoted on 102; P. Johnson, *Shopkeeper's Millennium*, 3–5, 95–127; Noll, *History of Christianity in the United States*, 174–78.

69. Howe, *What Hath God Wrought*, 166–68, 285–89, Lyman Beecher quoted on 166; Noll, *History of Christianity in the United States*, 193.

70. Howe, *What Hath God Wrought*, 289–92; Noll, *History of Christianity in the United States*, 192–93; Reynolds, *Waking Giant*, 155–56.

71. Appleby, *Inheriting the Revolution*, 203–4; Hatch, *Democratization of American Christianity*, 3–5; Noll, *America's God*, 204–7; G. Wood, *Empire of Liberty*, 582–83, 589–91, 611–12.

72. Baker, *Affairs of Party*, 269–74; Haselby, *Origins*, 18–20; Kersh, *Dreams of a More Perfect Union*, 109; Noll, *America's God*, 204–6; Jacob Gruber quoted

in Reynolds, *Waking Giant*, 128 ("O Lord"); G. Wood, *Empire of Liberty*, 613–14, Alexis de Tocqueville quoted on 614.

73. Appleby, *Inheriting the Revolution*, 204–15; Rorabaugh, *Alcoholic Republic*, 5–21, 237–40, Isaac Candler quoted on 7.

74. George Washington to Thomas Green, Mar. 31, 1789, in Abbott et al., eds., *Papers of George Washington, Presidential Series*, 1:467–69; Rorabaugh, *Alcoholic Republic*, 14–15, 47.

75. Freeman, *Field of Blood*, 38–39, 50–52; Larkin, *Reshaping of Everyday Life*, 284–85; Thomas Low Nichols quoted in Reynolds, *Waking Giant*, 176 ("There were"); Rorabaugh, *Alcoholic Republic*, 47–49, James T. Austin quoted on 18 ("American stage coach"), Joseph Story quoted on 103 ("brought up").

76. Reynolds, *Waking Giant*, 175–76; Rorabaugh, *Alcoholic Republic*, 19–20, 152–55, S. B. Cloudman quoted on 20 ("I can't make") and Humphrey Marshall quoted on 20 ("the way").

77. Foster, *Jeffersonian America*, 21–22; Hietala, *Manifest Design*, 95–96, John Godly quoted on 95 ("Americans"); Pessen, *Jacksonian America*, 21–22; Rorabaugh, *Alcoholic Republic*, 95–120, Frederick Marryat quoted on 97 ("It's very good"), unnamed traveler quoted on 118 ("As soon as").

78. Rorabaugh, *Alcoholic Republic*, 125, Henry Foote quoted on 151.

79. Gilje, *Rioting in America*, 73; Rorabaugh, *Alcoholic Republic*, 189–90.

80. P. Johnson, *Shopkeeper's Millennium*, 55–61, 79–93; Larkin, *Reshaping of Everyday Life*, 295–96; Rorabaugh, *Alcoholic Republic*, 8, 191–212; Ryan, *Cradle of the Middle Class*, 133–35.

81. P. Johnson, *Shopkeeper's Millennium*, 7–9; Larkin, *Reshaping of Everyday Life*, 296–97; Rorabaugh, *Alcoholic Republic*, 8, 214–17, 233; Watson, *Liberty and Power*, 179, 185–86.

82. Bushman, *Refinement of America*, 208–22, 404–5; Jaffee, *New Nation of Goods*, ix–xv; G. Wood, *Empire of Liberty*, 27–31, 355–56; Yokota, *Unbecoming British*, 92–95.

83. Bushman, *Refinement of America*, 222–27, 353–54, 381–82, 390–98; Jaffee, *New Nation of Goods*, 47–101; Larkin, *Reshaping of Everyday Life*, 300; McNamara, "Republican Art and Architecture," 509–10.

84. Bushman, *Refinement of America*, 420–25, 446–47; Pessen, *Jacksonian America*, 84–86; Rockman, *Scraping By*, 158–93; Stansell, *City of Women*, 6–10.

85. R. D. Brown, *Strength of a People*, 85–88, 92–114, 146–47; Haselby, *Origins*, 45–46, 48; James Madison quoted in Kloppenberg, *Toward Democracy*, 609 ("popular government"); Lepore, *A Is for American*, 17–18; Opal, *Beyond the Farm*, 97–109; G. Wood, *Empire of Liberty*, 469–75.

86. Balogh, *Government Out of Sight*, 220–26; R. D. Brown, *Strength of a People*, 91, 111–12; R. John, *Spreading the News*, 3–6, 17–18, 50–54; Larson, *Market Revolution in America*, 80–81; Pasley, *Tyranny of Printers*, 8–9; G. Wood, *Empire of Liberty*, 476–79.

87. Cohen, *Murder of Helen Jewett*, 23–25; Howe, *What Hath God Wrought*, 626–

28; Larson, *Market Revolution in America*, 67–68; Reynolds, *Waking Giant*, 241–43, James Gordon Bennett quoted on 242.

88. J. Green, *Mathew Carey*, 10–17; McNamara, "Republican Art and Architecture," 506–9; Pessen, *Jacksonian America*, 27–28; G. Wood, *Empire of Liberty*, 563–71.

89. Dickey, *Empire of Mud*, 63–65; Reynolds, *Waking Giant*, 298–99, includes the titles of melodramas and unspecified newspaper quoted on 298, New York audience quoted on 299.

90. Baker, *Affairs of Party*, 213–31, 241–43; Reiss, *Showman and the Slave*, 9–10, 218; Reynolds, *Waking Giant*, 298–300, Virginia Minstrels quoted on 299; Roediger, *Wages of Whiteness*, 115–27, minstrels quoted on 124 ("bobolashun"); Saxton, *Rise and Fall of the White Republic*, 165–81.

91. Davidson, *Revolution and the Word*, 15–37; Haynes, *Unfinished Revolution*, 54–58, Philip Lindsley quoted on 55 ("such as"); Reynolds, *Waking Giant*, 3, 236–38; G. Wood, *Empire of Liberty*, 543–55, Sydney Smith quoted on 543 ("Who reads"); Yokota, *Unbecoming British*, 8–18.

92. Gura, *Truth's Ragged Edge*, 39–40, 62–64; Haynes, *Unfinished Revolution*, 54–55, 60–69; Howe, *What Hath God Wrought*, 232–34; Meyers, *Jacksonian Persuasion*, 57–100; Pessen, *Jacksonian America*, 23–24; Reynolds, *Waking Giant*, 239–41, James Fenimore Cooper quoted on 241.

93. Howe, *What Hath God Wrought*, 632–33; Reynolds, *Waking Giant*, 244–48.

94. Reynolds, *Waking Giant*, 244–48, Edgar Allan Poe quoted on 247; Thomas and Jackson, eds., *Poe Log*, 843–46; Whalen, *Edgar Allan Poe and the Masses*, 29–30.

95. Howe, *What Hath God Wrought*, 617–21; H. Jackson, *American Radicals*, 97–105, Emerson quoted on 104 ("I was born"); Kersh, *Dreams of a More Perfect Union*, 137–40; Reynolds, *Waking Giant*, 249–50, Emerson quoted on 250 ("'Tis," and *"Manifest Destiny"*).

96. Howe, *What Hath God Wrought*, 618–19, 623–25, Henry David Thoreau quoted on 625; H. Jackson, *American Radicals*, 106–8; Reynolds, *Waking Giant*, 257–63.

97. Howe, *What Hath God Wrought*, 621–22; Lepore, *These Truths*, 252.

98. Lepore, *These Truths*, 258; M. Marshall, *Margaret Fuller*, 369–90.

99. Sophia Hawthorne quoted in M. Marshall, *Margaret Fuller*, 387.

100. Reynolds, *Waking Giant*, 278–86, Thomas Cole quoted on 285.

101. Reynolds, *Waking Giant*, 277–78, John Banvard quoted on 277.

102. Howe, *What Hath God Wrought*, 536–37; Larson, *Market Revolution in America*, 89–90, 101–2.

103. C. Clark, *Social Change in America*, 103–4; Feller, *Jacksonian Promise*, 27–28, Friedrich List quoted on 29; Jaffee, "One of the Primitive Sort," 103–38; Prude, "Town–Factory Conflicts," 74–76.

104. C. Clark, *Social Change in America*, 103–4, 162–64; Dublin, "Women and Outwork," 51–65.

105. C. Clark, *Social Change in America*, 161–65; Dublin, *Women at Work*, 14–17;

Larson, *Market Revolution in America*, 32–33, 112–13; Prude, "Town–Factory Conflicts," 71–72.

106. C. Clark, *Social Change in America*, 165–66; Dublin, *Women at Work*, 17–22; Larson, *Market Revolution in America*, 71–72; Reynolds, *Waking Giant*, 63–64.

107. C. Clark, *Social Change in America*, 165–66; Dublin, *Women at Work*, 23–85; Larson, *Market Revolution in America*, 72–73, 113–14.

108. C. Clark, *Social Change in America*, 185–86; Dublin, *Women at Work*, 86–164; Feller, *Jacksonian Promise*, 120–21; Larson, *Market Revolution in America*, 114–16.

109. C. Clark, *Social Change in America*, 167–68, 180; Larson, *Market Revolution in America*, 75–76.

110. C. Clark, *Social Change in America*, 171–74; Howe, *What Hath God Wrought*, 167–68, 550; Larson, *Market Revolution in America*, 64–65; Prude, "Town–Factory Conflicts," 79–80.

111. C. Clark, *Social Change in America*, 171; P. Johnson, *Shopkeeper's Millennium*, 41–42; Larson, *Market Revolution in America*, 61–64, 104–7; Tomlins, *Law, Labor, and Ideology*, 152–53.

112. Cohen, *Murder of Helen Jewett*, 61–76; Ryan, *Womanhood in America*, 122–23; Stansell, *City of Women*, 15–18, 105–12, 176–79, 191–92, Society for the Relief of Poor Women quoted on 71.

113. C. Clark, *Social Change in America*, 198–201; Cohen, *Murder of Helen Jewett*, 10–11, 202–15; Larson, *Market Revolution in America*, 139–40; Ryan, *Cradle of the Middle Class*, 13–14.

114. Philadelphian quoted in Ignatiev, *How the Irish Became White*, 144 ("after a hard day's"); P. Johnson, *Shopkeeper's Millennium*, 43–44; Stansell, *City of Women*, 41–42.

115. C. Clark, *Social Change in America*, 171–72, 194–96; Ignatiev, *How the Irish Became White*, 127–28, George Lippard quoted on 128; Stansell, *City of Women*, 3–6, 47–52, 63–70.

116. C. Clark, *Social Change in America*, 174–75, 193–96; Howe, *What Hath God Wrought*, 538–39; Pessen, *Jacksonian America*, 81–83, 87–88.

117. C. Clark, *Social Change in America*, 176–77; Prude, "Town–Factory Conflicts," 87–88; Wilentz, *Rise of American Democracy*, 282–83, Mechanics Union of Trade Associations quoted on 283.

118. Larson, *Market Revolution in America*, 108–9; Reynolds, *Waking Giant*, 64–65, *Mechanics Free Press* quoted on 65; Tomlins, *Law, Labor, and Ideology*, 9–10.

119. Hahn, *Nation Without Borders*, 72–73; Larson, *Market Revolution in America*, 110; Wilentz, *Rise of American Democracy*, 283–84, 353–54, Thomas Skidmore quoted on 354.

120. Larson, *Market Revolution in America*, 110–11; Tomlins, *Law, Labor, and Ideology*, 153–54; Watson, *Liberty and Power*, 189–91; Wilentz, *Rise of American Democracy*, 354–56.

121. Gunn, *The Decline of Authority*, ix–xi, 1–19; McCurdy, *Anti–Rent Era*, 332–35; Tomlins, *Law, Labor, and Ideology*, 38–39, 102–5, 218–19, 388–89, Peter O. Thacher quoted on 105.

122. Tomlins, *Law, Labor, and Ideology*, 102–5, 165–66, Ogden Edwards quoted on 165 ("Every American"), and Charles Grandison Thomas quoted on 389 ("sacred right").

123. Tomlins, *Law, Labor, and Ideology*, 9–11, 157–58, Workingmen of Charlestown quoted on 11.

124. Howe, *What Hath God Wrought*, 545–48; Stansell, *City of Women*, 76–79, 130–41; Stanley, "Marriage, Property, and Class," 201–2; Wilentz, *Rise of American Democracy*, 282–86, 415–16.

125. Larson, *Market Revolution in America*, 111–12; Stansell, *City of Women*, 137–38; Tomlins, *Law, Labor, and Ideology*, 156–59, 175, convention of National Trades' Union quoted on 159.

126. Feldberg, *Turbulent Era*, 18; Larson, *Market Revolution in America*, 106–7; Tomlins, *Law, Labor, and Ideology*, 9–10, Workingmen of Charlestown quoted on 10.

127. Feldberg, *Turbulent Era*, 62–64; Gilje, *Rioting in America*, 70–71; Tomlins, *Law, Labor, and Ideology*, 131–32, 144–52, 168–76, 217–18, *Philadelphia Public Ledger* quoted on 168 ("to annoy"); Wilentz, *Rise of American Democracy*, 416–18, handbill quoted on 417 ("The Freemen").

128. C. Clark, *Social Change in America*, 80–81, 181–83; Howe, *What Hath God Wrought*, 822–23; Ignatiev, *How the Irish Became White*, 140–41, Irish quoted on 140; Watson, *Liberty and Power*, 18–26.

129. Feldberg, *Turbulent Era*, 11–14, 35–36, *Native American* quoted on 20 ("bloody hand"); Gilje, *Rioting in America*, 64–66; Ignatiev, *How the Irish Became White*, 148–49; Lepore, *A is for American*, 148.

130. C. Clark, *Social Change in America*, 188–89; Feldberg, *Turbulent Era*, 76–80; Ignatiev, *How the Irish Became White,* 138; Watson, *Liberty and Power*, 194–95.

131. Haynes, *Unfinished Revolution*, 13–14; Ignatiev, *How the Irish Became White*, 69–70; Caleb Cushing quoted in Roediger, *Wages of Whiteness*, 142.

132. Ignatiev, *How the Irish Became White*, 75–81, 127–30, Frederick Douglass quoted on v.

133. Ignatiev, *How the Irish Became White*, 140 ("Blackbirders") and George Lippard quoted on 144; Roediger, *Wages of Whiteness*, 133–56.

134. Feldberg, *Turbulent Era*, 41–42, *Philadelphia Gazette* quoted on 42; Gilje, *Rioting in America*, 89; Ignatiev, *How the Irish Became White*, 124–27, Robert Smyth quoted on 136.

135. Feldberg, *Turbulent Era*, 39–40; Gilje, *Rioting in America*, 89–90; Ignatiev, *How the Irish Became White*, 136–38, Irish woman quoted on 137.

136. Baker, *Affairs of Party*, 245–48; Feldberg, *Turbulent Era*, 37–39, 43–44; Gilje, *Rioting in America*, 88–91; Grimsted, *American Mobbing*, 30–31; Horton and Horton, *In Hope of Liberty*, 243–44; Ignatiev, *How the Irish Became White*, 129–30; J. Jones, *Dreadful Deceit*, 97–101, 105–8.

137. Freeman, *Field of Blood*, 4–5; *Richmond Whig* quoted in Howe, *What Hath God Wrought*, 431; *Philadelphia Bulletin* quoted in Ignatiev, *How the Irish Became White*, 155.

138. Greenberg, *Cause for Alarm*, 92–93; Grimsted, *American Mobbing*, 8–32; Ignatiev, *How the Irish Became White*, 132–39, 159–60.

139. Haynes, *Unfinished Revolution*, 79–96; Reynolds, *Waking Giant*, 238, 303–6; Saxton, *Rise and Fall of the White Republic*, 114–16; Stansell, *City of Women*, 90–92, 96.

140. Gilje, *Rioting in America*, 74–75; Haynes, *Unfinished Revolution*, 100–105, handbill quoted on 102, rioter quoted on 105 ("America rules"); rioter quoted in Reynolds, *Waking Giant*, 306–7.

141. Grimsted, *American Mobbing*, 8–32; Howe, *What Hath God Wrought*, 431–34.

142. Dickey, *Empire of Mud*, 136–39; Feldberg, *Turbulent Era*, 76–80; Greenberg, *Cause for Alarm*, 84–92, 95, 107–8; Ignatiev, *How the Irish Became White*, 143–44.

143. Balogh, *Government Out of Sight*, 245–47; Gilje, *Rioting in America*, 75–76; Huston, "Popular Movements and Party Rule," 355–86; McCurdy, *Anti-Rent Era*, 234–59.

144. Cohen, *Murder of Helen Jewett*, 73–75; Feldberg, *Turbulent Era*, 73–74; Gilje, *Rioting in America*, 80–82; Ignatiev, *How the Irish Became White*, 131–33.

145. Sidney George Fisher quoted in Feldberg, *Turbulent Era*, 4 ("be destroyed"); Abraham Lincoln quoted in Guardino, *Dead March*, 15–16; Morley, *Snow-Storm in August*, 159–60.

146. Arrington and Bitton, *Mormon Experience*, 3–19; Bushman, *Joseph Smith*, 43–142; Remini, *Joseph Smith*, 18–74; Shipps, *Mormonism*, 25–33.

147. Arrington and Bitton, *Mormon Experience*, 20–43, Brigham Young quoted on 86; Bushman, *Joseph Smith*, 53–54, 143–70, Joseph Smith, Jr. quoted on 54; Shipps, *Mormonism*, 35–65.

148. Arrington and Bitton, *Mormon Experience*, 20–21; Bigler, *Forgotten Kingdom*, 22–23; Bushman, *Joseph Smith*, 171–77; Remini, *Joseph Smith*, 95–126.

149. Arrington and Bitton, *Mormon Experience*, 45–58, Clay County meeting quoted on 49; Howe, *What Hath God Wrought*, 318–19, Governor Lilburn Boggs quoted on 319; Remini, *Joseph Smith*, 127–39.

150. Arrington and Bitton, *Mormon Experience*, 21–22, 68–72; Bigler, *Forgotten Kingdom*, 27–28; Howe, *What Hath God Wrought*, 723–24, James Gordon Bennett quoted on 723; Remini, *Joseph Smith*, 140–49.

151. Arrington and Bitton, *Mormon Experience*, 51–52, 69–70, 77–78; Bigler, *Forgotten Kingdom*, 28–29; Hyde, *Empires, Nations, and Families*, 364–65; Pearsall, *Polygamy*, 174–78; Shipps, *Mormonism*, 160–61.

152. Arrington and Bitton, *Mormon Experience*, 22–23, 45–46, 58–59, 78–82, 94–95; Hyde, *Empires, Nations, and Families*, 365–67; Remini, *Joseph Smith*, 160–75; Shipps, *Mormonism*, 161–62.

153. Arrington and Britton, *Mormon Experience*, 86–88, 93–96, 114; Bigler, *Forgotten Kingdom*, 21–24, 62–63; Hyde, *Empires, Nations, and Families*, 359, 367–68.

CHAPTER 6: MONSTERS

1. Burstein, *Passions of Andrew Jackson*, 181–86, Francis Walker Gilmer quoted on 136 ("Mr. Clay's voice"); Dangerfield, *Era of Good Feelings*, 10–13, anecdote of Lucretia Clay quoted on 10; A. Greenberg, *Wicked War*, 4–6, 228, John C. Calhoun quoted on 6 ("a creator"); Heidler and Heidler, *Henry Clay*, xi–xv, 65–66.

2. Balogh, *Government Out of Sight*, 129–32, 134–35, Henry Clay quoted on 135 ("to make us"); Heidler and Heidler, *Henry Clay*, 78, 165–66, 179, 228–30; Watson, *Liberty and Power*, 76–77, 113–14.

3. A. Greenberg, *Wicked War*, 6–7; Heidler and Heidler, *Henry Clay*, 34–35, 131–32.

4. Dangerfield, *Era of Good Feelings*, 102–3, Harriet Martineau quoted on 102 ("cast-iron"); Freehling, *Road to Disunion*, 265–66, Henry Clay quoted on 266 ("careworn"); Heidler and Heidler, *Henry Clay*, 157–58; Howe, *What Hath God Wrought*, 401; Wilentz, *Rise of American Democracy*, 319 ("Whereas").

5. Burstein, *Passions of Andrew Jackson*, 124–26, 133, 151–55; Jackson to James Gadsden, Dec. 6, 1821, and Jackson to George Kremer, May 6, 1824, in Moser et al., eds., *Papers of Andrew Jackson*, 5:121–22 ("I have"), 402–3; Ratcliffe, *One-Party Presidential Contest*, 125–34; Watson, *Liberty and Power*, 47–49, Andrew Jackson quoted on 48–49 ("We are"); Wilentz, *Rise of American Democracy*, 243–48.

6. A. Greenberg, *Wicked War*, 25–26; Oakes, *Ruling Race*, 145–46; Remini, *Andrew Jackson and the Course of American Freedom*, 50, 53, 84–85.

7. Burstein, *America's Jubilee*, 145–46; Burstein, *Passions of Andrew Jackson*, 130–31, 149–51; Howe, *What Hath God Wrought*, 92–94, 203–6; Ratcliffe, *One-Party Presidential Contest*, 33–45, 234; Wilentz, *Rise of American Democracy*, 240–43.

8. Larson, *Internal Improvements*, 156–57; Ratcliffe, *One-Party Presidential Contest*, 233–34; Wilentz, *Rise of American Democracy*, 240–41, 250–51.

9. Heidler and Heidler, *Henry Clay*, 178–85; Ratcliffe, *One-Party Presidential Contest*, 232–33, 239, 252–54; Wilentz, *Rise of American Democracy*, 254–56, Henry Clay quoted on 255 ("fatal road").

10. Howe, *What Hath God Wrought*, 209; Andrew Jackson to John Overton, Feb. 10, 1825, and Jackson to William Berkeley Lewis, Feb. 14, 1825, in Moser et al., eds., *Papers of Andrew Jackson*, 6:28, 29–30 ("So you see"); Ratcliffe, *One-Party Presidential Contest*, 237, 254–57.

11. Balogh, *Government Out of Sight*, 139–43; Burstein, *America's Jubilee*, 150–54; Feller, *Jacksonian Promise*, 70–73; Larson, *Internal Improvements*, 156–80.

12. Burstein, *America's Jubilee*, 212–16, 226–27; Kloppenberg, *Toward Democracy*, 605–7; Ratcliffe, *One-Party Presidential Contest*, 59–61, 268–73, James Buchanan quoted on 61 ("His manners"); John Quincy Adams quoted in Reynolds, *Waking Giant*, 36 ("The best") and 46 ("They crawl");

Wilentz, *Rise of American Democracy*, 257–60, 293–94, Adams quoted on 259 ("liberty").

13. Baker, *Affairs of Party*, 125–27; Howe, *What Hath God Wrought*, 483–84, Amos Kendall quoted on 341 ("Van Buren glides"), Martin Van Buren quoted on 483 ("sun rise); Watson, *Liberty and Power*, 66–69; Van Buren quoted in Wilentz, *Rise of American Democracy*, 295 ("We must").

14. Baker, *Affairs of State*, 213, 248–55; James Silk Buckingham quoted in Oakes, *Ruling Race*, 142 ("more democratic"); Remini, *Andrew Jackson and the Course of American Freedom*, 72–73, 114–15, 135–37; Wilentz, *Rise of American Democracy*, 295–97, Martin Van Buren quoted on 295 ("clamour")

15. Freeman, *Field of Blood*, 19–20; Howe, *What Hath God Wrought*, 277–83, campaign ditty quoted on 279 ("Between"), Thomas B. Stevenson quoted on 283 ("man"); Wilentz, *Rise of American Democracy*, 306–7, anti–Jackson handbill quoted on 306 ("wild man").

16. Howe, *What Hath God Wrought*, 276–83; Remini, *Andrew Jackson and the Course of American Freedom*, 145–48; Wilentz, *Rise of American Democracy*, 308–9.

17. Howe, *What Hath God Wrought*, 328; Remini, *Andrew Jackson and the Course of American Freedom*, 149–57, Rachel Donelson Jackson quoted on 149 ("I assure you"); Wilentz, *Rise of American Democracy*, 301–9, includes Jackson quotation ("great").

18. Feller, *Jacksonian Promise*, 161–62, John Quincy Adams quoted on 161 ("electioneering"); Howe, *What Hath God Wrought*, 331–34; Remini, *Andrew Jackson and the Course of American Freedom*, 197–99; Wilentz, *Rise of American Democracy*, 315–17, William Marcy quoted on 316 ("to the victor").

19. Allgor, *Parlor Politics*, 1–3, 102–46.

20. Allgor, *Parlor Politics*, 48–101, 147–89, 239–46; C. M. Green, *Washington*, 48, 110–11, Charles Bagot quoted on 66 ("every inch"); Ratcliffe, *One-Party Presidential Contest*, 59–62; Wilentz, *Rise of American Democracy*, 257–58.

21. A. Greenberg, *Manifest Manhood*, 11–14; K. Wood, "'One Woman So Dangerous,'" 269–70; Zaeske, "'Nest of Rattlesnakes,'" 106–11. Greenberg coined the phrase "restrained manhood."

22. A. Greenberg, *Manifest Manhood*, 12–17; A. Greenberg, *Wicked War*, 118–19; Varon, *Disunion*, 92; Watson, *Liberty and Power*, 193–95, 236–37; K. Wood, "'One Woman So Dangerous,'" 268–69; Zaeske, "'Nest of Rattlesnakes,'" 106–11. Greenberg coined the phrase "martial manhood."

23. Burstein, *Passions of Andrew Jackson*, 174; Howe, *What Hath God Wrought*, 337.

24. Allgor, *Parlor Politics*, 198–200, Louis McLane quoted on 200 ("Eaton"); Burstein, *Passions of Andrew Jackson*, 173–75; Ezra Stiles Ely to Andrew Jackson, Mar. 18, 1829, in Moser et al., eds., *Papers of Andrew Jackson*, 7:101–104; K. Wood, "'One Woman So Dangerous,'" 238–39, 244–46, 252–54.

25. Allgor, *Parlor Politics*, 200–203; Howe, *What Hath God Wrought*, 336–37; Ezra Stiles Ely to Andrew Jackson, Mar. 18, 1829, in Moser et al., eds.,

Papers of Andrew Jackson, 7:101–104 ("She will"); K. Wood, "'One Woman So Dangerous,'" 241–42, 246–50, 256–57.

26. Allgor, *Parlor Politics*, 203–5; Burstein, *Passions of Andrew Jackson*, 177–80; Andrew Jackson to Andrew Jackson Donelson, n.d. in Moser et al., eds., *Papers of Andrew Jackson*, 7:415 ("I had not come"); Wilentz, *Rise of American Democracy*, 318; K. Wood, "'One Woman So Dangerous,'" 259.

27. Allgor, *Parlor Politics*, 205–6; Burstein, *Passions of Andrew Jackson*, 174–78, Margaret Eaton quoted on 175 ("He did not"); Howe, *What Hath God Wrought*, 335–37, Andrew Jackson quoted on 337 ("She is"), Henry Clay quoted on 339 ("Age"); Ezra Stiles Ely to Andrew Jackson, Mar. 18, 1829, and Jackson to Ely, Mar. 23, 1829, in Moser et al., eds., *Papers of Andrew Jackson*, 7:101–4, 113–18; K. Wood, "'One Woman So Dangerous,'" 260–61.

28. Allgor, *Parlor Politics*, 203–4; Burstein, *Passions of Andrew Jackson*, 179–80; Remini, *Andrew Jackson and the Course of American Freedom*, 239–40; Wilentz, *Rise of American Democracy*, 318–19, 329; K. Wood, "'One Woman So Dangerous,'" 242–43, 251–68.

29. Andrew Jackson to John Christmas McLemore, Dec. 25, 1830, and Jackson to John Coffee, Apr. 24, 1831, in Moser et al., eds., *Papers of Andrew Jackson*, 8:707–14, 9: 210–12 ("The plot"); Wilentz, *Rise of American Democracy*, 318–19, John C. Calhoun quoted on 318 ("great victory"); K. Wood, "'One Woman So Dangerous,'" 249–59.

30. Andrew Jackson to John Coffee, Apr. 24, 1831, in Moser et al., eds., *Papers of Andrew Jackson*, 9: 210–12 ("I *now know*"); Howe, *What Hath God Wrought*, 340–41; Remini, *Andrew Jackson and the Course of American Freedom*, 237–38; K. Wood, "'One Woman So Dangerous,'" 259–68.

31. *New York Courier* quoted in Allgor, *Parlor Politics*, 208 ("Well indeed"); Watson, *Liberty and Power*, 124–26; K. Wood, "'One Woman So Dangerous,'" 243–44, 271–73.

32. Freehling, *Road to Disunion*, 255–57; Howe, *What Hath God Wrought*, 274–75, 396–97; Remini, *Andrew Jackson and the Course of American Freedom*, 136–38; Schoen, *Fragile Fabric*, 131–32.

33. Freehling, *Road to Disunion*, 257–59; Howe, *What Hath God Wrought*, 396–99; Varon, *Disunion*, 57–58, John C. Calhoun quoted on 193 ("Ours"); Watson, *Liberty and Power*, 116–17, John C. Calhoun quoted on 117 ("An unchecked"); Wilentz, *Rise of American Democracy*, 319–21.

34. Kersh, *Dreams of a More Perfect Union*, 10, 110–12; Varon, *Disunion*, 58–59; Watson, *Liberty and Power*, 118–20; Wilentz, *Rise of American Democracy*, 320–22, Webster quoted on 321 ("Liberty").

35. Freehling, *Road to Disunion*, 273–78; McCurry, *Masters of Small Worlds*, 258–59, *Charleston Mercury* quoted on 258 ("wool–weavers" and "The man"); Schoen, *Fragile Fabric*, 141–42; Watson, *Liberty and Power*, 126–27; Wilentz, *Rise of American Democracy*, 374–79.

36. Freehling, *Road to Disunion*, 278–81; Howe, *What Hath God Wrought*, 409–

10, Andrew Jackson quoted on 410 ("soldiers"); Wilentz, *Rise of American Democracy*, 379–84.

37. Freehling, *Road to Disunion*, 278–79; Howe, *What Hath God Wrought*, 405–6, Andrew Jackson and Thomas Hart Benton quoted on 406 ("I will hang" and "I tell you"); Varon, *Disunion*, 89–90.

38. Freehling, *Road to Disunion*, 281–82; Schoen, *Fragile Fabric*, 142–43, Alabama legislature quoted on 142 ("anarchy"); Varon, *Disunion*, 59–60, 90–93, Robert J. Walker quoted on 90 ("and upon"); Watson, *Liberty and Power*, 128; Wilentz, *Rise of American Democracy*, 383–84.

39. Freehling, *Road to Disunion*, 284–86; Varon, *Disunion*, 90–91; Watson, *Liberty and Power*, 129; Wilentz, *Rise of American Democracy*, 385–87.

40. Balogh, *Government Out of Sight*, 215–16, James Petigru quoted on 216 ("Nullification"); Freehling, *Road to Disunion*, 285–86, Andrew Jackson quoted on 286 ("blow up"); Varon, *Disunion*, 93–94; Watson, *Liberty and Power*, 129–31; Wilentz, *Rise of American Democracy*, 388–89.

41. Burin, *Slavery and the Peculiar Solution*, 24; Schoen, *Fragile Fabric*, 134–35; Varon, *Disunion*, 87–89, 91–95, Lydia Maria Child quoted on 87 ("Who does not") and 91 ("third party"); Watson, *Liberty and Power*, 129–30.

42. Brown, *Self-Evident Truths*, 106–7, 131–34; Roger B. Taney quoted in Howe, *What Hath God Wrought*, 442 ("The African Race"); Richards, *Slave Power*, 95–96; Sinha, *Slave's Cause*, 58–59.

43. Freehling, *Road to Disunion*, 308; Grimsted, *American Mobbing*, 20–21, *Woodville Republican* quoted on 20 ("fiend-like").

44. Horton and Horton, *Slavery*, 120–21, John Quitman quoted on 121 ("thousand freedoms"); Libby, *Slavery and Frontier Mississippi*, 115–16, Quitman quoted on 116 ("The morality"); Schoen, *Fragile Fabric*, 157.

45. Feldberg, *Turbulent Era*, 46–47; Grimsted, *American Mobbing*, 18–19, 26–27; Hietala, *Manifest Design*, 19; R. John, *Spreading the News*, 275–77, James Henry Hammond quoted on 276 ("These men") John Forsyth quoted on 276–77 ("a little more" and "A portion"); Wilentz, *Rise of American Democracy*, 409–11, 451.

46. Baker, *Affairs of State*, 237–38; Feldberg, *Turbulent Era*, 43–45; Grimsted, *American Mobbing*, 18–22, [Boston] *Commercial Gazette* quoted on 22 ("property and standing"); McDaniel, *Problem of Democracy*, 55–56; Richard Brodhead quoted in Varon, *Disunion*, 181 ("The Union"); Wilentz, *Rise of American Democracy*, 408–9, 466–70, Anti-abolition committee quoted on 466 ("insurrection"); Richards, *Slave Power*, 107–33.

47. Feldberg, *Turbulent Era*, 45–47; Grimsted, *American Mobbing*, 4, 12–13; McDaniel, *Problem of Democracy*, 53–57; Richards, *Gentlemen of Property and Standing*, 20–123; unnamed witness quoted in Reiss, *Showman and the Slave*, 8 ("Throughout"); Sinha, *Slave's Cause*, 238–39; Varon, *Disunion*, 102–4, 133–34.

48. Asch and Musgrove, *Chocolate City*, 76–77, Arthur Bowen quoted on 76

("I've got"); Morley, *Snow-Storm in August*, 104–7, 121–38, Bowen quoted on 134–35 ("We *ought*").

49. Asch and Musgrove, *Chocolate City*, 77–78, 108–10, Francis Scott Key quoted on 77 ("to excite"); Morley, *Snow-Storm in August*, 139–47.

50. Asch and Musgrove, *Chocolate City*, 78–79; Corrigan, "'Whether They be Ours or No,'" 173–74; Curry, *Free Black in Urban America*, 98–100; Dickey, *Empire of Mud*, 127–28; Morley, *Snow-Storm in August*, 3–9, 96–97, 148–55, Julia Seaton quoted on 149 ("Snow will").

51. Curry, *Free Black in Urban America*, 98–100; Andrew Jackson quoted in Dickey, *Empire of Mud*, 128 ("promote"); Morley, *Snow-Storm in August*, 155–58, 209–10.

52. Asch and Musgrove, *Chocolate City*, 80–81, Francis Scott Key quoted on 81 ("the right" and "friends"); Corrigan, "'Whether They be Ours or No,'" 173–74; Dickey, *Empire of Mud*, 80–81; Finkelman, "Slavery in the Shadow of Liberty," 11; Morley, *Snow-Storm in August*, 173–203, 211–34.

53. Asch and Musgrove, *Chocolate City*, 78–82; C. M. Green, *Washington*, 142–43; Morley, *Snow-Storm in August*, 173–74, 241–45, *National Intelligencer* quoted on 174 ("If they wish").

54. Feldberg, *Turbulent Era*, 47–49; Sinha, *Slave's Cause*, 236–39; Varon, *Disunion*, 134–35; Wilentz, *Rise of American Democracy*, 408–9, 466–70.

55. Feldberg, *Turbulent Era*, 51–52; Grimsted, *American Mobbing*, 35–36; Ignatiev, *How the Irish Became White*, 134–36; H. Jackson, *American Radicals*, 74–76, handbill quoted on 74 ("right of property"), *Philadelphia Spirit of the Times* quoted on 76 ("open violation"), and *Niles National Register* quoted on 76 ("Whites and blacks").

56. Burstein, *Passions of Andrew Jackson*, 238–39; Delbanco, *War Before the War*, 38–39; Freehling, *Road to Disunion*, 308–10, Andrew Jackson quoted on 309 ("unconstitutional"); Howe, *What Hath God Wrought*, 426–29, Jackson quoted on 429 ("exciting"); R. John, *Spreading the News*, 257–75; Morley, *Snow-Storm in August*, 177–78, Jackson quoted on 177 ("peace within"); Sinha, *Slaves' Cause*, 250–51; Wilentz, *Rise of American Democracy*, 409–13.

57. Faust, *James Henry Hammond*, 169–80; Freehling, *Road to Disunion*, 310–34; Freeman, *Field of Blood*, 112–14; Rugemer, *Slave Law*, 300–301, Calhoun quoted on 301 ("Abolition"); Varon, *Disunion*, 109–11; Wilentz, *Rise of American Democracy*, 451–52, Martin Van Buren quoted on 452 ("harmony").

58. Zaeske, "'Nest of Rattlesnakes,'" 97–98, 111–18, Jesse Bynum quoted on 113 ("old grannies") and 116 ("imbecile"), and William C. Johnson quoted on 114 ("attend to").

59. Freeman, *Field of Blood*, 114–30, 139–41; John Quincy Adams quoted in Morley, *Snow-Storm in August*, 159 ("Slavery and democracy"); Isenberg and Burstein, *Problem of Democracy*, 409–21, 425–26; Richards, *Slave Power*, 129–33; Sinha, *Slave's Cause*, 251–53.

60. Thomas Marshall quoted in Hietala, *Manifest Design*, 190 ("I wish"); Henry

Wise quoted in Howe, *What Hath God Wrought*, 514 ("the acutest"); Varon, *Disunion*, 111–14; Zaeske, "'Nest of Rattlesnakes,'" 118–23.

61. Horton and Horton, *In Hope of Liberty*, 244–45; Horton and Horton, *Slavery*, 116–17; Isenberg and Burstein, *The Problem of Democracy*, 421–24; Sinha, *Slave's Cause*, 406–11; Wilentz, *Rise of American Democracy*, 473–78.

62. Morley, *Snow-Storm in August*, 174–76, Elizur Wright quoted on 174 ("thousand lecturers"); R. G. Williams quoted in Wilentz, *Rise of American Democracy*, 412 ("Instead").

63. Grimsted, *American Mobbing*, 16–17, 20–22; R. John, *Spreading the News*, 278–80; Sinha, *Slave's Cause*, 236–39, New York Antislavery Society quoted on 237 ("crucify"), 415–16; Richards, *Slave Power*, 85–91 ("doughfaces" and "northern men" from 86); Varon, *Disunion*, 113–15, *Weekly Advocate* quoted on 114 ("actual slavery").

64. Bodenhorn, *History of Banking*, 8–22; Lebergott, *Americans*, 59–62, 114–18; Schermerhorn, *Business of Slavery*, 26–27.

65. B. Hammond, *Banks and Politics*, 164–96; Howe, *What Hath God Wrought*, 382–83; Lebergott, *The Americans*, 118–19; Lepler, *Many Panics*, 15–16; Watson, *Liberty and Power*, 35–38.

66. Bodenhorn, *History of Banking*, 168–77; Feller, *Jacksonian Promise*, 169; Howe, *What Hath God Wrought*, 85–86, 374–75; Lepler, *Many Panics*, 16–17; Watson, *Liberty and Power*, 37–38.

67. B. Hammond, *Banks and Politics*, 258–62; Larson, *Market Revolution in America*, 40–41, William Gouge quoted on 40 ("The bank"); Watson, *Liberty and Power*, 38–39, Thomas Hart Benton quoted on 39 ("All the flourishing"); Wilentz, *Rise of American Democracy*, 206–9.

68. B. Hammond, *Banks and Politics*, 287–98; Howe, *What Hath God Wrought*, 373–76, Andrew Jackson quoted on 376 ("Monster"); Meyers, *Jacksonian Persuasion*, 121–41; Watson, *Liberty and Power*, 39–41

69. Feller, *Jacksonian Promise*, 163–64; Howe, *What Hath God Wrought*, 357–61, 375–76; Remini, *Andrew Jackson and the Course of American Freedom*, 251–56, 266–67; Watson, *Liberty and Property*, 132–37, unnamed congressman quoted on 136; Wilentz, *Rise of American Democracy*, 327–28.

70. Feller, *Jacksonian Promise*, 169; Howe, *What Hath God Wrought*, 376–79; Remini, *Andrew Jackson and the Course of American Freedom*, 337–44, 363–66; Watson, *Liberty and Property*, 142–43; Wilentz, *Rise of American Democracy*, 367–69, Andrew Jackson quoted on 369 ("The bank").

71. Meyers, *Jacksonian Persuasion*, 18–28, 103–8; Sexton, *Debtor Diplomacy*, 22–23; Watson, *Liberty and Property*, 143–50, Andrew Jackson quoted on 145 ("concentration"); Wilentz, *Rise of American Democracy*, 369–71, Jackson quoted on 370 ("The rich" and "make the rich").

72. Howe, *What Hath God Wrought*, 381–83; Lepler, *Many Panics*, 19–20; Remini, *Andrew Jackson and the Course of American Freedom*, 369–72; Watson, *Liberty and Property*, 150–51; Wilentz, *Rise of American Democracy*, 371–72, Nicholas Biddle quoted on 371 ("manifesto" and "all the fury").

73. Freeman, *Field of Blood*, 58; Howe, *What Hath God Wrought*, 383–84, Whigs quoted on 383 ("King Andrew"); Watson, *Liberty and Property*, 151–54; Wilentz, *Rise of American Democracy*, 372–73.

74. Howe, *What Hath God Wrought*, 386–95, Nicholas Biddle quoted on 391 ("This worthy"); Watson, *Liberty and Power*, 154–59; Wilentz, *Rise of American Democracy*, 392–95, Andrew Jackson quoted on 393 ("destroy[ing]").

75. B. Hammond, *Banks and Politics*, 452–62; Watson, *Liberty and Property*, 159–64, Andrew Jackson quoted on 161 ("paper system"); Wilentz, *Rise of American Democracy*, 438–46.

76. Howe, *What Hath God Wrought*, 436–37; Morley, *Snow-Storm in August*, 99–100, Jackson quoted on 99 ("Let me"); Wilentz, *Rise of American Democracy*, 436.

77. Howe, *What Hath God Wrought*, 436–37; Morley, *Snow-Storm in August*, 100–103.

78. Balogh, *Government Out of Sight*, 183–84; Feller, *Jacksonian Promise*, 166–67, Andrew Jackson quoted on 166 ("citizen"); Howe, *What Hath God Wrought*, 367–68, Thomas Hart Benton quoted on 367 ("The public lands") and 368 ("to check" and "the vast"); Schoen, *Fragile Fabric*, 136–38; Wilentz, *Rise of American Democracy*, 287, 443.

79. Baker, *Affairs of Party*, 35; Earle, *Jacksonian Antislavery*, 129–30, 135–38; A. Greenberg, *Manifest Manhood*, 13–14; Hietala, *Manifest Design*, 3–7, 95–131, Thomas Turner quoted on 119 ("White slavery"); Watson, *Liberty and Property*, 114.

80. Feller, *Jacksonian Promise*, 167; Hietala, *Manifest Design*, 3–4; Howe, *What Hath God Wrought*, 368–69, Richard Rush quoted on 368 ("The creation"), 592–93; Watson, *Liberty and Power*, 113–14.

81. S. Banner, *How the Indians Lost Their Land*, 215–16; Andrew Jackson, "First Annual Message to Congress," Dec. 8, 1829, in Moser et al., eds., *Papers of Andrew Jackson*, 7:609–10 ("mass"); Ostler, *Surviving Genocide*, 209–10, Jackson quoted on 288 ("extinguish"); Perdue and Green, *Columbia Guide*, 80–81, 89–90; Remini, *Andrew Jackson and His Indian Wars*, 228, Jackson quoted on 263 ("seek").

82. Andrew Jackson quoted in Guyatt, *Bind us Apart*, 317 ("wandering"); Jackson quoted in Hietala, *Manifest Design*, 136–37 ("would prefer"); Horsman, *Race and Manifest Destiny*, 202–3.

83. S. Banner, *How the Indians Lost Their Land*, 193–97, *North American Review* quoted on 227 ("would otherwise"); Lee, *Masters of the Middle Waters*, 223–24; Ostler, *Surviving Genocide*, 191–92, 215–16; Robertson, *Conquest by Law*, 118–19.

84. S. Banner, *How the Indians Lost Their Land*, 199; Demos, *Heathen School*, 211–16; Lepore, *A Is for American*, 63–81.

85. Cherokees quoted in S. Banner, *How the Indians Lost Their Land*, 199–200 ("that the Cherokees"); Ostler, *Surviving Genocide*, 188–93, 206–208; Per-

due and Green, *Columbia Guide*, 82–85; Saunt, *Unworthy Republic*, 12–14, 22–24; Witgen, "Seeing Red," 607–8.

86. Hendrickson, *Union, Nation, or Empire*, 157–58; Hahn, *Nation Without Borders*, 31–32; Horsman, *Race and Manifest Destiny*, 195–97, John C. Calhoun quoted on 196–97 ("great difficulty"); Ostler, *Surviving Genocide*, 208–9; Perdue and Green, *Columbia Guide*, 87–88.

87. Demos, *Heathen School*, 243–44; Ostler, *Surviving Genocide*, 248–50; Saunt, *Unworthy Republic*, 28–29, *Savannah Republican* quoted on 36 ("Our savage");

88. S. Banner, *How the Indians Lost Their Land*, 194–98; Green, *Politics of Indian Removal*, 86–97; Ostler, *Surviving Genocide*, 195–96; Perdue and Green, *Columbia Guide*, 85–86; Saunt, *Unworthy Republic*, 33–36; George M. Troup quoted in Watson, *Liberty and Power*, 107 ("unblushing").

89. S. Banner, *How the Indians Lost Their Land*, 198; Green, *Politics of Indian Removal*, 98–125; Horsman, *Race and Manifest Destiny*, 198–99, James Barbour quoted on 199 ("see that"); Perdue and Green, *Columbia Guide*, 86; Robertson, *Conquest by Law*, 118–19; Saunt, *Unworthy Republic*, 36–37.

90. S. Banner, *How the Indians Lost Their Land*, 198–201, Georgia state legislature quoted on 200; Dupre, *Alabama's Frontiers*, 284–85; Perdue and Green, *Columbia Guide*, 88–89; Robertson, *Conquest by Law*, 122–25; Saunt, *Unworthy Republic*, 37–41, 85–87.

91. S. Banner, *How the Indians Lost Their Land*, 200–201, 214–15; Dupre, *Alabama's Frontiers*, 283–84, unnamed Alabaman quoted on 284 ("now is"); Howe, *What Hath God Wrought*, 414–15, song quoted on 414 ("All I want"); Ostler, *Surviving Genocide*, 212–13, 266–67; Saunt, *Unworthy Republic*, 69–70, 93–96.

92. S. Banner, *How the Indians Lost Their Land*, 215–16; Andrew Jackson, "First Annual Message to Congress," Dec. 8, 1829, and Jackson to John Pitchlynn, Aug. 5, 1830, in Moser et al., eds., *Papers of Andrew Jackson*, 7:609–10 ("or submit"), and 8:465–66 ("that the Indians" and "I feel"); Perdue and Green, *Columbia Guide*, 89–90; Robertson, *Conquest by Law*, 126–27.

93. S. Banner, *How the Indians Lost Their Land*, 209–10, 216–18, Brown County, Ohio petition quoted on 217 ("cruel"); Howe, *What Hath God Wrought*, 349–50, petition quoted on 349–50 ("We are unwilling"); Saunt, *Unworthy Republic*, 65–68, 97–99, petition quoted on 320 ("the only").

94. S. Banner, *How the Indians Lost Their Land*, 206–13; Guyatt, *Bind Us Apart*, 300–305; Andrew Jackson to James Gadsden, Oct. 12, 1829, in Moser et al., eds., *Papers of Andrew Jackson*, 7:491–92 ("exercise"); Saunt, *Unworthy Republic*, 4–7, 14–15, 63–64, 70–71.

95. S. Banner, *How the Indians Lost Their Land*, 211–12, 218–19, Wilson Lumpkin quoted on 218 ("Northern fanatics"); Remini, *Andrew Jackson and His Indian Wars*, 234–35; Saunt, *Unworthy Republic*, 28–30, 46–47, 78–81; Jacksonian quoted in Watson, *Liberty and Power*, 110 ("general government").

96. S. Banner, *How the Indians Lost Their Land*, 201–2, 205–6, 217–18; Hors-

man, *Race and Manifest Destiny*, 201–202; Howe, *What Hath God Wrought*, 351–53; Ostler, *Surviving Genocide*, 211–12; Remini, *Andrew Jackson and His Indian Wars*, 236–38; Saunt, *Unworthy Republic*, 71–77, 84–85.

97. Andrew Jackson to William B. Lewis, Aug. 25, 1830, in Moser et al., eds., *Papers of Andrew Jackson*, 8:500–501 ("leave"); Ostler, *Surviving Genocide*, 250–56; Perdue and Green, *Columbia Guide*, 90–91; Remini, *Andrew Jackson and His Indian Wars*, 227–28, 239–40, Andrew Jackson quoted on 227 ("entail"); Saunt, *Unworthy Republic*, 82–83, 86–90, 96–97, 110–11, 124–26, Choctaw quoted on 126 ("white folks").

98. Hendrickson, *Union, Nation, or Empire*, 163–64, John Marshall quoted on 163 ("If"); Perdue and Green, *Columbia Guide*, 94–95; Robertson, *Conquest by Law*, 129–30.

99. S. Banner, *How the Indians Lost Their Land*, 218–21, John Marshall quoted on 221 ("Cherokee nation"); Howe, *What Hath God Wrought*, 412–13; Ostler, *Surviving Genocide*, 213–14, 264–65; Remini, *Andrew Jackson and His Indian Wars*, 255–57; Robertson, *Conquest by Law*, 133–35.

100. S. Banner, *How the Indians Lost Their Land*, 221–23; Ostler, *Surviving Genocide*, 265–66; Perdue and Green, *Columbia Guide*, 94–95; Remini, *Andrew Jackson and His Indian Wars*, 257; Robertson, *Conquest by Law*, 135–38.

101. S. Banner, *How the Indians Lost Their Land*, 223–24; Demos, *Heathen School*, 257–60; Ostler, *Surviving Genocide*, 248, 266–74, unnamed soldier quoted on 270 ("the Cherokee removal"); Perdue and Green, *Columbia Guide*, 95–97, John Ridge quoted on 96 ("I have signed"); Remini, *Andrew Jackson and His Indian Wars*, 261–70.

102. S. Banner, *How the Indians Lost Their Land*, 224–25; Dupre, *Alabama's Frontiers*, 280–90, John Horry Dent quoted on 280 ("redemption"); Green, *Politics of Indian Removal*, 174–86; Ostler, *Surviving Genocide*, 257–63, 287; Perdue and Green, *Columbia Guide*, 93–94; Remini, *Andrew Jackson and His Indian Wars*, 272–73; Saunt, *Unworthy Republic*, xi–xii, 120–24.

103. Ericson, *Slavery in the American Republic*, 20–21, 113–14; Hahn, *Nation Without Borders*, 34–35; Missall and Missall, *Seminole Wars*, 10–12, 83, Thomas Jesup quoted on 126 ("This"); Ostler, *Surviving Genocide*, 274–75; Perdue and Green, *Columbia Guide*, 92–93.

104. Ericson, *Slavery in the American Republic*, 112–13; Missall and Missall, *Seminole Wars*, 124–26, 171–73; Ostler, *Surviving Genocide*, 276–82, *Tallahassee Floridian* quoted on 282 ("tear to pieces"); Perdue and Green, *Columbia Guide*, 93; Porter, *Black Seminoles*, 36–52; Remini, *Andrew Jackson and His Indian Wars*, 274–75; Saunt, *Unworthy Republic*, 280–84, 289–94, W. W. Smith quoted on 284 ("one vast").

105. Missall and Missall, *Seminole Wars*, 134–42; Ostler, *Surviving Genocide*, 279–84; Porter, *Black Seminoles*, 84–86; Saunt, *Unworthy Republic*, 305–6, Velentine Mott quoted on 306 ("cabinet").

106. Missall and Missall, *Seminole Wars*, 146–51; Ostler, *Surviving Genocide*, 280–81; Porter, *Black Seminoles*, 94–96; Saunt, *Unworthy Republic*, 288–89.

107. Ericson, *Slavery in the American Republic*, 114-15; Missall and Missall, *Seminole Wars*, 126-27, 154-56, 203-6; Ostler, *Surviving Genocide*, 277-86; Porter, *Black Seminoles*, 106-7; Saunt, *Unworthy Republic*, 294-96.

108. A. Barr, *Black Texans*, 29-30; Ericson, *Slavery in the American Republic*, 99-100; Ostler, *Surviving Genocide*, 335-36; Perdue and Green, *Columbia Guide*, 102-3; Porter, *Black Seminoles*, 111-42.

109. Kahgegahbouh quoted in S. Banner, *How the Indians Lost their Land*, 232-33; Ostler, *Surviving Genocide*, 196-201, 224-26; Rockwell, *Indian Affairs*, 136-37; Saunt, *Unworthy Republic*, 90-93.

110. Bowes, *Land Too Good for Indians*, 19-20, 42-49, William Clark quoted on 45 ("faithless"); Ostler, *Surviving Genocide*, 233-34, 242-43, 297-99; Saunt, *Unworthy Republic*, 108-10.

111. Bowes, *Land Too Good for Indians*, 19-20, 42-49; Ostler, *Surviving Genocide*, 299-306, Henry Atkinson quoted on 302 ("crushed"); Saunt, *Unworthy Republic*, 144-47.

112. Remini, *Andrew Jackson and His Indian Wars*, 258-59, Andrew Jackson quoted on 259 ("drenching") and Fanny Kemble quoted on 259 ("shriveled"); Saunt, *Unworthy Republic*, 303-4; Turner, *Red Men Calling*, 88-101.

113. Bowes, *Land Too Good for Indians*, 154-56, 167-81; Joseph Balestier quoted on 177 ("miserable race"); Guyatt, *Bind Us Apart*, 321-22; Witgen, "Seeing Red," 596-98.

114. Fuller, *Summer on the Lakes*, 46-47, 52 ("the site"); Margaret Fuller to Richard F. Fuller, July 29, 1843, in Hudspeth, *Letters of Margaret Fuller*, 3:132-33 ("It is only" and "the body").

115. Fuller, *Summer on the Lakes*, 114-15.

116. S. Banner, *How the Indians Lost Their Land*, 226-27; Saunt, *Unworthy Republic*, 306-8, Senate Committee on Indian Affairs quoted on 314 ("They are").

117. Green, *Politics of Indian Removal*, 179; Ostler, *Surviving Genocide*, 260, 270-71; Perdue and Green, *Columbia Guide*, 97; Watson, *Liberty and Power*, 111; Witgen, "Seeing Red," 581-611.

118. Hietala, *Manifest Design*, 149-50; Rockwell, *Indian Affairs*, 132-53, 157-58; Tocqueville, *Democracy in America*, Phillips Bradley, ed., 1:341-45.

119. S. Banner, *How the Indians Lost Their Land*, 223-24; Demos, *Heathen School*, 256-57; Perdue and Green, *Columbia Guide*, 95-97, 101-2, John Ridge quoted on 96 ("I have signed"); Ostler, *Surviving Genocide*, 335-36; Andrew Jackson quoted in Watson, *Liberty and Power*, 111 ("philanthropist").

120. Bowes, *Exiles and Pioneers*, 89-90; Hine and Faragher, *American West*, 160-61, Stephen Long quoted on 160 ("Great American Desert"); Potawatomis quoted in Remini, *Andrew Jackson and His Indian Wars*, 280 ("too poor"); Saunt, *Unworthy Republic*, 21.

121. Ostler, *Surviving Genocide*, 215-28, 240, 247, Black Eagle quoted on 235 ("to push"); Perdue and Green, *Columbia Guide*, 100-101.

122. Bowes, *Exiles and Pioneers*, 140-41; Guyatt, *Bind Us Apart*, 316-23; Hendrickson, *Union, Nation, or Empire*, 162.

123. S. Banner, *How the Indians Lost Their Land*, 230–31; Faragher, *Women and Men*, 4–11; Lewis Linn quoted in Hietala, *Manifest Design*, 143 ("impeding"); Trennert, *Alternative to Extinction*, 185; Unruh, *Plains Across*, 119–20; White, *It's Your Misfortune*, 189–91.

124. Dickason, *Canada's First Nations*, 200; Schmalz, *Ojibwa of Southern Ontario*, 148–49, Sir Charles Bagot quoted on 167 ("encouraged").

125. Allen, *His Majesty's Indian Allies*, 178–84; Dickason, *Canada's First Nations*, 203–4; Morse, *Report to the Secretary of War*, 19 ("expressed"); Schmalz, *Ojibwa of Southern Ontario*, 167–68; Surtees, "Land Cessions," 112–19.

126. Schmalz, *Ojibwa of Southern Ontario*, 174–75, unnamed Ojibwa quoted on 175 ("to break").

127. Dickason, *Canada's First Nations*, 209–13; D. B. Smith, *Mississauga Portraits*, 59–61.

128. Bleasdale, "Manitowaning," 148–49, Sir Francis Bond Head quoted on 148 ("greatest") and 149 ("impeding"); Chute, *Legacy of Shingwaukonse*, 69–70; Schmalz, *Ojibwa of Southern Ontario*, 131–36; D. B. Smith, *Mississauga Portraits*, 62; D. B. Smith, *Sacred Feathers*, 162–64, Saugeen Ojibwas quoted on 163–64 ("their Great Father").

129. Bleasdale, "Manitowaning," 153–57; Chute, *Legacy of Shingwaukonse*, 69–70; Schmalz, *Ojibwa of Southern Ontario*, 162–64, George Copway quoted on 163 ("large rocks"), Laurence Oliphant quoted on 163 ("poverty-stricken"); D. B. Smith, *Sacred Feathers*, 162–64, 221–22.

130. Bleasdale, "Manitowaning," 148–49; Schmalz, *Ojibwa of Southern Ontario*, 134–35, 139–42, 168–74; D. B. Smith, *Mississauga Portraits*, 62–64; D. B. Smith, *Sacred Feathers*, 164–65, Peter Jones quoted on 165 ("the policy"), John Beverley Robinson quoted on 223 ("such lands").

131. Schmalz, *Ojibwa of Southern Ontario*, 120–25, 143–46; D. B. Smith, *Sacred Feathers*, 222–23; Surtees, *Canadian Indian Policy*, 33–34.

132. Baptist, *Half Has Never Been Told*, 256–57; Libby, *Slavery and Frontier Mississippi*, 102–3; J. Rothman, *Flush Times*, 2–7.

133. Libby, *Slavery and Frontier Mississippi*, 103–4; J. Rothman, *Flush Times*, 2–9, Burrell Fox quoted on 5 ("I like"), Joseph H. Ingraham quoted on 5 ("one vast"), and James Davidson quoted on 7 ("hell-carnival").

134. Stephen Duncan quoted in Baptist, *Half Has Never Been Told*, 208 ("we will"); Dupre, *Alabama's Frontiers*, 272–73; Libby, *Slavery and Frontier Mississippi*, 75–78; J. Rothman, *Flush Times*, 10–11, Joseph Holt Ingraham quoted on 10 ("to sell").

135. Libby, *Slavery and Frontier Mississippi*, 104–9, Virgil Stewart quoted on 107 ("that they are") and 108 ("how successful"); J. Rothman, *Flush Times*, 87–91, 117–18.

136. Baptist, *Half Has Never Been Told*, 211–12; Libby, *Slavery and Frontier Mississippi*, 109–12; J. Rothman, *Flush Times*, 92–118.

137. Baptist, *Half Has Never Been Told*, 212–13; Grimsted, *American Mobbing*,

15–16; Libby, *Slavery and Frontier Mississippi*, 112–14; J. Rothman, *Flush Times*, 118–53, 212–13.

138. Baptist, *Half Has Never Been Told*, 270–76; Libby, *Slavery and Frontier Mississippi*, 114–18, Clinton town meeting quoted on 114 ("blessing"); J. Rothman, *Flush Times*, 218–34.

139. Rothman, *Flush Times*, 270–304; Schoen, *Fragile Fabric*, 159–60; Sexton, *Debtor Diplomacy*, 24–28, Alexander McNutt quoted on 27 ("mortgage").

CHAPTER 7: REVOLUTIONS

1. Borneman, *Polk*, 5–12; Dusinberre, *Slavemaster President*, 5–6, 33–48, James K. Polk quoted on 25.

2. Borneman, *Polk*, 12–14; Dusinberre, *Slavemaster President*, 24–25; A. Greenberg, *Lady First*, xiii–xv; A. Greenberg, *Wicked War*, 29–31, 72–75, Sarah Preston Hale quoted on 75 ("perhaps").

3. A. Greenberg, *Wicked War*, 95–96, Sarah Childress Polk quoted on 9.

4. A. Greenberg, *Wicked War*, 32–33; Haynes, *Unfinished Revolution*, 252–53; Silbey, *Storm over Texas*, 53–60.

5. Lynch, *Spanish American Revolutions*, 18–20, 30–31; MacLachlan, *Spain's Empire*, 107–9; Avila and Tutino, "Becoming Mexico," 239–40.

6. Liss, *Atlantic Empires*, 142–45, 166–68, 191, Miranda quoted on 142 ("infallible preliminary") and 143 ("Good God").

7. Arana, *Bolívar*, 20–21, 69–70; Langley, *Americas in the Age of Revolution*, 167–69, Francisco de Miranda quoted on 167 ("Two great"); Lynch, ed., *Latin American Revolutions*, 29, 32, 36.

8. Adelman, *Sovereignty and Revolution*, 175–76; Arana, *Bolívar*, 70–71; Klooster, *Revolutions*, 137–38; Langley, *Americas in the Age of Revolution*, 167–69.

9. Lynch, *Spanish American Revolutions*, 22–23, 28–29, Simón Bolívar quoted on 23 ("great volcano").

10. Avila and Tutino, "Becoming Mexico," 243–45; Langley, *Americas in the Age of Revolution*, 166–67; Lynch, *Spanish American Revolutions*, 23–25, Simón Bolívar quoted on 24–25 ("Americans by birth"); Rodríguez O, *Independence of Spanish America*, 114–15.

11. Arana, *Bolívar*, 3–8, 14–25; Klooster, *Revolutions*, 138–39; Lynch, *Spanish American Revolutions*, 199–201; Rodríguez O, *Independence of Spanish America*, 117–19.

12. Langley, *Americas in the Age of Revolution*, 176–77, 187–90, 194–98, Simón Bolívar quoted on 177 ("to liberate"); Lynch, *Spanish American Revolutions*, 202–218, Bolívar quoted on 212 ("madness"); Rodríguez O, *Independence of Spanish America*, 121–22, 186–90.

13. Klooster, *Revolutions*, 140–41, 155; Simón Bolívar quoted in Krauze, *Mexico*, 134 ("He who serves"); Langley, *Americas in the Age of Revolution*, 199–

200; Lynch, *Spanish American Revolutions*, 222–26, Bolívar quoted on 265 ("although they speak").

14. Avila and Tutino, "Becoming Mexico," 234–37; Lynch, *Spanish American Revolutions*, 295–302.

15. Lynch, *Spanish American Revolutions*, 296–99, Fray Antonio de San Miguel quoted on 298 ("maldistribution") and Manuel Abad y Queipo quoted on 298 ("those who have"); Russell, *History of Mexico*, 113; Tutino, *From Insurrection to Revolution*, 119–26.

16. Langley, *Americas in the Age of Revolution*, 179–80; Lynch, *Spanish American Revolutions*, 302–305, Viceroy Iturrigaray quoted on 303; Russell, *History of Mexico*, 114–16.

17. Krauze, *Mexico*, 91–95; Langley, *Americas in the Age of Revolution*, 180, Hidalgo quoted on 182 ("Their God"); Lynch, *Spanish American Revolutions*, 297–99, 305–6.

18. Krauze, *Mexico*, 97–98; Langley, *Americas in the Age of Revolution*, 180–81; Russell, *History of Mexico*, 116–17; Tutino, *From Insurrection to Revolution*, 126–29.

19. Langley, *Americas in the Age of Revolution*, 181–82; Krauze, *Mexico*, 97–98, Hidalgo quoted on 97 ("much easier"); Lynch, *Spanish American Revolutions*, 307–10, Lucas Alaman quoted on 309; Russell, *History of Mexico*, 118 ("Death to the Spaniards"); Tutino, *From Insurrection to Revolution*, 129–33.

20. Krauze, *Mexico*, 98–103, Pedro Armendáriz quoted on 103 ("stared"); Langley, *Americas in the Age of Revolution*, 182–83; Lynch, *Spanish American Revolutions*, 311–12.

21. Krauze, *Mexico*, 103–14, Morelos quoted on 112; Langley, *Americas in the Age of Revolution*, 183–84; Lynch, *Spanish American Revolutions*, 312–18; Russell, *History of Mexico*, 122–23.

22. Avila and Tutino, "Becoming Mexico," 248–50; Krauze, *Mexico*, 112–17.

23. Avila and Tutino, "Becoming Mexico," 252–54; Krauze, *Mexico*, 119–26; Lynch, *Spanish American Revolutions*, 318–22, Simón Bolívar quoted on 322; Poinsett, *Notes on Mexico*, 67–69; Rodríguez O, *Independence of Spanish America*, 205–10; Russell, *History of Mexico*, 130–31, 142–43, 167.

24. Avila and Tutino, "Becoming Mexico," 253–54; Calderón de la Barca, *Life in Mexico*, 65–66; Krauze, *Mexico*, 126–30, Simón Bolívar quoted on 130 ("most perverse"); Lynch, *Spanish American Revolutions*, 322–24; Poinsett, *Notes on Mexico*, 52–53, 63–64; Russell, *History of Mexico*, 143–44.

25. Avila and Tutino, "Becoming Mexico," 256–58; DeLay, *War of a Thousand Deserts*, 23–25; Guardino, *Dead March*, 13–14; Hahn, *Nation Without Borders*, 13–14; Lynch, *Spanish American Revolutions*, 323–25; Russell, *History of Mexico*, 145–46; Torget, *Seeds of Empire*, 76–81, 150–51.

26. Avila and Tutino, "Becoming Mexico," 254–55; DeLay, *War of a Thousand Deserts*, 23–24; Lynch, *Spanish American Revolutions*, 331–34, Carlos Maria Bustamante quoted on 333.

27. Guardino, *Dead March*, 308–9; Hurtado, *Indian Survival*, 36–37; Reséndez, *Other Slavery*, 247–48; White, *"It's Your Misfortune,"* 39–42.

28. Hyde, *Empires, Nations, and Families*, 172–80, 312–13; Reséndez, *Other Slavery*, 247–50, Salvador Vallejo quoted on 248–49.

29. Hyde, *Empires, Nations, and Families*, 183–87.

30. Limerick, *Something in the Soil*, 129–30, Henrich Lienhard quoted on 138–39 ("the long"); J. M. O'Brien, "Indians and the California Gold Rush," 103–4; Reséndez, *Other Slavery*, 254–55.

31. Hurtado, *Indian Survival*, 55–71; Reséndez, *Other Slavery*, 255–58.

32. Avila and Tutino, "Becoming Mexico," 258–59; Haynes, *Unfinished Revolution*, 213; Lynch, *Spanish American Revolution*, 326–27; Reséndez, *Other Slavery*, 219; Russell, *History of Mexico*, 135–37.

33. Delay, *War of a Thousand Deserts*, 30–31, 38–49, 62–70, 114–17, 317–40; Reséndez, *Other Slavery*, 219–30; St. John, *Line in the Sand*, 31–32.

34. DeLay, *War of a Thousand Deserts*, 23–24; Krauze, *Mexico*, 129–33; Russell, *History of Mexico*, 120; St. John, *Line in the Sand*, 15–16.

35. DeLay, *War of a Thousand Deserts*, 71–72; Krauze, *Mexico*, 133–35, Alamán quoted on 135 ("The history") and 142 ("enterprising"); Russell, *History of Mexico*, 146–47.

36. John Adams to James Lloyd, Mar. 27, 1815, Founders Online, National Archives, (https://founders.archives,gov/documents/Adams/99-02-02-6440); Arana, *Bolívar*, 73–74; Fitz, *Our Sister Republics*, 1–16, 23–24, 36–43, 80–115; Johnson, *Hemisphere Apart*, 1–2, 21–28, 44–46.

37. Arana, *Bolívar*, 73–74; Bushnell, *Simón Bolívar*, 15–16, 71, 150–51; DeLay, *War of a Thousand Deserts*, 3–5; Simón Bolívar quoted in Fitz, *Our Sister Republics*, 246; Sexton, *Monroe Doctrine*, 57–58.

38. James Monroe to Thomas Jefferson, May 27, 1820, Founders Online, National Archives (http://founders.archives.gov/documents/Jefferson/98-01-02-1294).

39. Fitz, *Our Sister Republics*, 179–88; J. J. Johnson, *Hemisphere Apart*, 19–20; James Lewis, *American Union*, 177–78; Sexton, *Monroe Doctrine*, 39–44, 68–70, George Canning quoted on 68.

40. Fitz, *Our Sister Republics*, 157–58; Sexton, *Monroe Doctrine*, 6–7, 49–52, 63–69.

41. Fitz, *Our Sister Republics*, 158–59; Howe, *What Hath God Wrought*, 111–12; Sexton, *Monroe Doctrine*, 6–7, 19–21, Henry Clay quoted on 20.

42. Chambers, *No God but Gain*, 4–6; Sexton, *Monroe Doctrine*, 3–5, 11, 60–63, 66, 69.

43. Sexton, *Monroe Doctrine*, 9–13, 16–18, 35–37, 56–59, James Monroe quoted on 56 and John Quincy Adams quoted on 57 ("then") and 59 ("different").

44. Arana, *Bolívar*, 353; Bushnell, *Simón Bolívar*, 150–52; Fitz, *Our Sister Republics*, 194–200; Sexton, *Monroe Doctrine*, 73–78, Andrew Jackson quoted on 78.

45. Fitz, *Our Sister Republics*, 203–8, 212–13, Thomas Hart Benton quoted on

203, John Randolph quoted on 208; Karp, *Vast Southern Empire*, 13–14; Sexton, *Monroe Doctrine*, 76–78.

46. Fitz, *Our Sister Republics*, 205–24, John Floyd quoted on 219; Thomas Hart Benton quoted in J. J. Johnson, *Hemisphere Apart*, 77–78.

47. Fitz, *Our Sister Republics*, 214–15; John H. Marable quoted in Wilentz, *Rise of American Democracy*, 261.

48. Baptist, *Half Has Never Been Told*, 299–300; Karp, *Vast Southern Empire*, 4–7, 90, Abel P. Upshur quoted on 25; Winsboro and Knetsch, "Florida Slaves," 75–76.

49. Karp, *Vast Southern Empire*, 2–4, 57–58, 70–71, 81, William Harper quoted on 58 ("gone through"), William Lowndes Yancey quoted on 101 ("immense superiority"); Schoen, *Fragile Fabric*, 169–70.

50. Karp, *Vast Southern Empire*, 4–7, 48–49, 70–71, 88–89; Schoen, "Calculating the Price," 194–200.

51. Karp, *Vast Southern Empire*, 8, 12, 15–21, 41–42, *Richmond Enquirer*, Apr. 14, 1840 quoted on 20 ("the center"), J. G. F. Wurdemann quoted on 61 ("to form"), Henry Wise quoted on 75 ("the coils"), Francis Pickens quoted on 105 ("Our systems"); Schoen, *Fragile Fabric*, 160–61.

52. Karp, *Vast Southern Empire*, 17–21, Andrew Stevenson quoted on 18; Winsboro and Knetch, "Florida Slaves," 51–78.

53. Horton and Horton, *In Hope of Liberty*, 245; Karp, *Vast Southern Empire*, 17–21; Sinha, *Slave's Cause*, 411–14; Winsboro and Knetch, "Florida Slaves," 58–61.

54. Winsboro and Knetch, "Florida Slaves," 51–57, 61–63, 69–75, John C. Calhoun quoted on 75.

55. Fehrenbacher and McAfee, *Slaveholding Republic*, 156–68; Karp, *Vast Southern Empire*, 25–26.

56. Karp, *Vast Southern Empire*, 31, 40–41, 51–55, 105, Matthew Maury quoted on 55 ("raven").

57. Abel Upshur quoted in Hietala, *Manifest Design*, 13–14; Karp, *Vast Southern Empire*, 32–35, 38–41, 56–57, John Quincy Adams quoted on 34.

58. Chambers, *No God but Gain*, 18–20, 24–25, 83–84, 92–96, 121–22; Karp, *Vast Southern Empire*, 60–61; Schafer, *Anna Madgigine Jai Kingsley*, 20 ("Sugar"); Sartorius, "Cuban Counterpoint," 175–200.

59. Chambers, *No God but Gain*, 105–6, 109–11, 121–23, 166–68; Fitz, *Our Sister Republics*, 19–21, 204–5, John Randolph quoted on 205; J. J. Johnson, *Hemisphere Apart*, 4–5; Karp, *Vast Southern Empire*, 59–60; Sexton, *Monroe Doctrine*, 70–73.

60. Karp, *Vast Southern Empire*, 58–69, Robert Blair Campbell quoted on 64 ("No punishment") and 66 ("no sickly"); Reid-Vazquez, *Year of the Lash*, 1–2.

61. G. C. Anderson, *Conquest of Texas*, 18–42; Cantrell, *Stephen F. Austin*, 107–8; Reséndez, *Changing National Identities*, 19–22; St. John, *Line in the Sand*, 16–17; Torget, *Seeds of Empire*, 57–58, 67–68.

62. G. C. Anderson, *Conquest of Texas*, 46–48; Reséndez, *Changing National Identities*, 27–29, Francisco Ruiz quoted on 27 ("honest"); Torget, *Seeds of Empire*, 68–76; Weber, *Mexican Frontier*, 162–63.

63. Cantrell, *Stephen F. Austin*, 117–18, 124; Nugent, *Habits of Empire*, 142–44; Reséndez, *Changing National Identities*, 28–29; Weber, *Mexican Frontier*, 163.

64. Cantrell, *Stephen F. Austin*, 104–70, 176–77, 182–84; Hine and Faragher, *American West*, 163–64, Austin quoted on 164 ("I look"); Hyde, *Empires, Nations, and Families*, 204–7, 209, 212; Torget, *Seeds of Empire*, 59–66, 81–89, 92–96, 157–59; Weber, *Mexican Frontier*, 164–66.

65. Cantrell, *Stephen F. Austin*, 189–90; Torget, *Seeds of Empire*, 139–48, 157–58, José de las Piedras quoted on 147 ("her inhabitants"), Agustin Viesca quoted on 148 ("their entire"), Austin quoted on 155 ("Nothing is").

66. G. C. Anderson, *Conquest of Texas*, 60–64; DeLay, *War of a Thousand Deserts*, 5–6; Hyde, *Empires, Nations, and Families*, 212–13; Reséndez, *Changing National Identities*, 40–44 (Declaration of the Republic of Fredonia, quoted on 44); Torget, *Seeds of Empire*, 113–16

67. G. C. Anderson, *Conquest of Texas*, 64; Cantrell, *Stephen F. Austin*, 183–85, Austin quoted on 185 ("unnatural"); Reséndez, *Changing National Identities*, 44–45.

68. G. C. Anderson, *Conquest of Texas*, 72; Lucas Alamán quoted in Fitz, *Our Sister Republics*, 243 ("Where"); Hahn, *Nation Without Borders*, 21–22.

69. Henderson, *Glorious Defeat*, 51–55, 59–61, Manuel de Mier y Terán quoted on 59 ("They pull") and 61 ("execrable traitor"); St. John, *Line in the Sand*, 17–18, Mier y Terán quoted on 17 ("precarious"); Torget, *Seeds of Empire*, 137–38; Weber, *Mexican Frontier*, xvii–xviii, 31, 162.

70. Reséndez, *Other Slavery*, 218–19, 238–39; Torget, *Seeds of Empire*, 139–44, José María Tornel quoted on 144 ("It is not").

71. Torget, *Seeds of Empire*, 139–50, Ramón Músquiz quoted on 145 ("robust"),

72. R. Campbell, *An Empire for Slavery*, 23–24, Clarissa's contract quoted on 24, Stephen F. Austin quoted on 38 ("Texas"); Cantrell, *Stephen F. Austin*, 220–21; Reséndez, *Changing National Identities*, 22–25; Torget, *Seeds of Empire*, 151–55, Austin quoted on 153 ("to keep") and 155 ("to say").

73. G. C. Anderson, *Conquest of Texas*, 79; Krauze, *Mexico*, 138; Reséndez, *Changing National Identities*, 122–23; Torget, *Seeds of Empire*, 161–62; Weber, *Mexican Frontier*, 171–75, Mier y Terán quoted on 172 ("no physical force"), Stephen F. Austin quoted on 175 ("dam out").

74. G. C. Anderson, *Conquest of Texas*, 88, 95–6, and 97–107; Hyde, *Empires, Nations, and Families*, 216–18; Nugent, *Habits of Empire*, 150–52; Torget, *Seeds of Empire*, 156–57, 164–66.

75. Hine and Faragher, *American West*, 169–70, David Crockett quoted on 170; Reséndez, *Changing National Identities*, 165–69; Torget, *Seeds of Empire*, 168–69, 179–80.

76. F. Anderson and Cayton, *Dominion of War*, 266–67, Sam Houston quoted on 267; *Telegraph and Texas Register*, Oct. 17, 1835, quoted in Howe, *What*

Hath God Wrought, 662 ("to give"); Reséndez, *Changing National Identities*, 207–10; Torget, *Seeds of Empire*, 171–73.

77. Campbell, *Empire for Slavery*, 35; masters of Brazoria quoted in Hahn, *Nation Without Borders*, 40 ("on the tip–toe"); Torget, *Seeds of Empire*, 172–73, Santa Anna quoted on 173 ("Shall we").

78. F. Anderson and Cayton, *Dominion of War*, 266–68; Hine and Faragher, *American West*, 171–72; Krauze, *Mexico*, 139–40; Torget, *Seeds of Empire*, 168, 173–74, 180–82.

79. Brack, *Mexico Views Manifest Destiny*, 79–80; Haynes, *Unfinished Revolution*, 232–33; Henderson, *Glorious Defeat*, 124–25; Hyde, *Empires, Nations, and Families*, 356–57; Reséndez, *Changing National Identities*, 197–200; Torget, *Seeds of Empire*, 219–20, 224–27.

80. DeLay, *War of a Thousand Deserts*, 64–65; Hyde, *Empires, Nations, and Families*, 51–52; Nugent, *Habits of Empire*, 152–54; Torget, *Seeds of Empire*, 183–88.

81. Campbell, *Empire for Slavery*, 40–48, B. J. White quoted on 41 ("whipd"), Texas provisional legislators quoted on 45 ("infusion"); Foley, *White Scourge*, 19; Hahn, *Nation Without Borders*, 41–42.

82. Campbell, *Empire for Slavery*, 50–58; Torget, *Seeds of Empire*, 195–96.

83. Montejano, *Anglos and Mexicans*, 26–28, Edward Dwyer quoted on 28 ("not sufficiently"); Teja, *Revolution Remembered*, viii, 24–28, 34–35, 41–49, 73–74, 89–101, Juan N. Seguín quoted on 90; Torget, *Seeds of Empire*, 222, 256–57, Americans quoted on 204 ("the friends").

84. G. C. Anderson, *Conquest of Texas*, 169–75, 177–80, Mirabeau Lamar quoted on 174; Torget, *Seeds of Empire*, 203–6; Siegel, *Political History*, 49–50, 67–68, 100–104, 108–109.

85. DeLay, *War of a Thousand Deserts*, 76–77; Hyde, *Empires, Nations, and Families*, 303–4; Kennedy, *Cotton and Conquest*, 76–87, Warren Angus Ferris quoted on 82 ("land mania").

86. G. C. Anderson, *Conquest of Texas*, 176, 181–94; DeLay, *War of a Thousand Deserts*, 76–78; Hoig, *Tribal Wars*, 153–65; Hyde, *Empires, Nations, and Families*, 303–6; Torget, *Seeds of Empire*, 208–12.

87. Nugent, *Habits of Empire*, 153–54; Torget, *Seeds of Empire*, 183–85, 191–92, 204, 208–9, 223–24, L. A. McHenry quoted on 183 ("the most"), French visitors quoted on 193 ("detested" and "merely"), Washington Miller quoted on 244 ("We are").

88. Henderson, *Glorious Defeat*, 120–21; Silbey, *Storm over Texas*, 13–17.

89. Jackson, *American Radicals*, 161–62; Torget, *Seeds of Empire*, 212–15, 221–22, 242, James Morgan quoted on 215 ("Old Sam").

90. G. C. Anderson, *Conquest of Texas*, 195–97; Freehling, *Road to Disunion*, 378–81; Torget, *Seeds of Empire*, 237–41, Alphonse Dubois de Saligny quoted on 209 ("Slavery").

91. Freehling, *Road to Disunion*, 380–82; Karp, *Vast Southern Empire*, 11, 25–28,

86, John Quincy Adams quoted on 25; Torget, *Seeds of Empire*, 244–50, Ashbel Smith quoted on 241.

92. Haynes, *Unfinished Revolution*, 226, 230–39, unnamed Texas diplomat quoted on 239 ("You would be"); Hietala, *Manifest Design*, 17–25; Robert Walker quoted in Karp, *Vast Southern Empire*, 83; Torget, *Seeds of Empire*, 187, 240–41.

93. Freehling, *Road to Disunion*, 415–17, Andrew Jackson quoted on 416 ("hordes" and "servile"); Haynes, *Unfinished Revolution*, 226, 239–42, Jackson quoted on 226 ("iron hoop" and "oceans"); Hietala, *Manifest Design*, 13–15, Jackson quoted on 24 ("our slaves" and "I am gasping").

94. A. Greenberg, *Wicked War*, 11–12; Howe, *What Hath God Wrought*, 677–80; John Tyler quoted in Lepore, *These Truths*, 235–36; Silbey, *Storm over Texas*, 28–46; Torget, *Seeds of Empire*, 244.

95. A. Greenberg, *Wicked War*, 12–14, Abel P. Upshur quoted on 14; Hietala, *Manifest Design*, 13–15; Karp, *Vast Southern Empire*, 86–87; Torget, *Seeds of Empire*, 245–46.

96. A. Greenberg, *Wicked War*, 69–70; Hietala, *Manifest Design*, 26–27; Silbey, *Storm over Texas*, 33–34.

97. Haynes, *Unfinished Revolution*, 242; Hietala, *Manifest Design*, 26–33, Robert J. Walker quoted on 29–31; Schoen, *Fragile Fabric*, 188–89; Silbey, *Storm over Texas*, 34–35.

98. Hietala, *Manifest Design*, 33–34, Robert Owen quoted on 47 ("what modern"), and George Dallas quoted on 50 ("on Texas"); Silbey, *Storm over Texas*, 36–38, Charles Ingersoll quoted on 37–38.

99. Haynes, *Unfinished Revolution*, 240–41; Hietala, *Manifest Design*, 64–70, John B. Jones quoted on 66 ("fatal"), John Tyler quoted on 68, and John Chipman quoted on 180 ("starving"); Karp, *Vast Southern Empire*, 100–101. For Britain's cotton imports, see Torget, *Seeds of Empire*, 212.

100. John L. O'Sullivan, "Annexation," *Democratic Review*, 17 (July 1845): 5; Hietala, *Manifest Design*, 8–9; Horsman, *Race and Manifest Destiny*, 219–20; Howe, *What Hath God Wrought*, 705–6.

101. Lee, *Masters of the Middle Waters*, 197–99; Hietala, *Manifest Design*, 191–93, John L. O'Sullivan quoted on 193.

102. DeLay, *War of a Thousand Deserts*, 288; Howe, *What Hath God Wrought*, 708–11; Hyde, *Empires, Nations, and Families*, 392–93, Jose Castro quoted on 392 ("Americans").

103. A. Greenberg, *Wicked War*, 57–58; Hietala, *Manifest Design*, 59–62, Caleb Cushing quoted on 59–60; Hyde, *Empires, Nations, and Families*, 195–98; Karp, *Vast Southern Empire*, 44–45, *New Orleans Courier*, Feb. 18, 1840 quoted on 44–45 ("planting" and "all of").

104. Haynes, *Unfinished Revolution*, 213–14, 233–34; Hietala, *Manifest Design*, 55–76, John Harmanson quoted on 87 ("fifty years").

105. Hietala, *Manifest Design*, 86–88, 200–203, Asa Whitney quoted on 200

("would place"); Jones and Rakestraw, *Prologue to Manifest Destiny*, 239–40; E. West, *Essential West*, 47–48.

106. C. Clark, *Social Change in America*, 205–6; Guardino, *Dead March*, 20–21; Hietala, *Manifest Design*, 6–7, 98–100, 255–56; Silbey, *Storm over Texas*, 10–12, 26–27, Henry Clay quoted on 26.

107. A. Greenberg, *Wicked War*, 16–17; Haynes, *Unfinished Revolution*, 243; Karp, *Vast Southern Empire*, 92–93; Lepore, *These Truths*, 234–38.

108. Freehling, *Road to Disunion*, 407–10; A. Greenberg, *Wicked War*, 15–20, Henry Clay quoted on 18 ("I regard"); Silbey, *Storm over Texas*, 39–50; Torget, *Seeds of Empire*, 250–51.

109. A. Greenberg, *Wicked War*, 33–34, 41–43, Philip Hone quoted on 42 ("General Jackson's"), 59–63, Jackson quoted on 62 ("didn't shoot"); Haynes, *Unfinished Revolution*, 128–31, 246–47; Howe, *What Hath God Wrought*, 680–89, Andrew Jackson quoted on 689 ("I thank"); Silbey, *Storm over Texas*, 68–79.

110. Haynes, *Unfinished Revolution*, 246–50; Hendrickson, *Union, Nation, or Empire*, 173–74, John Quincy Adams quoted on 174; Hietala, *Manifest Design*, 46–49; Karp, *Vast Southern Empire*, 95–96; Silbey, *Storm over Texas*, 80–90; Sinha, *Slave's Cause*, 478–80.

111. Hyde, *Empires, Nations, and Families*, 92–97, 133–34, 403–4; Nugent, *Habits of Empire*, 164–75, Charles Elliot quoted on 183 ("Settlers"); Robbins, *Landscapes of Promise*, 64–65, 70–73, 77–78, James Douglas quoted on 70 ("restless Americans"); Stuart, *United States Expansionism*, 102–103.

112. Earle, *Jacksonian Antislavery*, 131–32; A. Greenberg, *Wicked War*, xiii; Hietala, *Manifest Destiny*, 180–84; Howe, *What Hath God Wrought*, 715–20, *New York Herald* quoted on 720 ("We can"); Jones and Rakestraw, *Prologue to Manifest Destiny*, 206, 243–63; Silbey, *Storm over Texas*, 111–20.

113. A. Barr, *Black Texans*, 29–32; Karp, *Vast Southern Empire*, 110; Torget, *Seeds of Empire*, 234.

114. Clary, *Eagles and Empire*, 68–73, 80–85, 96–99, Ethan Hitchcock quoted on 85 ("We have"); A. Greenberg, *Wicked War*, 77–78, 84, 95, 101–2; Guardino, *Dead March*, 31, 34–35, 71–76.

115. A. Greenberg, *Wicked War*, 103–5; Hietala, *Manifest Design*, 85–86; Howe, *What Hath God Wrought*, 739–43, James K. Polk quoted on 741 ("After reiterated") and 743 ("to defray").

116. A. Greenberg, *Wicked War*, 104–8; Hietala, *Manifest Design*, 187–88; William Duer quoted on 258 ("cant"); Lucas Alamán quoted in Krauze, *Mexico*, 143 ("most unjust war").

117. John C. Calhoun quoted in A. Greenberg, *Wicked War*, 108 ("It sets"); Hietala, *Manifest Design*, 117–18, 155–56, 242–43, Calhoun quoted on 242 ("Our people").

118. A. Greenberg, *Wicked War*, xvii, 110–14, *Illinois State Register*, quoted on 113 ("are reptiles") and 115 ("but little"); Horsman, *Race and Manifest Destiny*, 212–16; Texan master quoted in Oakes, *Ruling Race*, 131.

119. DeLay, *War of a Thousand Deserts*, 246–47, Waddy Thompson quoted on 247 ("I do not"); A. Greenberg, *Manifest Manhood*, 22–23.

120. Clary, *Eagles and Empire*, 128–29; Guardino, *Dead March*, 6–17; Nugent, *Habits of Empire*, 200–201.

121. Clary, *Eagles and Empire*, 135–38; Guardino, *Dead March*, 6–13, 170; Howe, *What Hath God Wrought*, 746–48; Nugent, *Habits of Empire*, 200–201; Russell, *History of Mexico*, 161–64, 206–7.

122. Clary, *Eagles and Empire*, 132–34; DeLay, *War of a Thousand Deserts*, 282–88, Chihuahua representatives quoted on 286 ("desolated"); A. Greenberg, *Wicked War*, 56–57.

123. Guardino, *Dead March*, 6–10, 67–69, 89–90, 169–74; A. Greenberg, *Manifest Manhood*, 25–26, Jane Swisshelm quoted on 25; Henderson, *Glorious Defeat*, 188–89.

124. A. Greenberg, *Wicked War*, 99, 115–16, Henry Clay quoted on 124 ("unhappy War"); Guardino, *Dead March*, 85–86; Thomas Hart Benton quoted in Russell, *History of Mexico*, 199.

125. Clary, *Eagles and Empire*, 88–92; A. Greenberg, *Wicked War*, 122–24; Guardino, *Dead March*, 311–13; Hyde, *Empires, Nations, and Families*, 392–95; Nugent, *Habits of Empire*, 192–93.

126. Clary, *Eagles and Empire*, 174–79, 206–8, 240–45, 255–57; A. Greenberg, *Wicked War*, 123–24, Robert Stockton quoted on 123; Guardino, *Dead March*, 309–10, 313–15.

127. Clary, *Eagles and Empire*, 179–88; DeLay, *War of a Thousand Deserts*, 265–66, George Ruxton quoted on 275 ("mountain"); Hyde, *Empires, Nations, and Families*, 380–83; Reséndez, *Changing National Identities*, 237–40, 249–53, Manuel Álvarez quoted on 250 ("far preferable").

128. Clary, *Eagles and Empire*, 245–47, 264–65; DeLay, *War of a Thousand Deserts*, 266–67, 278–79; Hyde, *Empires, Nations, and Families*, 384–86; Reséndez, *Changing National Identities*, 254–58.

129. Clary, *Eagles and Empire*, 68–69, 111–16, 191–203; A. Greenberg, *Wicked War*, 98–99, 119–21, 127–28, *Sangamo Journal* quoted on 120 ("The prowess"); Guardino, *Dead March*, 77–84, 134–41.

130. A. Greenberg, *Wicked War*, 143–44; Guardino, *Dead March*, 187; Nugent, *Habits of Empire*, 203–4.

131. Guardino, *Dead March*, 87–88; Henderson, *Glorious Defeat*, 130–32, crowd quoted on 132 ("Death"); Krauze, *Mexico*, 141, 143: Russell, *History of Mexico*, 150–53.

132. A. Greenberg, *Wicked War*, 148–49; Guardino, *Dead March*, 141–42; Howe, *What Hath God Wrought*, 766–67; Karp, *Vast Southern Empire*, 114–15; Russell, *History of Mexico*, 198.

133. Clary, *Eagles and Empire*, 271–82; A. Greenberg, *Wicked War*, 157–58; Guardino, *Dead March*, 145–57; Russell, *History of Mexico*, 198–99.

134. Clary, *Eagles and Empire*, 305–6; A. Greenberg, *Wicked War*, 160–61, Zachary Taylor quoted on 199.

135. Clary, *Eagles and Empire*, 119–20, Mexican broadside quoted on 120 ("Their motto"); Guardino, *Dead March*, 5–6, 26–27, 30, 212–22.

136. Clary, *Eagles and Empire*, 129–31; Guardino, *Dead March*, 91–101.

137. Guardino, *Dead March*, 101–7, Arkansas volunteer quoted on 112; Howe, *What Hath God Wrought*, 771–72.

138. A. Greenberg, *Wicked War*, 102, 131–34, Frank Hardy quoted on 132–33 ("They are"); Guardino, *Dead March*, 107–25, volunteers quoted on 116 ("greasers" and "greaseritas").

139. Clary, *Eagles and Empire*, 118–20, 283–84, anonymous soldier quoted on 119 ("The majority"), and Zachary Taylor quoted on 283; A. Greenberg, *Wicked War*, 130–31; Guardino, *Dead March*, 110–12, 157–58; Winfield Scott quoted in Russell, *History of Mexico*, 210.

140. Clary, *Eagles and Empire*, 165, 201–3, 268–69, 282–84; A. Greenberg, *Wicked War*, 156, 194–95, *St. Louis Republican*, quoted on 194; Guardino, *Dead March*, 128–30, 151.

141. Clary, *Eagles and Empire*, 120–22; A. Greenberg, *Wicked War*, xvii, 132–34; Guardino, *Dead March*, 1, 114–15, 125–26, 132–33; Hietala, *Manifest Design*, 157–58.

142. A. Greenberg, *Wicked War*, 101–102, 190–91, 205, 151, 153, 287n15, Ulysses S. Grant quoted on vii ("I do not"); Guardino, *Dead March*, 1–2, 116–17, 120–21, 208–10, Henry Smith Lane quoted on 121 ("a graveyard"); Grant quoted in Karp, *Vast Southern Empire*, 113 ("republic").

143. A. Greenberg, *Wicked War*, 203–4; Guardino, *Dead March*, 28–29, 36–38, 105–6, 213–14, 251–52.

144. A. Greenberg, *Wicked War*, 204–5; Guardino, *Dead March*, 250–59.

145. A. Greenberg, *Wicked War*, 116–17, 193, 196–98, Massachusetts legislature quoted on 196, and Jane Swisshelm quoted on 198; Guardino, *Dead March*, 203–6, Thomas Corwin quoted on 206 ("each chapter"); Sinha, *Slave's Cause*, 482–83.

146. Clary, *Eagles and Empire*, 299–304, Stephen F. Nunnalee quoted on 300 ("heart-rending"); A. Greenberg, *Wicked War*, 169–71, William Tobey quoted on 171 ("you would"); Guardino, *Dead March*, 189–92; Russell, *History of Mexico*, 199–200.

147. Clary, *Eagles and Empire*, 311–16, unnamed Mexican quoted on 315 ("continuous"); A. Greenberg, *Wicked War*, 200–205; Guardino, *Dead March*, 193–201; Russell, *History of Mexico*, 200–201.

148. Clary, *Eagles and Empire*, 359–60; A. Greenberg, *Wicked War*, 205–10; Guardino, *Dead March*, 229–31, 240–50, 260–67; Russell, *History of Mexico*, 201–3.

149. Clary, *Eagles and Empire*, 372–79, D. H. Hill quoted on 377 ("corrupted"); A. Greenberg, *Wicked War*, 210–13; Guardino, *Dead March*, 277–88; Henderson, *Glorious Defeat*, 172–73.

150. Clary, *Eagles and Empire*, 379–80, George Meade quoted on 379 ("five or

six"); A. Greenberg, *Wicked War*, 222–23; Guardino, *Dead March*, 294–300, 335–38.

CHAPTER 8: SOIL

1. Borneman, *Polk*, 261–66; Howe, *What Hath God Wrought*, 800–814; Ohrt, *Defiant Peacemaker*, x–xi, 13–17, 43–58.

2. A. Greenberg, *Wicked War*, 128–29, 221, James Buchanan quoted on 129; Guardino, *Dead March*, 323–24; Nugent, *Habits of Empire*, 207–9.

3. A. Greenberg, *Manifest Manhood*, 26; Guardino, *Dead March*, 324; Henderson, *Glorious Defeat*, 175–76; Hietala, *Manifest Design*, 155–67, *New York Herald* quoted on 155 ("inferior races"), William Wick quoted on 167 ("I do not want"); Karp, *Vast Southern Empire*, 120.

4. Castillo, *Treaty of Guadalupe Hidalgo*, 22–27; A. Greenberg, *Wicked War*, 77–78, 91–93, 173–75, 221–23, 246–47, 256, Nicholas P. Trist quoted on 218 ("a thing"); Ohrt, *Defiant Peacemaker*, 133–37.

5. Castillo, *Treaty of Guadalupe Hidalgo*, 36–41; A. Greenberg, *Wicked War*, 221–23; Henderson, *Glorious Defeat*, 172–73; Krauze, *Mexico*, 144; Russell, *History of Mexico*, 204.

6. A. Greenberg, *Wicked War*, 238–40, 258–59, Nicholas Trist quoted on 239, James K. Polk quoted on 240; Guardino, *Dead March*, 303–4, 325–26; Ohrt, *Defiant Peacemaker*, 138–42.

7. Borneman, *Polk*, 300–308; Castillo, *Treaty of Guadalupe Hidalgo*, 41–42; Guardino, *Dead March*, 326–27; Ohrt, *Defiant Peacemaker*, 142–46; Russell, *History of Mexico*, 204–6, 210, 212.

8. Borneman, *Polk*, 309–13; A. Greenberg, *Wicked War*, 260–61; Guardino, *Dead March*, 328; Nugent, *Habits of Empire*, 213–14; Ohrt, *Defiant Peacemaker*, 147–48.

9. Castillo, *Treaty of Guadalupe Hidalgo*, 44–46; John Quincy Adams quoted in Karp, *Vast Southern Empire*, 99 ("turning-point"); Nugent, *Habits of Empire*, 215–16; Ohrt, *Defiant Peacemaker*, 148–50.

10. A. Greenberg, *Wicked War*, 261–64, James K. Polk quoted on 264; Lepore, *These Truths*, 252–53; Ohrt, *Defiant Peacemaker*, 153–62.

11. Hietala, *Manifest Design*, 215–23, 245–49, Louis McLane quoted on 234 ("not the slightest"), John Fairfield quoted on 249 ("I had rather"); Sam Houston quoted in Borneman, *Polk*, 11.

12. Guardino, *Dead March*, 2–3; Sam Houston and William Worth quoted in Foley, *White Scourge*, 21; Hietala, *Manifest Design*, 2, 166, 251–52; E. West, *Essential West*, 46–47.

13. F. Anderson and Cayton, *Dominion of War*, 283–84, Abraham Lincoln quoted on 284; Lepore, *These Truths*, 252–53, James DeBow quoted on 253 ("nearly").

14. Carrigan and Webb, *Forgotten Dead*, 21–22, 28–29, 34–36, 44–45, 56; Cas-

tillo, *Treaty of Guadalupe Hidalgo*, 48–49, 51, 66–77, 83; Foley, *White Scourge*, 24–25; Varon, *Disunion*, 200.

15. Trennert, *Alternative to Extinction*, 118–127, James S. Calhoun quoted on 126.

16. G. C. Anderson, *Conquest of Texas*, 293–94; Carrigan and Webb, *Forgotten Dead*, 45–50, 98; Castillo, *Treaty of Guadalupe Hidalgo*, 83–85; Montejano, *Anglos and Mexicans*, 30–32, José María Rodríguez quoted on 31, and Emanuel Domench quoted on 31–32 ("The Americans").

17. Howe, *What Hath God Wrought*, 813–18; Rohrbough, "Mining," 114–18; White, *It's Your Misfortune*, 191–92, naval captain quoted on 192.

18. Howe, *What Hath God Wrought*, 813–16, 820; Rohrbough, "Mining," 114–18.

19. Carrigan and Webb, *Forgotten Dead*, 51–53, 58–60, Andrew Stone quoted on 98 ("You mentioned"); W. J. Ghent quoted in Trennert, *Alternative to Extinction*, 178 ("all the misfits").

20. Carrigan and Webb, *Forgotten Dead*, 34–41, Chauncey Canfield quoted on 35 ("It made them") and Thomas J. Green quoted on 36; Limerick, *Something in the Soil*, 215–17.

21. Carrigan and Webb, *Forgotten Dead*, 28, 33–34, 62–63, Clarence King quoted on 28 ("To shoot"); Hyde, *Empires, Nations, and Families*, 468–69; Rohrbough, "Mining," 117.

22. Hyde, *Empires, Nations, and Families*, 463–65; Madley, *American Genocide*, 67–172; J. M. O'Brien, "Indians and the California Gold Rush," 101–6; Reséndez, *Other Slavery*, 261–65.

23. Delay, *War of a Thousand Deserts*, 243–45, 288–310; Guardino, *Dead March*, 326–28; Russell, *History of Mexico*, 210, 212–13, Apache quoted on 212 ("We must steal"); St. John, *Line in the Sand*, 32–34; Trennert, *Alternative to Extinction*, 112–22, John M. Washington quoted on 113 ("They must").

24. Bigler, *Forgotten Kingdom*, 62–63; Hyde, *Empires, Nations, and Families*, 359.

25. Arrington and Britton, *Mormon Experience*, 86–88, 93–96, 114; Bigler, *Forgotten Kingdom*, 21–24; Howe, *What Hath God Wrought*, 726–27; Hyde, *Empires, Nations, and Families*, 367–68.

26. Bigler, *Forgotten Kingdom*, 40–45, Young quoted on 40–41; A. Greenberg, *Wicked War*, 121–22, James K. Polk quoted on 122; Hyde, *Empires, Nations, and Families*, 388–90.

27. Arrington and Britton, *Mormon Experience*, 96–105, 111–13; Bigler, *Forgotten Kingdom*, 29–30; E. E. Campbell, *Establishing Zion*, 5–9, 35–36, 41–55, 84–85, Brigham Young quoted on 44 ("There is no"); Hyde, *Empires, Nations, and Families*, 454–55.

28. Bigler, *Forgotten Kingdom*, 34–38, 43–45, 53; E. E. Campbell, *Establishing Zion*, 136–37.

29. E. E. Campbell, *Establishing Zion*, 58–59, 70–71, 135–39, Brigham Young quoted on 135.

30. Arrington and Britton, *Mormon Experience*, 96–105, 114–15, 121–26, 130–36;

Bigler, *Forgotten Kingdom*, 38–39; E. E. Campbell, *Establishing Zion*, 1–2, 13–14, 136–37; Hyde, *Empires, Nations, and Families*, 455–57.

31. Arrington and Britton, *Mormon Experience*, 101–19; E. E. Campbell, *Establishing Zion*, 9–10, 58–59.

32. Arrington and Britton, *Mormon Experience*, 112, 145–48, Brigham Young quoted on 148; E. E. Campbell, *Establishing Zion*, 93–95; Hyde, *Empires, Nations, and Families*, 458–59, Book of Mormon quoted on 458 ("to overthrow" and "become").

33. Arrington and Britton, *Mormon Experience*, 145–48, Brigham Young quoted on 148 ("you must not"); E. E. Campbell, *Establishing Zion*, 98–99, Brigham Young quoted on 99 ("dominion"), 101 ("take possession"), and 127 ("The land").

34. Arrington and Britton, *Mormon Experience*, 152–53; Bigler, *Forgotten Kingdom*, 65–73, Young quoted on 72 ("Let it be"); E. E. Campbell, *Establishing Zion*, 97–111.

35. Arrington and Britton, *Mormon Experience*, 150–51, Brigham Young quoted on 150; Bigler, *Forgotten Kingdom*, 66–67; E. E. Campbell, *Establishing Zion*, 132–33.

36. Arrington and Britton, *Mormon Experience*, 110–11; Bigler, *Forgotten Kingdom*, 40–41, 46–55, Brigham Young quoted on 47 ("as a sovereign"); E. E. Campbell, *Establishing Zion*, 78, 145–46, 201–15; Hyde, *Empires, Nations, and Families*, 452–58, Brigham Young quoted on 458 ("Would sooner").

37. Miller, *Prophetic Worlds*, 45–62, Spokane Prophet quoted on 45–53; Whaley, *Oregon*, 53.

38. Jetté, *Hearth of the Crossed Races*, 71–72; Miller, *Prophetic Worlds*, 45–62.

39. Whaley, *Oregon*, 99–107, Cyrus Shepard quoted on 126.

40. Stern, *Chiefs and Change*, 45–47; Whaley, *Oregon*, 108–13, Margaret Smith quoted on 113 ("Your heart"), Jason Lee quoted on 131 ("The truth"), George Gary quoted on 141 ("had experienced").

41. Whaley, *Oregon*, 122–23, 128, 134, 149–50.

42. Jetté, *Hearth of the Crossed Races*, 103.

43. Bunting, *Pacific Raincoast*, 52–61; Coleman, *Dangerous Subjects*, 6, 10, 55–46.

44. Bunting, *Pacific Raincoast*, 52–61, Gustavus Hines quoted on 57 ("give place"); Coleman, *Dangerous Subjects*, 74–77, Peter H. Burnett quoted on 76 ("We came"); Jetté, *Hearth of the Crossed Races*, 139–40, 169–70; Whaley, *Oregon*, 136–55, Philip Edwards quoted on 148 ("gaunt").

45. Bunting, *Pacific Raincoast*, 56–58; Jetté, *Hearth of the Crossed Races*, 147–48; Robbins, *Landscapes of Promise*, 71–78; Whaley, *Oregon*, 174.

46. Whaley, *Oregon*, 165–67, Chinook man quoted on 167.

47. David Douglas quoted in Calloway, *One Vast Winter Count*, 334 ("flocks"); Jetté, *Hearth of the Crossed Races*, 61–69; Morrison, *Outpost*, 209–12; Robbins, *Landscapes of Promise*, 58–60, 69–70; Whaley, *Oregon*, 91–94, 162–63.

48. Hyde, *Empires, Nations, and Families*, 404–5, 423–24; Jeffrey, *Converting the West*, 104–26, 148–49, Narcissa Whitman quoted on 108 ("thick darkness")

and 148–49 ("We must"); Ruby and Brown, *Cayuse Indians*, 70–83; Miller, *Prophetic Worlds*, 96–102.

49. Jeffrey, *Converting the West*, 205–21; Miller, *Prophetic Worlds*, 103–7, 127–28; Ruby and Brown, *Cayuse Indians*, 84–112; Stern, *Chiefs and Change*, 168–75.

50. Tilokaikt quoted in Jeffrey, *Converting the West*, 220; Miller, *Prophetic Worlds*, 109–10, H. A. G. Lee quoted on 110 ("declar[d]"); Morrison, *Outpost*, 449–52; Ruby and Brown, *Cayuse Indians*, 113–71, *New York Tribune* quoted on 171; Stern, *Chiefs and Change*, 176–225.

51. Bunting, *Pacific Raincoast*, 60–63, *Oregon Statesman* quoted on 61; Jetté, *Hearth of the Crossed Races*, 193–96; Whaley, *Oregon*, 176–84.

52. Bunting, *Pacific Raincoast*, 64–66; Robert Hull quoted in Hyde, *Empires, Nations, and Families*, 426 ("These Indians"); Robbins, *Landscapes of Promise*, 85–86; Whaley, *Oregon*, 14–15, 178–79.

53. Coleman, *Dangerous Subjects*, 4–7, 71–73, George B. Currey quoted on 73 ("to escape"); McLagan, *Peculiar Paradise*, 11, Robert W. Morrison quoted on 24 ("Unless"), Jesse Applegate quoted on 29 ("hated slavery"); Whaley, *Oregon*, 175–76.

54. Coleman, *Dangerous Subjects*, 5–7, 61–63, 102–3, 109–12, 119–21, 139–40, 145–46; Jetté, *Hearth of the Crossed Races*, 174–79; McLagan, *Peculiar Paradise*, 17–18; Robbins, *Landscapes of Promise*, 82–83.

55. Coleman, *Dangerous Subjects*, 61–63, 140–41; McLagan, *Peculiar Paradise*, 17–18, 24–31, Samuel Thurston quoted on 31.

56. Coleman, *Dangerous Subjects*, 155–58; McLagan, *Peculiar Paradise*, 27–28, petition quoted on 27.

57. Faragher, *Women and Men*, 16–20; Unruh, *Plains Across*, 90–117; White, *It's Your Misfortune*, 189–91.

58. Faragher, *Women and Men*, 27–39; Unruh, *Plains Across*, 49–50, 149–55; White, *It's Your Misfortune*, 202, 207.

59. Faragher, *Women and Men*, 31–32; Unruh, *Plains Across*, 177–89.

60. S. Banner, *How the Indians Lost their Land*, 231; Ostler, *Plains Sioux*, 32–34; Trennert, *Alternative to Extinction*, 25–26, 138–39, 163–65.

61. Ostler, *Plains Sioux*, 34–35; Trennert, *Alternative to Extinction*, 9, 14–15, 18–19, 160–61, 168–69, 179–80, Thomas Fitzpatrick quoted on 175–76.

62. Hietala, *Manifest Design*, 140–42, 151–52, Ambrose Sevier quoted on 151; Ostler, *Plains Sioux*, 35–36; Trennert, *Alternative to Extinction*, 29–31, 36–37, 58–60; White, *It's Your Misfortune*, 90–92.

63. Ostler, *Plains Sioux*, 37–38; Trennert, *Alternative to Extinction*, 187–92, Black Hawk quoted on 190.

64. Karp, *Vast Southern Empire*, 119–24, Solomon Northrup quoted on 123, William Gilmore Simms quoted on 124.

65. D. B. Davis, *Problem of Slavery in the Age of Emancipation*, 286–87; Karp, *Vast Southern Empire*, 128–130, Duff Green quoted on 128; Schoen, *Fragile Fabric*, 190–95.

66. Haynes, *Unfinished Revolution*, 278–81; Hietala, *Manifest Design*, 167–68, 245–47, William Wick quoted on 167; Richards, *Slave Power*, 152–53.

67. Hietala, *Manifest Design*, 168–69, William Sawyer quoted on 169.

68. Earle, *Jacksonian Antislavery*, 124–25, 132–34; Richards, *Slave Power*, 150–52; Silbey, *Storm over Texas*, 123–25; Sinha, *Slave's Cause*, 481–82; Varon, *Disunion*, 193–94.

69. Earle, *Jacksonian Antislavery*, 129–31, 135–36, David Wilmot quoted on 131 ("By God"); Hietala, *Manifest Design*, 122–25, Wilmot quoted on 125 ("sympathy" and "a fair"); Varon, *Disunion*, 181–86.

70. Earle, *Jacksonian Antislavery*, 136–37, David Wilmot quoted on 136.

71. Dusinberre, *Slavemaster President*, 142–48; Hietala, *Manifest Design*, 126–28, 228–29, Arthur Bagby quoted on 128 ("never consent"); Oakes, *Ruling Race*, 147–48; Varon, *Disunion*, 191–92.

72. Freeman, *Field of Blood*, 144–46, Robert Toombs quoted on 145; Silbey, *Storm over Texas*, 126–28; Varon, *Disunion*, 192–93; *Charleston Mercury* quoted in Wilentz, *Rise of American Democracy*, 600.

73. Haynes, *Unfinished Revolution*, 271; Hietala, *Manifest Design*, 133, 220, 231–32, 250–54, James Faran quoted on 237 ("The South"); Richards, *Slave Power*, 153–54, 159–60; Silbey, *Storm over Texas*, 124–25.

74. A. Greenberg, *Wicked War*, 196; Hietala, *Manifest Design*, 126–27.

75. Howe, *What Hath God Wrought*, 767–68, 832–33; Silbey, *Storm over Texas*, 136–40; Wilentz, *Rise of American Democracy*, 596–97, Free Soil motto quoted on 625 ("Free Soil").

76. Earle, *Jacksonian Antislavery*, 138–39, David Wilmot quoted on 138 ("white man's"); Wilentz, *Rise of American Democracy*, 596–97, James Russell Lowell quoted on 605, and Free Soiler quoted on 627.

77. A. Greenberg, *Manifest Manhood*, 34–35; Hietala, *Manifest Design*, 249–50; Richards, *Slave Power*, 179–80, Cass quoted on 180 ("cover"); Varon, *Disunion*, 199–201, *North Star* quoted on 201 ("Gross"); Wilentz, *Rise of American Democracy*, 615–28.

78. Borneman, *Polk*, 328–44; Clary, *Eagles and Empire*, 416; A. Greenberg, *Wicked War*, 266–68.

79. Wilentz, *Rise of American Democracy*, 629–31, George Julian quoted on 629.

80. Horton and Horton, *In Hope of Liberty*, 233–34; Ricks, "The 1848 *Pearl* Escape," 195–201, 211–12, unnamed slave quoted on 201; Sinha, *Slave's Cause*, 401–3, Daniel Drayton quoted on 401.

81. Asch and Musgrove, *Chocolate City*, 90–92; Fehrenbacher, *Slaveholding Republic*, 50–52, Joshua R. Giddings quoted on 52; Ricks, "The 1848 *Pearl* Escape," 200–17; Sinha, *Slave's Cause*, 401–4.

82. Fehrenbacher, *Slaveholding Republic*, 50–51, Abraham Venable quoted on 51; Ricks, "The 1848 *Pearl* Escape," 214–15; Sinha, *Slave's Cause*, 403–4.

83. Fehrenbacher, *Slaveholding Republic*, 49–51, Henry S. Foote quoted on 49 ("the age"); Grimsted, *American Mobbing*, 267–68, John C. Calhoun quoted

on 268 and Foote quoted on 268 ("grace"); Ricks, "The 1848 *Pearl* Escape," 215–16; Sinha, *Slave's Cause*, 403.

84. Fehrenbacher, *Slaveholding Republic*, 52–53, 81–82; Grimsted, *American Mobbing*, 268–69, John C. Calhoun and Stephen A. Douglas quoted on 269; Ricks, "The 1848 *Pearl* Escape," 218–19.

85. Freehling, *Road to Disunion*, 487–499; Holt, *Rise and Fall of the American Whig Party*, 461–62, 474–76; Varon, *Disunion*, 207–8.

86. Henry Clay quoted in Hendrickson, *Union, Nation, or Empire*, 195; Holt, *Rise and Fall of the American Whig Party*, 463–65; Schoen, *Fragile Fabric*, 197–200; Varon, *Disunion*, 209–11.

87. Freehling, *Road to Disunion*, 489–90, 495–502; Hendrickson, *Union, Nation, or Empire*, 195–96; Holt, *Rise and Fall of the American Whig Party*, 459–60, 476–84; Horton and Horton, *Slavery*, 146–47.

88. Varon, *Disunion*, 216–17; Wilentz, *Rise of American Democracy*, 639–41, Calhoun quoted on 639.

89. Deyle, *Carry Me Back*, 73–76; Freeman, *Field of Blood*, 148–49, *Boston Herald* quoted on 173.

90. Freehling, *Road to Disunion*, 493; Freeman, *Field of Blood*, 174; Hendrickson, *Union, Nation, or Empire*, 196–97; Holt, *Rise and Fall of the American Whig Party*, 517–52; Varon, *Disunion*, 227–28.

91. Freeman, *Field of Blood*, 174–76, unnamed onlooker quoted on 174 ("a night"); Holt, *Rise and Fall of the American Whig Party*, 566–97; Sinha, *Slave's Cause*, 490–91; Varon, *Disunion*, 207, 225–26; Wilentz, *Rise of American Democracy*, 642–45, Salmon P. Chase quoted on 644.

92. Foner, *Gateway to Freedom*, 25–26; Freehling, *Road to Disunion*, 502–5; Horton and Horton, *Slavery*, 148–49; Richards, *Slave Power*, 180–81; Wilentz, *Rise of American Democracy*, 645–50.

93. Hahn, *Political Worlds*, 38–40; Jackson, *American Radicals*, 182–88; Wilentz, *Rise of American Democracy*, 645–50, Pennsylvania newspaper quoted on 647, Frederick Douglass quoted on 650.

94. Delbanco, *War Before the War*, 42; Jackson, *American Radicals*, 171, 184–85, Theodore Parker quoted on 185 ("The South"); McDaniel, *Problem of Democracy*, 196–97; Varon, *Disunion*, 226–29.

95. Blackett, *Beating Against the Barriers*, 87–90; Delbanco, *War Before the War*, 267–68; Sinha, *Slave's Cause*, 436–38; Wilentz, *Rise of American Democracy*, 645–46.

96. Blackett, *Beating Against the Barriers*, 97–98, unnamed abolitionist quoted on 98 ("as ready").

97. Blackett, *Beating Against the Barriers*, 90–96, William Crafts quoted on 87 ("claws"), *Aberdeen Journal* quoted on 99; Sinha, *Slave's Cause*, 438.

98. Delbanco, *War Before the War*, 269–70, Wendell Phillips quoted on 269; Ralph Waldo Emerson quoted in Kersh, *Dreams of a More Perfect Union*, 151.

99. Ralph Orth and Alfred Ferguson, eds., *Miscellaneous Notebooks of Ralph*

Waldo Emerson, 1843–1847 (Cambridge: Harvard University Press, 1977), 9:430–31; Torget, *Seeds of Empire*, 267.

100. McCurry, *Masters of Small Worlds*, 259–60; Varon, *Disunion*, 186–89, 196–97, Robert W. Roberts quoted on 186 ("sickly morbid'), John Petit quoted on 186 ("fawning"), and David Wilmot quoted on 187 ("stamp").

101. Ulysses S. Grant quoted in F. Anderson and Cayton, *Dominion of War*, 283; Guardino, *Dead March*, 4–5; Varon, *Disunion*, 183.

EPILOGUE

1. Coleman, *Dangerous Subjects*, 48; Hyde, *Empires, Nations, and Families*, 97–104, John Work quoted on 102; Morrison, *Outpost*, 3–27, 38–57; Van Kirk, *"Many Tender Ties,"* 4–93.

2. Coleman, *Dangerous Subjects*, 50–52; Hyde, *Empires, Nations, and Families*, 104–23; Jetté, *Hearth of the Crossed Races*, 43–45; Morrison, *Outpost*, 37–38, 71–110; Whaley, *Oregon*, 84–85.

3. Hyde, *Empires, Nations, and Families*, 109–14, Eloisa McLoughlin quoted on 113; Rich, *Fur Trade*, 274–75; Whaley, *Oregon*, 83–84, 89–90, John McLoughlin quoted on 90.

4. Coleman, *Dangerous Subjects*, 51–53, Charles Wilkes quoted on 52; Hyde, *Empires, Nations, and Families*, 95–97, Thomas Farnham quoted on 96; McLagan, *Peculiar Paradise*, 12–13.

5. Hyde, *Empires, Nations, and Families*, 142–45, John McLoughlin quoted on 144; Jetté, *Hearth of the Crossed Races*, 7–11, 42–61, 91, 102, 141–42, 148–49, 181–82, 196–97, 210–13; Whaley, *Oregon*, 169–70, 175–76, John Minto quoted on 140 ("Indian families"), Joel Palmer quoted on 170 ("mongrel").

6. Coleman, *Dangerous Subjects*, 90; Hyde, *Empires, Nations, and Families*, 135–45, 406, 507–11; Morrison, *Outpost*, 385–86; Stern, *Chiefs and Change*, 48; Whaley, *Oregon*, 126.

7. Jetté, *Hearth of the Crossed Races*, 150–51, Elizabeth Miller Wilson quoted on 151.

8. Coleman, *Dangerous Subjects*, 144; Morrison, *Outpost*, 453–70, Thurston quoted on 462 ("triumphant"), John McLoughlin quoted on 470.

9. Hyde, *Empires, Nations, and Families*, 143–45; Morrison, *Outpost*, 477–78.

BIBLIOGRAPHY

Abbott, William W., et al., eds. *The Papers of George Washington, Confederation Series*, 6 vols. (Charlottesville: University Press of Virginia, 1992–97).

Abbott, William W., et al., eds. *The Papers of George Washington, Presidential Series*, 10 vols. to date (Charlottesville: University Press of Virginia, 1987–).

Ackerman, Bruce. *The Failure of the Founding Fathers: Jefferson, Marshall, and the Rise of Presidential Democracy* (Cambridge: Harvard University Press, 2005).

Adelman, Jeremy. *Sovereignty and Revolution in the Iberian Atlantic* (Princeton: Princeton University Press, 2006).

Allen, Robert S. *His Majesty's Indian Allies: British Indian Policy in the Defence of Canada, 1774–1815* (Toronto: Dundurn Press, 1992).

Allgor, Catherine. *Parlor Politics: In Which the Ladies of Washington Help Build a City and a Government* (Charlottesville: University Press of Virginia, 2000).

Ames, Kenneth M., and Herbert D. G. Machner, eds. *Peoples of the Northwest Coast: Their Archeology and Prehistory* (London: Thames & Hudson, 2000).

Anderson, Fred, and Andrew Cayton. *The Dominion of War: Empire and Liberty in North America, 1500–2000* (New York: Viking Penguin, 2005).

Anderson, Gary Clayton. *The Conquest of Texas: Ethnic Cleansing in the Promised Land, 1820–1875* (Norman: University of Oklahoma Press, 2005), 18–26.

Andrews, Dee E. *The Methodists and Revolutionary America, 1760–1800: The Shaping of an Evangelical Culture* (Princeton: Princeton University Press, 2000).

Antal, Sandy. *A Wampum Denied: Procter's War of 1812* (Ottawa: Carleton University Press, 1997).

Appleby, Joyce. *Inheriting the Revolution: The First Generation of Americans* (Cambridge: Harvard University Press, 2000).

Aptheker, Herbert. *American Negro Slave Revolts* (New York: Columbia University Press, 1943).

Arana, Marie. *Bolívar: American Liberator* (New York: Simon & Schuster, 2013).

Aron, Stephen. *American Confluence: The Missouri Frontier from Borderland to Border State* (Bloomington: Indiana University Press, 2006).

Aron, Stephen. *How the West Was Lost: The Transformation of Kentucky from Daniel Boone to Henry Clay* (Baltimore: Johns Hopkins University Press, 1996).

Arrington, Leonard, and Davis Bitton. *The Mormon Experience: A History of the Latter-Day Saints* (Urbana: University of Illinois Press, 1992).

Ash, Chris Myers, and George Derek Musgrove. *Chocolate City: A History of Race and Democracy in the Nation's Capital* (Chapel Hill: University of North Carolina Press, 2017).

Avila, Alfredo, and John Tutino. "Becoming Mexico: The Conflictive Search for a North American Nation," in Tutino, ed., *New Countries: Capitalism, Revolutions, and Nations in the Americas, 1750–1870* (Durham, NC: Duke University Press, 2016), 233–77.

Ayers, Edward L. *Vengeance and Justice: Crime and Punishment in the Nineteenth-Century American South* (New York: Oxford University Press, 1984).

Baker, Jean H. *Affairs of Party: The Political Culture of Northern Democrats in the Mid-Nineteenth Century* (New York: Fordham University Press, 1998).

Ball, Charles. *Fifty Years in Chains*, ed. Philip S. Foner (New York: Dover Publications, 1970 reprint of 1837).

Balogh, Brian. *A Government Out of Sight: The Mystery of National Authority in Nineteenth-Century America* (New York: Cambridge University Press, 2009).

Banner, James M., Jr. *To the Hartford Convention: The Federalists and the Origins of Party Politics in Massachusetts, 1789–1815* (New York: Alfred A. Knopf, 1970).

Banner, Stuart. *How the Indians Lost Their Land: Law and Power on the Frontier* (Cambridge: Harvard University Press, 2005).

Baptist, Edward E. *The Half Has Never Been Told: Slavery and the Making of American Capitalism* (New York: Basic Books, 2014).

Barr, Alwyn. *Black Texans: A History of African-Americans in Texas, 1528–1995* (Norman: University of Oklahoma Press, 1995).

Barr, Julianna. *Peace Came in the Form of a Woman: Indians and Spaniards in the Texas Borderlands* (Chapel Hill: University of North Carolina Press, 2007).

Barrett, Richard. *Richard Barrett's Journal: New York and Canada, 1816* (Winfield, KS: Wedgestone Press, 1983).

Bayly, C. A. *Imperial Meridian: The British Empire and the World, 1780–1830* (London: Addison, Wesley, Longman, 1989).

Beckert, Sven. *Empire of Cotton: A Global History* (New York: Alfred A. Knopf, 2014).

Beckert, Sven, and Seth Rockman, eds. *Slavery's Capitalism: A New History of American Economic Development* (Philadelphia: University of Pennsylvania Press, 2016).

Beeman, Richard R. *Plain, Honest Men: The Making of the American Constitution* (New York: Random House, 2009).

Ben-Atar, Doron, and Barbara B. Oberg. "Introduction: The Paradoxical Legacy of the Federalists," in Ben-Atar and Oberg, eds., *Federalists Reconsidered* (Charlottesville: University Press of Virginia, 1998), 1–16.

Benn, Carl. *The Iroquois in the War of 1812* (Toronto: University of Toronto Press, 1998).

Berkin, Carol. *A Brilliant Solution: Inventing the American Constitution* (New York: Harcourt, 2002).

Berkin, Carol. *Revolutionary Mothers: Women in the Struggle for America's Independence* (New York: Alfred A. Knopf, 2005).

Berlin, Ira. *Many Thousands Gone: The First Two Centuries of Slavery in North America* (Cambridge: Harvard University Press, 1998).

Bigler, David L. *Forgotten Kingdom: The Mormon Theocracy in the American West, 1847–1896* (Spokane: Arthur H. Clark, 1998).

Blackburn, Robin. *The Overthrow of Colonial Slavery, 1776–1848* (New York: Verso Press, 1988).

Blackett, Richard J. M. *Beating Against the Barriers: Biographical Essays in Nineteenth-Century Afro-American History* (Baton Rouge: Louisiana State University Press, 1986).

Blackett, Richard J. M. *Making Freedom: The Underground Railroad and the Politics of Slavery* (Chapel Hill: University of North Carolina Press, 2013).

Bleasdale, Ruth. "Manitowaning: An Experiment in Indian Settlement," *Ontario History* 66 (Sept. 1974): 147–57.

Blight, David W. *Frederick Douglass: Prophet of Freedom* (New York: Simon & Schuster, 2018).

Bodenhorn, Howard. *A History of Banking in Antebellum America: Financial Markets and Economic Development in an Era of Nation-Building* (New York: Cambridge University Press, 2000).

Bolster, W. Jeffrey. *Black Jacks: African American Seamen in the Age of Sail* (Cambridge: Harvard University Press, 1997).

Borneman, Walter R. *Polk: The Man Who Transformed the Presidency and America* (New York: Random House, 2008).

Bothwell, Robert. *The Penguin History of Canada* (Toronto: Penguin Canada, 2006).

Bouton, Terry. *Taming Democracy: "The People," the Founders, and the Troubled Ending of the American Revolution* (New York: Oxford University Press, 2007).

Bowes, John P. *Exiles and Pioneers: Eastern Indians in the Trans-Mississippi West* (New York: Cambridge University Press, 2007).

Bowes, John P. *Land Too Good for Indians: Northern Indian Removal* (Norman: University of Oklahoma Press, 2010).

Boyd, Julian P., et al., eds. *The Papers of Thomas Jefferson*, 43 vols. to date (Princeton: Princeton University Press, 1950–).

Boydston, Jeanne. "The Woman Who Wasn't There: Women's Market Labor and the Transition to Capitalism in the United States," in Paul A. Gilje, ed., *Wages of Independence: Capitalism in the Early American Republic* (Madison: Madison House, 1997), 23–47.

Brack, Gene M. *Mexico Views Manifest Destiny, 1821–1846: An Essay on the Origins of the Mexican War* (Albuquerque: University of New Mexico Press, 1975).

Bradburn, Douglas. *The Citizenship Revolution: Politics and the Creation of the American Union, 1774–1804* (Charlottesville: University of Virginia Press, 2009).

Breen, Patrick H. *The Land Shall be Deluged in Blood: A New History of the Nat Turner Revolt* (New York: Oxford University Press, 2015).

Brown, Richard D. *Self-Evident Truths: Contesting Equal Rights from the Revolution to the Civil War* (New Haven: Yale University Press, 2017).

Brown, Richard D. *The Strength of a People: The Idea of an Informed Citizenry in America, 1650–1870* (Chapel Hill: University of North Carolina Press, 1996).

Brown, Roger H. *The Republic in Peril: 1812* (New York: W. W. Norton, 1971).

Brown, Vincent. "A Vapor of Dread: Observations on Racial Terror and Vengeance in the Age of Revolution," in Thomas Bender, Lauren Dubois, and Richard Rabinowitz, eds., *Revolution!: The Atlantic World Reborn* (New York: New-York Historical Society, 2011), 177–98.

Bruce, Dickson D., Jr. *Violence and Culture in the Antebellum South* (Austin: University of Texas Press, 1979).

Bruce, William Cabell. *John Randolph of Roanoke, 1773–1833*, 2 vols. (New York: G. P. Putnam's Sons, 1922).

Brugger, Robert J., et al., eds. *Papers of James Madison, Secretary of State Series*, 11 vols. to date (Charlottesville: University of Virginia Press, 1986–).

Buel, Richard, Jr. *America on the Brink: How the Political Struggle over the War of 1812 Almost Destroyed the Young Republic* (New York: Palgrave Macmillan, 2005).

Bullock, Steven C. "A Pure and Sublime System: The Appeal of Post-Revolutionary Freemasonry," *Journal of the Early Republic* 9 (Fall 1989): 359–74.

Bullock, Steven C. *Revolutionary Brotherhood: Freemasonry and the Transformation of the American Social Order, 1730–1840* (Chapel Hill: University of North Carolina Press, 1996).

Bullock, Steven C. "The Revolutionary Transformation of American Freemasonry, 1752–1792," *William and Mary Quarterly*, 3rd ser., vol. 47 (July 1990): 347–69.

Bunting, Robert. *The Pacific Raincoast: Environment and Culture in an American Eden, 1778–1900* (Lawrence: University Press of Kansas, 1997).

Burin, Eric. *Slavery and the Peculiar Solution: A History of the American Colonization Society* (Gainesville: University Press of Florida, 2005).

Burstein, Andrew. *America's Jubilee* (New York: Vintage Books, 2001).

Burstein, Andrew. *The Passions of Andrew Jackson* (New York: Alfred A. Knopf, 2003).

Bushman, Richard L. *Joseph Smith and the Beginnings of Mormonism* (Urbana: University of Illinois Press, 1988).

Bushman, Richard L. *The Refinement of America: Persons, Houses, Cities* (New York: Alfred A. Knopf, 1992).

Bushnell, David. *Simón Bolívar: Liberation and Disappointment* (New York: Pearson, 2004).

Butler, Jon. "Coercion, Miracle, Reason: Rethinking the American Religious Experience in the Revolutionary Age," in Ronald Hoffman and Peter J. Albert, eds., *Religion in a Revolutionary Age* (Charlottesville: University Press of Virginia, 1994), 1–30.

Calderón de la Barca, Fanny. *Life in Mexico: The Letters of Fanny Calderón de la*

Barca, ed. Howard T. and Marion Hall Fisher (Garden City, NY: Doubleday & Co., 1966).

Calloway, Colin G. *The American Revolution in Indian Country: Crisis and Diversity in Native American Communities* (New York: Cambridge University Press, 1995).

Calloway, Colin G. *Crown and Calumet: British-Indian Relations, 1783–1815* (Norman: University of Oklahoma Press, 1987).

Calloway, Colin G. "The End of an Era: British-Indian Relations in the Great Lakes Region after the War of 1812," *Michigan Historical Review* 12 (Fall 1986): 1–20.

Calloway, Colin G. *The Indian World of George Washington: The First President, the First Americans, and the Birth of the Nation* (New York: Oxford University Press, 2018).

Calloway, Colin G. *One Vast Winter Count: The Native American West Before Lewis and Clark* (Lincoln: University of Nebraska Press, 2003).

Camp, Stephanie M. H. *Closer to Freedom: Enslaved Women and Everyday Resistance in the Plantation South* (Chapel Hill: University of North Carolina Press, 2004).

Campbell, Eugene E. *Establishing Zion: The Mormon Church in the American West, 1847–1869* (Salt Lake City: Signature Books, 1988).

Campbell, Randolph B. *An Empire for Slavery: The Peculiar Institution in Texas, 1821–1865* (Baton Rouge: Louisiana State University Press, 1989).

Candler, John. *Brief Notices of Hayti: With Its Condition, Resources, and Prospects* (London: Thomas Ward & Co., 1842).

Cantrell, Gregg. *Stephen F. Austin: Empresario of Texas* (New Haven: Yale University Press, 1999).

Careless, J. M. S. *The Union of the Canadas: The Growth of Canadian Institutions, 1841–1857* (Toronto: McClelland & Stewart, 1967).

Carp, Benjamin L. "Jefferson's Embargo: National Intent and Sectional Effects," in Joanne B. Freeman and Johann N. Neem, eds., *Jeffersonians in Power: The Rhetoric of Opposition Meets the Reality of Governing* (Charlottesville: University of Virginia Press, 2019), 128–47.

Carrigan, William D., and Clive Webb. *Forgotten Dead: Mob Violence Against Mexicans in the United States, 1848–1928* (New York: Oxford University Press, 2013).

Carroll, Francis M. *A Good and Wise Measure: The Search for the Canadian-American Boundary, 1783–1842* (Toronto: University of Toronto Press, 2001).

Carter, Clarence Edwin, ed. *The Territorial Papers of the United States*, 11 vols. (Washington, DC: Government Printing Office, 1940).

Castillo, Richard Griswold del. *The Treaty of Guadalupe Hidalgo: A Legacy of Conflict* (Norman: University of Oklahoma Press, 1990).

Cayton, Andrew R. L. *The Frontier Republic: Ideology and Politics in the Ohio Country, 1780–1825* (Kent, Ohio: Kent State University Press, 1986).

Cayton, Andrew R. L. "Radicals in the 'Western World': The Federalist Conquest of Trans-Appalachian North America," in Doron Ben-Atar and Barbara Oberg, eds., *Federalists Reconsidered* (Charlottesville: University of Virginia Press, 1998), 77–96.

Chambers, Stephen M. *No God but Gain: The Untold Story of Cuban Slavery, the Monroe Doctrine, and the Making of the United States* (New York: Verso, 2015).

Chase, Philander D., et al., eds. *The Papers of George Washington, Revolutionary War Series*, 22 vols. to date (Charlottesville: University of Virginia Press, 1985–).

Chernow, Ron. *Washington: A Life* (New York: Penguin Press, 2010).

Chopra, Ruma. *Choosing Sides: Loyalists in Revolutionary America* (New York: Rowman & Littlefield, 2013).

Chopra, Ruma. *Unnatural Rebellion: Loyalists in New York City During the Revolution* (Charlottesville: University of Virginia Press, 2011).

Chute, Janet E. *The Legacy of Shingwaukonse: A Century of Native Leadership* (Toronto: University of Toronto Press, 1998).

Clark, Christopher. *Social Change in America from the Revolution Through the Civil War* (Chicago: Ivan R. Dee, 2006).

Clavin, Matthew J. *The Battle of Negro Fort: The Rise and Fall of a Fugitive Slave Community* (New York: New York University Press, 2019).

Cogliano, Francis D. *Emperor of Liberty: Thomas Jefferson's Foreign Policy* (New Haven: Yale University Press, 2014).

Cohen, Patricia Cline. *The Murder of Helen Jewett: The Life and Death of a Prostitute in Nineteenth-Century New York* (New York: Alfred A. Knopf, 1998).

Coleman, Kenneth R. *Dangerous Subjects: James D. Saules and the Rise of Black Exclusion in Oregon* (Corvallis: Oregon State University Press, 2017).

Cook, Warren L. *Flood Tide of Empire: Spain and the Pacific Northwest, 1543–1819* (New Haven: Yale University Press, 1973).

Cornell, Saul. *The Other Founders: Anti-Federalism & the Dissenting Tradition in America, 1788–1828* (Chapel Hill: University of North Carolina Press, 1999).

Corrigan, Mary Beth. " 'Whether They Be Ours or No, They May be Heirs of the Kingdom': The Pursuit of Family Ties Among Enslaved People," in Paul Finkelman and Donald R. Kennon, eds., *In the Shadow of Freedom: The Politics of Slavery in the National Capital* (Athens: Ohio University Press, 2011), 169–94.

Costanzo, Adam. *George Washington's Washington: Visions for the National Capital in the Early American Republic* (Athens: University of Georgia Press, 2018).

Cotlar, Seth. *Tom Paine's America: The Rise and Fall of Transatlantic Radicalism in the Early Republic* (Charlottesville: University of Virginia Press, 2011).

Cott, Nancy F. *Bonds of Womanhood: 'Woman's Sphere' in New England, 1780–1835* (New Haven: Yale University Press, 1997).

Cox, Caroline. *A Proper Sense of Honor: Service and Sacrifice in George Washington's Army* (Chapel Hill: University of North Carolina Press, 2004).

Craig, Gerald M. *Upper Canada: The Formative Years, 1784–1841* (Toronto: McClelland & Stewart, 1963).

Crawford, Mark, ed. *Encyclopedia of the Mexican-American War* (Santa Barbara: ABC-Clio, 1999).

Crawford, Mary M., ed. "Mrs. Lydia B. Bacon's Journal, 1811–1812," *Indiana Magazine of History* 40 (Dec. 1944): 367–86, and vol. 41 (Mar. 1945): 59–79.

Cruikshank, E. A., ed. *The Correspondence of the Honourable Peter Russell*, 3 vols. (Toronto: Ontario Historical Society, 1932–36).

Cruikshank, E. A., ed. *The Correspondence of Lieut. Governor John Graves Simcoe, with Allied Documents Relating to His Administration of the Government of Upper Canada*, 5 vols. (Toronto: Ontario Historical Society, 1923–31).

Curry, Leonard P. *The Free Black in Urban America, 1800–1850: The Shadow of the Dream* (Chicago: University of Chicago Press, 1981).

Cusick, James G. *The Other War of 1812: The Patriot War and the American Invasion of Spanish East Florida* (Gainesville: University Press of Florida, 2003).

Dagenais, Maxime. "Introduction," in Maxime Dagenais and Julien Mauduit, eds., *Revolutions Across Borders: Jacksonian America and the Canadian Rebellion* (Montreal: McGill-Queen's University Press, 2019), 3–24.

Dangerfield, George. *The Era of Good Feelings* (New York: Harcourt, Brace & Co., 1952).

Davidson, Cathy N. *Revolution and the Word: The Rise of the Novel in America* (New York: Oxford University Press, 1987).

Davis, David Brion. *The Problem of Slavery in the Age of Emancipation* (New York: Alfred A. Knopf, 2014).

Davis, David Brion. *The Problem of Slavery in the Age of Revolution, 1770–1823* (Ithaca: Cornell University Press, 1975).

Daws, Gavan. *Shoal of Time: A History of the Hawaiian Islands* (New York: Macmillan, 1968).

DeLay, Brian. *War of a Thousand Deserts: Indian Raids and the U.S.-Mexican War* (New Haven: Yale University Press, 2008).

Delbanco, Andrew. *The War Before the War: Fugitive Slaves and the Struggle for America's Soul from the Revolution to the Civil War* (New York: Penguin, 2018).

Demos, John P. *The Heathen School: A Story of Hope and Betrayal in the Age of the Early Republic* (New York: Alfred A. Knopf, 2014).

Deyle, Steven. *Carry Me Back: The Domestic Slave Trade in American Life* (New York: Oxford University Press, 2005).

Dickason, Olive Patricia. *Canada's First Nations: A History of Founding Peoples from Earliest Times* (Don Mills, ON: Oxford University Press Canada, 2002).

Dickens, Charles. *American Notes* (New York: Modern Library, 1996).

Dickey, J. D. *Empire of Mud: The Secret History of Washington, D.C.* (Guilford, CT: Lyons Press, 2014).

Dierksheide, Christa. *Amelioration and Empire: Progress and Slavery in the Plantation Americas* (Charlottesville: University of Virginia Press, 2014).

Dillon, Elizabeth Maddock, and Michael J. Drexler. "Introduction: Haiti and the Early United States, Entwined," in Dillon and Drexler, eds., *The Haitian*

Revolution and the Early United States (Philadelphia: University of Pennsylvania Press, 2016), 1–15.

Din, Gilbert C. "The Immigration Policy of Governor Esteban Miró in Spanish Louisiana," *Southwestern Historical Quarterly* 73 (Oct. 1969): 155–75.

Din, Gilbert C. "Spain's Immigration Policy in Louisiana and the American Penetration, 1792–1803," *Southwestern Historical Quarterly* 76 (Jan. 1973): 255–76.

Diouf, Sylviane. *Slavery's Exiles: The Story of the American Maroons* (New York: New York University Press, 2014).

Donnan, Elizabeth, ed. "Papers of James A. Bayard, 1796–1815," in American Historical Association, *Annual Report for the Year 1913*, 2 vols. (Washington, DC: American Historical Association, 1915).

Dowd, Gregory Evans. *A Spirited Resistance: The North American Indian Struggle for Unity, 1745–1815* (Baltimore: Johns Hopkins University Press, 1992).

Drayton, Richard. *Nature's Government: Science, Imperial Britain, and the 'Improvement' of the World* (New Haven: Yale University Press, 2000).

Drescher, Seymour. *Abolition: A History of Slavery and Antislavery* (New York: Cambridge University Press, 2009).

Duane, William. "Selections from the Duane Papers," *Historical Magazine* 4 (Aug. 1868): 60–75.

Dublin, Thomas. *Women at Work: The Transformation of Work and Community in Lowell, Massachusetts, 1826–1860* (New York: Columbia University Press, 1979).

Dublin, Thomas. "Women and Outwork in a Nineteenth-Century New England Town: Fitzwilliam, New Hampshire: 1830–1850," in Steven Hahn and Jonathan Prude, eds., *The Countryside in the Age of Capitalist Transformation: Essays in the Social History of Rural America* (Chapel Hill: University of North Carolina Press, 1985), 51–69.

Dubois, Laurent. *A Colony of Citizens: Revolution & Slave Emancipation in the French Caribbean, 1787–1804* (Chapel Hill: University of North Carolina Press, 2004).

Dubois, Laurent. "Frederick Douglass, Anténor Firmin, and the Making of U.S.-Haitian Relations," in Elizabeth Maddock Dillon and Michael J. Drexler, eds., *The Haitian Revolution and the Early United States* (Philadelphia: University of Pennsylvania Press, 2016), 95–110.

Dubois, Laurent. *Haiti: The Aftershocks of History* (New York: Henry Holt, 2012).

Dubois, Laurent. "The Haitian Revolution and the Sale of Louisiana; or, Thomas Jefferson's (Unpaid) Debt to Jean-Jacques Dessalines," in Peter J. Kastor and Francois Weil, eds., *Empires of the Imagination: Transatlantic Histories of the Louisiana Purchase* (Charlottesville: University of Virginia Press, 2009), 93–116.

Dubois, Laurent. "Unworthy of Liberty?: Slavery, Terror, and Revolution in Haiti," in Isaac Land, ed., *Enemies of Humanity: The Nineteenth-Century War on Terrorism* (New York: Palgrave Macmillan, 2008), 45–62.

Dubois, Laurent, and Julius S. Scott. "An African Revolutionary in the Atlantic World," in Thomas Bender, Laurent Dubois, and Richard Rabinowitz, eds., *Revolution!: The Atlantic World Reborn* (New York: New-York Historical Society, 2011), 139–57.

Duffy, John J., ed. *Ethan Allen and His Kin: Correspondence, 1772–1819*, 2 vols. (Hanover, NH: University Press of New England, 1998).

Dunham, Aileen. *Political Unrest in Upper Canada, 1815–1836* (Toronto: McClelland & Stewart, 1963).

Dunn, Richard S. "Black Society in the Chesapeake, 1776–1810," in Ira Berlin and Ronald Hoffman, eds., *Slavery and Freedom in the Age of the American Revolution* (Urbana: University of Illinois Press, 1983), 49–82.

Dupre, Daniel S. *Alabama's Frontiers and the Rise of the Old South* (Bloomington: Indiana University Press, 2018).

Dusinberre, William. *Slavemaster President: The Double Career of James Polk* (New York: Oxford University Press, 2003).

DuVal, Kathleen. *Independence Lost: Lives on the Edge of the American Revolution* (New York: Random House, 2015).

Dye, Ira. *The Fatal Cruise of the Argus: Two Captains in the War of 1812* (Annapolis: Naval Institute Press, 1994).

Earle, Jonathan H. *Jacksonian Antislavery & the Politics of Free Soil, 1824–1854* (Chapel Hill: University of North Carolina Press, 2004).

Eckhardt, Celia Morris. *Fanny Wright: Rebel in America* (Cambridge: Harvard University Press, 1984).

Edling, Max M. *A Revolution in Favor of Government: Origins of the U.S. Constitution and the Making of the American State* (New York: Oxford University Press, 2003).

Edmunds, R. David. *The Shawnee Prophet* (Lincoln: University of Nebraska Press, 1983).

Egerton, Douglas R. *Death or Liberty: African Americans and Revolutionary America* (New York: Oxford University Press, 2009).

Egerton, Douglas R. *Gabriel's Rebellion: The Virginia Slave Conspiracies of 1800 and 1802* (Chapel Hill: University of North Carolina Press, 1993).

Egerton, Douglas R. *He Shall Go Out Free: The Lives of Denmark Vesey* (Madison, WI: Madison House, 1999).

Elkins, Stanley, and Eric McKitrick. *The Age of Federalism* (New York: Oxford University Press, 1993).

Ellis, Joseph J. *After the Revolution: Profiles of Early American Culture* (New York: W. W. Norton, 1979).

Engstrand, Iris H. W. "Seekers of the 'Northern Mystery': European Exploration of California and the Pacific," in Ramón A. Gutiérrez and Richard J. Orsi, eds., *Contested Eden: California Before the Gold Rush* (Berkeley: University of California Press, 1998), 78–110.

Ericson, David F. *Slavery in the American Republic: Developing the Federal Government, 1791–1861* (Lawrence: University Press of Kansas, 2011).

Errington, Jane. *The Lion, the Eagle, and Upper Canada: A Developing Colonial Ideology* (Montreal: McGill-Queen's University Press, 1987).

Esarey, Logan, ed. *Messages and Letters of William Henry Harrison*, 2 vols. (Indianapolis: Indiana Historical Commission, 1922).

Evans, Emory G. *A "Topping People": The Rise and Decline of Virginia's Old Political Elite, 1680–1790* (Charlottesville: University of Virginia Press, 2009).

Faber, Eberhard L. *Building the Land of Dreams: New Orleans and the Transformation of Early America* (Princeton: Princeton University Press, 2016).

Faragher, John Mack. *Women and Men on the Overland Trail* (New Haven: Yale University Press, 1979).

Faust, Drew Gilpin. *James Henry Hammond and the Old South: A Design for Mastery* (Baton Rouge: Louisiana State University Press, 1982).

Fedric, Francis. *Slave Life in Virginia and Kentucky: A Narrative by Francis Fedric, Escaped Slave* (Baton Rouge: Louisiana State University Press, 2010).

Fehrenbacher, Don E. *The Slaveholding Republic: An Account of the United States Government's Relations to Slavery* (New York: Oxford University Press, 2001).

Feldberg, Michael. *The Turbulent Era: Riot and Disorder in Jacksonian America* (New York: Oxford University Press, 1980).

Feller, Daniel. *The Jacksonian Promise: America, 1815–1840* (Baltimore: Johns Hopkins University Press, 1995).

Fenn, Elizabeth A. *Encounters at the Heart of the World: A History of the Mandan People* (New York: Hill & Wang, 2014).

Fenn, Elizabeth A. *Pox Americana: The Great Smallpox Epidemic of 1775–82* (New York: Hill & Wang, 2001).

Ferling, John E. *A Leap in the Dark: The Struggle to Create the American Republic* (New York: Oxford University Press, 2003).

Ferrer, Ada. "Haiti, Free Soil, and Antislavery in the Revolutionary Atlantic," *American Historical Review* 117 (Feb. 2012): 40–66.

Fick, Carolyn. "From Slave Colony to Black Nation: Haiti's Revolutionary Inversion," in John Tutino, ed., *New Countries: Capitalism, Revolutions, and Nations in the Americas, 1750–1870* (Durham, NC: Duke University Press, 2016), 138–74.

Finkelman, Paul. "Evading the Ordinance: The Persistence of Bondage in Indiana and Illinois," *Journal of the Early Republic* 9 (Spring 1989): 21–51.

Finkelman, Paul. "Slavery and the Constitutional Convention: Making a Covenant with Death," in Richard Beeman, Stephen Botein, and Edward C. Carter II, eds., *Beyond Confederation: Origins of the Constitution and American National Identity* (Chapel Hill: University of North Carolina Press, 1987), 188–225.

Finkelman, Paul. "Slavery in the Shadow of Liberty: The Problem of Slavery in Congress and the Nation's Capital," in Finkelman and Donald R. Kennon, eds., *In the Shadow of Freedom: The Politics of Slavery in the National Capital* (Athens: Ohio University Press, 2011), 3–15.

Firth, Edith G., ed. *The Town of York, 1793–1815: A Collection of Documents of Early Toronto* (Toronto: Champlain Society, 1962).

Fitz, Caitlin. *Our Sister Republics: The United States in an Age of American Revolutions* (New York: W. W. Norton, 2016).

Foley, Neil. *The White Scourge: Mexicans, Blacks, and Poor Whites in Texas Cotton Culture* (Berkeley: University of California Press, 1997).

Foley, William E. *The Genesis of Missouri: From Wilderness Outpost to Statehood* (Columbia: University of Missouri Press, 1989).

Foner, Eric. *The Fiery Trial: Abraham Lincoln and American Slavery* (New York: W. W. Norton, 2010).

Foner, Eric. *Gateway to Freedom: The Hidden History of the Underground Railroad* (New York: W. W. Norton, 2015).

Foner, Jack D. *Blacks and the Military in American History: A New Perspective* (New York: Praeger Publishers, 1974).

Ford, Lacy K. *Deliver Us from Evil: The Slavery Question in the Old South* (New York: Oxford University Press, 2009).

Foster, Augustus John. *Jeffersonian America: Notes on the United States of America*, ed. Richard Beale Davis (San Marino, CA: Huntington Library, 1954).

Franklin, James. *The Present State of Hayti (Saint Domingo), with Remarks on its Agriculture, Commerce, Laws, Religion, Finances, and Population* (London: John Murray, 1828).

Franklin, John Hope, and Loren Schweninger *Runaway Slaves: Rebels on the Plantation* (New York: Oxford University Press, 1999).

Freehling, William W. *The Road to Disunion: Secessionists at Bay, 1776–1854* (New York: Oxford University Press, 1990).

Freeman, Joanne B. *Affairs of Honor: National Politics in the New Republic* (New Haven: Yale University Press, 2001).

Freeman, Joanne B. *The Field of Blood: Violence in Congress and the Road to Civil War* (New York: Farrar, Straus & Giroux, 2018).

Freeman, Joanne B., and Johann N. Neem. "Introduction," in Freeman and Neem, eds., *Jeffersonians in Power: The Rhetoric of Opposition Meets the Reality of Governing* (Charlottesville: University of Virginia Press, 2019), 1–11.

Frey, Sylvia R. *Water from the Rock: Black Resistance in a Revolutionary Age* (Princeton: Princeton University Press, 1991).

Fryd, Vivien Green. *Art & Empire: The Politics of Ethnicity in the United States Capitol, 1815–1860* (Athens: Ohio University Press, 2001).

Fuller, Margaret. *Summer on the Lakes in 1843* (Boston: Charles C. Little & James Brown, 1844).

Furstenberg, François. "Beyond Freedom and Slavery: Autonomy, Virtue, and Resistance in Early American Political Discourse," *Journal of American History* 89 (Mar. 2003): 1295–1330.

Furstenberg, François. "The Significance of the Trans-Appalachian Frontier," *American Historical Review* 113 (June 2008): 647–77.

Gallagher, Gary W. *The Union War* (Cambridge: Harvard University Press, 2011).

Gascoigne, John. *Science in the Service of Empire: Joseph Banks, the British State, and the Uses of Science in the Age of Revolution* (New York: Cambridge University Press, 1998).

Gates, Lillian F. *Land Policies of Upper Canada* (Toronto: University of Toronto Press, 1968).

Gates, Lillian F. "Roads, Rivals, and Rebellion: The Unknown Story of Asa Danforth, Jr.," *Ontario History* 76 (Sept. 1984): 233–54.

Geggus, David Patrick. "Haiti and the Abolitionists: Opinion, Propaganda, and International Politics in Britain and France, 1804–1838," in David Richardson, ed., *Abolition and its Aftermath: The Historical Context, 1790–1916* (London: Frank Cass, 1985): 113–40.

Geggus, David Patrick. *Haitian Revolutionary Studies* (Bloomington: Indiana University Press, 2002).

Gibson, James R. *Imperial Russia in Frontier America: The Changing Geography of Supply of Russian America, 1784–1867* (New York: Oxford University Press, 1976).

Gilbert, Alan. *Black Patriots and Loyalists: Fighting for Emancipation in the War for Independence* (Chicago: University of Chicago Press, 2012).

Gilje, Paul A. *Liberty on the Waterfront: American Maritime Culture in the Age of Revolution* (Philadelphia: University of Pennsylvania Press, 2004).

Gilje, Paul A. *The Making of the American Republic, 1763–1815* (Upper Saddle River, NJ: Pearson, Prentice-Hall, 2006).

Gilje, Paul A. *Rioting in America* (Bloomington: Indiana University Press, 1996).

Ginzberg, Lori D. *Untidy Origins: A Story of Woman's Rights in Antebellum New York* (Chapel Hill: University of North Carolina Press, 2005).

Ginzberg, Lori D. *Women and the Work of Benevolence: Morality, Politics, and Class in the Nineteenth-Century United States* (New Haven: Yale University Press, 1992).

Girard, Philippe R. *Paradise Lost: Haiti's Tumultuous Journey from Pearl of the Caribbean to Third World Hot Spot* (New York: Palgrave Macmillan, 2005).

Giunta, Mary A., ed. *Documents of the Emerging Nation: U.S. Foreign Relations, 1775–1789* (Wilmington, DE: Scholarly Resources, 1998).

Glover, Lorri. *Southern Sons: Becoming Men in the New Nation* (Baltimore: Johns Hopkins University Press, 2007).

Goetzmann, William H. *Exploration and Empire: The Explorer and the Scientist in the Winning of the American West* (New York: Alfred A. Knopf, 1966).

Goetzmann, William H. *New Lands, New Men: America and the Second Great Age of Discovery* (New York: Viking, 1986).

Gonzalez, Johnhenry. "Defiant Haiti: Free-Soil Runaways, Ship Seizures and the Politics of Diplomatic Non-Recognition in the Early Nineteenth Century," *Slavery & Abolition* 36 (Spring 2015): 124–35.

Goodman, Paul. *Towards a Christian Republic: Antimasonry and the Great Transition in New England, 1826–1836* (New York: Oxford University Press, 1988).

Gordon-Reed, Annette. *The Hemingses of Monticello: An American Family* (New York: W. W. Norton, 2008).

Gorn, Elliott J. " 'Gouge and Bite, Pull Hair and Scratch': The Social Significance of Fighting in the Southern Backcountry," *American Historical Review* 90 (Feb. 1985): 18–43.

Gough, Barry M. *Distant Dominion: Britain and the Northwest Coast of North America* (Vancouver: University of British Columbia Press, 1980).

Gough, Barry M. *First Across the Continent: Sir Alexander Mackenzie* (Norman: University of Oklahoma Press, 1997).

Gould, Eliga H. "American Independence and Britain's Counter-Revolution," *Past and Present* 154 (Feb. 1997): 107–41.

Gould, Eliga H. *Among the Powers of the Earth: The American Revolution and the Making of a New World Empire* (Cambridge: Harvard University Press, 2012).

Gould, Eliga H. "Independence and Interdependence: The American Revolution and the Problem of Postcolonial Nationhood, circa 1802," *William and Mary Quarterly*, 3rd ser., vol. 74 (Oct. 2017): 729–52.

Gould, Eliga H. "The Making of an Atlantic State System: Britain and the United States, 1795–1825," in Julie Flavell and Stephen Conway, eds., *Britain and America Go to War: The Impact of War and Warfare in Anglo-America, 1754–1815* (Gainesville: University Press of Florida, 2004), 241–65.

Gourlay, Robert, ed. *Statistical Account of Upper Canada, Compiled with a View to a Grand System of Emigration*, 2 vols. (New York: Johnson Reprint Corp., reprint of London, 1822).

Grabbe, Hans-Jürgen. "European Immigration to the United States in the Early National Period, 1783–1820," *American Philosophical Society, Proceedings* 133 (June 1989): 190–214.

Graffagnino, J. Kevin. "'Twenty Thousand Muskets!!!': Ira Allen and the Olive Branch Affair, 1796–1800," *William and Mary Quarterly* 48 (July 1991): 409–31.

Gray, Edward G. *The Making of John Ledyard: Empire and Ambition in the Life of an Early American Traveler* (New Haven: Yale University Press, 2007).

Green, Constance McLaughlin. *Washington: Village and Capital, 1800–1878* (Princeton: Princeton University Press, 1962).

Green, James N. *Mathew Carey: Publisher and Patriot* (Philadelphia: Library Company of Philadelphia, 1985).

Green, Michael D. *The Politics of Indian Removal: Creek Government and Society in Crisis* (Lincoln: University of Nebraska Press, 1982).

Greenberg, Amy S. *Cause for Alarm: The Volunteer Fire Department in the Nineteenth-Century City* (Princeton: Princeton University Press, 1998).

Greenberg, Amy S. *Lady First: The World of First Lady Sarah Polk* (New York: Alfred A. Knopf, 2019).

Greenberg, Amy S. *Manifest Manhood and the Antebellum American Empire* (New York: Cambridge University Press, 2005).

Greenberg, Amy S. "The Practicability of Annexing Canada: Or, the Manifest Destiny of Canada, According to the United States," in Maxime Dagenais and Julien Mauduit, eds., *Revolutions Across Borders: Jacksonian America and the Canadian Rebellion* (Montreal: McGill-Queen's University Press, 2019), 276–86.

Greenberg, Amy S. *A Wicked War: Polk, Clay, Lincoln, and the 1846 U.S. Invasion of Mexico* (New York: Alfred A. Knopf, 2012).

Greenberg, Kenneth S. *Masters and Statesmen: The Political Culture of American Slavery* (Baltimore: Johns Hopkins University Press, 1985).

Greenwood, F. Murray. *Legacies of Fear: Law and Politics in Quebec in the Era of the French Revolution* (Toronto: University of Toronto Press, 1993).

Greer, Allan. "1837–38: Rebellion Reconsidered," *Canadian Historical Review* 76 (Mar. 1995): 1–18.

Griffin, Patrick. *American Leviathan: Empire, Nation, and Revolutionary Frontier* (New York: Hill & Wang, 2007).

Griffin, Patrick. *America's Revolution* (New York: Oxford University Press, 2013).

Grimes, William. *Life of William Grimes, the Runaway Slave* (New York: Oxford University Press, 2008, reprint of 1855).

Grimsted, David. *American Mobbing, 1828–1861: Toward Civil War* (New York: Cambridge University Press, 1998).

Guardino, Peter. *The Dead March: A History of the Mexican-American War* (Cambridge: Harvard University Press, 2017).

Guasco, Suzanne Cooper. *Confronting Slavery: Edward Coles and the Rise of Antislavery Politics in Nineteenth-Century America* (DeKalb: Northern Illinois University Press, 2013).

Gudmestad, Robert H. *A Troublesome Commerce: The Transformation of the Interstate Slave Trade* (Baton Rouge: Louisiana State University Press, 2003).

Gunn, L. Ray. *The Decline of Authority: Public Economic Policy and Political Development in New York State, 1800–1860* (Ithaca: Cornell University Press, 1988).

Gura, Philip F. *Truth's Ragged Edge: The Rise of the American Novel* (New York: Farrar, Straus & Giroux, 2013).

Guyatt, Nicholas. *Bind Us Apart: How Enlightened Americans Invented Racial Segregation* (New York: Basic Books, 2016).

Hadden, Sally E. *Slave Patrols: Law and Violence in Virginia and the Carolinas* (Cambridge: Harvard University Press, 2001).

Hahn, Steven. *A Nation Without Borders: The United States and Its World in an Age of Civil Wars, 1830–1910* (New York: Viking, 2016).

Hahn, Steven. *The Political Worlds of Slavery and Freedom* (Cambridge: Harvard University Press, 2009).

Hallowell, Gerald, ed. *The Oxford Companion to Canadian History* (Don Mills, ON: Oxford University Press, 2004).

Hamilton, Stanislaus Murray, ed. *The Writings of James Monroe: Including a Collection of his Public and Private Papers and Correspondence*, 7 vols. (New York: G. P. Putnam's Sons, 1901).

Hammond, Bray. *Banks and Politics in America from the Revolution to the Civil War* (Princeton: Princeton University Press, 1957).

Hammond, John Craig. "'Uncontrollable Necessity': The Local Politics, Geopolitics, and Sectional Politics of Slavery Expansion," in Hammond and

Matthew Mason, eds., *Contesting Slavery: The Politics of Bondage and Freedom in the New American Nation* (Charlottesville: University of Virginia Press, 2011), 138–60.

Hardin, Garrett. "The Tragedy of the Commons," *Science* 162 (Dec. 1968): 1243–48.

Harlow, Vincent T. *The Founding of the Second British Empire, 1763–1793*, 2 vols. (London: Longmans, Green, 1964).

Harris, Neil. *Humbug: The Art of P. T. Barnum* (Chicago: University of Chicago Press, 1973).

Harvey, Louis-Georges. "John L. O'Sullivan's 'Canadian Moment': The Democratic Review and the Canadian Rebellions," in Maxime Dagenais and Julien Mauduit, eds., *Revolutions Across Borders: Jacksonian America and the Canadian Rebellion* (Montreal: McGill-Queen's University Press, 2019), 209–38.

Haselby, Sam. *The Origins of American Religious Nationalism* (New York: Oxford University Press, 2015).

Hatch, Nathan O. *The Democratization of American Christianity* (New Haven: Yale University Press, 1989).

Hayes, Kevin J., ed. *Jefferson in His Own Time: A Biographical Chronicle of His Life, Drawn from Recollections, Interviews, and Memoirs by Family, Friends, and Associates* (Iowa City: University of Iowa Press, 2012).

Haynes, Sam W. *Unfinished Revolution: The Early American Republic in a British World* (Charlottesville: University of Virginia Press, 2010).

Heidler, David S., and Jeanne T. Heidler. *Henry Clay: The Essential American* (New York: Random House, 2010).

Heinl, Robert Debs, Jr., and Nancy Gordon Heinl. *Written in Blood: The Story of the Haitian People, 1492–1995* (New York: University Press of America, 1996).

Hendrickson, David C. "Escaping Insecurity: The American Founding and the Control of Violence," in Patrick Griffin et al., eds., *Between Sovereignty and Anarchy: The Politics of Violence in the American Revolutionary Era* (Charlottesville: University of Virginia Press, 2015), 216–42.

Hendrickson, David C. "The First Union: Nationalism versus Internationalism in the American Revolution," in Eliga H. Gould and Peter S. Onuf, eds., *Empire and Nation: The American Revolution in the Atlantic World* (Baltimore: Johns Hopkins University Press, 2005), 35–53.

Hendrickson, David C. *Peace Pact: The Lost World of the American Founding* (Lawrence: University Press of Kansas, 2003).

Hendrickson, David C. *Union, Nation, or Empire: The American Debate over International Relations, 1789–1941* (Lawrence: University Press of Kansas, 2009).

Hermann, Janet Sharp. *The Pursuit of a Dream* (New York: Oxford University Press, 1981).

Herschthal, Eric. "Slaves, Spaniards, and Subversion in Early Louisiana, 1803–1812," *Journal of the Early Republic* 36 (Summer 2016): 283–311.

Hewitt, Nancy A. "Religion, Reform, and Radicalism in the Antebellum Era," in Nancy A. Hewitt, ed., *A Companion to American Women's History* (New York: Blackwell, 2002), 117–31.

Heyrman, Christine Leigh. *Southern Cross: The Beginnings of the Bible Belt* (New York: Alfred A. Knopf, 1997).

Hickey, Donald R. "America's Response to the Slave Revolt in Haiti, 1791–1806," *Journal of the Early Republic* 2 (1982): 361–79.

Hickey, Donald R. *Don't Give Up the Ship!: Myths of the War of 1812* (Urbana: University of Illinois Press, 2006).

Hickey, Donald R. *The War of 1812: A Forgotten Conflict* (Urbana: University of Illinois Press, 1989).

Hietala, Thomas R. *Manifest Design: Anxious Aggrandizement in Late Jacksonian America* (Ithaca: Cornell University Press, 1985).

Hinderaker, Eric. *Elusive Empires: Constructing Colonialism in the Ohio Valley, 1673–1800* (New York: Cambridge University Press, 1997).

Hine, Robert V., and John Mack Faragher. *The American West: A New Interpretive History* (New Haven: Yale University Press, 2000).

Hoffer, Peter Charles. *The Treason Trials of Aaron Burr* (Lawrence: University Press of Kansas, 2008).

Hoig, Stan. *Tribal Wars of the Southern Plains* (Norman: University of Oklahoma Press, 1993).

Holt, Michael F. *The Rise and Fall of the American Whig Party: Jacksonian Politics and the Onset of the Civil War* (New York: Oxford University Press, 1999).

Holton, Woody. *Unruly Americans and the Origins of the Constitution* (New York: Hill & Wang, 2007).

Horsman, Reginald. *The Causes of the War of 1812* (Philadelphia: University of Pennsylvania Press, 1962).

Horsman, Reginald. *Expansion and American Indian Policy, 1783–1812* (East Lansing: Michigan State University Press, 1967).

Horsman, Reginald. "The Indian Policy of an 'Empire for Liberty,'" in Frederick E. Hoxie, Ronald Hoffman, and Peter J. Albert, eds., *Native Americans and the Early Republic* (Charlottesville: University Press of Virginia, 1999), 37–61.

Horsman, Reginald. *Race and Manifest Destiny: The Origins of American Racial Anglo-Saxonism* (Cambridge: Harvard University Press, 1981).

Horton, James Oliver, and Lois E. Horton. *In Hope of Liberty: Culture, Community, and Protest Among Northern Free Blacks, 1700–1860* (New York: Oxford University Press, 1997).

Horton, James Oliver, and Lois E. Horton. *Slavery and the Making of America* (New York: Oxford University Press, 2005).

Houck, Louis, ed. *The Spanish Regime in Missouri*, 2 vols. (Chicago: R. R. Donnelley & Sons, 1909).

Howe, Daniel Walker. *What Hath God Wrought: The Transformation of America, 1815–1848* (New York: Oxford University Press, 2007).

Howe, John R., Jr. "Republican Thought and the Political Violence of the 1790s," *American Quarterly* 19 (Summer 1967): 147–65.

Howison, John. *Sketches of Upper Canada: Domestic, Local, and Characteristic* (Edinburgh: Oliver & Boyd, 1821).

Hudspeth, Robert N., ed. *The Letters of Margaret Fuller*, 6 vols. (Ithaca: Cornell University Press, 1983).

Humboldt, Alexander von. *Political Essay on the Kingdom of New Spain* (New York: Alfred A. Knopf, 1972).

Hurtado, Albert L. *Indian Survival on the California Frontier* (New Haven: Yale University Press, 1988).

Huston, Reeve. "Popular Movements and Party Rule: The New York Anti-Rent Wars and the Jacksonian Political Order," in Jeffrey L. Pasley et al., eds., *Beyond the Founders: New Approaches to the Political History of the Early American Republic* (Chapel Hill: University of North Carolina Press, 2004), 355–86.

Hutchinson, William T., et al., eds. *The Papers of James Madison, Congressional Series*, 17 vols. to date (Chicago and Charlottesville: University of Chicago Press and University of Virginia Press, 1962–).

Hyde, Anne F. *Empires, Nations, and Families: A History of the North American West, 1800–1860* (Lincoln: University of Nebraska Press, 2011).

Igler, David. *The Great Ocean: Pacific Worlds from Captain Cook to the Gold Rush* (New York: Oxford University Press, 2013).

Ignatiev, Noel. *How the Irish Became White* (New York: Routledge, 1995).

Irvin, Benjamin H. *Clothed in Robes of Sovereignty: The Continental Congress and the People Out of Doors* (New York: Oxford University Press, 2011).

Isenberg, Andrew C. *The Destruction of the Bison: An Environmental History, 1750–1920* (New York: Cambridge University Press, 2000).

Isenberg, Nancy. *Fallen Founder: The Life of Aaron Burr* (New York: Viking, 2007).

Isenberg, Nancy. *Sex and Citizenship in Antebellum America* (Chapel Hill: University of North Carolina Press, 1998).

Isenberg, Nancy, and Andrew Burstein. *The Problem of Democracy: The Presidents Adams Confront the Cult of Personality* (New York: Viking, 2019).

Jackson, Donald, ed. *Letters of the Lewis and Clark Expedition, with Related Documents, 1783–1854*, 2 vols. (Urbana: University of Illinois Press, 1978).

Jackson, Donald. *Thomas Jefferson and the Stony Mountains: Exploring the West from Monticello* (Norman: University of Oklahoma Press, 1993).

Jackson, Holly. *American Radicals: How Nineteenth-Century Protest Shaped the Nation* (New York: Crown, 2019).

Jaffee, David. *A New Nation of Goods: The Material Culture of Early America* (Philadelphia: University of Pennsylvania Press, 2010).

Jaffee, David. "One of the Primitive Sort: Portrait Makers of the Rural North, 1760–1840," in Steven Hahn and Jonathan Prude, eds., *The Countryside in the Age of Capitalist Transformation: Essays in the Social History of Rural America* (Chapel Hill: University of North Carolina Press, 1985), 103–38.

Jasanoff, Maya. *Liberty's Exiles: American Loyalists in the Revolutionary World* (New York: Alfred A. Knopf, 2011).

Jeffrey, Julie Roy. *Converting the West: A Biography of Narcissa Whitman* (Norman: University of Oklahoma Press, 1991).

Jenkins, Brian. *Henry Goulburn, 1784–1856: A Political Biography* (Montreal: McGill-Queen's University Press, 1996).

Jensen, Merrill. *The New Nation: A History of the United States During the Confederation, 1781–1789* (New York: Alfred A. Knopf, 1950).

Jensen, Merrill. "The Sovereign States: Their Antagonisms and Rivalries and Some Consequences," in Ronald Hoffman and Peter J. Albert, eds., *Sovereign States in an Age of Uncertainty* (Charlottesville: University Press of Virginia, 1981), 226–50.

Jetté, Melinda Marie. *At the Heart of the Crossed Races: A French-Indian Community in Nineteenth-Century Oregon, 1812–1859* (Corvallis: Oregon State University Press, 2015).

John, Elizabeth A. H. *Storms Brewed in Other Men's Worlds: The Confrontation of Indians, Spanish, and French in the Southwest, 1540–1795* (Norman: University of Oklahoma Press, 1996).

John, Richard R. *Spreading the News: The American Postal System from Franklin to Morse* (Cambridge: Harvard University Press, 1995).

Johnson, David Alan. *Founding the Far West: California, Oregon, and Nevada, 1840–1890* (Berkeley: University of California Press, 1992).

Johnson, Herbert A., et al., eds. *Papers of John Marshall*, 12 vols. to date (Chapel Hill: University of North Carolina Press, 1974–).

Johnson, J. K. *Becoming Prominent: Regional Leadership in Upper Canada, 1791–1841* (Kingston and Montreal: McGill-Queen's University Press, 1989).

Johnson, John J. *A Hemisphere Apart: The Foundations of United States Policy Toward Latin America* (Baltimore: Johns Hopkins University Press, 1990).

Johnson, Michael. "Denmark Vesey and His Co-Conspirators," *William and Mary Quarterly*, 3rd ser., vol. 58 (Oct. 2001): 915–76.

Johnson, Paul E. *A Shopkeeper's Millennium: Society and Revivals in Rochester, New York, 1815–1837* (New York: Hill & Wang, 1978).

Johnson, Walter. *Soul by Soul: Life Inside the Antebellum Slave Market* (Cambridge: Harvard University Press, 1999).

Jones, Dorothy V. *License for Empire: Colonialism by Treaty in Early America* (Chicago: University of Chicago Press, 1982).

Jones, Howard, and Donald A. Rakestraw. *Prologue to Manifest Destiny: Anglo-American Relations in the 1840s* (Wilmington, DE: Scholarly Resources, 1997).

Jones, Jacqueline. *A Dreadful Deceit: The Myth of Race from the Colonial Era to Obama's America* (New York: Basic Books, 2013).

Jordan, Winthrop D. *White over Black: American Attitudes Toward the Negro, 1550–1812* (Chapel Hill: University of North Carolina Press, 1968).

Karp, Matthew. *This Vast Southern Empire: Slaveholders at the Helm of American Foreign Policy* (Cambridge: Harvard University Press, 2016).

Kastor, Peter J. *The Nation's Crucible: The Louisiana Purchase and the Creation of America* (New Haven: Yale University Press, 2004).

Kastor, Peter J. "'They Are All Frenchmen': Background and Nation in an Age of Transformation," in Kastor and Francois Weil, eds., *Empires of the Imagination: Transatlantic Histories of the Louisiana Purchase* (Charlottesville: University of Virginia Press, 2009), 239–67.

Kastor, Peter J. *William Clark's World: Describing America in an Age of Unknowns* (New Haven: Yale University Press, 2011).

Kelly, Catherine. "Gender and Class Formations in the Antebellum North," in Nancy A. Hewitt, ed., *A Companion to American Women's History* (New York: Blackwell, 2002), 100–116.

Kennedy, Roger G. *Cotton and Conquest: How the Plantation System Acquired Texas* (Norman: University of Oklahoma Press, 2013).

Kerber, Linda K. *Federalists in Dissent: Imagery and Ideology in Jeffersonian America* (Ithaca: Cornell University Press, 1970).

Kerber, Linda K. " 'History Can Do It No Justice': Women and the Reinterpretation of the American Revolution," in Ronald Hoffman and Peter J. Albert, eds., *Women in the Age of the American Revolution* (Charlottesville: University Press of Virginia, 1989), 3–42.

Kersh, Rogan. *Dreams of a More Perfect Union* (Ithaca: Cornell University Press, 2001).

Ketcham, Ralph. "The Dictates of Conscience: Edward Coles and Slavery," *Virginia Quarterly Review* 36 (Winter 1960): 46–62.

Ketcham, Ralph. *James Madison: A Biography* (Charlottesville: University Press of Virginia, 1990).

Kettner, James H. *The Development of American Citizenship, 1608–1870* (Chapel Hill: University of North Carolina Press, 1978).

King, Charles R., ed. *The Life and Correspondence of Rufus King*, 6 vols. (New York: G. P. Putnam's Sons, 1897).

Kirk, Russell. *John Randolph of Roanoke* (Indianapolis: Liberty Press, 1978).

Klein, Rachel N. *Unification of a Slave State: The Rise of the Planter Class in the South Carolina Backcountry, 1760–1808* (Chapel Hill: University of North Carolina Press, 1990).

Klinck, Carl F., and Malcolm Ross, eds. *Tiger Dunlop's Upper Canada* (Toronto: McClelland & Stewart, 1967).

Klooster, Wim. *Revolutions in the Atlantic World: A Comparative History* (New York: New York University Press, 2009).

Kloppenberg, James T. *Toward Democracy: The Struggle for Self-Rule in European and American Thought* (New York: Oxford University Press, 2016).

Kohn, Richard H. "The Inside History of the Newburgh Conspiracy: America and the Coup d'Etat," *William and Mary Quarterly*, 3rd ser., vol. 27 (Apr. 1970): 187–220.

Kolchin, Peter. *American Slavery, 1619–1877* (New York: Hill & Wang, 2003).

Kornblith, Gary J., and John M. Murrin. "The Making and Unmaking of an American Ruling Class," in Alfred F. Young, ed., *Beyond the American Revolution: Explorations in the History of American Radicalism* (DeKalb: Northern Illinois University Press, 1993), 27–79.

Krauze, Enrique. *Mexico Biography of Power: A History of Modern Mexico, 1810–1996* (New York: HarperCollins, 1997).

Kulikoff, Allan. *Tobacco and Slaves: The Development of Southern Cultures in the Chesapeake, 1660–1800* (Chapel Hill: University of North Carolina Press, 1986).

Kulikoff, Allan. "Uprooted Peoples: Black Migrants in the Age of the American Revolution," in Ira Berlin and Ronald Hoffman, eds., *Slavery and Freedom in the Age of the American Revolution* (Urbana: University of Illinois Press, 1983), 143–71.

Kulikoff, Allan. "The War in the Countryside," in Edward G. Gray and Jane Kamensky, eds., *The Oxford Handbook of the American Revolution* (New York: Oxford University Press, 2013), 216–33.

Kutolowski, John F., and Kathleen Smith Kutolowski. "Commissions and Canvasses: The Militia and Politics in Western New York, 1800–1845," *New York History* 63 (Jan. 1982): 5–38.

Kutolowski, Kathleen Smith. "Freemasonry and Community in the Early Republic: The Case for Antimasonic Anxieties," *American Quarterly* 34 (Winter 1982): 543–61.

Kuykendall, Ralph S. *The Hawaiian Kingdom, 1778–1854: Foundation and Transformation* (Honolulu: University of Hawaii Press, 1957).

Lachance, Paul. "The Louisiana Purchase in the Demographic Perspective of Its Time," in Peter J. Kastor and François Weil, eds., *Empires of the Imagination: Transatlantic Histories of the Louisiana Purchase* (Charlottesville: University of Virginia Press, 2009), 143–79.

Lamar, Howard R., ed. *The Reader's Encyclopedia of the American West* (New York: Thomas Y. Crowell Co., 1977).

Lambert, Andrew. *The Challenge: America, Britain, and the War of 1812* (London: Faber & Faber, 2012).

Lambert, Frank. *The Barbary Wars: American Independence in the Atlantic World* (New York: Farrar, Straus, & Giroux, 2005).

Lanctot, Gustave. *Canada and the American Revolution, 1774–1783* (Cambridge: Harvard University Press, 1967).

Langley, Lester D. *The Americas in the Age of Revolution, 1750–1850* (New Haven: Yale University Press, 1996).

Larkin, Jack. *The Reshaping of Everyday Life, 1790–1840* (New York: Harper & Row, 1988).

Larson, Edward J. *The Return of George Washington, 1783–1789* (New York: HarperCollins, 2014).

Larson, John Lauritz. *Internal Improvement: National Public Works and the Promise of Popular Government in the Early United States* (Chapel Hill: University of North Carolina Press, 2001).

Larson, John Lauritz. *The Market Revolution in America: Liberty, Ambition, and the Eclipse of the Common Good* (New York: Cambridge University Press, 2010).

Lebergott, Stanley. *The Americans: An Economic Record* (New York: W. W. Norton, 1984).

Lebsock, Suzanne. *The Free Women of Petersburg: Status and Culture in a Southern Town, 1784–1860* (New York: W. W. Norton, 1984).

Lee, Jacob F. *Masters of the Middle Waters: Indian Nations and Colonial Ambitions Along the Mississippi* (Cambridge: Harvard University Press, 2009).

Leichtle, Kurt E., and Bruce G. Carveth. *Crusade Against Slavery: Edward Coles, Pioneer of Freedom* (Carbondale: Southern Illinois University Press, 2011).

Lepler, Jessica M. *The Many Panics of 1837: People, Politics, and the Creation of a Transatlantic Financial Crisis* (New York: Cambridge University Press, 2013).

Lepore, Jill. *A is for American: Letters and Other Characters in the Newly United States* (New York: Alfred A. Knopf, 2002).

Lepore, Jill. *These Truths: A History of the United States* (New York: W. W. Norton, 2018).

Levine, Allan. *Toronto: Biography of a City* (Madeira Park, BC: Douglas & McIntyre, 2013).

Levine, Bruce. *Half Slave and Half Free: The Roots of Civil War* (New York: Hill & Wang, 2005).

Lewis, James E., Jr. *The American Union and the Problem of Neighborhood* (Chapel Hill: University of North Carolina Press, 1998).

Lewis, James E., Jr. *The Burr Conspiracy: Uncovering the Story of an Early American Crisis* (Princeton: Princeton University Press, 2017).

Lewis, James E., Jr. *The Louisiana Purchase: Jefferson's Noble Bargain?* (Charlottesville: Thomas Jefferson Foundation, 2003).

Lewis, Jan E. *The Pursuit of Happiness: Family and Values in Jefferson's Virginia* (New York: Cambridge University Press, 1983).

Lewis, Jan E. "The Republican Wife: Virtue and Seduction in the Early Republic," *William and Mary Quarterly*, 3rd ser., vol. 44 (Oct. 1987): 689–721.

Lewis, Michael. *A Social History of the Navy, 1793–1815* (London: George Allen & Unwin, 1960).

Libby, David J. *Slavery and Frontier Mississippi, 1720–1835* (Jackson: University Press of Mississippi, 2004).

Limerick, Patricia Nelson. *Something in the Soil: Legacies and Reckonings in the New West* (New York: W. W. Norton, 2000).

Lindert, Peter H., and Jeffrey G. Williamson. "American Incomes Before and After the Revolution," *Journal of Economic History* 73 (Sept. 2013): 725–65.

Liss, Peggy K. *Atlantic Empires: The Network of Trade and Revolution, 1713–1826* (Baltimore: Johns Hopkins University Press, 1983).

Litwack, Leon F. *North of Slavery: The Negro in the Free States, 1790–1860* (Chicago: University of Chicago Press, 1961).

Lobb, John, ed. *Uncle Tom's Story: An Autobiography of the Rev. Josiah Henson, 1789–1876* (London: Frank Cass & Co., 1971, reprint of London, Ont., 1881).

Longmore, Paul K. *The Invention of George Washington* (Charlottesville: University Press of Virginia, 1999).

Looney, J. Jefferson, et al., eds. *The Papers of Thomas Jefferson, Retirement Series*, 16 vols. to date (Princeton: Princeton University Press, 2005–).

Lurie, Shira. "Liberty Poles and the Fight for Popular Politics in the Early Republic," *Journal of the Early Republic* 38 (Winter 2018): 673–97.

Lynch, John. *The Spanish American Revolutions, 1808–1826* (London: Weidenfeld & Nicolson, 1973).

Mackay, David. *In the Wake of Cook: Exploration, Science, and Empire, 1780–1801* (London: Croom Helm, 1985).

Mackenzie, Charles. *Notes on Haiti, Made During a Residence in that Republic*, 2 vols. (London: Colburn & Bentley, 1830).

Madley, Benjamin. *An American Genocide: The United States and the California Indian Catastrophe* (New Haven: Yale University Press, 2017).

Maier, Pauline. *American Scripture: Making the Declaration of Independence* (New York: Alfred A. Knopf, 1997).

Maier, Pauline. *Ratification: The People Debate the Constitution, 1787–1788* (New York: Simon & Schuster, 2010).

Main, Jackson Turner. *The Antifederalists: Critics of the Constitution, 1781–1788* (New York: W. W. Norton, 1961).

Malcomson, Robert. *Capital in Flames: The American Attack on York, 1813* (Annapolis: Naval Institute Press, 2008).

Malcomson, Robert. *Lords of the Lake: The Naval War on Lake Ontario, 1812–1814* (Annapolis: Naval Institute Press, 1998).

Malcomson, Robert. *A Very Brilliant Affair: The Battle of Queenston Heights, 1812* (Annapolis: Naval Institute Press, 2003).

Malone, Dumas. *Jefferson and His Time*, 6 vols. (Boston: Little, Brown, 1948–1981).

Malone, Henry T. "New Echota: Capital of the Cherokee Nation, 1825–1830," *Early Georgia* 1 (Fall 1955): 6–13.

Manning, William R., ed. *Diplomatic Correspondence of the United States: Canadian Relations, 1784–1860*, 3 vols. (Washington, DC: Carnegie Endowment for International Peace, 1940).

Marini, Stephen A. "Religion, Politics, and Ratification," in Ronald Hoffman and Peter J. Albert, eds., *Religion in a Revolutionary Age* (Charlottesville: University Press of Virginia, 1994), 184–217.

Marshall, Megan. *Margaret Fuller: A New American Life* (Boston: Houghton Mifflin Harcourt, 2013).

Marshall, Peter J. *The Making and Unmaking of Empires: Britain, India, and America, c. 1750–1783* (Oxford: Oxford University Press, 2005).

Martin, Ged. *Britain and the Origins of Canadian Confederation, 1837–1867* (Vancouver, BC: UBC Press, 1995).

Martin, James Kirby, ed. *Ordinary Courage: The Revolutionary War Adventures of Joseph Plumb Martin* (St. James, NY: Brandywine Press, 1993).

Martin, James Kirby, and Mark E. Lender, eds. *A Respectable Army: The Military Origins of the Republic, 1763–1789* (Arlington Heights, IL: Harlan Davidson, 1982).

Masters, D. C. *The Rise of Toronto, 1850–1890* (Toronto: University of Toronto Press, 1947).

Matthewson, Tim. *A Proslavery Foreign Policy: Haitian-American Relations During the Early Republic* (Westport, CT: Praeger, 2003).

May, Robert E. "Invisible Men: Blacks and the U.S. Army in the Mexican War," in Darlene Clark Hine and Earnestine Jenkins, eds., *A Question of Manhood: A Reader in U.S. Black Men's History and Masculinity,* 2 vols. (Bloomington: Indiana University Press, 1999), 1:473–85.

McCalla, Douglas. *Planting the Province: The Economic History of Upper Canada, 1784–1870* (Toronto: University of Toronto Press, 1992).

McColley, Robert. *Slavery and Jeffersonian Virginia* (Urbana: University of Illinois Press, 1964).

McCoy, Drew R. "James Madison and Visions of American Nationality in the Confederation Period: A Regional Perspective," in Richard Beeman, Stephen Botein, and Edward C. Carter II, eds., *Beyond Confederation: Origins of the Constitution and American National Identity* (Chapel Hill: University of North Carolina Press, 1987), 226–58.

McCurdy, Charles. *The Anti-Rent Era in New York Law and Politics* (Chapel Hill: University of North Carolina Press, 2001).

McCurry, Stephanie. *Masters of Small Worlds: Yeoman Households, Gender Relations, and the Political Culture of the Antebellum South Carolina Low Country* (New York: Oxford University Press, 1995).

McCusker, John J., and Russell R. Menard. *The Economy of British America, 1607–1789* (Chapel Hill: University of North Carolina Press, 1985).

McDaniel, W. Caleb. *The Problem of Democracy in the Age of Slavery: Garrisonian Abolitionists & Transatlantic Reform* (Baton Rouge: Louisiana State University Press, 2013).

McLagan, Elizabeth. *A Peculiar Paradise: A History of Blacks in Oregon, 1788–1840* (Portland, OR: Georgian Press, 1980).

McNairn, Jeffrey L. *The Capacity to Judge: Public Opinion and Deliberative Democracy in Upper Canada, 1791–1854* (Toronto: University of Toronto Press, 2000).

McNamara, Martha J. "Republican Art and Architecture," in Edward G. Gray and Jane Kamensky, eds., *The Oxford Handbook of the American Revolution* (New York: Oxford University Press, 2013), 499–518.

Melish, Joanne Pope. *Disowning Slavery: Gradual Emancipation and "Race" in New England, 1780–1860* (Ithaca: Cornell University Press, 1998).

Merk, Frederick, and Lois Bannister Merk. *Slavery and the Annexation of Texas* (New York: Alfred A. Knopf, 1972).

Meyers, Marvin, ed. *The Mind of the Founder: Sources of the Political Thought of James Madison* (Hanover, NH: University Press of New England, 1981).

Miller, Christopher L. *Prophetic Worlds: Indians and Whites on the Columbia Plateau* (New Brunswick, NJ: Rutgers University Press, 1985).

Millett, Nathaniel. *The Maroons of Prospect Bluff and Their Quest for Freedom in the Atlantic World* (Gainesville: University Press of Florida, 2013).

Mills, David. *The Idea of Loyalty in Upper Canada, 1784–1850* (Kingston, ON: McGill-Queens University Press, 1988).

Milobar, David. "Conservative Ideology, Metropolitan Government, and the Reform of Quebec, 1782–1791," *International History Review* 12 (Feb. 1990): 45–64.

Missall, John, and Mary Lou Missall. *The Seminole Wars: America's Longest Indian Conflict* (Gainesville: University Press of Florida, 2004).

Montejano, David. *Anglos and Mexicans in the Making of Texas, 1836–1986* (Austin: University of Texas Press, 1987).

Moody, Robert E., ed. *The Saltonstall Papers, 1607–1815*, 2 vols. (Boston: Massachusetts Historical Society, 1972–74).

Moore, Christopher. *The Loyalists: Revolution, Exile, Settlement* (Toronto: McClelland & Stewart, 1994).

Morley, Jefferson. *Snow-Storm in August: Washington City, Francis Scott Key, and the Forgotten Race Riot of 1835* (New York: Doubleday, 2012).

Morris, Larry E. *The Fate of the Corps: What Became of the Lewis and Clark Explorers After the Expedition* (New Haven: Yale University Press, 2004).

Morris, Richard B. *The Forging of the Union: 1781–1789* (New York: Harper & Row, 1987).

Morris, Richard B. *The Peacemakers: The Great Powers and American Independence* (New York: Harper & Row, 1965).

Morrison, Dorothy Nafus. *Outpost: John McLoughlin & the Far Northwest* (Portland: Oregon Historical Society Press, 1999).

Morse, Jedidiah. *A Report to the Secretary of War of the United States on Indian Affairs, Comprising a Narrative of a Tour Performed in the Summer of 1820* (New Haven: S. Converse, 1822).

Morton, Louis. *Robert Carter of Nomini Hall: A Virginia Tobacco Planter of the Eighteenth Century* (Charlottesville: University Press of Virginia, 1964).

Moser, Harold D., et al., eds. *The Papers of Andrew Jackson,* 9 vols. to date (Knoxville: University of Tennessee Press, 1980–).

Moulton, Gary E., ed. *The Journals of the Lewis and Clark Expedition,* 13 vols. (Lincoln: University of Nebraska Press, 1979–2001).

Mullin, Gerald W. *Flight and Rebellion: Slave Resistance in Eighteenth-Century Virginia* (New York: Oxford University Press, 1972).

Murrin, John M. "A Roof Without Walls: The Dilemma of American National Identity," in Richard Beeman, Stephen Botein, and Edward C. Carter II, eds., *Beyond Confederation: Origins of the Constitution and American National Identity* (Chapel Hill: University of North Carolina Press, 1987), 333–48.

Narrett, David. *Adventurism and Empire: The Struggle for Mastery in the Louisiana-Florida Borderlands, 1762–1803* (Chapel Hill: University of North Carolina Press, 2015).

Nasatir, Abraham P. *Borderland in Retreat: From Spanish Louisiana to the Far Southwest* (Albuquerque: University of New Mexico Press, 1976).

Nash, Gary B. *Race and Revolution* (Madison, WI: Madison House, 1990).

Nash, Gary B., and Jean R. Soderlund. *Freedom by Degrees: Emancipation in Pennsylvania and Its Aftermath* (New York: Oxford University Press, 1991).

Neatby, Hilda. *Quebec: The Revolutionary Age, 1760–1791* (Toronto: McClelland & Stewart, 1966).

Newman, Richard S. *Freedom's Prophet: Bishop Richard Allen, the AME Church, and the Black Founding Fathers* (New York: New York University Press, 2008).

Newman, Richard S. *The Transformation of American Abolitionism: Fighting Slavery in the Early Republic* (Chapel Hill: University of North Carolina Press, 2002).

Newman, Simon P. "Paine, Jefferson, and Revolutionary Radicalism in Early National America," in Newman and Peter S. Onuf, eds., *Paine and Jefferson in the Age of Revolutions* (Charlottesville: University of Virginia Press, 2013): 71–94.

Newmyer, R. Kent. *John Marshall and the Heroic Age of the Supreme Court* (Baton Rouge: Louisiana State University Press, 2001).

Newmyer, R. Kent. *Supreme Court Justice Joseph Story: Statesman of the Old Republic* (Chapel Hill: University of North Carolina Press, 1985).

Nicholls, Michael L. "Passing Through This Troublesome World: Free Blacks in the Early Southside," *Virginia Magazine of History and Biography* 92 (Jan. 1984): 50–70.

Nicholls, Michael L. *Whispers of Rebellion: Narrating Gabriel's Conspiracy* (Charlottesville: University of Virginia Press, 2012).

Nichols, David Andrew. *Red Gentlemen & White Savages: Indians, Federalists, and the Search for Order on the American Frontier* (Charlottesville: University of Virginia Press, 2008).

Nobles, Gregory H. *American Frontiers: Cultural Encounters and Continental Conquest* (New York: Hill & Wang, 1997).

Noll, Mark A. *America's God: From Jonathan Edwards to Abraham Lincoln* (New York: Oxford University Press, 2002).

Noll, Mark A. *A History of Christianity in the United States and Canada* (Grand Rapids: William B. Eerdmans Publishing Co., 1992).

North, Douglass C., Terry L. Anderson, and Peter J. Hill. *Growth and Welfare in the American Past: A New Economic History* (Englewood Cliffs, NJ: Prentice-Hall, 1983).

Norton, Mary Beth. *Liberty's Daughters: The Revolutionary Experience of American Women, 1750–1800* (Boston: Little, Brown, 1980).

Oakes, James. *The Ruling Race: A History of American Slaveholders* (New York: Alfred A. Knopf, 1982).

Oakes, James. *Slavery and Freedom: An Interpretation of the Old South* (New York: Alfred A. Knopf, 1990).

O'Brien, Brendan. *Speedy Justice: The Tragic Last Voyage of His Majesty's Vessel Speedy* (Toronto: University of Toronto Press, 1992).

O'Brien, Jean M. "Indians and the California Gold Rush," in Susan Sleeper-Smith et al., eds., *Why You Can't Teach United States History Without American Indians* (Chapel Hill: University of North Carolina Press, 2015): 101–17.

Oertel, Kristen T. *Harriet Tubman: Slavery, the Civil War, and Civil Rights in the Nineteenth Century* (New York: Routledge, 2016).

Ohrt, Wallace. *Defiant Peacemaker: Nicholas Trist and the Mexican War* (College Station: Texas A&M University Press, 1997).

Onuf, Peter S. "The Empire of Liberty: Land of the Free and Home of the Slave," in Andrew Shankman, ed., *The World of the Revolutionary American Republic: Land, Labor, and the Conflict for a Continent* (New York: Routledge, 2014), 195–217.

Onuf, Peter S. "The Expanding Union," in David Thomas Konig, ed., *Devising Liberty: Preserving and Creating Freedom in the New American Republic* (Stanford, CA: Stanford University Press, 1995), 50–80.

Onuf, Peter S. "Imperialism and Nationalism," in Ian Tyrrell and Jay Sexton, eds., *Empire's Twin: U.S. Anti-Imperialism from the Founding Era to the Age of Terrorism* (Ithaca: Cornell University Press, 2015), 21–40.

Onuf, Peter S. *Jefferson's Empire: The Language of American Nationhood* (Charlottesville: University of Virginia Press, 2000).

Onuf, Peter S. *The Mind of Thomas Jefferson* (Charlottesville: University of Virginia Press, 2007).

Onuf, Peter S. *The Origins of the Federal Republic: Jurisdictional Controversies in the United States, 1775–1787* (Philadelphia: University of Pennsylvania Press, 1983).

Onuf, Peter S. "Prologue: Jefferson, Louisiana, and American Nationhood," in Peter J. Kastor and François Weil, eds., *Empires of the Imagination: Transatlantic Histories of the Louisiana Purchase* (Charlottesville: University of Virginia Press, 2009), 23–33.

Onuf, Peter S. "Settlers, Settlements, and New States," in Jack P. Greene, ed., *The American Revolution: Its Character and Limits* (New York: New York University Press, 1987), 179–213.

Onuf, Peter S. *Statehood and Union: A History of the Northwest Ordinance* (Bloomington: Indiana University Press, 1987).

Onuf, Peter S. "State-Making in Revolutionary America: Independent Vermont as a Case Study," *Journal of American History* 67 (Mar. 1981): 797–815.

Opal, Jason M. *Avenging the People: Andrew Jackson, the Rule of Law, and the American Nation* (New York: Oxford University Press, 2017).

Opal, Jason M. *Beyond the Farm: National Ambitions in Rural New England* (Philadelphia: University of Pennsylvania Press, 2008).

Orsi, Jared. *Citizen Explorer: The Life of Zebulon Pike* (New York: Oxford University Press, 2014).

O'Shaughnessy, Andrew Jackson. *An Empire Divided: The American Revolution and the British Caribbean* (Philadelphia: University of Pennsylvania Press, 2000).

O'Shaughnessy, Andrew Jackson. *The Men Who Lost America: British Leadership, the American Revolution, and the Fate of the Empire* (New Haven: Yale University Press, 2013).

Ostler, Jeffrey. *The Plains Sioux and U.S. Colonialism from Lewis and Clark to Wounded Knee* (New York: Cambridge University Press, 2004).

Ostler, Jeffrey. *Surviving Genocide: Native Nations and the United States from the American Revolution to Bleeding Kansas* (New Haven: Yale University Press, 2019).

Owsley, Frank L., Jr., and Gene A. Smith, *Filibusters and Expansionists: Jefferso-nian Manifest Destiny, 1800–1812* (Tuscaloosa, AL: University of Alabama Press, 1997).

Palmer, Bryan. "Popular Radicalism and the Theatrics of Rebellion: The Hybrid Discourse of Dissent in Upper Canada in the 1830s," in Nancy Christie, ed., *Transatlantic Subjects: Ideas, Institutions, and Social Experience in Post-Revolutionary British North America* (Montreal: McGill-Queen's University Press, 2008), 403–38.

Palmer, R. R. *The Age of Democratic Revolution: A Political History of Europe and America, 1760-1800*, 2 vols. (Princeton: Princeton University Press, 1959).

Parkinson, Richard. *A Tour in America in 1798, 1799, and 1800*, 2 vols (London: J. Harding, 1805).

Parkinson, Robert G. "'Manifest Signs of Passion': The First Federal Congress, Antislavery, and Legacies of the Revolutionary War," in John Craig Ham-mond and Matthew Mason, eds., *Contesting Slavery: The Politics of Bondage and Freedom in the New American Nation* (Charlottesville: University of Vir-ginia Press, 2011), 49–68.

Pasley, Jeffrey L. "1800 as a Revolution in Political Culture: Newspapers, Cel-ebrations, Voting, and Democratization in the Early Republic," in James Horn, Jan Ellen Lewis, and Peter S. Onuf, eds., *The Revolution of 1800: Democracy, Race, and the New Republic* (Charlottesville: University of Virginia Press, 2002), 121–52.

Pasley, Jeffrey L. *"The Tyranny of Printers": Newspaper Politics in the Early American Republic* (Charlottesville: University of Virginia Press, 2001).

Patrick, Rembert W. *Florida Fiasco: Rampant Rebels on the Georgia-Florida Border, 1810–1815* (Athens: University of Georgia Press, 1954).

Pearsall, Sarah M. S. *Polygamy: An Early American History* (New Haven: Yale Uni-versity Press, 2019).

Perdue, Theda, and Michael D. Green. *Columbia Guide to American Indians of the Southeast* (New York: Columbia University Press, 2001).

Perkins, Bradford. *Castlereagh and Adams: England and the United States, 1812–1823* (Berkeley: University of California Press, 1964).

Perkins, Bradford. *The First Rapprochement: England and the United States, 1795–1805* (Philadelphia: University of Pennsylvania Press, 1955).

Perkins, Bradford. *Prologue to War: England and the United States, 1805–1812* (Berke-ley: University of California Press, 1963).

Pessen, Edward. *Jacksonian America: Society, Personality, and Politics* (Homewood, IL: Dorsey Press, 1978).

Peterson, Merrill D. *The Great Triumvirate: Webster, Clay, and Calhoun* (New York: Oxford University Press, 1987).

Poinsett, Joel Roberts. *Notes on Mexico, Made in the Autumn of 1822* (New York: Frederick A. Praeger, 1969, reprint of 1824).

Porter, Kenneth W. *The Black Seminoles: History of a Freedom-Seeking People* (Gainesville: University Press of Florida, 1996).

Porter, Kenneth W. "Negroes and the East Florida Annexation Plot, 1811–1813," *Journal of Negro History* 30 (Jan. 1945): 9–29.

Potter, Janice. *The Liberty We Seek: Loyalist Ideology in Colonial New York and Massachusetts* (Cambridge: Harvard University Press, 1983).

Pratt, Julius W. *Expansionists of 1812* (New York: Peter Smith, 1949).

Prucha, Francis Paul. *The Sword of the Republic: The United States Army on the Frontier, 1783–1846* (Toronto: Macmillan Co., 1969).

Prude, Jonathan. "Town-Factory Conflicts in Antebellum Rural Massachusetts," in Steven Hahn and Jonathan Prude, eds., *The Countryside in the Age of Capitalist Transformation: Essays in the Social History of Rural America* (Chapel Hill: University of North Carolina Press, 1985), 71–102.

Pybus, Cassandra. *Epic Journeys of Freedom: Runaway Slaves of the American Revolution and Their Global Quest for Liberty* (Boston: Beacon Press, 2006).

Quimby, Robert S. *The U.S. Army in the War of 1812: An Operational and Command Study*, 2 vols. (East Lansing: Michigan State University Press, 1997).

Quist, John W. *Restless Visionaries: The Social Roots of Antebellum Reform in Alabama and Michigan* (Baton Rouge: Louisiana State University Press, 1998).

Ragosta, John. *Religious Freedom: Jefferson's Legacy, America's Creed* (Charlottesville: University of Virginia Press, 2013).

Rakove, Jack N. *The Beginnings of National Politics: An Interpretive History of the Continental Congress* (Baltimore: Johns Hopkins University Press, 1979).

Rakove, Jack N. *Original Meanings: Politics and Ideas in the Making of the Constitution* (New York: Random House, 1996).

Rakove, Jack N. *Revolutionaries: A New History of the Invention of America* (Boston: Houghton Mifflin Harcourt, 2010).

Randolph, Thomas Jefferson. *The Speech of Thomas J. Randolph in the House of Delegates of Virginia on the Abolition of Slavery* (Richmond: Samuel Shepherd & Co., 1832).

Rasmussen, Daniel. *American Uprising: The Untold Story of America's Largest Slave Revolt* (New York: HarperCollins, 2011).

Ratcliffe, Donald. *The One-Party Presidential Contest: Adams, Jackson, and 1824's Five-Horse Race* (Lawrence: University Press of Kansas, 2015).

Read, Colin, and Ronald J. Stagg, eds. *The Rebellion of 1837 in Upper Canada: A Collection of Documents* (Toronto: Champlain Society, 1985).

Read, James H. *Power Versus Liberty: Madison, Hamilton, Wilson, and Jefferson* (Charlottesville: University Press of Virginia, 2000).

Reid-Vazquez, Michele. *The Year of the Lash: Free People of Color in Cuba and the Nineteenth-Century Atlantic World* (Athens: University of Georgia Press, 2011).

Reiss, Benjamin. *The Showman and the Slave: Race, Death, and Memory in Barnum's America* (Cambridge: Harvard University Press, 2001).

Remini, Robert V. *Andrew Jackson and the Course of American Empire, 1767–1821* (New York: Harper & Row, 1977).

Remini, Robert V. *Andrew Jackson and the Course of American Freedom, 1822–1832* (New York: Harper & Row, 1981).

Remini, Robert V. *Andrew Jackson and His Indian Wars* (New York: Viking Penguin, 2017).

Remini, Robert V. *Joseph Smith* (New York: Viking Penguin, 2002).

Reséndez, Andrés. *Changing National Identities at the Frontier: Texas and New Mexico, 1800–1850* (New York: Cambridge University Press, 2005).

Reséndez, Andrés. *The Other Indian Slavery: The Uncovered Story of Indian Enslavement in America* (Boston: Houghton Mifflin Harcourt, 2016).

Reynolds, David S. *Waking Giant: America in the Age of Jackson* (New York: HarperCollins, 2008).

Rhodehamel, John, ed. *The American Revolution* (New York: Library of America, 2001).

Rhodehamel, John, ed. *George Washington: Writings* (New York: Library of America, 1997).

Rich, E. E. *The Fur Trade and the Northwest to 1857* (Toronto: McClelland & Stewart, 1967).

Richards, Leonard L. *Gentlemen of Property and Standing: Anti-Abolition Mobs in Jacksonian America* (New York: Oxford University Press, 1970).

Richards, Leonard L. *Shays's Rebellion: The American Revolution's Final Battle* (Philadelphia: University of Pennsylvania Press, 2002).

Richards, Leonard L. *The Slave Power: The Free North and Southern Domination, 1780–1860* (Baton Rouge: Louisiana State University, 2000).

Richards, Thomas, Jr. "The Lure of a Canadian Republic," in Maxime Dagenais and Julien Mauduit, eds., *Revolutions Across Borders: Jacksonian America and the Canadian Rebellion* (Montreal: McGill-Queen's University Press, 2019), 91–136.

Richardson, H. Edward. *Cassius Marcellus Clay: Firebrand of Freedom* (Lexington: University Press of Kentucky, 1976).

Richter, Daniel. *Facing East from Indian Country: A Native History of Early America* (Cambridge: Harvard University Press, 2003).

Ricks, Mary K. "The 1848 *Pearl* Escape from Washington, D.C.: A Convergence of Opportunity, Motivation, and Political Action in the Nation's Capital," in Paul Finkelman and Donald R. Kennon, eds., *In the Shadow of Freedom: The Politics of Slavery in the National Capital* (Athens: Ohio University Press, 2011), 195–219.

Ritcheson, Charles R. *Aftermath of Revolution: British Policy Toward the United States, 1783–1795* (Dallas: Southern Methodist University Press, 1969).

Robbins, William G. *Landscapes of Promise: The Oregon Story, 1800–1940* (Seattle: University of Washington Press, 1997).

Robertson, Lindsay G. *Conquest by Law: How the Discovery of America Dispossessed Indigenous Peoples of Their Lands* (New York: Oxford University Press, 2005).

Robinson, Donald. *Slavery in the Structure of American Politics, 1765–1820* (New York: W. W. Norton, 1979).

Rockman, Seth. *Scraping By: Wage Labor, Slavery, and Survival in Early Baltimore* (Baltimore: Johns Hopkins University Press, 2008).

Rockwell, Stephen J. *Indian Affairs and the Administrative State in the Nineteenth Century* (New York: Cambridge University Press, 2010).

Rodríguez O, Jaime E. *The Independence of Spanish America* (New York: Cambridge University Press, 1998).

Roediger, David R. *The Wages of Whiteness: Race and the Making of the American Working Class* (New York: Verso, 1991).

Rohrbough, Malcolm J. *The Land Office Business: The Settlement and Administration of American Public Lands, 1789–1837* (New York: Oxford University Press, 1968).

Rohrbough, Malcolm J. "Mining and the Nineteenth-Century American West," in William Deverell, ed., *A Companion to the American West* (Malden, MA: Blackwell Publishing, 2004), 112–29.

Romney, Paul. "From the Types Riot to Rebellion: Elite Ideology, Anti-Legal Sentiment, Political Violence, and the Rule of Law in Upper Canada," *Ontario History* 79 (June 1987): 113–44.

Romney, Paul. "Reinventing Upper Canada: American Immigrants, Upper Canadian History, English Law, and the Alien Question," in Roger Hall et al., eds., *Patterns of the Past: Interpreting Ontario History* (Toronto: Dundurn Press, 1988), 78–107.

Ronda, James P. *Astoria and Empire* (Lincoln: University of Nebraska Press, 1990).

Ronda, James P. "Dreams and Discoveries: Exploring the American West, 1760–1815," *William and Mary Quarterly*, 3rd ser., vol. 46 (1989): 145–62.

Ronda, James P. *Finding the West: Explorations with Lewis and Clark* (Albuquerque: University of New Mexico Press, 2001).

Ronda, James P. *Lewis and Clark Among the Indians* (Lincoln: University of Nebraska Press, 1984).

Roney, Jessica Choppin. "1776, Viewed from the West," *Journal of the Early Republic* 37 (Winter 2017): 655–700.

Rorabaugh, W. J. *The Alcoholic Republic: An American Tradition* (New York: Oxford University Press, 1979).

Rothman, Adam. *Slave Country: American Expansion and the Origins of the Deep South* (Cambridge: Harvard University Press, 2005).

Rothman, Joshua D. *Flush Times and Fever Dreams: A Story of Capitalism and Slavery in the Age of Jackson* (Athens: University of Georgia Press, 2012).

Ruby, Robert H., and John A. Brown. *The Cayuse Indians: Imperial Tribesmen of Old Oregon* (Norman: University of Oklahoma, 1972).

Rugeley, Terry. *Rebellion Now and Forever: Mayas, Hispanics, and Caste War Violence in Yucatan, 1800–1880* (Stanford, CA: Stanford University Press, 2009).

Rugemer, Edward. *Slave Law and the Politics of Resistance in the Early Atlantic World* (Cambridge: Harvard University Press, 2018).

Russell, Philip L. *The History of Mexico from Pre-Conquest to Present* (New York: Routledge, 2010).

Ryan, Mary P. *Cradle of the Middle Class: The Family in Oneida County, New York, 1790–1865* (New York: Cambridge University Press, 1981).

Ryan, Mary P. *Womanhood in America: From Colonial Times to the Present* (New York: Franklin Watts, 1983).

Ryan, Mary P. *Women in Public: Between Banners and Ballots, 1825–1880* (Baltimore: Johns Hopkins University Press, 1990).

Sartorius, David. "Cuban Counterpoint: Colonialism and Continuity in the Atlantic World," in John Tutino, ed., *New Countries: Capitalism, Revolutions, and Nations in the Americas, 1750–1870* (Durham, NC: Duke University Press, 2016), 175–200.

Saunt, Claudio. *A New Order of Things: Property, Power, and the Transformation of the Creek Indians, 1733–1816* (New York: Cambridge University Press, 1999).

Saunt, Claudio. *Unworthy Republic: The Dispossession of Native Americans and the Road to Indian Territory* (New York: W. W. Norton, 2020).

Saunt, Claudio. *West of the Revolution: An Uncommon History of 1776* (New York: W. W. Norton, 2014).

Saxton, Alexander. *P. T. Barnum: The Legend and the Man* (New York: Columbia University Press, 1989).

Saxton, Alexander. *The Rise and Fall of the White Republic: Class Politics and Mass Culture in Nineteenth-Century America* (New York: Verso, 2003).

Schafer, Daniel L. *Anna Madgigine Jai Kingsley: African Princess, Florida Slave, Plantation Slaveowner* (Gainesville: University Press of Florida, 2003).

Schafer, Daniel L. *Zephania Kingsley, Jr. and the Atlantic World: Slave Trader, Plantation Owner, Emancipator* (Gainesville: University Press of Florida, 2013).

Schermerhorn, Calvin. *The Business of Slavery and the Rise of American Capitalism* (New Haven: Yale University Press, 2015).

Schmalz, Peter S. *The Ojibwa of Southern Ontario* (Toronto: University of Toronto Press, 1991).

Schmidt, Fredrika Teute, and Barbara Ripel Wilhelm. "Early Proslavery Petitions in Virginia," *William and Mary Quarterly*, 3rd ser., vol. 30 (Jan. 1973): 133–46.

Schoen, Brian. "Calculating the Price of Union: Republican Economic Nationalism and the Origins of Southern Sectionlism, 1790–1828," *Journal of the Early Republic* 23 (Summer 2003): 173–206.

Schoen, Brian. *The Fragile Fabric of Union: Cotton, Federal Politics, and the Global Origins of the Civil War* (Baltimore: Johns Hopkins University Press, 2009).

Scott, Julius S. *The Common Wind: Afro-American Currents in the Age of the Haitian Revolution* (New York: Verso, 2018).

Scott, Winfield. *Memoirs of Lieut.-General Scott, L.L.D., Written by Himself* (New York: Sheldon & Co., 1864).

Sexton, Jay. *Debtor Diplomacy: Finance and American Foreign Relations in the Civil War Era, 1837–1873* (New York: Oxford University Press, 2005).

Sexton, Jay. *The Monroe Doctrine: Empire and Nation in Nineteenth-Century America* (New York: Hill & Wang, 2011).

Shankman, Andrew. *Crucible of American Democracy: The Struggle to Fuse Egalitarianism & Capitalism in Jeffersonian Pennsylvania* (Lawrence: University Press of Kansas, 2004).

Shankman, Andrew. "Toward a Social History of Federalism: The State and Capitalism to and from the American Revolution," *Journal of the Early Republic* 37 (Winter 2017): 615–54.

Sheriff, Carol. *The Artificial River: The Erie Canal and the Paradox of Progress, 1817–1862* (New York: Hill & Wang, 1996).

Shipps, Jan. *Mormonism: The Story of a New Religious Tradition* (Urbana: University of Illinois Press, 1985).

Shortt, Adam, and Arthur G. Doughty, eds. *Documents Relating to the Constitutional History of Canada, 1759–1791: Part Two, 1774–1791* (Ottawa: J. de L. Tache, 1918).

Shy, John. *A People Numerous and Armed: Reflections on the Military Struggle for American Independence* (Ann Arbor: University of Michigan Press, 1990).

Sidbury, James. *Ploughshares into Swords: Race, Rebellion, and Identity in Gabriel's Virginia, 1730–1810* (New York: Cambridge University Press, 1997).

Sidbury, James. "Saint Domingue in Virginia: Ideology, Local Meanings, and Resistance to Slavery, 1790–1800," *Journal of Southern History* 63 (1997): 531–52.

Sidbury, James. "Thomas Jefferson in Gabriel's Virginia," in James Horn, Jan Ellen Lewis, and Peter S. Onuf, eds., *The Revolution of 1800: Democracy, Race, and the New Republic* (Charlottesville: University of Virginia Press, 2002), 199–219.

Siegel, Stanley. *A Political History of the Texas Republic, 1836–1845* (Austin: University of Texas Press, 1956).

Sievens, Mary Beth. *Stray Wives: Marital Conflict in Early National New England* (New York: New York University Press, 2005).

Silbey, Joel H. *Storm over Texas: The Annexation Controversy and the Road to Civil War* (New York: Oxford University Press, 2005).

Simeone, James. *Democracy and Slavery in Frontier Illinois: The Bottomland Republic* (DeKalb: Northern Illinois University Press, 2000).

Simon, James F. *What Kind of Nation: Thomas Jefferson, John Marshall, and the Epic Struggle to Create a United States* (New York: Simon & Schuster, 2002).

Sinha, Manisha. *The Slave's Cause: A History of Abolition* (New Haven: Yale University Press, 2016).

Skelton, William B. *An American Profession of Arms: The Army Officer Corps, 1784–1861* (Lawrence: University Press of Kansas, 1992).

Skelton, William B. "High Army Leadership in the Era of the War of 1812: The Making and Remaking of the Officer Corps," *William and Mary Quarterly*, 3rd ser., vol. 51 (Apr. 1994): 253–74.

Slaughter, Thomas P. *The Whiskey Rebellion: Frontier Epilogue to the American Revolution* (New York: Oxford University Press, 1986).

Smith, Barbara Sweetland, and Redmond J. Barnett, eds. *Russian America: The Forgotten Frontier* (Tacoma: Washington State Historical Society, 1990).

Smith, Donald B. *Mississauga Portraits: Ojibwe Voices from Nineteenth-Century Canada* (Toronto: University of Toronto Press, 2013).

Smith, Donald B. *Sacred Feathers: The Reverend Peter Jones (Kahkewaquonaby) and the Mississauga Indians* (Toronto: University of Toronto Press, 2013).

Smith, Gene Allen. *The Slaves' Gamble: Choosing Sides in the War of 1812* (New York: Palgrave Macmillan, 2013).

Smith, Joshua M. *Borderland Smuggling: Patriots, Loyalists, and Illicit Trade in the Northeast, 1783–1820* (Gainesville: University Press of Florida, 2006).

Smith, Matthew J. *Liberty, Fraternity, Exile: Haiti and Jamaica After Emancipation* (Chapel Hill: University of North Carolina Press, 2014).

Smith, Michael. *A Geographical View of the Province of Upper Canada; and Promiscuous Remarks on the Government* (Philadelphia: Thomas and Robert DeSilver, 1813).

Smith, Rogers M. *Civic Ideals: Conflicting Visions of Citizenship in U.S. History* (New Haven: Yale University Press, 1997).

Snyder, Christina. *Great Crossings: Indians, Settlers, and Slaves in the Age of Jackson* (New York: Oxford University Press, 2017).

Snyder, Christina. *Slavery in Indian Country: The Changing Face of Captivity in Early America* (Cambridge: Harvard University Press, 2010).

Sobel, Mechal. *The World They Made Together: Black and White Values in Eighteenth-Century Virginia* (Princeton: Princeton University Press, 1987).

Stagg, J. C. A. "Between Black Rock and a Hard Place: Peter B. Porter's Plan for an American Invasion of Canada in 1812," *Journal of the Early Republic* 19 (Fall 1999): 383–422.

Stagg, J. C. A. *Borderlines in Borderlands: James Madison and the Spanish American Frontier, 1776–1821* (New Haven: Yale University Press, 2009).

Stagg, J. C. A. "Enlisted Men in the United States Army, 1812–1815: A Preliminary Survey," *William and Mary Quarterly*, 3rd ser., vol. 43 (1986): 615–45.

Stagg, J. C. A. *Mr. Madison's War: Politics, Diplomacy, and Warfare in the Early American Republic, 1783–1830* (Princeton: Princeton University Press, 1983).

Stanley, Amy Dru. "Marriage, Property, and Class," in Nancy A. Hewitt, ed., *A Companion to American Women's History* (New York: Blackwell, 2002), 193–205.

Stansell, Christine. *City of Women: Sex and Class in New York, 1789–1860* (New York: Alfred A. Knopf, 1986).

Stanton, Lucia C. *"Those Who Labor for My Happiness": Slavery at Thomas Jefferson's Monticello* (Charlottesville: University of Virginia Press, 2012).

Stanton, Lucia C. " 'Those Who Labor for My Happiness': Thomas Jefferson and His Slaves," in Peter S. Onuf, ed., *Jeffersonian Legacies* (Charlottesville: University Press of Virginia, 1993), 147–80.

Steele, Ian K. *Warpaths: Invasions of North America* (New York: Oxford University Press, 1994).

Stern, Theodore. *Chiefs and Change in the Oregon Country* (Corvallis: Oregon State University Press, 1996).

Steward, Austin. *Twenty-Two Years a Slave and Forty Years a Freeman* (Canandaigua, NY: A. Steward, 1867).

Stewart, James B. "Christian Statesmanship, Codes of Honor, and Congressional Violence: The Antislavery Travails and Triumphs of Joshua Giddings," in Paul Finkelman and Donald R. Kennon, eds., *In the Shadow of Freedom: The Politics of Slavery in the National Capital* (Athens: Ohio University Press, 2011), 36–57.

Stinchcombe, William C. *The American Revolution and the French Alliance* (Syracuse: Syracuse University Press, 1969).

St. John, Rachel. *Line in the Sand: A History of the Western U.S.–Mexico Border* (Princeton: Princeton University Press, 2011).

Stowell, Daniel W., ed. *Balancing Evils Judiciously: The Proslavery Writings of Zephaniah Kingsley* (Gainesville: University Press of Florida, 2000).

Strachan, John. *A Sermon Preached at York Before the Legislative Council and House of Assembly, August 2nd 1812* (York: John Cameron, 1812).

Stuart, Reginald C. *United States Expansionism and British North America, 1775–1871* (Chapel Hill: University of North Carolina Press, 1988).

Sugden, John. *Tecumseh: A Life* (New York: Henry Holt, 1997).

Surtees, Robert J. *Canadian Indian Policy: A Critical Bibliography* (Bloomington: Indiana University Press, 1982).

Surtees, Robert J. "Land Cessions, 1763–1830," in Edward S. Rogers and Donald B. Smith, eds., *Aboriginal Ontario: Historical Perspectives on the First Nations* (Toronto: Dundurn Press, 1994), 92–121.

Syrett, Harold C., ed. *The Papers of Alexander Hamilton*, 27 vols. (New York: Columbia University Press, 1961–87).

Szatmary, David P. *Shays' Rebellion: The Making of an Agrarian Insurrection* (Amherst: University of Massachusetts Press, 1980).

Tallant, Harold D. *Evil Necessity: Slavery and Political Culture in Antebellum Kentucky* (Lexington: University Press of Kentucky, 2003).

Taylor, Alan. "The Alien and Sedition Acts," in Julian E. Zelizer, ed., *The American Congress: The Building of Democracy* (Boston: Houghton Mifflin, 2004), 63–76.

Taylor, Alan. *The Civil War of 1812: American Citizens, British Subjects, Irish Rebels & Indian Allies* (New York: Alfred A. Knopf, 2010).

Taylor, Alan. *The Divided Ground: Indians, Settlers, and the Northern Borderland of the American Revolution* (New York: Alfred A. Knopf, 2006).

Taylor, Alan. "From Fathers to Friends of the People: Political Personas in the Early Republic," *Journal of the Early Republic* 11 (Winter 1991): 465–91.

Taylor, Alan. *The Internal Enemy: Slavery and War in Virginia, 1772–1832* (New York: W. W. Norton, 2013).

Taylor, Alan. "A Northern Revolution of 1800?: Upper Canada and Thomas Jefferson," in James Horn, Jan Ellen Lewis, and Peter S. Onuf, eds., *The Revolution of 1800: Democracy, Race, and the New Republic* (Charlottesville: University of Virginia Press, 2002), 383–409.

Teja, Jesús F. de la, *A Revolution Remembered: The Memoirs and Selected Correspondence of Juan N. Seguín* (Austin, TX: State House Press, 1991).

Thomas, Dwight, and David K. Jackson, eds. *The Poe Log: A Documentary Life of Edgar Allan Poe, 1809–1849* (Boston: G. K. Hall & Co., 1987).

Thompson, John Herd, and Stephen J. Randall. *Canada and the United States: Ambivalent Allies* (Athens: University of Georgia Press, 1997).

Tocqueville, Alexis de. *Democracy in America*, ed. Phillip Bradley, 2 vols. (New York: Vintage Books, 1945).

Tomlins, Christopher L. *Freedom Bound: Law, Labor, and Civic Identity in Colonizing English America, 1580–1865* (New York: Cambridge University Press, 2010).

Tomlins, Christopher L. *Law, Labor, and Ideology in the Early American Republic* (New York: Cambridge University Press, 1993).

Torget, Andrew J. *Seeds of Empire: Cotton, Slavery, and the Transformation of the Texas Borderlands, 1800–1850* (Chapel Hill: University of North Carolina Press, 2015).

Townshend, William H. *Lincoln and the Bluegrass: Slavery and Civil War in Kentucky* (Lexington: University of Kentucky Press, 1955).

Trennert, Robert A., Jr. *Alternative to Extinction: Federal Indian Policy and the Beginnings of the Reservation System, 1846–1851* (Philadelphia: Temple University Press, 1975).

[Tucker, George]. *Letters from Virginia, Translated from the French* (Baltimore: Fielding Lucas, Jr., 1816).

Tucker, Robert W., and David C. Hendrickson. *Empire of Liberty: The Statecraft of Thomas Jefferson* (New York: Oxford University Press, 1990).

Tucker, Spencer C., and Frank T. Reuter. *Injured Honor: The Chesapeake-Leopard Affair, June 22, 1807* (Annapolis: Naval Institute Press, 1996).

Turner, Katharine C. *Red Men Calling on the Great White Father* (Norman: University of Oklahoma Press, 1951).

Turner, Wesley B. *British Generals in the War of 1812: High Command in the Canadas* (Montreal: McGill-Queen's University Press, 1999).

Tutino, John. *From Insurrection to Revolution in Mexico: Social Bases of Agrarian Violence, 1750–1940* (Princeton: Princeton University Press, 1986).

Tyler-McGraw, Marie. *An African Republic: Black and White Virginians in the Making of Liberia* (Chapel Hill: University of North Carolina Press, 2007).

Unruh, John D., Jr. *The Plains Across: The Overland Emigrants and the Trans-Mississippi West, 1840–1860* (Urbana: University of Illinois Press, 1979).

Upton, Dell. *Another City: Urban Life and Urban Spaces in the New American Republic* (New Haven: Yale University Press, 2008).

Upton, Leslie F. S. *The Loyal Whig: William Smith of New York & Quebec* (Toronto: University of Toronto Press, 1969).

Utley, Robert M. *A Life Wild and Perilous: Mountain Men and the Paths to the Pacific* (New York: Henry Holt, 1997).

Van Cleve, George William. "Founding a Slaveholders' Union, 1770–1797," in John Craig Hammond and Matthew Mason, eds., *Contesting Slavery: The Politics of Bondage and Freedom in the New American Nation* (Charlottesville: University of Virginia Press, 2011), 117–37.

Van Cleve, George William. *A Slaveholders' Union: Slavery, Politics, and the Constitution in the Early Republic* (Chicago: University of Chicago Press, 2010).

Van Cleve, George William. *We Have Not a Government: The Articles of Confederation and the Road to the Constitution* (Chicago: University of Chicago Press, 2017).

Van Kirk, Sylvia. *"Many Tender Ties": Women in Fur Trade Society, 1670–1870* (Norman: University of Oklahoma Press, 1983).

Van Young, Eric. *The Other Rebellion: Popular Violence, Ideology, and the Mexican Struggle for Independence, 1810–1821* (Stanford, CA: Stanford University Press, 2001).

Varon, Elizabeth R. *Disunion!: The Coming of the American Civil War, 1789–1859* (Chapel Hill: University of North Carolina Press, 2008).

Vernet, Julien. *Strangers on Their Native Soil: Opposition to United States' Governance in Louisiana's Orleans Territory, 1803–1809* (Jackson: University Press of Mississippi, 2013).

Vinkovetsky, Ilya. *Russian America: An Overseas Colony of a Continental Empire, 1804–1867* (New York: Oxford University Press, 2011).

Viola, Herman J. *Diplomats in Buckskins: A History of Indian Delegations in Washington City* (Washington, DC: Smithsonian Institution Press, 1981).

Virgil, Ralph H., Frances W. Kaye, and John R. Wunder, eds. *Spain and the Plains: Myths and Realities of Spanish Exploration and Settlement on the Great Plains* (Niwot: University Press of Colorado, 1994).

Waldstreicher, David. *Slavery's Constitution: From Revolution to Ratification* (New York: Hill & Wang, 2009).

Walker, David. *David Walker's Appeal to the Coloured Citizens of the World*, ed. Peter P. Hinks (State College: Pennsylvania State University Press, 2008).

Walsh, Lorena S. "Work & Resistance in the New Republic: The Case of the Chesapeake, 1770–1820," in Mary Turner, ed., *From Chattel Slaves to Wage Slaves: The Dynamics of Labour Bargaining in the Americas* (Bloomington: Indiana University Press, 1995), 97–122.

Waterhouse, Benjamin, ed. *A Journal of a Young Man of Massachusetts, Late a Surgeon on Board an American Privateer* (New York: William Abbott, 1911).

Watson, Harry L. *Liberty and Power: The Politics of Jacksonian America* (New York: Noonday Press, 1990).

Watson, Samuel J. *Jackson's Sword: The Army Officer Corps on the American Frontier, 1810–1821* (Lawrence: University Press of Kansas, 2012).

Watts, Steven. *The Republic Reborn: War and the Making of Liberal America, 1790–1820* (Baltimore: Johns Hopkins University Press, 1987).

Weber, David J. *Barbaros: Spaniards and Their Savages in the Age of Enlightenment* (New Haven: Yale University Press, 2005).

Weber, David J. *The Mexican Frontier, 1821–1846* (Albuquerque: University of New Mexico Press, 1982).

Weber, David J. *The Spanish Frontier in North America* (New Haven: Yale University Press, 1992).

Weld, Isaac. *Travels Through the States of North America and the Provinces of Upper and Lower Canada During the Years 1795, 1796, and 1797*, 2 vols. (New York: Johnson Reprint Co., 1968, reprint of London, 1807).

West, Elliott. *The Essential West: Collected Essays* (Norman: University of Oklahoma Press, 2012).

West, Elliott. *The Way to the West: Essays on the Central Plains* (Albuquerque: University of New Mexico Press, 1995).

Whalen, Terence. *Edgar Allan Poe and the Masses: The Political Economy of Literature in Antebellum America* (Princeton: Princeton University Press, 1999).

Whaley, Gray H. *Oregon and the Collapse of Illahee: U.S. Empire and the Transformation of an Indigenous World, 1792–1859* (Chapel Hill: University of North Carolina Press, 2010).

White, Ashli. *Encountering Revolution: Haiti and the Making of the Early Republic* (Baltimore: Johns Hopkins University Press, 2010).

White, Deborah Gray. *Ar'n't I a Woman?: Female Slaves in the Plantation South* (New York: W. W. Norton, 1999).

White, G. Edward. *The Marshall Court and Cultural Change, 1815–35* (New York: Macmillan, 1988).

White, Richard. *"It's Your Misfortune and None of My Own": A New History of the American West* (Norman: University of Oklahoma Press, 1991).

White, Richard. "The Louisiana Purchase and the Fictions of Empire," in Peter J. Kastor and François Weil, eds., *Empires of the Imagination: Transatlantic Histories of the Louisiana Purchase* (Charlottesville: University of Virginia Press, 2009), 37–61.

White, Richard. *The Middle Ground: Indians, Empires, and Republics in the Great Lakes Region, 1650–1815* (New York: Cambridge University Press, 1991).

White, Richard. "The Winning of the West: The Expansion of the Western Sioux in the Eighteenth and Nineteenth Centuries," *Journal of American History* 65 (Sept. 1978): 319–43.

White, Shane. *Somewhat More Independent: The End of Slavery in New York City, 1770–1810* (Athens: University of Georgia Press, 1991).

Wilbur, J. B. *Ira Allen, Founder of Vermont*, 2 vols. (Boston: Houghton Mifflin, 1928).

Wilentz, Sean. *The Rise of American Democracy: Jefferson to Lincoln* (New York: W. W. Norton, 2005).

Williams, Glyndwr. "The Pacific: Exploration and Exploitation," in P. J. Marshall, ed., *The Oxford History of the British Empire*, 2 vols. (New York: Oxford University Press, 1998), 2:552–75.

Wilton, Carol. *Popular Politics and Political Culture in Upper Canada, 1800–1850* (Montreal: McGill-Queen's University Press, 2000).

Winks, Robin W. *The Blacks in Canada: A History* (Montreal: McGill-Queen's University Press, 1997).

Winsboro, Irvin D. S., and Joe Knetch. "Florida Slaves, the 'Saltwater Railroad' to the Bahamas, and Anglo-American Diplomacy," *Journal of Southern History* 79 (Feb. 2013): 51–78.

Wise, S. F, and Robert Craig Brown. *Canada Views the United States: Nineteenth-Century Political Attitudes* (Seattle: University of Washington Press, 1967).

Witgen, Michael. "Seeing Red: Race, Citizenship, and Indigeneity in the Old Northwest," *Journal of the Early Republic* 38 (Winter 2018): 581–612.

Withey, Lynne. *Voyages of Discovery: Captain Cook and the Exploration of the Pacific* (New York: Morrow, 1987).

Wolf, Eva Sheppard. *Race and Liberty in the New Nation: Emancipation in Virginia from the Revolution to Nat Turner's Rebellion* (Baton Rouge: Louisiana State University Press, 2006).

Wong, Edlie. "In the Shadow of Haiti: The Negro Seamen Act, Counter-Revolutionary St. Domingue, and Black Emigration," in Elizabeth Maddock Dillon and Michael J. Drexler, eds., *The Haitian Revolution and the Early United States* (Philadelphia: University of Pennsylvania Press, 2016), 162–88.

Wood, Gordon S. *The Creation of the American Republic, 1776–1787* (Chapel Hill: University of North Carolina Press, 1969).

Wood, Gordon S. *Empire of Liberty: A History of the Early Republic, 1789–1815* (New York: Oxford University Press, 2009).

Wood, Gordon S. *The Radicalism of the American Revolution* (New York: Alfred A. Knopf, 1992).

Wood, Kirsten E. " 'One Woman So Dangerous to Public Morals': Gender and Power in the Eaton Affair," *Journal of the Early Republic* 17 (Summer 1997): 237–75.

Wright, Barry. "Sedition in Upper Canada: Contested Legality," *Labour/Le Travail* 29 (Spring 1992): 7–57.

Wright, J. Leitch, Jr. *Britain and the American Frontier, 1783–1815* (Athens: University of Georgia Press, 1975).

Wright, J. Leitch, Jr. *William Augustus Bowles: Director General of the Creek Nation* (Athens: University of Georgia Press, 1967).

Yokota, Kariann Akemi. *Unbecoming British: How Revolutionary America Became a Postcolonial Nation* (New York: Oxford University Press, 2014).

Young, Alfred F. *The Democratic Republicans of New York: The Origins, 1763–1797* (Chapel Hill: University of North Carolina Press, 1967).

Zaeske, Susan. " 'A Nest of Rattlesnakes Let Loose Among Them': Congressional Debates over Women's Antislavery Petitions, 1835–1845," in Paul Finkelman and Donald R. Kennon, eds., *In the Shadow of Freedom: The Politics of Slavery in the National Capital* (Athens: Ohio University Press, 2011), 97–124.

Zagarri, Rosemarie. "The American Revolution and a New National Politics," in Edward G. Gray and Jane Kamensky, eds., *The Oxford Handbook of the American Revolution* (New York: Oxford University Press, 2013), 483–98.

Zagarri, Rosemarie. *Revolutionary Backlash: Women and Politics in the Early American Republic* (Philadelphia: University of Pennsylvania Press, 2007).

Zilberstein, Anya. "Objects of Distant Exchange: The Northwest Coast, Early

America, and the Global Imagination," *William and Mary Quarterly*, 3rd ser., vol. 64 (July 2007): 591–620.

Zilversmit, Arthur. *The First Emancipation: The Abolition of Slavery in the North* (Chicago: University of Chicago Press, 1967).

Zimmerman, James Fulton. *Impressment of American Seamen* (Port Washington, NY: Kennikat Press, 1966).

INDEX